T0281019

Lecture Notes in Computer Science 14360

Founding Editors

Gerhard Goos
Juris Hartmanis

The series Lecture Notes in Computer Science (LNCS), including its subseries Lecture Notes in Artificial Intelligence (LNAI) and Lecture Notes in Bioinformatics (LNBI), has established itself as a medium for the publication of new developments in computer science and information technology research, teaching, and education.

LNCS enjoys close cooperation with the computer science R & D community, the series counts many renowned academics among its volume editors and paper authors, and collaborates with prestigious societies. Its mission is to serve this international community by providing an invaluable service, mainly focused on the publication of conference and workshop proceedings and postproceedings. LNCS commenced publication in 1973.

Frank de Boer · Ferruccio Damiani ·
Reiner Hähnle · Einar Broch Johnsen ·
Eduard Kamburjan
Editors

Active Object Languages: Current Research Trends

Springer

Editors
Frank de Boer
Centrum Wiskunde & Informatica
Amsterdam, The Netherlands

Ferruccio Damiani
University of Turin
Turin, Italy

Reiner Hähnle
Darmstadt University of Technology
Darmstadt, Hessen, Germany

Einar Broch Johnsen
University of Oslo
Oslo, Norway

Eduard Kamburjan
University of Oslo
Oslo, Norway

ISSN 0302-9743   ISSN 1611-3349 (electronic)
Lecture Notes in Computer Science
ISBN 978-3-031-51059-5   ISBN 978-3-031-51060-1 (eBook)
https://doi.org/10.1007/978-3-031-51060-1

This Springer imprint is published by the registered company Springer Nature Switzerland AG
The registered company address is: Gewerbestrasse 11, 6330 Cham, Switzerland

Paper in this product is recyclable.

Preface

Our interest in active object languages started almost twenty years ago and continued through a series of European research projects: CREDO (FP6, during 2006–2009), HATS (FP7, during 2010–2013), ENVISAGE (FP7, during 2013–2016), UpScale (FP7, during 2014–2017), and HyVar (H2020, during 2015–2018). At the time, we were attracted to the concurrency model of Actors and the code structuring mechanisms of Object-Oriented Programming. These projects developed the active object paradigm in the context of service-oriented distributed systems, software variability, cloud computing, multicore computing and IoT-driven dynamic software reconfiguration. Many of the problems that were explored in this work remain relevant in research today, e.g., asynchronous method calls and futures, asynchronous distributed workflows, parallel programs with explicit units of composition and deployment, resource-sensitive systems, software modularity and variability, programming and reasoning techniques for asynchronous systems.

Active objects is a programming paradigm that supports a non-competitive, data-driven concurrency model, a generalization of the popular actor paradigm. Active object languages study how actor-like concurrency can be combined with object-oriented structuring concepts. This makes active object languages well-suited for simulation, data race-free programming, and formal verification. For a comprehensive discussion of different active object languages and their design choices, we refer to the state-of-the-art survey[1]. Concepts from active objects made their way into languages such as Rust, ABS, Akka, JavaScript, and Go.

Today, we can say that we were intrigued by the compositionality mechanisms at play in active object languages, and their application in language semantics and formal reasoning techniques as well as in the executable modelling and analysis of complex, distributed systems. This volume collects a series of articles on recent trends on the topic of programming and reasoning about asynchronous and distributed systems, with active objects at its core but also touching on related techniques. For this volume, we took the opportunity to invite researchers, inside and outside of the projects, to reflect on some state-of-the-art developments in the field. We feel very lucky that so many of our peers responded. The result is a book whose chapters identify and address some of the latest challenges in active objects and asynchronous distributed systems. It captures aspects of novel programming techniques, modelling solutions and reasoning challenges for modern actor and active object languages, and the related field of asynchronous, distributed and decentralised systems.

We thank all authors for accepting our invitation and putting a lot of effort into producing the high-quality content we are proud to present here. With this book, we

---

[1] Frank S. de Boer, Vlad Serbanescu, Reiner Hähnle, Ludovic Henrio, Justine Rochas, Crystal Chang Din, Einar Broch Johnsen, Marjan Sirjani, Ehsan Khamespanah, Kiko Fernandez-Reyes, Albert Mingkun Yang: A Survey of Active Object Languages. ACM Comput. Surv. 50(5): 76:1–76:39 (2017).

hope to provide the community with insights into recent and latest developments in important subareas of active object languages and related research.

October 2023

Frank de Boer
Ferruccio Damiani
Reiner Hähnle
Einar Broch Johnsen

Organization

Editors

Frank de Boer	CWI, Amsterdam
Ferruccio Damiani	University of Turin, Italy
Reiner Hähnle	Technical University of Darmstadt, Germany
Einar Broch Johnsen	University of Oslo, Norway
Eduard Kamburjan	University of Oslo, Norway

Reviewers

Wolfgang Ahrendt	Chalmers University, Sweden
Lorenzo Bacchiani	University of Bologna, Italy
Richard Bubel	Technical University of Darmstadt, Germany
Sara Capecchi	University of Turin, Italy
Elias Castegren	Uppsala University, Sweden
Samir Genaim	Universidad Complutense de Madrid, Spain
Saverio Giallorenzo	University of Bologna, Italy
Stijn de Gouw	Open Universiteit, The Netherlands
Ludovic Henrio	Inria, France
Asmae Heydari Tabar	Technical University of Darmstadt, Germany
Hans-Dieter Hiep	CWI, Amsterdam
Ramtin Khosravi	University of Tehran, Iran
Paul Kobialka	University of Oslo, Norway
Olaf Owe	University of Oslo, Norway
Danilo Pianini	University of Bologna, Italy
Gabriel Radanne	Inria, France
Marco Scaletta	Technical University of Darmstadt, Germany
Rudolf Schlatte	University of Oslo, Norway
Christophe Scholliers	Ghent University, Belgium
Marjan Sirjani	Mälardalen University, Sweden
Jeremy Sproston	University of Turin, Italy
Martin Steffen	University of Oslo, Norway

Volker Stolz   Western Norway University of Applied Sciences,
                                        Norway
S. Lizeth Tapia Tarifa   University of Oslo, Norway
Martin Vassor   University of Oxford, UK
Gianluigi Zavattaro   University of Bologna, Italy

Contents

Analysis

Programming

Active Objects Based on Algebraic Effects

Martin Andrieux[1]◉, Ludovic Henrio[2](✉)◉, and Gabriel Radanne[2]◉

[1] ENS Rennes, Rennes, France
`martin.andrieux@ens-rennes.fr`
[2] Université Lyon, EnsL, UCBL, CNRS, Inria, LIP, Lyon, France
{`ludovic.henrio,gabriel.radanne`}`@ens-lyon.fr`

Abstract. Algebraic effects are a long-studied programming language construct allowing the implementation of complex control flow in a structured way. With OCaml 5, such features are finally available in a mainstream programming language, giving us a great opportunity to experiment with varied concurrency constructs implemented as simple libraries. In this article, we explore how to implement concurrency features such as futures and active objects using algebraic effects, both in theory and in practice. On the practical side, we present a library of active objects implemented in OCaml, with futures, cooperative scheduling of active objects, and thread-level parallelism. On the theoretical side, we formalise the compilation of a future calculus that models our library into an effect calculus similar to the primitives available in OCaml; we then prove the correctness of the compilation scheme.

1 Introduction

A *future* [1,9] is a standard synchronisation artefact used in programming languages with concurrency. It provides a data-flow oriented synchronisation at a higher level of abstraction than locks or monitors. A future is a promise of a result from a spawned task: it is a cell, initially empty, and filled with a value when the task finishes. Accessing this value synchronises the accessor with the end of the task. Promises [17] is a notion similar to futures except that a promise must be filled explicitly by the programmer. Promises are more flexible but also more difficult to use because one could try to fill a promise several times and this raises many issues.

Future pay a crucial role in the implementation of asynchronous computations, particularly in object-oriented languages. ABCL/f [23] proposed the first occurrence of typed futures as a mean for *asynchronous method invocation*, where a spawned task fills the future later. Then Creol [13] and ProActive [4] introduced *active objects* [3]; which are both an object (in the sense of object oriented programming) and an actor. As a consequence, an active object has its own logical thread and communications between active objects is done by asynchronous method invocations, using futures to represent the result of asynchronous calls.

Futures, promises, and concurrency primitives in general, have been implemented using a wide variety of techniques, often via dedicated runtime support.

© The Author(s), under exclusive license to Springer Nature Switzerland AG 2024
F. de Boer et al. (Eds.): *Active Object Languages: Current Research Trends*,
LNCS 14360, pp. 3–36, 2024.
https://doi.org/10.1007/978-3-031-51060-1_1

Many concurrency primitives require suspending, manipulating and resuming arbitrary computations. This need for non-local control flow appears as soon as task scheduling is not trivial. It turns out that *effect handlers* [2] precisely enable users to define new control-flow operators. This was quickly identified as a potential technique to implement concurrency primitives while developing Multicore OCaml. Multicore OCaml [21,22] is an ensemble of new features, including effect handlers, which enable parallel and concurrent programming in OCaml. Crucially, since effects are user-defined, they allow implementing concurrency operators such as futures as *libraries*. This remark is not a contribution of this article, and seems to be well known folklore among algebraic effects practitioners. It is also how `eio` [15], the new concurrency library for OCaml, is implemented.

This article expands beyond this folklore in two direction: First, we showcase how to use effects to implement other concurrency primitives, active objects, that were not previously explored. Second, we formalise the translation between futures and algebraic effects, and prove it correct.

Contribution 1: An Actor Library Based on Algebraic Effects. On the practical side, we present *a new implementation of active objects based on algebraic effects.* It takes the form of an OCaml library that features all the characteristics of active objects, adapted to the OCaml ecosystem. The implementation heavily relies on effect handlers. The library is presented in Sect. 3.

Our implementation only requires effect handlers and objects. To our knowledge and at the time of writing, both are only conjointly present in OCaml. However, as effect handlers are gaining interest and are developed in different contexts, we believe our methodology is applicable to develop active object libraries in any language that support both features.

Contribution 2: A Formalised Translation from Actors into Effect Handlers and Its Proof of Correctness. On the theoretical side, we present the formal arguments showing that our implementation of active objects by effect handlers fully follows the paradigms of active object languages, more precisely:

- In Sect. 4 we describe our calculi: first, an imperative λ-calculus similar to what can be found in the literature; second, FUT, which expands this λ-calculus with operations on futures: *parallelism, tasks, futures, cooperative scheduling inside a thread*; finally, EFF which expands the λ-calculus with *effects and effect handlers* in a *parallel* setting.
- Section 5 defines *a compilation scheme from* FUT *to* EFF that expresses the principles of the implementation of our active object library based on effects. We formally prove the correctness of our translation and show that the behaviours of the effect compilation of futures mimics exactly the future semantics. Our main theorem states that the compiled program faithfully behaves like the original one.

2 Context and Positioning: Futures, Promises, Effects

We start by revisiting, in a streamlined fashion, the context of our works. We first present the formal models that exist to define semantics of futures and effects, explaining why we need a new semantics to formalise our work. Then we present the programming patterns we rely on: an API for promises as it would appear in OCaml, and how to implement such API using algebraic effects.

2.1 Formal Model for Futures and Effects

In order to formalise our translation, we need a calculus modeling the core of active objects. Compared to existing active object languages, we base our work on a simple λ-calculus enhanced with imperative operations and futures featuring cooperative scheduling. This calculus does not reflect the object-oriented nature of active object languages. Indeed, while the object layer provides an effective programming abstraction and strong static guarantees, we are mostly interested in operational aspects where objects play little role. Conversely, we consider that cooperative scheduling is essential, as it precisely captures the dynamic behavior we want to reproduce after translation to algebraic effects.

Among previously existing calculi, we position ourselves compared to the following ones. On one hand, several previous calculi [6,7] rely on a pure λ-calculus, lacking any imperative features. We consider modeling imperative code essential, as it allows us to encode the stateful nature of active objects. In particular pure calculi are not able to represent cycles of futures [10]. On the other hand, a concurrent λ-calculus with futures [18] and the DeF calculus [5] feature imperative aspects but no cooperative scheduling, which is crucial to many active objects languages. Additionally, DeF separates cleanly global state and local variables and uses a notion of functions closer to object methods instead of λ-calculus. We do not believe these features are needed in our context. Finally, some formalisation efforts such as ABS [14] cover much more ground, including a full-blown object system and "concurrent object groups" to model the concurrent semantics. We believe such semantics can also be modeled by simpler mechanisms, such as threads and remote execution of pieces of code.

In the remaining of this work, we use a minimal λ-calculus that includes the following features, that are, from our point of view, the core runtime characteristics of actors and active object languages with futures:

- Impure λ-calculus with a store and memory locations,
- Cooperative scheduling among tasks on the same parallelisation entity.
- Request-reply interaction mechanism based on asynchronous calls targeting a given thread, and replies by mean of futures. Without loss of generality, asynchronous calls are simply performed by remote execution of a given λ-calculus expression.

One crucial aspect of actors and active objects that we omit in this work is the separation of the memory into separate entities manipulated by a single thread (like e.g. ABS "concurrent object groups"). While this feature is crucial and allows reasoning about the deterministic nature of some active object languages [11] we would not use it in our developments. We also believe this crucial separation could be added by separating the memory in our configurations into a single memory per thread, either syntactically or using some kind of separation logic.

On the algebraic effect side, we use an imperative λ-calculus with *shallow* effect handlers, similar to Hillerström and Lindley [12]. This fits well with OCaml, which supports both imperative and functional features. Note that both deep and shallow handlers are available in OCaml.

2.2   Promises in OCaml

Promises are not a new addition to OCaml. Historically, the libraries *Lwt* [24] and *Async* implemented monadic promise-based cooperative multitasking in OCaml. Due to OCaml's limitation at the time, neither library implemented parallelism. Multicore OCaml introduced parallelism (with a new garbage collector and supporting libraries for thread parallelism) [21] along with algebraic effects [22], with the objective for users to implement their own concurrency primitives. In recent time, several libraries implement their own flair of futures and promises, this time using a direct-style instead of the previous monadic one. Most of them, including the most developed library eio [15], and our own implementation, use a core API summarised in Fig. 1.

```
1 type 'a Promise.t
2 (** Promises containing values of type ['a] *)
3
4 val Promise.create : unit -> 'a Promise.t * ('a -> unit)
5 (** [Promise.create ()] creates a promise explicitly and
       returns both the promise and the function to be called
       for its resolution *)
6
7 val Promise.async : (unit -> 'a) -> 'a Promise.t
8 (** [Promise.async (fun () -> e)] executes [e] in a
       promise *)
9
10 val Promise.get : 'a Promise.t -> 'a
11 (** [Promise.get p] makes a blocking read on promise [p]
       *)
12
13 val Promise.await : 'a Promise.t -> 'a
14 (** [Promise.get p] makes a non-blocking read on promise [
       p] *)
```

Fig. 1. A simple API for promises

The different elements of the API are commented in the figure. The type Promise.t is parameterised by its content (denoted by the type variable 'a).

There are two ways to create a promise: `Promise.create` creates a promise and also returns the resolution function, while `Promise.async` associates a computation to the promise, actually creating a future. This library can be used in any setting, we thus differentiate between *non-blocking* operations such as `await`, which yield to another task, and *blocking* operations such as `get`, whose evaluation is stuck and blocks the current logical thread. It is then up to the invoker of this function and the scheduler to deal with this blocked state conveniently.

2.3   Promising Effects

Following [20], we now summarise a simplistic implementation of the `get` primitive for promises or futures using effects, as a way to introduce effects in the context of concurrency. As noted before, A promise, denoted here by the `promise` type is an atomic mutable box containing a status. The status is either `Resolved`, containing a value of type `'a`, or `Empty` waiting for a value.

```
1 type 'a status = Resolved of 'a | Empty
2 type 'a promise = 'a status Atomic.t
```

Using effects, Fig. 2 showcases the implementation of blocking reads (`get` primitive) as explained below. On Line 1, we declare a new effect, called `Get`. From the usage perspective, an effect is a parameterised operation whose semantics is not specified, but whose typing is fixed: here, performing the `Get` effect takes as parameter a promise and returns the content. The `get` function, on Line 4, directly returns the value if the promise is fulfilled, or performs the `Get` effect otherwise. We still need to define what performing `Get` actually does. This is done via an *effect handler*, one Line 9. From the definition perspective, effects behave similarly to exceptions, except they allow resumption. The `exec` function executes a task in the context of a handler. When an effect is performed, it

```
 1 effect Get : 'a promise -> 'a (** A new 'Get' effect *)
 2
 3 (** User-level function for blocking reads on promises *)
 4 let get (p : 'a promise) : 'a = match Atomic.get p with
 5   | Resolved v -> v
 6   | Empty -> perform (Get p)
 7
 8 (** Underlying implementation of Get *)
 9 let exec task = handle task() with
10   ...
11   | Promise.Get p, (k : 'a continuation) ->
12     let rec poll () = match Atomise.get p with
13       | Empty -> Domain.cpu_relax (); poll ()
14       | Resolved v -> continue k v
15     in poll ()
16   ...
```

Fig. 2. Function `Promise.get` and its effect handler

triggers the evaluation of the appropriate branch in the handler (here, Line 11) and binds the value contained in the effect (here, variable p is the promise to get). The handler also gives access to the *continuation* k at the point where the effect was performed. To implement get, we repeatedly poll the content of the promise until a value is obtained, and resume the continuation k with the value, thus resuming the execution of the task.

The continuation k, which is applied directly here, is in fact a first class value and can be passed around and stored. This allows implementing other operations on promises and other concurrency primitives, by defining a scheduler that manipulates continuations directly in user-land.

As indicated before, this implementation exactly mirrors (albeit with some simplifications) the ones in the current OCaml ecosystem. We now move on to a novel usage of algebraic effects by combining them with objects to implement active objects in OCaml.

3   An OCaml Library for Active Objects

Our first contribution is an OCaml library, actors-ocaml available at https:// github.com/Marsupilami1/actors-ocaml, which implements promises and active objects on top of OCaml's new features: effect handlers, to handle concurrency; and "domains", threads accompanied by their memory-managed heap, which acts as OCaml's parallelism units. We start by a showing our overlay for active objects before presenting its translation to effects.

3.1   Active Objects

We showcase a first example of active object in OCaml in Fig. 3. To create a new active object, we introduce a new dedicated syntax[1] object%actor[2]. It functions similarly to an OCaml object, with private fields, introduced by val and public methods. Here, we create an active object with one local field x initialised to 0, and three methods to set the local field, get it, and multiply it by a provided integer. Accessing private fields is transparent inside the active object, as if it was a normal variable, but forbidden outside the active object. We will see below that we use OCaml domains to implement such a local memory.

In OCaml, objects are typed structurally, with a type that reflects all their methods. Our active objects follow a similar trend: the object type is delimited by < ... > and contains a list of all methods. For instance, get : int (Line 3), indicates that the method get takes no argument and returns an integer. set : int -> unit marks a method taking an integer and returning nothing. Note that the field is not shown in the type, since it represents internal state.

---

[1] In our implementation we choose to adopt the *Actor* terminology instead of active objects because we believe actors are better known in the functional programming community.

[2] For this purpose, we use PPX, a specific hook that allow to extend OCaml with new lightweight syntax extensions.

```
1 let a = object%actor              1 val a : <
2   val mutable state = 0           2     set : int -> unit;
3   method set n = state <- n       3     get : int;
4   method get = state             4     multiply : int -> int
5   method multiply n = state*n    5 > Actor.t
6 end
                                            (b) Inferred type
            (a) Object definition
```

```
1 a#.set 10;
2 let x : int Promise.t = a#!get in
3 let y : int Promise.t = a#!multiply (Promise.await x) in
4 let z : unit Promise.t = a#!set (Promise.await x) in
5 a#.get + Promise.get y
```

(c) Example of use

Fig. 3. A simple example using active object

This is crucial for active objects, as local fields are stored locally and shouldn't be accessed by other active objects. To distinguish active objects from normal objects, the structural type that consists of the methods is wrapped, giving the type `< .. > Actor.t`.

Actual usage of active objects is where we depart from traditional OCaml objects. Indeed, active objects support two types of method calls: `a#.get`, in Line 1, is *synchronous*. Such calls are either blocking if made externally, similarly to `Promise.get`, or direct if made internally by the actor itself. `a#!get` in Line 2 is *asynchronous*, which wraps the result in a Promise. `Promise.create` is called to create the promise and associates a dedicated resolver with the triggered call. The promise is returned to the invoker that can then perform `Promise.get` and `Promise.await` on it. The programmer cannot explicitly resolve the promise and can only access its value: promises returned by active objects are in fact *futures*, similarly to other active object languages.

3.2   Encapsulation and Data-Race Freedom

Our library takes advantage of the OCaml type system to provide safe encapsulation of state and safe abstraction. Indeed, local variables, such as the `state` field in Fig. 3, are hidden. Access can thus only be made inside methods. This ensures proper abstraction since only fields that are exposed through getters and setters can be accessed. It also ensures the absence of data-races, since methods are not executed concurrently (unless programmer explicitly use lower-level constructs, such as shared memory). Naturally, this is only true if two crucial properties are ensured: mutable access cannot be captured, and it is impossible to return mutable values shared with the internal state.

Capture. Methods calls in OCaml are currified by default. For instance a#! multiply returns a closure of type int -> (int Promise.t) encapsulating message sending to a and retrieval of a result from a. Furthermore, functions are first class, and can be returned by methods. While this provides great integration into the rest of the language, this means that we need to be particularly careful with captures in methods. We illustrate this in Fig. 4, with an incorrect implementation of the multiply method. Here, we return a closure capturing an access to the internal field state. Such closure should never be executed in the context of another active object. We detect such ill-conceived code and return the error shown below, instructing the user to first access the state before capturing the value.

In theory, this is a simple matter of name resolution. In practice, name resolution in OCaml is complex, and relies on typing information which can't be accessed by syntax extensions such as the one we develop. We implement a conservative approximation.

```
1 let a = object%actor
2   val mutable state = 0
3   method multiply = let f n = state * n in f
4 end
```

(a) An incorrect implementation of multiply

```
1 Closures cannot capture internal mutable state, you may
    want to use something like:
2 |
3 | let a = state in fun _ -> ... a ...
4 |
5 Instead of:
6 |
7 | fun _ -> ... state ...
8 |
```

(b) The error message for an illegal capture

Fig. 4. An example of illegal capture and its error message

Mutability and Sharing. Code that respects the criterion mentioned above can still exhibit data-races, for instance by returning the content of a field which manifest internal mutability, such as arrays. Preventing such mistakes is a bit more delicate: with the strong abstraction of OCaml, the implementation of a data-structure can be completely hidden, and hence its potential mutability. A static type analysis is therefore insufficient. A dynamic analysis of the value is similarly insufficient (mutable and immutable records are represented similarly in OCaml). The last common solution to this problem, to make a deep copy of returned values, is costly both in terms of time and loss of sharing.

So far, we opted to only support immutable values in fields, and do not provide any guarantees when mutable values are used. Thankfully, immutable values are the default in OCaml and are largely promoted for most use-cases. In the future, we plan to combine static and dynamic analysis to inform where to insert deep copies.

3.3 Active Object Desugaring

We now have all the ingredients to explain how the OCaml code for the active object is generated from the programmer's input. An example of such translation is given in Fig. 5. The first important notion is to use memory local to the domain to store the internal fields. Using domains, this is done via the DLS (for Domain Local Storage, analogous to thread local storage), see for instance line 2 of the translated code. All reads and writes are then replaced by DLS functions. The second transformation aims to separate method calls (i.e., message sent), and execution, and can be observed on line 3 and 4: Each method is split in two. The first *hidden* method, shown on line 3, contains the computational content. The second is the actual entry point: it proceeds by creating a promise; launch a

```
1 let a = object%actor
2   val mutable state = 0
3   method set n = state <- n
4   method get = state
5 end
```

⇓

```
1  let a = object (self)
2    val __state = DLS.new_key (fun _ -> 0)
3    method __meth_set n = DLS.set __state n
4    method set n =
5      let p, resolver = Promise.create () in
6      Actor.send self
7        (Scheduler.process resolver
8          (fun _ -> self#__meth_set n)) ;
9      p
10   method __meth_get = DLS.get __state
11   method get =
12     let p, resolver = Promise.create () in
13     Actor.send self
14       (Scheduler.process resolver
15         (fun _ -> self#__meth_get)) ;
16     p
17 end
```

Fig. 5. Simple active object code (top) and its translation (bottom)

```
1 object%actor (self)
2    method syracuse n =
3      if n = 1 then 1
4      else
5        let next = if n mod 2 = 0 then n/2 else 3*n+1 in
6        self#!!syracuse next
7 end
```

Fig. 6. Simple use of delegation

new task; and return the promise. The goal of the task is to queue a message in the actor's mailbox, via `Actor.send`, and then launch a process which eventually resolves the promise; this is done by `Scheduler.process`.

3.4 Forward

While handling a method, one might want to delegate the computation to another active object or method. With traditional asynchronous calls such as `#!` or `await`, this would involve unwrapping and rewrapping the promises. Dealing efficiently with delegation in asynchronous invocations is a well-studied problem [5–7]. In [6], one construct called *forward* was suggested for such delegations; it was then shown that directly forwarding an asynchronous invocation (`return(async(e))`) could be efficiently and safely implemented using promises.

We can easily adapt this approach to our actors. We also implement delegation calls by syntactically identifying such optimisable situation with the primitive: `actor#!!m`. Figure 6 illustrates a simple program using such method delegation; the statement `self#!!syracuse next` delegates the current invocation to another one. These calls act as `return` in many languages, and ignore any computations that would come after in the method. From the functional programming point of view, this is analogous to tail-calls. Tail-calls exploit synchronous calls in return positions to eschew using additional stack space. Forward statement exploits asynchronous calls in return position to eschew indirection of promises.

In a more general case, we can simply forward[3] a promise as the future resolution of the current promise. A statement similar to the one of Encore, `Actors.forward p` performs such a shortcut where p is a `'a Promise.t`.

We implement the two forwarding constructs presented above as *effects* in the library. Similarly to capturing issues highlighted in previous sections, delegation calls should not be captured in a closure: indeed, it wouldn't be clear which indirection to avoid[4]. We forbid such situations (dynamically, via a runtime test).

---

[3] In the future, we hope to turn asynchronous calls in a `forward` into delegation automatically.

[4] Already in [6], the authors prevented forward from appearing inside a closure.

3.5   Runtime Support

From a parallelism point of view, we rely on domains, which are threads equipped with a private heap and a garbage collector. There is also a global, shared heap. In practice, we spawn a pool of domains at the start of the execution. This pool of domains is fixed for the whole execution. Similarly to many other implementations, multiple actors may share a domain, and will use cooperative scheduling together.

Cooperative scheduling is implemented using effects and continuations, similarly to the one implemented in the introduction. To make this scheduler more realistic and fair, we implement the following optimisations:

- Each domain contains a first round-robin scheduler in charge of scheduling between active objects hosted on the same domain. Spawning of new actors is implemented at this layer, enabling the choice of an arbitrary domain to spawn it. Synchronous method calls in the same domain are transparently turned into direct calls (instead of asynchronous calls followed by a synchronisation when the domain is different).
- Each active object contains an OCaml object with the methods of the object, as described above, and a second round-robin scheduler which schedules the promises currently executed by this actor. Instead of a traditional mailbox of messages, active objects contain a queue of thunks to be executed. In the case of method calls, each thunk contains a call to the underlying OCaml object as a closure. Forwards and delegation calls are implemented at this second layer, which is aware of all the details pertaining to the actor.
- Unresolved promises contain a list of *callbacks*, i.e., other promises that are currently waiting on it. This allows the implementation of passive waits for unresolved promise reads.

Note that this implies we have *two* effects handlers, both providing slightly differing implementation of the base effects related to promises (`Async`, `Get`, `Await`). Indeed, promises can appear outside of actors, but should be handled locally if they appear inside one.

4   Future and Effect λ-Calculi

The rest of this article is dedicated to the formal description of the compilation of Futures to Effects. For this purpose, we first introduce our protagonists: A common imperative base (Sect. 4.1), the source future calculus (Sect. 4.2) often characterised in green, and the target effect calculus (Sect. 4.3) often characterised in blue. For all these calculi, we define small-step operational semantics in the sequential and parallel cases.

4.1   A Functional-Imperative Base

We define a standard λ-calculus with imperative operations that will be the base language for our other definitions and semantics. The syntax is given in Fig. 7. As meta-syntactic notations, we use overbar for lists ($\bar{e}$ a list of expressions) and brackets for association maps ($[\overline{\ell \mapsto e}]$). $\text{Dom}(M)$ is the domain of M and $\emptyset$ is the empty map. $M[v \mapsto v']$ is a copy of M where v is associated to v', $M \setminus v$ is a copy of M where v is not mapped to anything ($v \notin \text{Dom}(M \setminus v)$).

Most expression and values are classical. The substitution of x by e' in e is denoted $e[x \leftarrow e']$. Stores are maps indexed by location references, denoted ℓ. **Id** denotes unique identifiers that can be crafted during execution, which will be useful in our two main calculi. Location references and identifiers should not occur in the source programs and only appear during evaluation. We also define evaluation contexts C that are expressions with a single hole $\square$. Evaluation contexts are used in the semantics to specify the point of evaluation in every term, ensuring a left-to-right call-by-value evaluation. We classically rely on evaluation contexts, $C[e]$ is the expression made of the context C where the hole is filled with expression e. Figure 8 defines a semantics for this base calculus; it is similar to what can be found in the literature. It expresses a reduction relation, denoted $\longrightarrow$, of pairs store$\times$expression.

Important Note. The rules of Fig. 8 act on the syntax of imperative λ-calculus. However, in the next section we will re-use $\longrightarrow$ on terms of bigger languages, with the natural embedding that $\longrightarrow$ rules only are able to handle the λ-calculus primitives but will manipulate terms and reduction contexts of the other languages. The alternative would be to define from the beginning the syntax and reduction contexts of our language as the largest syntax including all the three

$$
\begin{array}{llll}
& & v ::= \ell \in \textbf{Loc} & \text{(References)} \\
e ::= v & \text{(Values)} & \mid \lambda x.e & \text{(Functions)} \\
\mid x \in \textbf{Var} & \text{(Variables)} & \mid i \in \textbf{Id} & \text{(Identifiers)} \\
\mid () & \text{(Unit)} & \mid c \in \textbf{Const} & \text{(Constants)} \\
\mid \lambda x.e \mid (e_1 \ e_2) & \text{(Functions)} & & \\
\mid \textbf{newref}(e) \mid \ !x \mid x := e & \text{(References)} & \sigma ::= [\overline{\ell \mapsto v}] & \text{(Store)}
\end{array}
$$

$$C ::= \square \mid (C\ e) \mid (v\ C) \mid \textbf{newref}(C) \mid C := e \mid \ell := C \qquad \text{(Eval. context)}$$

Fig. 7. Syntax for the base impure λ-calculus

$$\frac{\ell \notin \text{Dom}(\sigma)}{\sigma, \textbf{newref}(v) \longrightarrow \sigma[\ell \mapsto v], \ell} \qquad \frac{(\ell \mapsto v) \in \sigma}{\sigma, !\ell \longrightarrow \sigma, v} \qquad \frac{}{\sigma, (\ell := v) \longrightarrow \sigma[\ell \mapsto v], ()}$$

$$\frac{\sigma, e \longrightarrow \sigma', e'}{\sigma, C[e] \longrightarrow \sigma', C[e']} \qquad \frac{}{\sigma, (\lambda x.e\ v) \longrightarrow \sigma, e[x \leftarrow v]}$$

Fig. 8. Semantics for the base impure λ-calculus

considered languages (λ-calculus, FUT, and EFF). We chose here to adopt a more progressive presentation despite the slight abuse of notation this involves on the formal side.

In the rest of this article, we also assume additional constructs which can be classically encoded in the impure λ-calculus:

- Let-declaration: `let x = ... in ...`
- Sequence: `e; e'`
- Mutually recursive declarations: `let rec ... and ...`
- Mutable maps indexed by values: empty map {}, reads $M[e]$, writes $M[e] \leftarrow e'$, and deletions `del` $M[e]$
- Pattern matching on simple values: `match ... with ...`

4.2 Futures and Cooperative Scheduling

Our λ-calculus with futures shares some similarities with the concurrent λ-calculus with futures [18], but without future handlers or explicit future name creation and scoping, resulting in a simpler calculus. Our calculus can also be compared to the one of Fernandez-Reyes et al. [6] but with cooperative scheduling with multiple threads, and imperative aspects.

The λ-calculus of previous section is extended as shown in Fig. 9. Four new constructs are added to the syntax: `spawn()` spawns a new processing unit; `asyncAt(e, e')` starts a new task e in the processing unit e' and creates a future identifier f, when the task finishes, this *resolves* the future f; `get(e)`, provided e is a future identifier, blocks the current processing unit until the future in e is resolved; `await(e)` is similar but releases the current processing unit until the future is resolved. Evaluation contexts are trivially extended.

As shown in Fig. 9, we suppose that *future identifiers* have a specific shape of the form $fut = (tid, lf)$ where tid is a thread identifier and lf is a local future identifier. Tasks map expressions to future identifiers, when the expression is fully evaluated (to a value) the future is *resolved*.

The dynamic syntax is expressed in two additional layers: above the λ-calculus layer of Fig. 8, Fig. 10 expresses the reduction relation in a given processing unit, and Fig. 11 extends this local semantics to a parallel semantics with several processing units.

The local semantics in Fig. 10 is based on configurations of the form σ, F, s where σ is a shared mutable store, F is the map of futures, and s is a state. If the expression in the current task is fully evaluated to a value, the task is finished, the future is resolved and put back into the task list, the state of the processing unit is `Idle` (rule RETURN). Rule STEP performs a λ-calculus step (see Fig. 8). $get(f)$ can only progress if the future f has been resolved, in which case the value associated with the future is fetched (rule GET). There are two rules

$$e ::= \ldots \qquad \text{(Base language)}$$
$$\mid \texttt{asyncAt}(e, e) \qquad \text{(Creation)}$$
$$\mid \texttt{get}(e) \qquad \text{(Blocking read)}$$
$$\mid \texttt{await}(e) \qquad \text{(Non-blocking read)}$$
$$\mid \texttt{spawn}() \qquad \text{(Spawn process)}$$

$$C ::= \cdots \mid \texttt{asyncAt}(C, e) \mid \texttt{asyncAt}(v, C)$$
$$\mid \texttt{await}(C) \mid \texttt{get}(C)$$
$$\text{(Evaluation Contexts)}$$

$$tid \in \textbf{ThreadId} \subset \textbf{Id}$$
$$\textit{lf} \in \textbf{LocalFutures} \subset \textbf{Id}$$
$$f ::= (tid, \textit{lf}) \in \textbf{Id} \qquad \text{(Future Ids)}$$

$$F ::= \boxed{f \mapsto e} \qquad \text{(Tasks)}$$
$$s ::= \texttt{Idle} \mid (f \mapsto e) \qquad \text{(Exec. State)}$$

$$P ::= \|_{i \in I} s^i \qquad \text{(Parallel exec. state)}$$
$$I \subseteq \textbf{ThreadId}$$

Fig. 9. Syntax for the FUT language

STEP
$$\frac{\sigma, e \longrightarrow \sigma', e'}{\sigma, F, (f \mapsto e) \longrightarrow \sigma', F, (f' \mapsto e')}$$

GET
$$\frac{(f' \mapsto v) \in F}{\sigma, F, (f \mapsto C[\texttt{get}(f')]) \longrightarrow \sigma, F, (f \mapsto C[v])}$$

AWAIT-VAL
$$\frac{(f' \mapsto v) \in F}{\sigma, F, (f \mapsto C[\texttt{await}(f')]) \longrightarrow \sigma, F, (f \mapsto C[v])}$$

AWAIT-YIELD
$$\frac{\nexists v. (f' \mapsto v) \in F}{\sigma, F, (f \mapsto C[\texttt{await}(f')]) \longrightarrow \sigma, F\left[f \mapsto C[\texttt{await}(f')]\right], \texttt{Idle}}$$

RETURN
$$\frac{}{\sigma, F, (f \mapsto v) \longrightarrow \sigma, F\left[f \mapsto v\right], \texttt{Idle}}$$

ASYNC
$$\frac{f' = (tid, \textit{lf}) \qquad f' \notin \text{Dom}(F)}{\sigma, F, (f \mapsto C[\texttt{asyncAt}(e, tid)]) \longrightarrow \sigma, F\left[f' \mapsto e\right], (f \mapsto C[f'])}$$

Fig. 10. Semantics for FUT—$\sigma, F, s \longrightarrow \sigma, F, s$

for $\texttt{await}(f)$: if the future is resolved $\texttt{await}(f)$ behaves like $\texttt{get}(f)$; if it is not resolved the task is interrupted (it returns to the task pool), the processing unit becomes $\texttt{Idle}$. Finally, rule ASYNC starts a new task: the effect of $\texttt{asyncAt}(e, tid)$ is first to forge a future identifier containing the thread identifier tid and another identifier $\textit{lf}$ so that the pair $(tid, \textit{lf})$ is fresh, a task is created, associating e to the new future.

The management of processing units and thread identifiers is the purpose of the parallel semantics in Fig. 11. It expresses the evaluation of configurations of the form σ, F, P where P is a parallel composition of processing units. $P \| s^i$ is used both to extract the execution state of thread i form the parallel composition P and to add it back. Rule ONE-STEP simply triggers a rule of the local semantics in Fig. 11. Rule SPAWN spawns a new thread, creating a fresh thread identifier that will be used in an AsyncAt statement to initiate work on this thread (the new thread is initially $\texttt{Idle}$). Finally, if s^i is $\texttt{Idle}$, no task is currently running and a new task can be started on the processing unit i by the rule SCHEDULE.

ONE-STEP

$$\frac{\sigma, F, s \longrightarrow \sigma_2, F_2, s_2}{\sigma, F, P \parallel s^i \longrightarrow_{\parallel} \sigma_2, F_2, P \parallel s_2{}^i}$$

SPAWN

$$\frac{tid \notin tids(P) \cup \{i\}}{\sigma, F, P \parallel (f \mapsto C[\texttt{spawn}()])^i \longrightarrow_{\parallel}}$$
$$\sigma, F, P \parallel (f \mapsto C[tid])^i \parallel \texttt{Idle}^{tid}$$

SCHEDULE

$$\frac{((i, lf) \mapsto e) \in F \qquad e \text{ is not a value}}{\sigma, F, P \parallel \texttt{Idle}^i \longrightarrow_{\parallel} \sigma, F \setminus (i, lf), P \parallel ((i, lf) \mapsto e)^i}$$

Fig. 11. Parallel semantics for FUT—$\sigma, F, \parallel_{i \in I} s^i \longrightarrow_{\parallel} \sigma, F, \parallel_{i \in I} s^i$

An initial configuration for an FUT program e_p consists of the program associated with a fresh task identifier i and a fresh future identifier f, with an empty store and future map: $\emptyset, \emptyset, (f \rightarrow e_p)^i$.

4.3   Effects

We now extend the base calculus of Sect. 4.1 with effects. For the moment this extension is independent of the previous one, they are used separately in this article even though composing the two extensions would be perfectly possible. Indeed, we transform programs with only futures into programs with only effects but having a language with at the same time futures and effects would also make sense.

Figure 12 shows the syntax of the parallel and imperative λ-calculus with effects. Parallelism is obtained by the keyword $\texttt{spawn}(e)$ that creates a new thread in the same spirit as in the previous section. $\texttt{handle}(e)\{h\}$ runs the expression e under the handler h, if an effect is thrown by $\texttt{throw}(E(C))$ inside e, and if h can handle this effect, the handler is triggered. Rule HANDLE-EFFECT in Fig. 13 specifies the semantics of effect handling. Suppose an effect E is thrown, the first encompassing handler that can handle this effect is triggered: if a rule $(E(x), k \mapsto e)$ is in the handler, then the handler e is triggered with x assigned to the effect value v and k assigned to the continuation of the expression that triggered the effect. The interplay between evaluation contexts and the captured_effects() function captures the closest matching effect. Rule HANDLE-STEP handles the case where the term e performs a reduction not related to effect handling. If e finally returns a value, Finally, rule HANDLE-RETURN deals with the case where the handled expression can be fully evaluated without throwing an effect; it triggers the expression corresponding to the success case $x \mapsto e$ in the handler definition. Note that we don't reinstall the handler after triggering the rule, corresponding to the *shallow* interpretation of effect handlers [12].

Figure 14 shows the parallel semantics of effects. The only specific rule is SPAWN, which spawns a new thread with a fresh identifier. Note that in EFF, the parameter of $\texttt{spawn}$ is the expression to be evaluated in the new thread, with its own thread identifier as argument.

$$e ::= \ldots$$
$$| \; \mathtt{handle}(e)\{h\} \; | \; \mathtt{throw}(E(e))$$
$$| \; \mathtt{spawn}(e)$$
$$C ::= \; \cdots \; | \; \mathtt{handle}(C)\{h\} \; | \; \mathtt{throw}(E(C))$$
$$| \; \mathtt{spawn}(e) \qquad \text{(Evaluation Contexts)}$$

$$E \in \mathbf{Symbol}$$
$$k \in \mathbf{Var}$$

$$h ::= \left[E(x), k \mapsto e; \; x \mapsto e \right]$$

Fig. 12. EFF Syntax

HANDLE-STEP
$$\frac{\sigma, e \longrightarrow \sigma', e'}{\sigma, e \longrightarrow \sigma', e'}$$

HANDLE-RETURN
$$\frac{(x \mapsto e) \in h}{\sigma, \mathtt{handle}(v)\{h\} \longrightarrow \sigma, e\,[x \leftarrow v]}$$

HANDLE-EFFECT
$$\frac{(E(x), k \mapsto e) \in h \qquad E \notin \text{captured\_effects}(C)}{\sigma, \mathtt{handle}(C[\mathtt{throw}(E(v))])\{h\} \longrightarrow \sigma, e\,[x \leftarrow v]\,[k \leftarrow \lambda y.C[y]]}$$

$$\text{captured\_effects}(\square) = \emptyset$$
$$\text{captured\_effects}(\mathtt{handle}(C)\{h\}) = \text{captured\_effects}(C) \cup \{E \mid (E(x), k \mapsto e) \in h\}$$
$$\text{captured\_effects}(\ldots) = \ldots \quad \text{(by immediate recursion otherwise)}$$

Fig. 13. Semantics for EFF—$\sigma, e \longrightarrow \sigma, e$

SEQ
$$\frac{\sigma, e \longrightarrow \sigma', e'}{\sigma, P \parallel e^i \longrightarrow_{\parallel} \sigma', P \parallel e'^i}$$

SPAWN
$$\frac{tid \notin tids(P) \cup \{i\}}{\sigma, P \parallel C[\mathtt{spawn}(e)]^i \longrightarrow_{\parallel} \sigma, P \parallel C[tid]^i \parallel (e \; tid)^{tid}}$$

Fig. 14. Parallel semantics for EFF—$\sigma, \parallel_{i \in I} e^i \longrightarrow \sigma, \parallel_{i \in I} e^i$

An initial configuration for an EFF program e_p simply consists of the program associated with a fresh task identifier i and with an empty store: $\emptyset, e_p^i$.

5   Compilation of Futures into Effects

In this section we define a transformation from FUT to EFF that translates from our concurrent λ-calculus with futures into the calculus with effect handlers. We then prove its correctness.

5.1   Translating FUT into EFF

Figure 15 shows the translation $[\![e]\!]_p$ that transforms a FUT program e into an EFF program with the same semantics. The color highlighting in the definition can be ignored at first. It will be used in the proof in the next section. $[\![e]\!]_p$ is the top level **program** transformation while $[\![e]\!]_e$ is used to compile **expression**; this transformation simply replaces FUT specific expressions into expressions

$[\![e]\!]_p \triangleq$ **let** $tasks = \{\}$ **in**
  let rec $poll(fut) = Poll$ **in**
  let rec $continue(fut, k, t) = Continue$
  and $run(t) = Run$ **in**
  $continue(fresh(), \lambda().\,[\![e]\!]_e\,, t_0)$

$[\![\texttt{asyncAt}(e,t)]\!]_e = \texttt{throw}(Async(\,\lambda().\;[\![e]\!]_e\,, [\![t]\!]_e))$

$[\![\texttt{await}(e)]\!]_e = \texttt{throw}(Await([\![e]\!]_e))$

$[\![\texttt{get}(e)]\!]_e = \texttt{throw}(Get([\![e]\!]_e))$

$[\![\texttt{spawn}()]\!]_e = \texttt{throw}(Spawn())$

$[\![x]\!]_e = x \qquad [\![v]\!]_e = v$

$[\![e]\!]_e = \ldots$ (immediate recursion otherwise)

Where
$Continue \triangleq$
  $\texttt{handle}(\ k()\ )\{$
  $\mid x \mapsto$
    $tasks[fut] \leftarrow \mathbb{V}(x);$
    $run(t)$
  $\mid Async(job, t'), k' \mapsto$
    let $fut' = (t', fresh())$ **in**
    $tasks[fut'] \leftarrow \mathbb{C}(job);$
    $continue(fut, \lambda().k'(fut'), t)$
  $\mid Await(fut_a), k' \mapsto$
    match $tasks[fut_a]\{$
      $\mid \mathbb{V}(v) \mapsto continue(fut, \lambda().k'(v))$
      $\mid \_ \mapsto$ **let** $k''() = k'(\texttt{throw}(Await(fut_a)))$ **in**
        $tasks[fut] \leftarrow \mathbb{C}(k'');$
        $run(t)$
    $\};$
  $\mid Spawn(), k' \mapsto$
    let $t' = \texttt{spawn}(run)$ **in**
    $continue(fut, \lambda().k'(t'), t)$
  $\mid Get(fut_a), k' \mapsto$
    let $v = poll(fut_a)$ **in**
    $continue(fut, \lambda().k'(v), t)$
  $\}$

$Run \triangleq$
  let $(fut, k) =$
    $pop(tasks, t)$
  in
  $tasks[fut] \leftarrow None;$
  $continue(fut, k, t)$

$Poll \triangleq$
  match $tasks[fut]\{$
    $\mid \mathbb{V}(v) \mapsto v$
    $\mid \_ \mapsto poll(fut)$
  $\}$

POP
$$\frac{fut = (tid, lf) \qquad tasks[fut] = \mathbb{C}(k)}{pop(tasks, tid) \longrightarrow (fut, k)}$$

Fig. 15. Translation from FUT to EFF

throwing an effect with adequate name and parameters. The handling of effects is defined at the top level, i.e. when translating the source program.

$[\![e]\!]_p$ creates a program that uses a pool of tasks called *tasks* and three functions that manipulate it. *tasks* is implemented by a mutable map from future identifiers to tasks, which can be of two kinds: continuations of the form $\mathbb{C}(k)$ or values of the form $\mathbb{V}(v)$.

The main function is *continue*, it sets up a handler dealing with all the effects of FUT. It first evaluates the thunk continuation parameter k. Then it reacts to the different possible effects as follows. The first branch describes the behavior when $k()$ throws no effect and simply returns a value. In this case, the task is saved as a value $\mathbb{V}(v)$ (the future is resolved). The *Async* effect adds a new task to the task pool and *continues* the execution of the current task with the continuation k' and the newly created future fut'. The *Await* effects checks whether the future fut_a in the task pool has been resolved or not; if it is resolved the task continues with the future value, otherwise the task is put back in the pool of tasks (keeping the *Await* effect at the head of the continuation). The *Get* effect is similar to the resolved case of *Await* but does not allow the task to be returned to the pool of tasks. Instead, if the future is not resolved the thread actively polls the matching task until the future is finally resolved using the auxiliary *poll* function. The *Spawn* effect case spawns a new thread that runs the *run* function. In each case where the task does not continue, the body of the function *run* is triggered.

The function $run(t)$ uses the external function $pop(tasks, t)$ to fetch a new unresolved task that should run on thread t, the task is thus of the form $\mathbb{C}(k)$ and the thread continues by evaluating the thunk continuation k.

5.2   Correctness of the Compilation of Actors into Effects

We define in this section a hiding semantics and will prove strong bisimulation between the source program and the hiding semantics of the transformed program.

5.2.1   Hiding Semantics

In translation such as the one defined here, the compiled program must often take several more "administrative" steps than the source program. This makes proof by bisimulation more complex, and requires using weak bisimulation that ignores some steps marked as internal.

In this article we take a stronger approach and prove strong bisimilarity on a derived transition relation. The principle is that internal steps of the transformed program are called silent, and they are by nature deterministic and terminating. We can thus consider that we "normalise" the runtime configuration of the transformed program by systematically applying as many internal steps as possible until a stable state is reached. We discuss this idea further in Sect. 6.

We first state that $hidden(e)$ is true if the top level node in the syntax of e is *colored*; where colored means the term is surrounded by a colored box: $\boxed{e}$. There should be no ambiguity on the node of the syntax that is colored (at least in our translation).

Definition 1 (Hiding semantics). *We define a hiding operation to hide parts of the reduction. It works as follows. We can define a h-reduction $\longrightarrow_h$ that puts a τ label on the transitions that target a node of the syntax that is hidden:*

$$\frac{\sigma, e \longrightarrow_{||} \sigma', e' \quad hidden(e)}{\sigma, e \xrightarrow{\tau}_h \sigma', e'} \qquad \frac{\sigma, e \longrightarrow_{||} \sigma', e' \quad \neg hidden(e)}{\sigma, e \longrightarrow_h \sigma', e'}$$

We finally define the hiding semantics as one non-hidden step followed by any number of hidden step, until no further hidden step can be performed[5]:

$$\sigma, e \Longrightarrow_{||} \sigma, e \iff \sigma, e \longrightarrow_{\mathrm{h}} \xrightarrow{\tau}_{\mathrm{h}}^{*} \sigma', e' \not\xrightarrow{\tau}_{\mathrm{h}}$$

Note that, considering the nodes colored in our translation, the transitions marked as τ should only have a local and deterministic effect on the program state. In practice there are some hidden statements that spawn a thread or launches task for example, but they are immediately and deterministically preceded by a decision point that is visible, here the reaction to an effect. The interleaving of the tau transition have no visible effect on the global state, only the state along the visible transitions is important. This property will be made explicit in our proof of correctness. As a consequence, because the hidden step commutes with all the other steps, each execution of a FUT program compiled into EFF can be seen as a succession of $\Longrightarrow_{||}$. Additionally, except when polling futures the transitive closure of hidden steps terminate. We have the following property, relating our middle-step and small-step semantics.

Theorem 1 (Middle-step semantics). *Consider $e_1 = [\![e_f]\!]_p$. Any EFF reduction of e_1 can be seen as a hiding semantics reduction, modulo a few hidden steps, and a few get operations on unresolved futures:*

$$\sigma_1, e_1 \longrightarrow_{||}^{*} \sigma_2, e_2 \implies \exists \sigma_3, e_3, \sigma_4, e_4. \bigwedge \begin{array}{l} \sigma_1, e_1 \Longrightarrow_{||}^{*} \sigma_3, e_3 \\[4pt] \sigma_2, e_2 \xrightarrow{\tau}_{\mathrm{h}}^{*} \sigma_4, e_4 \\[4pt] \sigma_3, e_3 \xrightarrow{\text{handle-get}}_{||}^{*} \sigma_4, e_4 \end{array}$$

Where $\sigma_3, e_3 \xrightarrow{\text{handle-get}}_{||}^{*} \sigma_4, e_4$ is application (inside an appropriate context) of a HANDLE-EFFECT rule with a Get effect on an unresolved future. In particular, if all futures are resolved, $\sigma_3, e_3 = \sigma_4, e_4$.

This theorem is true because the hidden semantic steps commute, only a special case is needed for handling the polling of unresolved futures.

5.2.2 Bisimulation Definition To help with our bisimulation definition, we now define a few execution contexts that appear commonly in the proof. C_{rec} is the context that corresponds to the recursive knot introduced by `let rec`. Indeed, since `let rec` expresses recursion as an encoding into λ-calculus, the encoding will appear again in each task and can be sugared/de-sugared at will. In addition, C_c and C_r are the contexts in the translated program where *continue* and *run* are respectively executed, parameterised by all their free variables. In the following we thus start each task by C_{rec}, C_c or C_r. More precisely:

---

[5] $\longrightarrow^{*}$ denotes the reflexive transitive closure of the relation $\longrightarrow$.

$$C_{rec}[\ell_{threads}] \triangleq \left(\begin{array}{l} \texttt{let rec } poll(fut) = Poll \texttt{ in} \\ \texttt{let rec } continue(fut, k, t) = Continue \\ \texttt{and } run(t) = Run \texttt{ in} \\ \square \end{array} \right) [tasks \leftarrow \ell_{threads}]$$

$$C_c[\ell_{threads}, fut, K', t] \triangleq C_{rec}[\ell_{threads}][continue(fut, k, t)[k() \leftarrow K']]$$

$$C_r[\ell_{threads}, t] \triangleq C_{rec}[\ell_{threads}][run(t)]$$

Definition 2 (Relation over configurations). *Let R be a relation over pairs of a* FUT *configuration C_{FUT} and a* EFF *configuration C_{EFF}. We also note R_e a relation over pairs of configuration states in* FUT *(i.e., $(\sigma, \ell_{threads})$) and in* EFF *(i.e., (σ, F)).*

Figure 16 defines both relations. The purpose of the relation is to prove the correctness of our compilation scheme. We will prove that R is a strong bisimulation. R is indexed either by $\|$ for parallel configurations, and by a given t to reason about single-threaded configurations of thread t. For single-threaded configurations, the computation can either be in the CONTINUE *case, or the* RUN *case. The most complex relation is on the environments, which details the content of the $\ell_{threads}$ values.*

The translation $[\![ ]\!]_e$ can straightforwardly be extended to contexts (where $[\![\square]\!]_e = \square$). Consequently, we have the following property:

Lemma 1 (Context compilation). $[\![C[e]]\!]_e \equiv [\![C]\!]_e [\![e]\!]_e]$

Proof. By case analysis on the translation rules (and on contexts). $\square$

ENV
$$F_e = F_{e,1} \uplus F_{e,2}$$
$$\forall f \in \mathrm{Dom}(F_v).\, F_v(f) \text{ is a value} \qquad \forall f \in \mathrm{Dom}(F_e).\, F_e(f) \text{ is not a value}$$
$$T_{e,1} = \big[f' \mapsto \mathbb{C}(\lambda().\, [\![e]\!]_e) \mid F_{e,1}(f') = e\big]$$
$$T_{e,2} = \big[f' \mapsto \mathbb{C}\,(\lambda().((\lambda x.C[x])\; e)) \mid [\![F_{e,2}(f')]\!]_e = C[e]\big]$$
$$T_v = \big[f' \mapsto \mathbb{V}([\![v]\!]_e) \mid F_v(f') = v\big]$$
$$\overline{\sigma_{base} \cup \{\ell_{threads} \mapsto T_{e,1} \uplus T_{e,2} \uplus T_v\}, \ell_{threads} \;\; \mathrm{R}_e \;\; \sigma_{base}, F_e \uplus F_v}$$

CONTINUE
$$\frac{\sigma, \ell_{threads} \;\; \mathrm{R}_e \;\; \sigma', F}{\sigma, C_c[\ell_{threads}, f, [\![e]\!]_e, t] \;\; \mathrm{R}_t \;\; \sigma', F, (f \rightarrow e)}$$

RUN
$$\frac{\sigma, \ell_{threads} \;\; \mathrm{R}_e \;\; \sigma', F}{\sigma, C_r[\ell_{threads}, t] \;\; \mathrm{R}_t \;\; \sigma', F, \texttt{Idle}}$$

PAR
$$\frac{\forall t \in T.\;\; \sigma, e_t \;\; \mathrm{R}_t \;\; \sigma', F, s_t}{\sigma, \|_{t \in T}(e_t)^t \;\; \mathrm{R}_\| \;\; \sigma', F, \|_{t \in T}(s_t)^t}$$

Fig. 16. Relation between FUT terms and their compiled version

5.2.3   Correctness of the Compilation Scheme We now establish the correctness of our translation by proving that the relation we exhibited in the previous section is a bisimulation.

Theorem 2 (Correctness of the compilation scheme). *The relation* $R_\parallel$ *is a strong bisimulation where the transition on the* EFF *side is the hiding transition relation, and the transition on the* FUT *side is* $\longrightarrow_\parallel$. *Formally, for all configurations the following holds:*

$$
\sigma_1, P_1 \ R_\parallel \ \sigma_1', F_1, P_1' \ \wedge \ \sigma_1, P_1 \Longrightarrow_\parallel \sigma_2, P_2
$$
$$
\Longrightarrow \exists \sigma_2', F_2, P_2'. \quad \sigma_1', F_1, P_1' \longrightarrow_\parallel \sigma_2', F_2, P_2' \ \wedge \ \sigma_2, P_2 \ R_\parallel \ \sigma_2', F_2, P_2'
$$

and

$$
\sigma_1, P_1 \ R_\parallel \ \sigma_1', F_1, P_1' \wedge \sigma_1', F_1, P_1' \longrightarrow_\parallel \sigma_2', F_2, P_2'
$$
$$
\Longrightarrow \exists \sigma_2, P_2. \quad \sigma_1, P_1 \Longrightarrow_\parallel \sigma_2, P_2 \wedge \sigma_2, P_2 \ R_\parallel \ \sigma_2', F_2, P_2'
$$

so that for any FUT *program p the initial configuration of the program and of its effect translation are bisimilar (with t_0 fresh, and f_0 is the fresh future identifier that has been chosen when triggering the first continue function.).*

$$
\emptyset, (\llbracket e_p \rrbracket_p \, [\mathit{fresh}() \leftarrow f_0])^{t_0} \ R_\parallel \ \emptyset, \emptyset, (f_0 \mapsto e_p)^{t_0}
$$

Proof (sketch). The proof of bisimulation follows a standard structure. For each pair of related configurations we show that the possible reductions made by one configuration can be simulated by the equivalent configuration (in the other calculus). Then a case analysis is performed depending on the rule applied. The set of rules is different between FUT and EFF calculi but on the EFF side, we need to distinguish cases based on the name of the triggered effect, leading to a proof structure similar to the different rules of FUT. Appendix A details the proof that the compiled program simulates the original one. By case analysis on the rule that makes the relation true and the involved reduction. This leads to seven different main cases; we prove simulation in each case.   □

Finally, Theorems 1 and 2 allow us to conclude regarding the correctness of our compilation scheme. Indeed, each execution of a compiled program is equivalent to a middle-step reduction that itself simulates one of the possible executions of our FUT program. Conversely, any execution of our FUT program corresponds (modulo polling of unresolved futures) to a middle-step execution of its compilation, which is in fact one of the EFF executions of the compiled program.

6   Conclusion and Discussion

We have presented an active object library based on effect handlers and proved the correctness of its implementation principles. To prove this correctness, we expressed the implementation as a translation from a future calculus to an effect calculus and proved a bisimulation relation between the source and the transformed program. This illustrates that effects are a very general and versatile construct which can be leveraged to implement concurrency constructs as libraries, including futures. We discuss below a few alternatives that we considered and, more generally, extensions of this work we envision.

Deep and Shallow Handlers. As highlighted at multiple points, we use *shallow* effect handlers, both in our implementation and in our formal development. Shallow effect handlers are not automatically reinstalled upon resuming a continuation, while deep handlers are automatically reinstalled.

In theory, Hillerström and Lindley [12] show that both deep and shallow handlers are equivalent, and showcase code transformation from one to the other. In addition, OCaml provides both versions. In practice, however, for the purpose of implementing a scheduler, shallow handlers offer numerous advantages. First, they make recursion in the *continue* function uniform over all tasks, be they continuations or new tasks. Furthermore, since they allow precise control over when handlers are installed, we can ensure that we never install nested handlers. In our implementation, this was essential to make *continue* and *run* tail-recursive.

Unfortunately, shallow handlers are a bit more delicate to implement for language designers. Furthermore, deep handlers admit a more precise small-step semantics [19]. It remains to be seen if the deep version of our scheduler can be expressed as elegantly as the one showcased in our formalisation.

Relation to Existing Promise-as-Effect Libraries. To develop our active object library, we made our own implementation of promises. This was convenient, as full-control allowed us to tie both together, which was essential for implementing *forward*, notably.

However, implementing an industrial-strength promise library with efficient scheduling, parallelism, and system integration is a significant task. Making several such libraries work together is delicate. In practice, `eio` [15] is trending towards being the standard promise library in OCaml.

Now that we formalised our semantics independently, one of the next steps is to adapt our developments to rely on an existing scheduling library. There are two difficulties here:

- Adapting to different underlying primitives (`eio` uses "suspend", similar to a form of yielding, and "fork" to create new promises).
- Finding a way to extend the scheduler implemented by an existing library, accessing its internal state, without completely breaking its invariants, nor breaking abstraction.

Optimisation on Forward. As we mentioned in Sect. 3, forward is a construct that allows efficient delegation of asynchronous method invocations by making shortcuts when a future is resolved with another one [6]. For simplicity, we decided not to specify forward in our formal development. Its specification and proof is rather straightforward, by introducing an additional effect. In the future, in addition to this formal aspect, we would like to experiment with introducing delegated method calls automatically, following the analogy with tail-call optimisations.

Hiding Semantics and Middle-Step Reductions. Proof of correctness of translations between languages and calculi often reduce to simulation or bisimulation proofs [5,6,16] between a source program and a transformed program. Often, it is however necessary for the transformed program to do more steps than the original one. These additional internal steps are necessary to maintain internal information on the program state. Sometimes, even the source program must also do some internal steps. The usual tool to prove the equivalence in this case is to use a weak bisimulation that "ignores" some steps marked as internal. However, weak bisimulations do not guarantee the preservation of all program properties, in particular liveness properties [8]. In such situations, some previous work prove branching bisimilarity which is stronger but not always sufficient.

In this article, we developed a new "hiding" semantics and a middle-step reduction which executes one non-hidden step, followed by as many hidden steps as possible. This allows us to decide exactly in the specification of the translation which code is "administrative" and which code must really be synchronised. Naturally, in our context, such code is deterministic.

While we developed this in an ad-hoc manner here, we believe this approach can be adapted to many other program translations, simplifying simplifying the proof of correctness for compilers, and program transformations in general.

A   Proof of the Bisimulation Theorem (Theorem 2)

A proof of bisimulation involves two simulation proofs for the same relation. We detail the proof for the first direction: the behaviour of the compiled program is one of the behaviours of the original one. This direction is more complex because of the middle-step semantics and is also more important as it states that the behaviour of the compiled program is a valid one. The other direction is done very similarly with the same arguments as the ones used in the first direction. It however has a different structure as the SOS semantics provides more different cases (but the proof below often needs to distinguish cases according to the current state of the configuration, leading to a similar set of cases overall). We omit the other direction.

Consider $\sigma_1, P_1 \; \mathrm{R}_{\parallel} \; \sigma_1', F_1, P_1'$, and $\sigma_1, P_1 \Longrightarrow_{\parallel} \sigma_2, P_2$. Let i be the thread identifier of the thread involved in the reduction $\Longrightarrow_{\parallel}$ (in case of spawn i is the thread that performs the spawn).

We have $P_1 = Q_1 \parallel e^i$ and $P_1' = Q_1' \parallel s^i$ for some Q_1 and Q_1'. Additionally, $\sigma_1, Q_1 \; \mathrm{R}_{\parallel} \; \sigma_1', F_1, Q_1'$ and $\sigma_1, e \; \mathrm{R}_i \; \sigma_1', F_1, s$.

We do a case analysis on the rule used to prove the R_i relation; two cases are possible:

Continue:

CONTINUE

$$\frac{\sigma_1, \ell_{threads} \; R_e \; \sigma_1', F_1}{\sigma_1, C_c[\ell_{threads}, f, [\![e']\!]_e, i] \; R_i \; \sigma_1', F_1, (f \mapsto e')}$$

In this case, the top level of continue is a *handle* thanks to the context C_c. $\sigma_1, P_1 \Longrightarrow_{||} \sigma_2, P_2$ can result from three possible rules (modulo a SEQ rule at the configuration level and a λ-calculus context rule to reach the reducible statement):

HANDLE-RETURN $[\![e']\!]_e$ must be of the form v (and is inside a handle because of C_c).

We have $\sigma_1, P_1 \Longrightarrow_{||} \sigma_2, P_2$. Its first visible reduction rule must be:

$$\frac{\dfrac{(x \mapsto e_2) \in h}{\sigma_1, \mathtt{handle}(v)\{h\} \longrightarrow \sigma_1, e_2\,[x \leftarrow v]} \; \text{HANDLE-RETURN}}{\dfrac{\sigma_1, C_{rec}\,[\mathtt{handle}(v)\{h\}] \longrightarrow \sigma_1, C_{rec}\,[e_2\,[x \leftarrow v]]}{\sigma_1, Q_1 \,\|\, e^i \longrightarrow_{||} \sigma_1, Q_1 \,\|\, C_{rec}\,[e_3]^i} \; \text{SEQ}} \; \text{CONTEXT}}$$

Where:

C_{rec} the "let ... rec" context

h the effect handlers defined in Continue

$$e = C_c[\ell_{threads}, f, [\![e']\!]_e, i]$$
$$= C_{rec}[\mathtt{handle}(v)\{h\}]$$

$$e_3 = \;\; \ell_{threads}[f] \leftarrow \mathbb{V}(v);$$
$$\qquad run(i)$$

The hidden rules then update the appropriate task in the store and start the *run* function. Overall, we obtain:

$$\sigma_1, Q_1 \,\|\, C_c[\ell_{threads}, f, [\![e']\!]_e, i] \Longrightarrow_{||} \sigma_2, Q_1 \,\|\, C_r[\ell_{threads}, i]^i$$

Where

$$\sigma_2 = \sigma_1\Big[\ell_{threads} \mapsto \sigma_1(\ell_{threads})\,\big[f \mapsto \mathbb{V}(v)\big)\big]\Big]$$

Since $e = C_{rec}[\mathtt{handle}(v)\{h\}]$, by case analysis on the compilation rules, we must have the source expression $e' = v'$ be a FUT value with $v = [\![v']\!]_e$. Then we have:

$$\frac{\dfrac{\sigma_1', F_1, (f \mapsto v')^i \longrightarrow \sigma_1', F_1[f \mapsto v'], \mathtt{Idle}^i}{\sigma_1', F_1, Q_1' \,\|(f \mapsto v')^i \longrightarrow_{||} \sigma_1', F_1[f \mapsto v'], Q_1' \,\|\, \mathtt{Idle}^i} \; \text{ONE-STEP}} \; \text{RETURN}$$

We then need to establish that the new future map and stores are in relation, i.e., $\sigma_2, \ell_{threads} R_e \sigma_1', F_1[f \mapsto v']$.
We recall the ENV rule below:

ENV
$$F_e = F_{e,1} \uplus F_{e,2}$$
$$\forall f \in \mathrm{Dom}(F_v). \, F_v(f) \text{ is a value}$$
$$\forall f \in \mathrm{Dom}(F_e). \, F_e(f) \text{ is not a value}$$
$$T_{e,1} = [f' \mapsto \mathbb{C}(\lambda(). \llbracket e \rrbracket_e) \mid F_{e,1}(f') = e]$$
$$T_{e,2} = \left[f' \mapsto \mathbb{C}\left(\lambda().((\lambda x.C[x]) \, e) \right) \mid \llbracket F_{e,2}(f') \rrbracket_e = C[e] \right]$$
$$T_v = [f' \mapsto \mathbb{V}(\llbracket v \rrbracket_e) \mid F_v(f') = v]$$
$$\overline{\sigma_{base} \cup \{\ell_{threads} \mapsto T_{e,1} \uplus T_{e,2} \uplus T_v\}, \ell_{threads} \ R_e \ \sigma_{base}, F_e \uplus F_v}$$

By inversion on $\sigma_1, \ell_{threads} \, R_e \, \sigma_1', F_1$, we obtain three maps $T_{e,1} \uplus T_{e,2} \uplus T_v$ that ensure the relation. We extend T_v so that $T_v[f] \mapsto \mathbb{V}(v)$ to obtain the relation.
Recall that $v = \llbracket v' \rrbracket_e$; this is sufficient to conclude that

$$\sigma_2, Q_1 \parallel C_r[\ell_{threads}, i]^i \qquad R_\parallel \qquad \sigma_1', F_1[f \mapsto v'], Q_1' \parallel \texttt{Idle}^i$$

HANDLE-STEP $\llbracket e' \rrbracket_e$ must be of the form e_1 where e_1 can only be reduced by a λ-calculus reduction.
We have $\sigma_1, P_1 \Longrightarrow_\parallel \sigma_2, P_2$. Its first visible reduction rule must be:

$$\cfrac{\cfrac{\cfrac{\sigma_1, e_1 \longrightarrow \sigma_2, e_2}{\sigma_1, e_1 \longrightarrow \sigma_2, e_2} \text{ HANDLE-STEP}}{\sigma_1, C_{rec}\,[\texttt{handle}(e_1)\{h\}] \longrightarrow \sigma_2, C_{rec}\,[\texttt{handle}(e_2)\{h\}]} \text{ CONTEXT}}{\sigma_1, Q_1 \parallel e^i \longrightarrow_\parallel \sigma_2, Q_1 \parallel C_{rec}\,[e_3]^i} \text{ SEQ}$$

Where:

C_{rec} the "let ... rec" context

h the effect handlers defined in Continue

$e = C_c[\ell_{threads}, f, \llbracket e' \rrbracket_e, i] = C_{rec}[\texttt{handle}(e_1)\{h\}]$

$e_3 = \texttt{handle}(e_2)\{h\}$

The translation leave λ-calculus terms unchanged, without any hiding, thus there are no follow up hidden rules.
Overall, we obtain:

$$\cfrac{\sigma_1, \llbracket e' \rrbracket_e \longrightarrow \sigma_2, e_2}{\sigma_1, Q_1 \parallel C_c[\ell_{threads}, f, \llbracket e' \rrbracket_e, i] \Longrightarrow_\parallel \sigma_2, Q_1 \parallel C_c[\ell_{threads}, f, e_2, i]}$$

We know that $\sigma_1, \ell_{threads}$ R_e σ_1', F_1. By definition, this means that $\sigma_1 = \sigma_1' \cup \{\ell_{threads} \mapsto T\}$ for some map T. By definition of the translation, $\ell_{threads}$ is not accessible by user code, and thus left unchanged by the reduction on $[\![e']\!]_e$. As such, we have:

$$\sigma_2 = \sigma_2' \cup \{\ell_{threads} \mapsto T\} \qquad \sigma_1', [\![e']\!]_e \longrightarrow \sigma_2', e_2$$

By case analysis on the translation and the λ-calculus reduction rules, e' must be reduced by the same λ-calculus reduction rule than $[\![e']\!]_e$. Thus:

$$\frac{\dfrac{\sigma_1', e' \longrightarrow \sigma_2', e_2'}{\sigma_1', F_1, (f \mapsto e')^i \longrightarrow \sigma_2', F_1, (f \mapsto e_2')^i} \text{ STEP}}{\sigma_1', F_1, Q_1' \,\|\, (f \mapsto e')^i \longrightarrow_{\|} \sigma_2', F_1, Q_1' \,\|\, (f \mapsto e_2')^i} \text{ ONE-STEP}$$

This case analysis and by determinism of our λ-calculus, we have $[\![e_2']\!]_e = e_2$. We also have $\sigma_2, \ell_{threads} R_e \sigma_2', F_1$.
This is sufficient to conclude that

$$\sigma_2, Q_1 \,\|\, C_c[\ell_{threads}, f, [\![e']\!]_e, i]^i \quad R_{\|} \quad \sigma_2', F_1, Q_1' \,\|\, C_c[\ell_{threads}, f, [\![e_2']\!]_e, i]$$

HANDLE-EFFECT $[\![e']\!]_e$ must be of the form $C[\texttt{throw}(E(x))]$ (and is inside a handle because of C_c). We distinguish by the effect captured:
   $Async(job, t')$. We have $\sigma_1, P_1 \Longrightarrow_{\|} \sigma_2, P_2$. Its first visible reduction rule must be:

SEQ+HANDLE-EFFECT+CONTEXT
$$\frac{(Async(job, t'), k' \mapsto e_2) \in h \qquad Async \notin \text{captured\_effects}(C)}{\begin{array}{c} \sigma_1, C_{rec}\Big[\texttt{handle}(C[\texttt{throw}(Async(\, \lambda(). \ e'', t))])\{h\}\Big] \\ \longrightarrow \sigma_1, C_{rec}\Big[e_2 \, [t' \leftarrow t] \Big[job \leftarrow \, \lambda(). \ e''\Big] [k' \leftarrow \lambda y.C[y]]\Big] \end{array}}{\sigma_1, Q_1 \,\|\, e^i \longrightarrow_{\|} \sigma_1, Q_1 \,\|\, C_{rec}[e_3]^i}$$

Where:

C_{rec} the "let ... rec" context

h the effect handlers defined in Continue

$e = C_c[\ell_{threads}, f, [\![e']\!]_e, i]$
$\quad = C_{rec}[\texttt{handle}(C[\texttt{throw}(Async(\, \lambda(). \ e'', t))])\{h\}]$

$e_3 = \texttt{let } fut' = (t, fresh()) \texttt{ in}$

$\quad\quad \ell_{threads}[fut'] \leftarrow \mathbb{C}(\, \lambda(). \ e'');$

$\quad\quad continue(f, \lambda().(\lambda y.C[y])(fut'), i)$

By definition of the translation, and because the reduction is possible, the arguments of the `Async` effect must be a thunk task, and its second argument must be a thread identifier (it can be an expression but this one is entirely evaluated before triggering the effect). This as some consequences on the considered FUT configuration, e.g. e' is of the form $\texttt{AsyncAt}(e_0, t)$. Additionally, t is the same on both side as thread identifiers are preserved by the translation (this can be proven by case analysis on the definition of R_i).

The hidden rules apply then update the suspended tasks in the store and start the *continue* function. The last hidden reduction rule is the beta-reduction that de-thunks the continuation $\lambda().(\lambda y.C[y])(\mathit{fut}')$ inside the handler of continue and puts fut' back into the invocation context.

Overall, we obtain:

$$\sigma_1, Q_1 \parallel C_c[\ell_{threads}, f, [\![e']\!]_e, i] \Longrightarrow_{\parallel} \sigma_2, Q_1 \parallel C_c[\ell_{threads}, f, C[\mathit{fut}'], i]^i$$

Where

$$\sigma_2 \;=\; \sigma_1\Big[\ell_{threads} \;\mapsto\; \sigma_1(\ell_{threads})\big[\mathit{fut}' \mapsto \mathbb{C}(\lambda(). \, e'')\big]\Big]$$

Since $e = C_{rec}[\texttt{handle}(C[\texttt{throw}(Async(\lambda(). \, e'', t))])]\{h\}]$, by case analysis on the compilation rules, we must have the source expression $e' = C_1[\texttt{asyncAt}(e_1', t)]$ where $C = [\![C_1]\!]_e$ and $e'' = [\![e_1']\!]_e$ by Lemma 1. Note also that the set of future identifiers are the same in the FUT program and in its translation, and thus $\mathit{fut}' = (t, \mathit{fresh}())$ is a fresh future in the FUT configuration. Then we have:

ASYNC+ONE-STEP
$$\frac{\mathit{fut}' = (t, \mathit{lf}) \qquad \mathit{fut}' \notin \mathrm{Dom}(F_1)}{\sigma_1', F_1, Q_1' \parallel (f \mapsto C_1[\texttt{asyncAt}(e_1', t)])^i \longrightarrow_{\parallel} \sigma_1', F_1\big[\mathit{fut}' \mapsto e_1'\big], Q_1' \parallel (f \mapsto C_1[\mathit{fut}'])^i}$$

We then need to establish that the new future map and stores are in relation, i.e., $\sigma_2, \ell_{threads} R_e \sigma_1', F_1\big[\mathit{fut}' \mapsto e_1'\big]$.

We recall the ENV rule below:

ENV
$$F_e = F_{e,1} \uplus F_{e,2}$$
$$\forall f \in \mathrm{Dom}(F_v). \, F_v(f) \text{ is a value}$$
$$\forall f \in \mathrm{Dom}(F_e). \, F_e(f) \text{ is not a value}$$
$$T_{e,1} = [f' \mapsto \mathbb{C}(\lambda(). \, [\![e]\!]_e) \mid F_{e,1}(f') = e]$$
$$T_{e,2} = [f' \mapsto \mathbb{C}\,(\lambda().((\lambda x.C[x])\; e)) \mid [\![F_{e,2}(f')]\!]_e = C[e]]$$
$$T_v = [f' \mapsto \mathbb{V}([\![v]\!]_e) \mid F_v(f') = v]$$
$$\overline{\sigma_{base} \cup \{\ell_{threads} \mapsto T_{e,1} \uplus T_{e,2} \uplus T_v\}, \ell_{threads} \; R_e \; \sigma_{base}, F_e \uplus F_v}$$

By inversion on $\sigma_1, \ell_{threads} \; R_e \; \sigma_1', F_1$, we obtain tree maps $T_{e,1} \uplus T_{e,2} \uplus T_v$ that ensure the relation. We then extend $T_{e,1}$ so that $\ell_{threads}[fut'] \mapsto \mathbb{C}(\lambda().\,[\![e_1']\!]_e)$ to obtain the relation. This is sufficient to conclude that

$$\sigma_2, Q_1 \parallel C_c[\ell_{threads}, f, C[fut'], i]^i \quad R_{\parallel}$$
$$\sigma_1', F_1\left[fut' \mapsto e_1'\right], Q_1' \parallel (f \mapsto C_1[fut'])^i$$

$Get(f')$. We have $\sigma_1, P_1 \Longrightarrow_{\parallel} \sigma_2, P_2$. Its first visible reduction rule must be:

$$\text{SEQ+HANDLE-EFFECT+CONTEXT}$$

$$\frac{\begin{array}{c}(Get(fut_g), k' \mapsto e_2) \in h \qquad Get \notin \text{captured\_effects}(C) \\ \hline \sigma_1, C_{rec}\left[\text{handle}(C[\text{throw}(Get(f'))])\{h\}\right] \\ \longrightarrow \sigma_1, C_{rec}\left[e_2\left[fut_g \leftarrow f'\right]\left[k' \leftarrow \lambda y.C[y]\right]\right]\end{array}}{\sigma_1, Q_1 \parallel e^i \longrightarrow_{\parallel} \sigma_1, Q_1 \parallel C_{rec}[e_3]^i}$$

Where[6]:

C_{rec} the "let ... rec" context

h the effect handlers defined in Continue

$e = C_c[\ell_{threads}, f, [\![e']\!]_e, i]$
$\quad = C_{rec}[\text{handle}(C[\text{throw}(Get(f'))])\{h\}]$

$e_3 = \;$ `let `$v = poll(f')$` in`
$\qquad continue(f, \lambda().((\lambda y.C[y])\; v), i)$

The argument of the `Get` effect must be a future reference that is totally evaluated for the rule to succeed. If it is not a future the evaluation of *poll* fails. If it is not fully evaluated, the reduction should first occur inside the argument of the `Get` effect.

Details on Poll Reductions. At this point, we look at hidden reductions, which must start in the body of *poll*. If the future is unresolved, *poll* loops forever and the medium step reduction diverges. This means either that the future never resolves, and this divergence in EFF simulates a deadlock in FUT; or that we could make reductions in other threads to resolve the deadlock. In the second case, the semantics for EFF would interleave loops in *poll* and reduction in other threads.

---

[6] A few substitutions have occurred inside *poll* by definition of C_c. We omit them here not to clutter the proof.

Such interleaving is equivalent to triggering the Get event at the end, with a single loop in *poll*. The current theorem only consider this last interleaving. Overall, if there is a medium step reduction it means that the future is resolved.

In this case, the future has been resolved, and, by bisimilarity on the stores (R_e) we have $F_1(f') = v$ and $\sigma_1(\ell_{threads})[f'] = v$ for some v. We obtain after a couple of steps of beta-reduction:

$$\sigma_1, Q_1 \parallel C_c[\ell_{threads}, f, [\![e']\!]_e, i] \Longrightarrow_{\parallel} \sigma_1, Q_1 \parallel C_c[\ell_{threads}, f, C[v], i]^i$$

Since $e = C_{rec}[\texttt{handle}(C[\texttt{throw}(Get(f'))])h]$, by case analysis on the compilation rules, we have $e' = C_1[\texttt{get}(f')]$ where $C = [\![C_1]\!]_e$ by Lemma 1. Then we have:

GET+ONE-STEP
$$\frac{(f' \mapsto v) \in F_1}{\sigma_1', F_1, Q_1' \parallel (f \mapsto C_1[\texttt{get}(f')])^i \longrightarrow_{\parallel} \sigma_1', F_1, Q_1' \parallel (f \mapsto C_1[v])^i}$$

This is sufficient to conclude that

$$\sigma_1, Q_1 \parallel C_c[\ell_{threads}, f, C[v], i]^i \quad R_{\parallel} \quad \sigma_1', F_1, Q_1' \parallel (f \mapsto C_1[v])^i$$

$Await(f')$. The case when the awaited future is resolved is similar to the case of the Get effect just above. We only detail the proof in case the future is still unresolved.

We have $\sigma_1, P_1 \Longrightarrow_{\parallel} \sigma_2, P_2$. Its first visible reduction rule must be:

SEQ+HANDLE-EFFECT+CONTEXT
$$\frac{(Await(fut_a), k' \mapsto e_2) \in h \qquad Await \notin \text{captured\_effects}(C)}{\dfrac{\sigma_1, C_{rec}[\texttt{handle}(C[\texttt{throw}(Await(f'))])\{h\}]}{\longrightarrow \sigma_1, C_{rec}[e_2[fut_a \leftarrow f'][k' \leftarrow \lambda y.C[y]]]}}{\sigma_1, Q_1 \parallel e^i \longrightarrow_{\parallel} \sigma_1, Q_1 \parallel C_{rec}[e_3]^i}$$

Where:

C_{rec} the "let ... rec" context

h the effect handlers defined in Continue

$$e = C_c[\ell_{threads}, f, [\![e']\!]_e, i]$$
$$= C_{rec}[\texttt{handle}(C[\texttt{throw}(Await(f'))])\{h\}]$$

$$e_3 = \texttt{match } \ell_{threads}[f']\{$$
$$\mid \mathbb{V}(v) \mapsto continue(f, \lambda().((\lambda y.C[y])\; v))$$
$$\mid {}_{\_} \mapsto \texttt{let } k''() = (\lambda y.C[y])\; (\texttt{throw}(Await(f'))) \texttt{ in}$$
$$\ell_{threads}[f] \leftarrow \mathbb{C}(k''); run(i)$$
$$\}$$

Like in the Get case, the argument of the Await effect must be a future reference that is totally evaluated for the rule to succeed.
When the future is unresolved, $\ell_{threads}[f']$ is not a value (it is not mapped or mapped to a $\mathbb{C}$). By definition of R_e we necessarily have: $\nexists v.\,(f' \mapsto v) \in F_1$. Then a few hidden beta reduction steps lead to the following configuration:

$$\sigma_1, Q_1 \parallel C_c[\ell_{threads}, f, [\![e']\!]_e, t] \Longrightarrow_{\parallel} \sigma_2, Q_1 \parallel C_r[\ell_{threads}, i]^i$$

Where

$$\sigma_2 = \sigma_1 \Big[\ell_{threads} \mapsto \sigma_1(\ell_{threads})$$
$$[f \mapsto \mathbb{C}(\lambda().((\lambda y.C[y])\; (\texttt{throw}(Await(f')))))]\Big]$$

Since $e = C_{rec}[\texttt{handle}(C[\texttt{throw}(Await(f'))])h]$, by case analysis on the compilation rules, we have $e' = C_1[\texttt{await}(f')]$ where $C = [\![C_1]\!]_e$ by Lemma 1. Thus on the FUT side, we have:

AWAIT-YIELD+ONE-STEP
$$\frac{\nexists v.\,(f' \mapsto v) \in F_1}{\begin{array}{c}\sigma_1', F_1, Q_1' \parallel (f \mapsto C_1[\texttt{await}(f')])^i \\ \longrightarrow_{\parallel} \sigma_1', F_1\,[f \mapsto C_1[\texttt{await}(f')]], Q_1' \parallel \texttt{Idle}^i\end{array}}$$

We easily obtain that $\sigma_2, \ell_{threads} \; R_e \; \sigma_1', F_1\,[f \mapsto C_1[\texttt{await}(f')]]$ by expanding the environment $T_{e,2}$ in the ENV rule.
With the arguments above and the case RUN of $R_{\parallel}$ we conclude:

$$\sigma_2, Q_1 \parallel C_r[\ell_{threads}, i]^i \quad R_{\parallel} \quad \sigma_1', F_1\,[f \mapsto C_1[\texttt{await}(f')]], Q_1' \parallel \texttt{Idle}^i$$

Spawn(). We have $\sigma_1, P_1 \Longrightarrow_{\|} \sigma_2, P_2$. Its first visible reduction rule must be:

SEQ+HANDLE-EFFECT+CONTEXT

$$\frac{(Spawn(), k' \mapsto e_2) \in h \qquad Spawn \notin \text{captured\_effects}(C)}{\sigma_1, C_{rec}[\texttt{handle}(C[\texttt{throw}(Spawn())])\{h\}] \longrightarrow \sigma_1, e_2\,[k' \leftarrow \lambda y.C[y]]}$$
$$\sigma_1, Q_1 \parallel e^i \longrightarrow_{\|} \sigma_1, Q_1 \parallel e_2^i$$

With: C_{rec} the "let ... rec" context of the continue handler inside C_c, h the effect handlers defined in Continue, additionally:

$$e = C_{rec}[\texttt{handle}(C[\texttt{throw}(Spawn())])\{h\}]$$
$$= C_c[\ell_{threads}, f, \llbracket e' \rrbracket_e, t]$$
$$e_2 = \texttt{let } t' = \texttt{spawn}(run) \texttt{ in } continue(fut, \lambda().k'(t'), t)$$

The first hidden rule applied is

SPAWN (HIDDEN)

$$\frac{tid \notin tids(P) \cup \{i\}}{\sigma_1, Q_1 \parallel C_2[\texttt{spawn}(run)]^i \longrightarrow_{\|} \sigma_1, Q_1 \parallel C_2[tid]^i \parallel C_c[(run\ tid)]^{tid}}$$

Where $e_2 = C_2[\texttt{spawn}(run)]$. This is followed by steps of beta reduction to reduce the $\texttt{let } t' = \dots$ construct, trigger continue, pass the associated tid and de-thunk the $\lambda().\lambda y.C[y](tid)$ inside continue. We obtain the following configuration

$$\sigma_1, Q_1 \parallel C_c[\ell_{threads}, f, C[tid], t]^i \parallel C_c[(run\ tid)]^{tid}$$

Finally, by a step of beta reduction in the thread tid we obtain the right evaluation context C_r

$$\sigma_1, Q_1 \parallel C_c[\ell_{threads}, f, C[tid], t]^i \parallel C_r[\ell_{threads}, tid]^{tid}$$

This configuration is not reducible by a hidden transition. Thus

$$\sigma_1, C_{rec}[\texttt{handle}(C[\texttt{throw}(Spawn())])\{h\}]$$
$$\Longrightarrow_{\|} \sigma_1, Q_1 \parallel C_c[\ell_{threads}, f, C[tid], t]^i \parallel C_r[\ell_{threads}, tid]^{tid}$$

By case analysis on the terms involved in $\sigma_1, P_1 \ \text{R}_{\|} \ \sigma_1', F_1, P_1'$ we have $e' = C_1[\texttt{spawn}()]$ where $C = \llbracket C_1 \rrbracket_e$ by Lemma 1. We then have:

SPAWN

$$\frac{tid \notin tids(Q_1') \cup \{i\}}{\sigma_1', F_1, Q_1' \parallel (f \mapsto C_1[\texttt{spawn}()])^i \longrightarrow_{\|}}$$
$$\sigma_1', F_1, Q_1' \parallel (f \mapsto C_1[tid])^i \parallel \texttt{Idle}^{tid}$$

Note that by definition of $R_{\parallel}$ the set of used thread identifiers is the same in both configurations, wo we can take the same fresh tid. Note also that the store and the future map are unchanged. Comparing thread by thread, we can directly apply rule RUN and rule CONT for the two processes tid and i, which leads to the conclusion:

$$\sigma_1, Q_1 \parallel C_c[\ell_{threads}, f, C[tid], t]^i \parallel C_r[\ell_{threads}, tid]^{tid}$$
$$R_{\parallel} \quad \sigma_1', F_1, Q_1' \parallel (f \mapsto C_1[tid])^i \parallel \mathtt{Idle}^{tid}$$

Run:

$$\frac{\text{RUN}}{\sigma_1, \ell_{threads} \quad R_e \quad \sigma_1', F_1}{\sigma_1, C_r[\ell_{threads}, i] \quad R_i \quad \sigma_1', F_1, \mathtt{Idle}}$$

The only first applicable rule is the pop operation reduction that picks a new available thread:

$$\sigma, C_r[\ell_{threads}, i] \xrightarrow{\text{pop}}_h Run\,[t \leftarrow i]$$
$$\xrightarrow{\tau}{}_h^* \sigma_2, C_c[\ell_{threads}, f_2, e_2, i]$$

Note that pop ensures that f_2 is of the form $f_2 = (i, lf)$. Using only reductions in the thread i and such that: $\sigma_1(\ell_{threads})[f_2] = \mathbb{C}(\lambda(). \llbracket F_1(f_2) \rrbracket_e)^7$ by definition of R_i and $e_2 = \llbracket F_1(f_2) \rrbracket_e{}^8$ by definition of pop. Note that the last step of reduction is inside continue and de-thunks the new task $((\lambda().e_2()) \longrightarrow e_2)^9$. We additionally have:

$$\sigma_2 = \sigma_1[\ell_{threads} \mapsto \sigma_1(\ell_{threads}) \setminus f_2]$$

From the points above, we obtain (with $f_2 = (i, lf)$):

$$\frac{\text{SCHEDULE}}{(f_2 \mapsto F_1(f_2)) \in F_1 \qquad F_1(f_2) \text{ is not a value}}{\sigma_1', F_1, Q_1' \parallel \mathtt{Idle}^i \longrightarrow_{\parallel} \sigma_1', F_1 \setminus f_2, Q_1' \parallel (f_2 \mapsto F_1(f_2))^i}$$

Note that $F_1(f_2)$ is not a value by construction of the equivalence on stores (Fig. 16). Finally (the equivalence on the store can be trivially checked):

$$\frac{\text{CONTINUE}}{\sigma_2, \ell_{threads} \quad R_e \quad \sigma_1', F_1 \setminus f_2}{\sigma_2, C_c[\ell_{threads}, f_2, \llbracket F_1(f_2) \rrbracket_e, i] \quad R_i \quad \sigma_2', F_1 \setminus f_2, (f_2 \mapsto F_1(f_2))}$$

This immediately concludes by adding the other threads (in Q_1 and Q_1') and obtaining the $R_{\parallel}$ relation on the obtained configurations. □

---

[7] Resp. $\sigma_1(\ell_{threads})[f_2] = \mathbb{C}\,(\lambda().((\lambda x.C[x])\ e))$.

[8] Resp. $\llbracket F_1(f_2) \rrbracket_e = C[e]$ and $e_2 = \mathbb{C}\,(\lambda().((\lambda x.C[x])\ e))$.

[9] Resp. with two steps of beta-reductions.

References

1. Baker Jr., H.G., Hewitt, C.: The incremental garbage collection of processes. In: Proceedings Symposium on Artificial Intelligence and Programming Languages, New York, NY, USA, pp. 55–59 (1977)
2. Bauer, A., Pretnar, M.: Programming with algebraic effects and handlers. J. Log. Algebraic Methods Program. **84**(1), 108–123 (2015). https://doi.org/10.1016/j.jlamp.2014.02.001
3. de Boer, F., et al.: A survey of active object languages. ACM Comput. Surv. **50**(5), 76:1–76:39 (2017). Article 76
4. Caromel, D., Henrio, L., Serpette, B.: Asynchronous and deterministic objects. In: Proceedings of the 31st ACM SIGPLAN-SIGACT Symposium on Principles of Programming Languages, pp. 123–134. ACM Press (2004)
5. Chappe, N., Henrio, L., Maillé, A., Moy, M., Renaud, H.: An optimised flow for futures: from theory to practice. CoRR abs/2107.07298 (2021). https://arxiv.org/abs/2107.07298
6. Fernandez-Reyes, K., Clarke, D., Castegren, E., Vo, H.P.: Forward to a promising future. In: Di Marzo Serugendo, G., Loreti, M. (eds.) COORDINATION 2018. LNCS, vol. 10852, pp. 162–180. Springer, Cham (2018). https://doi.org/10.1007/978-3-319-92408-3_7
7. Fernandez-Reyes, K., Clarke, D., Henrio, L., Johnsen, E.B., Wrigstad, T.: Godot: all the benefits of implicit and explicit futures. In: Donaldson, A.F. (ed.) 33rd European Conference on Object-Oriented Programming (ECOOP 2019). Leibniz International Proceedings in Informatics (LIPIcs), vol. 134, pp. 2:1–2:28. Schloss Dagstuhl-Leibniz-Zentrum fuer Informatik, Dagstuhl (2019). https://drops.dagstuhl.de/opus/volltexte/2019/10794. Distinguished artefact
8. Graf, S., Sifakis, J.: Readiness semantics for regular processes with silent actions. In: Ottmann, T. (ed.) ICALP 1987. LNCS, vol. 267, pp. 115–125. Springer, Heidelberg (1987). https://doi.org/10.1007/3-540-18088-5_10
9. Halstead, R.H., Jr.: MULTILISP: a language for concurrent symbolic computation. ACM Trans. Program. Lang. Syst. (TOPLAS) **7**(4), 501–538 (1985)
10. Henrio, L.: Data-flow explicit futures. Research report, I3S, Université Côte d'Azur (2018). https://hal.archives-ouvertes.fr/hal-01758734
11. Henrio, L., Johnsen, E.B., Pun, V.K.I.: Active objects with deterministic behaviour. In: Dongol, B., Troubitsyna, E. (eds.) IFM 2020. LNCS, vol. 12546, pp. 181–198. Springer, Cham (2020). https://doi.org/10.1007/978-3-030-63461-2_10
12. Hillerström, D., Lindley, S.: Shallow effect handlers. In: Ryu, S. (ed.) APLAS 2018. LNCS, vol. 11275, pp. 415–435. Springer, Cham (2018). https://doi.org/10.1007/978-3-030-02768-1_22
13. Johnsen, E.B., Blanchette, J.C., Kyas, M., Owe, O.: Intra-object versus inter-object: concurrency and reasoning in Creol. In: Proceedings of the 2nd International Workshop on Harnessing Theories for Tool Support in Software (TTSS 2008). Electronic Notes in Theoretical Computer Science, vol. 243, pp. 89–103. Elsevier (2009)
14. Johnsen, E.B., Hähnle, R., Schäfer, J., Schlatte, R., Steffen, M.: ABS: a core language for abstract behavioral specification. In: Aichernig, B.K., de Boer, F.S., Bonsangue, M.M. (eds.) FMCO 2010. LNCS, vol. 6957, pp. 142–164. Springer, Heidelberg (2011). https://doi.org/10.1007/978-3-642-25271-6_8
15. Leonard, T., et al.: Eio 1.0 - effects-based IO for OCaml 5. OCaml Workshop (2023)

16. Leroy, X.: Formal certification of a compiler back-end, or: programming a compiler with a proof assistant. In: 33rd ACM Symposium on Principles of Programming Languages, pp. 42–54. ACM Press (2006). https://xavierleroy.org/publi/compiler-certif.pdf
17. Liskov, B., Shrira, L.: Promises: linguistic support for efficient asynchronous procedure calls in distributed systems. In: PLDI 1988, pp. 260–267. Association for Computing Machinery, New York (1988). https://doi.org/10.1145/53990.54016
18. Niehren, J., Schwinghammer, J., Smolka, G.: A concurrent lambda calculus with futures. Theor. Comput. Sci. **364**(3), 338–356 (2006)
19. Sieczkowski, F., Pyzik, M., Biernacki, D.: A general fine-grained reduction theory for effect handlers. Proc. ACM Program. Lang. **7**(ICFP) (2023). https://doi.org/10.1145/3607848
20. Sivaramakrishnan, K.C.: https://github.com/kayceesrk/ocaml5-tutorial. Accessed 30 May 2023
21. Sivaramakrishnan, K.C., et al.: Retrofitting parallelism onto OCaml. Proc. ACM Program. Lang. **4**(ICFP), 113:1–113:30 (2020). https://doi.org/10.1145/3408995
22. Sivaramakrishnan, K.C., Dolan, S., White, L., Kelly, T., Jaffer, S., Madhavapeddy, A.: Retrofitting effect handlers onto OCaml. In: Freund, S.N., Yahav, E. (eds.) PLDI 2021: 42nd ACM SIGPLAN International Conference on Programming Language Design and Implementation, Virtual Event, Canada, 20–25 June 2021, pp. 206–221. ACM (2021). https://doi.org/10.1145/3453483.3454039
23. Taura, K., Matsuoka, S., Yonezawa, A.: ABCL/f: a future-based polymorphic typed concurrent object-oriented language - its design and implementation. In: Proceedings of the DIMACS Workshop on Specification of Parallel Algorithms, pp. 275–292. American Mathematical Society (1994)
24. Vouillon, J.: LWT: a cooperative thread library. In: Sumii, E. (ed.) Proceedings of the ACM Workshop on ML, 2008, Victoria, BC, Canada, 21 September 2008, pp. 3–12. ACM (2008). https://doi.org/10.1145/1411304.1411307

Actor-Based Designs for Distributed Self-organisation Programming

Roberto Casadei[1] , Ferruccio Damiani[2](✉) , Gianluca Torta[2] ,
and Mirko Viroli[1]

[1] Alma Mater Studiorum–Università di Bologna, Cesena, Italy
{roby.casadei,mirko.viroli}@unibo.it
[2] Università degli Studi di Torino, Turin, Italy
{ferruccio.damiani,gianluca.torta}@unito.it

Abstract. Self-organisation and collective adaptation are highly desired features for several kinds of large-scale distributed systems including robotic swarms, computational ecosystems, wearable collectives, and Internet-of-Things systems. These kinds of distributed processes, addressing functional and non-functional aspects of complex socio-technical systems, can emerge in an engineered/controlled way from (re)active decentralised activity and interaction across all physical and logical system devices. In this work, we study how the Actors programming model can be adopted to support collective self-organising behaviours. Specifically, we analyse the features of the Actors model, such as reactivity, asynchrony, and locality, that are instrumental for implementing the adaptive coordination of large-scale systems, and discuss potential actor-based designs, from simple ad-hoc implementation of algorithms to a full-fledged general toolkit. In particular, the approach is incarnated in the aggregate computing paradigm, which stands as a comprehensive engineering approach for self-organisation. This is based on Akka, and can be fully programmed in the Scala programming language thanks to the ScaFi aggregate computing toolkit.

Keywords: Actors · Collective intelligence · Collective adaptive systems · Self-organisation · Programming models · Aggregate computing

1 Introduction

In the last decades, two key trends have been taking place in computer science and technology. First, more and more heterogeneous computing-enabled devices are being deployed into our environments, with larger scales and densities expected in the future, eventually creating enormous socio-technical ensembles. Secondly, there is an increasing need towards automation, demanding software systems to be more *autonomous* [30] (or *autonomic* [36]), and to exhibit so-called *self-* properties* [47] (e.g., self-managing, self-adaptive, self-repairing,

F. de Boer et al. (Eds.): *Active Object Languages: Current Research Trends*,
LNCS 14360, pp. 37–58, 2024.
https://doi.org/10.1007/978-3-031-51060-1_2

etc.). These two trends together give rise to new potential applications and corresponding challenges, addressed through various approaches. In particular, a prominent *nature-inspired* [16] technique for the decentralised self-management of large ensembles of computing devices is *self-organisation*, the process whereby a system autonomously (i.e., without external control) seeks and sustains its order or structures [29], which is studied and implemented across different subfields of computer science [28,32,44,49]. Self-organisation can be an important component (or outcome) of collective intelligence [21]. A main classification of self-organisation engineering [17] is based on the distinction between *automatic* (i.e., based on learning and evolution) and *manual* approaches (where programmers use languages to express self-organisation programs—cf. *macroprogramming* [22]).

In this chapter, we focus on the latter approach and, in particular, we are interested in how *programming abstractions and paradigms* may support *self-organisation programming*. Specifically, we investigate how the *Actor model* can contribute to address the emergence of collective and self-organising behaviour. Indeed, self-organisation is generally related to particular aspects of actor systems, including reactivity, asynchrony, and locality. To do so, we develop actor-based solutions of well-known self-organising behaviours (*gradients* [7,41] and derived ones), and relate them with corresponding programs expressed in the *aggregate computing* paradigm [54] which is, currently and to the best of our knowledge, the most powerful and researched approach to self-organisation programming. What we find is that the plain Actor model has a relevant *abstraction gap* (distance between the problem and the solution), making it more suitable as a paradigm for the development of a middleware of a more high-level and declarative approach like aggregate computing, than as a solution for end-to-end design of self-organising behaviour. Still, research should be carried out to investigate what kinds of Actor extensions may help in the design and implementation of self-organisation, or what features of actors may improve aspects of aggregate computations (e.g., fine-grained scheduling of sub-computations).

The presentation is organised as follows. Section 2 provides background on self-organisation programming, reference examples of self-organising behaviour, and the Actor model (also through the Akka implementation [46]). Section 3 discusses actor-based designs of the self-healing gradient. Section 4 presents the actor-based design of the ScaFi aggregate computing middleware [26]. Finally, Sect. 5 provides a discussion and delineates directions for further research.

2   Background

In this section, we recall background information about self-organisation engineering and describe in detail two example self-adaptive algorithms (Sect. 2.1); then, we briefly recall the Actors model and its Akka implementation (Sect. 2.2). While other actor languages, such as Erlang [5], could have worked as well as Akka, we consider Akka since it is based on Scala, which is also the host language of the ScaFi aggregate programming domain-specific language (DSL) considered in this work (cf. Sect. 2.1) .

2.1 Self-organisation and Collective Adaptive Systems

Self organization is often meant as a bottom-up decentralised process where macro-level structures and behaviours *emerge* from micro-level activities and interactions.

In modern cyber-physical systems such as the Internet of Things [6] and swarm robotics [17], self-organisation directly concerns the collective behaviour of large sets of computing and interacting devices. Engineering such systems is therefore a challenge of great practical importance, that can be addressed drawing from research areas such as *collective adaptive systems* [28], *macroprogramming* [22], *multi-agent systems* [57], and *aggregate computing* [54].

A main distinction in self-organisation engineering can be made between *automatic* approaches, whereby self-organising behaviour is learned (cf. multi-agent reinforcement learning [19,58]), evolved (cf. evolutionary robotics [51]), or synthesised [48]; and *manual* approaches [39], which are based on the definition of programs by programmers, e.g., in terms of control rules or designs involving patterns of information flow [56]. The manual approaches tend to differ based on the levels of *heterogeneity* and *scale*: small-scale heterogeneous systems can be programmed using *multi-agent programming* [15] or *choreographic* [40] approaches, whereas large-scale homogeneous systems are generally programmed using *macroprogramming* [22] approaches, such as *ensemble computing* [42], or *aggregate computing* [54] approaches. Note that *hybrid* automatic/manual approaches also exist—cf. approaches where program sketches are filled with automatically generated/searched behaviours [2].

In this chapter, we focus on *manual approaches for programming large homogeneous systems*. In particular, this activity can be supported by suitable *programming abstractions* supporting declarative specifications of collective behaviours. Examples of abstractions include first-class *ensembles* [42] or collective data structures like *computational fields* [38,54], In the following, we will focus on the computational field abstraction, offered by *Aggregate Computing (AC)*.

Aggregate Computing (AC). AC systems consist of a (possibly large) number of computational devices, connected in a network, and all operating at asynchronous *rounds* of execution, each round consisting of *sense–compute–act* steps, where the compute step involves the evaluation of an aggregate program against the currently sensed contextual information. An output or state of a whole or part of a distributed system can then be represented as a *field* of values computed by all the device constituting its domain. For instance, the movement of a swarm may be described by a field of velocity vectors; or, the temperature in a room may be denoted by the field of temperature readings of all the sensors there. The computational field is the fundamental abstraction for AC, and programming AC systems roughly means describing how such fields are manipulated in space-time. The essence of the programming model is captured by a minimal core language called the *field calculus* (FC) [8], which provides a set of functional constructs for handling the stateful evolution of fields and neighbour-based communications. A device can only directly communicate (in broadcast) with its *neighbours*, as defined by an application-specific logical or physical (ad-hoc) proximity relation. In each device, a round of computations consists mainly of three steps: (i) creation/update of the execution context, consisting of previous device state, the most recent messages received from neighbours, and values sampled from local sensors; (ii) local execution of the aggregate program, which produces a logically single result (*output*); (iii) broadcast of part of the output to all the neighbours (this part is called the *export*), and possible activation of the actuators on the basis of the provided output.

Reference Example #1: Self-healing Gradient. As a first, simple example of a self-organising computation, we consider the *gradient* [7,41], namely the self-healing field of minimum path distances from any node to a source node. A simple implementation is based on the distributed Bellman-Ford algorithm, to be executed by all the devices repeatedly in rounds (where the rounds serve to integrate and propagate up-to-date information):

$$g(\delta, src) := \begin{cases} 0 & \text{if } src(\delta) \\ \min\{g(\delta', src) + d(\delta, \delta') : \delta' \in N(\delta)\} & \text{otherwise.} \end{cases} \tag{1}$$

The algorithm estimates the minimum distance of a device from a *source* device (i.e., a device where predicate $src()$ is true). We assume that function $d()$ returns the *current* distance between two devices, and $N()$ returns the set of current neighbours of a device. At each round, a device δ which is not a source, estimates $g()$ by considering the set of distances $g(\delta', src) + d(\delta, \delta')$ that separate it from the source through each one of its neighbours δ', and taking the minimum of those.

Two observations are in order: first of all, it is easy to see that, if the network is stable (i.e., devices do not crash, do not move, and do not join/leave the network), the algorithm actually converges to the correct value in each device δ. Secondly, after *any* of the above changes happen, if the network stabilises again for enough time, the values in each device δ are updated with the new correct values. In other words, the algorithm is *self-stabilising* [53]. Even if simple, the algorithm is both *collective*, i.e., fully distributed among the participating devices, and *adaptive*, i.e., resilient to the relevant changes in the system and the environment.

The following code is the implementation of the algorithm in the ScaFi language [26], a Scala-based implementation of Field Calculus.

```
1  def gradient(source: Boolean): Double =
2    rep(Double.PositiveInfinity) { dist =>
3      mux(source){ 0.0 } { minHood(nbr{dist} + nbrRange()) }
4    }
```

The **rep** construct propagates the computed gradient value between rounds (in this case, the value computed by mux[1]). The **nbr** construct, returns the neigh-

---

[1] The mux(c){t}{e} ScaFi built-in operator evaluates all the arguments and returns the value of t if c is true or the value of e otherwise.

bouring field with the last values of `dist` received from the neighbours (whose set, implicitly managed by the execution platform, corresponds to the N operator in Eq. (1)). Finally, `nbrRange()` returns a neighbouring field with the distance estimates to the neighbours, and `minHood()` returns the minimum value of a field. Also, note that the `gradient` function directly takes a Boolean value indicating whether the current device δ is a source, and that the δ parameter is not passed explicitly to `gradient` (since the program is evaluated locally to each device, there is always an implicit current device).

Reference Example #2: Self-healing Channel. A more complex example of self-organising computation is the *self-healing channel*, namely the construction of a path of devices across the network connecting a source device to a destination device, where the fact of belonging or not to the channel can be denoted by a local Boolean output (i.e., the channel consists of all the devices of the network the output `true`). Since this can be implemented on top of (a generalisation of) gradients, it is instrumental to convey the idea of *compositionality* of self-organising behaviours.

Taking inspiration from [53], let us generalize the D function to a higher-order operator G as follows:

$$G(\delta, src, ini, acc, met)$$

where src is the source of the field to be constructed, ini is the input value of the field to be considered, acc is the function expressing how to accumulate values starting from the source outwards (i.e., how to integrate local values ini to the accumulated value taken from the neighbour minimising the gradient in the neighbourhood), and met the metric of the distance between two devices. The G operator returns a pair (x, y), where x is the distance of δ from the source, estimated with met, and y is the value accumulated with acc along the gradient.

The self-healing gradient above can then be expressed as:

$$D(\delta, src) := 2nd(G(\delta, src, 0, \lambda x.(x + d), d))$$

where we have used the lambda calculus notation for defining the acc function, and $2nd$ returns the second element of a pair. We exploit the G operator to define another function, broadcast (B):

$$B(\delta, src, val) := 2nd(G(\delta, src, val, \lambda x.x, d))$$

Assuming a single source device δ_{SRC} for which $src(\delta_{SRC})$ is true, this function broadcasts a value val defined in δ_{SRC} unaltered (thanks to using the identity function for acc) to all the other nodes, at increasing distances.

Let us consider the problem of establishing a robust communication channel between a source device δ_{SRC} and a destination/target device δ_{TRG} in a network with proximity-based communication. Starting from the B and D functions defined above, we can first of all define a function which broadcasts everywhere the distance between a source and a target, where src and trg are predicates that are true, respectively in the source and target of the communication channel:

$$BTW(\delta, src, trg) := B(\delta, src, D(\delta, trg))$$

Then, we can define a function that, for every device δ, is true iff δ belongs to the communication channel between the source and target devices:

$$CH(\delta, src, trg, w) := D(\delta, src) + D(\delta, trg) \leq BTW(\delta, src, trg) + w$$

Note that a device belongs to the channel iff it falls within an ellipse whose foci are the source and target devices. The w parameter determines the "stretch" of the ellipse, which reduces to a linear path in case $w = 0$. In particular, to determine which devices are part of the channel between δ_{SRC} and δ_{TRG}, we execute in every node:

$$CH(\delta, \lambda x.(x == \delta_{SRC}), \lambda x.(x == \delta_{DST}), w)$$

The following code is the implementation of the algorithm in the ScaFi language.

```
1   def broadcast[V:OB](source: Boolean, init: V): V =
2     G[V](source, init, x=>x, nbrRange())
3
4   def distanceTo(source: Boolean): Double =
5     G[Double](source, 0, _ + nbrRange(), nbrRange())
6
7   def distBetween(source: Boolean, target: Boolean): Double =
8     broadcast(source, distanceTo(target))
9
10  def isSource = sense[Boolean]("source")
11  def isTarget = sense[Boolean]("target")
12
13  def channel(src: Boolean, dest: Boolean, width: Double) =
14    distanceTo(src) + distanceTo(dest) <=
15    distBetween(src, dest) + width
16
17  channel(isSource, isTarget)
```

2.2 The Actors Programming Model

The *Actor model* [1,33,37] puts *actors* at the core of the design and implementation of distributed systems. Actors are *reactive* agents that communicate with each other through *asynchronous message passing* (i.e., no shared memory is allowed).

It is worth noting that each message is directed to a specific actor through a *target address*, and that a mailbox system buffers messages until they are processed by their target actors. The actors in the distributed system execute in parallel. In particular, each actor iteratively and asynchronously processes the messages in its mailbox received from the other actors.

The fundamental part of the behaviour of an actor is specified in terms of how it handles incoming messages. In response to a message, an actor can:

- perform local computations;
- send messages to other actors;
- create new actors;
- choose the behaviour for handling the next message.

Handling of multiple messages is not interleaved or, analogously, handling of a single message is atomic.

Then, the Actor model can be formalised and implemented in different ways, possibly bringing in particular extensions. An example of implementation is provided by the *Akka toolkit* [46], whose user interface is briefly described in the following.

2.3   The Akka Toolkit: A Short Primer

We briefly illustrate the user *Application Program Interface (API)* of *Akka* [46], focussing on the *Akka Typed* version, which will be useful to understand the code provided in Sect. 3.

Actor Behaviour. Actor behaviour is dynamically represented through values of type `Behavior[M]`, which encapsulate the logic for handling messages of type `M`. So, an actor behaviour can be defined by extending `AbstractBehavior[M]` and overriding method `onMessage` (*OOP-style*), or by functions yielding a `Behavior[M]` (*functional style*). The Akka API provides a factory object `Behaviors` for specifying behaviours as functions mapping messages to the next behaviour, e.g., using pattern matching. Actors can be addressed through a reference of type `ActorRef[T]`: e.g., given a reference `r`, instruction `r ! m` denotes the sending of a message `m` of type `T` to the actor denoted by reference `r`.

Actor Systems. An actor system is created by instantiating an `ActorSystem[T]` with the `Behavior[T]` of the top-level actor; such a top-level actor would be responsible for *spawning* new actors by calling `ActorContext[T].spawn(behavior)`. Indeed, actor systems consist of a *hierarchy* of actors (enabling *supervision*), where each actor has a position in this hierarchy that can be denoted by a *path* of *actor names*, starting from the *top-level actor* `/user` (for user – i.e., non-system-level – actors): e.g., `/user/a/b` is the path of actor `b` which is a child of `a` (which is in turn a child of the top-level actor).

3   Actor-Based Designs for Aggregate Computations

In this section, we discuss possible actor-based designs for building the paradigmatic self-organising behaviours covered in Sect. 2.1. The produced source code has been made available at a permanent public repository [23][2] with a permissive licence, equipped with the build infrastructure for simple execution.

---

[2] https://github.com/metaphori/experiment-actor-design-selforg.

```
 1  object Device {
 2    def apply(src: Boolean,
 3               g: Double,
 4               nbrs: Map[ActorRef[Msg],Long],
 5               distances: Map[ActorRef[Msg],Double],
 6               nbrGs: Map[ActorRef[Msg],Double],
 7               pos: Point3D = Point3D(0,0,0)): Behavior[Msg] = Behaviors.setup { ctx =>
 8      val getPositionAdapter: ActorRef[NbrPos] =
 9        ctx.messageAdapter(m => SetDistance(m.pos.distance(pos), m.nbr))
10      val getGradientAdapter: ActorRef[NbrGradient] =
11        ctx.messageAdapter(m => SetNeighbourGradient(m.g, m.nbr))
12
13      Behaviors.withTimers { timers => Behaviors.receive { case (ctx,msg) => msg match {
14        case SetSource(s) =>
15          Device(s, 0, nbrs, distances, nbrGs, pos)
16        case AddNeighbour(nbr) =>
17          Device(src, g, nbrs + (nbr -> currTime()), distances, nbrGs, pos)
18        case RemoveNeighbour(nbr) =>
19          Device(src, g, nbrs - nbr, distances, nbrGs, pos)
20        case SetPosition(p) =>
21          Device(src, g, nbrs, distances, nbrGs, p)
22        case GetPosition(replyTo) =>
23          replyTo ! NbrPos(pos, ctx.self)
24          Behaviors.same
25        case SetDistance(d, from) =>
26          Device(src, g, nbrs + (from -> currTime()), distances + (from -> d), nbrGs, pos)
27        case ComputeGradient =>
28          val newNbrGradients = nbrGs + (ctx.self -> g)
29          val disalignedNbrs = nbrs.filter(nbr => currTime() -
30            nbrs.getOrElse(nbr._1, Long.MinValue) > RETENTION_TIME).keySet
31          val alignedNbrGradients = newNbrG -- disalignedNbrs
32          val alignedDistances = distances -- disalignedNbrs
33          timers.startSingleTimer(Round, 1.second)
34          if(src){
35            Device(src, 0, nbrs, distances, newNbrG, pos)
36          } else {
37            val updatedG = (alignedNbrGradients - ctx.self).map(n => n -> (n._2 +
38              alignedDistances.get(n._1).getOrElse(Double.PositiveInfinity))
39              ).values.minOption.getOrElse(Double.PositiveInfinity)
40            Device(src, updatedG, nbrs, distances, nbrGs + (ctx.self -> updatedG), pos)
41          }
42        case QueryGradient(replyTo) =>
43          replyTo ! NbrGradient(g, ctx.self)
44          Behaviors.same
45        case SetNeighbourGradient(d, from) =>
46          Device(src, g, nbrs + (from -> currTime()), distances, nbrGs + (from -> d), pos)
47        case Round =>
48          nbrs.keySet.foreach(nbr => {
49            nbr ! GetPosition(getPositionAdapter) // query nbr for nbrsensors
50            nbr ! QueryGradient(getGradientAdapter) // query nbr for app data
51          })
52          timers.startSingleTimer(ComputeGradient, 1.seconds)
53          Behaviors.same
54        case Stop => Behaviors.stopped
55    } } } }
56  }
```

Fig. 1. A naive Akka implementation where a single actor encapsulates all the concerns.

3.1   A Naive Actor-Based Implementation of the Self-healing Gradient Example

Figure 1 shows a possible implementation of the self-healing gradient within the Akka framework. This version is deliberately naive, and serves mainly as a baseline that will be refined in the next sections.

The application contains a single type of actor named `Device`. The actor defines a behaviour that matches several types of messages (note the use of `Behaviors.withTimers`, needed to schedule self messages that simulate the scheduling of computation rounds). The code executed to handle a `Round` serves as the initiation of a round of computation (cf. the aggregate computing execution model—see Sect. 2.1). More specifically:

- for each neighbour `nbr`, it requests the current value of the position (`GetPosition`) and of the gradient (`QueryGradient`)
- a timer is set to expire in one second and send a `ComputeGradient` message to the actor itself.

The neighbour actors would reply to the `GetPosition` and `QueryGradient` requests, and the current actor stores the retrieved information in its state (specifically, in the `distances` and `nbrGs` maps). When the `QueryGradient` is received, further operations are performed to complete the round of computation:

- neighbours whose latest messages are expired (i.e., older than the constant `RETENTION_TIME`) are discarded (e.g., in order to become aware of device failing or quitting the system);
- a timer is set to expire in one second and send a `Round` message to the actor itself (i.e., to initiate the next round and possibly detect new information from the environment);
- if the actor is a `src` of the gradient computation, it just propagates its behaviour with the gradient set to constant `g = 0`;
- otherwise, the gradient is updated to the new value `updatedG` computed from the information retrieved from the neighbours, according to the logic of the gradient implementation illustrated in Sect. 2.1.

3.2   An Improved Design

The naive design of the previous section has several issues. The main issue is that the `Device` actor is not *reusable* but rather specific to the computation at hand: this is witnessed by application-specific messages (e.g., `ComputeGradient` and `SetNeighbourGradient`). Another issue is that the `Device` encapsulates all the concerns, including e.g. the scheduling concern (cf. the use of `timers` to schedule rounds and computations).

In Fig. 2, an improved design is presented. It is also coded with a different style: the OOP style, instead of the functional style as in Fig. 1, which is mainly a matter of taste, and in this case is more suitable to avoid encoding state into a large parameter list. In particular, the `DeviceActor` is an abstract class: to be implemented, the abstract `compute` method has to be defined (cf. the *Template Method* design pattern [31]). Additionally, the responsibility of scheduling has been moved outside of the actor: it will compute reactively upon reception of a `Compute` message; it is straightforward to define a scheduler actor that keeps the

```
1   abstract class DeviceActor[T](c: ActorContext[DeviceProtocol]) extends AbstractBehavior(c) {
2     var sensors = Map[String, Any]()
3
4     def senseOrElse[T](name: String, default: => T): T =
5       sensors.getOrElse(name, default).asInstanceOf[T]
6     def nbrValue[T](name: String): Map[Nbr, T] =
7       senseOrElse[Map[Nbr, T]](name, Map.empty).filter(tp => neighbors.contains(tp._1))
8     def neighbors: Set[ActorRef[DeviceProtocol]] =
9       senseOrElse[Map[Nbr, Long]](Sensors.neighbors, Map(context.self -> currentTime()))
10      .filter(tp => currentTime() - tp._2 < RETENTION_TIME).keySet
11    def updateNbrTimestamp(nbr: Nbr, t: Long = currentTime()): Unit =
12      sensors += Sensors.neighbors -> (nbrValue[Long](Sensors.neighbors) + (nbr -> t))
13
14    def compute(what: String, d: DeviceActor[T]): T // cf. template method's abstract method
15
16    override def onMessage(msg: DeviceProtocol): Behavior[DeviceProtocol] = msg match {
17      case SetSensor(sensorName, value) =>
18        sensors += (sensorName -> value)
19        this
20      case SetNbrSensor(name, nbr, value)Behaviors.withTimers { timers =>
21        =>
22        val sval = sensors.getOrElse(name, Map.empty).asInstanceOf[Map[Nbr, Any]]
23        sensors += name -> (sval + (nbr -> value))
24        updateNbrTimestamp(nbr)
25        this
26      case Compute(what) =>
27        val result = compute(what, this)
28        neighbors.foreach(_ ! SetNbrSensor(what, context.self, result))
29        this
30      case AddNeighbour(nbr) =>
31        context.self ! SetNbrSensor(Sensors.neighbors, nbr, currentTime())
32        context.self ! SetNbrSensor(Sensors.nbrRange, nbr, 1.0)
33        this
34      case RemoveNeighbour(nbr) =>
35        context.self ! SetNbrSensor(Sensors.neighbors, nbr, 0)
36        this
37      case Stop =>
38        Behaviors.stopped
39      }
40    }
41  }
42
43  // then, a DeviceActor computing a gradient can be launched as follows
44  val a = ctx.spawn(DeviceActor[Double]((ctx,w,d) => {
45    val nbrg = d.nbrValue[Double]("gradient")
46      .map(n => n._2 + d.nbrSense[Double](Sensors.nbrRange)(n._1)
47              .getOrElse(Double.PositiveInfinity))
48      .minOption.getOrElse(Double.PositiveInfinity)
49    if(d.senseOrElse("source", false)) 0.0 else nbrg
50  }), "device-1")
51  a ! SetSensor("source", true)
52  a ! AddNeighbour(...)
53  a ! Compute("gradient")
```

Fig. 2. An improved Akka implementation of a reusable device.

references of the device(s) to be scheduled, and implements a basic scheduling logic (e.g., to let each schedulable compute once per second). Another element of generality is given by keeping all contextual data into a single data structure sensors, where the basic idea is that any access to context is mediated by a sensor.

More in detail, the behaviour of DeviceActor is defined in terms of reactions to a few message types. The acquisition of contextual information is handled through a push-style interface based on two main incoming messages: SetSensor for *local sensors* (e.g., position sensors or temperature sensors), and SetNbrSensor for *neighbouring sensors* (i.e., those associating data to neighbours). Neighbouring sensors are used to access the current set of neighbours, information relative to neighbours (e.g., the distance to neighbours), and information shared by neighbours (e.g., their gradient value). Upon these, behaviours associated to specific control messages like `AddNeighbour` and `RemoveNeighbour` can be easily implemented. Then, the `Compute(what)` message, carrying an indication of `what` has to be computed (to enable multiple computations), is handled by calling the `compute` abstract method, and then communicating the corresponding result to the neighbours by sending a `SetNbrSensor` message. Finally, at the bottom of Fig. 2 it is shown how the gradient computation can be specified, and how an actor computing the gradient can be configured.

4 The ScaFi Akka-Based Distributed Middleware

In this section, we present an implementation of a general self-organisation programming system, based on the aggregate computing paradigm [54] and integrated into the *ScaFi toolkit* [26], whose *runtime* (also called a *middleware*) is based on actors, along the lines of the improved design presented in Sect. 3.2. The ScaFi toolkit can be exploited to simulate and build self-organizing systems distributed on heterogenous computational resources. Interestingly, the design is organised in order to support *distributed* execution of aggregate systems, also according to multiple *architectural styles* (cf. [24,25])—which is important to fully exploit modern infrastructures like the heterogeneous multi-scale computing continua of which the *edge-cloud continuum* is a prominent example [13].

4.1 System Design

A simplified view of the elements participating in an actor-based aggregate computing application is provided by Fig. 3.

Essentially, the key types of elements are:

- `AggregateApplication` – It represents, in any subsystem, a particular aggregate application, as specified by some `Settings`. Also, it works as a supervisor for all the other application-specific actors. This notion is required to properly handle the management of multiple aggregate computations on the same infrastructure.
- `Scheduler` – Optionally, a scheduler may be used to centralise system execution at a system- or subsystem-level.
- `ComputationDevice` – It is a device which is able to carry out some local computation. It communicates with other devices and interacts with `Sensors` and `Actuators` (which may be actors as well or not).

Also, note how all these entities are specific to a particular *platform incarnation*, i.e., a concrete set of implementations for the defined types (see also the notion of "incarnation" as an instantiated "family of types" in ScaFi [26]).

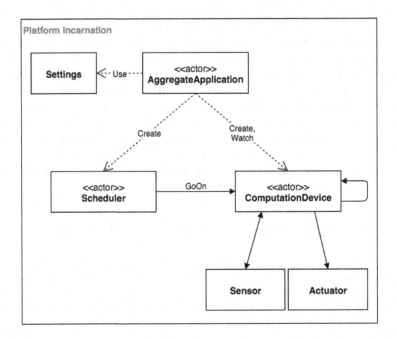

Fig. 3. Structure diagram of the main entities of an aggregate computing system.

Devices. Figure 4 shows how devices are modelled. A first key distinction is between actors and actor behaviours. In fact, one design goal is to split a big, articulated behaviour into many small, reusable, composable behaviours. The convention in the diagram is to express message-based interfaces by means of incoming and outcoming messages which are represented as arrows with a filled arrowhead.

By a conceptual point of view, a device must, at minimum, manage its sensors and actuators. Then, in the context of aggregate computing, a device must also interact with its neighbours (`BaseNbrManagementBehavior`); such interaction has not been detailed yet, as it may be somehow different in the peer-to-peer and server-based cases. Also, a computation device executes some program with a certain frequency (here represented by a tick message called `GoOn`, externally or self-sent).

4.2 Server-Based Actor Platform

The *server-based platform*, following the client/server architectural style, is depicted in Fig. 5. The devices are clients of a central server that owns the information about the *topology* of the aggregate system and is responsible for the propagation of the exports of the devices.

Figure 5 statically describes the message interfaces of device and server:

– Each device registers itself with the server at startup (`Registration`).

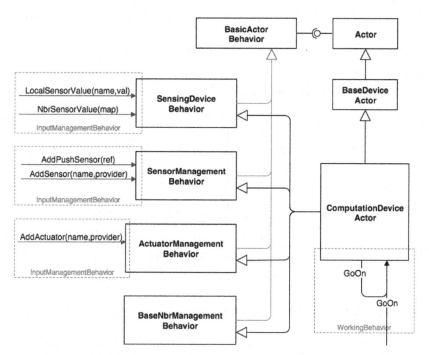

Fig. 4. Structure and interface of device actors.

- After a computation, a device communicates its newly computed state to the server (`Export`).
- Each device asks the server (`GetNeighbourhoodExports`) for the most recent states of its neighbours (`NeighbourhoodExports`), with some frequency.

4.3 Peer-to-Peer Actor Platform

The *peer-to-peer platform*, following an ad-hoc architectural style, is shown in Fig. 6. Each device, at the end of each computation, propagates its newly computed state (`MsgExport`) directly to all its neighbour actors. Here, the critical point concerns how a device gets acquainted with its neighbours, i.e., by receiving information about a neighbour (`NbrInfo`).

The choice of the particular architectural style (peer-to-peer vs. server-based vs. hybrid deployments) essentially depends on the infrastructure and requirements for the specific application at hand. Generally speaking, different architectures may involve different patterns of information exchange and system management that may affect the costs and efficiency of running applications. For instance, the server-based solution may simplify the enaction of neighbouring policies. Recent work has been carried out to estimate (e.g., via simulation) and compare different deployments for the same aggregate computing system [24, 25].

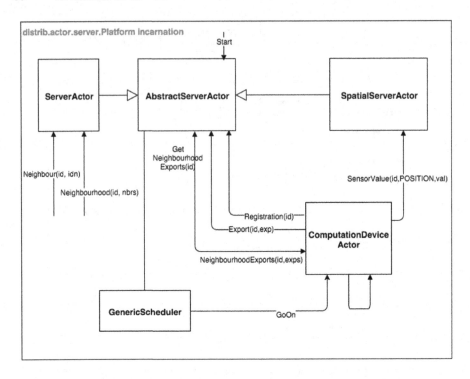

Fig. 5. Key elements and relationships in a server-based actor platform.

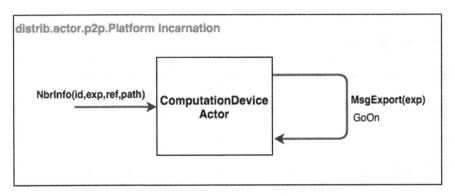

Fig. 6. Key elements and relationships in a peer-to-peer actor platform.

4.4 Actors and Reactive Behaviour

The ScaFi actor platform was implemented using *Akka Classic* framework [46]. In Akka Classic, actors are defined by extending the `akka.actor.Actor` trait and implementing the `receive` method, of type `Receive=PartialFunction[Any,Unit]`, that associates reactions to incoming messages.

An interesting implication of having (reactive) behaviours expressed by PartialFunctions is that they *compose*. This composability feature has been extensively used to promote separation of concerns. For example, the device behaviour related to the management of sensors can be kept separated from the behaviour aimed at handling actuators:

```
1   def SensorManagementBehavior: Receive = {
2     case MsgAddPushSensor(ref) => { ref ! MsgAddObserver(self); ref ! GoOn }
3     case MsgAddSensor(name, provider) => setLocalSensor(name, provider)
4   }
5
6   def ActuatorManagementBehavior: Receive = {
7     case MsgAddActuator(name, consumer) => setActuator(name, consumer)
8   }
9
10  def CompositeBehavior: Receive =
11    SensorManagementBehavior
12    .orElse(ActuatorManagementBehavior)
```

Moreover, it is also possible to leverage on *trait stacking* to automatically extend some behaviour by mixing in behaviour traits. In the following example, the behavior of DeviceActor is obtained by mixing-in SensorManagementBehavior and ActuatorManagementBehavior:

```
1   trait BasicActorBehavior { selfActor: Actor =>
2
3     def receive: Receive =
4       workingBehavior
5         .orElse(inputManagementBehavior)
6         .orElse(queryManagementBehavior)
7         .orElse(commandManagementBehavior)
8
9     def inputManagementBehavior: Receive = Map.empty
10    def queryManagementBehavior: Receive = Map.empty
11    def commandManagementBehavior: Receive = Map.empty
12    def workingBehavior: Receive = Map.empty
13  }
14
15  trait SensorManagementBehavior extends BasicActorBehavior { selfActor: Actor =>
16    def SensorManagementBehavior: Receive = { ... }
17
18    override def inputManagementBehavior: Receive =
19      super.inputManagementBehavior.orElse(SensorManagementBehavior)
20
21    // ...
22  }
23
24  trait ActuatorManagementBehavior extends BasicActorBehavior { selfActor: Actor =>
25    def ActuatorManagementBehavior: Receive = { ... }
26
27    override def inputManagementBehavior: Receive =
28      super.inputManagementBehavior.orElse(ActuatorManagementBehavior)
29
30    // ...
31  }
32
33  class DeviceActor extends Actor
34    with SensorManagementBehavior
35    with ActuatorManagementBehavior { ... }
```

Finally, ScaFi provides an object-oriented façade API for setting up, launching, and managing a running system upon the described actor-based middleware. Please refer to the ScaFi repository[3] and website[4] for further details.

5 Discussion and Future Work

The development of actor-based designs and implementations of self-organising behaviours like the gradient, as well as the experience in research and development of aggregate computing systems, provided some general insights about self-organisation programming. These suggest some general principles (as also indicated by modern software engineering practice) or desiderata for implementations. In particular, we emphasise the following.

Declarativity. The program logic expressing how self-organisation is carried out should be as declarative as possible. This means that the program should abstract from a number of details, e.g. including the following: (i) scheduling of context retrieval and update, (ii) scheduling of computation, (iii) neighbourhood management, (iv) details of message passing (cf. the naive actor design vs. the improved design vs. the ScaFi program), and (iv) application partitioning and deployment (cf. [25]). Aggregate programming in general and ScaFi in particular do support a programming model where such details are abstracted away: this provides great operational flexibility [24].

Composability of Behaviour. Another benefit of aggregate programming is compositionality, namely the ability of connecting basic self-organising behaviours (e.g., gradients—cf. Sect. 2.1) in order to build more complex self-organising behaviours (e.g., channels—cf. Sect. 2.1). The problem with the actor-based design proposed in Sect. 3 is that explicitly managing the relationships between computations in terms of message-passing is cumbersome and error-prone[5].

Separation of Concerns. Separating different concerns is a well-known design principle in software engineering, fostering modular design. It is also related to the *Single Responsibility Principle (SRP)*, which suggests that a module (e.g., a class or an actor) should handle a single piece of functionality. As we have seen, it is good to separate certain concerns: e.g., the scheduling concern may be encapsulated into a scheduler (actor)—cf. Sect. 3.2. However, there is the risk of too much separation, possibly leading to over-complication and inefficiency. In the provided repository, for instance, a "fully destructured" device actor is provided, encapsulating the different concerns (sensor management, neighbourhood management, scheduling management, context management, communication management, and computation) into separate child actors; however, this design turns out to be very complex, due to the need of properly managing the interaction among those inter-related sub-actors.

---

[3] https://github.com/scafi/scafi.

[4] https://scafi.github.io/.

[5] A sketch of an actor-based implementation of the channel is given in the provided repository.

Propensity to Openness and Reconfiguration. The kinds of systems we are considering in this chapter, i.e., large homogeneous systems (e.g., swarms, IoT systems, etc.), are generally *open* systems, where devices may easily enter or exit the system (also due to failure, user decisions, and environmental dynamics). Additionally, the execution of such systems may need to be *reconfigured* [27] into different architectural styles (cf. Sect. 4) in order to optimise for or opportunistically exploit available infrastructure by re-deployment [4,24]. Reconfiguration is typically based on *component models* [12,25,43], but also actors have shown their suitability for dynamically reconfigurable open systems [52]. In [55], the prelude of the *pulverisation model* of aggregate computing systems [25], it was proposed to split the behaviour of a device into sub-actors (handling sensors, actuators, communication, and computation), to be potentially deployable (and relocatable) across different architectures. Different approaches may leverage other kinds of components, e.g., based on microservices or containers [27], hence possibly leveraging actors at the level of their implementation.

Fine-Grained Execution Model. Aggregate computing systems typically work in a round-based fashion, where devices repeatedly execute asynchronous rounds atomically performing *sense–compute–act* steps. Actors, instead, promote the construction of asynchronous reactive dataflow graphs, that may in principle support a finer-grained definition of the execution model where, e.g., the only computations that are re-evaluated are those whose inputs have changed. A first reactive extension to aggregate computing, based on reactive policies and explicit program graphs, has been proposed in [45]. A different approach may exploit the functional reactive programming paradigm [11]. A comparison between these approaches and potential actor-based design may be an interesting future work, to determine more efficient and finely controllable execution strategies, and to possibly also provide general insights about the relationship between self-organisation and reactivity.

Abstraction Gap. Even though the Actors model and technologies like the Akka actor-based toolkit provide some support for the implementation of a middleware for aggregate systems, it is important to consider if and how more advanced Actors and Active Objects models [14], could further reduce the abstraction gap for such systems. Some well-known *Active Objects Languages (AOLs)* include Rebeca [50], ABS [34], ASP [20], and Encore [18].

For instance, [14] considers the offered *degree of synchronisation* and corresponding *synchronisation mechanisms* as one of the dimensions along which to compare AOLs. These mechanism may be useful for structuring control flow and the collaboration among middleware components, possibly in a more fine-grained and verifiable way. Indeed, AOLs like Rebeca and ABS are designed for *verifiability*, and can support the analysis of the correctness of a middleware implementation—e.g., to ensure that the middleware enacts the desired execution model for the system. The support in ABS for time, resource, and deployment modelling can also be instrumental for assessing the cost of an aggregate computing system deployment. Indeed, there exist works [3,35] that have exploited the ABS language to study the performance of a given system for different deployment architectures; the same approach could be applied to aggregate computing deployments (cf. pulverisation [24,25]).

Future Work. In the present paper, we have considered actor-based solutions for the design and implementation of self-organising behaviours. Some interesting work has been conducted about implementing self-organising systems with actor languages through *coordinated actor models* [9,10], which would be worth comparing to our approach in future work.

As previously mentioned, one interesting future work also amounts to investigating whether specialised Actors and Active Objects models/language can better support the development of component or layers within an aggregate computing system.

Acknowledgements. This work has been partially supported by the MUR PRIN 2020 Project "COMMON-WEARS" (2020HCWWLP) and the EU/MUR FSE REACT-EU PON R&I 2014–2020. This study was carried out within the Agritech National Research Center and received funding from the European Union Next-GenerationEU (PIANO NAZIONALE DI RIPRESA E RESILIENZA (PNRR) - MISSIONE 4 COMPONENTE 2, INVESTIMENTO 1.4 - D.D. 1032 17/06/2022, CN00000022). This publication is also part of the project NODES which has received funding from the MUR - M4C2 1.5 of PNRR with grant agreement no. ECS00000036. This manuscript reflects only the authors' views and opinions, neither the European Union nor the European Commission can be considered responsible for them.

References

1. Agha, G.: Actors: A Model of Concurrent Computation in Distributed Systems. MIT Press, Cambridge (1986)
2. Aguzzi, G., Casadei, R., Viroli, M.: Towards reinforcement learning-based aggregate computing. In: ter Beek, M.H., Sirjani, M. (eds.) COORDINATION 2022. IFIP Advances in Information and Communication Technology, vol. 13271, pp. 72–91. Springer, Cham (2022). https://doi.org/10.1007/978-3-031-08143-9_5
3. Albert, E., et al.: Formal modeling and analysis of resource management for cloud architectures: an industrial case study using real-time ABS. Serv. Orient. Comput. Appl. **8**, 323–339 (2014)
4. Arcangeli, J., Boujbel, R., Leriche, S.: Automatic deployment of distributed software systems: definitions and state of the art. J. Syst. Softw. **103**, 198–218 (2015). https://doi.org/10.1016/j.jss.2015.01.040
5. Armstrong, J.: Programming erlang: software for a concurrent world. Program. Erlang 1–548 (2013)
6. Atzori, L., Iera, A., Morabito, G.: The internet of things: a survey. Comput. Netw. **54**(15), 2787–2805 (2010). https://doi.org/10.1016/j.comnet.2010.05.010
7. Audrito, G., Casadei, R., Damiani, F., Viroli, M.: Compositional blocks for optimal self-healing gradients. In: SASO, pp. 91–100. IEEE (2017). https://doi.org/10.1109/SASO.2017.18
8. Audrito, G., Viroli, M., Damiani, F., Pianini, D., Beal, J.: A higher-order calculus of computational fields. ACM Trans. Comput. Log. **20**(1), 5:1–5:55 (2019). https://doi.org/10.1145/3285956

9. Bagheri, M., Akkaya, I., Khamespanah, E., Khakpour, N., Sirjani, M., Movaghar, A., Lee, E.A.: Coordinated actors for reliable self-adaptive systems. In: Kouchnarenko, O., Khosravi, R. (eds.) FACS 2016. LNCS, vol. 10231, pp. 241–259. Springer, Cham (2017). https://doi.org/10.1007/978-3-319-57666-4_15

10. Bagheri, M., et al.: Coordinated actor model of self-adaptive track-based traffic control systems. J. Syst. Softw. **143**, 116–139 (2018). https://doi.org/10.1016/j.jss.2018.05.034

11. Bainomugisha, E., Carreton, A.L., Cutsem, T.V., Mostinckx, S., Meuter, W.D.: A survey on reactive programming. ACM Comput. Surv. **45**(4), 52:1–52:34 (2013). https://doi.org/10.1145/2501654.2501666

12. El Ballouli, R., Bensalem, S., Bozga, M., Sifakis, J.: Four exercises in programming dynamic reconfigurable systems: methodology and solution in DR-BIP. In: Margaria, T., Steffen, B. (eds.) ISoLA 2018, Part III. LNCS, vol. 11246, pp. 304–320. Springer, Cham (2018). https://doi.org/10.1007/978-3-030-03424-5_20

13. Bittencourt, L.F., et al.: The internet of things, fog and cloud continuum: integration and challenges. Internet Things **3–4**, 134–155 (2018). https://doi.org/10.1016/j.iot.2018.09.005

14. de Boer, F.S., et al.: A survey of active object languages. ACM Comput. Surv. **50**(5), 76:1–76:39 (2017). https://doi.org/10.1145/3122848

15. Boissier, O., Bordini, R.H., Hubner, J., Ricci, A.: Multi-agent Oriented Programming: Programming Multi-agent Systems Using JaCaMo. MIT Press, Cambridge (2020)

16. Bonabeau, E., Dorigo, M., Theraulaz, G.: Swarm Intelligence: From Natural to Artificial Systems. Santa Fe Institute Studies in the Sciences of Complexity. Oxford University Press, Inc., Oxford (1999)

17. Brambilla, M., Ferrante, E., Birattari, M., Dorigo, M.: Swarm robotics: a review from the swarm engineering perspective. Swarm Intell. **7**(1), 1–41 (2013). https://doi.org/10.1007/s11721-012-0075-2

18. Brandauer, S., et al.: Parallel objects for multicores: a glimpse at the parallel language Encore. In: Bernardo, M., Johnsen, E.B. (eds.) SFM 2015. LNCS, vol. 9104, pp. 1–56. Springer, Cham (2015). https://doi.org/10.1007/978-3-319-18941-3_1

19. Busoniu, L., Babuska, R., Schutter, B.D.: A comprehensive survey of multiagent reinforcement learning. IEEE Trans. Syst. Man Cybern. Part C **38**(2), 156–172 (2008). https://doi.org/10.1109/TSMCC.2007.913919

20. Caromel, D., Henrio, L.: A Theory of Distributed Objects: Asynchrony-Mobility-Groups-Components. Springer, Heidelberg (2005). https://doi.org/10.1007/b138812

21. Casadei, R.: Artificial collective intelligence engineering: a survey of concepts and perspectives. Artif. Life 1–35 (2023). https://doi.org/10.1162/artl_0408

22. Casadei, R.: Macroprogramming: concepts, state of the art, and opportunities of macroscopic behaviour modelling. ACM Comput. Surv. (2023). https://doi.org/10.1145/3579353

23. Casadei, R.: Metaphori/experiment-actor-design-selforg: actor- based Designs for self-organising systems (2023). https://doi.org/10.5281/zenodo.8377727

24. Casadei, R., Fortino, G., Pianini, D., Placuzzi, A., Savaglio, C., Viroli, M.: A methodology and simulation-based toolchain for estimating deployment performance of smart collective services at the edge. IEEE Internet Things J. **9**(20), 20136–20148 (2022). https://doi.org/10.1109/JIOT.2022.3172470

25. Casadei, R., Pianini, D., Placuzzi, A., Viroli, M., Weyns, D.: Pulverization in cyber-physical systems: engineering the self-organizing logic separated from deployment. Future Internet **12**(11), 203 (2020). https://doi.org/10.3390/fi12110203
26. Casadei, R., Viroli, M., Aguzzi, G., Pianini, D.: ScaFi: a scala DSL and toolkit for aggregate programming. SoftwareX **20**, 101248 (2022). https://doi.org/10.1016/j.softx.2022.101248
27. Coullon, H., Henrio, L., Loulergue, F., Robillard, S.: Component-based distributed software reconfiguration: a verification-oriented survey. ACM Comput. Surv. (2023). https://doi.org/10.1145/3595376
28. De Nicola, R., Jähnichen, S., Wirsing, M.: Rigorous engineering of collective adaptive systems: special section. Int. J. Softw. Tools Technol. Transf. **22**(4), 389–397 (2020). https://doi.org/10.1007/s10009-020-00565-0
29. De Wolf, T., Holvoet, T.: Emergence versus self-organisation: different concepts but promising when combined. In: Brueckner, S.A., Di Marzo Serugendo, G., Karageorgos, A., Nagpal, R. (eds.) ESOA 2004. LNCS (LNAI), vol. 3464, pp. 1–15. Springer, Heidelberg (2005). https://doi.org/10.1007/11494676_1
30. Franklin, S., Graesser, A.: Is it an agent, or just a program?: A taxonomy for autonomous agents. In: Müller, J.P., Wooldridge, M.J., Jennings, N.R. (eds.) ATAL 1996. LNCS, vol. 1193, pp. 21–35. Springer, Heidelberg (1997). https://doi.org/10.1007/BFb0013570
31. Gamma, E., Helm, R., Johnson, R., Johnson, R.E., Vlissides, J.: Design Patterns: Elements of Reusable Object-Oriented Software. Pearson Deutschland GmbH (1995)
32. Gershenson, C.: Design and Control of Self-organizing Systems. CopIt Arxives (2007)
33. Hewitt, C.: A universal modular actor formalism for artificial intelligence. In: Proceedings of IJCAI (1973)
34. Johnsen, E.B., Hähnle, R., Schäfer, J., Schlatte, R., Steffen, M.: ABS: a core language for abstract behavioral specification. In: Aichernig, B.K., de Boer, F.S., Bonsangue, M.M. (eds.) FMCO 2010. LNCS, vol. 6957, pp. 142–164. Springer, Heidelberg (2011). https://doi.org/10.1007/978-3-642-25271-6_8
35. Johnsen, E.B., Schlatte, R., Tapia Tarifa, S.L.: Integrating deployment architectures and resource consumption in timed object-oriented models. J. Log. Algebraic Methods Program. **84**(1), 67–91 (2015). https://doi.org/10.1016/j.jlamp.2014.07.001
36. Kephart, J.O., Chess, D.M.: The vision of autonomic computing. Computer **36**(1), 41–50 (2003). https://doi.org/10.1109/MC.2003.1160055
37. Koster, J.D., Cutsem, T.V., Meuter, W.D.: 43 years of actors: a taxonomy of actor models and their key properties. In: Clebsch, S., Desell, T., Haller, P., Ricci, A. (eds.) Proceedings of the 6th International Workshop on Programming Based on Actors, Agents, and Decentralized Control, AGERE 2016, Amsterdam, The Netherlands, 30 October 2016, pp. 31–40. ACM (2016). https://doi.org/10.1145/3001886.3001890
38. Mamei, M., Zambonelli, F., Leonardi, L.: Co-fields: a physically inspired approach to motion coordination. IEEE Pervasive Comput. **3**(2), 52–61 (2004). https://doi.org/10.1109/MPRV.2004.1316820
39. Martius, G., Herrmann, J.M.: Variants of guided self-organization for robot control. Theory Biosci. **131**(3), 129–137 (2012). https://doi.org/10.1007/s12064-011-0141-0
40. Montesi, F.: Choreographic programming. Ph.D. thesis (2014). https://pure.itu.dk/ws/files/78733848/m13_phd.pdf

41. Nagpal, R., Shrobe, H., Bachrach, J.: Organizing a global coordinate system from local information on an ad hoc sensor network. In: Zhao, F., Guibas, L. (eds.) IPSN 2003. LNCS, vol. 2634, pp. 333–348. Springer, Heidelberg (2003). https://doi.org/10.1007/3-540-36978-3_22
42. Nicola, R.D., Loreti, M., Pugliese, R., Tiezzi, F.: A formal approach to autonomic systems programming: the SCEL language. ACM Trans. Auton. Adapt. Syst. **9**(2), 7:1–7:29 (2014). https://doi.org/10.1145/2619998
43. Nicola, R.D., Maggi, A., Sifakis, J.: The DReAM framework for dynamic reconfigurable architecture modelling: theory and applications. Int. J. Softw. Tools Technol. Transf. **22**(4), 437–455 (2020). https://doi.org/10.1007/s10009-020-00555-2
44. Parunak, H.V.D., Brueckner, S.A.: Software engineering for self-organizing systems. Knowl. Eng. Rev. **30**(4), 419–434 (2015). https://doi.org/10.1017/S0269888915000089
45. Pianini, D., Casadei, R., Viroli, M., Mariani, S., Zambonelli, F.: Time-fluid field-based coordination through programmable distributed schedulers. Log. Methods Comput. Sci. **17**(4) (2021). https://doi.org/10.46298/lmcs-17(4:13)2021
46. Roestenburg, R., Williams, R., Bakker, R.: Akka in Action. Simon and Schuster (2016)
47. Salehie, M., Tahvildari, L.: Self-adaptive software: landscape and research challenges. ACM Trans. Auton. Adapt. Syst. **4**(2), 14:1–14:42 (2009). https://doi.org/10.1145/1516533.1516538
48. Samarasinghe, D., Lakshika, E., Barlow, M., Kasmarik, K.: Automatic synthesis of swarm behavioural rules from their atomic components. In: Aguirre, H.E., Takadama, K. (eds.) Proceedings of the Genetic and Evolutionary Computation Conference, GECCO 2018, Kyoto, Japan, 15–19 July 2018, pp. 133–140. ACM (2018). https://doi.org/10.1145/3205455.3205546
49. Singh, V.K., Singh, G., Pande, S.: Emergence, self-organization and collective intelligence - modeling the dynamics of complex collectives in social and organizational settings. In: UKSim, pp. 182–189. IEEE (2013). https://doi.org/10.1109/UKSim.2013.77
50. Sirjani, M., Movaghar, A., Shali, A., De Boer, F.S.: Modeling and verification of reactive systems using Rebeca. Fund. Inform. **63**(4), 385–410 (2004)
51. Trianni, V.: Evolutionary Swarm Robotics - Evolving Self-organising Behaviours in Groups of Autonomous Robots. Studies in Computational Intelligence, vol. 108. Springer, Heidelberg (2008). https://doi.org/10.1007/978-3-540-77612-3
52. Varela, C.A., Agha, G.: Programming dynamically reconfigurable open systems with SALSA. ACM SIGPLAN Not. **36**(12), 20–34 (2001). https://doi.org/10.1145/583960.583964
53. Viroli, M., Audrito, G., Beal, J., Damiani, F., Pianini, D.: Engineering resilient collective adaptive systems by self-stabilisation. ACM Trans. Model. Comput. Simul. **28**(2) (2018). https://doi.org/10.1145/3177774
54. Viroli, M., Beal, J., Damiani, F., Audrito, G., Casadei, R., Pianini, D.: From distributed coordination to field calculus and aggregate computing. J. Log. Algebraic Methods Program. **109** (2019). https://doi.org/10.1016/j.jlamp.2019.100486
55. Viroli, M., Casadei, R., Pianini, D.: On execution platforms for large-scale aggregate computing. In: Lukowicz, P., Krüger, A., Bulling, A., Lim, Y., Patel, S.N. (eds.) Proceedings of the 2016 ACM International Joint Conference on Pervasive and Ubiquitous Computing, UbiComp Adjunct 2016, Heidelberg, Germany, 12–16 September 2016, pp. 1321–1326. ACM (2016). https://doi.org/10.1145/2968219.2979129

56. Wolf, T.D., Holvoet, T.: Designing self-organising emergent systems based on infor-
    mation flows and feedback-loops. In: SASO, pp. 295–298. IEEE Computer Society
    (2007). https://doi.org/10.1109/SASO.2007.16
57. Wooldridge, M.J.: An Introduction to MultiAgent Systems, 2nd edn. Wiley, Hobo-
    ken (2009)
58. Zhang, K., Yang, Z., Basar, T.: Multi-agent reinforcement learning: a selective
    overview of theories and algorithms. CoRR abs/1911.10635 (2019). http://arxiv.
    org/abs/1911.10635

Encore: Coda

Elias Castegren⬤ and Tobias Wrigstad$^{(\boxtimes)}$⬤

Department of Information Technology, Uppsala University, Uppsala, Sweden
{elias.castegren,tobias.wrigstad}@it.uu.se

Abstract. Encore is a programming language that was developed between 2014 and 2019. Encore was designed following the principle of inversion of defaults: computations are concurrent (rather than sequential) by default; data is isolated (rather than freely sharable) by default. The language worked as a seedbed for a large number of research ideas aimed at making programming with active objects safe, expressive and efficient.

Encore allows active objects to share data but statically ensures the absence of data races and allows fully concurrent garbage collection. Active objects can synchronize using first-class futures, which are also used to delegate and coalesce computations across active objects. The type system also supports orchestration of intra-object parallelism, expressed using composable units of computation. Active objects which see a lot of traffic can turn themselves into passive objects protected by lock-free synchronization mechanisms to avoid performance bottle-necks, while still facilitating safe sharing and concurrent garbage collection.

This paper gives an overview of these features of Encore, reflecting on lessons learned from trying to fit all of these research ideas into a single language.

1 Introduction

The Encore programming language was developed in the context of the UPSCALE project from 2014 to 2019. The UPSCALE project was funded by the EU Future and Emerging Technologies X-Track and focused on delivering object-oriented programming on multicore architectures.

This paper serves as an introduction to the Encore language and sets out to survey the many ideas that make up the Encore programming language. We delimit ourselves to work that has been integrated with the Encore language in one form or other, or direct descendents of such work that has yet to be integrated.

In terms of research output, the project was a success with more than 40 papers published on various aspects of the language (many of which are cited here), 15 undergraduate theses [35,37,48,49,52,57,58,61,63,64,66,70,71,76,77], as well as the production of several successful PhD candidates (which will be described on the next page). The PhD student who worked extensively on efficient array-like data layout now works at DeepMind on machine learning, where

© The Author(s), under exclusive license to Springer Nature Switzerland AG 2024
F. de Boer et al. (Eds.): *Active Object Languages: Current Research Trends*,
LNCS 14360, pp. 59–91, 2024.
https://doi.org/10.1007/978-3-031-51060-1_3

such aspects are key for performance; the PhD student working on mining existing software for insights now works in the code query team at GitHub; the PhD student working on the low-level details of the language runtime and garbage collection now works in the Java GC team at Oracle; the PhD student working on parallel combinators now works in the Erlang team at Ericsson; finally the PhD student leading the development work on the compiler secured a postdoctoral position at KTH working on the compiler for the Miking [14] language, and now works as assistant professor at Uppsala University, and is an author of this paper.

Yet, in terms of producing a long-term research artefact, the project was a failure: Encore simply grew too fast, and with too little control.

In retrospect, the Encore language development was very chaotic and lacked a clear steward, let alone a rigid development process, or complete formal semantics.[1] This made it very difficult for all the consortium members to contribute. Furthermore, the availability of additional, well-aligned funding to one member in particular—Uppsala University—contributed to Uppsala's unintentional, de-facto domination of the development of the language (it was difficult to keep up). Uppsala's choice of implementation languages (Haskell and C) further contributed to difficulties for students from other members to contribute. Thus, few contributions from other members made it into the Encore language.

Encore: Cast. From the Uppsala side, the Encore programming language was developed by Dave Clarke and Tobias Wrigstad as senior co-principal investigators. The project enjoyed effective co-funding from the Swedish Research Council through its Linnæus Excellence Centre UPMARC (Uppsala Programming for Multicore Architectures Research Centre) as well as a project grant *SCADA: Scalable Data for Pervasive Parallelism* held by Dave Clarke, and *Structured Aliasing* held by Wrigstad, plus a mobility grant from the the Swedish Foundation for Strategic Research through which Wrigstad spent part of his time embedded at Spotify. Together, these grants funded the following PhD students: Elias Castegren [15], Stephan Brandauer [10], Albert Mingkun Yang, Francisco Fernandez-Reyez [67], and Huu Phuc Vo, in the order they were added to the project. From the Imperial side, the principal investigator was Sophia Drossopoulou. Sophia employed Juliana Franco [44] as a PhD student. At the time, she also had Sylvan Clebsch [29]—the creator of the Pony programming language—working as a PhD student, which is how Encore came to share lots of its underlying runtime with Pony (a language with which Encore had considerable mind-share).

The main concepts of the Encore programming language were quite clear early in the project and were published [11] in conjunction with a 2015 project workshop held in Bertinoro. Many of these ideas were influenced by insights from earlier work on the programming languages Joelle [26,62], ABS [54] and Thorn [8,79]. Two main strands of directions were already clear: the use of

---

[1] The title of this paper hides a pun within a pun: *koda* in Swedish is the colloquial for *hacking*, in its MIT 1960's code-cutting sense.

ownership types to enforce encapsulation and guarantee data-race freedom [26] and the use of futures to get from actors to active objects where message sends were made to resemble method calls by returning first-class futures [32].

Outline. In the following sections, we will start by giving an overview of Encore and the motivations and intentions behind its design (Sect. 2). We then move on to describe the type system of Encore and how it prevents data-races (Sect. 3), followed by a description of how Encore uses futures for synchronisation and delegation (Sect. 4). We then discuss other ways to express concurrency and parallelism in Encore (Sect. 5), how Encore was evaluated (Sect. 6) and how the information provided by the type system can be used to achieve efficient data-layout (Sect. 7). We reflect on the surprisingly large role that garbage collection had on the development of Encore (Sect. 8), give an overview of the implementation work of the Encore compiler and runtime (Sect. 9) and finally conclude with some of the lessons we learned from the Encore project (Sect. 10).

2 Encore and the "Principle of Inversion"

At an early stage, the Encore language was guided by the so-called "principle of inversion", which can be described loosely as an intention of breaking with tradition. In the Encore project, the "ideal" was to not carry any past design decisions forward without a strong reason for doing so.

Looking at imperative, object-oriented programming languages, we found that they were predominantly sequential with parallelism or concurrency added as an afterthought; to make matters worse (at least if one's goal is safe parallelism), data was by default mutable, aliasable, fields nullable, etc. In a break with this design, Encore was supposed to be parallel or concurrent by default, use immutable data by default, mutable data non-aliasable, and variables and fields non-nullable. These ideas were roughly summarised in a paper, *Inversion in Programming Language Design: The Encore Way* [27], presented at NOOL—New Object-Oriented Languages, in conjunction with OOPSLA 2015.

In many ways, these ideas reflected many ideals from purely functional programming languages, but retaining an imperative mindset. The importance of the latter was a key selling point in the Encore project proposal: could we avoid paying the cost of rewriting two decades of object-oriented software in functional programming languages?

While the principle of inversion served its purpose well as a license to think fresh, it failed to materialise as an organised design principle for the Encore language. The main reason for this is not easy to pin-point, but likely, the strongest reason was that the team in Uppsala was so eager to get started, that it did not pause to work out a grand design for the language we were so eager to build. In other words, the team solved the problem of getting started at the expense of not having an even remotely clear roadmap for the language. Thus, the entire Encore project never reached a state of convergence. This was well-known even during the project as exemplified by the subtitle of Wrigstad's 2018 AGERE keynote "Encore: Let 1024 Flowers Bloom".

2.1 Concurrency and Parallelism

Encore implements the active object model as its concurrency model. Due to their mind-share, active objects and actors are often confused, so let us begin by quickly discussing both models.

The *Actor Model* is a theoretical framework for concurrent computation, proposed by Hewitt et al. in 1973 [51]. The actor model views computation as a collection of autonomous actors that communicate with each other by sending messages. An actor is a computational entity that encapsulates its own state and behavior and can execute its tasks sequentially but concurrently with other actors in the system. Actors can create new actors, send messages to other actors, and change their internal state upon receiving messages. Importantly, actors are independent and do not share mutable data, ensuring a high degree of concurrency and minimizing the need for explicit synchronization. A survey of actor-based languages can be found in [56].

The *Active Object Model*, also known as the Active Method or Active Object Design Pattern, is a design pattern for concurrent and asynchronous programming proposed by Schmidt and Stal in the mid-1990s [69]. In the active object model, objects encapsulate their own state and behavior, but their methods are executed asynchronously in separate threads or processes. Akin to actors, active objects maintain a message queue (aka mailbox), which contains requests for method invocations. These requests are processed sequentially by the object, ensuring that the object's state is updated consistently. Some active object languages (including Encore) support for suspending processing of a request to be resumed later. This is powerful, but forces programmers to reason about the possible changes to the state of the active object between suspending and resuming.

A survey of active object-based languages, including several members of the UPSCALE project, can be found in [33]. This survey was a initial activity in the UPSCALE project and should probably have fed into Encore more than it did.

In summary, both models provide abstractions for concurrent and distributed computation. The actor model focuses on autonomous actors communicating via message passing, while the active object model emphasizes encapsulation and asynchronous method invocations. A key difference, discussed further in Sect. 4, is how the result of a method call is propagated back to its caller.

Thus, the key source of concurrency in Encore stemmed from asynchronous method calls between active objects. An alternative source of concurrency came later in the form of bestowed references (*cf.* Sect. 5.1) which are similar to the far references in *e.g.,* AmbientTalk [34] and E [60]. Initially, parallelism in Encore stemmed from architecting your programs so that there were enough active objects scheduled in the system at all times to (ideally) saturate the machine. Thus, like task-based systems and unlike threads, parallelism was not mandatory and thus composable. To further unlock parallelism, Encore added a sublanguage of parallel combinators (*cf.* Sect. 5.2) as well as a notion of active objects which supported internal parallelism (*cf.* Sect. 5.3).

2.2 A Brief Introduction to Encore

Encore is an imperative, class-based, object-oriented programming language built on active objects [69], which is a specialisation of the actor model [1]. A class can be marked as **active**, meaning any instance of it will logically have its own thread of control and can only be communicated with asynchronously via message passing. The type system (*cf.* Sect. 3.1) ensures that any data shared between two active objects is safe from data-races: only active and immutable objects can be shared between active objects.

Figure 1 shows a slightly elaborated version of "Hello, World!". Execution starts in the main method of the Main class, where an active PrintServer object is created and passed an immutable Document object (its class is marked as **read**). The expression ps ! print(d) denotes passing the message print with the argument d to ps. Message sends are asynchronous and immediately returns a *future*, which acts as a placeholder for the result of the computation. The get() operation blocks until the future is *fulfilled* by the callee. Futures are expanded on in Sect. 4.

In the PrintServer class, the print method receives a Document, formats the carried string (note that synchronous method calls are written with a period rather than a bang) and prints the string. Since the Main thread is waiting for the print message to finish, the program will always print "Hello, World!" before "Success".

Subtyping and code reuse in Encore is achieved via traits [68]—there is no class inheritance. A trait is similar to a Java 8-style interface with default methods, with the addition that it can also require the presence of fields in the including class. A class must provide all the required fields and methods of its included traits, either by declaring them or by including them from other traits.

Figure 2 shows the PrintServer class from Fig. 1, but with the printing functionality extracted to a trait Printer. The Printer trait requires the presence of a field p of type Printer and a method print taking a String and returning a String. When included in a class that provides these members, as in the class PrintServer, the trait provides the method print.

The semantics is the same as if we had copy-pasted the print method from the trait to the class[2]. Importantly, we are now able to reuse the Printer functionality in a different class, for example one that provides another format method. Additionally, it may be used for classes have not been marked as active (meaning the interaction is synchronous).

In Sect. 3.1, we go into details on how Encore facilitates code reuse across different sharing and concurrency scenarios.

3 Types for Safe Concurrency and Parallelism

Encore's type system statically prevents data races. This means that whenever two active objects have access to the same passive object, neither of them can

---

[2] This is known as the *flattening property* [68].

```
 1  active class Main
 2    def main() : unit
 3      val ps = new PrintServer
 4      val d = new Document("Hello, World!")
 5      val fut = ps ! print(d)
 6      get(fut)
 7      println("Success")
 8    end
 9  end
10
11  active class PrintServer
12    val p : Printer
13    // The 'init' method is the constructor
14    def init(p : Printer) : unit
15      this.p = p
16    end
17    def format(s : String) : String
18      ...
19    end
20    def print(doc : Document) : unit
21      val s = this.format(doc.str)
22      this.p.print(s)
23    end
24  end
25
26  read class Document
27    val str : String
28      def init(str : String) : unit
29        this.str = str
30      end
31  end
```

Fig. 1. A slightly elaborated Hello World example in Encore.

mutate that object. One of the design goals of Encore was to achieve this without giving up on staple features of object-oriented languages, such as subtyping and code reuse. We based Encore's type system on the Kappa type system [15, 19, 20].

3.1 Subtyping and Code Reuse Across Concurrency Scenarios

In Encore, each class or trait type has a *capability*[3] which denotes what makes an object of that type safe to access. The following capabilities are available for use:

- **local**: the object is local to the current active object and can never be shared
- **read**: the object will not be mutated, and so can be freely shared

---

[3] The origin Kappa work referred these properties "mode", but "capability" is more in line with recent terminology.

```
1   trait Printer
2     require val p : Printer
3     require def format(s : String) : String
4     def print(s : String) : String
5       val s = this.format(doc.str)
6       this.p.print(s)
7     end
8   end
9
10  active class PrintServer : Printer
11    val p : Printer
12    def init(p : Printer) : unit
13      this.p = p
14    end
15    def format(s : String) : String
16      ...
17    end
18  end
```

Fig. 2. The example from Figure 1 with the printer functionality broken out as a trait.

- **linear**[4]: the object has at most one reference to it, so it is never shared
- **subord**: the object is *strongly encapsulated* inside the current class
- **active**: the object is an active object and can only be passed messages

Note that while **read** and **active** objects are the only ones that can be *shared*, **linear** objects can be *passed* between active objects and retain their mutability. This is because the active object sending a **linear** object necessarily gives up its only reference to that object in doing so. Using the **subord** capability it is possible for a **linear** object to encapsulate other objects [25], making it possible to send entire object aggregates as long as the entry point is **linear**. **local** objects are the closest thing to "regular" objects, with the only restriction that they cannot be passed between active objects.

In Fig. 1 the capabilities are given where classes are declared. This means that the type of **this** is known, allowing for example a Document object to pass itself to an active object. Classes can include any number of traits and must give each trait a capability. Classes with a declared capability implicitly give that capability to all its included traits (as is the case with the **active** PrintServer class in Fig. 2). Classes without a declared capability can only define a constructor method and otherwise has to rely on methods from included traits (which necessarily have been given capabilities explaining why their provided methods are safe to use).

When a capability is not given to a trait, as is the case with the Printer trait in Fig. 2, the body of the trait is type checked as if the capability was **subord**. This prevents **this** from escaping, either via an external method call or message send, by returning it in a method, or by capturing it in an object or closure

---

[4] A better name would be unique, as a linear capability does not imply that a reference is used exactly once, as with linear types.

```
1    subord class PrivateList : ...        25   linear class Token : HasLog
2      ...                                 26     val log : PrivateLog
3    end                                   27     val id : String
4                                          28     def init(id : String) : unit
5    trait Loggable                        29       this.log = new PrivateLog
6      require val backend : PrivateList    30       this.id = id
7      def append(entry : String)          31     end
8        this.backend.append(entry)        32   end
9      end                                 33
10   end                                   34   local class Ledger : HasLog
11                                         35     val log : PrivateLog
12   subord class PrivateLog : Loggable    36     def init() : unit
13     val backend : PrivateList           37       this.log = new PrivateLog
14     def init() : unit                   38     end
15       this.backend = new PrivateList    39   end
16     end                                 40
17   end                                   41   active class Worker
18                                         42     val id : String
19   trait HasLog                          43     val ledger : Ledger
20     require val log : PrivateLog        44     val next : Worker
21     def log(entry : String) : unit     45     def handleToken(token : Token) : unit
22       this.log.append(entry)           46       token.log(this.id)
23     end                                 47       this.ledger.log(token.id)
24   end                                   48       this.next ! handleToken(consume token)
                                           49     end
                                           50   end
```

Fig. 3. The HasLog trait is re-used for both the **linear** Token class and the **local** Ledger class.

which later escapes. Importantly, this enables us to give any capability to the trait when it is used, allowing traits to be reused for both active objects (*e.g.,* the **active** PrintServer class in Fig. 2) and passive objects. The exception to this rule is the **read** capability, which requires all fields to be immutable (**val** rather than **var**) and have types which do not allow direct mutation (**read** or **active**). Because of this, the **read** capability can only be given at trait (or class) declaration site[5].

Figure 3 shows a scenario where a trait HasLog, which provides a log method is reused both for a **linear** Token class and for a **local** Ledger class. On Line 45 an **active** Worker object receives a Token in a message. It logs its own ID in the log of the Token, and then logs the ID of the token in its Ledger, before passing the Token on to another Worker (the **consume** keyword tells the type checker that we will not use the token variable again). Note how the class PrivateLog is marked as **subord**, meaning it cannot escape the scope in which it is used. This makes it safe to pass the Token class around, even though it has access to mutable state in the list backend of the PrivateLog class—the only way to access the internal state is by going via the Token itself.

---

[5] It is possible to check this also at use site, but it makes type checking less modular.

It would be possible to also type check classes without capabilities as if they were subordinate, as for traits. However, making classes without capabilities rely entirely on their traits enables the pattern shown in Fig. 4. Here a `Cell` class is built from a **read** trait for reading a value and a **linear** trait for setting the value. The + on line 15 is used for including multiple traits, and the since one of the included traits is **linear** the whole class is treated as **linear**. As long as the `Cell` is **linear**, it can be mutated and even passed around between active objects. On Line 29 the **linear** part is forgotten via an upcast, and with it the ability to mutate the object. The remaining value can be shared safely since it now only allows reading, and we just forgot the *only* way to cause mutation to the object. The original Kappa paper shows how to recover mutability after turning a reference read-only [20], while in Encore, forgetting a **linear** trait is permanent.

```
1   read trait Gettable
2     require val value : int
3     def getValue() : int
4       return this.value
5     end
6   end
7
8   linear trait Settable
9     require var value : int
10    def setValue(value : int) : unit
11      this.value = value
12    end
13  end
14
15  class Cell : Gettable + Settable
16    var value : int
17    def init(value : int) : unit
18      this.value = value
19    end
20  end

21  class Main
22    def main() : unit
23      val cell = new Cell(0)
24      // Mutate the cell while it is linear
25      cell.setValue(42)
26      ...
27
28      // Forget mutability and linearity...
29      val g : Gettable = cell
30      // ...allowing the cell to be shared
31      val w1 = new Worker
32      val w2 = new Worker
33      w1 ! doWork(g)
34      w2 ! doWork(g)
35    end
36  end
```

Fig. 4. A `Cell` object built from a **read** part and a (mutable) **linear** part can be initialised and changed until the **linear** part is forgotten, after which it can be freely shared.

Encore's type system also supports method overriding and parametric polymorphism, neither of which are trivial when capabilities are involved. For example, an overridden method of a **read** trait must not be allowed to cause mutation, and a polymorphic method that sends its argument to an active object must not be called with a **local** reference. See Castegren's PhD thesis (Chap. 6) for a treatise on these two topics [15].

3.2 Attached and Detached Closures

Since Encore supports higher-order functions in the form of closures, an important question is how to handle transfer of closures which capture references to local state. Intuitively, a closure that is created by some active object A and which closes over A's local state can not be safely sent to another active object B, as running the closure would mean that B gets access the local state of A, causing potential data-races. We say that a closure that can only (safely) be run by some active object *attached* to that object. In contrast, a *detached* closure is one that can (in principle) be run by any active object.

Because the type system already tracks which objects can be safely shared and not, Encore similarly tracks which closures are attached (and therefore cannot be shared) and which closures are detached. Rather than just a single capability, the type of a closure has several capabilities denoting what kind of references have been captured. A closure that captures a **local** reference is **local** (and cannot be shared), a closure that captures a **linear** reference is **linear** (and can only be called once) and a closure that captures both a **local** and a **linear** reference is both **local** and **linear**.

The concept of attached and detached closures in the context of Encore was further explored in a paper which also discusses the possibility of running attached closures asynchronously by delegating back to the active object that created it [16].

The bestowed references discussed in Sect. 5.1 relax the type system and uses attached closures to ensure that operations on an active object's representation is always performed by the active object's thread of control by lifting operations into closures attached to the owning active object.

3.3 Capabilities for Safe Array Programming

The Kappa type system was later extended to support programming with arrays [2,3]. In addition to treating arrays as objects and applying the same capabilities as listed in Sect. 3.1 (with a **read** array meaning an array that can not be assigned to), it is also possible to make use of the regular structure of arrays to split one array reference into several non-overlapping *views* (or slices) of the same array. Each view appears as a zero-indexed array, but during runtime indices are translated to access the corresponding part the original array. These disjoint views can then be operated on concurrently without data-races. Let c be the array [A, B, C, D, E] and apply a split operation splitting at the 3rd element:

```
a, b = split(c, 2, strided=false)  -- a = [A, B, C], b = [D, E]
```

As long as elements in a and b cannot alias (a crude but simple typed-driven check due to capabilities), a and b can be operated on safely in parallel.

The most important operations for manipulating array views—split and merge—are surprisingly expressive. For example, the following line of code performs matrix rotation (more examples in [3]):

—— a is a 2d matrix of type T[rows][cols]
```
merge(split(a, cols, strided=true), concatenate=true)
```

The inner `split` operation splits a into individual columns, which are then logically concatenated using the `merge` operation. A third operation `align` (not shown) was introduced to reorganise an array's physical layout to conform with the logical layout stemming from split and merge operations. This removes translations that are otherwise needed for individual element access, and can be key to unlocking improved cache utilisation.

Both actors and active objects are typically associated by a single thread of control operating inside each actor or active object. In such a model, being able to turn an array into a set of disjoint views does not immediately solve the problem of how to express a parallel operation on them. The simplest solution in Encore is to capture the views in separate detached closures. This however creates two new problems. First, the ownership of the views move from the actor to the closures and must be explicitly moved back again. Second, how to balance scheduling of tasks for parallelism vs. tasks for concurrency is unclear. In an effort to address both these problems, parallel abstractions were introduced in Encore (*cf.* Sect. 5.2).

An implementation of splittable array capabilities was prototyped, but never implemented for Encore, partly because the underlying concurrent garbage collector (*cf.* Sect. 8) did not easily support partial tracing of objects, *e.g.*, when disjoint parts of a single array are held by different active objects.

3.4 Letting Go of Static Types

The data-race safety offered by type systems such as Encore's comes with the overhead of having to annotate your program with capabilities. As with any static type system, there will always be safe programs that are rejected by the capability system due to lack of precision or flexibility in the available annotations. An attempt at addressing this problem comes in the shape of Dala [43], a language which sprung out of the work on Encore and James Noble's work on the teaching language Grace [5]. In Dala, capability annotations are optional, but an object which is created with a capability remembers it for the rest of its lifetime. This allows writing code without capability annotations which interacts with annotated code. Whenever an annotated part of a program expects an object with unknown origins to have a certain capability it can be checked dynamically—similar to how static and dynamic code interacts in gradually typed languages.

As an explicit goal, the Dala capability system is simpler than Encore's, supporting only three capabilities: **local**, **imm**(utable), similar to Encore's **read**, and **iso**(lated), similar to Encore's **linear**. Immutable objects can only refer to immutable objects; isolated objects to isolated and immutable objects; and local objects to all of the above. References that violate these constraints give rise to run-time exceptions.

Objects without capabilities are considered **unsafe**, and **unsafe** objects can refer to any object. The main safety property provided by Dala is that data-races can only happen through operations on **unsafe** objects. A gradual type system allows a programmer to annotate parts of a Dala programs with type annotations that can guarantee that well-typed programs do not violate the aforementioned reference constraints. This is in contrast to Encore, where the whole program needs to be annotated with capabilities in order to get any safety guarantees. Dala was implemented as an extension to the gradually typed language Grace [5] by Michael Homer.

4   The Futures of Encore

The Encore design ideal was an object-oriented look and feel. Thus, a message send is a bidirectional operation: the caller passes a message and a payload to the callee, and the callee eventually returns a result back to the caller. Contrast this with the actor model where a message is from the caller to the callee; returns are handled by message passing in the opposite direction. This is considerably more difficult to understand and maintain, *i.e.*, programmers having to manually sort out what incoming message is a response to what outgoing message (if any). Some languages (*e.g.*, Erlang) simplify this by a selective receive operation that only permits some messages to be received at a particular program point, but processing messages out-of-order is also challenging and loses causality.

In Fig. 1 a future is created as an effect of the message send at Line 5. Unlike synchronous method calls, control immediately returns to the call site and the active object that sent the message can continue working. In this example however, already at Line 6 the active Main object blocks until the value of the future is available using the **get** operation. Here, the contents of the future is an uninteresting unit value (*i.e.*, the future is only used for synchronization of active objects), but in general calling **get** on a future of type Future[t] results in a value of type t.

4.1   Forward Delegation

Encore forced explicit manipulation of future values. A method which ended in **return** 42 would have return type **int** when called synchronously and Future[int] when called asynchronously. Making futures explicit was a design choice motivated by a desire to reason about performance. In languages like E [60], AmbientTalk [34] and Newspeak [9], it is not generally possible to see if an operation is performed synchronously or asynchronously, which can have detrimental effects on a system, *i.e.*, because asynchronous indirections can have a several orders of magnitude slowdown.

As more and more Encore code was being written, a pattern emerged with a considerable code smell: actors which were orchestrating computations found themselves on the critical path on computation simply because future values needed unpacking to satisfy return types. Figure 5 illustrates this. Because the return type on Line 1 is **int**, d must also have type **int** on Line 4, which necessitates Line 3's forced wait for the future value to materialise.

There are several problems with this pattern, all related to performance:

```
1  def example(a: int, b: int, x: Calc) : int
2    var c = x ! add(a, b)
3    var d = get(c) // unwrap future value
4    return d // return value
5  end
```

Fig. 5. Delegation example

1. It adds unnecessary work and garbage to the system: more futures must be created and destroyed;
2. It adds latency on method returns: when Calc is finished adding a and b, the result does not directly flow to its final destination—instead it must wait for all intermediate steps to become scheduled to unwrap and then re-wrap the result in and out of futures; and
3. It blocks actors from doing useful work: a call to example will block the caller on Line 3 until Calc is scheduled and able to perform the addition. During this time, the caller is unable to respond to any other messages for fear of interference with its ongoing operations in example.

To mitigate this problem, Encore introduces a concept called *forwarding* [39]. Forwarding allows the entire body of example in Fig. 5 to be written like so: **forward** x ! add(a, b). The **forward** keyword behaves like a **return**, *i.e.*, it aborts the current method and returns a result. Thus, it preserved the existing Encore guarantee that a future would be fulfilled exactly once.

In the Encore implementation, a future is created by the caller to be fulfilled by the callee. A call wrapped in a **forward** would reuse the existing future ensuring that a long pipeline of actors delegating work would only create one future, at the start of the message pipeline.

4.2 Futures: Explicit or Implicit, and Control Flow or Data Flow?

The work on forward delegation continued with a joint effort with Ludovic Henrio (who had been exploring similar ideas [50]) and Einar Broch Johnsen, leading to a publication at ECOOP [40] and an accompanying artefact [41]. In this work, we defined two dimensions of futures: control-flow vs. data-flow futures, how each of them can be used to encode the other, and explicit vs. implicit futures. Futures in Joelle and ABS were explicit: visible to the programmer and unpacked with a get() operation. Futures in *e.g.*, AmbientTalk are implicit: a future value (*e.g.*, a to-be-computed integer) is indistinguishable from its materialised value (*e.g.*, 42). Accessing a data-flow future will block until a non-future value has materialised, regardless of any nesting of futures. Control-flow futures allow the incremental unravelling of future indirections, meaning nested futures must be multiply unpacked, which enables writing code that explicitly wants to handle *future* values, *e.g.*, scheduling code, multiplexers and load-balancers. Through the **forward** mechanism, control-flow futures can be used to encode data-flow futures in most cases. This is why, in the end, Encore settled for explicit control-flow futures using **forward** to avoid nested futures where those were not needed. Chappe *et al.* later extended Encore with data-flow futures [23], implementing control-flow futures as a library and thus realising the second encoding first presented in [40].

4.3 Future Chaining

To build computational pipelines, Encore supported the concept of future chaining, *i.e.*, adding a callback to a future to be executed upon its fulfilment. Figure 6 illustrates this: instead of forcing the future result from the calculation server to be fulfilled before printing the result, we chain a continuation on the future result in the form of a closure. The result of the entire expression in Fig. 6 is a future unit (Future[**Unit**]). Thus, we could chain another continuation on the future to report that the printing was completed, etc.

```
calcServer ! add(a, b) -> fun v => print("{a}+{b}={v}")
```

Fig. 6. Future chaining. The printing closure will be executed when the future result from the calculation server is fulfilled.

Future chaining is strongly connected to the concept of attached and detached closures discussed in Sect. 3.2. In Fig. 6, the closure that is chained on the future result from the calculation server captures a and b; thus the closure must be attached if at least one of a and b is a mutable value.

There were many discussions about the semantics of future chaining, especially who performs the chained closure? Chaining something on an already fulfilled closure naturally could be executed immediately at the call-site (the active object producing the future value may no longer exist), but what happens to a closure chained on an unfulfilled future? One possibility is to have the active object that fulfils the future execute the closure. This would shorten the latency between fulfilling the future and executing the continuation, but also allows anyone to inject code into any active object. An example that illustrates the point is shown in Fig. 7, where the continuation, a never ending loop, will cause the calculation service to never finish processing the add() message, effectively causing a form of denial-of-service attack.

```
calcServer ! add(a, b) -> fun _
                      while true
                      end
                  end
```

Fig. 7. Denial of service attack using a detached closure.

Furthermore, if the calculation server was able to fulfil the future before the chaining operation was executed, the caller would loop forever. While this code is clearly contrived, it is easy to conceive of isomorphic accidents in real code, looping forever or slowing a critical active object down.

In the end, Encore adopted the following semantics for future chaining: chaining a closure on a future always leads to an asynchronous operation, regardless of whether the future is fulfilled at the time of chaining. The closure is sent to an active object in the system together with the value of the fulfilled future to be executed. The Encore compiler infers whether a closure is attached or detached at compile-time. If it is attached, the active object it will be sent to for execution is its creator. If it is detached, it will be sent to a system service that processes detached closures. In the case of Fig. 6, the closure is detached (because a and b are integers which can be captured safely). Thus, the current actor will be able to define a continuation of the add() operation in terms of printing the result, take itself out of the control-flow path to this printing, and not be scheduled again while still having the value printed.

5   More Concurrency and Parallelism

Encore's *concurrency abstractions* are to a large extent about enabling a program structure that permits responding to events or requests whose distribution is not known ahead-of-time. Encore's *parallel abstractions* instead deal with problem decomposition and orchestration of multiple (typically identical) operations operating on different data, or how to support contention on data crucial to multiple operations.

5.1   New Concurrency Abstractions: Bestowed References

Active objects in Encore present an interface of available messages. When processing a message, an active object operates on its own local state (consisting of passive objects). This local state must be encapsulated to avoid data-races. Thus, the only means by which to interact with state of another active object is through the interface of that active object. This is akin to how strong encapsulation in *e.g.,* ownership types [28] prevent useful patterns such as iterators of linked lists: there is no way for an external entity to even learn of the existence of the internal objects (links) of the list. This impacts the structure of programs, and favours *e.g.,* transfer of code via closures instead of direct knowledge of objects inside another active object enclosure. Staying with our iterator analogy, there is no straightforward way to store the state of the iterator, unless the iterator itself is encapsulated inside the list, and therefore not accessible externally.

To simplify programs where external access to objects residing in another active object leads to simpler design with less indirect manipulation, Encore supports a principled relaxation of encapsulation of **local** objects by *bestowing* *them with activity* and having them appear as active objects [18,21][6]. If x is a reference of type **local** T, the operation **bestow** x returns a reference of type **bestowed** T. This reference has the same interface as T, but can only be interacted with via message sends. These messages are delegated to the actor that bestowed the object with activity, and which can safely operate on the object. This is similar to far references in AmbientTalk [34] and E [60], but with delegation being visible in the type of the reference rather than being implicit.

As an example of bestowed references, consider the code in Fig. 8 where Server objects store local Database objects. Through the shareDatabase method, a Client can ask for asynchronous access to a Database—the local Database object is bestowed on Line 9. Note how the owner of the Database accesses it synchronously (Line 8) while a Client can only send it messages (Line 19). These messages will be delegated to be processed by the Server that shared the Database.

```
1   local class Database
2     ...
3   end
4
5   active class Server
6     var db : local Database
7     def shareDatabase(client : Client) : bestowed Database
8       this.db.addClient(client)
9       return bestow this.db
10    end
11  end
12
13  active class Client
14    var server : Server
15    def run(socket : Socket) : unit
16      val db = this.server.shareDatabase(this)
17      while (socket.hasMore()) do
18        val entry = socket.getEntry()
19        db!addEntry(entry)
20      end
21    end
22  end
```

Fig. 8. The Server class bestows its local Database object with activity. Messages sent to the Database will be delegated to the Server object that owns it.

The motivation behind bestowed references is to allow relaxing the strong encapsulation required by the active object model. From a software engineering standpoint, this is useful to avoid duplicating the interface of a passive class when an asynchronous interface is required. For example, in Fig. 8 the Server class does not need to repeat the (possibly very large) interface of its internal Database object.

---

[6] This feature was implemented, but was never merged into mainline Encore.

5.2   New Parallel Abstractions: Building Parallel Pipelines with Par[T]-Types

The programming model described so far has focused on *concurrent* programs, where a message being processed by an active object serves as the unit of computation, where active objects run independently from each other, and one active object can be involved in multiple "computations". Sometimes however, it is desirable to express *parallel* computations, where a single result is calculated by several units of computation for performance reasons. While it is possible to express parallel computations with the active object model, because the active object model is fundamentally unstructured, inability to express dependencies between "tasks" makes it difficult to efficiently partition work and joining the results of multiple computations without introducing artificial latency due to suboptimal scheduling.

For example, recursive problem decomposition in a fork-join model naturally constructs a dependency tree of computations towards a common goal, where work-stealing higher up in the tree is able to efficiently move considerable amounts of work across cores. This is in contrast to the scheduling of active objects, where a message from one active object to another typically pulls the second onto the same core as the first for efficient communication and cache utilisation (unless the second was already scheduled elsewhere). Put differently: when using a single abstraction, it becomes difficult for a language runtime to distinguish between a "normal call chain", where computation is essentially sequential but may be interleaved with other computations at points that arise naturally due to asynchronous indirections brought on by decomposition of state, and "a fork-join call chain", where (some of) the asynchronous indirections morally give rise to new "sub-computations" that should be distributed across multiple cores for efficient processing.

To express situations like the latter, Encore supports building pipelines of parallel computations using a domain-specific expression language [38,42]. A parallel computation of type Par[T] (pronounced "party", with an Australian accent) results in zero or more values of type T. Parallel computations are expressed using the following basic combinators (other derived combinators are also available):

- liftv : T → Par[T] – lift a value to a (trivial) parallel computation
- || : Par[T] → Par[T] → Par[T] – merge two parallel computations into one
- >> : Par[T] → (T → T') → Par[T'] – apply a function (in parallel) to each value of a parallel computation
- join : Par[Par[T]] → Par[T] – "flatten" a nested parallel computation
- extract : Par[T] → [T] – gather all values of a parallel computation into an array (this blocks the active object until the computation is complete)

Spawning a new parallel computation is different from an asynchronous message send, in that it expresses an operation that is *intended* to be parallelised, modulo resource availability.

Figure 9 shows a simple example of a parallel pipeline calculating the square of each prime smaller than 100. The helper function liftUpTo builds a Par[**int**] holding the first n values (note the function `empty` on line 2 which returns an empty parallel computation). On line 10 we spawn a parallel computation starting with the numbers 0–100. On line 12, we pass each of these numbers (in parallel) to a function that only keeps the numbers which are prime. We then pass the remaining values to a function that squares them. While this parallel computation is running, the active object is free to do other work, including passing messages to other active objects (we could even store the parallel computation in a field and get back to it in another method). Finally, on line 20 we block until the result is available in the array `result`. Note that the order of the elements in the array will be determined by the order in which the computations finished.

```
1   fun liftUpTo(n : int) : Par[int]
2     var p = empty[int]() // An empty computation of zero values
3     for i <- [1..n] do
4       p = p || liftv(i)
5     end
6   end
7
8   active class Main
9     def main() : unit
10      val par =
11        // Get the first 100 integers
12        liftUpTo(100) >>
13        // Keep only primes
14        (fun v => if isPrime(v) then v else empty[int]()) >>
15        // Square the numbers
16        (fun p => p * p)
17        // Do some independent work (potentially) in parallel with the above
18        ... // don't access the result in par
19        // (Potentially) Block on the availability of the result in par
20      val result = extract(par)
21    end
22  end
```

Fig. 9. A parallel pipeline calculating the square of primes with Par[T] types

The parallel combinators are based on the orchestration language Orc [55]. The main difference between the implementations in Encore and Orc is that parallel computations in Encore are statically typed (Orc is dynamically typed, with an optional static type checker) and run asynchronously with the rest of the program, allowing e.g., spawning a parallel computation and performing some other work before waiting for the result. Encores parallel computations are also integrated with futures; any future can be lifted into a parallel computation using the function `liftf : Future[T] → Par[T]`. This allows involving other active objects in a parallel computation but with the same type system restrictions that ensure the absence of data-races.

Using Encore's type system it is possible to identify immutable (**read**) objects, which means that it is simple to build functional pipelines that do not modify shared state. However, there is no support for temporarily turning mutable objects immutable, meaning that it is not possible to create parallel pipelines that operate on mutable (*e.g.,* **local**) objects, even if they would be functional (and therefore free from data-races). This is further complicated by the fact that an active object can perform operations concurrently with a parallel computation. While solutions for turning **linear** objects temporarily immutable exist (*cf.* the discussion around Fig. 4), they were never implemented in Encore, and so the implementation of Par[T] types were somewhat stymied.

5.3 Dealing with Hot Objects

Programs whose concurrency is built on threads and locks eventually must decide on lock granularity. Too fine-grained locks can hurt performance due to excessive locking and unlocking, and may make it harder to establish the necessary atomicity guarantees. Too coarse-grained locking instead hurts parallel performance by forcing unnecessary waiting, and may lead to deadlocks.

The enforced isolation of active objects in Encore gives a natural lock granularity: a single active object. This is a good choice if the messages in the system are sufficiently uniformly distributed, and require roughly the same processing time. Otherwise, objects that are critical to many operations become bottlenecks that may serialise computation.

For example, if the server active object in Fig. 8 ends up getting disproportionally many messages in a system, it will affect the parallelism of the system negatively, and may cause the server's mailbox to grow unboundedly.

Broadly speaking, there are two solutions for dealing with such "hot" objects. The first solution is to distribute different parts of the database over multiple different active objects, and use *e.g.,* some hashing strategy to send messages directly to the right database shard. This works well, but complicates database queries that require access to multiple active objects. This might force bespoke implementations of two-phase commits or other synchronisation protocols on-top of the active objects.

The second solution is to permit simultaneous accesses to the contended data without compromising safety: for example using a multiple readers–single writer lock to permit simultaneous read access, or transactions to optimistically synchronise concurrent writes to (hopefully) different parts of the database.

The Kappa type system included a hot capability which provided an asynchronous interface like a regular active object, but could be implemented using a synchronous access model in the backend [78]. The only implementation of hot objects used Kappa's type system for lock-free algorithms [22] and was supported by a special garbage collector that could handle the simultaneous access by multiple threads of control [82]. By permitting the run-time to turn accesses to hot objects into synchronous accesses, the hot objects would scale with their contention. There were plans to support hot objects using transactional memory in addition to lock-free algorithms, but this was never implemented. Asynchronous message sends from inside transactions require special treatment. An interesting paper combining actors and transactions can be found in the works of Swalens et al. [72].

6   Benchmarking and Evaluation

To understand Encore's performance, we relied on the de-facto standard benchmark suite for actor languages: Savina [53]. We implemented all the Savina benchmarks including *e.g.*, ThreadRing, Fib, Chameneos, Big, concdict, Dining-Philosophers, NQueens, and ParallelQuickSort. In this work, Uppsala had the help of several other consortium members, most notably Einar Broch Johnsen, Sophia Drossopoulou and Juliana Franco. In addition to the Savina benchmarks, we also implemented a SAT solver, a Support Vector Machine, a CRDT framework, several prime sieves, preferential attachment, and ported ProRail, an agent-based control system for train scheduling, which had been used for evaluation in a prior project. The latter was not able to stress the system meaningfully, but provided insights about the "programming experience" of Encore.

The ThreadRing benchmark led to an interesting discovery in the Pony runtime: the benchmark turned out to be a pathological case for the cycle detector which is instrumental in automatically collecting actors in Pony and active objects in Encore. Analysing several of the benchmarks made clear shortcomings of the Savina suite, as many supposedly actor programs directly accessed other actors' state using atomic operations. This made an apples-to-apples comparison with existing Savina benchmarks difficult. This work continued in a collaboration with Sebastian Blessing [7], and subsequently with Sebastian Blessing, Stefan Marr, Rudolf Schlatte, and the implementers of CAF on a new malleable benchmark called "ChatApp" with implementations in ABS, CAF, Erlang, Newspeak and Pony.[7]

Our overall conclusion from benchmarking was that Encore performed on-par with Akka; slightly better on a saturated machine, and slightly worse on an undersaturated machine. When the final benchmarking was performed, the Akka baseline was run using the G1 garbage collector which is mostly concurrent. Today, it would make more sense to use the new ZGC garbage collector where GC work is never on the critical path of performance (assuming sensible deployment).

As one goal of Encore was to provide a path of migration for existing object-oriented software, we undertook a substantial mining effort using trace-based analysis in a tool named Spencer, constructed for this purpose by Stephan Brandauer from Uppsala University [13]. We analysed the entire DaCapo benchmark suite [6] in Spencer, to see the extent to which programmers were writing programs which were compatible with the constraints enforced by the Encore compiler, even though the Java language would not be able to leverage this at compile-time or run-time.

The results of this undertaking are summarised in [12] as well as in Brandauer's PhD thesis [10]. We found that while Java allows aliasing and mutation

---

[7] Available at https://github.com/sblessing/chat-app.

by default, objects are often unique, unique modulo references from the stack, immutable, or stack-bound (*i.e.,* not pointed to from fields in the heap): 97.7% of objects enjoy at least one of these properties. Furthermore, uniqueness and immutability, or their absence, are per-class properties, not per-object properties, meaning that it is very rare for classes to produce both immutable and mutable instances. This latter result confirmed the design of Kappa, which argued the simplicity of class-level annotations (*i.e.,* at declaration-site) over object-level annotations (*i.e.,* at use-site), although both kinds were supported.

7 Type-Driven Optimisations for Data Layout

Efficient data utilisation plays a crucial role in optimising program performance in modern computer systems. One significant factor that greatly impacts performance is how data is organised in memory. Understanding and carefully designing the data layout can have a substantial influence on cache performance, which directly affects the speed of data access and processing due to the performance gap between memory systems and processors.

Managed programming languages, which abstract away the low-level details of memory management, pose challenges when it comes to optimising data layout. Such languages (exemplified by *e.g.,* C#, Java, and Python) provide memory management features like garbage collection which relieve developers from manual memory allocation and deallocation tasks. This avoids whole classes of bugs, and simplifies the management of object ownership from the perspective of who is responsible for deallocating a datum. This is especially crucial in concurrent programming. (For more on garbage collection Encore *cf.* Sect. 8.)

A downside of such abstractions is that programmers have limited control over how data is laid out in memory. In particular, the aforementioned optimisation of data layout becomes difficult when runtime system manages memory allocation and placement. Ultimately, this leads to an inability to fully exploit cache performance and optimise memory access patterns.

A classic example in this context is the choice between using an array of structures (AoS) or a structure of arrays (SoA), a decision which can have a profound impact on cache utilisation. In an AoS layout, each element of the array contains a complete structure, while in an SoA layout, the components of the structure are stored in separate arrays. Going from the former to the latter in *e.g.,* Java means "exploding" an object and scattering its data across multiple places in memory. This creates new opportunities for errors as programmers may mistakenly combine data belonging to different objects giving rise to spurious values in the system. Furthermore, distributing data across multiple locations can greatly complicate synchronisation in a concurrent program.

Several members of the Encore team had worked previously on ownership types [28]. Ownership types places objects in *ownership contexts*, which previously had not been reified. By reifying the ownership contexts (now called "pools"), the contexts could be associated with layout information that could be used to control placement of objects as well as object layout. Consider the following type of a stack object in pool a with T-typed elements in pool b:

```
s : Stack[a, T[b]]
```

The stack object s lives itself in pool a and thus the object layout and placement is controlled by a. The elements in the stack live in the pool b which may impose different layout. For example, we might decide that objects in b are allocated using a bump allocator to get locality of consecutive pushes, or if T is a pair of fst and snd, we might allocate all pairs so that all fst's are consecutive and snd's separately consequtive, or both in combination. Our prototype implementation implemented pools using a 4 Gb alignment so that each pool had room to grow. (This also permitted intra-pool references to be stored as 32-bit addresses, fitting more discrete objects into cache.)

The example above shows how one can decouple the layout of a class from its definition – the properties of a and b are determined by where in the code the stack type is declared, not where the stack is defined. Thus, it is possible to instantiate multiple versions of the stack class in different places of the code, laid out according to the needs for those particular use cases. Our starting point was the memory of individual active objects, which would simplify the problem by restricting access to one single thread. The SHAPES programming model [46,47] document these efforts further. It aims to present a programmer with a familiar pointer-based abstraction but control how data was distributed by placement of objects in pools. These ideas were later continued by Alexandros Tasos who explored fusing these ideas with vectorisation [73–75].

An runtime extension was constructed as part of a master thesis project [48], but sadly this runtime was never properly integrated with the rest of Encore.

8   Garbage Collection

A substantial effort of the Encore project was devoted to garbage collection, despite the early consortium agreement to *not* do so. This can be chalked up to not fully understanding the impact of concurrent garbage collection for performance and the consortium's lack of understanding of how little actor isolation had been explored in the mainstream for performance gains in garbage collection. The choice of Pony as a runtime for Encore was made to piggyback on its memory management [30,31], but the growing collaboration with the Pony team pushed efforts in the direction of proving the correctness of its collector for passive objects [45] to the point of this becoming the subject of Juliana Franco's dissertation [44].

Pony's collector for passive objects relied on a combination of tracing and reference counting. Inside the heap of an actor (or active object), liveness was determined by tracing. Upon sending a message, the sending actor would trace through the payload of the message and record all the references. For each reference shared with the world, the actor would increment a reference count to keep track of "external stake" in the object. When a reference to an object in another actor was dropped, it would eventually be discovered and communicated in terms of a decrement message to the owning actor. In this way, actors could further share a reference to another actor's innards, and the system would keep in sync through passing increment and decrement messages on the same channels used for normal message sends. Thus, each actor had a conservative approximation of external stake in its objects, that it could use together with trace-based liveness information to maintain its heap. Importantly, this design allows an actor to do garbage collection whenever it chooses, without the need to synchronise with any other agent in the system.

The Pony philosophy was to keep actors' individual heaps down so that tracing an actor's heap did not cause unreasonable delays for its messages. The lack of large standard benchmarks in Pony made these results very difficult to publish, given the maturity of mainstream GC research, which typically takes place in the context of well-established languages with commercial applications available for evaluation.

In a system with large number of actors, Pony's GC design has excellent tail-latency properties as demonstrated by Fig. 10, which shows a comparison between Pony, Erlang and Java (using C4 a fully-concurrent collector, and G1 which is mostly concurrent) (taken from [31] which discusses this experiment further). The decreasing GC concurrency of Erlang, C4 and G1 clearly materialises as worse outliers. Given its mostly-concurrent nature, G1 is surprisingly good in comparison with Erlang and C4.

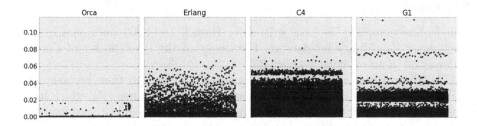

Fig. 10. Comparing jitter/latency variance in a synthetic benchmark across Pony, Erlang and Java (C4 and G1).

In a system with few larger actors, the inability to GC in an actor while the actor is running will change the above figure considerably, highlighting the bad fit of a collector designed for highly concurrent actor-based programs and applications with very limited concurrency.

Pony's GC was minimalistic and served Pony's needs perfectly. It would only allow an actor to perform GC between processing messages to save itself the trouble of scanning the stack. This pragmatic choice was motivated by its implementation as a C library and a desire to have exact information about references on the stack. In theory, this caused problems for Encore programs due to its extended synchronisation mechanisms: an active object blocking on a future could not perform GC as it had an attached stack; the same was true for an active object which has cooperatively suspended itself to perform another message.

Finally, Pony's GC was designed for a sequential actor model where only a single thread of control manipulates an actor's innards. The hot object parallel abstraction provided by Encore broke away from this design. Since sending a message to a hot object was guaranteed to not block, garbage collection in hot objects was forced to be fully concurrent at a lower granularity than Pony's GC. This materialised itself as an entirely new collector, Isolde [82], that was used internally inside hot objects. Its implementor, Albert Mingkun Yang, continued in fully concurrent memory management [80,81,83] in the context of the ZGC garbage collector, and today works in the GC team at Oracle.

Experiences with Pony's garbage collector in production have been incorporated in the Verona programming language by decoupling management of object lifetimes from particular "threads", and also managed immutable objects differently from mutable objects [4].

9   Implementation

In this section we give an overview of the implementation work, focusing in turn on the Encore compiler, and the Encore runtime.

9.1   Compiler

The Encore compiler [36] was written in Haskell (∼14,000 lines), using the megaparsec [59] library for parsing. The design of the type checker of Encore is described in an experience paper [17].

The Encore compiler compiles Encore to C, which can then be compiled with a C compiler of choice and linked with the Pony runtime [65], which handles creation and destruction of actors, message sends, scheduling, and memory management of passive objects. In addition to the Pony runtime, the Encore runtime consists of ∼3600 lines of C code for primitive constructs, such as arrays, closures, algebraic data types, futures, *etc.*

Because the compilation target is C, a lot of early prototyping in Encore could be done by using **embed** blocks with literal C code. Embedded C code can in turn embed Encore code, for example in order to refer to variables in the Encore program:

```
1   def print(s : string): void
2     embed unit
3       puts(#{s}); // #{s} Refers to the Encore variable s
4     end
5   end
```

For similar reasons, debugging the compiler was as simple as inspecting the outputted C code. We made an effort to generate readable C which saved copious amounts of time.

The entire repository with compiler and runtime extension was hosted on GitHub [36] and saw 1923 commits from a total of 18 contributors. The top three contributors were all PhD students in the project. These PhD students (among others) were also heavily involved in reviewing pull requests from other members of the project, and the >20 undergraduate students that worked on various aspects of the language at different times. The pull request reviewing model was great for keeping a >1 "bus factor", and for ensuring code consistency. However, contributors at times attempted to "brute force" their commits into the compiler, or submitted patches of very low quality. This led to frustration among the top-committer PhD students who saw too much of their time spent on software engineering as opposed to research. This also at times caused friction in the team, especially among PhD students, when pull requests were not merged. In hindsight, the senior researchers could have done a better job of protecting these students by inserting themselves in the process or creating a more formal process for the reviewing PhD students to point to. Guidelines for contributing should also have been posted sooner including encouragement to engage with the developers before *e.g.,* issuing a patch removing trailing whitespace across the entire project.

9.2 Runtime

By building on the Pony runtime, Encore got a runtime that came with built-in support for many of the things the language enforced statically through its type system and design: garbage collection took advantage of actor isolation, message passing took advantage of uniqueness information, etc. However, the tight fit of Pony's runtime to a language that was not Encore ended up complicating essentially every Encore feature. In hindsight, it would have been considerably better to compile Encore to say the JVM—at least initially—and ignore performance until the key design elements were firmly in place (read: not while the project lasted).

For example, Pony's runtime did not have futures, only promises, and furthermore, its promises were implemented as actors under the hood, meaning that it added additional latency when returning a value. This design was probably right for Pony, which relied on unidirectional message sends as its main model of communication. As a result, a scheduler thread in Pony was never blocking, and the scheduler defaulted to using exactly as many threads as there were cores on the machine. This was an oversight that was not clearly understood at the time when the decision was made to use the Pony runtime as a basis for Encore.

This forced the first extention of the Pony runtime in the Encore compiler, which continued to be problematic whenever we sought to pull recent updates from Pony into the main Encore repository. Conceptually the change is simple: perform a userland context switch when blocking on a future and maintain a pool of suspended actors that can be scheduled once the futures they are blocking on are fulfilled. However, there were a number of technical challenges related to futures, as well as cooperative scheduling primitives in Encore that had no Pony equivalent. One example was an invariant on Pony's multi-producer single-consumer queue that implemented the actor mailbox, which meant that pushing a message directly at the front of an actor's message queue—to get it to resume a suspended operation—was not directly supported.

One PhD student spent a significant amount of time maintaining the Encore version of the Pony runtime and interacting with the Pony developers. From a research career perspective, this time could have been more well spent.

10   Lessons Learned

In this section, we discuss important lessons learned from the Encore project regarding how to run (and not run) a programming language project.

First, the open sourcing of Encore happened much too late. There is essentially no reason to not develop projects like Encore in the open, and it would possibly have connected the project wider, for example to curious students, and hobbyists. The literature on software engineering teaches us that writing code to be read by external people improves code quality, even if it might have slowed down the language development a little. A key to building a long-term research artefact is to not try to cut as much code as possible in as short a time as possible. By devoting effort to a more stable core language, we could have continued to support just as many offshoots as we did, but without compromising the integrity of the core language. Over time, battle-tested offshoots could be integrated in the core language, and enjoy a better understanding of their impact on the total complexity budget, in relation to the importance of their delivered features. For Encore, the desire to have as many features as possible make it into the mainline caused growth pains which eventually killed progress on the language. (On the other hand, one should not under-estimate the motivation that comes from desire to have a patch merged into the mainline.)

On a similar note, assigning a language steward would have been very helpful. Ideally, this person would have been located outside of Uppsala, thereby forcing communication in the project and more committment from non-Uppsala members. The stewardship might even be a rotating function, injecting some democracy into the process, and incentives to "play fair" at all times. That said, it seems plausible that not all decisions about a research language can be driven by democratic processes, at least not in a time-limited project. For example, there may be compelling technical reasons for choosing, say Haskell or C, as technologies to build on, *e.g.,* because of availability of key libraries. Having an external steward and a process for extending the code language would naturally have created incentives for better documentation of both code and language features. To this day, the Encore documentation is distributed over a large number of papers, and more often than one would like, the implementation has come to diverge to some extent with what is the described in the paper. A language project will do well by spending substantial effort early on laying down some ground rules for documentation as well as setting up infrastructure for gathering and curating documentation. Preferably a tool that allows the documentation to be stored in the same repository as the language to facilitate linking different versions of the documentation to different versions (or branches) of the language.

The choice of implementation language was in many ways poor. We certainly do not wish to throw any shade on Haskell, but it has a steep learning curve, especially for those who are new to purely functional programming or lazy evaluation. The choice to go with Haskell seems to have denied senior project members—*i.e.,* those with fewer available cycles—entry into the programming, which is not a great strategy for a project that is intended to survive the graduation of the current batch of PhD students. Also, consortium-wide decisions really should not be made at the whim of individual consortium members, regardless whether the decision is right or wrong.

The UPLANG group at the department of information technology at Uppsala university thrived during the Encore years, and the weekly meeting revolving around Encore created a feeling of the group coming together. It set a gold standard that we have since strived to re-create. PhD students with widely different projects collaborated on each others' patches, either directly by contributing logic, or indirectly through code reviews. A handful of undergraduate students were actively involved at any moment in time giving the PhD students hands-on experience with supervision, and in total 15 undergraduate theses were published that worked directly on the language implementation or provided input for design decisions [35, 37, 48, 49, 52, 57, 58, 61, 63, 64, 66, 70, 71, 76, 77]. Given that the length of a Swedish PhD is four years of research interleaved with one year of teaching over a five year period, it was typically not difficult for the PhD students to balance research time vs. student supervision time. The PhD students also got hands-on experience with maintaining a "large" body of code, and first-hand experience with the joys of unchecked technical debt. The main negative time sink for PhD students was time spent reviewing a small number of pull requests time and time again. This happened when the issuer of the pull request seemed unwilling (or unable) to respond to criticism. The main problem here was that the custodian of quality was (also, typically) a PhD student who did not want to block the progress of a peer. Thus, instead of simply refusing to re-review code which had not morally changed, they worked hard on giving more feedback to the student on the other side. On a few occasions, this led to friction between PhD students, and senior people had to step in to make sure that conflicts did not escalate. Introducing tools like Slack that offered a fast backchannel for these kinds of discussions was great, and also ensured that the distance between all team members was equal. This helped distributing sensitive or complicated questions unsuitable for email more uniformly across the team.

In hindsight, picking the Pony runtime as the language backend was a stupid move due to its high level of complexity stemming from optimisation. This made changes that broke with the Pony design unnecessarily hard and made us spend time on irrelevant details. A better idea would have been to target a less opinionated backend, or at least compile to a less heavily optimised backend that was easier to change. While compiling to a higher-level language would complicate optimisation, it would facilitate experimentation. Having two backends for compiling both to a high-level language and a low-level language would be ideal, although adding more complexity and increasing the maintenance costs. "Transpiling" and linking with an externally developed runtime worked really well for prototyping implementations, where we would often write Encore code to generate code that could then manually be edited and experimented with to create a goal for the compiler extensions.

In the end, there are many things that we would do again given the opportunity, but also many things that we would try to do differently. Clearly some things were done right, as is apparent from the research output of the project, but we also think that if we had done things differently, Encore would not be effectively dead as a language today.

11   Concluding Remarks, or Encore: Fine

The Encore project failed to deliver a long-term research artefact, but succeeded in producing a wide range of research outputs in a multitude of directions. Insights into the weaknesses of the actor and active object models, and the challenges of combining parallelism and concurrency in a single language are carefully curated by the authors of this paper and are informing the development of the Verona language, whose concurrency abstractions [24] and type-driven isolation [4] mechanisms draw heavily on experiences with Encore.

References

1. Agha, G.A.: ACTORS - A Model of Concurrent Computation in Distributed Systems. MIT Press Series in Artificial Intelligence, MIT Press (1990)
2. Åkerblom, B., Castegren, E., Wrigstad, T.: Parallel programming with arrays in kappa. In: Scholz, S.-B., Shivers, O. (eds.) Proceedings of the 5th ACM SIGPLAN International Workshop on Libraries, Languages, and Compilers for Array Programming, ARRAY@PLDI 2018, Philadelphia, PA, USA, 19 June 2018, pp. 24–33. ACM (2018)
3. Åkerblom, B., Castegren, E., Wrigstad, T.: Reference capabilities for safe parallel array programming. Art Sci. Eng. Program. 4(1), 1 (2019)
4. Arvidsson, E., et al.: Reference capabilities for flexible memory management. In: Proceedings of the ACM on Programming Languages, vol. 7 (OOPSLA2) (2023)
5. Black, A.P., Bruce, K.B., Homer, M., Noble, J.: Grace: the absence of (inessential) difficulty. In: ACM Symposium on New Ideas in Programming and Reflections on Software, Onward!, Part of SPLASH 2012, Tucson, AZ, USA, 21–26 October 2012, pp. 85–98 (2012)
6. Blackburn, S.M., et al.: The DaCapo benchmarks: Java benchmarking development and analysis. In: Proceedings of the 21st Annual ACM SIGPLAN Conference on Object-Oriented Programming Systems, Languages, and Applications, OOPSLA 2006, New York, NY, USA, pp. 169–190. Association for Computing Machinery (2006)
7. Blessing, S., Fernandez-Reyes, K., Yang, A.M., Drossopoulou, S., Wrigstad, T.: Run, actor, run: towards cross-actor language benchmarking. In: Bergenti, F., Castegren, E., De Koster, J., Franco, J. (eds.) Proceedings of the 9th ACM SIGPLAN International Workshop on Programming Based on Actors, Agents, and Decentralized Control, AGERE!@SPLASH 2019, Athens, Greece, 22 October 2019, pp. 41–50. ACM (2019)

8. Bloom, B., et al.: Thorn: robust, concurrent, extensible scripting on the JVM. In: Arora, S., Leavens, G.T. (eds.) Proceedings of the 24th Annual ACM SIGPLAN Conference on Object-Oriented Programming, Systems, Languages, and Applications, OOPSLA 2009, Orlando, Florida, USA, 25–29 October 2009, pp. 117–136. ACM (2009)

9. Bracha, G., von der Ahé, P., Bykov, V., Kashai, Y., Maddox, W., Miranda, E.: Modules as objects in newspeak. In: D'Hondt, T. (ed.) ECOOP 2010. LNCS, vol. 6183, pp. 405–428. Springer, Heidelberg (2010). https://doi.org/10.1007/978-3-642-14107-2_20

10. Brandauer, S.: Structured Data. Ph.D. thesis, Uppsala University, Sweden (2018)

11. Brandauer, S., et al.: Parallel objects for multicores: a glimpse at the parallel language ENCORE. In: Bernardo, M., Johnsen, E.B. (eds.) SFM 2015. LNCS, vol. 9104, pp. 1–56. Springer, Cham (2015). https://doi.org/10.1007/978-3-319-18941-3_1

12. Brandauer, S., Wrigstad, T.: Mining for safety using interactive trace analysis. In: Pre-proceedings - Fifteenth International Workshop on Quantitative Aspects of Programming Languages and Systems, no. 15 (2017)

13. Brandauer, S., Wrigstad, T.: Spencer: interactive heap analysis for the masses. In: González-Barahona, J.M., Hindle, A., Tan, L. (eds.) Proceedings of the 14th International Conference on Mining Software Repositories, MSR 2017, Buenos Aires, Argentina, 20–28 May 2017, pp. 113–123. IEEE Computer Society (2017)

14. Broman, D.: A vision of miking: interactive programmatic modeling, sound language composition, and self-learning compilation. In: Proceedings of the 12th ACM SIGPLAN International Conference on Software Language Engineering, pp. 55–60 (2019)

15. Castegren, E.: Capability-Based Type Systems for Concurrency Control. Ph.D. thesis, Uppsala University, Sweden (2018)

16. Castegren, E., Clarke, D., Fernandez-Reyes, K., Wrigstad, T., Yang, A.M.: Attached and detached closures in actors. In: De Koster, J., Bergenti, F., Franco, J. (eds.) Proceedings of the 8th ACM SIGPLAN International Workshop on Programming Based on Actors, Agents, and Decentralized Control, AGERE!@SPLASH 2018, Boston, MA, USA, 5 November 2018, pp. 54–61. ACM (2018)

17. Castegren, E., Fernandez-Reyes, K.: Developing a monadic type checker for an object-oriented language: an experience report. In: Nierstrasz, O., Gray, J., Oliveira, B.C.S. (eds.) Proceedings of the 12th ACM SIGPLAN International Conference on Software Language Engineering, SLE 2019, Athens, Greece, 20–22 October 2019, pp. 184–196. ACM (2019)

18. Castegren, E., Wallin, J., Wrigstad, T.: Bestow and atomic: concurrent programming using isolation, delegation and grouping. J. Log. Algebraic Methods Program. 100, 130–151 (2018)

19. Castegren, E., Wrigstad, T.: Kappa: insights, current status and future work. In: 7th International Workshop on Aliasing, Capabilities and Ownership (IWACO) (2016)

20. Castegren, E., Wrigstad, T.: Reference capabilities for concurrency control. In: Krishnamurthi, S., Lerner, B.S. (eds.) 30th European Conference on Object-Oriented Programming, ECOOP 2016, Rome, Italy, 18–22 July 2016. LIPIcs, vol. 56, pp. 5:1–5:26. Schloss Dagstuhl - Leibniz-Zentrum für Informatik (2016)

21. Castegren, E., Wrigstad, T.: Actors without borders: amnesty for imprisoned state. In: Vasconcelos, V.T., Haller, P. (eds.) Proceedings Tenth Workshop on Programming Language Approaches to Concurrency- and Communication-cEntric Soft-

ware, PLACES@ETAPS 2017, Uppsala, Sweden, 29 April 2017. EPTCS, vol. 246, pp. 10–20 (2017)

22. Castegren, E., Wrigstad, T.: Relaxed linear references for lock-free data structures. In: Müller, P. (ed.) 31st European Conference on Object-Oriented Programming, ECOOP 2017, Barcelona, Spain, 19–23 June 2017. LIPIcs, vol. 74, pp. 6:1–6:32. Schloss Dagstuhl - Leibniz-Zentrum für Informatik (2017)

23. Chappe, N., Henrio, L., Maillé, A., Moy, M., Renaud, H.: An optimised flow for futures: from theory to practice. Art Sci. Eng. Program. **6**(1) (2022)

24. Cheeseman, L., et al.: When concurrency strikes. Under submission (2023)

25. Clarke, D., Wrigstad, T.: External uniqueness is unique enough. In: Cardelli, L. (ed.) ECOOP 2003. LNCS, vol. 2743, pp. 176–200. Springer, Heidelberg (2003). https://doi.org/10.1007/978-3-540-45070-2_9

26. Clarke, D., Wrigstad, T., Östlund, J., Johnsen, E.B.: Minimal ownership for active objects. In: Ramalingam, G. (ed.) APLAS 2008. LNCS, vol. 5356, pp. 139–154. Springer, Heidelberg (2008). https://doi.org/10.1007/978-3-540-89330-1_11

27. Clarke, D., Wrigstad, T., Yoshida, N., de Boer, F.S., Johnsen, E.B.: Inversion in programming language design: the Encore way. In: NOOL 2015, October 2015

28. Clarke, D.G., Potter, J., Noble, J.: Ownership types for flexible alias protection. In: Proceedings of the 1998 ACM SIGPLAN Conference on Object-Oriented Programming Systems, Languages & Applications (OOPSLA 1998), Vancouver, British Columbia, Canada, 18–22 October 1998, pp. 48–64 (1998)

29. Clebsch, S.: 'Pony': co-designing a type system and a runtime. Ph.D. thesis, Imperial College London, UK (2017)

30. Clebsch, S., Drossopoulou, S.: Fully concurrent garbage collection of actors on many-core machines. In: Hosking, A.L., Eugster, P.Th., Lopes, C.V. (eds.) Proceedings of the 2013 ACM SIGPLAN International Conference on Object Oriented Programming Systems Languages & Applications, OOPSLA 2013, Part of SPLASH 2013, Indianapolis, IN, USA, 26–31 October 2013, pp. 553–570. ACM (2013)

31. Clebsch, S., Franco, J., Drossopoulou, S., Yang, A.M., Wrigstad, T., Vitek, J.: Orca: GC and type system co-design for actor languages. Proc. ACM Program. Lang. **1**(OOPSLA), 72:1–72:28 (2017)

32. de Boer, F.S., Clarke, D., Johnsen, E.B.: A complete guide to the future. In: De Nicola, R. (ed.) ESOP 2007. LNCS, vol. 4421, pp. 316–330. Springer, Heidelberg (2007). https://doi.org/10.1007/978-3-540-71316-6_22

33. de Boer, F.S., et al.: A survey of active object languages. ACM Comput. Surv. **50**(5), 76:1–76:39 (2017)

34. Dedecker, J., Van Cutsem, T., Mostinckx, S., D'Hondt, T., De Meuter, W.: Ambient-oriented programming in AmbientTalk. In: Thomas, D. (ed.) ECOOP 2006. LNCS, vol. 4067, pp. 230–254. Springer, Heidelberg (2006). https://doi.org/10.1007/11785477_16

35. Eklund, L., Nikamo, K., Strömberg, C.: Improving the developer experience by implementing syntax in the Encore language. Bachelor's thesis, Uppsala University, Department of Information Technology (2017)

36. GitHub repository for Encore. https://github.com/parapluu/encore, May 2023

37. Escher, D.: Parallel performance comparison between Encore and OpenMP using pedestrian simulation. Bachelor's thesis, Uppsala University, Department of Information Technology (2017)

38. Fernandez-Reyes, K., Clarke, D.: Affine killing: semantics for stopping the ParT. In: Proceedings of 2nd International Workshop on Type-Driven Development (2017)

39. Fernandez-Reyes, K., Clarke, D., Castegren, E., Vo, H.P.: Forward to a Promising Future. In: Di Marzo Serugendo, G., Loreti, M. (eds.) COORDINATION 2018. LNPSE, vol. 10852, pp. 162–180. Springer, Cham (2018). https://doi.org/10.1007/978-3-319-92408-3_7

40. Fernandez-Reyes, K., Clarke, D., Henrio, L., Johnsen, E.B., Wrigstad, T.: Godot: all the benefits of implicit and explicit futures. In: Donaldson, A.F. (ed.) 33rd European Conference on Object-Oriented Programming, ECOOP 2019, London, United Kingdom, 15–19 July 2019. LIPIcs, vol. 134, pp. 2:1–2:28. Schloss Dagstuhl - Leibniz-Zentrum für Informatik (2019)

41. Fernandez-Reyes, K., Clarke, D., Henrio, L., Johnsen, E.B., Wrigstad, T.: Godot: all the benefits of implicit and explicit futures (artifact). Dagstuhl Artifacts Ser. 5(2), 01:1–01:2 (2019)

42. Fernandez-Reyes, K., Clarke, D., McCain, D.S.: ParT: an asynchronous parallel abstraction for speculative pipeline computations. In: Lluch Lafuente, A., Proença, J. (eds.) COORDINATION 2016. LNCS, vol. 9686, pp. 101–120. Springer, Cham (2016). https://doi.org/10.1007/978-3-319-39519-7_7

43. Fernandez-Reyes, K., Gariano, I.O., Noble, J., Greenwood-Thessman, E., Homer, M., Wrigstad, T.: Dala: a simple capability-based dynamic language design for data race-freedom. In: Proceedings of the 2021 ACM SIGPLAN International Symposium on New Ideas, New Paradigms, and Reflections on Programming and Software (ONWARD!), pp. 1–17 (2021)

44. Franco, J.: Orca: Ownership and Reference Count Collection for Actors. Ph.D. thesis, Imperial College London, UK (2018)

45. Franco, J., Clebsch, S., Drossopoulou, S., Vitek, J., Wrigstad, T.: Correctness of a concurrent object collector for actor languages. In: Ahmed, A. (ed.) ESOP 2018. LNCS, vol. 10801, pp. 885–911. Springer, Cham (2018). https://doi.org/10.1007/978-3-319-89884-1_31

46. Franco, J., Hagelin, M., Wrigstad, T., Drossopoulou, S., Eisenbach, S.: You can have it all: abstraction and good cache performance. In: Torlak, E., van der Storm, T., Biddle, R. (eds.) Proceedings of the 2017 ACM SIGPLAN International Symposium on New Ideas, New Paradigms, and Reflections on Programming and Software, Onward!, Vancouver, BC, Canada, 23–27 October 2017, pp. 148–167. ACM (2017)

47. Franco, J., Tasos, A., Drossopoulou, S., Wrigstad, T., Eisenbach, S.: Safely abstracting memory layouts. CoRR, abs/1901.08006 (2019)

48. Hagelin, M.: Optimizing memory management with object-local heaps. Master's thesis, Uppsala University, Department of Information Technology (2015)

49. Karakoca, J.H.: Big data types: internally parallel in an actor language. Bachelor's thesis, Uppsala University, Department of Information Technology (2018)

50. Henrio, L.: Data-flow Explicit Futures. Research report, I3S, Université Côte d'Azur, April 2018

51. Hewitt, C., Bishop, P., Steiger, R.: A universal modular actor formalism for artificial intelligence. In: Proceedings of the 3rd International Joint Conference on Artificial Intelligence, IJCAI 1973, San Francisco, CA, USA, pp. 235–245. Morgan Kaufmann Publishers Inc. (1973)

52. Hillert, J.: A comparison of the capability systems of Encore, Pony and Rust. Bachelor's thesis, Uppsala University, Department of Information Technology (2019)

53. Imam, S.M., Sarkar, V.: Savina - an actor benchmark suite: enabling empirical evaluation of actor libraries. In: Proceedings of the 4th International Workshop on Programming Based on Actors Agents & Decentralized Control, AGERE! 2014, New York, NY, USA, pp. 67–80. Association for Computing Machinery (2014)

54. Johnsen, E.B., Hähnle, R., Schäfer, J., Schlatte, R., Steffen, M.: ABS: a core language for abstract behavioral specification. In: Aichernig, B.K., de Boer, F.S., Bonsangue, M.M. (eds.) FMCO 2010. LNCS, vol. 6957, pp. 142–164. Springer, Heidelberg (2011). https://doi.org/10.1007/978-3-642-25271-6_8
55. Kitchin, D., Quark, A., Cook, W., Misra, J.: The Orc programming language. In: Lee, D., Lopes, A., Poetzsch-Heffter, A. (eds.) FMOODS/FORTE -2009. LNCS, vol. 5522, pp. 1–25. Springer, Heidelberg (2009). https://doi.org/10.1007/978-3-642-02138-1_1
56. De Koster, J., Van Cutsem, T., De Meuter, W.: 43 years of actors: a taxonomy of actor models and their key properties. In: Clebsch, S., Desell, T., Haller, P., Ricci, A. (eds.) Proceedings of the 6th International Workshop on Programming Based on Actors, Agents, and Decentralized Control, AGERE 2016, Amsterdam, The Netherlands, 30 October 2016, pp. 31–40. ACM (2016)
57. Lundin, G.: Pattern matching in Encore. Bachelor's thesis, Uppsala University, Department of Information Technology (2016)
58. Manning, J.E.: For-comprehension: an Encore compiler story. Bachelor's thesis, Uppsala University, Department of Information Technology (2019)
59. Martini, P., Leijen, D., Megaparsec Contributors: Megaparsec: monadic parser combinators. https://hackage.haskell.org/package/megaparsec, May 2023
60. Miller, M.S.: Robust Composition: Towards a Unified Approach to Access Control and Concurrency Control. Ph.D. thesis, Johns Hopkins University, Baltimore, Maryland, USA, May 2006
61. Olander, J.: Design & implementation of separate compilation for Encore. Bachelor's thesis, Uppsala University, Department of Information Technology (2017)
62. Östlund, J.: Language Constructs for Safe Parallel Programming on Multi-Cores. Ph.D. thesis, Uppsala University, Sweden (2016)
63. Östlund, M.: Benchmarking parallelism and concurrency in the Encore programming language. Bachelor's thesis, Uppsala University, Department of Information Technology (2016)
64. Pedersen, O.: Implementing and evaluating the performance of CRDTs in Encore. Bachelor's thesis, Uppsala University, Department of Information Technology (2018)
65. The pony programming language. https://www.ponylang.org. Accessed May 2023
66. Remmers, A.: Enhancing functionality with assistive error visualisations in Encore. Bachelor's thesis, Uppsala University, Department of Information Technology (2019)
67. Reyes, F.R.F.: Abstractions to Control the Future. Ph.D. thesis, Uppsala University, Sweden (2021)
68. Schärli, N., Ducasse, S., Nierstrasz, O., Black, A.P.: Traits: composable units of behaviour. In: Cardelli, L. (ed.) ECOOP 2003. LNCS, vol. 2743, pp. 248–274. Springer, Heidelberg (2003). https://doi.org/10.1007/978-3-540-45070-2_12
69. Schmidt, D.C., Stal, M., Rohnert, H., Buschmann, F.: Pattern-Oriented Software Architecture. Patterns for Concurrent and Networked Objects, vol. 2. Wiley, New York (2000)
70. Taher, S.S.: Exceptional actors implementing exception handling for -Encore. Bachelor's thesis, Uppsala University, Department of Information Technology (2017)
71. Sommerland, H.: An implementation of the vat programming abstraction. Bachelor's thesis, Uppsala University, Department of Information Technology (2016)
72. Swalens, J., De Koster, J., De Meuter, W.: Transactional actors: communication in transactions. In: Proceedings of the 4th ACM SIGPLAN International Workshop

on Software Engineering for Parallel Systems, SEPS 2017, New York, NY, USA, pp. 31–41. Association for Computing Machinery (2017)

73. Tasos, A., Franco, J., Drossopoulou, S., Wrigstad, T., Eisenbach, S.: Reshape your layouts, not your programs: a safe language extension for better cache locality. Sci. Comput. Program. **197**, 102481 (2020)

74. Tasos, A., Franco, J., Drossopoulou, S., Wrigstad, T., Eisenbach, S.: Reshape your layouts, not your programs: a safe language extension for better cache locality (SCICO journal-first). In: Hirschfeld, R., Pape, T. (eds.) 34th European Conference on Object-Oriented Programming, ECOOP 2020, Berlin, Germany (Virtual Conference), 15–17 November 2020. LIPIcs, vol. 166, pp. 31:1–31:3. Schloss Dagstuhl - Leibniz-Zentrum für Informatik (2020)

75. Tasos, A., Franco, J., Wrigstad, T., Drossopoulou, S., Eisenbach, S.: Extending SHAPES for SIMD architectures: an approach to native support for struct of arrays in languages. In: Felgentreff, T., Zendra, O. (eds.) Proceedings of the 13th Workshop on Implementation, Compilation, Optimization of Object-Oriented Languages, Programs and Systems, ICOOOLPS@ECOOP 2018, Amsterdam, Netherlands, 16–21 July 2018, pp. 23–29. ACM (2018)

76. Tönqvist, C.: Finding patterns in lock-free algorithms. Bachelor's thesis, Uppsala University, Department of Information Technology (2017)

77. Wallin, J.: Implementing safe sharing features for Encore. Bachelor's thesis, Uppsala University, Department of Information Technology (2017)

78. Wrigstad, T., Fritzon, T.: Actors and hot objects. In: NOOL (2016)

79. Wrigstad, T., Nardelli, F.Z., Lebresne, S., Östlund, J., Vitek, J.: Integrating typed and untyped code in a scripting language. In: Hermenegildo, M.V., Palsberg, J. (eds.) Proceedings of the 37th ACM SIGPLAN-SIGACT Symposium on Principles of Programming Languages, POPL 2010, Madrid, Spain, 17–23 January 2010, pp. 377–388. ACM (2010)

80. Yang, A.M., Österlund, E., Wilhelmsson, J., Nyblom, H., Wrigstad, T.: ThinGC: complete isolation with marginal overhead. In: Ding, C., Maas, M. (eds.) 2020 ACM SIGPLAN International Symposium on Memory Management, ISMM 2020, Virtual, London, UK, 16 June 2020, pp. 74–86. ACM (2020)

81. Yang, A.M., Österlund, E., Wrigstad, T.: Improving program locality in the GC using hotness. In: Donaldson, A.F., Torlak, E. (eds.) Proceedings of the 41st ACM SIGPLAN International Conference on Programming Language Design and Implementation, PLDI 2020, London, UK, 15–20 June 2020, pp. 301–313. ACM (2020)

82. Yang, A.M., Wrigstad, T.: Type-assisted automatic garbage collection for lock-free data structures. In: Kirsch, C.M., Titzer, B.L. (eds.) Proceedings of the 2017 ACM SIGPLAN International Symposium on Memory Management, ISMM 2017, Barcelona, Spain, 18 June 2017, pp. 14–24. ACM (2017)

83. Yang, A.M., Wrigstad, T.: Deep dive into ZGC: a modern garbage collector in OpenJDK. ACM Trans. Program. Lang. Syst. **44**(4), 22:1–22:34 (2022)

Bridging Between Active Objects: Multitier Programming for Distributed, Concurrent Systems

Guido Salvaneschi$^{(\boxtimes)}$ (ID) and Pascal Weisenburger (ID)

University of St. Gallen, St. Gallen, Switzerland
{pascal.weisenburger,guido.salvaneschi}@unisg.ch
https://programming-group.com/

Abstract. Programming distributed and concurrent systems is notoriously hard. Active objects, which encapsulate operations, state and control flow, have been investigated by researchers to alleviate this issue. In a distributed system, message exchange among active objects or actors often coincides with network boundaries, and determines a major modularization direction for the application. Yet, certain application functionalities naturally crosscut such modularization direction. For those, structuring the application architecture around network boundaries is purely accidental and does not help reasoning about programs.

Recently, multitier programming has been proposed as a programming paradigm that enables code that belongs to different peers to be developed together, in the same compilation unit. The compiler then splits the code and generates the required deployment components.

In this work we explore the relation between multitier programming and active objects. Multitier programming can be considered a programming paradigm based on active objects with a focus on application domains where functionalities span multiple active objects, and allows such functionalities to be encapsulated into a single object. The multitier approach keeps the asynchronous model of active objects and actors but provides a holistic view of distributed components and their interactions. Multitier programming addresses the use cases where separating components into different active objects or actors hinders encapsulation and modularization across functional boundaries. In such use cases, multitier programming can increase the level of abstraction, improve software design, simplify code maintenance, aid program comprehension and enable formal reasoning. A number of features of active objects are directly visible to programmers also in the multitier programming, resulting in an interesting combination of language abstractions available to developers.

1 Introduction

Modern-day ubiquitous services – including search engines, online social networks and streaming platforms – run on a network of interconnected computers. Typically, the components of such distributed systems are developed as

© The Author(s), under exclusive license to Springer Nature Switzerland AG 2024
F. de Boer et al. (Eds.): *Active Object Languages: Current Research Trends*,
LNCS 14360, pp. 92–122, 2024.
https://doi.org/10.1007/978-3-031-51060-1_4

separate modules. This separation, however, comes with a number of difficulties [23]. Composing the modules correctly into a complete distributed system is a highly difficult challenge that requires intensive integration work and the manual implementation of communication protocols. Thus, programmers are faced with the complex task of implementing complicated communication schemes between hosts, which frequently involves low-level operations prone to errors. As a result, the distributed data flows that arise from the approach are in many cases convoluted and scattered among several modules, making it difficult to fully comprehend the behavior of the system as a whole. Despite the prevalence of distributed software, the design and development of distributed systems remains an extremely challenging task.

Multitier programming [95] presents a promising approach for taming the complexities of developing distributed systems through language abstractions focusing on interacting distributed components, i.e., interacting active objects where distributed objects are bound to different threads of control and communicate asynchronously with other objects.

Active Objects. Active objects [16] build on top of object-oriented abstractions which encapsulate operations and state, and, in addition, encapsulate execution flow. Active objects have been successfully adopted to program distributed systems, which are concurrent by nature. This programming abstraction defines clear boundaries among concurrency units, making them coincide with those naturally defined by the object structure. Also, because of asynchronous message passing, active objects simplify developing concurrent systems where different parts are decoupled and progress independently. Yet, in the case of distributed systems, active objects and their derivatives (e.g., actors) encourage programmers to develop software that is modularized according to network boundaries – where the remote communication occurs. While this has been necessary for technical reasons, software functionalities can logically span over several system components and such separation may be not ideal [37,72,84].

Multitier Programming. In multitier programming, distributed functionalities that cross different components are developed in a single compilation unit [95]. As a result, programmers do not need to arrange the implementation along network boundaries but along logical functions. Since the distributed parts of such a function naturally run concurrently in a distributed system, multitier programming languages typically further abstract over active objects and rely on active objects for an efficient implementation. Yet, multitier languages provide features to deal with concurrent execution – either by exposing standard concurrency abstractions such as futures or by abstracting concurrency away from the developer through a compilation scheme that ensures that code that appears sequentially in the multitier program is also executed in sequence.

Using a single (distributed) program relieves the developer from having to break down a functionality into the parts that should be executed on different machines. Instead of reasoning in terms of distributed components (that may mix different functions together), developers can reason in terms of different modules that functionally belong together (even though they are distributed themselves) – leaving the splitting into the components to be distributed to different machines to the compiler [93].

Active Objects and Multitier Programming. While multitier programming provides linguistic abstractions to reason about distribution at the language level and lets the compiler handle the actual partitioning of code and the insertion of remote calls and handlers, the underlying execution model is fundamentally distributed active objects that asynchronously invoke methods on remote objects. Multitier programming, however, goes beyond active objects – and actor systems in particular – and solves some of the issues that often arise in actor-based implementations of distributed systems. In particular, control flow between actors can get quite involved and hard to follow for developers due to the fact that actors are highly decoupled and behavior of actors that interact to provide a logically combined function is modeled through complex message-passing schemes. Such functions can be expressed more directly using multitier programming. Hence, multitier programming can be seen as both an evolution and a combination of active objects for distributed systems.

In this work, we explore the connection between active objects and multitier programming. We show that multitier programming addresses some of the design issues that emerge with active objects, and we show that active objects complement multitier programming when reasoning about concurrency in a distributed system.

2   Background

This sections provides a short overview about (1) active objects and actors as a state-of-the-art programming model for concurrent and distributed systems and (2) multitier programming, a programming paradigm designed to ease the development of distributed applications where functionality spans across multiple components.

2.1   Active Objects and Actors

The actor model [47] is based on independent computational entities – so-called *actors* – that encapsulate both behavior and state and communicate with each other by sending and receiving messages. An actor's internal state can only be modified by processing incoming messages. When an actor receives a message, it can perform computations, modify its state, create new actors or send messages to other actors [44]. Actors process one message at a time – messages are processed sequentially – and do not share their state or memory, which eliminates many of the pitfalls of traditional multithreaded programming.

Active objects extend the actor paradigm with structured communication: Instead of message-passing, they use method calls and futures. Futures represent asynchronous return values that will be available at some point in the

Listing 1. Akka Typed actor summing up a list of numbers.

```
1  object SumActor {
2    sealed trait Request
3    case class Shutdown() extends Request
4    case class Calculate(
5      numbers: List[Int], replyTo: ActorRef[Result]) extends Request
6
7    case class Result(result: Int)
8
9    def apply(): Behavior[Request] =
10     Behaviors.receive { (context, message) =>
11       message match {
12         case Calculate(numbers, replyTo) =>
13           replyTo ! Result(numbers.sum)
14           Behaviors.same
15         case Shutdown() =>
16           Behaviors.stopped
17       }
18     }
19 }
```

future. Usually, method calls on active objects look like "normal" method calls on (non-active) objects. They thus remove the fraction in actor systems of fragmenting programs into (1) sending messages to emulate method invocations and (2) sending other messages to emulate their return values. Hence, active object became popular as an improved way to structure concurrent code.

Yet, not being able to easily distinguish synchronous and asynchronous method invocations can also be a disadvantage. Especially in – not only concurrent, but also – distributed systems, remote methods often should not only be executed asynchronously but they also have more fundamentally different invocation semantics. In particular, a remote method may even never return in case of partial failures (i.e., the remote system crashes) or network partitions (i.e., the remote system is not reachable over the network anymore). Due to these differences between local and remote methods, actors – that distinguish between local method calls and remote message-passing – remain widely used for distributed systems.

Listing 1 shows an actor implemented in Akka Typed [59]. Lines 2 to 7 define the messages that the actor can send and receive. Line 10 defines the actor's message handler that has to pattern-match on every type message the actor could receive (Lines 11 to 17). In case the actor receives a Calculate message with a list of numbers (Line 12), it calculates the sum of the numbers and sends out the result using the ! send operator (Line 13). In the example, the Calculate message includes an actor reference replyTo to which to send the result – a common pattern to model returning values in actor systems.

Another reason for using actors for implementing distributed systems is their support for fault tolerance using supervision hierarchies. Supervision hierarchies organize actors into a tree, where an actor acts as a supervisor for its children and monitors their behavior [24]. Supervisors can then take appropriate actions to handle errors in supervised actors, such as restarting a failed actor, stopping it or propagating the error up the hierarchy.

Whereas actors proved effective to implement fault-tolerant distributed systems and actor systems are widely deployed, such systems may fall short of achieving encapsulation of distributed functionalities because the scope of a component in a distributed system is tied to an object or actor, i.e., to call a method asynchronously, it has to be part of the public interface of an object. Remote calls across objects or messages sent across actors often lead to code with obscured data and control flow that is hard to read and follow.

2.2   Multitier Programming

Multitier programming is an approach for developing distributed systems, which provides language abstractions to reason about different tiers of a distributed system – for example, a client, server and a database tier – in the same compilation unit. The code for the different tiers is either generated at run time or created by the compiler. Code annotations, static analysis, types, or a combination of these approaches are used to separate the code into components that correspond to the various tiers.

A distributed application is composed of several tiers that can run on various computers connected through a network. A typical three-tier architecture, for example, consists of the presentation, application logic, and data management tiers, each of which runs at a different network location. The benefit of this approach is that each tier's functionality can be updated independently.

However, because of this architectural choice, a functionality that cuts across multiple tiers is now scattered across numerous compilation units. For instance, functionality on the Web is frequently spread across the client and the server. The tiers of a Web application are further typically implemented using different programming languages, such as JavaScript for the browser interface, Java for the server-side application logic and SQL for the database. Multitier languages aim to reduce the separation between client and server by compiling client-side code to JavaScript or by running JavaScript on the server.

In a multitier programming language, the different tiers can be programmed in a single language. Depending on the target tier, different compilation backends (such as Java for the server and JavaScript for the browser) are used. Consequently, functionality that spans multiple tiers can be developed within a single compilation unit. The compiler automatically adds the communication code necessary for components to interact while the program is being executed, generating numerous deployable units from a single multitier program (Fig. 1).

The multitier approach's ultimate goal is to improve program comprehension, make maintenance easier and enable formal reasoning about the entire distributed application. A number of research languages that adopt multitier

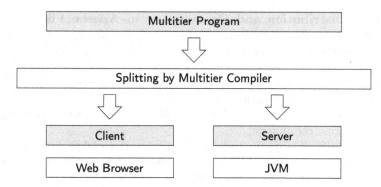

Fig. 1. Multitier programming [adopted from [95]].

concepts have been proposed and show the advantages of the approach, such as improving software comprehension, design, reasoning and maintenance. As a result, ideas from multitier programming have been included into a number of industrial solutions, demonstrating the potential of this approach, such as Ocsigen [12], Opa [83], WebSharper [14], Meteor [89] or GWT [52]. Different multitier languages cover different areas of the design space, integrating various techniques (such as compile time vs. run time splitting) and design choices (such as the placement of compilation units vs. individual functions), which frequently depend on the application domain and the software stack.

3 Modular Structuring of Asynchronous Communication

This section illustrates how developers structure asynchronous communication in distributed systems, comparing actor systems and multitier programming. For both approaches, we first describe them conceptually and then we demonstrate how these concepts are applied in a real-world stream processing system.

Active objects and actors proved to be an effective abstraction for developers to organize concurrent code [2]. They allow developers to reason in terms of a sequential execution environment within an active object or actor and communicating with others through asynchronous method calls or message-passing. Although actor framework implementations can reuse threads across actors, processing messages sequentially in every actors hides a potentially multithreaded execution environment.

The downside of this approach is that concurrency boundaries are closely tied to objects boundaries. This means that the concurrent parts of a system need to be separated into different objects. In some cases, splitting concurrent parts into separate objects aligns naturally with the problem domain and allows for independent reasoning about the concurrency aspects. In other application scenarios, however, this separation may increase the complexity of the implementation. Dependencies and interactions between concurrent objects can become intricate, making it harder to comprehend and maintain the system.

A Peak at Distribution and Concurrency in Apache Flink. To support the discussion about the design enabled by actor systems, we introduce a concrete application which makes extensive use of actors. Apache Flink [4] is a widely-used stream processing system. It features a distributed data-flow engine implemented in Scala and Java, which can pipeline and execute data-parallel programs. To increase performance, Flink is able to run different components on different machines in a computer cluster to distribute the load for processing a data stream across computers.

We look specifically into the task distribution system of Apache Flink, which provides Flink's core task scheduling and deployment logic. The task distribution system is based on Akka actors [58] and consists of 23 remote procedures in six *gateways* – an API that encapsulates sending actor messages into asynchronous RPCs – amounting to ~ 500 source lines of Scala code with complex interaction patterns. In the Flink task distribution system, a *JobManager* actor is responsible for assigning data processing tasks to *TaskManager* actors.

3.1 The Actor Approach

Actor languages provide dedicated features to represent different concurrently executing components of a distributed system – so-called actors. Actors naturally capture the concurrent nature of distributed systems and significantly simplify the development of such systems in several ways, making them suitable for building distributed and highly available systems.

Concurrency Abstraction. The primary feature of the actor model – both for distributed and for local concurrent systems – is that it offers a structured way to manage concurrency without worrying about low-level synchronization primitives [1]. Further, the model ensures that actors operate in isolation and their internal state is not directly accessible by other actors. This isolation simplifies concurrent programming as actors do not need to be aware of each other's internal state or execution details.

Fault Tolerance and Scalability. A notable benefit of the actor model, in particular in a distributed setting, is its fault tolerance [64]. Since actors are isolated from each other, failures in one actor do not directly impact others. If an actor crashes or becomes unresponsive, it can be restarted or replaced without affecting the overall system. For the same reason, the actor model also promotes scalability. New actors can be added or removed dynamically without affecting the overall system, enabling flexible scaling of the application to changing demands or requirements.

Modularity. The actor model also fosters modularity since actors are independent entities, which both encapsulate their private state and can be tested individually. However, an important aspect of the behavior of the entire distributed system stems from the communication and interaction between the actors, which can become quite complex, especially in systems with a large number of actors and

Listing 2. Communicating Flink actors [adopted from 93].

(**a**) Message definition.

```
1  package flink.runtime
2
3  case class SubmitTask(td: TaskDeployment)
```

(**b**) Calling side.

```
1  package flink.runtime.job
2
3  case class SubmitTask(td: TaskDeployment)
4
5  class TaskManagerGateway {
6    def submitTask(td: TaskDeployment, mgr: ActorRef) =
7      (mgr ? SubmitTask(td)).mapTo[Acknowledge]
8  }
```

(**c**) Responding side.

```
1  package flink.runtime.task
2
3  class TaskManager extends Actor {
4    def receive = {
5      case SubmitTask(td) =>
6        val task = new Task(td)
7        task.start()
8        sender ! Acknowledge()
9    }
10 }
```

intricate dependencies. Understanding the behavior of individual actors in a complex system can be challenging [94]. As actors operate independently and asynchronously, tracing the flow of messages and identifying the root cause of issues can be more difficult compared to more traditional programming models.

The Actor Version of Apache Flink. As it is commonly done in actor-based distributed systems today, the different distributed components of Apache Flink are implemented as different actors. As usual, communication between Flink actors is based on message-passing. Besides Flink, a number of other open-source projects (e.g., the Play Framework for web applications [57] or the Gatling load- and performance-testing framework [40]) and companies (e.g., PayPal [60] or Capital One [61]) use Akka actors.

Concurrency Abstraction. Listing 2 shows an excerpt of the – extensively simplified – interaction of the `TaskManagerGateway` with the `TaskManager`, taken from Apache Flink's task distribution system. The snippets show an example of sending and receiving of only a single message. The `TaskManagerGateway` is used by the *JobManager* actor to communicate with the *TaskManager* actor to submit data processing tasks to the *TaskManager*. Note that, in contrast to Listing 1, Flink uses the untyped version of Akka with a slightly different syntax. Listing 2a defines the `SubmitTask` message that is exchanged between the actors and which contains the meta data for the task to be executed by the TaskManager. Listing 2b shows the sending of the message (Line 7) from the JobManager using the ? send operator. As opposed to the fire-and-forget style of the ! send operator (shown in Listing 1), the ? operator implements a request-response pattern. With this operator, the next message from the addressed actor is treated as a response, which is then made available as result of ? in the form of a future containing the response message. Listing 2c shows the receiving of the message on the TaskManager. The TaskManager defines the actor message loop as its `receive` method (Line 4) that pattern-matching on the received messages (Line 5) and carries out a computation that depends on he received message (Lines 6 to 8), e.g., starting the task that was assigned by the JobManager.

The full `receive` methods of course contains a multitude of cases for the different messages which the actor can handle. While messages can be sent to an actor concurrently, programmers can safely assume that only one message is processed in the message loop at a time, relieving them from the complexities of handling intricate concurrency problems such as race conditions when accessing the actor's internal state from inside the message loop.

Fault Tolerance and Scalability. The actor-based design allows Flink to easily scale up to a large number of nodes to keep up with an increasing incoming stream of data to be processed. To achieve this, Flink can spawn actors on additional computer node to handle processing parts of the stream. For example, if the system requires additional computing power to process increased amounts of data, the JobManager can submit processing task to additional TaskManagers to carry out the processing work. Further, thanks to the actor model, if nodes fail or become unresponsive, Flink can re-spawn the respective actor (potentially on another node), making the system highly tolerant to faults.

Modularity. A potential issue of the actor model's message-passing scheme – where messages sent in some part of the code are processed by a completely separated part – in terms of code comprehension and maintenance is that it is not straightforward to map call sites modeled by sending messages to the sites where the messages are handled, which convolutes the control flow between the different actors, making it hard for developers to keep track.

The small code excerpt (Listing 2), illustrates how the task submission functionality is scattered over different modules, making it difficult to correlate sent messages (Listing 2b, Line 7) with the remote computations they initiate by pattern-matching on the received message (Listing 2c, Lines 6 to 8). Further, it

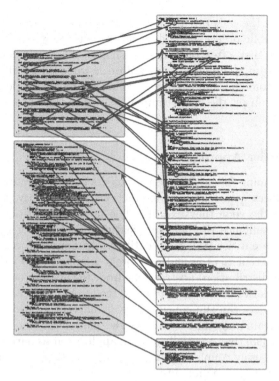

Fig. 2. Communication of two actors in Apache Flink [adopted from [94]].

is worth noting that the message loop of the TaskManager does not only handle a single type of message sent via the TaskManagerGateway. Due to the modularization enforced by the actor's remote communication boundaries, the message loop also needs to handle messages belonging to unrelated functions that should be executed on the TaskManager.

To provide a broader overview of the scattered control flow in Apache Flink, Fig. 2 depicts a larger portion of the communication between the two actors. The figure shows a part of the JobManager implementation (dark gray boxes, left), the TaskManager implementation (light gray boxes, right) and their communication (arrows). Every box is an actor which is confined by network boundaries. Thus, cross-host data flow belonging to the same (distributed) functionality is scattered over multiple objects.

Notably, Flink implements its own abstraction over message-passing that encapsulates the sending of messages into asynchronous remote procedure calls. As such, Flink is essentially using active objects, built on top of actors. Most of these calls are processed in a different compilation unit within another package, making it difficult to correlate the messages sent with the remote computations they trigger.

A closer look at the code reveals that the reason these remote procedures are implemented as public object methods is not because they represent a reusable function – in fact they often only have a single call site. Instead, the reason is that this structure to organize distribution is imposed by the actor model, which tempts to combine unrelated functionalities into a single actor because they incidentally run on the same component rather than properly separating them.

3.2   The Multitier Approach

Multitier programming follows the active objects or actor systems approach of providing developers with language abstractions for explicitly defining concurrent entities and the code they execute. The focus of multitier programming is to provide and enhance the language features for handling the communication between these entities [85]. Such entities, like active object or actors, are represented by different *tiers* in multitier programming [30]. Tiers decouple the concurrency (and distribution) abstractions from the objects/actors. Hence, the concurrency boundaries do not need to be at the level of objects. Different methods of the same object can run concurrently at different locations.

Multitier programming thus addresses the modularization issues of active objects and actors [93] that especially arise in application scenarios where remote functions are not loosely coupled but work closely together to achieve a common goal and provide a joint functionality.

Basic Multitier Language Features. Multitier languages typically give the developer full control over where values are placed and computations are executed using a variety of different techniques such as annotations, types or multistage programming. For illustration, we will use a language where placement is expressed in the types. For example, a value of type Int on Server represents an integer value that lives on the server, and a method of type String on Client represents a method that will execute on the client and return a string. A main method, which runs on the client when it starts, has the signature main(): Unit on Client – i.e., the method receives no arguments, has a void return value (i.e., it returns the singleton unit value) and lives on the client. Calling methods that live on other tiers looks similar to traditional (local) method calls. In particular, remote calls are fully type-checked across distributed components and remote methods are looked up according to the usual scoping rules (e.g., defined in the same lexical scope, imported, inherited, etc.). In the following presentation, remote calls are explicit through the remote call marker. Note that there also exist multitier languages in which remote calls are transparent.

Listing 3 places the main method on the client (Line 1), where it keeps reading line-by-line from standard input (Line 2). For every line, it calls the fire method on the server remotely (Line 3), which in turn calls the show method on the client remotely (Line 6) to print the line to standard output (Line 9). The remote call to fire (Line 3) requires the remote call marker since the fire method is placed on the server (Line 5) but is invoked within the main method placed on

Listing 3. Method with specified placement.

```
1  def main(): Unit on Client =
2    for (line <- io.Source.stdin.getLines)
3      remote call fire(line)
4
5  def fire(message: String): Unit on Server =
6    remote call show(line)
7
8  def show(message: String): Unit on Client =
9    println(line)
```

Listing 4. Nested code blocks with specified placement.

```
1  def main(): Unit on Client =
2    for (line <- io.Source.stdin.getLines)
3      on[Server].run.capture(line) {
4        on[Client].run.capture(line) {
5          println(line)
6        }
7      }
```

the client (Line 1). Hence, it is statically known where remote calls appear and which method is invoked to handle them.

As the example illustrates, multitier programming brings programming distributed applications closer to the development of "traditional" non-distributed applications. Both method definitions and calls look similar to the usual way of defining and calling methods – with the only new language features being the ones required for distribution, namely the specification of the placement and marking remote accesses.

Multitier languages typically take the possibility to compose code on different tiers one step further and do not only allow methods to be placed on tiers but also expressions inside methods. For example, Listing 4 implements the same logic as the snippet above but nests the expressions to be run on the client (Lines 1 and 4) and on the server (Line 3) inside each other.

In our example language, an expression of the form on[T].run is used to divert the control flow to another tier. In this language design, we also require developers to explicitly list the values that should be transferred to another tier using the capture clause. This design choice aims to avoid accidental captures which are distinctively more costly in a distributed setting – compared to captures in local closures, for example – as they require additional data to be transmitted over the network. The compiler issues an error if variables are used in a nested placed block without being explicitly captured, as this situation may indicate a potentially expensive programming mistake.

Listing 5. Distributed architecture specification.

```
1  @multitier object Chat {
2    @peer type Server <: { type Tie <: Multiple[Client] }
3    @peer type Client <: { type Tie <: Single[Server] }
4
5    def main(): Unit on Client = /* ... */
6    def fire(message: String): Unit on Server = /* ... */
7    def show(message: String): Unit on Client = /* ... */
8  }
```

Distributed Architectures. Multitier languages use different underlying system architectures or application topologies. Historically, multitier programming focused on client–server Web applications. Hence, most approaches have a server and a client – and sometimes a database – as the only supported tiers baked into the language model. They differ in whether they treat the server side as the single instance of the server code that serves a connected client or as one server instance serving all connected clients. The former case leads to a one-to-one connection between server and client sides. In such case, the example presented in Listing 3 will lead to the server echoing the message from the client back to the same client that sent the message. The latter case leads to a one-to-many connection between server and clients. In the example (Listing 3), the server would then forward the message from one client to all connected clients, essentially implementing a simple command line chat.

While the underling topology may be implicit and built into the language, we will use a multitier language that makes the involved peers and their architectural connection explicit – extending the scope beyond the Web and the client–server model. In Listing 5, we assume that the main, fire and show methods are implemented as before (Listing 3) and part of the Chat object. Lines 2 and 3 define the peers and their relation: A server that can handle multiple clients and a client that is connected to a single server.

Modularization, Encapsulation, Composition. Separating the distribution aspect from the object structure in multitier programming allows developers to return to using OOP abstractions for structuring, modularizing and composing their code based on distinguishing functionalities rather than locations. A single module – e.g., an object, class, trait, mixin, depending on the abstractions offered by the language – can contain functionalities that are themselves distributed. Hence, a module can abstract also over distributed functionalities: Distribution will not leak if it should not be exposed as part of the public interface. To integrate functionality defined in different modules, developers can use the usual techniques such as inheritance, delegation, composition or mixins.

For example, we can define different variants for the chat examples, e.g., one using a command line interface (like before, Listings 3 and 5) and another one using a graphical user interface. First, as shown in Listing 6, we can factor out

Listing 6. Abstract multitier module.

```
1   @multitier trait Chat {
2     @peer type Server <: { type Tie <: Multiple[Client] }
3     @peer type Client <: { type Tie <: Single[Server] }
4
5     def main(): Unit on Client
6
7     protected def fire(message: String): Unit on Server =
8       remote call show(line)
9
10    protected def show(message: String): Unit on Client
11  }
```

Listing 7. Concrete implementation of abstract multitier module.

```
1   @multitier object CommandLineChat extends Chat {
2     def main(): Unit on Client =
3       for (line <- io.Source.stdin.getLines)
4         remote call fire(line)
5
6     protected def show(message: String): Unit on Client =
7       println(line)
8   }
```

the architecture (Lines 2 and 3) and the common methods (Lines 5, 7 and 10), leaving the implementation of the methods abstract (Lines 5 and 10) that are to be implemented by a specific variant.

The command line chat variant (Listing 7) then only needs to implement the abstract methods (Lines 2 and 6), inheriting the architecture and the distributed functionalities form the Chat trait defined in Listing 6. In the example, the methods that are only relevant to the module or its sub-modules are access-protected using the usual protected visibility modifier.

Multitier programming goes beyond active objects and the actor model by enabling the separation of distribution concerns and OOP mechanisms used for modularization and composition. The ability to declare placement as an orthogonal dimension in the language relieves the developer from having to manually model placement and being forced to align the structure of the program with the boundaries of active objects or actors. Multitier objects can be composed like standard objects but different parts of their code can be run across different distributed components.

A Multitier Version of Apache Flink. In the case of Apache Flink, many remote procedures could be expressed more directly using nested remote expressions. Listing 8 shows a multitier variant of the interaction between JobMan-

Listing 8. Communicating Flink peers [adopted from 93].

```
1   @multitier object TaskManagerGateway {
2     @peer type JobManager <: { type Tie <: Multiple[TaskManager] }
3     @peer type TaskManager <: { type Tie <: Single[JobManager] }
4
5     def submitTask(td: TaskDeployment, tm: Remote[TaskManager]) =
6       on[JobManager] {
7         on(tm).run.capture(td) {
8           val task = new Task(td)
9           task.start()
10          Acknowledge()
11        }
12      }
13   }
```

ager and the TaskManager of Listing 2. The multitier version uses an intra-module cross-peer remote call (Line 7) to execute the data processing task on the TaskManager (Lines 8 to 10). Thus, related functionalities are kept inside the same TaskManagerGateway module and the multitier module contains the functionality that is executed on both the JobManager and the TaskManager peer.

Figure 3 shows a reimplementation of Fig. 2 using the multitier approach. The cross-peer data flow in the system is much more regular – thanks to the reorganization of the same code in a single unit – and thus much easier to track.

In the Flink example, the different distributed sub-functionalities of the task distribution system can be encapsulated into their own module. Besides the module already shown in Figs. 2 and 3, the task distribution system consists of five further individual functionalities. Figure 4 shows the task distribution system module (background), composed by mixing together the modules for the different sub-functionalities (foreground). Cross-peer data flow (arrows) is encapsulated within modules and is not split over different modules. As before, the data flow in each module spans across the JobManager (dark gray) and TaskManager (light gray) peers.

4 Discussion

This section discusses the similarities and differences among active objects, actors and multitier programming. Finally, we highlight the areas where multitier programming strives for improvement compared to alternative approaches.

4.1 Active Objects vs. Actors vs. Tiers

Multitier programming adopts the same approach of actors and active objects to decouple method invocation and method execution. Invoking a method on an active object – or sending a message to an actor – returns immediately. The method itself is executed – or the message is dispatched – asynchronously. Hence, the multitier approach retains the basic asynchronous execution model of active objects and actors. In fact, every tier can be thought of as an active object on which the methods that are placed on the tier can be executed. The execution of a remote method is necessarily asynchronous since the threads of execution of the different tiers are – even physically – separated. Some languages hide the asynchronicity from the developer by compiling the multitier code to continuation-passing style and invoking the continuation only when the remote result becomes locally available [30]. Other languages make the asynchronicity of the result explicit by having remote methods return futures [94] – similar to how asynchronicity is often handled in active objects – or by employing coroutine-based approaches for cooperative multitasking [29].

Multitier languages, however, provide a holistic view on the distributed components and their interaction. They tackle situations where the interaction between active objects or actors hinders encapsulation and proper modularization along meaningful functional boundaries, when different places are treated as different objects or actors. To achieve this goal, the multitier paradigm is characterized by linguistic features for expressing different tiers and their interaction. Therefore, multitier programming especially focuses on application scenarios where systems that are designed "as a whole" and a holistic view simplifies the reasoning about the system for the developer. In these scenarios, multitier programming can serve to bridge the communication across distributed active entities.

Fig. 3. Flink: Multitier approach [from [94]].

4.2   Development Benefits

In summary, the development benefits of the multitier programming paradigm revolve mainly around the following aspects.

Higher Abstraction Level. Multitier programming simplifies software development for distributed systems by abstracting away low-level details such as network communication, serialization, and data format conversions [82], allowing

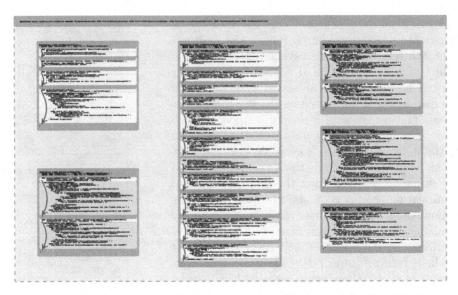

Fig. 4. Communication of two actors in Apache Flink: Multitier modularization [adopted from [93]].

developers to work at a higher level of abstraction [94]. With multitier programming, there is no need for manual design of inter-tier APIs, as the underlying technologies used for inter-tier communication are transparent to the developer [85].

Improved Software Design. In distributed applications, the boundaries between hosts and functionalities may not always align, with functionalities spanning multiple locations and a single location hosting multiple functionalities. Programming each location separately introduces two issues: compromised modularity and code repetition. Multitier programming addresses these problems by enabling the development of a functionality once and placing it where needed [36].

Formal Reasoning. Multitier design improves formal reasoning by explicitly modeling distributed applications and capturing important aspects such as placement, system components, and tier boundaries. This approach enables thorough analysis of software properties across the entire system, instead of treating components in isolation. It supports reasoning about concurrency [76], security [13], performance optimization [26], as well as domain-specific properties like reachability in software-defined networks [75].

Code Maintenance. Multitier programming simplifies the process of modifying software systems in two notable ways. First, it allows for migrating functionality between different tiers without the need for a rewrite in a different language [43] (i.e., validating user input on both the client and server sides without code duplication). Second, it provides easier migration of applications across different platforms [46] (e.g., simply changing the compilation target to JavaScript for a Web client).

Program Comprehension. Multitier programming simplifies program comprehension – i.e., the complexity that programmers face to develop a correct mental model of a program [88] – by enabling seamless data flow across multiple hosts, eliminating communication code details and interruptions from forcing modularization along peer boundaries. Thereby, multitier programming simplifies development and debugging [66]. Yet, so far, we lack empirical studies or controlled experiments measuring the specific advantage of multitier programming in terms of program comprehension.

5   A Research Roadmap

This section outlines open challenges and opportunities for future research on multitier programming.

Dynamic Placement. Existing multitier languages assign the application functionalities to the nodes in the system based on various mechanisms, such as user annotations, types, and static analysis. Serrano et al. [85] and Cooper et al. [30] introduced multitier languages that incorporate two places as annotations on functions: client and server. Murphy et al. [74] developed a type system based on modal logic to represent different places as *possible worlds*. Type-based approaches have also been used to describe the interaction of places. Notably, multiparty session types [49] provide static specifications for communication protocols. Choreographic programming [41] ensures safe communication protocols across different locations encoded by different type parameters. Information flow type systems have been employed to define the placement of data and computation, preventing the leakage of private data to untrusted parties [99].

All these mechanisms are based on *compile time* assignment of functionalities to nodes. Yet, in distributed systems, often, functionalities need to be assigned to nodes during the program execution, usually to improve performance.

Dynamic placement decisions play a crucial role in various computing domains. First, both computation and the resulting data placement can be dynamically decided. For instance, in a master–worker system, the master leverages information about the execution environment and the job's parameters to determine the most suitable worker [97]. In this scenario, the computed result is dynamically placed at the location where it was generated. Second, computation can depend on data that is being transferred between different places. For instance, data that is frequently accessed in a remote database is often stored in a cache for access speed [7,101]. An application that operates on data should be able to handle both the database-stored data and the data residing in the cache. Conversely, data that does not exist in either the database or the cache may require distinct handling, e.g., when dealing with data received from a client, it is necessary to sanitize the data prior to storage.

Developers need to tackle the lack of programming abstractions for dynamic placement themselves by manually encoding placement information into the program. The first option is to extract a common interface, treating the system as homogeneous, consisting of a single type of place. This approach, however, leads to a loss of precision necessary to distinguish between various types of places. Consequently, this approach can potentially cause run time errors as the distinctions among nodes are abstracted away. The second option involves not explicitly extracting any interface but relying solely on the programmer's awareness of equivalent functionalities across different places. This approach, however, does not support dynamic placement efficiently as the same functionality needs to be implemented multiple times for the different places, resulting in code repetitions.

Active objects provide a high degree of flexibility to decide their placement dynamically. Actor systems in particular typically provide location transparency, i.e., they abstract away the actors' placement. However, these models lack the static reasoning about placement and the automatic compiler checks found in multitier languages. So far, we lack programming models that combine the strength of both approaches. Finding a practical language abstractions to trade-off static safety guarantees and the ability to decide placement dynamically is still an open problem.

Error Handling. In software execution, error occurs in various circumstances, for example when dealing with the external environment (e.g., I/O). Another class of errors occurs in the case of software bugs (e.g., in the case of null values). In distributed systems, software applications are executed on several nodes. Hence the overall probability that (at least) one of the nodes fails increases with the number of nodes. In addition, network connections can also fail, leading to packet loss and system partitioning. These potential errors need to be modeled in the application to give developers the opportunity to execute a reaction. This mechanism can be implemented in various ways. Actor systems provide supervision hierarchies where certain actors that "supervise", i.e., monitor, other actors – the supervisor can react to failing supervised actors. Different actor systems can offer different means to setup supervisors.

In Akka, supervision trees are defined by configuring parent actors with supervisor strategies, which dictate the parent's response to child failures. Akka provides several built-in strategies, such as the `OneForOneStrategy`, which restarts only the failing child, or the `AllForOneStrategy`, which restarts all children upon a single child's failure. Erlang OTP [8] utilizes a similar approach with its supervisor behavior, where a supervisor process is responsible for starting, stopping, and monitoring its child processes. In this case, supervision trees are built by composing supervisors and worker processes, with supervisors specifying restart strategies and intensity, allowing for fine-grained control over failure handling.

Supervision trees offer several advantages for fault-tolerant systems. First, the hierarchical organization of actors provides a clear structure for error handling, with each level of the tree responsible for a specific subset of actors. Second, the isolation between actors prevents errors from cascading uncontrollably through the system. Also, supervision trees enable self-healing capabilities in a system by restarting failed actors, often allowing the system to recover from failures without manual intervention. This promotes system resilience, as the impact of isolated errors can be minimized and the system can continue functioning despite component failures.

As most multitier languages make the underlying actors visible, e.g., as types or annotations, it is conceivable that a multitier language can provide similar features to define supervision relations. So far, however, multitier languages have not developed such specific fault tolerance mechanisms yet. This is partly due to their origins as languages for web development, where neither the server has the ability to stop or restart clients nor the other way around. Yet, with multitier languages expanding their scope beyond web applications, dedicated features for fault tolerance will become more important. For example, a multitier programming framework could allow developers to specify whether only the failed or all supervised peers should be automatically restarted in case of failures, while also deciding whether to wipe or retain their state – akin to supervision strategies in actor systems.

Consistency. Message ordering guarantees vary in different actor systems. One basic requirement is that messages sent by the same source actor are processed in the same receiving actor in the exact order they were sent. This ordering property transitively holds true even when messages are relayed through multiple actors. For example, if actor A sends messages to actor B, and B forwards them to actor C, actor C receives the messages in the same order they were generated by actor A. However, actor systems like Erlang, do not provide ordering guarantees when actor A sends two messages to actors B and C, and both B and C forward these messages to the same actor D. In such cases, there is no guarantee on the order in which messages are received by D.

Generally, this kind of non-deterministic message ordering can introduce inconsistencies if the processing order of messages affects the outcome. Yet, in distributed systems based on message-passing, guaranteeing a specific sequence of messages may incur overhead, both in terms of maintenance complexities for the developers and in terms of potential run time performance implications.

Further, in distributed actor systems, issues like network problems or node failures can cause delays in message transmission or even result in message loss. If a particular actor relies on a specific message to carry out its operations, the loss of that message can introduce inconsistencies and disrupt the desired behavior. Actor systems are typically stateful with each actor maintaining its own private state. An actor's state can only be modified by the actor itself, usually in response to received messages. Hence, when different actors receive messages in a different order or miss certain messages, their internal states can diverge. These data inconsistencies across actors can lead to unexpected behavior and undesired outcomes. Thus, handling message loss is crucial to maintaining consistency.

Traditionally, synchronization techniques such as locks are used to prevent such inconsistencies. To ensure that state changes are carried out consistently across multiple operations, operations are grouped into transactions, which are executed atomically, guaranteeing that either all operations take effect or none of them do. Such concurrency control mechanisms, however, are challenging in distributed actor systems. The distributed nature of actor systems, where actors work independently and communicate through message passing, adds complexity to the coordination process. Coordinating multiple actors to achieve consistent outcomes throughout the system requires careful design and synchronization.

These issues often render strong consistency impractical in distributed systems. Instead, these systems often resort to a weaker consistency model, such as eventual consistency. In an eventual consistency model, a certain level of consistency is guaranteed over time but is not enforced immediately.

Reasoning about consistency in distributed system is still an active area of research. To aid developers in understanding the behavior and the consistency of distributed systems, multitier programming offers a valuable approach by providing a holistic view of the system and the interactions among the different actors, multitier programming facilitates reasoning about consistency in distributed systems. One promising direction yet to be explored is the automatic generation of consistency schemes based on a hypothetical sequential execution of multitier code. This approach could offer insights into effectively achieving consistency in distributed systems by automatically deriving suitable consistency mechanisms from the code structure. Additionally, consistency types [48,53] are a promising technique for statically reasoning about consistency properties. They allow developers to analyze and reason about the expected consistency of distributed systems at compile-time, catching potential inconsistencies early on.

6   Related Work

Programming Languages and Calculi for Distributed Systems. Multitier programming emerged from a rich lineage of programming language design for distributed systems, influenced by notable distributed languages such as Argus [62], Emerald [15], Distributed Oz [45,90], Dist-Orc [5] and Jolie [73]. Additionally, various frameworks for big data processing have emerged in recent years, including Flink [20], Spark [98], Dryad [51], PigLatin [77] and FlumeJava [25]. These frameworks refine and generalize the original MapReduce [35] model, transparently handling fault tolerance, replication, and task distribution. Further, significant contributions have been made towards designing programming languages that cater to specific aspects of distributed systems. For example, conflict-free replicated data types (CRDT) [86,87] or cloud types [18] ensure eventual consistency, Ericsson's Calvin [79] provides a programming frameworks for mixed IoT/Cloud development and Spores [68] provide language support for distribution of computations and fault tolerance [69].

Formal calculi have been developed to model distributed systems. They provide varying levels of abstraction for placement and communication across peers.

Process calculi such as the π-calculus [70, 71] are especially common to model the behavior of distributed systems. In the π-calculus and its variants, different processes represent the execution threads of the different peers. In particular, the join-calculus [38] defines processes communicating through asynchronous message-passing over channels. The Ambient calculus [21] describes concurrent systems involving mobile devices and computation. It allows the definition of named places where computations take place, with the ability to move ambients between nested places, representing administrative domains and access control. The Cloud Programming Language (CPL) [17] serves as a core calculus for composing services in cloud computing environments. CPL employs an event-based approach and provides combinators that enable secure composition of cloud applications.

Choreographies. Choreographic programming defines a concurrent system as a unified compilation unit, which provides a global description of the interactions and computations among connected components within a distributed system, known as a *choreography* [56, 73, 92]. Similar to multitier programming, the compiler automatically generates implementations for each component [19]. However, choreographic programming differs in that it makes the communication protocol between peers explicit. The compiler ensures that the generated code strictly adheres to this defined flow. The foundations of choreographic programming lie in process calculi [11], which has been used to explore novel techniques in information flow control [63], deadlock-free distributed algorithms [32], and protocols for dynamic run time code updates for components [81]. Giallorenzo et al. [42] make a first attempt to systematically compare choreographic programming and multitier programming.

Aggregate Programming. The concept behind aggregate programming is to allow the specification of global behaviors for distributed systems by defining local computations. The Field calculus [9] is designed to specify and execute distributed computations over devices embedded in a spatial environment. This environment might include diverse entities like sensor networks, mobile robots, or other distributed systems where there is a notion of spatial distribution. In Field calculus, computations are expressed in terms of fields, which are functions from space-time to data values. Devices can read and modify the local values of these fields and use the information from neighboring devices to compute new field values. The paradigm promotes the idea that by providing the right local interactions and computations, more complex global behaviors can emerge without the need for central coordination. *Field-based computing* [54, 65, 91] is a programming model where the overall distributed system behavior is understood as producing a *computational field*, i.e., a map from network nodes to values. Among the most important advantages, by abstracting over the role of individual devices, it is possible to define a programming paradigm where concurrency, asynchronicity, network communication, message loss and failures do not need to be handled explicitly [10]. Both aggregate and multitier programming aim to improve the development of complex distributed systems. In multitier programming, the system architecture is explicitly defined, composed of heterogeneous tiers, each representing a specific function or component. Aggregate computing, on the other hand, builds on a network of homogeneous devices that execute localized computations, which collectively contribute to the overall behavior of the system.

PGAS Languages. Partitioned global address space languages (PGAS) [34] offer a programming model designed for high-performance parallel execution. The X10 language [27], for example, parallelizes task execution using a work-stealing scheduler, enabling developers to write highly scalable code. The X10 programming model features explicit fork/join operations to make the communication cost visible. The language's advanced dependent type system [26] captures the specific place to which a reference points. While both PGAS and multitier languages aim to reduce host boundaries between places for simplified development, their scopes differ significantly. PGAS languages primarily target high-performance computing in dedicated clusters, whereas multitier programming focuses on networked distributed systems on the Internet. Hence, places in multitier programming represent the different peers of a distributed system, whereas places in PGAS refer to partitions in a shared global heap address space.

Software Architectures. Software architectures [39,78] organize software systems into components with defined connections and interaction constraints. Architecture description languages (ADLs) [67] specify components, connectors, architectural invariants, and a mapping of architectural models to implementation infrastructure. ArchJava [3] aims to combine architecture specification in the style of ADLs with the actual system implementation in a single language. Hilda [96] is a language at the intersection of multitier and modeling languages and enables automatic partitioning of data-driven multitier software using a declarative language similar to UML. Component models [31], influenced by ADLs and object-oriented design, separate concerns in the entire software system, defining component interfaces and composition mechanisms, and enforcing strong interfaces with other modules. In the distributed setting, component-based development typically models the distributed system components as separate units, forcing developers to modularize along network boundaries.

Big Data Processing Systems. A significant factor contributing to the success of modern big data systems is the availability of a programming interface that – similar to multitier programming – enables developers to program components running on different hosts within the same compilation unit, with the big data processing framework handling communication and scheduling. This kind of systems includes batch processing frameworks like Hadoop [35] and Spark [98] and stream processing systems such as Flink [4] and Storm [6]. Yet, the domain of big data processing systems is limited enough that they can completely abstract distribution concerns away. Further, the language semantics of these systems visibly differs, e.g., mutable shared variables are transformed into non-shared separated copies.

Operator Placement. In contrast to explicit placement methods – such as using annotations as typically found in multitier programming – the operator placement problem focuses on determining the best host for deploying each operator in a distributed system. In this domain, the best placement is the one that maximizes a specific metric like throughput [33,55] or load [28]. Various approaches have been proposed to address the operator placement problem, including the use of overlay networks where operators are assigned to hosts through random selection [50], network modeling [80] and linear optimization techniques for finding the optimal solution to a constraint problem [22]. While these systems typically consider operators as the deployment unit, Zhou et al. [100] suggest a coarser granularity approach where query fragments, i.e., groups of operators, are deployed to reduce the load on the placement algorithm.

7 Conclusion

Active objects have been studied for long as a language abstraction that encapsulates not only state and operations, like objects, but also a process. This work delved into the multitier programming language paradigm, which is rooted in active objects and improves on some aspects of active objects when a distributed system is conceived as a cohesive unit. In multitier programming, code that belongs to different peers within a distributed system can coexist within the same compilation unit. It is the responsibility of the compiler to split the code into deployment components and add the necessary networking code. We showed that multitier programming achieves positive results in modularizing distributed and concurrent applications, abstracting over network communication and host boundaries, and outlined areas that present open challenges. As active objects are the ideal compilation target for multitier languages and their execution model of such languages is based on interacting active entities, active objects remain visible for developers when they implement data exchange across peers using multitier programming.

Acknowledgements. This work has been supported by the Swiss National Science Foundation (SNSF), grant 200429.

References

1. Agha, G.: Actors: A Model of Concurrent Computation in Distributed Systems. MIT Press, Cambridge, MA, USA (1986). ISBN 0-262-01092-5
2. Agha, G., Hewitt, C.: Concurrent programming using actors: exploiting large-scale parallelism. In: Maheshwari, S.N. (ed.) FSTTCS 1985. LNCS, vol. 206, pp. 19–41. Springer, Heidelberg (1985). https://doi.org/10.1007/3-540-16042-6_2. ISBN 978-3-540-39722-9
3. Aldrich, J., Chambers, C., Notkin, D.: Archjava: connecting software architecture to implementation. In: Proceedings of the 24th International Conference on Software Engineering, ICSE '02, pp. 187–197, New York, NY, USA. ACM (2002). ISBN 1-58113-472-X, https://doi.org/10.1145/581339.581365
4. Alexandrov, A., et al.: The stratosphere platform for big data analytics. VLDB J. **23**(6), 939–964 (2014). ISSN 1066-8888, https://doi.org/10.1007/s00778-014-0357-y

5. AlTurki, M., Meseguer, J.: DIST-ORC: a rewriting-based distributed implementation of Orc with formal analysis. In: Proceedings First International Workshop on Rewriting Techniques for Real-Time Systems, RTRTS '10, pp. 26–45 (2010). https://doi.org/10.4204/EPTCS.36.2

6. Apache Software Foundation. Storm (2011). http://storm.apache.org/

7. Arani, Z., Chapman, D., Wang, C., Gruenwald, L., d'Orazio, L., Basiuk, T.: A scored semantic cache replacement strategy for mobile cloud database systems. In: Bellatreche, L., et al. (eds.) TPDL/ADBIS -2020. CCIS, vol. 1260, pp. 237–248. Springer, Cham (2020). https://doi.org/10.1007/978-3-030-55814-7_20, ISBN 978-3-030-55814-7

8. Armstrong, J.: Erlang. Commun. ACM **53**(9), 68–75 (2010). ISSN 0001–0782. https://doi.org/10.1145/1810891.1810910

9. Audrito, G., Viroli, M., Damiani, F., Pianini, D., Beal, J.: A higher-order calculus of computational fields. ACM Trans. Comput. Log. **20**(1) (2019). ISSN 1529–3785. https://doi.org/10.1145/3285956

10. Audrito, G., Roberto, C., Damiani, F., Guido, S., Mirko, V.: Functional programming for distributed systems with XC. In: Ali, K., Vitek, J. (eds.), Proceedings of the 36th European Conference on Object-Oriented Programming (ECOOP '22), volume 222 of Leibniz International Proceedings in Informatics (LIPIcs), pp. 20:1–20:28, Dagstuhl, Germany, June 2022. Schloss Dagstuhl - Leibniz-Zentrum für Informatik. ISBN 978-3-95977-225-9. https://doi.org/10.4230/LIPIcs.ECOOP. 2022.20

11. Baeten, J.C.M.: A brief history of process algebra. Theor. Comput. Sci. **335**(2–113), 131–146 (2005). ISSN 0304–3975. https://doi.org/10.1016/j.tcs.2004.07.036

12. Balat, V.: Ocsigen: typing web interaction with objective CAML. In: Proceedings of the 2006 Workshop on ML, ML '06, pp. 84–94, New York, NY, USA, ACM (2006). ISBN 1-59593-483-9. https://doi.org/10.1145/1159876.1159889

13. Baltopoulos, I.G., Gordon, A.D.: Secure compilation of a multi-tier web language. In: Proceedings of the 4th International Workshop on Types in Language Design and Implementation, TLDI '09, pp. 27–38, New York, NY, USA, 2009. ACM (2009). ISBN 978-1-60558-420-1. https://doi.org/10.1145/1481861.1481866

14. Bjornson, J., Tayanovskyy, A., Granicz, A.: Composing reactive GUIs in F# using websharper. In: Hage, J., Morazán, M.T. (eds.) IFL 2010. LNCS, vol. 6647, pp. 203–216. Springer, Heidelberg (2011). https://doi.org/10.1007/978-3-642-24276-2_13, ISBN 978-3-642-24275-5

15. Black, A.P., Hutchinson, N.C., Jul, E., Levy, H.M.: The development of the emerald programming language. In: Proceedings of the Third ACM SIGPLAN Conference on History of Programming Languages, HOPL III, pp. 11:1–11:51, New York, NY, USA, 2007. ACM (2007). ISBN 978-1-59593-766-7. https://doi.org/10. 1145/1238844.1238855

16. Boer, F.D., et al.: A survey of active object languages. ACM Comput. Surv. **50**(5) (2017). ISSN 0360–0300. https://doi.org/10.1145/3122848

17. Bračevac, O., Erdweg, S., Salvaneschi, G., Mezini, M.: CPL: a core language for cloud computing. In: Proceedings of the 15th International Conference on Modularity, MODULARITY '16, pp. 94–105 (2016). https://doi.org/10.1145/2889443. 2889452

18. Burckhardt, S., Fähndrich, M., Leijen, D., Wood, B.P.: Cloud types for eventual consistency. In: Noble, J. (ed.) ECOOP 2012. LNCS, vol. 7313, pp. 283–307. Springer, Heidelberg (2012). https://doi.org/10.1007/978-3-642-31057-7_14, ISBN 978-3-642-31056-0

19. Carbone, M., Montesi, F.: Deadlock-freedom-by-design: multiparty asynchronous global programming. In: Proceedings of the 40th Annual ACM SIGPLAN-SIGACT Symposium on Principles of Programming Languages, POPL '13, pp. 263–274, New York, NY, USA, 2013. ACM (2013). ISBN 978-1-4503-1832-7. https://doi.org/10.1145/2429069.2429101

20. Carbone, P., Katsifodimos, A., Ewen, S., Markl, V., Haridi, S., Tzoumas, K.: Apache Flink^{TM}: stream and batch processing in a single engine. IEEE Data Eng. Bull. **38**(4), 28–38 (2015). http://sites.computer.org/debull/A15dec/p28.pdf

21. Cardelli, L., Gordon, A.D.: Mobile ambients. In: Nivat, M. (ed.) FoSSaCS 1998. LNCS, vol. 1378, pp. 140–155. Springer, Heidelberg (1998). ISBN 978-3-540-64300-5, https://doi.org/10.1007/BFb0053547

22. Cardellini, V., Grassi, V., Lo Presti, F., Nardelli, M.: Optimal operator placement for distributed stream processing applications. In: Proceedings of the 10th ACM International Conference on Distributed and Event-Based Systems, DEBS '16, pp. 69–80, New York, NY, USA, 2016. ACM (2016). ISBN 978-1-4503-4021-2. https://doi.org/10.1145/2933267.2933312

23. Cavage, M.: There's just no getting around it: you're building a distributed system: building a distributed system requires a methodical approach to requirements. Queue **11**(4), 30–41 (2013). ISSN 1542-7730. https://doi.org/10.1145/2466486.2482856

24. Cesarini, F., Thompson, S.: Erlang Programming – A Concurrent Approach to Software Development. O'Reilly, Sebastopol, CA, USA (2009). ISBN 978-0-596-51818-9

25. Chambers, C., et al.: Flumejava: easy, efficient data-parallel pipelines. In: Proceedings of the 31st ACM SIGPLAN Conference on Programming Language Design and Implementation, PLDI '10, pp. 363–375, New York, NY, USA, 2010. ACM (2010). ISBN 978-1-4503-0019-3. https://doi.org/10.1145/1806596.1806638

26. Chandra, S., Saraswat, V., Sarkar, V., Bodik, R.: Type inference for locality analysis of distributed data structures. In: Proceedings of the 13th ACM SIGPLAN Symposium on Principles and Practice of Parallel Programming, PPoPP '08, pp. 11–22, New York, NY, USA, 2008. ACM (2008). ISBN 978-1-59593-795-7. https://doi.org/10.1145/1345206.1345211

27. Charles, P., et al.: X10: an object-oriented approach to non-uniform cluster computing. In: Proceedings of the 20th Annual ACM SIGPLAN Conference on Object-Oriented Programming, Systems, Languages, and Applications, OOPSLA '05, pp. 519–538, New York, NY, USA, 2005. ACM (2005). ISBN 1-59593-031-0. https://doi.org/10.1145/1094811.1094852

28. Cherniack, M., et al.: Scalable distributed stream processing. In: Proceedings of the First Biennial Conference on Innovative Data Systems Research, CIDR '03, January 2003. http://nms.csail.mit.edu/papers/CIDR_CRC.pdf

29. Choi, K., Chang, B.-M.: A theory of RPC calculi for client-server model. J. Funct. Program. **29** (2019). https://doi.org/10.1017/S0956796819000029

30. Cooper, E., Lindley, S., Wadler, P., Yallop, J.: Links: web programming without tiers. In: de Boer, F.S., Bonsangue, M.M., Graf, S., de Roever, W.-P. (eds.) FMCO 2006. LNCS, vol. 4709, pp. 266–296. Springer, Heidelberg (2007). ISBN 978-3-540-74791-8, https://doi.org/10.1007/978-3-540-74792-5_12

31. Crnkovic, I., Sentilles, S., Vulgarakis, A., Chaudron, M.R.: A classification framework for software component models. IEEE Trans. Softw. Eng. **37**(5), 593–615 (2011). ISSN 0098-5589. https://doi.org/10.1109/TSE.2010.83

32. Cruz-Filipe, L., Montesi, F.: Choreographies in practice. In: Albert, E., Lanese, I. (eds.) FORTE 2016. LNCS, vol. 9688, pp. 114–123. Springer, Cham (2016). ISBN 978-3-319-39569-2. https://doi.org/10.1007/978-3-319-39570-8_8

33. Cugola, G., Margara, A.: Deployment strategies for distributed complex event processing. Computing **95**(2), 129–156 (2013). ISSN 0010–485X. https://doi.org/10.1007/s00607-012-0217-9

34. De Wael, M., Marr, S., De Fraine, B., Van Cutsem, T., De Meuter, W.: Partitioned global address space languages. ACM Comput. Surv. **47**(4), 62:1–62:27 (2015). ISSN 0360–0300. https://doi.org/10.1145/2716320

35. Dean, J., Ghemawat, S.: MapReduce: simplified data processing on large clusters. Commun. ACM **51**(1), 107–113 (2008). ISSN 0001–0782. https://doi.org/10.1145/1327452.1327492

36. Delaval, G., Girault, A., Pouzet, M.: A type system for the automatic distribution of higher-order synchronous dataflow programs. In: Proceedings of the 2008 ACM SIGPLAN-SIGBED Conference on Languages, Compilers, and Tools for Embedded Systems, LCTES '08, pp. 101–110, New York, NY, USA, 2008. ACM (2008). ISBN 978-1-60558-104-0. https://doi.org/10.1145/1375657.1375672

37. Drechsler, J., Mogk, R., Salvaneschi, G., Mezini, M.: Thread-safe reactive programming. Proc. ACM Program. Lang. **2**(OOPSLA) (2018). https://doi.org/10.1145/3276477

38. Fournet, C., Gonthier, G.: The reflexive CHAM and the join-calculus. In: Proceedings of the 23rd ACM SIGPLAN-SIGACT Symposium on Principles of Programming Languages, POPL '96, pp. 372–385, New York, NY, USA, 1996. ACM (1996). ISBN 0-89791-769-3. https://doi.org/10.1145/237721.237805

39. Garlan, D., Shaw, M.: An introduction to software architecture. Technical report, Pittsburgh, PA, USA (1994). http://www.cs.cmu.edu/afs/cs/project/vit/ftp/pdf/intro_softarch.pdf

40. Gatling Corp. Gatling (2011). https://gatling.io/

41. Giallorenzo, S., Montesi, F., Peressotti, M.: Choreographies as objects, 2020

42. Giallorenzo, S., Montesi, F., Peressotti, M., Richter, D., Salvaneschi, G., Weisenburger, P.: Multiparty languages: the choreographic and multitier cases. In: Møller, A., Sridharan, M. (eds.), Proceedings of the 35th European Conference on Object-Oriented Programming (ECOOP '21), volume 194 of Leibniz International Proceedings in Informatics (LIPIcs), pp. 22:1–22:27, Dagstuhl, Germany, July 2021. Schloss Dagstuhl - Leibniz-Zentrum für Informatik. ISBN 978-3-95977-190-0. https://doi.org/10.4230/LIPIcs.ECOOP.2021.22

43. Groenewegen, D.M., Hemel, Z., Kats, L.C., Visser, E.: WebDSL: a domain-specific language for dynamic web applications. In: Companion to the 23rd ACM SIGPLAN Conference on Object-Oriented Programming Systems Languages and Applications, OOPSLA Companion '08, pp. 779–780, New York, NY, USA, 2008. ACM (2008). ISBN 978-1-60558-220-7. https://doi.org/10.1145/1449814.1449858

44. Haller, P., Odersky, M.: Scala actors: unifying thread-based and event-based programming. Theor. Comput. Sci. **410**(2–3), 202–220 (2009). ISSN 0304–3975. https://doi.org/10.1016/j.tcs.2008.09.019

45. Haridi, S., Van Roy, P., Smolka, G.: An overview of the design of distributed Oz. In: Proceedings of the Second International Symposium on Parallel Symbolic Computation, PASCO '97, pp. 176–187, New York, NY, USA, 1997. ACM (1997). ISBN 0-89791-951-3. https://doi.org/10.1145/266670.266726

46. Haxe Foundation. Haxe cross-platform toolkit, 2005. http://haxe.org

47. Hewitt, C., Bishop, P., Steiger, R.: A universal modular actor formalism for arti- ficial intelligence. In: Proceedings of the 3rd International Joint Conference on Artificial Intelligence, IJCAI '73, pp. 235–245, San Francisco, CA, USA (1973). Morgan Kaufmann Publishers Inc. http://ijcai.org/Proceedings/73/Papers/027B. pdf

48. Holt, B., Bornholt, J., Zhang, I., Ports, D., Oskin, M., Ceze, L.: Disciplined incon- sistency with consistency types. In: Proceedings of the Seventh ACM Symposium on Cloud Computing, SoCC '16, pp. 279–293, New York, NY, USA, 2016. ACM (2016). ISBN 978-1-4503-4525-5. https://doi.org/10.1145/2987550.2987559

49. Honda, K., Yoshida, N., Carbone, M.: Multiparty asynchronous session types. In: Proceedings of the 35th Annual ACM SIGPLAN-SIGACT Symposium on Prin- ciples of Programming Languages, POPL '08, pp. 273–284, New York, NY, USA, 2008. ACM (2008). ISBN 978-1-59593-689-9. https://doi.org/10.1145/1328438. 1328472

50. Huebsch, R., Hellerstein, J.M., Lanham, N., Loo, B.T., Shenker, S., Stoica, I.: Querying the internet with PIER. In: Proceedings of the 29th International Con- ference on Very Large Data Bases, VLDB '03, pp. 321–332. VLDB Endowment (2003). ISBN 0-12-722442-4. https://doi.org/10.1016/B978-012722442-8/50036-7

51. Isard, M., Yu, Y.: Distributed data-parallel computing using a high-level pro- gramming language. In: Proceedings of the 2009 ACM SIGMOD International Conference on Management of Data, SIGMOD '09, pp. 987–994, New York, NY, USA, 2009. ACM (2009). ISBN 978-1-60558-551-2. https://doi.org/10.1145/ 1559845.1559962

52. Kereki, F.: Essential GWT: Building for the Web with Google Web Toolkit 2, 1st edn. Addison-Wesley Professional, Boston (2010). ISBN 978-0-321-70514-3

53. Köhler, M., Eskandani, N., Weisenburger, P., Margara, A., Salvaneschi, G.: Rethinking safe consistency in distributed object-oriented programming. Proc. ACM Program. Lang. 4(OOPSLA), 1–30 (2020) https://doi.org/10.1145/3428256

54. Lafuente, A.L., Loreti, M., Montanari, U.: Asynchronous distributed execution of fixpoint-based computational fields. Log. Methods Comput. Sci. 13 (2017). https://doi.org/10.23638/LMCS-13(1:13)2017

55. Lakshmanan, G.T., Li, Y., Strom, R.: Placement strategies for internet-scale data stream systems. IEEE Internet Comput. 12(6), 50–60 (2008). ISSN 1089–7801. https://doi.org/10.1109/MIC.2008.129

56. Lanese, I., Guidi, C., Montesi, F., Zavattaro, G.: Bridging the gap between interaction- and process-oriented choreographies. In: Proceedings of the 6th IEEE International Conference on Software Engineering and Formal Methods, SEFM '08, pp. 323–332, Washington, DC, USA. IEEE Computer Society (2008). ISBN 978-0-7695-3437-4. https://doi.org/10.1109/SEFM.2008.11

57. Lightbend. Play Framework, 2007. http://playframework.com/

58. Lightbend. Akka Classic Actors, 2009. https://doc.akka.io/docs/akka/current/ actors.html

59. Lightbend. Akka Typed Actors, 2015. https://doc.akka.io/docs/akka/current/ typed.html

60. Lightbend. Case study: Capital one scales real-time auto loan decisioning with lightbend's akka platform, 2017. https://www.lightbend.com/case-studies/ paypal-blows-past-1-billion-transactions-per-day-using-just-8-vms-and-akka- scala-kafka-and-akka-streams

61. Lightbend. Case study: Capital one scales real-time auto loan decisioning with lightbend's akka platform, 2020. https://www.lightbend.com/case-studies/real- time-decision-making-for-auto-loans

62. Liskov, B.: Distributed programming in Argus. Commun. ACM **31**(3), 300–312 (1988). ISSN 0001–0782. https://doi.org/10.1145/42392.42399

63. Lluch Lafuente, A., Nielson, F., Nielson, H.R.: Discretionary information flow control for interaction-oriented specifications. In: Martí-Oliet, N., Ölveczky, P.C., Talcott, C. (eds.) Logic, Rewriting, and Concurrency. LNCS, vol. 9200, pp. 427–450. Springer, Cham (2015). ISBN 978-3-319-23164-8. https://doi.org/10.1007/978-3-319-23165-5_20

64. Logan, M., Merritt, E., Carlsson, R.: Erlang and OTP in Action. Manning Publications, Shelter Island, NY, USA (2010). ISBN 1-933988-78-9

65. Mamei, M., Zambonelli, F.: Programming pervasive and mobile computing applications with the TOTA middleware. In: Proceedings of the Second IEEE Annual Conference on Pervasive Computing and Communications, pp. 263–273, Piscataway, NJ, USA, 2004. IEEE Press (2004). ISBN 0-7695-2090-1. https://doi.org/10.1109/PERCOM.2004.1276864

66. Manolescu, D., Beckman, B., Livshits, B.: Volta: developing distributed applications by recompiling. IEEE Softw. **25**(5), 53–59 (2008). ISSN 0740–7459. https://doi.org/10.1109/MS.2008.131

67. Medvidovic, N., Taylor, R.N.: A classification and comparison framework for software architecture description languages. IEEE Trans. Softw. Eng. **26**(1), 70–93 (2000). ISSN 0098–5589. https://doi.org/10.1109/32.825767

68. Miller, H., Haller, P., Odersky, M.: Spores: a type-based foundation for closures in the age of concurrency and distribution. In: Jones, R. (ed.) ECOOP 2014. LNCS, vol. 8586, pp. 308–333. Springer, Heidelberg (2014). ISBN 978-3-662-44201-2. https://doi.org/10.1007/978-3-662-44202-9_13

69. Miller, H., Haller, P., Muller, N., Boullier, J.: Function passing: a model for typed, distributed functional programming. In: Proceedings of the 2016 ACM International Symposium on New Ideas, New Paradigms, and Reflections on Programming and Software, Onward! 2016, pp. 82–97, New York, NY, USA, 2016. ACM (2016). ISBN 978-1-4503-4076-2. https://doi.org/10.1145/2986012.2986014

70. Milner, R., Parrow, J., Walker, D.: A calculus of mobile processes, i. Inf. Comput. **100**(1), 1–40 (1992). ISSN 0890–5401. https://doi.org/10.1016/0890-5401(92)90008-4

71. Milner, R., Parrow, J., Walker, D.: A calculus of mobile processes, ii. Inf. Comput. **100**(1), 41–77 (1992). ISSN 0890–5401. https://doi.org/10.1016/0890-5401(92)90009-5

72. Mogk, R., Drechsler, J., Salvaneschi, G., Mezini, M.: A fault-tolerant programming model for distributed interactive applications. Proc. ACM Program. Lang. **3**(OOPSLA) (2019). https://doi.org/10.1145/3360570

73. Montesi, F.: Kickstarting choreographic programming. In: Hildebrandt, T., Ravara, A., van der Werf, J.M., Weidlich, M. (eds.) WS-FM 2014-2015. LNCS, vol. 9421, pp. 3–10. Springer, Cham (2016). ISBN 978-3-319-33611-4. https://doi.org/10.1007/978-3-319-33612-1_1

74. Murphy VII, T., Crary, K., Harper, R.: Type-safe distributed programming with ML5. In: Barthe, G., Fournet, C. (eds.) TGC 2007. LNCS, vol. 4912, pp. 108–123. Springer, Heidelberg (2008). ISBN 978-3-540-78662-7. https://doi.org/10.1007/978-3-540-78663-4_9

75. Nelson, T., Ferguson, A.D., Scheer, M.J., Krishnamurthi, S.: Tierless programming and reasoning for software-defined networks. In: Proceedings of the 11th USENIX Conference on Networked Systems Design and Implementation, NSDI '14, pp. 519–531, Berkeley, CA, USA, 2014. USENIX Associa-

tion (2014). ISBN 978-1-931971-09-6. http://usenix.org/system/files/conference/nsdi14/nsdi14-paper-nelson.pdf

76. Neubauer, M., Thiemann, P.: From sequential programs to multi-tier applications by program transformation. In: Proceedings of the 32nd ACM SIGPLAN-SIGACT Symposium on Principles of Programming Languages, POPL '05, pp. 221–232, New York, NY, USA, 2005. ACM (2005). ISBN 978-1-58113-830-6. https://doi.org/10.1145/1040305.1040324

77. Olston, C., Reed, B., Srivastava, U., Kumar, R., Tomkins, A.: Pig Latin: a not-so-foreign language for data processing. In: Proceedings of the 2008 ACM SIGMOD International Conference on Management of Data, SIGMOD '08, pp. 1099–1110, New York, NY, USA, 2008. ACM (2008). ISBN 978-1-60558-102-6. https://doi.org/10.1145/1376616.1376726

78. Perry, D.E., Wolf, A.L.: Foundations for the study of software architecture. ACM SIGSOFT Softw. Eng. Notes 17(4), 40–52 (1992). ISSN 0163–5948. https://doi.org/10.1145/141874.141884

79. Persson, P., Angelsmark, O.: Calvin - merging Cloud and IoT. Procedia Comput. Sci. 52(The 6th International Conference on Ambient Systems, Networks and Technologies, the 5th International Conference on Sustainable Energy Information Technology), 210–217 (2015). ISSN 1877–0509. https://doi.org/10.1016/j.procs.2015.05.059

80. Pietzuch, P., Ledlie, J., Shneidman, J., Roussopoulos, M., Welsh, M., Seltzer, M.: Network-aware operator placement for stream-processing systems. In: Proceedings of the 22nd International Conference on Data Engineering, ICDE '06, pp. 49–60, Washington, DC, USA. IEEE Computer Society (2006). ISBN 0-7695-2570-9. https://doi.org/10.1109/ICDE.2006.105

81. Dalla Preda, M., Gabbrielli, M., Giallorenzo, S., Lanese, I., Mauro, J.: Dynamic choreographies: theory and implementation. Log. Methods Comput. Sci. 13(2) (2017). https://doi.org/10.23638/LMCS-13(2:1)2017

82. Radanne, G., Vouillon, J., Balat, V.: Eliom: a core ML language for tierless web programming. In: Igarashi, A. (ed.) APLAS 2016. LNCS, vol. 10017, pp. 377–397. Springer, Cham (2016). ISBN 978-3-319-47957-6. https://doi.org/10.1007/978-3-319-47958-3_20

83. Rajchenbach-Teller, D., Sinot, F.R.: OPA: language support for a sane, safe and secure web. In: Proceedings of the OWASP AppSec Research (2010). http://owasp.org/www-pdf-archive/OWASP_AppSec_Research_2010_OP_by_Rajchenbach-Teller.pdf

84. Salvaneschi, G., Drechsler, J., Mezini, M.: Towards distributed reactive programming. In: De Nicola, R., Julien, C. (eds.) COORDINATION 2013. LNCS, vol. 7890, pp. 226–235. Springer, Heidelberg (2013). ISBN 978-3-642-38493-6. https://doi.org/10.1007/978-3-642-38493-6_16

85. Serrano, M., Gallesio, E., Loitsch, F.: Hop, a language for programming the web 2.0. In: Companion to the 21th ACM SIGPLAN Conference on Object-Oriented Programming, Systems, Languages, and Applications, OOPSLA Companion '06, New York, NY, USA, 2006. ACM (2006). https://www.lri.fr/~conchon/TER/2012/3/dls06.pdf

86. Shapiro, M., Preguiça, N., Baquero, C., Zawirski, M.: A comprehensive study of convergent and commutative replicated data types, p. 47, January 2011. http://hal.inria.fr/inria-00555588

87. Shapiro, M., Preguiça, N., Baquero, C., Zawirski, M.: Conflict-free replicated data types. In: Défago, X., Petit, F., Villain, V. (eds.) SSS 2011. LNCS, vol. 6976, pp.

386–400. Springer, Heidelberg (2011). ISBN 978-3-642-24549-7. https://doi.org/10.1007/978-3-642-24550-3_29

88. Soloway, E., Ehrlich, K.: Empirical studies of programming knowledge. IEEE Trans. Softw. Eng. **10**(5), 595–609 (1984). ISSN 0098–5589. https://doi.org/10.1109/TSE.1984.5010283

89. Strack, I.: Getting Started with Meteor.js JavaScript Framework, 1st edn. Packt Publishing, Birmingham (2012). ISBN 978-0-321-70514-3

90. Van Roy, P., Haridi, S., Brand, P., Smolka, G., Mehl, M., Scheidhauer, R.: Mobile objects in distributed Oz. ACM Trans. Program. Lang. Syst. **19**(5), 804–851 (1997). ISSN 0164–0925. https://doi.org/10.1145/265943.265972

91. Viroli, M., Beal, J., Damiani, F., Audrito, G., Casadei, R., Pianini, D.: From distributed coordination to field calculus and aggregate computing. J. Log. Algebr. Methods Program. **109** (2019). ISSN 2352–2208. https://doi.org/10.1016/j.jlamp.2019.100486

92. W3C WS-CDL Working Group. Web services choreography description language version 1.0, 2005. http://www.w3.org/TR/ws-cdl-10/

93. Weisenburger, P., Salvaneschi, G.: Multitier modules. In: Donaldson, A.F. (ed.), Proceedings of the 33rd European Conference on Object-Oriented Programming (ECOOP '19), volume 134 of Leibniz International Proceedings in Informatics (LIPIcs), pp. 3:1–3:29, Dagstuhl, Germany (2019). Schloss Dagstuhl - Leibniz-Zentrum für Informatik. ISBN 978-3-95977-111-5. https://doi.org/10.4230/LIPIcs.ECOOP.2019.3

94. Weisenburger, P., Köhler, M., Salvaneschi, G.: Distributed system development with ScalaLoci. Proc. ACM Program. Lang. **2**(OOPSLA), 129:1–129:30 (2018). ISSN 2475–1421. https://doi.org/10.1145/3276499

95. Weisenburger, P., Wirth, J., Salvaneschi, G.: A survey of multitier programming. ACM Comput. Surv. **53**(4) (2020). ISSN 0360–0300. https://doi.org/10.1145/3397495

96. Yang, F., et al.: A unified platform for data driven web applications with automatic client-server partitioning. In: Proceedings of the 16th International Conference on World Wide Web, WWW '07, pp. 341–350, New York, NY, USA, 2007. ACM (2007). ISBN 978-1-59593-654-7. https://doi.org/10.1145/1242572.1242619

97. Yang, F., Li, J., Cheng, J.: Husky: towards a more efficient and expressive distributed computing framework. Proc. VLDB Endow. **9**(5), 420–431 (2016). ISSN 2150–8097. https://doi.org/10.14778/2876473.2876477

98. Zaharia, M., et al.: Resilient distributed datasets: a fault-tolerant abstraction for in-memory cluster computing. In: Proceedings of the 9th USENIX Conference on Networked Systems Design and Implementation, NSDI '12, Berkeley, CA, USA, 2012. USENIX Association (2012). http://www.usenix.org/system/files/conference/nsdi12/nsdi12-final138.pdf

99. Zdancewic, S., Zheng, L., Nystrom, N., Myers, A.C.: Secure program partitioning. ACM Trans. Comput. Syst. **20**(3), 283–328 (2002). ISSN 0734–2071. https://doi.org/10.1145/566340.566343

100. Zhou, Y., Ooi, B.C., Tan, K.-L., Wu, J.: Efficient dynamic operator placement in a locally distributed continuous query system. In: Meersman, R., Tari, Z. (eds.) OTM 2006. LNCS, vol. 4275, pp. 54–71. Springer, Heidelberg (2006). ISBN 978-3-540-48287-1. https://doi.org/10.1007/11914853_5

101. Zulfa, M.I., Hartanto, R., Permanasari, A.E.: Caching strategy for web application – a systematic literature review. Int. J. Web Inf. Syst. (2020). https://doi.org/10.1108/IJWIS-06-2020-0032

A Survey of Actor-Like Programming Models for Serverless Computing

Jonas Spenger[1,2] , Paris Carbone[1,2] , and Philipp Haller[1(✉)]

[1] Digital Futures and EECS, KTH Royal Institute of Technology, Stockholm, Sweden
{jspenger,parisc,phaller}@kth.se
[2] Computer Systems, RISE Research Institutes of Sweden, Stockholm, Sweden
{jonas.spenger,paris.carbone}@ri.se

Abstract. Serverless computing promises to significantly simplify cloud computing by providing Functions-as-a-Service where invocations of functions, triggered by events, are automatically scheduled for execution on compute nodes. Notably, the serverless computing model does not require the manual provisioning of virtual machines; instead, FaaS enables load-based billing and auto-scaling according to the workload, reducing costs and making scheduling more efficient. While early serverless programming models only supported stateless functions and severely restricted program composition, recently proposed systems offer greater flexibility by adopting ideas from actor and dataflow programming. This paper presents a survey of actor-like programming abstractions for stateful serverless computing, and provides a characterization of their properties and highlights their origin.

Keywords: Actor Model · Active Objects · Serverless Computing · Dataflow · Stateful Serverless · Distributed Programming · Cloud Computing

1 Introduction

Serverless computing has greatly simplified building cloud applications by providing Functions-as-a-Service (FaaS), a programming model consisting of *functions* and *event triggers*. These functions are automatically scheduled for execution on compute nodes, elastically scaling with the load [22]. In effect, the serverless model fully abstracts away the underlying computing infrastructure, billing and running user code on-demand. As a consequence, serverless computing can reduce costs and make scheduling more efficient.

While early serverless models were restricted, recent developments have introduced more flexible abstractions. The first major serverless frameworks, such as AWS Lambda [6] and similar [31,40,51], were restricted to: 1) *stateless functions*; and 2) limited compositional primitives such as no direct function-to-function messaging, often-cited challenges with serverless computing [12,36,42]. Recent developments, however, have seen programming models supporting stateful serverless that overcome these challenges through abstractions closely related

F. de Boer et al. (Eds.): *Active Object Languages: Current Research Trends*,
LNCS 14360, pp. 123–146, 2024.
https://doi.org/10.1007/978-3-031-51060-1_5

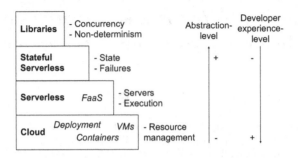

Fig. 1. Levels of abstraction for distributed programming.

to dataflow programming and the actor model [17,18,29,47,53,61–63]. We refer to these as *actor-like programming models for serverless computing*, this can also be referred to as *stateful serverless*.

These stateful serverless programming models are an abstraction of the underlying computing infrastructure. Conceptually, we can represent the abstraction levels of utility computing for distributed applications as a step-ladder, as shown in Fig. 1, ranging from low-level cloud resources to abstract, virtualized applications.

In this representation, *stateful serverless* is on the third layer, aiming to abstract away application state and masking failures, providing abstractions for deploying failure-free stateful functions with powerful compositional primitives. The stateful serverless layer provides powerful abstractions for building distributed applications and is used increasingly to build libraries or compose stronger abstraction levels (*e.g.,* level 4, abstracting from concurrency and non-determinism). In contrast to lower layers, it abstracts away failure and state management, which are difficult to get right.

This paper surveys actor-like programming models for serverless computing. The purpose is to provide a background on the development of these models; provide a characterization thereof; describe their challenges with respect to a serverless execution (state management and fault tolerance); highlight the similarities and differences of popular implementations; and provide an outlook on research directions. For this purpose, we survey eight implementations in detail [17,18,29,47,53,61–63], and include other relevant works in the whole analysis. In particular, we find three key enabling principles for their serverless execution to be of importance: they are virtualized, decoupled; they are data-parallel; they are slightly less dynamic than traditional actors.

Recent surveys have studied serverless computing [12,22,26,36,42,49], the actor model [43], the active objects model [14], and other related fields [11,50]. In contrast to surveys on serverless computing [12,22,26,36,42,49], the presented analysis puts more focus on the programming model and its properties. Actor systems have been studied extensively [43], whereas this survey sheds more light on properties at the intersection of actors and serverless such as per-key execution semantics, fault tolerance, and execution guarantees. Similarly, this applies also

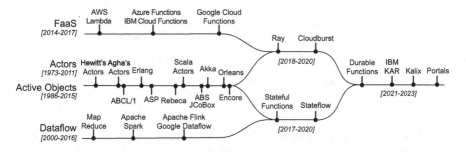

Fig. 2. An overview over related programming models and systems with effective periods.

to active object languages [14]. Reactive programming [11], and vertex-centric programming [50], also share some similarities with the discussed topics here, yet they lack some of the dynamic messaging properties of actors.

The rest of this paper is structured as follows. In Sect. 2, we provide a background on the development of the actor model, active object model, dataflow processing, serverless, and actor-like serverless models. Section 3 discusses the main challenges of programming systems for stateful serverless computing. Next, in Sect. 4, we analyse the distinctive characteristics of these systems, and compare their properties with respect to programming model (Subsect. 4.1) and serverless execution (Subsect. 4.2). Finally, we outline promising research directions (Sect. 5), and provide a conclusion (Sect. 6).

2   Background

This section provides a background on the development of actor-like programming models in the context of serverless computing, traced back to Actor and Active Object systems, Dataflow platforms, and Functions-as-a-Service (FaaS). To that end, Fig. 2 presents a timeline of related systems in their respective areas. We discuss the main directions in more detail with the aim to identify distinct characterizations and their development.

2.1   Actors

The Actor Model is a programming model for distributed, concurrent programming. It was invented in 1973 by Carl Hewitt [39], originally as a formalism for reasoning agents (in the context of artificial intelligence) and distributed parallel computations [38]. Additional significant work on the Actor Model was performed by Gul Agha, who provided a semantic formalization [3], and proposed the model as a "framework for concurrent systems" [1]. Since then it has seen a myriad of implementations with heavy industry adoption [43]. Notable actor implementations include Erlang [9], Scala Actors [33,34], Akka [46], and Pony [24].

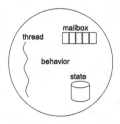
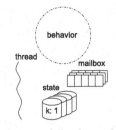

(a) Non-virtual actor: coupled mailbox, thread, behavior, and state.

(b) Virtual actor: fully decoupled and externalized mailbox, thread, behavior, and state.

Fig. 3. Regular and virtual actor types.

In essence, an actor is a concurrent object that can perform three different actions [2]: 1) *create* other actors; 2) *message* other actors; and 3) modify its *state* (or behavior) for the next received message. This style of actor corresponds to the non-virtual actor in Fig. 3a: an actor consists of an executing thread, mailbox, state and behavior.

A key principle of actor execution is the "isolated turn principle" [43], that is, the processing of a message by an actor (*i.e.*, a turn) can be viewed as a single isolated step. This is because actors do not share state, and actors process one message at a time. As a result, reasoning about concurrent actor programs is simplified. Another key property of actor systems is their hierarchical supervision for failure-management, which greatly influenced the design of fault-tolerant systems [8].

The actor model was later, in 2011, adapted for cloud programming in pioneering work on the *Virtual Actor* model (Fig. 3b) in Microsoft's Orleans framework [13,18] (created at Microsoft Research). This influential work proposed three core distinctions: 1) actors are virtual, *i.e.*, they always exist, they are not created; 2) the framework manages the actor life-cycle, *i.e.*, actors are activated on-demand (and passivated when there is no demand), and transparently recover from failures; and 3) actor references are virtual (logical), *i.e.*, they can be created and serialized, and are always valid. Importantly, a virtual actor's *virtual identity* consists of a type/class tag and a key: `identity` = `type` + `key`. With this new identity, multiple actor instances (one for each key) can exist for the same type of actor, enabling a form of data parallelism. As a result, virtual actors are suitable for the cloud setting, and have consequently been adopted and further extended in the cloud and serverless realm [17,29,46,47,56,61,63].

> Actor Model characterization:
>
> – Actor-to-actor communication
> – Stateful computation
> – Dynamic topology: actors can create new actors; actors can create new connections

The Actor and Virtual Actor models share similarities with other models. The Active Object model [65] is closely related to the Actor Model, and is discussed in the next section. The Virtual Actor model bears much similarity with the *Entity* model developed by Pat Helland in 2007 [35]. In fact, many incarnations of the virtual actor model bear the name entity [17,46,56].

2.2 Active Objects

The Active Object model is an object-oriented concurrent programming model which evolved from the actor model and was developed in 1986 for the programming language ABCL/1 [65]. The model consists of *active objects* with a single thread of control and local state, which interact through *asynchronous method calls* [14]. These method calls usually return a *future* of the return value (implicitly or explicitly). Within the method, the active objects can suspend and wait (await) for a guard (*i.e.,* a conjunction of futures or boolean expressions) to be satisfied [32]. Important systems in this space include the ABCL/1 language [65], the ABS language [32,41], ASP/ProActive [10,21], Rebeca [60], JCoBox [59], and Encore [15], providing a spectrum of implementations and flavours.

The active object model can be understood as an integration of object oriented concepts with the actor model [14]. This allows for compositional object-oriented program constructions through the supported interface abstractions. Still, there are notable differences. Method calls to active objects are statically guaranteed to be executed. Whereas in the actor model, the actor's behavior and its implicit interface may change dynamically such that a message is ignored. Method calls in the active object model, moreover, are tightly integrated with *futures* [65], whereas futures are optional features in actor systems. One such example is future forwarding (avoiding creating nested futures), and future sharing [14]. Another example are nested blocking receives, as seen in some actor models [34]. In contrast, active objects process further method calls even when the called method was suspended. Overall, active objects have sophisticated mechanisms for process suspension and process scheduling beyond the run-to-completion model of actors.

We can understand the term actor-like, for the purpose of this survey, to encompass programming models that resemble the actor model and active object model. In fact, Orleans [13,18], Durable Functions' Entities [17], IBM KAR [63], Ray [53], Cloudburst [62], and Kalix [47], resemble the object oriented style in the active object model.

2.3 Dataflow Processing

Dataflow Processing has become the de-facto standard for processing large amounts of data. It defines computations as static, acyclic computational graphs. One of the most influential early systems was *MapReduce* [25], developed in part as a reaction to the complexity of managing computations over large data, dispersed across thousands of machines. The MapReduce framework enabled computations to be programmed as sequences of Map/Reduce steps, introducing two key innovations. Firstly, the framework fully managed *fault tolerance*. If any machine failed, it would recover and redo any lost computations. As a result of this, the system guaranteed *exactly-once processing*: meaning, that everything was processed and delivered exactly once, or, in other words, the system behaved observably equivalent to a failure-free execution [17,61]. Failures, in effect, became completely transparent to the user; a hallmark of dataflow processing systems. Providing exactly-once processing out-of-the-box was a great relief for the programmer because of how notoriously difficult it is to implement manually. Secondly, the computations were performed over data sharded by their keys. This enabled *data-parallelism* by distributing the computation such that data/events for the same keys were processed by the same computing nodes using local state.

Subsequent dataflow processing models have inherited much from MapReduce, such as the vertex centric model [50], Apache Spark [66], Apache Kafka [45], Apache Flink [20], Google Dataflow [5], and Naiad [54]. While these frameworks have improved in terms of performance as well as expressiveness, they still adhere to the same characteristics as MapReduce did: they provide transparent fault-tolerance (typically, a distributed two-phase commit); and computations occur over a per-key context.

Dataflow Processing characterization:

– Transparent fault-tolerance, exactly-once processing guarantees
– Scalability, data-parallelism, computations over a per-key context
– Static, directed acyclic computational graphs (DAGs)

2.4 Functions-as-a-Service (FaaS)

Serverless computing would come to offer even more convenience for developing scalable and distributed services: a fully-managed runtime that would execute Functions-as-a-Service (FaaS). These services are specified by two components [22]: 1) the *functions* which are to be executed; and 2) the types of events that *trigger* the functions. These functions are executed on a serverless platform: the code is run on-demand, the billing is only per-use, abstracting away any of the servers and infrastructure from the user [22]. The computing model no longer requires manual provisioning of virtual machines or servers (hence, "serverless"), instead, the serverless platform fully manages the execution.

The major cloud vendors started adopting this new trend [12], with AWS Lambda [6] introduced in 2014, and other similar services right after [49] (Azure Functions [51], IBM Cloud Functions [40], Google Cloud Functions [31]).

Functions-as-a-Service are typically restricted to stateless functions with limited composition beyond step-like workflows, which are commonly cited challenges with serverless computing [12,36,42]. In reaction to this, recent programming models have started to support stateful serverless applications with more flexible communication and composition primitives [4,17,29,47,53,56,61–63]. These models utilize abstractions closely resembling actors, active objects, entities, and virtual actors.

Functions-as-a-Service (Serverless) characterization:

- Stateless functions triggered by events
- Elastic scalability, code is run on-demand, billing is per-use
- Fully-managed runtime/platform

2.5 Actor-Like Serverless Computing

Actor-like programming models for serverless computing, sometimes also referred to as *stateful serverless*, are a combination of actor, dataflow, and serverless principles; they provide the flexibility of stateful computations with actor-to-actor communication; together with the fault-tolerance and data-parallel scalability of dataflow processing; with the serverless, fully-managed execution platform, run on-demand.

These combinations require the *virtualization* (decoupling) of the following components: function, compute, state, and event queue (mailbox) (see Fig. 3b). Similarly to FaaS, the functions can be considered stateless: the function signature has both a stateful context and an event as parameters: F: Ctx => Event => Unit. The provided context Ctx gives the function access to state (Ctx.state) as well as the capabilities to interact with its environment (*e.g.,* Ctx.send). This decoupling, in turn, enables the on-demand scalability through replicating the functions and migrating state, and the transparent fault-tolerance through capturing any side-effects in terms of state and events from the context.

Systems in this space have adopted some of these new principles. The Virtual Actor model in Orleans [13,18], created at Microsoft Research, provided many of these features but lacked strong fault-tolerance guarantees such as exactly-once processing, or a fully-managed platform. Ray [53] and Cloudburst [62], incorporated actor principles with serverless (FaaS), forming decoupled (non-virtual) actors with automatic failure recovery providing at-least-once (and, tunable, at-most-once) guarantees. Another direction towards stateful functions, as seen on Flink [4,29], merged principles from dataflow processing with actors: scalable, data-parallel, stateful functions with function-to-function messaging and exactly-once processing guarantees.

Listing 1. A *bank account* entity that can get, deposit, withdraw, and transfer.

```
1   class Account(ctx: Context):
2     val balance = PersistentState[Int](ctx).withDefault(0)
3
4     def get(): Int =
5       balance.get()
6
7     def deposit(amount: Int): Unit =
8       balance.set(balance.get() + amount)
9
10    def withdraw(amount: Int): Unit =
11      balance.set(balance.get() − amount)
12
13    def transfer(amount: Int, to: String): Unit =
14      val otherAccount = EntityRef[Account](ctx).withKey(to)
15      if balance.get() > amount then
16        balance.set(balance.get() − amount)
17        otherAccount.deposit(amount)
```

More recently, proposals for stateful serverless programming models have emerged, merging actors, dataflow processing, and serverless, enabling the writing of stateful services with powerful compositional abstractions, while providing exactly-once processing guarantees. Notable systems include Microsoft's Durable Functions [17], IBM KAR [63], Portals [61], Stateful Entities [56], and Kalix [47].

An example entity representing a bank account is shown in Listing 1 in a style inspired by various systems [4,17,18,29,47,56,61,63]. It shows a bank account class that takes the runtime context as a parameter in its constructor (line 1). The runtime context is used to provide access to the side-effects of the entity: the state and the outgoing messages. The persisted state of the entity is explicitly declared on line 2, representing the account's balance with initial value 0. The entity defines methods, for getting, depositing to, and withdrawing from the account. It also defines a method for *transferring* an amount from the account to another account. Creating a reference to the other account (receiving the transfer), is achieved through the EntityRef factory, which takes the runtime context as well as a parameter for the other accounts *key* (line 14). This way a reference can be created, and later used for depositing the transferred amount (line 17). This example highlights some of the features of entities: the persistent explicit state, and the per-key identity. Note that the balance is not shared between different keys, rather, every key has its own balance value. The example also highlights potential issues due to the asynchronous nature of the method invocations on these actors: concurrently issued withdraw invocations may cause an overdraft on the account. In order to overcome this, some transactional mechanisms or similar would be needed.

Characterization. In general, we would characterize these actor-like serverless systems through five characteristics.

Actor-like serverless computing characterization:

1. Actor-like (Virtual Actors, Entities)
2. Data-parallel, keyed, scalable
3. Transparent fault-tolerance, exactly-once processing
4. Decoupled / externalized state, virtualization
5. Serverless execution, managed runtime

The execution model of serverless actor-like systems resemble the *isolated turn principle* [43] from actors with an additional *per-key* execution context: the execution of actors can be thought of an execution over isolated turns, in which a turn consists of an actor instance, identified by its *type* and *key*, consuming a message from its mailbox (mailboxes are disjoint over keys), executing the statements in the behavior, and possibly producing output messages and/or a state/behavior change. These turns are executed serially for a key, so that no two events are processed at the same time for a given actor type and key.

3   Challenges of Serverless Actors and Active Objects

Stateful serverless programming aims to provide several desirable properties which, in combination, are challenging without sacrificing the fault tolerance, flexibility, or performance. In particular, the following properties are essential: (a) serverless state management, enabling the provisioning of compute resources on demand; (b) fault tolerance with corresponding execution guarantees, providing the illusion of a failure-free execution in the presence of faulty computers and networks. In the following, we discuss the challenges of providing these properties in the context of actor and active object languages.

3.1   Serverless State Management

Serverless computing abstracts from the underlying computing infrastructure, providing load-based scaling of computing resources on demand. The automatic provisioning of compute resources affects the state management of the programming system. To illustrate some resulting challenges, consider the example shown in Listing 1. Suppose the `deposit` method of an `Account` is called by a different entity. When the `deposit` method is invoked on an entity reference, the corresponding entity instance must be activated on a suitable compute resource (*e.g.*, a virtual machine running in a data center). Note that we cannot assume that the entity instance is already loaded into the memory of a specific virtual machine. Instead, load-based scaling requires dynamically *loading/activate* a varying number of entity instances into a varying number of compute nodes. Likewise, in case demand for requests to certain entities drop, it must be possible to *passivate* entity instances by persisting their state to stable storage and

Listing 2. An *account* entity with a *guard* on its withdraw method (replacing the withdraw method for the account entity from Listing 1).

```
1   class Account(ctx: Context):
2     ... // (see Listing 1)
3     val balance = PersistentState[Int](ctx).withDefault(0)
4     def withdraw(amount: Int): Unit =
5       await balance.get() >= amount
6       balance.set(balance.get() − amount)
```

deallocating their memory. This means that all state of an entity must support *serialization* and the runtime system must be able to manage this state to support automatic passivation and activation.

Passivating the state of an entity is challenging in cases the programming model supports *guards* (*e.g.,* ABS [41]), or blocking receive statements (*e.g.,* Erlang [9]). To illustrate this, consider the `withdraw` method in Listing 2. On line 5, an ABS-style guard, `await balance.get() >= amount`, ensures that any call is *suspended* until the guard evaluates to true, ensuring a non-negative balance. This means that passivated entities might contain suspended calls. For this reason, the suspended calls and their *execution state* must be passivated as well, so that they subsequently can fully restore the suspended calls and be activated. Depending on the concrete programming model, execution states of suspended calls might consist of coroutines (*e.g.,* ABS [41], JCoBox [59]) or stackful continuations which are challenging to serialize (*e.g.,* due to embedded, non-portable memory addresses). In case the execution state of a suspended call or a suspended receive statement consists of just a continuation *closure* (*e.g.,* Scala Actors [34]), it is possible to support safe serialization using Spores [52] or other constructs that ensure the serializability of a closure's environment. For the reasons mentioned above, it is challenging to support the passivation and activation of actors and active objects in the context of serverless.

3.2   Fault Tolerance

Building distributed systems, *i.e.,* applications executing across multiple interconnected computers, requires handling faults such as machine crashes and unreliable or disconnected network connections. Consequently, distributed programming systems have long supported this through abstractions and constructs for fault handling. For example, Erlang's constructs for actor monitoring and supervision have been used successfully for building highly available distributed systems in the telecom industry [7]. Despite this, building distributed systems that completely mask failures has remained challenging, except for restricted computation patterns and system architectures (*e.g.,* Dataflow Processing).

The challenges of providing transparent fault tolerance in the context of actors and active objects are due to the combination and interplay of the following dimensions.

Stateful Computation. To enable recovering from faults, mutable state must be distributed across multiple *replicas* running on different computers. These replicas must be synchronized whenever the state is updated. Furthermore, state updates must be *transactional:* recovering from faults must not inadvertently repeat a state update that was already applied.

Non-deterministic Behavior. General concurrent programming models, such as active objects and actors, support writing non-deterministic programs. For example, when two concurrent active objects each call a method on a third active object, the two method calls are concurrent and thus their execution order is non-deterministic. In general, the behavior may also include non-deterministic computations, such as random number generation or the use of local time/clocks. Supporting non-determinsitic behavior in fault-tolerant systems is challenging, since computations might have to be re-executed when recovering from faults. However, re-executing non-deterministic code can change the outcome of computations, thereby failing to provide the illusion of a failure-free execution. Supporting non-deterministic behavior thus requires the use of implementation techniques that do not make use of re-execution (such as rollback-recovery [28]), or logging all sources of non-determinism [30], making state management more complex and potentially increasing runtime overhead. This is further complicated by the dynamic topology of actor systems.

Interaction with External Systems. In practice, distributed systems typically interact with various *external systems*, such as database management systems, distributed file systems, message queues. Requests submitted to external systems must not be tentative (and subject to potential rollback recovery); since such requests, in general, cannot be undone, they can only be submitted if the present system ensures that they are *never* going to be repeated, even during fault recovery.

Due to the above challenges, some stateful serverless programming systems trade flexibility for fault-tolerance guarantees. For example, instead of providing Exactly-Once Processing, some systems only provide At-Most-Once or At-Least-Once fault-tolerance guarantees. The latter significantly increases the complexity of the programming model, since events need to be either idempotent or deduplicated manually. On the other hand, At-Most-Once requires dealing with dropped events without support from the programming system. Although there are no fundamental limitations to execute the classic actor and active object model serverlessly, doing so comes at a tradeoff between the expressiveness, guarantees, performance, and cost of the model. The next section will explore various systems to highlight their variations among these dimensions.

4   Analysis of Actor-Like Serverless Systems

In this section we analyze the properties of a selection of systems at the intersection of actors, dataflow processing, and serverless. The analysis is structured around two questions. First, we analyze their specific properties with respect to the programming model. Second, we analyze their properties with respect to serverless execution. The purpose is to give an overview of similarities and dissimilarities between the programming models and implementations. The systems under survey are the following.

- The *Orleans* system [13,18], pioneering the virtual actor model.
- *Durable Functions' Entities* [16,17], virtual actors that can be used together with other abstractions such as Orchestrations and Activities within Microsoft's Durable Functions framework.
- *Apache Flink Stateful Functions* [4,29], an abstraction of virtual actor-like stateful functions running on Apache Flink, independently developed by different groups [4,29].
- *IBM KAR* [63], a polyglot scalable and fault-tolerant virtual actor system.
- *Kalix* [47], a serverless platform for deploying microservices consisting of entities, actions, and views.
- *Portals* and *Portals' Actors* [61], a research project and programming model which unifies the actor model with the dataflow processing model.
- *Ray* [53], a framework for scaling actor-like computational tasks, focused on reinforcement learning.
- *Cloudburst* [62], a stateful functions research project which leverages CRDT state for its execution.

Although not all systems fit the characterization from Sect. 2.5, *e.g.*, through a lack of a fully-managed platform with per-use billing, they are included in this survey as they are closely related and provide valuable insights.

4.1   Programming Model

We analyze the programming models of the systems across three categories: actor style; communication; and state and computation. The analysis is reflected in Table 1.

Actor Style. The actor-like systems can be divided into two groups based on their style: virtual; and non-virtual (see Table 1). These two groups differ quite uniformly over the properties in our analysis.

Life-Cycle. Virtual actors have a virtual life-cycle, they exist by definition rather than through creation. Non-virtual actors, in contrast, exist through creation.

Identity and References. Identifying a virtual actor is achieved through a *virtual identity*. *Virtual actor references* are constructed from identities using factories.

Table 1. Programming model properties.

		Dyn. Topology (Int/Ext)			
	Actor Style	Application	Comm	Ext. State	Fault-Transp
Orleans	virtual	✗ / ✓	✓ / ✓	✓	✓–
Durable Functions	virtual	✗ / ✓	✓ / ✓	✓	✓
Flink StateFun	virtual	✗ / ✓	✓ / ✓	✓	✓
IBM KAR	virtual	✗ / ✓	✓ / ✓	✓	✓–
Kalix	virtual	✗ / ✓	✓ / ✓	✓	✓–
Portals	virtual	✗ / ✓	✗ / ✓	✓	✓
Ray	non-virtual	✓ / ✓	✓ / ✓	✓	✓–
Cloudburst	non-virtual	✓ / ✓	✓ / ✓	✓	✓–

The virtual actor references are not strictly *always valid* when references can be forged from nonsensical user-provided strings [17,29,47,63]: if there is no corresponding actor definition for the provided string then this may cause a runtime error. Other systems ensure that references are valid either through compilation checks [61] or through reference factories constructed from existing actor types [18]. Non-virtual actors, in contrast, have references bound to lifetimes, which become invalidated if the referenced actor ceases to exist [53,62].

Actor Topology. The topology consists of the actors and how they are connected. We distinguish between *Application* and *Communication* topologies. The application topology consists of the actors, *i.e.*, if actors can be created and destroyed. The communication topology is the set of connections between actors, *i.e.*, if new connections can be formed, through exchanges of actor references. On another dimension, we also distinguish between *Internal* and *External* changes. *Internal* changes are triggered by the actors themselves, *e.g.*, an actor creating another actor; *External* changes are triggered by an outside force, *e.g.*, the driving application creating new actors or creating new connections (dynamic reconfiguration). The non-virtual actor systems are dynamic in all four cases (Table 1) [53,62]. The virtual actor systems, in contrast, have dynamic communication topologies, and partially dynamic application topologies (actors cannot create new actors, but the external force can do so) [17,18,29,47,61,63]. All of the systems have *first-class references*. The Portals system is an exception, it restricts actors from creating new connections dynamically through exchanging references; actor references are only usable by actors with the right capabilities, these capabilities are assigned statically through the actor definitions [61].

Communication. Actors communicate by exchanging messages either in the form of *message sends* or *method calls* (*cf.*, actors/active objects [43]) (see Table 2). Out of the selected systems, five had method-based communication, and three had message-based communication. The difference between the two is mostly syntactical, and some systems even provide both styles of interfaces

Table 2. Communication properties.

	Msg Ops	Msg Futures	Futures Retrieve Ops
Orleans	Send, Call, Reply	✓	Tunable
Durable Functions	Send, Reply-	✗	–
Flink StateFun	Send, Reply	✗	–
IBM KAR	Send, Call, TailCall, Reply	✓	Blocking
Kalix	Send, Call, Reply, Forward	–	–
Portals	Send, Call, Reply	✓	Non-blocking
Ray	Call, Reply	✓	Blocking
Cloudburst	Call, Reply	✓	Blocking

for the actor communication [17]. For this reason we will not further distinguish between these interfaces; we will consider a *Method Invocation* to correspond to a *Send* operation if it does not return a value, and to a *Call* operation if it returns a future of the return value. Similarly, we consider *Return* to correspond to the *Reply* operation.

Message Operations. All systems support the *Send* and *Reply* communication primitives. The exception, here, is Durable Functions [17], which can only reply to calls from *Orchestrations*. The *TailCall* primitive supported by IBM KAR, is for orchestrating guarantees across a chain of invocations: the previous call has to have finished/committed before the subsequent calls in the tail call are executed [63]. This can be used for higher fault-tolerance guarantees beyond what is provided. The *Forward* call in Kalix is a special operation which can forward a replyable message to another service [47].

State and Computation. The serverless computing paradigm is built on the decoupling of execution from side-effects and state. The programming models all provide explicit external state abstractions for this (Table 1), accessible through either a KV store-like interface [62,63], an object-store [53], or typed coarse-grained [18,47] or fine-grained [17,29,61] factories/annotations. Local variables, in contrast, do not survive a crash or migration, and are re-initialized upon activation of the actor.

Shared Memory. Although uncommon in actor-like abstractions, we found some instances of shared memory. Ray [53] has shared memory in the form of an external immutable first-writer-wins object store with distributed futures. Cloudburst [62] functions, on the other hand, share access to an eventually consistent key-value store, with additional mechanisms to enforce causal session consistency. Kalix [47] has replicated entity types backed by CRDTs which can be used as a form of highly available replicated shared state.

Concurrent Processing and Futures. Most systems provide futures for messaging and awaiting the completion of futures as a concurrency abstraction (see

Table 2). An exception is Durable Functions [17] which does not provide futures for their Entities but for the Orchestrations. Similarly, Kalix supports futures (async effects) on Actions with operations reminiscent of chaining futures [47], it was unclear if this also applies to Entities, for this reason the entry was left blank. Flink Stateful Functions [29] provides futures for asynchronous operations, but not for asynchronous message calls expecting a reply. In the table, we only consider futures that are created from inter-actor messages/method invocations.

While the actor model is traditionally continuous and non-blocking (re-entrant) to ensure liveness [43], processing an *await* command on a future forces the system to choose between blocking or re-entrant execution. The Blocking mode blocks the execution of further events of the same key until the await command completes [53,62,63]. Whereas the Re-entrant mode interleaves the processing of subsequent events before the await command has completed, enabling increased concurrency and avoiding potential issues associated with blocking [29,61]. This choice is also a tunable setting in some systems [18]. Further, IBM KAR provide a mode for re-entrant execution for method calls on itself with the same session-id [63].

Failure Transparency. Failure transparency enables the developer to write applications without having to reason about certain failures (Table 1). The system is completely failure transparent if it provides exactly-once processing (marked as *ExO* in Table 3): the application does not have to manage anything related to failures [17,29,61]. If the system is partially failure transparent, that is, it provides at-most-once/at-least-once guarantees and some failure support (marked as *AMO/ALO*), then the application must manually perform certain actions for failure tolerance. For example, Orleans [18] and Ray [53] provide methods for asynchronously persisting and reading state, and it is up to the developer to implement it for the required guarantees. Whereas IBM KAR [63], Kalix [47], and Cloudburst [62] automatically retry function invocations (at-least-once), and the developer must ensure that the function is idempotent. For these reasons, exactly-once processing make programs significantly easier to write and reason about.

4.2   Serverless Execution

In this section we analyze properties related to the serverless execution and runtime. The analysis is structured around four categories: fault-tolerance; state management; scalability; and platform management (Table 3).

Fault Tolerance and Guarantees. Fault-tolerance guarantees are crucial for distributed systems, commonly expressed as one of the following: Exactly-Once (ExO), At-Most-Once (AMO), and At-Least-Once (ALO) (Table 3). Out of these, *Exactly-Once* is the strongest guarantee, guaranteeing that every event is delivered and processed exactly-once, implemented by three of the studied

Table 3. Serverless execution properties.

	Proc. Guarantees	State	Parallelism	Plaftform Mgmt
Orleans	AMO/ALO	Ext	Data	✗
Durable Functions	ExO	Embedded	Data	✓
Flink StateFun	ExO	Ext	Data	✓
IBM KAR	ALO	Ext	Data	✗
Kalix	ALO	Ext	Data	✓
Portals	ExO	Embedded	Data	✗
Ray	AMO/ALO	Ext	Task	✓
Cloudburst	ALO	Ext	Task	✗

systems [17,29,61]. Exactly-once can also be regarded as observably failure-free, that is, the execution, and what is observed by the user, behaves as though it is failure-free. This greatly simplifies reasoning about distributed programs, eliminating the need for manual deduplication and the need to ensure that functions are idempotent. At-Most-Once, in contrast, guarantees that every event is delivered and processed at most once (failed invocations are not retried); whereas, At-Least-Once, guarantees that every event is delivered and processed at least once (failed invocations are continually retried until success). The choice between the latter two may be tunable in some cases [18,53], whereas others only provide At-Least-Once semantics [47,62,63].

Failure-Recovery. Failure-recovery enables the system to effectively mask failures such as crashes or message loss from the observed execution. The exactly-once processing systems [16,17,19,29,61] use a checkpointing and recovery strategy [28]. This approach involves the system periodically creating checkpoints that comprise: 1) the actor state; and 2) the event queues. In the event of a failure, recovery proceeds by restarting the actors from the most recent checkpointed state and replaying events from the last checkpointed event queues. The challenge of establishing consistent checkpoints lies in taking causally-consistent snapshots of the system. This is done in Flink [19] and Portals [61] with a snapshotting protocol similar to the one presented by Chandy and Lamport [23]. In the Netherite runtime for Durable Functions, in contrast, a distributed snapshot is avoided by isolating the processing nodes and blocking events from being observed until they have been committed [16]. Other implementations that do not provide exactly-once processing guarantees restart from the latest checkpointed state, but may potentially replay events more than once (at-least-once), or drop events (at-most-once) [13,18,47,53,62,63].

State Management. The runtime necessarily manages the state in order to ensure strong fault-tolerance guarantees. This state is either external, *i.e.,* primarily on some external storage, cached locally for quicker access [18,47,53,62,

63]; or embedded, *i.e.*, hosted in-full locally on the computing nodes, and persisted externally for durability (Table 3). There is a trade-off between the two. External state offers a higher decoupling, making it easier to scale up and down, as external state does not need to be migrated during reconfiguration. Embedded state, on the contrary, yields higher processing throughput and lower latency for stateful computations [16,17,61].

Scalability and Parallelism. All systems under discussion offer elastic scalability, enabling the runtime to flexibly scale up or down in response to demand. In this context, two forms of parallelism emerge (Table 3). The Non-Virtual Actors frameworks facilitate task-level parallelism. This is achieved by spawning new actors assigned to perform specific tasks and subsequently terminating them upon task completion. The Virtual Actors frameworks, on the other hand, support data-level parallelism, as a single actor definition is applied to many events but over different keys.

Platform Management. Platform management entails managing all aspects related to the runtime and the servers. That is, the user should only need to supply the stateful functions definitions and event triggers, and the platform should manage everything else, billing per-use. Of the selected systems, only Durable Functions [17] and Kalix [47] are purposefully built for that (Table 3). Concerning the other systems, both Flink (the Ververica Platform) and Ray (the Anyscale Platform) have hosted platforms available.

4.3 Related Work

This section concludes the analysis through summarizing other systems that were not included in the main analysis. *Data-Parallel Actors* [44] is a research project for writing data-parallel query systems, it is used to distribute otherwise non-distributed systems, such as databases and analytics systems. It does so by using an actor-like abstraction, which manages a partition of the wrapped system, for which the data-parallel actor must serve user-defined composable queries over the partitioned data, such as *Map, FlatMap, Scatter, Gather*; these queries apply to all partitions. *Crucial* [55] is a stateful serverless system for programming parallel applications. It executes on top of existing FaaS platforms, and provides a shared memory abstraction for fine-grained synchronization primitives and sharing larger state which can be used by the deployed functions. It executes on existing FaaS infrastructure with at-least-once guarantees. *Beldi* [67] enables writing fault-tolerant stateful serverless functions. It does so by providing primitives for consistently reading and writing from a shared memory, for transactional workloads with locking and transactions, and invoking other functions from within the function. It provides exactly-once processing guarantees using existing FaaS frameworks together with a strongly consistent storage provider. *A.M.B.R.O.S.I.A.* [30] is a system for transparent fault-tolerant non-deterministic applications. Ambrosia services are executed by actor-like abstractions called "immortals" using event sourcing and replay recovery for exactly-once guarantees, for which non-determinism are captured through impulses. For a replay to recover to a consistent state, it is important that the application adheres to a "weak language binding contract": from some state, any execution of inputs must result in an equivalent final state, outgoing events must be for the same destinations and in the same order, but may differ in content. *AEON* [57] is a scalable and elastic actor framework which guarantees strict serializability for events across actors using an ownership hierarchy. In follow-up work [58], the runtime is extended with programmable elasticity policies. The ABS model [41] has been used in the context of modelling distributed computing models, for example Spark Streaming [48], and Kubernetes deployments [64], making use of suspending guards for expressing the logic.

5   Research Directions

In this section we highlight some research directions with actor-like models for serverless computing.

Static Guarantees, Formal Proofs. There are two main challenges with deploying serverless actor-like models: 1) ensuring that the user application is statically sound, and 2) ensuring that the runtime is fault-tolerant. For the first, a common error in user code is due to user-defined functions capturing non-serializable state from the environment [52]. This may cause errors which are hard to debug due to the distributed execution, and consequently crash. This and similar issues, such as well-typed channels, existing dependencies, may be caught statically at compile-time, and thus prevent the user from deploying the application. For the second challenge, it is important to provide formal proofs for the fault-tolerance guarantees. There has been some work in this area proving the failure-guarantees [17,63]; future research efforts should focus on formally proving more implementations, and providing new proof-techniques and frameworks. Beside formal proofs, it is also an important research direction to continue the exploration of fault-tolerance mechanisms used in this context.

End-to-End Exactly-Once Processing with External Systems. Distributed systems are rarely used in isolation. Especially the types of systems presented in this survey are likely to be used together with other services. For this reason it is important to ensure that certain guarantees, such as exactly-once processing, are provided end-to-end, across the external systems. The problem, however, is that the side-effects to external systems are typically not tracked by the system itself. In the context of dataflow processing, end-to-end guarantees are achieved through using transactional sinks, for example, connecting Flink [20] and Kafka [45]. Similarly, Portals suggests connecting external systems via atomic streams (transactional streams) for preserving the end-to-end guarantees [61]. More research in this area is warranted, both formal proofs and abstractions, as well as implementations and primitives for interacting with external systems.

New Abstractions and Primitives. First, the presented actor-like abstractions may not be suitable for all types of applications. This is especially problematic as the serverless paradigm restricts the application developer from implementing their own core abstractions. Examples include the *Orchestrations* in Durable Functions used for orchestrating workflows with the capability to perform blocking calls to and transactions across entities [17]. Another abstraction is a stateless function or actor as a way to distributed work in a task-parallel fashion [17,18,47]. Second, new communication and compositional primitives can be explored. One example here, are data-parallel operations over actors [44], which allow applying Map, FlatMap, Scatter, and Gather operations over all instances of a data-parallel actor. Third, libraries present an interesting opportunity to leverage the implementations and provide higher-level abstractions (*e.g.,* level four in Fig. 1). Examples of this include numerous machine learning libraries on top of Ray [53], transactional libraries for Orleans [27] and Flink Stateful Functions [37], and streaming libraries [13]. Lastly, with the advancement of machine learning models, the importance of incorporating robust model serving capabilities within serverless frameworks has grown. Exploring this avenue presents interesting research opportunities.

6 Conclusion

This study has explored actor-like programming models within the context of serverless computing by providing a background, extracting distinctive features, outlining challenges, analyzing popular implementations within the field, concluding with suggestions for research directions.

In this paper, the development of actor-like models for serverless computing is traced back to the roots of Actors, Active Objects, Dataflow Processing, and Functions-as-a-Service, and presents a case for how merging principles of these three fields are expressed in the actor-like stateful serverless programming models as seen today: actor-like, virtual, data-parallel with decoupled state and transparent fault-tolerance in a serverless execution model. The core challenges of implementing serverless actors are the serverless state management and the fault tolerant execution. This includes managing the execution state of suspended objects, and providing fault-tolerance of non-deterministic functions in a dynamic environment. The analysis highlights similarities and differences between the implementations. One important difference is the choice between different fault-tolerance levels provided by the systems: at-least-once; at-most-once; exactly-once, as it affects many aspects surrounding the programming model and the implementation thereof. As future research directions, we suggest further exploring methods for static guarantees, end-to-end fault-tolerance, and new programming abstractions.

In summary, this survey of actor-like models in serverless computing has revealed a diverse and evolving field. Further work in this field can make future serverless systems more expressive and robust, resulting in more reliable and efficient software.

Acknowledgements. This work was partially funded by Digital Futures, the Swedish Foundation for Strategic Research (under Grant No.: BD15-0006), Horizon Europe (SovereignEdge.Cognit under Grant No.: 101092711), as well as RISE AI.

References

1. Agha, G.: Concurrent object-oriented programming. Commun. ACM **33**(9), 125–141 (1990). https://doi.org/10.1145/83880.84528
2. Agha, G.A.: Actors: a model of concurrent computation in distributed systems (parallel processing, semantics, open, programming languages, artificial intelligence). Ph.D. thesis, University of Michigan, USA (1985). http://hdl.handle.net/2027.42/160629
3. Agha, G.A.: ACTORS: A Model of Concurrent Computation in Distributed Systems. Series in Artificial Intelligence, The MIT Press, Cambridge (1986)
4. Akhter, A., Fragkoulis, M., Katsifodimos, A.: Stateful functions as a service in action. Proc. VLDB Endow. **12**(12), 1890–1893 (2019). https://doi.org/10.14778/3352063.3352092. http://www.vldb.org/pvldb/vol12/p1890-akhter.pdf
5. Akidau, T., et al.: The dataflow model: a practical approach to balancing correctness, latency, and cost in massive-scale, unbounded, out-of-order data processing. Proc. VLDB Endow. **8**(12), 1792–1803 (2015). https://doi.org/10.14778/2824032.2824076. http://www.vldb.org/pvldb/vol8/p1792-Akidau.pdf
6. Amazon Web Services: AWS Lambda (2023). https://aws.amazon.com/lambda/. Accessed 20 Mar 2023
7. Armstrong, J.: Erlang-a survey of the language and its industrial applications. In: Proceedings of the INAP, vol. 96, pp. 16–18 (1996)
8. Armstrong, J.: Making reliable distributed systems in the presence of software errors. Ph.D. thesis, KTH Royal Institute of Technology, Stockholm, Sweden (2003). https://nbn-resolving.org/urn:nbn:se:kth:diva-3658
9. Armstrong, J., Virding, R., Williams, M.: Concurrent Programming in ERLANG. Prentice Hall, Hoboken (1993)
10. Baduel, L., et al.: Programming, composing, deploying for the grid. In: Cunha, J.C., Rana, O.F. (eds.) Grid Computing: Software Environments and Tools, pp. 205–229. Springer, London (2006). https://doi.org/10.1007/1-84628-339-6_9
11. Bainomugisha, E., Carreton, A.L., Cutsem, T.V., Mostinckx, S., Meuter, W.D.: A survey on reactive programming. ACM Comput. Surv. **45**(4), 52:1–52:34 (2013). https://doi.org/10.1145/2501654.2501666
12. Baldini, I., et al.: Serverless computing: current trends and open problems. In: Chaudhary, S., Somani, G., Buyya, R. (eds.) Research Advances in Cloud Computing, pp. 1–20. Springer, Singapore (2017). https://doi.org/10.1007/978-981-10-5026-8_1
13. Bernstein, P., Bykov, S., Geller, A., Kliot, G., Thelin, J.: Orleans: distributed virtual actors for programmability and scalability. Technical report MSR-TR-2014-41 (2014). https://www.microsoft.com/en-us/research/publication/orleans-distributed-virtual-actors-for-programmability-and-scalability/
14. de Boer, F.S., et al.: A survey of active object languages. ACM Comput. Surv. **50**(5), 76:1–76:39 (2017). https://doi.org/10.1145/3122848
15. Brandauer, S., et al.: Parallel objects for multicores: a glimpse at the parallel language ENCORE. In: Bernardo, M., Johnsen, E.B. (eds.) SFM 2015. LNCS, vol. 9104, pp. 1–56. Springer, Cham (2015). https://doi.org/10.1007/978-3-319-18941-3_1

16. Burckhardt, S., et al.: Netherite: efficient execution of serverless workflows. Proc. VLDB Endow. **15**(8), 1591–1604 (2022). https://www.vldb.org/pvldb/vol15/p1591-burckhardt.pdf

17. Burckhardt, S., Gillum, C., Justo, D., Kallas, K., McMahon, C., Meiklejohn, C.S.: Durable functions: semantics for stateful serverless. Proc. ACM Program. Lang. **5**(OOPSLA), 1–27 (2021). https://doi.org/10.1145/3485510

18. Bykov, S., Geller, A., Kliot, G., Larus, J.R., Pandya, R., Thelin, J.: Orleans: cloud computing for everyone. In: Chase, J.S., Abbadi, A.E. (eds.) ACM Symposium on Cloud Computing in Conjunction with SOSP 2011, SOCC '11, Cascais, Portugal, 26–28 October 2011, p. 16. ACM (2011). https://doi.org/10.1145/2038916.2038932

19. Carbone, P., Ewen, S., Fóra, G., Haridi, S., Richter, S., Tzoumas, K.: State management in Apache Flink®: consistent stateful distributed stream processing. Proc. VLDB Endow. **10**(12), 1718–1729 (2017). https://doi.org/10.14778/3137765.3137777. http://www.vldb.org/pvldb/vol10/p1718-carbone.pdf

20. Carbone, P., Katsifodimos, A., Ewen, S., Markl, V., Haridi, S., Tzoumas, K.: Apache Flink™: stream and batch processing in a single engine. IEEE Data Eng. Bull. **38**(4), 28–38 (2015). http://sites.computer.org/debull/A15dec/p28.pdf

21. Caromel, D., Henrio, L., Serpette, B.P.: Asynchronous and deterministic objects. In: Jones, N.D., Leroy, X. (eds.) Proceedings of the 31st ACM SIGPLAN-SIGACT Symposium on Principles of Programming Languages, POPL 2004, Venice, Italy, 14–16 January 2004, pp. 123–134. ACM (2004). https://doi.org/10.1145/964001.964012

22. Castro, P.C., Ishakian, V., Muthusamy, V., Slominski, A.: The rise of serverless computing. Commun. ACM **62**(12), 44–54 (2019). https://doi.org/10.1145/3368454

23. Chandy, K.M., Lamport, L.: Distributed snapshots: Determining global states of distributed systems. ACM Trans. Comput. Syst. **3**(1), 63–75 (1985). https://doi.org/10.1145/214451.214456

24. Clebsch, S., Drossopoulou, S., Blessing, S., McNeil, A.: Deny capabilities for safe, fast actors. In: Boix, E.G., Haller, P., Ricci, A., Varela, C.A. (eds.) Proceedings of the 5th International Workshop on Programming Based on Actors, Agents, and Decentralized Control, AGERE! 2015, Pittsburgh, PA, USA, 26 October 2015, pp. 1–12. ACM (2015). https://doi.org/10.1145/2824815.2824816

25. Dean, J., Ghemawat, S.: MapReduce: simplified data processing on large clusters. Commun. ACM **51**(1), 107–113 (2008). https://doi.org/10.1145/1327452.1327492

26. Dragoni, N.: Microservices: yesterday, today, and tomorrow. In: Present and Ulterior Software Engineering, pp. 195–216. Springer, Cham (2017). https://doi.org/10.1007/978-3-319-67425-4_12

27. Eldeeb, T., Bernstein, P.: Transactions for distributed actors in the cloud. Technical report MSR-TR-2016-1001 (2016). https://www.microsoft.com/en-us/research/publication/transactions-distributed-actors-cloud-2/

28. Elnozahy, E.N., Alvisi, L., Wang, Y., Johnson, D.B.: A survey of rollback-recovery protocols in message-passing systems. ACM Comput. Surv. **34**(3), 375–408 (2002). https://doi.org/10.1145/568522.568525

29. The Apache Software Foundation: Apache Flink stateful functions (2023). https://nightlies.apache.org/flink/flink-statefun-docs-stable/. Accessed 18 May 2023

30. Goldstein, J., et al.: A.M.B.R.O.S.I.A: providing performant virtual resiliency for distributed applications. Proc. VLDB Endow. **13**(5), 588–601 (2020). https://doi.org/10.14778/3377369.3377370.   http://www.vldb.org/pvldb/vol13/p588-goldstein.pdf

31. Google Cloud: Google Cloud Functions (2023). https://cloud.google.com/functions. Accessed 28 May 2023

32. Hähnle, R.: The abstract behavioral specification language: a tutorial introduction. In: Giachino, E., Hähnle, R., de Boer, F.S., Bonsangue, M.M. (eds.) FMCO 2012. LNCS, vol. 7866, pp. 1–37. Springer, Heidelberg (2013). https://doi.org/10.1007/978-3-642-40615-7_1

33. Haller, P.: On the integration of the actor model in mainstream technologies: the Scala perspective. In: Agha, G.A., Bordini, R.H., Marron, A., Ricci, A. (eds.) Proceedings of the 2nd Edition on Programming Systems, Languages and Applications Based on Actors, Agents, and Decentralized Control Abstractions, AGERE! 2012, 21–22 October 2012, Tucson, Arizona, USA, pp. 1–6. ACM (2012). https://doi.org/10.1145/2414639.2414641

34. Haller, P., Odersky, M.: Scala actors: unifying thread-based and event-based programming. Theor. Comput. Sci. **410**(2–3), 202–220 (2009). https://doi.org/10.1016/j.tcs.2008.09.019

35. Helland, P.: Life beyond distributed transactions: an apostate's opinion. In: Third Biennial Conference on Innovative Data Systems Research, CIDR 2007, Asilomar, CA, USA, 7–10 January 2007, Online Proceedings, pp. 132–141 (2007). http://www.cidrdb.org/, http://cidrdb.org/cidr2007/papers/cidr07p15.pdf

36. Hellerstein, J.M., et al.: Serverless computing: one step forward, two steps back. In: 9th Biennial Conference on Innovative Data Systems Research, CIDR 2019, Asilomar, CA, USA, 13–16, January 2019, Online Proceedings (2019). http://www.cidrdb.org/, http://cidrdb.org/cidr2019/papers/p119-hellerstein-cidr19.pdf

37. de Heus, M., Psarakis, K., Fragkoulis, M., Katsifodimos, A.: Transactions across serverless functions leveraging stateful dataflows. Inf. Syst. **108**, 102015 (2022). https://doi.org/10.1016/j.is.2022.102015

38. Hewitt, C., Baker, H.G.: Laws for communicating parallel processes. In: Gilchrist, B. (ed.) Information Processing, Proceedings of the 7th IFIP Congress 1977, Toronto, Canada, 8–12 August 1977, pp. 987–992. North-Holland (1977)

39. Hewitt, C., Bishop, P.B., Steiger, R.: A universal modular ACTOR formalism for artificial intelligence. In: Nilsson, N.J. (ed.) Proceedings of the 3rd International Joint Conference on Artificial Intelligence. Stanford, CA, USA, 20–23 August 1973, pp. 235–245. William Kaufmann (1973). http://ijcai.org/Proceedings/73/Papers/027B.pdf

40. IBM Corp.: IBM Cloud Functions (2020). https://cloud.ibm.com/functions/. Accessed 28 May 2023

41. Johnsen, E.B., Hähnle, R., Schäfer, J., Schlatte, R., Steffen, M.: ABS: a core language for abstract behavioral specification. In: Aichernig, B.K., de Boer, F.S., Bonsangue, M.M. (eds.) FMCO 2010. LNCS, vol. 6957, pp. 142–164. Springer, Heidelberg (2011). https://doi.org/10.1007/978-3-642-25271-6_8

42. Jonas, E., et al.: Cloud programming simplified: A Berkeley view on serverless computing. CoRR abs/1902.03383 (2019). http://arxiv.org/abs/1902.03383

43. Koster, J.D., Cutsem, T.V., Meuter, W.D.: 43 years of actors: a taxonomy of actor models and their key properties. In: Clebsch, S., Desell, T., Haller, P., Ricci, A. (eds.) Proceedings of the 6th International Workshop on Programming Based on Actors, Agents, and Decentralized Control, AGERE 2016, Amsterdam, The Netherlands, 30 October 2016, pp. 31–40. ACM (2016). https://doi.org/10.1145/3001886.3001890

44. Kraft, P., Kazhamiaka, F., Bailis, P., Zaharia, M.: Data-parallel actors: a programming model for scalable query serving systems. In: Phanishayee, A., Sekar, V.

(eds.) 19th USENIX Symposium on Networked Systems Design and Implementation, NSDI 2022, Renton, WA, USA, 4–6 April 2022, pp. 1059–1074. USENIX Association (2022). https://www.usenix.org/conference/nsdi22/presentation/kraft

45. Kreps, J., Narkhede, N., Rao, J.: Kafka: a distributed messaging system for log processing. In: Proceedings of the NetDB, vol. 11, pp. 1–7. Athens, Greece (2011)

46. Lightbend Inc: Akka (2022). https://akka.io/. Accessed 07 July 2022

47. Lightbend Inc: Kalix (2023). https://www.kalix.io/. Accessed 18 May 2023

48. Lin, J., Lee, M., Yu, I.C., Johnsen, E.B.: Modeling and simulation of Spark Streaming. In: Barolli, L., Takizawa, M., Enokido, T., Ogiela, M.R., Ogiela, L., Javaid, N. (eds.) 32nd IEEE International Conference on Advanced Information Networking and Applications, AINA 2018, Krakow, Poland, 16–18 May 2018, pp. 407–413. IEEE Computer Society (2018). https://doi.org/10.1109/AINA.2018.00068

49. Mampage, A., Karunasekera, S., Buyya, R.: A holistic view on resource management in serverless computing environments: taxonomy and future directions. ACM Comput. Surv. **54**(11s), 222:1–222:36 (2022). https://doi.org/10.1145/3510412

50. McCune, R.R., Weninger, T., Madey, G.: Thinking like a vertex: a survey of vertex-centric frameworks for large-scale distributed graph processing. ACM Comput. Surv. **48**(2), 25:1–25:39 (2015). https://doi.org/10.1145/2818185

51. Microsoft: Azure Functions (2023). https://azure.microsoft.com/en-us/products/functions. Accessed 28 May 2023

52. Miller, H., Haller, P., Odersky, M.: Spores: a type-based foundation for closures in the age of concurrency and distribution. In: Jones, R. (ed.) ECOOP 2014. LNCS, vol. 8586, pp. 308–333. Springer, Heidelberg (2014). https://doi.org/10.1007/978-3-662-44202-9_13

53. Moritz, P., et al.: Ray: a distributed framework for emerging AI applications. In: Arpaci-Dusseau, A.C., Voelker, G. (eds.) 13th USENIX Symposium on Operating Systems Design and Implementation, OSDI 2018, Carlsbad, CA, USA, 8–10 October 2018, pp. 561–577. USENIX Association (2018). https://www.usenix.org/conference/osdi18/presentation/nishihara

54. Murray, D.G., McSherry, F., Isaacs, R., Isard, M., Barham, P., Abadi, M.: Naiad: a timely dataflow system. In: Kaminsky, M., Dahlin, M. (eds.) ACM SIGOPS 24th Symposium on Operating Systems Principles, SOSP '13, Farmington, PA, USA, 3–6 November 2013, pp. 439–455. ACM (2013). https://doi.org/10.1145/2517349.2522738

55. Pons, D.B., Sutra, P., Artigas, M.S., París, G., López, P.G.: Stateful serverless computing with Crucial. ACM Trans. Softw. Eng. Methodol. **31**(3), 39:1–39:38 (2022). https://doi.org/10.1145/3490386

56. Psarakis, K., Zorgdrager, W., Fragkoulis, M., Salvaneschi, G., Katsifodimos, A.: Stateful entities: object-oriented cloud applications as distributed dataflows. In: Tanca, L., Luo, Q., Polese, G., Caruccio, L., Oriol, X., Firmani, D. (eds.) Proceedings 27th International Conference on Extending Database Technology, EDBT 2024, Paestum, Italy, March 25–March 28, pp. 15–21. OpenProceedings.org (2024). https://doi.org/10.48786/edbt.2024.02

57. Sang, B., Petri, G., Ardekani, M.S., Ravi, S., Eugster, P.: Programming scalable cloud services with AEON. In: Proceedings of the 17th International Middleware Conference, Trento, Italy, 12–16 December 2016, p. 16. ACM (2016). https://doi.org/10.1145/2988336.2988352

58. Sang, B., Roman, P., Eugster, P., Lu, H., Ravi, S., Petri, G.: PLASMA: programmable elasticity for stateful cloud computing applications. In: Bilas, A.,

Magoutis, K., Markatos, E.P., Kostic, D., Seltzer, M.I. (eds.) EuroSys '20: Fifteenth EuroSys Conference 2020, Heraklion, Greece, 27–30 April 2020, pp. 42:1–42:15. ACM (2020). https://doi.org/10.1145/3342195.3387553

59. Schäfer, J., Poetzsch-Heffter, A.: JCoBox: generalizing active objects to concurrent components. In: D'Hondt, T. (ed.) ECOOP 2010. LNCS, vol. 6183, pp. 275–299. Springer, Heidelberg (2010). https://doi.org/10.1007/978-3-642-14107-2_13

60. Sirjani, M., de Boer, F.S., Movaghar-Rahimabadi, A.: Modular verification of a component-based actor language. J. Univers. Comput. Sci. 11(10), 1695–1717 (2005). https://doi.org/10.3217/jucs-011-10-1695

61. Spenger, J., Carbone, P., Haller, P.: Portals: an extension of dataflow streaming for stateful serverless. In: Scholliers, C., Singer, J. (eds.) Proceedings of the 2022 ACM SIGPLAN International Symposium on New Ideas, New Paradigms, and Reflections on Programming and Software, Onward! 2022, Auckland, New Zealand, 8–10 December 2022, pp. 153–171. ACM (2022). https://doi.org/10.1145/3563835.3567664

62. Sreekanti, V., et al.: Cloudburst: stateful functions-as-a-service. Proc. VLDB Endow. 13(11), 2438–2452 (2020). http://www.vldb.org/pvldb/vol13/p2438-sreekanti.pdf

63. Tardieu, O., Grove, D., Bercea, G., Castro, P., Cwiklik, J., Epstein, E.A.: Reliable actors with retry orchestration. Proc. ACM Program. Lang. 7(PLDI), 1293–1316 (2023). https://doi.org/10.1145/3591273

64. Turin, G., Borgarelli, A., Donetti, S., Damiani, F., Johnsen, E.B., Tarifa, S.L.T.: Predicting resource consumption of Kubernetes container systems using resource models. J. Syst. Softw. 203, 111750 (2023). https://doi.org/10.1016/j.jss.2023.111750

65. Yonezawa, A., Briot, J., Shibayama, E.: Object-oriented concurrent programming in ABCL/1. In: Meyrowitz, N.K. (ed.) Conference on Object-Oriented Programming Systems, Languages, and Applications, OOPSLA 1986, Portland, Oregon, USA, Proceedings, pp. 258–268. ACM (1986). https://doi.org/10.1145/28697.28722

66. Zaharia, M., et al.: Resilient distributed datasets: a fault-tolerant abstraction for in-memory cluster computing. In: Gribble, S.D., Katabi, D. (eds.) Proceedings of the 9th USENIX Symposium on Networked Systems Design and Implementation, NSDI 2012, San Jose, CA, USA, 25–27 April 2012, pp. 15–28. USENIX Association (2012). https://www.usenix.org/conference/nsdi12/technical-sessions/presentation/zaharia

67. Zhang, H., Cardoza, A., Chen, P.B., Angel, S., Liu, V.: Fault-tolerant and transactional stateful serverless workflows. In: 14th USENIX Symposium on Operating Systems Design and Implementation, OSDI 2020, Virtual Event, 4–6 November 2020, pp. 1187–1204. USENIX Association (2020). https://www.usenix.org/conference/osdi20/presentation/zhang-haoran

Programming Language Implementations with Multiparty Session Types

Nobuko Yoshida[(✉)] [iD]

University of Oxford, Oxford, UK
nobuko.yoshida@cs.ox.ac.uk

Abstract. Session types provide a typing discipline for communication systems, and a number of programming languages are integrated with session types. This paper provides a survey of programming language implementations which use the structuring mechanism from *multiparty session types* (*MPST*). The theory of MPST guarantees that processes following a predefined communication protocol (a *multiparty session*) are free from communication errors and deadlocks. We discuss the *top-down*, *bottom-up* and *hybrid* MPST frameworks, and compare their positive and negative aspects, through a Rust MPST implementation framework, RUMPSTEAK. We also survey MPST implementations with dynamic (runtime) verification which target active object programming languages.

1 Introduction

Since the first implementation work which integrates session types [27,68] into the mainstream programming language, Java [32], the session types community has been actively engaged with implementations or integration of session types into various programming languages and tools. This survey focuses on the programming language implementations and tools based on *multiparty session types* (MPST) [28,29].

Initially, session types had a main open problem, repeatedly posed by industry partners and researchers: whether the original *binary* session types [27,68] can be extended to multiparty (i.e. more than two parties). This is a natural question since most of business and distributed protocols and parallel computations are written in multiparty communications. The hint to discover a multiparty session type theory had come from an abstract version of "choreography" developed in W3C Web Service Choreography Description Language (WS-CDL) group [10]. Since the idea was first published in [28], it has been studied and used from many different theoretical and practical aspects in the research community, such as the automata theory, model checking, runtime verification, linear logic, workflows, contracts and mechanisation. With RedHat, multiparty session types

This research was funded in whole, or in part, by EPSRC EP/T006544/2, EP/K011715/1, EP/K034413/1, EP/L00058X/1, EP/N027833/2, EP/N028201/1, EP/T014709/2, EP/V000462/1, EP/X015955/1, NCSS/EPSRC VeTSS and Horizon EU TaRDIS 101093006.

F. de Boer et al. (Eds.): *Active Object Languages: Current Research Trends*,
LNCS 14360, pp. 147–165, 2024.
https://doi.org/10.1007/978-3-031-51060-1_6

have opened their way to industry with the new JBoss SCRIBBLE Project (a language to *describe* multiparty session types). In the U.S., Ocean Observatories Initiative (OOI) [64] deployed dynamic runtime checking using SCRIBBLE for historically large cyberinfrastructures. A new industry-led application domain of MPST is *microservices*– Estafet commercialised a tool which generates Go code for microservices from SCRIBBLE [17].

After nearly 15 years from the birth of MPST, as far as we have known, MPST is integrated over 16 different programming languages. Moreover, for some languages, several MPST tools exist: for example, research came up with various MPST tools integrated in Java, and that has led to different MPST-flavoured Java versions or related technologies such as SCRIBBLE.

Among the wide range of formal methods for verifying communicating systems, the MPST framework offers a direct link to programming primitives that *digest* the structures and dynamics of multiple communicating components. Specifically:

1. Multiparty session types offer clean abstractions of communicating behaviour as a *protocol*, defining a fundamental *Application Programming Interface* (API) of components, aiding modular development and well-structured engineering;
2. Multiparty session types give a *scalable* automatic verification method without *state-space explosion problems*, extensible to check more advanced/general properties, applying model-checking tools; and
3. Multiparty session types offer a foundation for more refined verification methods, such as the elaboration of components' type signature with assertions and monitoring and tracing behaviours of the systems.

The key element of MPST is a *global type*, which globally (i.e. in a bird's eye view) describes how message exchanges in a conversation (or *session*) proceed among its participants (*end-points*). To obtain the local protocol which an end-point should obey from a global protocol, we project the local portion of a global protocol onto each end-point, giving the end-point's *interface* with respect to that protocol. This local interface generalises the familiar notion of API, which can be regarded as the server-side projection of a two-party call-return protocol. One can then use, at each end-point, these projected local protocols to concurrently build and test an end-point system conforming to the local protocols so that the original global protocols are obeyed in the interactions among these systems.

The first part of this paper outlines three different MPST frameworks using a MPST Rust toolchain, RUMPSTEAK, as an example. The second part gives a summary of all MPST programming language implementations since 2008 and compares them through several criteria. The first part of this paper is an extended version of a short paper which appeared in [12]. A part of a survey of the top-down framework explained in § 3.1 is an expansion from [41, § 6.2], including the recent MPST implementations published after [41].

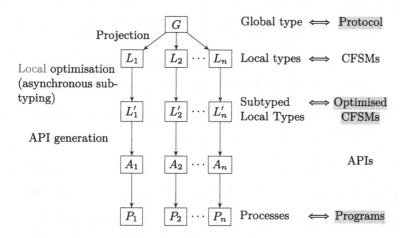

Fig. 1. Top-down MPST methodology: Highlight is supplied/done by user.

2   Multiparty Session Type Frameworks

This section explains the three frameworks of the multiparty session types (MPST), which combine the asynchronous message optimisation. We use the Rust framework, RUMPSTEAK [13], for the illustration as the toolchain implements the three frameworks. We start from the most standard and commonly used *top-down* framework, which can ensure *correctness by construction*.

2.1   Top-Down Multiparty Session Type Framework

Workflow. Figure 1 presents the top-down MPST methodology. As the first step, we write a *global type* G to describe the interactions between all roles, and project it onto each role to obtain an *endpoint local type* L_i; then we apply *asynchronous subtyping* [21] to optimise each L_i to obtain L_i' (denoted by $L_i' \leqslant L_i$); and finally, we type-check each process P_i by L_i'. Hence the group of processes $P_1...P_n$ created in this way are free from communication errors such as deadlocks.

In the RUMPSTEAK tool-chain (its stages correspond to the right-hand side in Fig. 1), a global type is written as a *protocol*, each local type is represented as a *communicating finite state machine* (CFSM) [5] (we denote a CFSM by M). The highlight denotes the part supplied by the user. More specifically, the implementation is conducted by the following steps: in

Step 1 we write a protocol to describe the interactions, and project it onto each role to obtain an endpoint communicating finite state machine (CFSM) M_i;
Step 2 we optimise each M_i to obtain M_i';
Step 3 we *generate* an API A_i from each M_i'; and
Step 4 we use each A_i to create an asynchronous Rust process P_i.

$$G = \mu t.\mathbf{A} \rightarrow \mathbf{B} : \left\{ add(\mathtt{i32}).\mathbf{B} \rightarrow \mathbf{C} : \left\{ \begin{array}{l} add(\mathtt{i32}).\mathbf{C} \rightarrow \mathbf{A} : \{ add(\mathtt{i32}).\mathbf{t} \} \\ sub(\mathtt{i32}).\mathbf{C} \rightarrow \mathbf{A} : \{ sub(\mathtt{i32}).\mathbf{t} \} \end{array} \right\} \right\}$$

$$L_{\mathbf{B}} = \mu t.\mathbf{A}?add(\mathtt{i32}).\{\mathbf{C}!add(\mathtt{i32}).\mathbf{t} \oplus \mathbf{C}!sub(\mathtt{i32}).\mathbf{t}\}$$

$$L'_{\mathbf{B}} = \mu t.\{\mathbf{C}!add(\mathtt{i32}).\mathbf{A}?add(\mathtt{i32}).\mathbf{t} \oplus \mathbf{C}!sub(\mathtt{i32}).\mathbf{A}?add(\mathtt{i32}).\mathbf{t}\}$$

Fig. 2. Global type (top) and the original $L_{\mathbf{B}}$ and optimised $L'_{\mathbf{B}}$ local types (bottom) for the `ring-choice` protocol

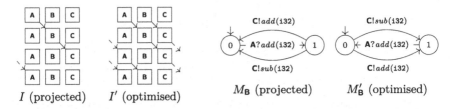

I (projected) I' (optimised) $M_{\mathbf{B}}$ (projected) $M'_{\mathbf{B}}$ (optimised)

Fig. 3. Ring protocol: (Left) Projected and optimised interactions; (Right) Projected and optimised session CFSMs.

End-Point Projection. For illustration, we use a ring protocol extended with choice (`ring-choice`) whose global type G is given in Fig. 2 (top). Role **B** chooses between sending an *add* or a *sub* message to role **C**, which must in turn send the same label to role **A**. We then project G into each role to obtain a set of local types. Figure 2 (bottom) gives a local type of role **B** (denoted by $L_{\mathbf{B}}$) where ! and ? denote send and receive respectively, and $\oplus$ denotes the output (internal) choice.

In the implementation, for [**Step 1**], RUMPSTEAK uses νSCR [63,75], which is a new lightweight and extensible Scribble toolchain implemented in OCaml. The Scribble language [26,73] is widely used to describe multiparty protocols, agnostic to target languages. Then the tool generates a CFSM for each role. The generated CFSM for role **B** (denoted by $M_{\mathbf{B}}$) is given in Fig. 3 (right).

Asynchronous Message-Reordering Optimisation. A protocol G is *synchronous*—i.e., naïvely projecting it onto **B** produces an overly synchronised local type $L_{\mathbf{B}}$. If **A** is slow to send its value to **B** then the entire interaction is blocked (as shown in I in Fig. 3). Instead, assuming each process begins with its own initial value, **B** could send its value to **C** in the meantime, allowing **C** to begin its next iteration (as shown in I' in Fig. 3).

Therefore, in [**Step 2**], we transform $L_{\mathbf{B}}$ into the optimal $L'_{\mathbf{B}}$ in Fig. 2. Importantly, we ensure that (**1**) no data dependencies exist between interactions, allowing their order to be changed; and (**2**) $L'_{\mathbf{B}}$ is an *asynchronous subtype* [21] of $L_{\mathbf{B}}$ ($L'_{\mathbf{B}} \leqslant L_{\mathbf{B}}$), allowing it to *safely* be used as a substitution while preserving deadlock-freedom. The CFSM representations of $L_{\mathbf{B}}$ and $L'_{\mathbf{B}}$ are given in $M_{\mathbf{B}}$ and $M'_{\mathbf{B}}$ in Fig. 3, respectively. While the asynchronous subtyping is proven undecidable [45], RUMPSTEAK implements the sound decidable algorithm which calculates approximately whether $M_\mathbf{B}'$ is a subtype of $M_\mathbf{B}$ [13].

Code Generation. While in the theory, we do not have this step, RUMPSTEAK includes a code generator to produce an API in **[Step 3]**. Listing 1 shows the API $A_\mathbf{B}$ corresponding to the CFSM $M_\mathbf{B}'$, from which we have elided other participants. To ensure that our API remains readable by developers and to eliminate extensive boilerplate code, we make use of Rust procedural macros [69]. By decorating types with #[...], these macros perform additional compile-time code generation. For each role, we generate a struct storing its communication channels with other roles. For example, **B** (line 3) contains unidirectional channels from **A** and to **C** as per the protocol. We use #[derive(Role)] to retrieve channels from the struct.

We build a set of *generic primitives* to construct a simple API—reducing the amount of generated code and avoiding arbitrarily named types. For instance, the **Receive** primitive (line 22) takes a role, label and continuation as generic parameters. For readability, we elide two additional parameters used to store channels at runtime with #[session].

Each choice generates an enum, as seen in **RingBChoice** (line 21), allowing processes to pattern match when branching to determine which label was received. Methods allowing the enum to be used with **Branch** or **Select** primitives are also generated with #[session]. An enum is required since Rust's lack of variadic generics means choice cannot be easily implemented as a primitive. We show how the **RingBChoice** type can be used with selection in the **Ring** type (line 18).

Our API requires only one session type for each role, internally sending a **Label** enum (line 9) over reusable channels. We create a type for each label (lines 14 and 15) and use #[derive(Message)] to generate methods for converting to and from the **Label** enum.

Process Implementation. In theory, this final step has been done by implementing an end-point process P_i and type-checking it against a local type L_i. In RUMPSTEAK, we use the API to implement a Rust process. Using the API $A_\mathbf{B}$, we give a possible implementation of the process $P_\mathbf{B}$, shown in Listing 2, for **[Step 4]**. Linear usage of channels is checked by Rust's *affine type system* to prevent channels from being used multiple times. When a primitive is executed, it consumes itself, preventing reuse, and returns its continuation.

To warn the programmer when a session is discarded without use, we ensure this *statically* by harnessing the type checker. Developers are prevented from constructing primitives directly using visibility modifiers and must instead use **try_session** (line 5). Its closure argument accepts the input session type and returns the terminal type **End**. If a session is discarded, breaking linearity, then the developer will have no **End** to return and the type checker will complain. Even so, we can implement processes with infinitely recursive types (containing no **End**) such as **RingB**.

```
1   #[derive(Role)]
2   #[message(Label)]
3   struct B {
4     #[route(A)] a: Receiver,
5     #[route(C)] c: Sender,
6   }
7
8   #[derive(Message)]
9   enum Label {
10    Add(Add),
11    Sub(Sub),
12  }
13
14  struct Add(i32);
15  struct Sub(i32);
16
17  #[session]
18  type RingB = Select<C, RingBChoice>;
19
20  #[session]
21  enum RingBChoice {
22    Add(Add, Receive<A, Add, RingB>),
23    Sub(Sub, Receive<A, Add, RingB>),
24  }
```

```
1   async fn ring_b(
2     role: &mut B,
3     mut input: i32,
4   ) -> Result<Infallible> {
5     try_session(
6       role,
7       |mut s: RingB<'_, _>| async {
8         loop {
9           let x = input * 2;
10          s = if x > 0 {
11            let s = s.select(Add(x)).await?;
12            let (Add(y), s) = s.receive().await?;
13            input = y + x;
14            s
15          } else {
16            let s = s.select(Sub(x)).await?;
17            let (Add(y), s) = s.receive().await?;
18            input = y - x;
19            s
20          };
21        }
22      },
23    ).await
24  }
```

Listing 1. Rust session type API for $M'_\mathbf{B}$ ($A_\mathbf{B}$)

Listing 2. Possible Rust implementation for process **B** ($P_\mathbf{B}$) using $A_\mathbf{B}$

We use an infinite loop (line 8) which is assigned `Infallible`: Rust's never (or bottom) type. `Infallible` can be implicitly cast to any other type, including `End`, allowing the closure to pass the type checker as before.

We allow roles to be reused across sessions since the channels they contain can be expensive to create. Crucially, to prevent communication mismatches between different sessions, `try_session` takes a *mutable* reference to the role. The same role, therefore, cannot be used multiple times at once because Rust's borrow checker enforces this requirement for mutable references.

2.2 Bottom-Up Multiparty Session Type Framework

A bottom-up framework applies the *global analysis* to check a set of local types or CFSMs satisfy a certain safety property such as communication safety or deadlock-freedom. For this, we require to use an additional general-purpose verification tool such as the *k-multiparty compatibility tool* (KMC) [46] or the mCRL2 [50].

Figure 4 depicts the two ways to perform the bottom-up strategies. In the left hand side, the user writes local types or CFSMs and generates APIs; and in the right hand side, each CFSM is generated from the API. In this approach, the user does not start from a global protocol, but starts from a set of local types/CFSMs or APIs.

The theory which corresponds to the bottom-up approach is given in [66]. This theory develops both synchronous and asynchronous semantics, but the model checking tool (mCRL2) is only usable for the synchronous version. This is

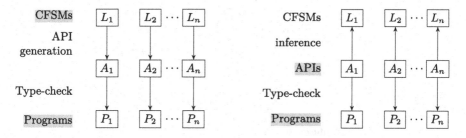

Fig. 4. Bottom-up MPST methodology: The tool globally analyses whether the set $\{L_i\}_{i \in I}$ satisfies a property. (Left) The user writes CFSMs and the tool generates APIs; (Right) the CFMSs are inferred from user-written APIs. Highlight is supplied/done by the user.

because checking a safety property in asynchronous CFSMs with infinite FIFO queues is undecidable.

To realise the bottom-up approach (right) in the RUMPSTEAK implementation, we first *serialise* each API A_i to obtain a CFSM M'_i. Next, we use KMC on the set of CFSMs $M'_{1...n}$. If they are indeed compatible, then the processes $P_{1...n}$, which implement their respective APIs, are free from communication-mistmatch and deadlocks. KMC takes a set of CFSMs for all participants and verifies deadlock freedom. To perform the serialisation of an API to a CFSM, we provide a Rust function `serialize<S>() -> Fsm` (this is a simplified version). It takes a session type API as a generic type parameter `S` and returns its corresponding CFSM. This CFSM can be printed in a variety of formats and passed into the KMC tool for verification.

Top-Down Vs Bottom-Up Frameworks. The benefit of the bottom up approach is that the user does not have to write down a global type. On the other hand, the bottom-up approach has a number of disadvantages:

Complexity KMC and mCRL2 conduct a *global analysis* of a set of CFSMs. The complexity of global verification is high–in general, the complexity of a safety property checking by mCRL2 is exponential w.r.t. the size of CFSMs. Checking k-multiparty compatibility is PPRIME [46]. From the implementation side, analysing the endpoint CFSMs for all participants in the protocol at once is challenging to do scalablely. The asynchronous subtyping checks the optimisation of *a single participant's CFSM in isolation*, performing a local analysis of a single participant. Hence the top-down framework has much less complexity. See [13, Theorem 9] for detailed complexity analysis;

Expressiveness while KMC allows a bounded verification for asynchronous CFSMs, mCRL2 is not applicable to asynchronous CFSMs.

Implementations it is often very tedious to implement a tool which can infer CFSMs or local types from a user-written real-world program [59]. In RUMP-STEAK, the inference is doable from a specialised API which takes a similar form to a CFSM; and

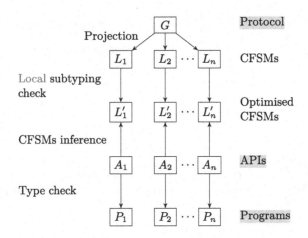

Fig. 5. Hybrid MPST methodology: Highlight is supplied/done by user.

Debugging when a KMC or mCRL2 analysis fails, it is difficult to determine how a programmer should update a complex protocol to make it free from deadlocks. Safety by construction, as used in the top-down approach, is easier to work with since verification is done locally on each participant.

2.3 Hybrid Multiparty Session Type Framework

The third framework, *hybrid*, approach (Fig. 5) is a combination of these two approaches. In this workflow, a global type G is provided by the developer and projected to obtain the CFSMs $M_{1...n}$ as before. Rather than the developers proposing the optimised CFSMs $M'_{1...n}$ directly, they simply write the APIs $A_{1...n}$ (as in the bottom-up approach). These are serialised to $M'_{1...n}$ which can (as in the top-down approach) be checked for safety against $M_{1...n}$ using asynchronous subtyping. In essence, the hybrid approach uses the same theory as the top-down approach, but presents a more programmer-friendly interface that uses serialisation rather than code generation.

The paper [13] gives more detailed complexity analysis and benchmark results which compare the local optimisation (in the top-down and hybrid frameworks) and the global analysis (in the bottom-up approach).

3 Multiparty Session Type Language Implementations

This section gives a survey of the programming language implementations based on multiparty session types (MPST). The previous section has discussed the *static* top-down, bottom-up and and hybrid approaches. The term *"static"* means that we verify safety of a program at the compile time. There is another approach, called *dynamic* where a program conformance against a specification (session type) is checked at runtime. The dynamic approach is often called *runtime verification*, and this framework also fits well for active object and actor languages. We discuss (1) the static top-down approach (Sect. 3.1); (2) the dynamic top-down approach (Sect. 3.2); and (3) the static bottom-up approach (Sect. 3.3). In (3), we also include the bottom-up tools which use behavioural types.

3.1 Static Top-Down Multiparty Session Type Framework

Table 1 gives a summary of the programming language implementations based on MPST, ordered by date of publication, focusing on statically typed languages.

The table is composed as follows, row by row:

Languages lists the programming languages introduced or used.

Mainstream language states if the language is broadly used among developers or not.

Linearity checking describes whether the linear usage of channels is not checked, checked at compile-time (*static*) or checked at runtime (*dynamic*).

Exhaustive choices check indicates whether the implementation can *statically* enforce the correct handling of potential input types. ✗ denotes implementations that do not support pattern-matching to carry out choices (branching) which are encoded into switch statements on enum types.

Formalism defines the theoretical foundations of the implementations, such as (1) the end point calculus (the π-calculus (noted as π-cal.), FJ [33]) or Mini-MPI; (2) the (global) types formalism without any endpoint calculi (no typing system is given, and no subject reduction theorem is proved); (3) the formalism based on CFSMs or (4) no formalism is given (no theory is developed).

Communication safety outlines the presence or the absence of session type-soundness demonstration. The languages, marked as $\triangle$, provide the type safety only at type or CFSM level. ✗• means that the theoretical formalism does not provide linear types, therefore only type safety of base values is proved.

Deadlock-freedom is a property guaranteeing that all components are progressing or ultimately terminate (which correspond to deadlock-freedom in MPST). The languages marked by $\triangle$ proved deadlock-freedom only at the type level. ✓• implies the absence of a formal link with the local configurations reduced from the projection of a global type. [24] did not prove that any typing context reduced from a projection of a well-formed global type satisfies a safety property. Hence, deadlock-freedom is not provided for processes initially typed by a given global type.

Liveness is a property which ensure that all actions are eventually communicated with other parties (unless killed by an exception in those which treat failures [3, 41]).

Notice that the *termination* property is a subset of safety but not deadlock-freedom. For example, the ring protocol given in the previous section does not terminate but deadlock-free and live. See [66].

Most of the MPST implementations [3,4,6,9,13,20,31,39,41,51,55,65,71,76] follow the API generation methodology from SCRIBBLE introduced by [30], which was explained in Sect. 2.1. One of the main benefits of this methodology [30] is that it empowers IDEs to provide auto-completion for developers. See [51, Fig. 6] for an example.

Notice that the implementations denoted by "dynamic" in the row of "linearity check" are not completely static: they dynamically check linearity of channels at runtime.

The tool [58] automatically generates paralleled endpoint MPI-C programs, using the aspect oriented tool which takes a sequential kernel and a MPST protocol as the input. Another MPI-C implementation [47] uses a global type extended with the indexed dependent types to statically type check the MPI code without the end-point projection (hence two cells are marked as N/A).

The earlier tool [40] implements static type-checking of communication protocols by linking Java classes and their respective typestate definitions generated from SCRIBBLE. Objects declaring a typestate should be used linearly, but a linear usage of channels is not statically enforced. Rust implementations in [13,41] can check linearity using the built-in affinity type checking from Rust.

The functional language implementation [35] uses type-level embedding of multiparty channels in OCaml. Their library relies on OCaml-specific parametric polymorphism for variant types to ensure type-safety and the implementation uses a non-trivial, comprehensive encoding of polymorphic variant types and lenses. The survey [39] gives the detailed explanations about the advantages of functional languages to handle linearity of session channels.

Recent works [3,9,24,51,71,76] use the *call-back style* API generations to statically guarantee channel linearity. The recent Scala tool [11] guarantees channel linearity by a new API generation based on the pomsets theory (instead of the FSM-based generation [30] explained in Sect. 2.1), exploring a facility provided by the matched types in Scala 3.

Built on the actor language framework Ensemble, the work [24] builds EnsembleS which generates a skeleton code based on the StMungo tool [40]. Static session typechecking is supported by modifying the original Ensemble typechecker to ensure that each communication action is permitted by the actor's declared session type. Notice that other actor programming languages based on MPST use dynamic verification, and they are discussed in Sect. 3.2.

Other Implementations Based on Top-Down Multiparty Session Types. There are several implementations which use the top-down MPST framework, targeting domain-specific applications. The early works in [16,61] implement prototypes of the MPST π-calculus with symmetric sums and dynamic roles in C and Standard ML, respectively.

Apart from the MPI-C implementations [47,58] mentioned above, the MPST is not only effective to provide the specifications of concurrent and distributed message passing programming languages, but also it is useful to provide the guidance to parallelise processes onto the HPC architectures. The earliest work

Table 1. MPST top-down implementations

	[60]	[58]	[47]	[30,31]	[40]	[65]	[55]	[6]	[39]	[35]
Language	C	MPI-C	MPI-C	Java	Java	Scala	F#	Go	PureScript	OCaml
Mainstream language	✓	✓	✓	✓	✓	✓	✓	✓	✓	✓
Linearity check	✗	✗	N/A	dynamic	✗	dynamic	dynamic	dynamic	static	static
Exhaustive choices check	✓	✗	N/A	✗	✗	✓	✗	✗	✓	✓
Formalism	✗	✗	mini-MPI	types	FJ	π-cal.	✗	types	✗	π-cal.
Comm. safety	✗	✗	✓	△	✓	✓	✗	△	✗	✗*
Deadlock freedom	✗	✗	✗	△	✗	✓	✗	△	✗	✗
Liveness	✗	✗	✗	✗	✗	✗	✗	✗	✗	✗

	[51]	[76]	[24]	[71]	[13]	[41]	[11]	[20]	[9]	[3]	[4]
Language	TypeScript	F*	EnsembleS	Scala	Rust	Rust	Scala	TypeScript	Go	Scala	Java
Mainstream language	✓	✓	✗	✓	✓	✓	✓	✓	✓	✓	✓
Linearity check	static	static	dynamic	static	static	static	dynamic	static	static	static	static
Exhaustive choices check	✓	✓	✓	✓	✓	✓	✓	✓	✓	✓	✓
Formalism	types	types	π-cal.	π-cal.	types	π-cal.	✗	CFSMs	types	π-cal.	✗
Comm. safety	△	△	✓	✓	△	✓	✗	△	△	✓	✗
Deadlock freedom	△	△	✓*	✓	△	✓	✗	△	△	✓	✗
Liveness	✗	✗	✗	✗	✓	✗	✗	✗	△	✓	✗

is [74] which maps the double-buffering algorithm specified as a MPST protocol to a multicore architecture. The tool [62] uses SCRIBBLE protocols to generate the deadlock-free MPI code to run on the specialised FPGA EURECA architecture. The work [53] designs a typing system inspired by global types for specifying the communication protocols among modern Systems-on-a-Chip (SoC). The algebraic protocol programming of MPST in Haskell is used for compiling sequential functional code into the low-level parallel C code in [8]. The work [7] proposes a cost theory which can predict the cost of message passing by analysing the MPST protocols annotated by the size of data and distance, and compared the difference between the predicted cost and the real execution of the benchmarks in the literature.

The work [25] uses the multiparty session types to implement workflows for healthcare protocols. Recent works in [48,49] develop the concurrent robotics framework where specifications extended from the multiparty session types are compiled into the robotics framework, PGCD [1], which can coordinate physical robots moving around in 3D space. The tool ensures not only deadlock-freedom but also collision-freedom of the concurrent robotics systems.

Another emergent topic of MPST is a *mechanisation*: the Zooid is a domain-specific language for certified asynchronous multiparty session types, embedded in Coq, with fully mechanised metatheory for global and local types. MPGV [36] is a strictly more expressive extension of GV (Wadler's 'Good Variation') [72] to multiparty session types. All results such as type safety and global progress in [36] are mechanised in Coq. A recent work in [70] implements a mechanised proof to proposes the sound and complete inductive endpoint projection algorithm against co-inductive endpoint projection, and proves its correctness by Coq.

3.2 Dynamic Top-Down Multiparty Session Type Framework

The static top-down approaches are suitable for the programming languages with the static type checking. The first application of MPST to the real-world systems was the runtime monitor of the cyberinfrustracture of the Ocean Observatories Initiative [64]. Since their architecture is built on Python, we have developed several dynamic checking systems based on MPST for Python. In essence, the tool monitors sending and receiving messages written in the specialised session APIs (called *conversation APIs*) against the CFSMs to check the local conformance. Along this line, the first work was a development of a monitoring tool in Python with the extensions to interrupts [15].

This Python framework was extended to *the multiparty session-actor framework* in [57]. In the previous work for runtime monitoring discussed above, each end-point process is monitored by a single monitor, which checks messages to conform to its local type. In the actor model, processes (actors) are *event-driven*: upon processing a message from a mailbox, an actor can send messages and *spawn* a set of new actors; and change its behaviour upon receiving the next message. The key point of the framework in [57] that actors are independent entities that can take part in *multiple interleaved sessions*. This enables (1) actors can be involved in multiple sessions (conversations) simultaneously; (2) actors can play multiple roles (one role per each multiparty session); and (3) actors can influence another session by receiving a message from a different session. This Python framework is later extended to the timed MPST in [54].

Later the MPST actor-based framework is applied to Erlang by Folwer [18]. His toolkit handles an extended version of Scribble with *subsessions* [14], which enables to invite new participants midway of the running session. The work [56] develops the sound recovery of supervision trees in Erlang using the causal analysis of the MPST protocols, and builds runtime monitoring.

Another important thread of work in the context of active objects is an application of MPST to the actor domain specific language, *ABS* [37]. The work [22] implements a framework in ABS where local atomic segments are verified *statically*, but global interactions among local objects are monitored *dynamically* against a global type. The work investigates various performance overhead related to object communications, synchronisation between peers, and scheduling. The implementation faithfully follows a theoretical work [38] which designs the MPST theory targeting a core ABS with futures.[1]

Recent work in [23] proposes the runtime monitoring framework called Discourje (as an extension of Courje) for monitoring more advanced MPST protocols.

---

[1] The work in [22] is categorised as "dynamic verification" as its workflow is close to the approaches by Erlang and Python discussed in this subsection.

3.3   Bottom-Up Behavioural Type Framework

The bottom-up approach uses a general-purpose model checking tool for verifying the properties directly against a set of CFSMs or local types. The first work which uses the bottom-up approach is [59]. This work infers the CFSMs directly from Go source code, and builds a global type so that the constructed global protocol gives the guidance for amending the unsafe code. It uses the GMC Syn tool [44] for synthesising a generalised global type from multiparty compatible CFSMs. However, the tool handles a very limited subset of Go program. The work in [42,43] uses a more general-purpose model-checking tool, mCRL2 [50], to verify properties of Go code such as safety, deadlock-freedom, liveness and termination, inferring *behavioural types* from Go source code. This tool was extended to verify shared memory concurrency in Go in [19]. In general, inferring behavioural types from source code requires non-trivial engineering efforts, and is not straightforward. The work [67] uses mCLR2 to directly verify message-passing behavioural types of a Scala-based DSL to check safety properties. This toolchain corresponds to the l.h.s. in Fig. 4.

The work in [66] extends the MPST theory to adapt the bottom-up approach and develops the verification tool for the MPST π-calculus based on mCRL2. Since this approach does not have to start from the global type, it can type more processes than the top-down approach in [29], but has several disadvantages, see § 2.2. The tool in [66] was extended to verify crash-failure semantics of the MPST π-calculus in [2].

Similarly to RUMPSTEAK, the Rust toolchain in [41] also includes the bottom-up approach based on the KMC-checker. The OCaml tool in [34] infers local types directly from OCaml source code using the OCaml built-in type inference system, and takes the bottom-up approach applying the KMC-checker to verify safety properties. The tools which use the KMC-checker and RUMPSTEAK which uses the asynchronous subtyping algorithm are only static behavioural typed programming language tools which can verify asynchronous optimised message-passing programs.

4   Conclusion

This paper gives a short survey of the programming language implementations based on multiparty session types (MPST). There are important related implementations which are not included in this paper—for examples, many works using model checking tools of session types, and choreography programming languages [52]. The author wishes to be informed if there is any omission in this survey.

From the author's viewpoint, the most practical innovative idea is the API generation from local CFSMs introduced by [30], which has been adapted to many different mainstream languages. This method is not only engineering useful (for example, integrating with IDEs for the auto-completion), but also theoretically important to motivate the researchers to seek the links between the MPST theory and the CFSM theory [75].

One of the most important future work is a deep adaptation of MPST to active object framework. An effective integration of *futures* and *await* primitives into MPST needs to be investigated. The challenge is to examine a trade-off between low-level preemptive concurrency and fully distributed actors, using the guidance from the MPST specification.

The practical development of MPST is still an infant, and its commercialisation is far beyond the state-of-the-art. We hope that more unforeseen, inventive ideas for "session types in practice" will be emerged from researchers and developers of parallel computing, concurrent and distributed systems.

Acknowledgements. We deeply thank the AOL reviewers for helpful and detailed comments, pointing out several missing literature.

References

1. Banusic, G.B., Majumdar, R., Pirron, M., Schmuck, A., Zufferey, D.: PGCD: robot programming and verification with geometry, concurrency, and dynamics. In: Liu, X., Tabuada, P., Pajic, M., Bushnell, L. (eds.) Proceedings of the 10th ACM/IEEE International Conference on Cyber-Physical Systems, ICCPS 2019, Montreal, QC, Canada, 16–18 April 2019, pp. 57–66. ACM (2019)
2. Barwell, A., Scalas, A., Yoshida, N., Zhou, F.: Generalised multiparty session types with crash-stop failures. In: 33rd International Conference on Concurrency Theory. LIPIcs, vol. 243, pp. 35:1–35:25. Dagstuhl (2022)
3. Barwell, A.D., Hou, P., Yoshida, N., Zhou, F.: Designing asynchronous multiparty protocols with crash-stop failures. In: 37th European Conference on Object-Oriented Programming. LIPIcs, Schloss Dagstuhl-Leibniz-Zentrum f'ur Informatik (2023)
4. Bouma, J., de Gouw, S., Jongmans, S.S.: Multiparty session typing in Java, deductively. In: Sankaranarayanan, S., Sharygina, N. (eds.) TACAS 2023. LNCS, vol. 13994, pp. 19–27. Springer, Cham (2023)
5. Brand, D., Zafiropulo, P.: On communicating finite-state machines. J. ACM **30**(2), 323–342 (1983). https://doi.org/10.1145/322374.322380
6. Castro-Perez, D., Hu, R., Jongmans, S.S., Ng, N., Yoshida, N.: Distributed programming using role-parametric session types in Go: statically-typed endpoint apis for dynamically-instantiated communication structures. Proc. ACM Program. Lang. **3**(POPL), 29:1–29:30 (2019). https://doi.org/10.1145/3290342
7. Castro-Perez, D., Yoshida, N.: CAMP: cost-aware multiparty session protocol. In: OOPSLA 2020: Conference on Object-Oriented Programming Systems, Languages and Applications. PACMPL, vol. 4, pp. 155:1–155:30. ACM (2020)
8. Castro-Perez, D., Yoshida, N.: Compiling first-order functions to session-typed parallel code. In: 29th International Conference on Compiler Construction, CC 2020, pp. 143–154. ACM (2020)
9. Castro-Perez, D., Yoshida, N.: Dynamically updatable multiparty session protocols. In: 37th European Conference on Object-Oriented Programming (ECOOP 2023). Leibniz International Proceedings in Informatics (LIPIcs), Schloss Dagstuhl-Leibniz-Zentrum für Informatik, Dagstuhl, Germany (2023)
10. W3C Web Services Choreography. http://www.w3.org/2002/ws/chor/

11. Cledou, G., Edixhoven, L., Jongmans, S.S., Proença, J.: API generation for multiparty session types, revisited and revised using scala 3. In: Ali, K., Vitek, J. (eds.) 36th European Conference on Object-Oriented Programming (ECOOP 2022). Leibniz International Proceedings in Informatics (LIPIcs), vol. 222, pp. 27:1–27:28. Schloss Dagstuhl - Leibniz-Zentrum für Informatik, Dagstuhl, Germany (2022). https://doi.org/10.4230/LIPIcs.ECOOP.2022.27. https://drops.dagstuhl.de/opus/volltexte/2022/16255

12. Cutner, Z., Yoshida, N.: Safe session-based asynchronous coordination in rust. In: Damiani, F., Dardha, O. (eds.) COORDINATION 2021. LNCS, vol. 12717, pp. 80–89. Springer, Cham (2021). https://doi.org/10.1007/978-3-030-78142-2_5

13. Cutner, Z., Yoshida, N., Vassor, M.: Deadlock-free asynchronous message reordering in rust with multiparty session types. In: 27th ACM SIGPLAN Symposium on Principles and Practice of Parallel Programming. ACM (2022). arxiv:2112.12693

14. Demangeon, R., Honda, K.: Nested protocols in session types. In: Koutny, M., Ulidowski, I. (eds.) CONCUR 2012. LNCS, vol. 7454, pp. 272–286. Springer, Heidelberg (2012). https://doi.org/10.1007/978-3-642-32940-1_20

15. Demangeon, R., Honda, K., Hu, R., Neykova, R., Yoshida, N.: Practical interruptible conversations: distributed dynamic verification with multiparty session types and python. Formal Methods Syst. Des. **46**(3), 197–225 (2015). https://doi.org/10.1007/s10703-014-0218-8

16. Deniélou, P., Yoshida, N.: Dynamic multirole session types. In: Ball, T., Sagiv, M. (eds.) Proceedings of the 38th ACM SIGPLAN-SIGACT Symposium on Principles of Programming Languages, POPL 2011, Austin, TX, USA, 26–28 January 2011, pp. 435–446. ACM (2011). https://doi.org/10.1145/1926385.1926435

17. Estafet: Managing distributed systems using Scribble (2017). https://www.youtube.com/watch?v=_qB2jV5SKwA

18. Fowler, S.: An erlang implementation of multiparty session actors. Electron. Proc. Theor. Comput. Sci. **223**, 36–50 (2016). https://doi.org/10.4204/eptcs.223.3

19. Gabet, J., Yoshida, N.: Static race detection and mutex safety and liveness for go programs. In: 34th European Conference on Object-Oriented Programming. LIPIcs, vol. 166, pp. 4:1–4:30. Schloss Dagstuhl-Leibniz-Zentrum f'ur Informatik (2020)

20. Gheri, L., Lanese, I., Sayers, N., Tuosto, E., Yoshida, N.: Design-by-contract for flexible multiparty session protocols. In: 36th European Conference on Object-Oriented Programming. LIPIcs, vol. 222, pp. 8:1–8:28. Schloss Dagstuhl-Leibniz-Zentrum fur Informatik (2022)

21. Ghilezan, S., Pantović, J., Prokić, I., Scalas, A., Yoshida, N.: Precise subtyping for asynchronous multiparty sessions. ACM Trans. Comput. Log. (2023). https://doi.org/10.1145/3568422

22. Hähnle, R., Haubner, A.W., Kamburjan, E.: Locally static, globally dynamic session types for active objects. In: de Boer, F.S., Mauro, J. (eds.) Recent Developments in the Design and Implementation of Programming Languages. OpenAccess Series in Informatics (OASIcs), vol. 86, pp. 1:1–1:24. Schloss Dagstuhl-Leibniz-Zentrum für Informatik, Dagstuhl, Germany (2020). https://doi.org/10.4230/OASIcs.Gabbrielli.1. https://drops.dagstuhl.de/opus/volltexte/2020/13223

23. Hamers, R., Jongmans, S.-S.: Discourje: runtime verification of communication protocols in clojure. In: TACAS 2020. LNCS, vol. 12078, pp. 266–284. Springer, Cham (2020). https://doi.org/10.1007/978-3-030-45190-5_15

24. Harvey, P., Fowler, S., Dardha, O., J. Gay, S.: Multiparty session types for safe runtime adaptation in an actor language. In: Møller, A., Sridharan, M. (eds.)

35th European Conference on Object-Oriented Programming (ECOOP 2021). Leibniz International Proceedings in Informatics (LIPIcs), vol. 194, p. 30. Schloss Dagstuhl - Leibniz-Zentrum für Informatik, Dagstuhl (2021). https://doi.org/10. 4230/LIPIcs.ECOOP.2021.12. https://2021.ecoop.org/details/ecoop-2021-ecoop-research-papers/12/Multiparty-Session-Types-for-Safe-Runtime-Adaptation-in-an-Actor-Language

25. Henriksen, A.S., Nielsen, L., Hildebrandt, T.T., Yoshida, N., Henglein, F.: Trust-worthy pervasive healthcare services via multiparty session types. In: Weber, J., Perseil, I. (eds.) FHIES 2012. LNCS, vol. 7789, pp. 124–141. Springer, Heidelberg (2013). https://doi.org/10.1007/978-3-642-39088-3_8

26. Honda, K., Mukhamedov, A., Brown, G., Chen, T.-C., Yoshida, N.: Scribbling interactions with a formal foundation. In: Natarajan, R., Ojo, A. (eds.) ICDCIT 2011. LNCS, vol. 6536, pp. 55–75. Springer, Heidelberg (2011). https://doi.org/10. 1007/978-3-642-19056-8_4

27. Honda, K., Vasconcelos, V.T., Kubo, M.: Language primitives and type discipline for structured communication-based programming. In: Hankin, C. (ed.) ESOP 1998. LNCS, vol. 1381, pp. 122–138. Springer, Heidelberg (1998). https://doi.org/ 10.1007/BFb0053567

28. Honda, K., Yoshida, N., Carbone, M.: Multiparty asynchronous session types. In: POPL, pp. 273–284. ACM Press (2008). https://doi.org/10.1145/1328438.1328472

29. Honda, K., Yoshida, N., Carbone, M.: Multiparty asynchronous session types. JACM **63**, 1–67 (2016)

30. Hu, R., Yoshida, N.: Hybrid session verification through endpoint API generation. In: Stevens, P., Wasowski, A. (eds.) FASE 2016. LNCS, vol. 9633, pp. 401–418. Springer, Heidelberg (2016). https://doi.org/10.1007/978-3-662-49665-7_24

31. Hu, R., Yoshida, N.: Explicit connection actions in multiparty session types. In: Huisman, M., Rubin, J. (eds.) FASE 2017. LNCS, vol. 10202, pp. 116–133. Springer, Heidelberg (2017). https://doi.org/10.1007/978-3-662-54494-5_7

32. Hu, R., Yoshida, N., Honda, K.: Session-based distributed programming in java. In: Vitek, J. (ed.) ECOOP 2008. LNCS, vol. 5142, pp. 516–541. Springer, Heidelberg (2008). https://doi.org/10.1007/978-3-540-70592-5_22

33. Igarashi, A., Pierce, B.C., Wadler, P.: Featherweight java: a minimal core calculus for java and GJ. ACM TOPLAS **23**(3), 396–450 (2001). https://doi.org/10.1145/ 503502.503505

34. Imai, K., Lange, J., Neykova, R.: Kmclib: automated inference and verification of session types from OCaml programs. In: TACAS 2022. LNCS, vol. 13243, pp. 379–386. Springer, Cham (2022). https://doi.org/10.1007/978-3-030-99524-9_20

35. Imai, K., Neykova, R., Yoshida, N., Yuen, S.: Multiparty session programming with global protocol combinators. In: Hirschfeld, R., Pape, T. (eds.) 34th European Conference on Object-Oriented Programming (ECOOP 2020). Leibniz International Proceedings in Informatics (LIPIcs), vol. 166, pp. 9:1–9:30. Schloss Dagstuhl-Leibniz-Zentrum für Informatik, Dagstuhl (2020). https://doi.org/10.4230/LIPIcs. ECOOP.2020.9. https://drops.dagstuhl.de/opus/volltexte/2020/13166

36. Jacobs, J., Balzer, S., Krebbers, R.: Multiparty GV: functional multiparty session types with certified deadlock freedom. Proc. ACM Program. Lang. **6**(ICFP) (2022). https://doi.org/10.1145/3547638

37. Johnsen, E.B., Hähnle, R., Schäfer, J., Schlatte, R., Steffen, M.: ABS: a core lan-guage for abstract behavioral specification. In: Aichernig, B.K., de Boer, F.S., Bonsangue, M.M. (eds.) FMCO 2010. LNCS, vol. 6957, pp. 142–164. Springer, Heidelberg (2011). https://doi.org/10.1007/978-3-642-25271-6_8

38. Kamburjan, E., Din, C.C., Chen, T.-C.: Session-based compositional analysis for actor-based languages using futures. In: Ogata, K., Lawford, M., Liu, S. (eds.) ICFEM 2016. LNCS, vol. 10009, pp. 296–312. Springer, Cham (2016). https://doi.org/10.1007/978-3-319-47846-3_19

39. King, J., Ng, N., Yoshida, N.: Multiparty session type-safe web development with static linearity. In: Programming Language Approaches to Concurrency and Communication-cEntric Software, vol. 291, pp. 35–46. Open Publishing Association (2019)

40. Kouzapas, D., Dardha, O., Perera, R., Gay, S.J.: Typechecking protocols with mungo and StMungo. In: Proceedings of the 18th International Symposium on Principles and Practice of Declarative Programming, PPDP 2016, pp. 146–159. Association for Computing Machinery, New York (2016). https://doi.org/10.1145/2967973.2968595

41. Lagaillardie, N., Neykova, R., Yoshida, N.: Stay safe under panic: affine rust programming with multiparty session types. In: 36th European Conference on Object-Oriented Programming. LIPIcs, vol. 222, pp. 4:1–4:29. Schloss Dagstuhl-Leibniz-Zentrum f'ur Informatik (2022)

42. Lange, J., Ng, N., Toninho, B., Yoshida, N.: Fencing off go: liveness and safety for channel-based programming. In: 44th ACM SIGPLAN Symposium on Principles of Programming Languages, pp. 748–761. ACM (2017)

43. Lange, J., Ng, N., Toninho, B., Yoshida, N.: A static verification framework for message passing in go using behavioural types. In: 40th International Conference on Software Engineering, pp. 1137–1148. ACM (2018)

44. Lange, J., Tuosto, E., Yoshida, N.: From communicating machines to graphical choreographies. In: POPL, pp. 221–232 (2015). https://doi.org/10.1145/2676726.2676964

45. Lange, J., Yoshida, N.: On the undecidability of asynchronous session subtyping. In: Esparza, J., Murawski, A.S. (eds.) FoSSaCS 2017. LNCS, vol. 10203, pp. 441–457. Springer, Heidelberg (2017). https://doi.org/10.1007/978-3-662-54458-7_26

46. Lange, J., Yoshida, N.: Verifying asynchronous interactions via communicating session automata. In: Dillig, I., Tasiran, S. (eds.) CAV 2019. LNCS, vol. 11561, pp. 97–117. Springer, Cham (2019). https://doi.org/10.1007/978-3-030-25540-4_6

47. López, H.A., et al.: Protocol-based verification of message-passing parallel programs. In: 2015 ACM International Conference on Object Oriented Programming Systems Languages and Applications/SPLASH 2015, pp. 280–298. ACM (2015)

48. Majumdar, R., Pirron, M., Yoshida, N., Zufferey, D.: Motion session types for robotic interactions. In: Proceedings of the 33rd European Conference on Object-Oriented Programming (ECOOP 2019). LIPIcs, Schloss Dagstuhl - Leibniz-Zentrum fuer Informatik (2019)

49. Majumdar, R., Yoshida, N., Zufferey, D.: Multiparty motion coordination: from choreographies to robotics programs. In: OOPSLA 2020: Conference on Object-Oriented Programming Systems, Languages and Applications. PACMPL, vol. 4, pp. 134:1–134:30. ACM (2020)

50. MCRL2 home page. https://www.mcrl2.org/web/user_manual/index.html

51. Miu, A., Ferreira, F., Yoshida, N., Zhou, F.: Communication-safe web programming in typescript with routed multiparty session types. In: International Conference on Compiler Construction, pp. 94–106. CC (2021)

52. Montesi, F.: Introduction to Choreographies. CUP (2023)

53. de Muijnck-Hughes, J., Vanderbauwhede, W.: A typing discipline for hardware interfaces. In: Donaldson, A.F. (ed.) 33rd European Conference on Object-Oriented

Programming (ECOOP 2019). Leibniz International Proceedings in Informatics (LIPIcs), vol. 134, pp. 6:1–6:27. Schloss Dagstuhl-Leibniz-Zentrum fuer Informatik, Dagstuhl (2019). https://doi.org/10.4230/LIPIcs.ECOOP.2019.6. http:// drops.dagstuhl.de/opus/volltexte/2019/10798

54. Neykova, R., Bocchi, L., Yoshida, N.: Timed runtime monitoring for multiparty conversations. Formal Asp. Comput. **29**(5), 877–910 (2017)

55. Neykova, R., Hu, R., Yoshida, N., Abdeljallal, F.: A session type provider: compile-time API generation for distributed protocols with interaction refinements in F#. In: 27th International Conference on Compiler Construction, pp. 128–138. ACM (2018)

56. Neykova, R., Yoshida, N.: Let it recover: multiparty protocol-induced recovery. In: Compiler Construction, pp. 98–108. ACM (2017)

57. Neykova, R., Yoshida, N.: Multiparty session actors. Logical Methods Comput. Sci. **13**(1) (2017). https://doi.org/10.23638/LMCS-13(1:17)2017

58. Ng, N., de Figueiredo Coutinho, J.G., Yoshida, N.: Protocols by default. In: Franke, B. (ed.) CC 2015. LNCS, vol. 9031, pp. 212–232. Springer, Heidelberg (2015). https://doi.org/10.1007/978-3-662-46663-6_11

59. Ng, N., Yoshida, N.: Static deadlock detection for concurrent go by global session graph synthesis. In: 25th International Conference on Compiler Construction, pp. 174–184. ACM (2016)

60. Ng, N., Yoshida, N., Honda, K.: Multiparty session C: safe parallel programming with message optimisation. In: Furia, C.A., Nanz, S. (eds.) TOOLS 2012. LNCS, vol. 7304, pp. 202–218. Springer, Heidelberg (2012). https://doi.org/10.1007/978-3-642-30561-0_15

61. Nielsen, L., Yoshida, N., Honda, K.: Multiparty symmetric sum types. In: Fröschle, S.B., Valencia, F.D. (eds.) Proceedings 17th International Workshop on Expressiveness in Concurrency, EXPRESS 2010, Paris, France, 30 August 2010. EPTCS, vol. 41, pp. 121–135 (2010). https://doi.org/10.4204/EPTCS.41.9

62. Niu, X., Ng, N., Yuki, T., Wang, S., Yoshida, N., Luk, W.: EURECA compilation: automatic optimisation of cycle-reconfigurable circuits. In: 26th International Conference on Field Programmable Logic and Applications, pp. 1–4. IEEE (2016)

63. nuScr home page. http://nuscr.dev/nuscr/

64. Ocean Observatories Initiative home page. https://oceanobservatories.org/

65. Scalas, A., Dardha, O., Hu, R., Yoshida, N.: A linear decomposition of multiparty sessions for safe distributed programming. In: ECOOP. LIPIcs, vol. 74, pp. 24:1–24:31. Schloss Dagstuhl - Leibniz-Zentrum fuer Informatik (2017). https://doi.org/10.4230/LIPIcs.ECOOP.2017.24

66. Scalas, A., Yoshida, N.: Less is more: multiparty session types revisited. Proc. ACM Program. Lang. **3**(POPL), 30:1–30:29 (2019). https://doi.org/10.1145/3290343

67. Scalas, A., Yoshida, N., Benussi, E.: Verifying message-passing programs with dependent behavioural types. In: Programming Language Design and Implementation, pp. 502–516. ACM (2019)

68. Takeuchi, K., Honda, K., Kubo, M.: An interaction-based language and its typing system. In: PARLE 1994, LNCS, vol. 817, pp. 398–413 (1994). https://doi.org/10.1007/3540581847118

69. The Rust Project Developers: Procedural Macros. https://doc.rust-lang.org/reference/procedural-macros.html

70. Tirore, D., Bengtson, J., Carbone, M.: A sound and complete projection for global types. In: ITP 2023. LIPIcs, Schloss Dagstuhl (2023)

71. Viering, M., Hu, R., Eugster, P., Ziarek, L.: A multiparty session typing discipline for fault-tolerant event-driven distributed programming. Proceedings of the ACM on Programming Languages 5(OOPSLA), 1–30 (2021). https://doi.org/10.1145/3485501
72. Wadler, P.: Propositions as sessions. JFP **24**(2–3), 384–418 (2014). https://doi.org/10.1017/S095679681400001X
73. Yoshida, N., Hu, R., Neykova, R., Ng, N.: The scribble protocol language. In: Abadi, M., Lluch Lafuente, A. (eds.) TGC 2013. LNCS, vol. 8358, pp. 22–41. Springer, Cham (2014). https://doi.org/10.1007/978-3-319-05119-2_3
74. Yoshida, N., Vasconcelos, V., Paulino, H., Honda, K.: Session-based compilation framework for multicore programming. In: de Boer, F.S., Bonsangue, M.M., Madelaine, E. (eds.) FMCO 2008. LNCS, vol. 5751, pp. 226–246. Springer, Heidelberg (2009). https://doi.org/10.1007/978-3-642-04167-9_12
75. Yoshida, N., Zhou, F., Ferreira, F.: Communicating finite state machines and an extensible toolchain for multiparty session types. In: Bampis, E., Pagourtzis, A. (eds.) FCT 2021. LNCS, vol. 12867, pp. 18–35. Springer, Cham (2021). https://doi.org/10.1007/978-3-030-86593-1_2
76. Zhou, F., Ferreira, F., Hu, R., Neykova, R., Yoshida, N.: Statically verified refinements for multiparty protocols. Proc. ACM Program. Lang. **4**(OOPSLA) (2020). https://doi.org/10.1145/3428216

Modelling

Integrated Timed Architectural Modeling/Execution Language

Lorenzo Bacchiani[1]([✉]), Mario Bravetti[1], Saverio Giallorenzo[1,2],
Jacopo Mauro[3], and Gianluigi Zavattaro[1,2]

[1] Università di Bologna, Bologna, Italy
`lorenzo.bacchiani2@unibo.it`
[2] Focus Team, INRIA, Sophia Antipolis, France
[3] University of Southern Denmark, Odense, Denmark

Abstract. We discuss an integrated approach for the design, specification, automatic deployment and simulation of microservice-based applications based on the ABS language. In particular, the integration of architectural modeling inspired by TOSCA (component types/port dependencies/architectural invariants) into the ABS language (static and dynamic aspects of ABS, including component properties, e.g., speed, and their use in timed/probabilistic simulations) via dedicated annotations. This is realized by the integration of the ABS toolchain with a dedicated tool, called Timed SmartDepl. Such a tool, at ABS code compile time, solves (starting from the provided architectural specification) the optimal deployment problem and produces ABS deployment orchestrations to be used in the context of timed simulations. Moreover, the potentialities and the expressive power of this approach are confirmed by further integration with external tools, e.g.: the Zephyrus tool, used by Timed SmartDepl to solve the optimal deployment problem via constraint solving, and a machine learning-based predictive module, that generates in advance data to be used in a timed ABS simulation exploiting such predicted data (e.g., simulating the usage, during the day, of predicted data generated during the preceding night).

1 Introduction

Inspired by service-oriented computing, microservices structure software system as highly modular and scalable compositions of fine-grained and loosely-coupled services [23]. These features support modern software engineering practices, like continuous delivery/deployment [27] and autoscaling [8]. A significant problem in these practices is the automation of the deployment process of non-trivial microservice systems: cost-optimal distribution of components over the available Virtual Machines (VMs) and dynamic reconfiguration. Indeed, the ability to modify the system architecture during execution is a fundamental property to cope with adaptation needs, e.g., fluctuating peaks of user requests.

Although these practices are already beneficial, they can be further improved by exploiting the interdependencies within an architecture (interface functional

F. de Boer et al. (Eds.): *Active Object Languages: Current Research Trends*,
LNCS 14360, pp. 169–198, 2024.
https://doi.org/10.1007/978-3-031-51060-1_7

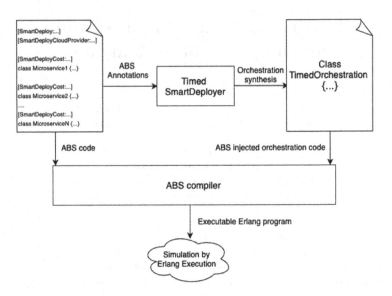

Fig. 1. Integrated timed architectural modeling/execution language toolchain.

dependences), instead of focusing on the single microservice. For instance, in the case of time-varying workload peaks w.r.t. traditional local scaling techniques [26], architecture-level dynamic deployment orchestration can avoid "domino" effects of unstructured scaling, i.e., single services scaling one after the other (cascading slowdowns) due to local workload monitoring.

In this paper, we thoroughly present the *integrated timed architectural modeling/execution language* introduced in [10]. The combination of modeling and execution capabilities makes it possible, in the context of a single language, to both (*i*) declaratively describe the architecture, its invariants, and the allowed reconfigurations and (*ii*) simulate system execution. Such an integrated language relies on an extension of the actor-based timed object-oriented Abstract Behavioral Specification (ABS) language [3]. In particular, it crucially exploits the twofold nature of ABS, which is both a process algebra (with probabilistic/timed formal semantics) and a programming language (compiled and executed, e.g., with the Erlang backend), allowing for timed simulations. As can be seen in Fig. 1, we extend the ABS language with *Timed SmartDeployer* tool [10] annotations, which make it possible to express: *architectural properties* of the modeled distributed system (global architectural invariants and allowed reconfigurations), of its VMs (their characteristics and the resource they provide) and of its software components/services (their resource/functional requirements). Timed SmartDeployer, at compile-time, checks the satisfiability of such annotations accounting for the desired target configuration requirements, modeled using the *Declarative Requirement Language* (DRL) [20], and architectural invariants. Once the annotations have been validated, it synthesizes the *deployment* orchestrations that build the system architecture and each of its specified reconfigurations (via

DRL). Simmetrically, it also generates the *undeployment* orchestrations to undo such reconfigurations. More precisely, Timed SmartDeployer uses ABS itself as an orchestration language and makes (un)deployment ABS code available via methods with conventional names. In this way, such methods can be invoked by the ABS code of services, thus simulating run-time adaptation. Technically, such (un)deployment orchestrations are *timed (un)deployment orchestrations*, which also manage time aspects of the simulation, e.g., dynamically adjusting VM speeds, based on actually used cpu cores, and setting VM startup times. Therefore, Timed SmartDeployer integrates architectural annotations and timed ABS, used as an execution language.

The fact that, besides combining them in a single language, we also integrate (via orchestration generation) modeling and execution capabilities, makes it possible to anticipate at design level performance-related issues. This fosters an approach where the analysis of the consequences of deployment decisions are available early on. Timed SmartDeployer checks (at compile-time) the synthesizability of deployment orchestrations that, at run-time, will ensure the system to be always capable of reaching the desired reconfiguration (specified via DRL). For example, in the case of time-varying workload such desired reconfigurations would aim at globally incrementing the computational power via service replication. In this way, we would have the guarantee that the system is always capable of adapting to positive/negative peaks of user requests, respecting the imposed Quality of Service. On the contrary, run-time deployment decisions, if left to loosely-coupled reactive scaling policies, could lead to a chaotic behavior.

Timed SmartDeployer has to solve the problem of synthesizing timed deployment orchestrations starting from a declarative description of desired reconfiguration requirements. Such a problem, called *optimal deployment problem*, has been proved to be algorithmically treatable for microservices only [16,17]. Timed SmartDeployer provides an interface with ABS, reading ABS annotations with DRL declarations and injecting code of synthesized (un)deployment orchestrations into the initial annotated ABS program. To do this, it relies on a pluggable external solver which outputs the synthesized architectural configuration (cost-optimal distribution of components over the available VMs), which is, then, translated by Timed SmartDeployer into (un)deployment orchestrations expressed as timed ABS code. Notice that, being the solver pluggable, Zephyrus2 can be replaced with any other (not necessarily constraint-based) solver, which takes as input a DRL declaration and produces an architectural configuration.

Concerning the simulation of a modeled microservice system, executable ABS code is·based on a set of hard-coded data (ABS array), which is divided into two parts: the actual and predicted workload for the simulated time period. Concerning the predicted workload, such data is generated at compile-time using a pluggable predictive module. Specifically, we make use of a machine learning predictive-based module implementing a neural network, which generates the workload data performing inference on a previously trained network. The idea is that the simulation represents system execution during the daytime and the neural network is trained during the preceding night. Notice that, being the predictive module pluggable, such a machine learning-based one can be replaced with any other module which produces predicted workload data.

Finally, we show our modeling execution language to be capable of expressing architecture-level adaptable systems. In particular, we consider, as a running example, a realistic microservice application, i.e., the Email Message Analysis Pipeline taken from Iron.io [24]. In such an application scenario, we use, as a reconfiguration requirement, some given increment or decrement of the system Maximum Computational Load (MCL), i.e., the maximum supported frequency for inbound requests (workload). Such global reconfigurations are used, in the context of an algorithm for architecture-level run-time adaptation [10] (also referred to as global scaling algorithm) to reach any target MCL (target workload), which overcomes the shortcomings of the traditional local scaling approach [26].

As we show in [10], the idea is that by monitoring at run-time the inbound workload, our algorithm causes the system to be always in the reachable configuration that better fits such workload (and that has the minimum number of deployed microservice instances). As a matter of fact, it is advantageous (see [9]) to consider as a target workload for the algorithm not merely the monitored one, but also the predicted workload (generated by the predictive module). Thus, we devised a run-time technique, based on past observed differences (where the most recent ones are given the highest weight) between monitored and predicted workload, to combine them into a single target workload.

Concerning the Email Message Analysis Pipeline itself, its model is built by considering static aspects of the architecture (annotations) and ABS code modeling the behavior of services. We simulate system execution using inbound traffic inspired to the real Enron dataset in [28], representing the frequency of emails entering the system. In order to show the effectiveness of our global scaling algorithm and show the advantages of using a predictive module and a technique to mix forecasted data with monitored ones, we run comparison experiments to show its advantages w.r.t. other approaches. The obtained code fully exploits the expressive power of ABS, e.g., using both its timed and probabilistic features. [1]

The paper is structured as follows. In Sect. 2, we briefly introduce our approach to the automatated deployment of microservice applications and we present the Email Pipeline Processing system that we use as a running example. In Sect. 3, we describe the Architectural Modeling/Execution Language, including Timed SmartDeployer and how we model service MCL. In Sect. 4, we present how external tools, i.e., Zephyrus2 and our machine learning based predictive module, can be integrated with this language. In Sect. 5, we test the expressive power of the Architectural Modeling/Execution Language, showing the implementation of the global scaling. Finally, in Sect. 6, we conclude the paper and discuss related work.

---

[1] Complexity of our ABS process algebraic models is also witnessed by the fact that they led us to discover an error in the Erlang backend: it caused interferences in time evolution between unrelated VMs (it was solved thanks to our code).

2   Microservices Deployment and Running Example

We now introduce our approach to the automatated deployment of microservice applications and illustrate it with our running example, the Email Message Analysis Pipeline.

2.1   Automated Deployment of Microservices

In [16,17], Bravetti et al. formalize component-based software systems and the problem of their automated deployment as the synthesis of deployment orchestrations (which allocate instances of software components on VMs) to reach a given target system configuration. In particular, the deployment life-cycle of each component type is formalized as a finite-state automaton, whose states denote a deployment stage. Each state corresponds to a set of *provided ports* (operations exposed by a component that other components can use) and a set of *required ports* (operations of other components needed by a component to work at that deployment stage). More specifically, Bravetti et al. [16,17] consider the case of microservices, components whose deployment life cycle consists of two phases: (*i*) creation, which entails the *mandatory* establishment of initial connections, via so-called *strongly required ports*, with other available microservices, and (*ii*) binding/unbinding, which corresponds to the establishment of *optional* connections, specified as so-called *weakly required ports*, to other available microservices. The two phases make it possible to manage circular dependencies among microservices.

The notions of strongly and weakly required ports are present also in state-of-the-art deployment technologies like Docker Compose [22], which is a language for the definition of multi-container deployments. In Docker Compose users specify different relationships among containers using, e.g., the depends_on (resp. external_links) relations. Then, these relations impose (resp. do not impose) a specific startup order among the containers, similar to how the combination of strong (resp. weak) dependencies induce an ordering in the orchestration of microservices deployment.

In addition, Bravetti et al. [16,17] consider resource/cost-aware deployments by modeling also memory and computational resources—i.e., the number of virtual CPU cores (vCores in Azure), sometimes simply called virtual CPUs as in Amazon EC2 and Kubernetes [26]. In particular, the authors enrich both microservice specifications and VM descriptions with the number of resources they, respectively, need and supply.

A microservice *deployment orchestration* is a program in an *orchestration language* that includes primitives for (*i*) creating/removing a certain microservice together with its strongly required bindings and (*ii*) adding/removing weak-required bindings between some created microservices. Given an initial microservice system, a set of available VMs, and a new target system configuration (corresponding to the set of microservices to be deployed), the *optimal deployment problem* is the problem of finding the deployment orchestration that (*a*) satisfies core and memory requirements, (*b*) leads to a new system configuration where

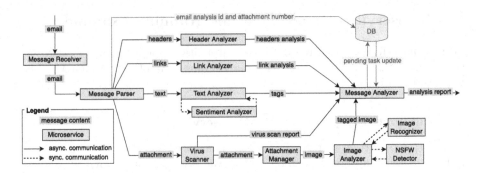

Fig. 2. Microservice Architecture of the Email Message Analysis Pipeline.

the target microservices are deployed, and (c) chooses the solution that optimizes resource usage, if more than one is available. As a typical example of an objective function to optimize, the reader can consider *cost minimization*, i.e., select among all possible deployment orchestrations the one which minimizes the sum of the cost-per-hour of the virtual machines used for microservice deployment.

While Di Cosmo et al. [18] proved that allowing components to have arbitrary deployment life-cycles makes the optimal deployment problem undecidable, Bravetti et al. showed that the latter becomes decidable when considering the simplified life-cycle of microservices described above, consisting of the two *creation* and *binding/unbinding* phases [16,17]. In particular, the authors presented a constraint-solving algorithm whose result is the new system configuration, i.e., the microservices to be deployed, their distribution over the VMs, and the bindings to be established among their strong/weak required and provided ports.

2.2 The Email Message Analysis Pipeline

In Fig. 2 (similar to that in [16,17]) we show a representation of the Email Message Analysis Pipeline [24]. The architecture includes 12 types of microservices, each equipped with its dedicated load balancer. Each load balancer distributes inbound requests among the set of microservice instances, whose number can change at runtime. We can logically partition our exemplary microservice application into four pipelines, each dedicated to the analysis or different parts of an email, namely its headers, links, text, and attachments (we detail each pipeline in Sect. 2.3). Messages enter the system through the *MessageReceiver*, which forwards them to the *MessageParser*. This microservice, in turn, extracts data from the email and routes them to the proper pipeline. Once each email component has been processed asynchronously (each taking its specific processing time), the *MessageAnalyzer* aggregates the outputs of each pipeline corresponding to the same email, and it produces a single analysis report for that email.

Before illustrating, in the next section, how one can apply to this example our approach for the automated deployment and scaling of microservice applications (cf. Sect. 2.1), we briefly present our representation of cloud resources.

We consider virtual CPU cores both for machines (providing them) and for microservices (requiring them). In particular, here, we assume microservices to be deployed on Amazon EC2 VMs of type *large*, *xlarge*, *2xlarge*, and *4xlarge*, each respectively providing 2, 4, 8, and 16 virtual CPU cores (following the Azure vCore terminology), simply called vCPUs in Amazon EC2. Notice that we model computational resources supplied by VMs (and required by microservices) using *virtual* cores with some speed fixed by the Cloud provider. Providers commonly use this kind of abstraction to uncouple the underlying hardware from the specifics exposed to users. Moreover, this level of indirection lets providers maximise the use of physical processors by delegating to the runtime (the VM/OS) the mapping of virtual cores and the scheduling of instructions. Each microservice type has a *number of required virtual cores*. Assigning the required virtual cores to a given microservice so that it achieves some expected performance (e.g., an estimated throughput) is a problem orthogonal to the one we investigate in this paper. While in practice programmers/operators perform this assignment as guesswork informed by their experience (as we do in this example), techniques like instruction counting [13] and profiling [14] can help in providing principled estimations.

2.3   Scaling Microservices

One of the pre-requisites to configure the deployment of microservice architecture is that each microservice should be defined by having a strongly required port towards the microservices which follow it in the pipeline. For instance, the *MessageParser* strongly requires connections with the *HeaderAnalyzer*, *LinkAnalyzer*, *TextAnalyzer*, and *VirusScanner* microservices since these services follow it in the pipeline (cf. Fig. 2).

More precisely, the ports should not be directly connected to instances of such microservices, but to their corresponding load balancers. In turn, each load balancer has a weakly required port that must be connected to all the available instances of the corresponding microservice, so that the load balancer can forward requests among them. The reasons behind this choice is that by establishing strongly requires connections to a microservice proxy it is possible to deploy first for example the load balancer of the *HeaderAnalyzer* and then deploy the instances of *MessageParser*, which are installable since they can be immediately connected to the load balancer they strongly require. Finally, it is possible to establish the connection of the load balancers to their instances through the weakly required port.

An advantage of using strongly and weakly required ports is that it is possible to easily capture dynamic adaptation of the pipeline deployment. A new microservice instance can be easily added to react to an increase workload by creating it and immediately connecting it to the (strongly required) load balancer of the microservice following in the pipeline. Then, the load balancer of the instance added binds to the new instance via the weakly required port. The removal of microservice instances instead follows the opposite order. First, we remove the binding between the load balancer of the microservice instances that we want to remove and, second, we safely de-allocate the interested instances.

Another advantage following from the knowledge of the microservice dependencies is that we can automatically adapt the whole architecture to provide the needed resources. Imagine for example the scenario in which an increase workload will require three new instances of *MessageParser* and two new instances of *HeaderAnalyzer* to proper handle all the traffic. If autoscaling [8] is used, scaling out and in decisions are taken locally by every service. As a consequence, the two services will be scaled out in sequence: first the *MessageParser* that comes first in the pipeline (and therefore witness for first the effects of the increase of the traffic) and then the *HeaderAnalyzer* that will start to be invoked more often by the *MessageParser*. Luckily, as shown in Sect. 5, having a global knowledge of the microservice dependencies allows to exploit the information that more than one service can be scale out at once and therefore perform a global adaptation. In our scenario, both the *MessageParser* and the *HeaderAnalyzer* would be scaled out at the same time, thus allowing the avoidance of the domino effects typical of autoscaling strategies.

2.4 Microservice Maximum Computational Load

We now introduce an important property of microservices, which characterizes their throughput: Maximum Computational Load (MCL), i.e., the maximum number of requests that a *microservice instance* of that type can handle within a second. As we will see, it is important to consider such a property to assess the correctness w.r.t. time behaviour of our integrated timed architectural modeling/execution language.

More precisely, the MCL of a microservice is computed as follows:

$$\mathsf{MCL} = 1/(\tfrac{\mathsf{size_{request}}}{\mathsf{data\_rate}} + \mathsf{pf})$$

where $\mathsf{size_{request}}$ is the average request size of the microservice in MB. Moreover, $\mathsf{data\_rate}$ is the microservice rate in MB/sec for managing request data. We determine such a value, based on the number of microservice requested cores, from Nginx server data in [31] (considering Nginx servers with that number of vCPUs). Finally, pf is a penalty factor that expresses an additional amount of time that a microservice needs to manage its requests, e.g., the *ImageRecognizer*, which needs Machine Learning techniques to fulfill its tasks.

3 Architectural Modeling/Execution Language

3.1 Abstract Behavioral Specification Language

Abstract Behavioral Specification (ABS) [3] is an actor-based object-oriented specification language (a process algebra) offering algebraic user-defined data types, side effect-free functions and immutable data. Since ABS is not directly executable, its toolchain [4] contains several backends that compile algebraic models into an executable programming language, e.g., Erlang in the case of the Erlang backend, and execute it. ABS objects are organized into Concurrent Object Groups (COGs) representing software components or services. Objects belonging to different COGs communicate with each other using asynchronous method calls [15], expressed as *object!method(...)* instructions. Asynchronicity is realized by means of the future mechanism: asynchronous method calls return a future that can be used to wait for the result using the *await* statement [5]. *Timed ABS* [7] is an extension to the ABS core language that introduces a notion of *abstract time*. In particular, evolution of time in ABS is modeled by means of discrete time: during execution system time is expressed as the number of *time units* that have passed since system start. The modeler decides what a time unit represents for a specific application. Such a feature makes it possible to perform simulations analysing the time-related behavior of systems. Timed ABS has also *probabilistic* features that allow modelers to create uniform distributions, e.g., the average number of attachments per email in our case study.

To represent VMs (and simulate them, e.g., inside the Erlang backend) ABS introduces the notion of Deployment Component (DC) [6] as a *location* where a COG can be deployed. As VMs, ABS DCs are associated with several kinds of resources, expressed via a dedicated annotations. In particular virtual cpu speed is represented in ABS by the DC *speed*: it models the amount of *computational resource* per time unit a DC can supply to the hosted COGs. This resource is consumed by ABS instructions that are marked with the *Cost* tag, e.g., *[Cost: 30] instruction*. COG instructions tagged with a cost consume the hosting DC computational resource still available for the current time unit (the instruction above consumes 30 from the DC speed resource): if not enough computational resource is left in the current time unit, then the instruction terminates its execution in the next one.

Concerning our approach to automated microservice deployment, based on strong and weak dependencies, in ABS we represent microservice types as classes and microservice instances as objects, each executed in an independent COG. Moreover, we represent strong dependencies as mandatory parameters required by class constructors: such parameters contain the references to the objects corresponding to the microservices providing the strongly required ports. Weak required ports are expressed by means of specific methods that allow an existing object to receive the references to the objects providing them.

3.2   Timed SmartDeployer

Timed SmartDeployer is executed at ABS compile time: it statically solves the optimal deployment problem described at the end of Sect. 2.1, i.e., synthesis of deployment orchestrations that reach a given target system configuration. Timed SmartDeployer takes its input from dedicated ABS annotations, which are present in the compiled ABS program, and produces its output as ABS code—synthesized timed (un)deployment orchestration—which is added to the initial annotated ABS program.

Timed SmartDeployer ABS Annotations. The JSON based ABS annotations from which Timed SmartDeployer extracts its input are:

- *[SmartDeployCost : JSONstring]* class annotation. This annotation is bound to an ABS class representing a given microservice type. It describes the functional dependencies (provided and weak/strong required ports) and the resources (e.g., number of cores and amount of memory) a microservice needs.
- *[SmartDeployCloudProvider : JSONstring]* global annotation. It defines the properties (e.g., *Cores, Bandwidth, Memory, Speed, StartupTime*) and cost-per-hour of the DCs created in the synthesized orchestration execution.
- *[SmartDeploy : JSONstring]* global annotation. It describes the desired properties and constraints of the deployment orchestration, e.g.:
  - The `id` property, which sets the name for the class that is going to include the ABS code of the synthesized orchestration.
  - The `cloud_provider_DC_availability` property, which fixes the maximum number of VMs the orchestration can allocate.

Some of these properties can have, as JSON value, a string whose content is a declarative specification (a formula of a logic language that is based on first-order logic), e.g.:

  - The `specification` property, which contains the declarative specification of the desired configuration in DRL. A value for this property, taken from our running example (orchestration with id `Scale2` in [1], see Sect. 5 for its description), can be:

```
SentimentAnalyser = 3 and VirusScanner = 2 and
    AttachmentsManager = 1 and ImageAnalyser = 1 and
NSFWDetector = 2 and ImageRecognizer = 2 and
    MessageAnalyser = 2
```

    meaning that 3 instances of the *SentimentAnalyser* must be (additionally) deployed, etc.
  - The `bind preferences` property, which is used to specify preferences about *weak* bindings among service instances (using the declarative language of [20]). A value for this property, taken from our running example (orchestration with id `BaseScale` in [1], see "B" configuration in Sect. 5), can be:

```
forall ?x of type MessageReceiver in '.*' :
    forall ?y of type MessageReceiver_LoadBalancer in '.*'
    : ?x used by ?y
```

    meaning that each instance (variable `?x`) of the *Message Receiver* service has to be bound to each *MessageReceiver_LoadBalancer* service instance (variable `?y`). Given that there exists only 1 instance of the *MessageReceiver_LoadBalancer* service in the system, this just means that each instance of the *MessageReceiver* service has to be bound to its load balancer. More precisely, the `in` keyword is used to set the scope for the indicated service: services considerd are only those located inside the DCs whose names are declared after `in`. Such a declaration can be made with a regular expression like *'.*'* (meaning any string), i.e., the service can be located in any running DC.

Synthesized Timed (Un)deployment Orchestration. Timed SmartDeployer produces as output the desired *timed (un)deployment orchestration*: a timed ABS program, injected in the initial annotated one, containing the set of *orchestration language* instructions (expressed as timed ABS code). The execution of the newly synthesized orchestration causes the system to reach a deployment configuration with the desired properties.

Internal Details. As detailed above, Timed SmartDeployer provides an interface with ABS, reading ABS annotations with DRL declarations and injecting the synthesized (un)deployment orchestrations code into the initial annotated program. To do this, it relies on a pluggable external solver, e.g., the Zephyrus2 constraint solver [2].

The external solver outputs the synthesized architectural *configuration* (cost-optimal distribution of components over the available VMs), which is, then, translated by Timed SmartDeployer into (un)deployment orchestrations expressed as timed ABS code. Such *timed* deployment orchestrations additionally encompass (w.r.t. untimed ones, see Sect. 2.1) dynamic management of overall DC *startup time* and *speed* (computational resources per time unit, see Sect. 3.1), based on the number of DC virtual cores that are actually used by some microservice after enacting the synthesized deployment sequence. As we will show, this allows us to correctly model time (microservice MCL). Timed SmartDeployer *dynamically* assigns a speed and a startup_time to each DC that is created during a deployment orchestration. Such timed properties of created DCs are evaluated, starting from the speed and startup_time annotations (see Sect. 3.2) in the original ABS code, as follows. The speed property is dynamically evaluated, during orchestration execution, taking into account the number of DC cores that are actually used: speed - speed_per_core · unused_cores. Concerning startup_time, we dynamically set an overall startup time such that it is the *maximum* among those of the DCs created during a deployment orchestration. The above is realized by automatically synthesizing timed orchestrations, whose language additionally includes (w.r.t. untimed ones) two primitives *explicitly* managing time aspects

- One to decrement the speed of a DC: *decrementResources(...)* in ABS.
- One to set overall the startup time of created DCs: *duration(...)* in ABS.

3.3   Modeling Service MCL

We now show how Time SmartDeployer allows us to correctly simulate the service MCL we want to model (see Sect. 2.4), independently of the VM (DC) in which it is deployed. An example is considering, as we do in our case study, the ABS time unit to be $1/30$ *sec* and setting VMs to supply 5 speed_per_core. According to the calculation we presented in Sect. 2.4, it turns out that the MCL of an actual implementation of the *ImageRecognizer* service is 91 requests per second. In the ABS code, to model service MCL, we make use of the *Cost* instruction tag (see Sect. 3.1). E.g., in the case of the *ImageRecognizer*, which requires 6 cores to be deployed, we obtain the MCL of 91 *req/s* as follows:

```
1    class ImageRecognizer() implements ImageRecognizerInterface {
2       Int mcl = 91;
3       String recognizeImage(ImageRecognizer_LoadBalancerInterface
                balancer){
4       [Cost: 5 * 6 * 30 / mcl] balancer!removeMessage();
5       Int category = random(9);
6       return "Category Recognized: " + toString(category);
7    }
8    }
```

where the method *recognizeImage*(...) is executed at each request.

Due to our SmartDeployer timed extension, the amount of VM speed used by *ImageRecognizer* is always $5 \cdot 6$ (speed_per_core · cores_required), independently of the VM in which it is deployed, i.e., *ImageRecognizer* can use up to $5 \cdot 6$ computational resources per time unit. The *Cost* tag above causes each request to consume speed_per_core · cores_required · 30/MCL computational resources. Therefore, since MCL/30 is the *ImageRecognizer* MCL expressed in requests per time unit, this realizes the desired (deployment independent) service MCL.

4 Integration with External Tools

In this section, we discuss external tools (w.r.t. ABS) that we have used in our work. First, we need a tool to solve the problem of synthesizing timed deployment orchestrations, starting from the deployment information contained in the ABS annotations. Second, given that we plan to use the executable semantics of ABS to simulate deployment and scaling policies for microservice systems that include also predictions of the incoming workload fluctuations, we also need a tool for workload prediction. Concerning the first tool, we have used the Zephyrus2 [2] solver based on constraint-solving technology, while for the latter we have adopted a well-established Machine Learning (ML) techniques. It is interesting to observe that, being such tools pluggable, Zephyrus2 and the ML predictive module could be replaced with any other (not necessarily constraint- or ML-based) tools.

4.1 The Zephyrus Deployment Engine

As described in Sect. 3.2, Timed SmartDeployer extracts, from ABS code, deployment information of different kinds: (*i*) *class annotations* that describe the requirements of objects which represent the resources and dependencies of the microservice instances modeled by such objects and (*ii*) *global annotations* that describes the available computing resources and the desired properties that the deployment should satisfy. Such annotations are processed by the deployment engine that automatically synthesizes a microservice architecture allocating the various microservices on available computing resources. This is done taking into account both local (e.g., single microservice dependencies) and the global (e.g., minimize the total number of allocated resources) constraints.

The deployment engine which is currently used in our Timed SmartDeployer prototype is Zephyrus2 [2]. Zephyrus2 is a tool for optimal deployment of software components over virtual machines that exploits SMT (Satisfiability Modulo Theories) and CP (Constraint Programming) technologies. More precisely, Zephyrus2 expects in input three different kinds of deployment information:

- a description of the components that can be deployed (which includes the consumed computing/memory resources as well as the functionalities required/provided from/to other components),
- a description of the virtual machines where the components can run (which includes the resources offered by the virtual machines as well as other information, like their cost), and
- the specific requirements on the component-based software architecture to be computed and deployed over the available virtual machines.

Notably, the last item could include also objective functions to be optimized, e.g., the request to minimize the total cost of the used virtual machines. Zephyrus2 then produces as output a description of the components to deploy, the allocation of such components over the available virtual machine, and the bindings among the components that reciprocally require/offer functionalities. The computed deployment satisfies the constraints and requirements specified in input.

Zephyrus2 computes its output as a solution to an optimization problem encoded in MiniZinc [29], a solver independent language for modeling constraint satisfaction and optimization problems. The interested reader can find in [2] details about how Zephyrus2 produces the MiniZinc specification of the deployment problem and how it exploits state-of-the-art tools to solve such problem. Here, we simply give an idea of how to translate deployment requirements into constraints on a couple of simple examples.

As a first example, we consider the allocation of memory to the components. Consider the constraint

$$\bigwedge_{v \in VM} \sum_{C \in CompTypes} \mathtt{inst}(C, v) \cdot C.mem \leq v.mem$$

where VM denotes the set of all the available virtual machines, $CompTypes$ the possibile component types, $\mathtt{inst}(C, v)$ the number of instances of components of type C allocated on the virtual machine v, $C.mem$ the memory consumed by a component of type C, and $v.mem$ the memory available on the virtual machine v. This constraint enforces the requirement that it is not possible, on every virtual machine, to allocate to components strictly more than the available memory.

As an additional example, we consider how it is possible to require the deployment which minimizes the total cost. For all the virtual machines v, a new boolean variable $\mathtt{used}(v)$ is introduced and bound to be true if at least a component is deployed on the v by the following constraints:

$$\bigwedge_{v \in VM} (\sum_{C \in CompTypes} \mathtt{inst}(C, v) > 0) \Leftrightarrow \mathtt{used}(v)$$

Then to minimize the total cost is is possible to minimize the following objective function:

$$\min \sum_{v \in VM,\, \mathtt{used}(v)} v.cost$$

where $v.cost$ is the cost of the virtual machine v.

4.2   ML-Based Predictive Module

When simulating a modeled microservice system using executable ABS code, we use a set of hard-coded data points in the form of an ABS array. While the most straightforward option is to run the simulation on actual traffic workload, our modular approach allows us to also integrate other components, such as *predictive modules*, which forecast traffic fluctuations, and *actuation modules*, which regulate how the logic for the architectural adaptation weights the different sources of information (e.g., the simulated traffic and its prediction).

Focusing on the role of prediction modules, we can distinguish between two types of information: the actual workload and the predicted workload. The latter is generated at compile-time using some pluggable predictive modules. For instance, one can implement the predictive module through neural networks, where the predictive module generates workload data by performing inference on the previously trained network. While this approach is apt for a simulation environment, it does not depart sensibly from real-world applications, e.g., where one can collect daytime information on the traffic and feed it to the neural model and obtain the forecast for the next day during the night.

Predicting the Traffic of the Email Message Analysis Pipeline. As an example, we describe how one can use data analytics to predict traffic fluctuations in our running example (cf. Sect. 2.2).

Dataset. The prediction module requires a datasat for training. Since the execution context of the Email Pipeline architecture is that of email correspondence, we draw our data from Enron corpus dataset [28]. This dataset has been made public by the Federal Energy Regulatory Commission during investigations concerning the Enron corporation (version of May 7th, 2015). The dataset contains 517,431 emails from 151 users, without attachments, distributed over a time window of about 10 years (1995–2005).

We processed the dataset to extract the attributes for predicting the number of incoming emails for a given time. We assume that time is discretized in one-hour intervals. For every email we extracted the *datetime* attribute, and then we summed the number of emails in the desired monitored time. Every email was associated with five new attributes: *month, day, weekday, hour,* and *counter* giving us a representation of the email flow in the system at a given hour.

Predictions. There are many techniques that one can apply to predict the traffic load. For our use case, as detailed in [9], the off-the-shelf Multi-Layer Perceptron is used. For the training, the dataset has been partitioned into a training set, a validation set, and a testing set—the latter, to estimate the error rate of the model. Specifically, a neural network with three fully-connected layers have been used, applying the Rectified Linear Unit (ReLU) nonlinear activation function to the output of each layer. Each level of the neural network compressed the input into a smaller representation. The first level reduced the input from 70 to 64 attributes, while the second level reduced it from 64 to 32 attributes. Finally, they linearly projected the 32 attributes into a single value that corresponds to the regression target. To compute the error rate, the Mean Squared Error (MSE) loss function is used while to optimize the network parameters the Adaptive Moment Estimation (Adam) has been used. The training process had a learning rate of 0.1 and an exponential decay scheduler with $\gamma = 0.9$.

5   Simulation of Architecture-Level Adaptable Systems

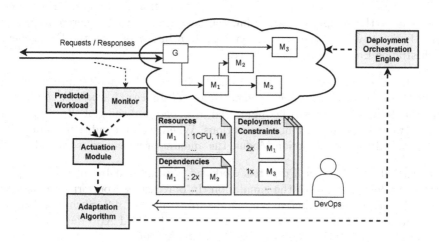

Fig. 3. Simulating proactive-reactive architecture-level system adaptation.

To test the expressive power of our modeling execution language, we simulate the platform depicted in Fig. 3. Such platform is made of two kinds of elements: the microservice system to be adapted (labelled G, M_1, M_2, M_3) and the element of the platform itself (depicted with orange boxes). Since the platform sees microservices as instance parameters, we abstract from their actual behaviour. We now describe each element of the platform. Before doing so, we highlight the three kinds of flows in Fig. 3: $\rightarrow$ showing the inbound workload reaching the microservice architecture; dashed-line arrows $-\rightarrow$ regarding the runtime execution of an architecture-level adaptation process; the thick arrow $\Leftarrow$ indicating the compilation time of deployment orchestrations.

Deployment Orchestration Engine. This component receives a deployment orchestration and enacts all the operations it contains, e.g., (de)allocating VMs, microservice replications. It is a loosely-coupled component of the platform, taken from existing solutions (the only requirement is that it provides a programming interface for the application of deployment plans), such as Kubernetes. In our simulated environment, the deployment orchestration engine is represented by the Erlang backend, which is in charge of executing the whole simulation.

Adaptation Algorithm The Adaptation Algorithm implements an architecture-level adaptation algorithm that computes the deployment orchestrations to be applied in order to cope with inbound workload peaks. To do that, such module takes into account two inputs. The first one, represented by $\Leftarrow$, regards the deployment orchestrations statically computed by Timed SmartDeployer (see Sect. 3.2) by means of a constraint solver, e.g., Zephyrus2. These orchestrations are computed such that they satisfy the specifications given by the user (DevOps in Fig. 3), i.e., Resources, Dependencies and Deployment Constraints in Fig. 3, respectively included in the *SmartDeployCloudProvider, SmartDeployCost* and *SmartDeploy* annotations, see Sect. 3.2. The second input, represented by $-->$, regards the workload the system has to support, after the adaptation process. In this case, the Adaptation Algorithm acts as a service that other components call. Upon activation, the Adaptation Algorithm interacts with the Deployment Orchestration Engine to perform the scaling.

Monitor. The monitor tracks the traffic flowing on the architecture within a prefixed *time window* and checks the possible occurrence of a *workload deviation*, e.g., the difference between the monitored workload and the globally supported one, as we will see in the following sections. When such a condition occurs, the Monitor sends to the Actuation Module the amount of measured workload.

Predicted Workload. The Predicted Workload is computed by means of a predictive module external to the simulation. In our case, we perform predictions using the ML-based predictive module described in Sect. 4.2. Such workload is statically injected in the simulation exploiting a standard ABS data structure, i.e., arrays, and it is forwarded to the Actuation Module.

Actuation Module. The Actuation Module computes the amount of workload given as input, i.e., the *target workload*, to the Adaptation Algorithm. Depending on how such workload is computed, we distinguish 3 modalities: (*i*) *reactive* mode, if the target workload is the one measured by the monitor (this modality has no predicted workload); (*ii*) *proactive* mode, if the target workload is represented by the predictions in the Predicted Workload (this modality has no monitor); and (*iii*) *proactive-reactive* mode, if the target workload is computed as a combination of the signals coming from the Monitor and Predicted Workload, according to the mixing technique implemented in this module.

Concretely, we model the architecture platform and the scaling approaches via ABS, compiling it into a system of Erlang programs that run the simulation. Then, the simulation receives three kinds of inputs, which are statically defined within a simulation run: *deployment orchestrations* (generated by Timed SmartDeployer at compile-time, see Sect. 3.2), an *actual* and a *predicted workload* (generated by the Predictive Module, see Sect. 4.2) both hard-coded in the simulation in the form of arrays. We model a real-world request flow sent to the simulated microservice architecture via an ad-hoc generating service, which distributes requests as specified in the actual workload array. The simulation uses these inputs to evaluate the performance of a target microservices architecture.

5.1 Application to Global Scaling

In the following sections, we use the above presented architecture (see Fig. 3) to simulate the algorithm for global run-time adaptation that we introduced in [10]. Such an algorithm, which we could conceive and simulate thanks to our integrated timed architectural modeling/execution language, finds application in the context of cloud-computing platforms endowed with orchestration engines. The algorithm reaches, by performing global reconfigurations, a target *system Maximum Computational Load (MCL)*, i.e., the maximum supported frequency for inbound requests. The idea is that, by monitoring at run-time the inbound workload, our algorithm causes the system to be always in the reachable configuration that better fits such a workload (and that has the minimum number of deployed microservice instances). This is achieved by enacting global reconfigurations, which are targeted at guaranteeing a given increment/decrement of the system MCL.

In particular, in the next section, we introduce the concept of microservice Multiplicative Factor (MF), which is needed by the algorithm. We already observed that each microservice type is characterized by a MCL (see Sect. 2.4), i.e., the maximum number of requests that a *microservice instance* of that type can handle in a second. We additionally observe that each microservice type is also characterized by a MF, i.e., the mean number of requests that a single request (i.e., an email) entering the system generates for that *microservice type*.

In the remaining sections, we introduce all the building blocks needed to realize our global scaling approach. We start from the mathematical calculation of the global scaling reconfigurations incrementing/decrementing the system MCL. This is done by showing how system MCL can be computed by the MCL of single service instances, which, in turn, are mathematically calculated based on the microservice data rate (we use, e.g., real data in [31] for Nginx servers) and the role it plays in the application architecture (which determines its MF and the size of its requests for each incoming message). Such global reconfigurations are synthesized into deployment orchestrations by Timed SmartDeployer. We then show a technique to combine the monitored and predicted workload into a unique target workload, used in our proactive-reactive global scaling approach. We finally introduce the scaling algorithm showing its implementation via ABS code excerpts. We then simulate the introduced global scaling approach by applying it to our example (cf. Sect. 2.2) and present simulation results: a set of comparisons that, not only shows that our global scaling approach overcomes the limitations of the traditional local one, but also the extent of improvements brought by our predictive module (see in Sect. 4.2) and our technique for computing the target workload to a purely reactive global scaling approach.

5.2   Microservice Multiplicative Factor

The Multiplicative Factor (MF) of a microservice type is determined from the role it plays in the whole architecture, e.g., in the running example, by the email part it receives. As a consequence it is strictly related to the (average) structure of emails entering the system. In particular, we estimate an email to have: (i) a single header; (ii) a set of links (treated collectively as a single information, received by the *LinkAnalyser*); (iii) a single text body (received by the *TextAnalyser*), which is split, on average, into $N_{blocks} = 2.5$ text blocks (individually analysed by *SentimentAnalyser*); and (iv) on average $N_{attachments} = 2$ attachments (individually sent to the attachment sub-pipeline starting with the *VirusScanner*), each having average size of $size_{attachment} = 7MB$ and containing a virus with probability $P_V = 0.25$ (which determines whether a virus scan report is sent to the *MessageAnalyser* or, in case of no virus, the attachment is forwarded to the *AttachmentManager*).

The average numbers above are estimated ones: the MF of microservices can be easily recomputed in case different numbers are considered. In particular, MFs are calculated as follows. Since emails have a single header, a set of links that are sent together and a single text body, the microservices that analyze these elements, i.e., *HeaderAnalyser, LinkAnalyser* and *TextAnalyser*, have $MF = 1$. As text blocks and attachments are individually sent, each of them generates a request to the *SentimentAnalyser* and the *VirusScanner*, therefore they have $MF = N_{blocks}$ and $MF = N_{attachments}$ respectively. The microservices that follow the *VirusScanner* in the architecture, i.e., *AttachmentManager, ImageAnalyzer, ImageRecognizer* and *NSFWDetector* have a MF equal to the number of virus-free attachments, which can be computed as $MF = N_{attachments} \cdot (1 - P_V)$. Finally, the MF of the *MessageAnalyser* is the sum of the email parts (1 header, 1 set of links, 1 text body and $N_{attachments}$ attachments).

From a timing viewpoint, considering microservice type Maximum Computational Load (MCL) and MF is important because it allows us to calculate the minimum number of instances of that type needed to guarantee a given overall system MCL sys_MCL, i.e.[2]

$$N_{instances} = \left\lceil \frac{\text{sys\_MCL} \cdot \text{MF}}{\text{MCL}} \right\rceil$$

Notice that, a microservice MF is also important in order to determine its request size $size_{request}$, which, in turn, as we showed in Sect. 2.4, is needed to calculate its MCL. More precisely, we compute microservice $size_{request}$ as follows. In our running example, for all microservices receiving attachments but the *MessageAnalyser* we have:

$$size_{request} = N_{attach\_per\_req} \cdot size_{attachment}$$

---

[2] $\lceil x \rceil$ is the ceil function that takes as input a real number and gives as output the least integer greater than or equal to x.

where $N_{attach\_per\_req} = N_{attachments}$ for microservices receiving entire emails and $N_{attach\_per\_req} = 1$ for the others. For *HeaderAnalyser, LinkAnalyser* and *TextAnalyser* we consider $size_{request}$ to be neglectable, thus (since their pf is also 0) their MCL is infinite. Concerning *MessageAnalyser* request size, we need instead to also consider its MF. In particular, we compute the average size of the MF requests that en email entering the system generates (since we consider only attachments to have a non-negligible size), i.e.

$$size_{request\_MA} = \frac{N_{attachments} \cdot (1 - P_V) \cdot size_{attachment}}{MF}.$$

5.3   Calculation of Scaling Configurations

We consider a base **B** system configuration, see Table 1, which guarantees a system MCL of 60 emails/sec. In the corresponding column of Table 1 we present the number of instances for each microservice type, calculated according to the formula in Sect. 2.4. Moreover, we consider four incremental configurations $\Delta1$, $\Delta2$, $\Delta3$ and $\Delta4$, synthesized via Timed SmartDeployer, each adding a number of instances to each microservice type, see Table 1. Those incremental configurations are used as target configurations for deployment/undeployment orchestration synthesis in order to perform run-time architecture-level reconfiguration. As shown in Table 2, $\Delta1$, $\Delta2$, $\Delta3$ and $\Delta4$ are used, in turn, to build (summing them up element-wise as arrays) the incremental configurations Scale1, Scale2, Scale3 and Scale4 that guarantee an additional system MCL of +60, +150, +240 and +330 emails/sec, respectively.

The reason for not considering our Scales as monolithic blocks and defining them as combinations of the Δ incremental configurations is the following. Let us suppose the system to be, e.g., in a **B** + Scale1 configuration and the increase in incoming workload to require the deployment of Scale2 and the undeployment of Scale1. If we had not introduced Δ configurations and we had synthesized orchestrations directly for Scale configurations, we would have needed to perform an undeployment of Scale1 followed by a deployment of Scale2. With Δ configurations, instead, we can simply additionally deploy $\Delta2$. Moreover, notice that dealing with such an incoming workload increase by naively deploying another Scale1 additional configuration, besides the already deployed one, would not lead the system MCL to be increased of another +60 emails/sec. This is because the maximum number of email per seconds that can be handled by individual microservices composing the obtained **B**+2·Scale1 configuration would be unbalanced. Such an effect worsens if the system incoming workload keeps slowly increasing and further additional Scale1 configurations are deployed. Since Scale1 for some microservices (*AttachmentManager, ImageAnalyser*) does not provide additional instances, such microservices would eventually become the bottleneck of the system and the system MCL would no longer increase. Moreover, Δ configurations yield, w.r.t. monolithic Scale ones, a finer granularity that makes Timed SmartDeployer orchestration synthesis faster.

For each microservice type, the number of additional instances considered in Tables 1 and 2 for the Scale configurations has been calculated as follows.

Table 1. Base **B** ($60 \frac{emails}{sec}$) and incremental Δ configurations.

Microservice	B	Δ1	Δ2	Δ3	Δ4	Microservice	B	Δ1	Δ2	Δ3	Δ4
Message Receiver	1	+1	+0	+1	+1	Virus Scanner	1	+1	+2	+1	+2
Message Parser	1	+1	+0	+1	+1	Attachment Manager	1	+0	+1	+0	+1
Header Analyser	1	+0	+0	+0	+0	Image Analyser	1	+0	+1	+0	+1
Link Analyser	1	+0	+0	+0	+0	NSFW Detector	1	+1	+2	+1	+2
Text Analyser	1	+0	+0	+0	+0	Image Recognizer	1	+1	+2	+1	+2
Sentiment Analyser	2	+1	+3	+2	+2	Message Analyser	1	+1	+2	+1	+2

Table 2. Incremental Scale configurations.

Scale 1 (+60 $\frac{emails}{sec}$)	Scale 2 (+150 $\frac{emails}{sec}$)	Scale 3 (+240 $\frac{emails}{sec}$)	Scale 4 (+330 $\frac{emails}{sec}$)
Δ1	Δ1 + Δ2	Δ1 + Δ2 + Δ3	Δ1 + Δ2 + Δ3 + Δ4

Given the additional system MCL to be guaranteed, the number $N_{deployed}$ of instances of that microservice already deployed and its MF and MCL, we have:

$$N_{instances} = \left\lceil \frac{(\text{base\_sys\_MCL}+\text{additional\_sys\_MCL})\cdot\text{MF}}{\text{MCL}} - N_{deployed} \right\rceil$$

In the following section we will present the algorithm for global adaptation. The algorithm is based on the principles described here, i.e., it has the following *invariant* property: if N Scale configurations are considered (N = 4 in our case study) and are indexed in increasing order of additional system MCL they guarantee, the system configuration reached after adapting to the monitored inbound workload is either **B** or **B** + (n · ScaleN) + scale, or some scale $\in$ {Scale1, Scale2, . . . , ScaleN} and n $\geq$ 0. The invariant property indeed shows, as we explained above, that the deployment of sequences of the same Scale configuration is not allowed, except for sequences of ScaleN. This is because, the biggest configuration ScaleN should be devised, for the system being monitored, in such a way that the inbound workload rarely yields to additional scaling needs. Moreover, even if a sequence of ScaleN occurs, the system would be sufficiently balanced. This is because, differently from smaller Scale configurations, ScaleN is assumed to add, at least, an instance for each microservice having non-infinite MCL (as for Scale4 in our case study).

5.4   Calculation of the Mixed Monitored and Predicted Workload

The fact that predictors are weak against exceptional events is well-known and affects approaches that just rely on predictions: in the case of global scaling, it would result in the execution of inappropriate deployment orchestrations (either wasting resources or degrading the QoS). In this section, we propose a solution mixing proactive and reactive global scaling (reactive and proactive mode of the Actuation Module, see above): we program the Actuation Module to calculate a *target workload* by combining the monitored and predicted ones.

Our algorithm does not rely on comparing the estimated and actual number of inbound requests in a given time window. The reason is that the dynamic interaction between message queues and scaling times makes it difficult to reliably estimate the accuracy of the predicted scaling configuration w.r.t. traffic fluctuations. Thus, we introduce a new, stable estimation, rooted in the workload measure defined below.

Our idea is to use the system MCL of the current configuration (reached by applying some incremental Δ configurations to the base **B** one) and to consider the difference (in terms of number of incremental Δ configurations added) between the system MCL induced by the monitored and predicted traffic. In this way, we can estimate both over- and under-scaling of proactive global scaling.

More precisely, our estimation considers a statically-defined score s for each type Δ configuration, based on the amount of system MCL increment it provides. Following Sect. 5.3, we have $i \in [1,4]$ different Δi applied sequentially (in the exceptional case $\Delta 4$ is not enough, we restart from $\Delta 1$). For each Δi we have a differential system MCL increment of: $\Delta MCL_1 = 60$ for $\Delta 1$ and $\Delta MCL_i = 90$ for Δi with $2 \le i \le 4$. Given ΔMCL_i, we compute $s_i = \frac{\Delta MCL_i}{\sum_{j=1}^{4} \Delta MCL_j}$. Notice that this yields $\sum_{i=1}^{4} s_i = 1$.

Then, for each time window tw, we compute our estimation following these 3 steps. In step 1, we calculate, for each index i, the absolute value $|diff_i|$ of the difference between the applications number of Δi induced by the predicted and monitored workload at time window tw. Then, we compute a weight $w \in [0,1]$ that we later use to combine both workloads. Since $|diff_i| > 1$ only happens in exceptional cases (when $\Delta 4$ is not enough), we compute $w = min\left(\sum_{i=1}^{4} s_i \cdot |diff_i|, 1\right)$.

We keep track of the values w computed in the last 3 time windows using function $h = \{(1, w_{tw-2}), (2, w_{tw-1}), (3, w_{tw})\}$, where w_{tw} is the weight computed for the current time window and w_{tw-2}, w_{tw-1} are the preceding ones. The pairs $(1, w_{tw-2}), (2, w_{tw-1})$ are included in h only if the system was already running at those times.

In step 2, we compute the overall weight $w_{ov} = \frac{\sum_{(i,w) \in h} w \cdot i}{\sum_{(i,\_) \in h} i}$ of tw. In particular, $w \cdot i$ means that the most recent w is the most influential one in the sum. The overall weight indicates the distance between the monitored and predicted one. Specifically, the closer the overall weight is to 1 the more distant the prediction is from the monitored workload.

In step 3, we use w_{ov} to linearly combine the predicted and monitored workload to estimate the target workload passed as input to the Adaptation Algorithm $target\_workload = (w_{ov} \cdot monitored\_workload) + ((1 - w_{ov}) \cdot predicted\_workload)$.

5.5   Scaling Algorithm

We now present the algorithm for global adaptation. As a matter of fact, for comparison purposes, we also realized an algorithm for local adaptation simulating the mainstream approach, e.g., Kubernetes [26]. In both of them we use a scaling condition on monitored inbound workload involving two constants called K and k. K is used to leave a margin under the guaranteed MCL, so to make sure that the system can handle the inbound workload. k is used to prevent fluctuations, i.e., sequences of scale up and down.

The condition for scaling up is $(\text{target\_workload} + \mathsf{K}) - \text{total\_MCL} > \mathsf{k}$ and the one for scaling down is $\text{total\_MCL} - (\text{target\_workload} + \mathsf{K}) > \mathsf{k}$. The interpretation of such conditions changes, depending on whether they are used for the local or global adaptation algorithm. In the case of local adaptation the conditions would be applied by monitoring a single microservice type: target_workload would be the number of requests per second received by the microservice load balancer and total_MCL would be the MCL of a microservice instance of that type (calculated as explained in Sect. 2.4) multiplied by the number of deployed instances. In the global adaptation case that we detail in the following, the conditions are, instead, applied by monitoring the whole system: target_workload is the number of requests (emails in our case study) per second entering the system and total_MCL is the system MCL. Notice that the target_workload is computed according to the mode in which the system is used, i.e., reactive (the monitored workload is the target one), proactive (the predicted workload is the target one) and proactive-reactive (mixing the monitored and predicted workload according to the technique presented in Sect. 5.4).

Concerning global adaptation, we have a single monitor that periodically executes the global scaling algorithm presented in code excerpt below. Notice that $kbig()$ and $k()$ are respectively the K and k constants described above, implemented as constant functions mimicking global variables in the code; scaler is a previously instantianted object that implements the methods *computeConfiguration* and *scale*, presented afterwards.

```
1    if(target_workload - (mcl - kbig())) > k() || (mcl - kbig()) -
         target_workload > k()) {
2      List<Int> target_config = scaler.computeConfiguration(
         target_workload);
3      scaler.scale(target_config);
4    }
```

The *computeConfiguration* method, whose code is presented below, aims at computing the system configuration needed to cope with the *target_workload* passed as input. Such configuration is expressed in the form of a List where index i represents Δi and the i-th element is the number of Δi applications.

```
1    List<Int> computeConfiguration(Rat target_workload) {
2      List<Int> configDeltas = this.createEmpty(numScales);
3      printableconfig = configDeltas;
4      List<Int> config = baseConfig;
5      mcl = this.mcl(config);
6      Bool configFound = (mcl - kbig()) - target_workload  >= 0;
7      while(!configFound) {
8        List<Int> candidateConfig = baseConfig;
9        Int i = -1;
10       while(i < numScales - 1 && !configFound) {
11         i = i + 1;
12         candidateConfig = this.vSum(config, nth(scaleComponents,i));
13         mcl = this.mcl(candidateConfig);
14         configFound = (mcl - kbig()) - target_workload  >= 0;
```

```
15        }
16        config = candidateConfig;
17        printableconfig = this.incrementValue(i,printableconfig);
18        configDeltas = this.addDeltas(i,configDeltas);
19      }
20      return configDeltas;
21    }
```

The code above uses constants numScales, representing the number of Scale configurations (4 in our case study), and scaleComponents: an array[3] of numScales elements (corresponding to Table 2) that stores in each position an array representing a Scale configuration (i.e., specifying, for each microservice, the number of additional instances to be deployed). Moreover, the code uses the variable mcl, containing the current system MCL (assumed to be initially set to the **B** configuration MCL, see Table 1). At first, the code applies the above described scale up/down conditions. Then it loops, starting from the **B** configuration in variable config (an array that stores, for each microservice, the number of instances we currently consider), and selecting Scale configurations to add to config, until a configuration c is found such that its system MCL satisfies mcl − K − target_workload ≥ 0. The system MCL of a configuration c is calculated with method *mcl*, which yields

$$\min_{1 \leq i \leq \text{length(config)}} \text{nth}(\text{config}, i-1) \cdot \text{MCL}_i/\text{MF}_i$$

with MCL_i/MF_i denoting the MCL/MF of the i-th microservice. More precisely the algorithm uses an external loop updating variables config and configDeltas according to the incremental Scale selected by the internal loop: configDeltas is an array of numScales elements that keeps track of the number of currently deployed Δ incremental configurations (assumed to be initially empty, i.e., with all 0 values). Every time a Scale configuration is selected, configDeltas is updated by incrementing the amount of the corresponding Δ configurations (as described in Table 2). The internal loop selects a Scale configuration by looking for the first one that, added to config, yields a candidate configuration whose system MCL satisfies the condition above. If such Scale configuration is not found then it just selects the last (the biggest) Scale configuration (Scale4 in our case study), thus implementing the invariant presented in Sect. 5.3.

The *scale* method presented below enacts the scaling operations required to reach the system configuration passed as input.

```
1    Unit scale(List<Int> configDeltas) {
2      Int i = 0;
3      while(i < numScales) {
4        Int diff = nth(configDeltas,i) - nth(deployedDeltas,i);
5        Rat num = abs(diff);
6        while(num > 0) {
7          if (diff > 0) {nth(orchestrationDeltas,i)!deploy();}
8          else {nth(orchestrationDeltas,i)!undeploy();}
9          num = num - 1;
10       }
```

---

[3] The ABS instructions nth(a, i) and length(a) retrieve the i-th element and the length of the a array, respectively.

```
11        i = i + 1;
12    }
13    deployedDeltas = configDeltas;
14    scalingAct = this.recordAction(scalingTrace, printableconfig);
15    scalingTrace = printableconfig;
16  }
```

Given the target Δ configurations configDeltas to be reached and the current deployedDeltas (an array with the same structure of configDeltas) ones, the *scale* method performs the difference between them so to find the Δ orchestrations that have to be (un)deployed. We use methods *deploy/undeploy* of the object in the position $i-1$ of the array orchestrationDeltas to execute the orchestration of the i-th Δ configuration. In our model such an orchestration is the ABS code generated by Timed SmartDeployer at compile-time: it makes use of ABS primitives *duration(...)* and *decrementResources(...)* to *dynamically* set, respectively, the overall startup time to the maximum of those of deployed DCs and the speed of such DCs accounting for the virtual cores actually being used (by decrementing the DC static speed, see Sect. 3.2). In this way we are guaranteed that each microservice always preserves the desired fixed MCL we want to model (see Sect. 2.4). Moreover, we remind that, besides speed, also constraints related to other resources (memory) are considered in the Timed SmartDeployer synthesis process. Notice that the variables scalingAct, scalingTrace as well as the *recordAction* method are only used for debug purpose.

5.6 Benchmarking the Performance of Global Scaling Approaches

In this section we present simulation results obtained with our ABS programs [1] modeling reactive local scaling and the three variants of the global one, i.e., reactive, proactive and proactive-reactive. In particular, at first, we show the impact of reactive global scaling on system performance w.r.t. the reactive local one; then we show how the reactive global scaling can be further improved endowing it with proactive capabilities, e.g., making use of a workload predictor. Finally, we show the risks of just relying on workload predictions to enact scaling actions and the need of mixing reactiveness and proactiveness. We make use of (part of) the Enron dataset [28] as the inbound workload inputed to the simulations, to test the performance of reactive and proactive global scaling and the local one. All benchmark tests shown in this section are performed on email traffic on a weekday in May 2001. To prove the effectivenss of our proactive-reactive global scaling, we selectively picked outliers from the Enron dataset to produce a traffic flow that our predictor would struggle to forecast, thus the workload inputed to this simulation differs from the one inputed to the others. In our simulations we consider the following metrics: (i) latency (considered as the average time for completely processing an email that enters the system), (ii) message loss, (iii) number of deployed microervices and (iv) monetary costs. Notice that in the comparison between reactive local scaling and the reactive global one, we do not consider monetary costs, since Timed SmartDeployer orchestrations are such that costs are minimized.

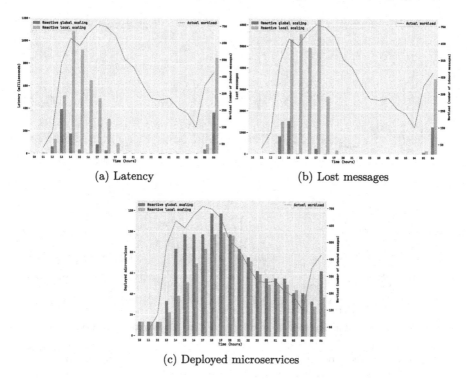

(a) Latency   (b) Lost messages

(c) Deployed microservices

Fig. 4. Comparison between reactive local scaling and the reactive global one.

Reactive Local vs Reactive Global Scaling. Considering the flow of incoming emails in the workload inputed to the simulation, it is clear the extent of the improvement introduced by our approach: our global adaptation [10] makes the system adapting much faster than the local approach. This is caused by the ability of the global adaptation strategy of detecting in advance the scaling needs of all system microservices. This is shown in Figs. 4a and 4b, where our reactive global scaling approach outperforms the local one: latency and message loss are restored in much shorter time w.r.t. the reactive local scaling.

Comparing the number of deployed microservices helps to have a deeper understanding of the reasons why the global adaptation performs better. As shown in Fig. 4c, our approach reaches the target configuation, needed to handle the monitored workload, faster than the local scaling approach. As expected, this makes the adaptation process slower and worsens the performance. The local adaptation slowness in reaching such a target configuration is caused by a scaling chain effect: local monitors periodically check the workload, thus single services scale one after the other. Hence, w.r.t. global adaptation, where the architecture is replicated as a single block, the number of instances grows slower. For example, considering the attachment pipeline in Fig. 2, the first microservice to become a bottleneck is the *Virus Scanner*: it starts losing requests, which will never arrive to the *Attachment Manager*. Therefore, this component will not

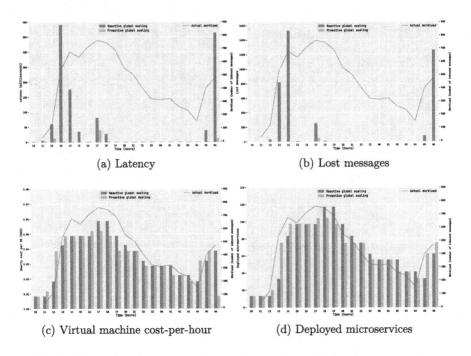

(a) Latency

(b) Lost messages

(c) Virtual machine cost-per-hour

(d) Deployed microservices

Fig. 5. Comparison between reactive and proactive global scaling approaches.

perceive the increment in the inbound requests until the *Virus Scanner* will be
replicated, thus causing a scaling chain effect that delays adaptation. This is the
main cause for the large deterioration in performances observed.

Proactive vs Reactive Global Scaling. To give an intuition of the effectiveness of
our proactive global scaling approach [9], we test its performance against reactive
global scaling [10]. This comparison mainly aims at showing the improvement
brought in the global scaling technique thanks to the use of a workload predictor,
i.e., endowing it with proactive capabilities.

Considering latency, as shown in Figs. 5a and 5b, the proactive scaling is
barely visible given that it performs in advance the scaling operations needed
to manage workload peaks, with negligible latency. The small visible spikes are
imputable to inaccuracies in the workload predictions. On the other hand, the
reactive approach suffers the most at sudden peaks of workload because of
the time needed to complete the adaptation process, e.g., VMs startup time.
As seen in Figs. 5c and 5d, despite the signifante difference in performance,
the costs/number of deployed instances are the same, although shifted by a
time-unit backwards. The reason is that, since the traffic is the same, resource
(de)allocations are the same across all the approaches, although these happen
one time-unit in advance in the proactive case.

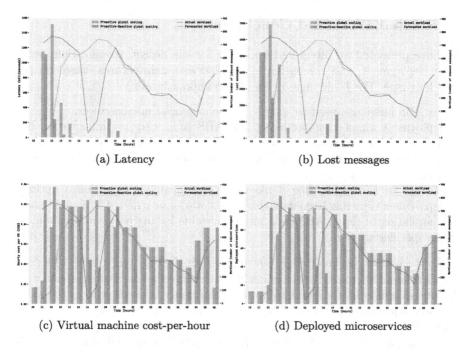

Fig. 6. Comparison between proactive-reactive and proactive global scaling, on the outliers test set.

Proactive-Reactive vs Proactive Global Scaling. The presented proactive approach proved to be quite effective. However, predictors are not infallible: if the traffic greatly deviates from the historical data, due to some unprecedented occurrence, the predictor can fail to provide an accurate estimation of the traffic. This fact, considered in the context of proactive global scaling (like the one implemented above) where scaling decisions neglect actual traffic fluctuations, can result in over- (wasted resources) or under-scaling (latency, request loss) of the system. To illustrate how much this phenomenon can affect performance, we selectively picked outliers from the test set described in Sect. 4.2 and used these to produce a traffic flow that our predictor struggles to forecast. From Figs. 6a and 6b, the proactive-reactive global scaling rapidly recovers from wrong predictions, while the proactive one neglects unexpected traffic fluctuations. This is visible, e.g., in the interval 11–13, where the proactive approach expects fewer requests and endures high latency. Also the proactive-reactive global scaling initially undergoes high latency, but, detecting the diverge with the predictions, it assumes a reactive stance and quickly adapts. Note that the latency of the proactive-reactive approach in the timespan 18–19 is "good". Indeed, while the workload drops between 15–17, the proactive approach allocates a high number of microservices (cf. Figures 6c and 6d), wasting resources. Contrarily, the other one (reacting to unforeseen changes) trades some minor latency off resource savings.

6   Related Work and Conclusion

We have presented an integrated approach for the design, specification, automatic deployment, and simulation of microservice architectures, based on the ABS language. The basic ingredients of this approach are:

- the ABS language, used to specify the behaviour of microservices;
- deployment annotations added to the ABS code, carrying information like the available computing resources and their costs, the resources consumed by each microservice instance, and constraints about the minimum number of instances for each microservice;
- the use of a compile-time deployment engine able to synthesize optimal deployments starting from deployment annotations extracted from ABS code;
- compilation of timed ABS code into executable Erlang program, to simulate the specified system.

To the best of our knowledge, our approach is the only one mixing a) formal specification of microservice behaviour, b) the usage of a language equipped with executable semantics for simulation and performance analysis, and c) the modeling and automatic synthesis of deployment orchestrations. Specifically, related work addressed the above aspects separately. Concerning executable semantics for simulation, [12] instead of compiling ABS into Erlang, makes use of a real-time Haskell backend: this makes it possible for the simulation to communicate with real services, thus mixing external execution and simulation at run-time. In our case, the communication between the simulated system and external systems (during simulation) is not needed, thus we avoid the complexities of the approach in [12] related to synchronizing real and simulated time. Another line of work encompasses the usage of timed/stochastic process algebras by integrating them in the software development process, with the aim of analysing the performances of the modeled system (see, e.g., the surveys [11,25]). Finally, other proposals adopt specific models for cloud deployment specification, e.g., TOSCA (Topology and Orchestration Specification for Cloud Applications) [30] or AEOLUS [21], to describe the components of a cloud service system and their deployment/orchestration process. The interested reader can find a recent survey of the model-based methodologies used to ensure the correctness of reconfigurations in component-based systems at [19].

In this presentation, we applied our integrated approach to the analysis of different techniques to deal with the problem of dynamic scaling of microservices applications. In particular, we have considered a rather sophisticated technique based on a mixture of predicted and monitored inbound workload, with subsequent global adaptations of the entire system (i.e., all the microservices that will be influenced by the modified workload will coordinate their scaling). A similar technique has been already investigated by Urgaonkar et al. [32]. Differently from our approach, [32] only focuses on adjusting under-estimations of the actual workload, to guarantee a given QoS. In the case of over-estimation, their approach simply considers the predicted workload as the target one, ending up wasting resources (and money), see [9] for a detailed comparison.

References

1. Code repository for the email processing examples. https://github.com/LBacchiani/ABS-Simulations-Comparison
2. Ábrahám, E., Corzilius, F., Johnsen, E.B., Kremer, G., Mauro, J.: Zephyrus2: on the fly deployment optimization using SMT and CP technologies. In: Fränzle, M., Kapur, D., Zhan, N. (eds.) SETTA 2016. LNCS, vol. 9984, pp. 229–245. Springer, Cham (2016). https://doi.org/10.1007/978-3-319-47677-3_15
3. ABS. ABS documentation. http://docs.abs-models.org/
4. ABS. ABS toolchain. https://www.sciencedirect.com/science/article/pii/S0167642322000946
5. ABS. Core ABS. https://www.sciencedirect.com/science/article/pii/S2352220814000479
6. ABS. Deployment component in ABS. https://link.springer.com/chapter/10.1007/978-3-642-25271-6_8
7. ABS. Real time ABS. https://link.springer.com/article/10.1007/s11334-012-0184-5
8. Amazon, AWS auto scaling. https://aws.amazon.com/autoscaling/
9. Bacchiani, L., Bravetti, M., Gabbrielli, M., Giallorenzo, S., Zavattaro, G., Zingaro, S.P.: Proactive-reactive global scaling, with analytics. In: Troya, J., Medjahed, B., Piattini, M., Yao, L., Fernández, P., Ruiz-Cortés, A. (eds.) Service-Oriented Computing - 20th International Conference, ICSOC 2022, Seville, Spain, 29 November–2 December 2022, Proceedings, vol. 13740 of Lecture Notes in Computer Science, pp. 237–254. Springer, Heidelberg (2022). https://doi.org/10.1007/978-3-031-20984-0_16
10. Bacchiani, L., Bravetti, M., Giallorenzo, S., Mauro, J., Talevi, I., Zavattaro, G.: Microservice dynamic architecture-level deployment orchestration. In: Damiani, F., Dardha, O. (eds.) COORDINATION 2021. LNCS, vol. 12717, pp. 257–275. Springer, Cham (2021). https://doi.org/10.1007/978-3-030-78142-2_16
11. Balsamo, S., Di Marco, A., Inverardi, P., Simeoni, M.: Model-based performance prediction in software development: a survey. IEEE Trans. Softw. Eng. **30**(5), 295–310 (2004)
12. Bezirgiannis, N., de Boer, F., de Gouw, S.: Human-in-the-loop simulation of cloud services. In: De Paoli, F., Schulte, S., Broch Johnsen, E. (eds.) ESOCC 2017. LNCS, vol. 10465, pp. 143–158. Springer, Cham (2017). https://doi.org/10.1007/978-3-319-67262-5_11
13. Binder, W., Hulaas, J., Camesi, A.: Continuous bytecode instruction counting for cpu consumption estimation. In: Third International Conference on the Quantitative Evaluation of Systems-(QEST 2006), pp. 19–30. IEEE (2006)
14. Binder, W., Hulaas, J., Moret, P., Villazón, A.: Platform-independent profiling in a virtual execution environment. Softw. Pract. Exp. **39**(1), 47–79 (2009)
15. Bravetti, M., Carbone, M., Zavattaro, G.: Undecidability of asynchronous session subtyping. Inf. Comput. **256**, 300–320 (2017)
16. Bravetti, M., Giallorenzo, S., Mauro, J., Talevi, I., Zavattaro, G.: Optimal and automated deployment for microservices. In: Hähnle, R., van der Aalst, W. (eds.) FASE 2019. LNCS, vol. 11424, pp. 351–368. Springer, Cham (2019). https://doi.org/10.1007/978-3-030-16722-6_21
17. Bravetti, M., Giallorenzo, S., Mauro, J., Talevi, I., Zavattaro, G.: A formal approach to microservice architecture deployment. In: Microservices, pp. 183–208. Springer, Cham (2020). https://doi.org/10.1007/978-3-030-31646-4_8

18. Di Cosmo, R., Zacchiroli, S., Zavattaro, G.: Towards a formal component model for the cloud. In: Eleftherakis, G., Hinchey, M., Holcombe, M. (eds.) SEFM 2012. LNCS, vol. 7504, pp. 156–171. Springer, Heidelberg (2012). https://doi.org/10.1007/978-3-642-33826-7_11

19. Coullon, H., Henrio, L., Loulergue, F., Robillard, S.: Component-based distributed software reconfiguration: a verification-oriented survey. ACM Comput. Surv. **56**(1), 1–37 (2023)

20. de Gouw, S., Mauro, J., Zavattaro, G.: On the modeling of optimal and automatized cloud application deployment. J. Logical Algebr. Methods Program. **107**, 108–135 (2019)

21. Di Cosmo, R., Mauro, J., Zacchiroli, S., Zavattaro, G.: Aeolus: a component model for the cloud. Inf. Comput. **239**, 100–121 (2014)

22. Docker. Docker compose documentation. https://docs.docker.com/compose/

23. Dragoni, N., et al.: Microservices: yesterday, today, and tomorrow. In: Present and Ulterior Software Engineering, pp. 195–216. Springer, Cham (2017). https://doi.org/10.1007/978-3-319-67425-4_12

24. Fromm, K.: Thinking Serverless! How New Approaches Address Modern Data Processing Needs. https://medium.com/a-cloud-guru/thinking-serverless-how-new-approaches-address-modern-data-processing-needs-part-1-af6a158a3af1

25. Hermanns, H., Herzog, U., Katoen, J.-P.: Process algebra for performance evaluation. Theor. Comput. Sci. **274**(1–2), 43–87 (2002)

26. Hightower, K., Burns, B., Beda, J.: Kubernetes: Up and Running Dive into the Future of Infrastructure, 1st edn. O'Reilly Media Inc., Sebastopol (2017)

27. Humble, J., Farley, D.: Continuous Delivery: Reliable Software Releases Through Build, Test, and Deployment Automation. Addison-Wesley Professional, Boston (2010)

28. Klimt, B., Yang, Y.: The enron corpus: a new dataset for email classification research. In: Machine Learning: ECML 2004, Berlin, pp. 217–226 (2004)

29. Nethercote, N., Stuckey, P.J., Becket, R., Brand, S., Duck, G.J., Tack, G.: MiniZinc: towards a standard CP modelling language. In: Bessière, C. (ed.) CP 2007. LNCS, vol. 4741, pp. 529–543. Springer, Heidelberg (2007). https://doi.org/10.1007/978-3-540-74970-7_38

30. OASIS. Topology and Orchestration Specification for Cloud Applications (TOSCA) Version 1.0. http://docs.oasis-open.org/tosca/TOSCA/v1.0/cs01/TOSCA-v1.0-cs01.html. Accessed May 2020

31. Rawdat, A.: Testing the performance of nginx and nginx plus web servers. https://www.nginx.com/blog/testing-the-performance-of-nginx-and-nginx-plus-web-servers/

32. Urgaonkar, B., Shenoy, P., Chandra, A., Goyal, P., Wood, T.: Agile dynamic provisioning of multi-tier internet applications. ACM Trans. Auton. Adapt. Syst. (TAAS) **3**(1), 1–39 (2008)

Simulating User Journeys with Active Objects

Paul Kobialka[1], Rudolf Schlatte[1], Gunnar Rye Bergersen[1,2],
Einar Broch Johnsen[1](✉), and Silvia Lizeth Tapia Tarifa[1]

[1] Department of Informatics, University of Oslo, Oslo, Norway
{paulkob,rudi,gunnab,einarj,sltarifa}@ifi.uio.no
[2] GrepS B.V., Utrecht, The Netherlands

Abstract. The servitization of business makes companies increasingly
dependent on providing carefully designed user experiences for their service offerings. User journeys model services from the user's perspective,
but user journeys are today mainly constructed and analyzed manually.
Recent work analyzing user journeys as games enable optimal service-
provider strategies to be automatically derived, assuming a restricted
user behavior. Complementing this work, we here develop an actor-based
modeling framework for user journeys that is parametric in user behavior and service-provider strategies, using the active-object modeling language ABS. Strategies for the service provider, such as those derived for
user journey games, can be automatically imported into the framework.
Our work enables prescriptive simulation-based analyses, as strategies
can be evaluated and compared in scenarios with rich user behavior.

1 Introduction

Companies increasingly offer services to enhance their product range, a development termed the *servitization of business* [48]. The success of these services
is highly dependent on user satisfaction: If the users are satisfied with how they
experience the offered service, the companies are rewarded financially without
increasing their risk [23]. Therefore, to provide successful services, companies
need to adjust and improve their services from the *users'* perspective. However,
services are usually analyzed from the *managerial* perspective, centered on the
company and not on the users.

User journeys allow services to be analyzed from the user perspective, with
the aim of understanding and hopefully improving the user's experience of a
service. User journeys model a user's actual path through a service by capturing
so-called touchpoints; these reflect communication between the user and the service provider, or actions performed by the user. Due to lacking formalization and

This work is part of the *Smart Journey Mining* project (Research Council of Norway,
grant no. 312198) and the SIRIUS Centre for Scalable Data Access (Research Council
of Norway, grant no. 237889).

F. de Boer et al. (Eds.): *Active Object Languages: Current Research Trends*,
LNCS 14360, pp. 199–225, 2024.
https://doi.org/10.1007/978-3-031-51060-1_8

tool support, the analysis of user journeys is today mainly a manual process [25]: analysts collect feedback on a service from a representative group of users (e.g., by means of questionnaires) to manually construct a user journey map, look for typical pain points, and possibly suggest improvements to the user journey. Because the user journey analysis is manual, the process is not easily applied to complex services or analyzed with respect to many users.

The interaction between a service provider and a user can be formalized as a game [31,32]. Users interact with the service provider to achieve a specific goal and the service provider may adopt different strategies to handle the users. Strategies for these games can be automatically analyzed using model checking tools such as UPPAAL [21] and PRISM [16] to reveal insights about the user journey. The analysis of user journey games can identify pain points in the user journeys (e.g., states where users abandon their journey), where the user journey could be improved. User journey games assume that all users are equally antagonistic, i.e., users always choose the worst possible action. However, in a real scenario users are not always uniformly antagonistic to the service provider, which makes it interesting to consider approaches that can relax this assumption.

In this paper, we propose to model user journeys by means of actors, to explore more diverse user behavior, complementing previous work on user journey games. We model a service provider and concurrent users as independent actors. The resulting actor model allows us to capture richer interaction scenarios between users and a service provider, and facilitates more realistic models than with user journey games, e.g., to explore several different service-provider strategies. Further, we consider parameterized and randomized user models to differentiate user behavior and explore the effect of service-provider strategies under different assumptions about such user behavior. Specifically, we investigate a user compliance parameter expressing the probability of a user waiting for the service provider's guidance instead of just taking a random action (e.g., the willingness or capability of users to follow instructions). Our model supports prescriptive analysis of user journeys by varying service-provider strategies and comparing the consequences of strategic decisions in the user journey.

We implement the user journey model as an actor-based simulation framework, using the active objects of ABS [27,29]. ABS is a timed actor-based modeling language, which supports cooperative scheduling and the specification of timing- and resource-aware behavior. Cooperative scheduling allows a process, executing in an actor, to be suspended while waiting for an event to occur, such that another process that is able to make progress can execute. Timed semantics allow the specification of the temporal behavior in the model. Resource-aware behavior takes a supply-and-demand perspective of execution, relating locations that provide resources to actors that require them for executing their active processes and modeling part of a system that has limited resources.

In this paper, we focus on the development of the core framework using ABS constructs without time and resources. We envision exploiting the time and resource aspects of ABS to reveal the bottlenecks of the service due to the waiting times of users and limited resources in the service (e.g., waiting for telephone calls or manual checks in the service). Towards this aim, we now focus on capturing the functional aspects of our proposed actor framework, which is parametric in both user behavior and the service provider's strategy. For example, service provider strategies derived using the above-mentioned model checking techniques can be automatically imported into our simulation framework.

Recent extensions to the ABS simulation tool [42], implemented in Erlang [3], allow the parameters of the framework to be instantiated in a data-driven way by means of SQL queries to instantiate user behavior and service-provider strategies into user-defined datatypes in ABS, that later can be used to drive the execution of the model. We then use simulations to conduct experiments on the resulting user journey model for different user parameters, i.e. we investigate user journeys for varying probabilities of user compliance on randomized users. We evaluate our actor model of user journeys on an industrial case study; the results are reviewed by a long-term employee of the cooperating company, who is also the third author of this paper.

In short, the contributions of this paper are:

1. an active-object model for user journeys that is parametric in user behavior and in service-provider strategies,
2. a data-driven simulation framework to evaluate and compare different strategies for the service-provider, and
3. an application of the simulation framework to an industrial case study.

2   Motivating Scenario

Consider an imaginary company TESTME ltd. that offers evaluations of programming skills. Companies searching for new developers commission TESTME to conduct tests of their applicants to determine their level of programming skills. TESTME is paid per user (i.e., a user is here an applicant to the commissioning company) that completes the evaluation and does not withdraw in the middle of the evaluation process. Therefore, TESTME wants to investigate the user experience when users engage in the tests of the evaluation process and hires a team of analysts to analyze the user journey. The analysts start by conducting questionnaires with selected users and manually generate, based on the answers, a so-called user journey map outlining the experiences and feedback from the questionnaires. The user journey map may reveal pain points in the user journey, i.e., interactions hindering a successful completion of the skill evaluation.

To improve the user journey and engage the user more actively, TESTME may consider different changes in the evaluation process based on the information gained from the user journey analysis. Further, the company would like to differentiate the user journey analysis depending on the users' skill level, assuming that users at different skill levels behave differently during the evaluation process. To facilitate a continuous evaluation of user journeys, the analysts need an automated process of user journey analysis that does not depend on the manual processing of questionnaires. To address this bottleneck, previous work by the authors proposes the use of recorded logs from the system to automatically generate a model of the user journey, called a *user journey game* [32]. This approach drastically reduces the time until realistic models are available. User journey games and strategies that ensure (or increase the chances for) a successful outcome of these games are introduced in Sect. 4.1.

The user journey games can be used by the team of analysts at TESTME to derive (winning) strategies suitable for the service provider, i.e., strategies that guide users toward completing the evaluation. However, the analysts struggle with the strict assumptions in user journey games, needed for successful analysis. User journey games do not distinguish users with, e.g., different skill levels, preventing the desired prescriptive analysis based on different users. To overcome these limitations, we here propose to model user journeys using active objects in the Abstract Behavioural Specification (ABS) language [27] (ABS is summarized in Sect. 4.2), and integrate the strategies derived from user journey games in an active object setting. The resulting workflow is outlined in Fig. 2.

Sections 5.1 and 5.2 discuss how to model user journeys as active objects (*Step 1* in Fig. 2), where we describe the transfer from UPPAAL [34] models to ABS and the intermediate steps needed to encode generated strategies. Section 5.3 introduces parameterized user behavior to differentiate users and expands on the model generation. The model is further specified with additional user parameters so that assumptions needed for games are removed (*Step 2*). Further, we simulate different kinds of users to evaluate possible changes to the service provider's behavior (*Step 3*). Our simulation model is parameterized in the user behavior and allows adaptations to reflect different user behavior, corresponding to the different kinds of users encountered by the company. Section 6 describes the conducted simulations and evaluates our approach on a real case study. We summarize our work in Sect. 7 and outline future work.

3   Related Work

We discuss related work with respect to the data-driven analysis of user journeys and the modeling capabilities provided by the active object language ABS. To the best of our knowledge, this is the first work on modeling user journeys in an actor or active object language, giving all actors an operative role.

User journeys express the interactions between a service provider and its users from the users' perspective [22,46]. Various modeling notations have been proposed to support the blueprinting process [13], establishing a model of the planned interactions between the user and service provider for a service. Approaches to create user journey diagrams include [5,18,26,33,39,40]; in most of these approaches, diagrams are created by hand after conducting surveys and questionnaires. Digital support exists in e.g. [33] to visualize static information of the interactions such as the time spent from the user's perspective, the experience per interaction, etc.

The *Customer Journey Modeling Language* (CJML) [24,26] offers two diagram types to highlight different aspects of the users' perspective: *customer journey network diagrams* display the interaction between the user and all sub-contractors, *customer journey diagrams* display the impressions from the users' point of view. CJML highlights deviations in the actual journey, the actual impressions a user has in the service, from the planned journey, the planned impressions. The *Smart Journey Mining* project aims to build data-driven tool support for user journeys [25]. Therefore, CJML was actively extended for digital support; CJML v2.0 provides an XML format for the in- and export of actual and planned user journeys [26].

Data-driven methods from process mining [1] for process discovery have been successfully applied to discover user journeys from recorded logs. Bernard *et al.* [8,10] investigate the possibility of using process mining for user journeys, they use hierarchical clustering and user-defined goals to abstract from a large number of journeys [7], and propose a method to discover user journeys from logs at varying levels of granularity [9]. Terragni and Hassani [44] investigate user journeys in the form of web logs and their optimization by building recommender systems proposing user-specific actions optimizing key performance indicators [45]. In contrast, our work focuses on the modeling aspect of user journeys with active objects and simulations to gain prescriptive insights into the service provider behavior and user journeys.

Formal methods allow the verification and analysis of discovered models for desired properties. David *et al.* present TAPAAL [19], a model checker for timed-arc Petri nets, which has been used by Bertolini *et al.* [11] to verify requirements in the healthcare domain. Kobialka *et al.* [31,32] proposed *user journey games* as a formal model for user journeys, where the user and service provider are independent actors competing for a successful user journey. In [31] the approach is applied to a large process mining benchmark log and a state reduction method on event level is proposed.

Challenges for leveraging formal, compositional language semantics to industrially applicable tools, including how to input/output real-world data, have been discussed in the context of ABS in [43]. The simulation tool of ABS has previously been used to model and analyze large use cases (e.g., [2,12,30,36,37,42]); in particular, Turin *et al.* [47] use ABS to build and analyze a formal model for cloud deployment in Kubernetes, illustrating the impact of large loads of users.

4   Preliminaries

4.1   User Journeys as Weighted Games

A game [4,15,16,21] consists of players that alternate in deciding on the action to take as the game transitions from one state to the next. Players may have strategies to try to force a specific outcome of the game; e.g., a player may try to reach a desired outcome of the game or to ensure that certain states are never reached. Actions in a game can have weights, e.g., to express rewards or penalties when taking an action, transforming the game into a weighted game.

A *weighted game* [15] is a tuple $(\Gamma, A_c, A_u, E, s_0, T, w)$ with a set Γ of states, sets A_c, A_u of *controllable* and *uncontrollable* actions (or labels) with $A_c \cap A_u = \emptyset$, a transition relation $E \subseteq \Gamma \times A_c \cup A_u \times \Gamma$, an initial state $s_0 \in \Gamma$, a set $T \subseteq \Gamma$ of final states, and a weight function $w : E \to \mathbb{R}$ that assigns weights to transitions. When analyzing a two-player game in which one player (the controller) takes controllable actions and the other player takes uncontrollable actions, it is assumed that only the controllable actions in A_c can be selected by the analyzer — the actions in A_u are nondeterministically decided by an adversarial environment, playing against the controller. If both players have actions available, the uncontrollable actions have precedence over the controllable actions.

In *user journey games* [32], the service provider and user are modeled as players in a two-player game, each with their own set of actions. Formally, a user journey game is a weighted game $(\Gamma, A_c, A_u, E, s_0, T, T_s, w)$, where $T_s \subseteq T$ are the successful final states. By using games as the user journey model, we inherently assume that (1) no player performs more than one activity concurrently, and that (2) user journeys are goal-driven processes where the user and service provider have the incentive to achieve the journey's goal, i.e., to reach a successful final state. For a user-centric analysis, the user is modeled as the adversarial environment that takes uncontrollable actions and the service provider as the controller that takes controllable actions. We require that the service provider has suitable responses for all user interactions and does not constrain the user.

The weights in user journey games reflect the users' experience as reflected in the system logs in the following way: interactions that only occur in successful journeys receive a positive weight, interactions that only occur in unsuccessful journeys receive a negative weight, and interactions that occur in both successful and unsuccessful journeys receive a neutral weight. The sum of weights along a (partial) user journey is called *gas*, and reflects the aggregated experiences of the respective users. In the games, a unique start state is introduced to ensure that all users start from the same state, and positive and negative final states are introduced to differentiate successful from unsuccessful journeys.

User journey games are generated from logs by (1) mining a transition system from the traces in the log, (2) transforming the transition system into a game by defining *controllable* and *uncontrollable* actions, and (3) adding user feedback by computing weights on the transitions. An entropy-based function assigns high positive weights to actions that primarily occur in successful journeys, high negative weights to actions that primarily occur in unsuccessful journeys and neutral weights to actions in successful and unsuccessful journeys. The generation of user journey games from event logs is detailed in [32].

A *strategy* [20] assigns a set of possible actions to every state in a game. Formally, given a game $G = (\Gamma, A_c, A_u, E, s_0, T, w)$, a strategy for G is a partial function $\sigma : \Gamma \to 2^{A_c \cup \{\lambda\}} / \{\emptyset\}$ from states in Γ to the power-set of controllable actions A_c; here, λ denotes the "wait" action (i.e., no controllable action is taken and the controller gives the next move to the environment) and the possibility of "no action" (expressed by $\{\emptyset\}$) is removed. We say that a player follows a strategy σ if, in every state $s \in \Gamma$, the player only selects actions in $\sigma(s)$. If there is a strategy that guarantees a desired property, the controller can enforce the desired outcome by following this strategy, preventing the adversary from making a choice that violates the property.

We here consider *memoryless* strategies, i.e., strategies where the choice of the next action only depends on the last state. Maler *et al.* [38] have shown that memoryless strategies suffice for reachability properties. Note that strategies can be nondeterministic; i.e., there might be more than one possible action available to enforce the desired outcome. We call a strategy *deterministic* if only one possible action can be selected in any state (i.e., $|\sigma(s)| = 1$ for all $s \in \Gamma$).

UPPAAL STRATEGO [21] is a model checker for games in the UPPAAL tool suite [34], which combines UPPAAL TIGA [4] with the stochastic model checker UPPAAL SMC to stochastically model check games; i.e., it verifies properties in a game setting through random simulations and hypothesis testing until sufficient statistical evidence is reached. UPPAAL STRATEGO allows refining a strategy towards an expected goal, e.g., to find the shortest path to a successful final state [20]. UPPAAL STRATEGO constructs strategies for adversarial users. When refining or evaluating strategies with respect to numerical criteria, e.g. estimating the expected number of steps in a user journey under a certain strategy, UPPAAL STRATEGO uses stochastic simulations.

4.2   The ABS Modeling Language

The *Abstract Behaviour Specification* [27] language (ABS) is a language for behavioral modeling of distributed systems. ABS is an active object language [14], combining executable actor-based semantics with asynchronous method calls and first-class futures. Data is modeled via a functional, side-effect-free layer of algebraic data types and parametric functions. The actor behavior is expressed in a sequential, imperative way, with explicit suspension points for cooperative scheduling in each actor. ABS has a Java-like syntax and is supported by a range of analysis tools (see, e.g., [41, 49]). The internal state of each actor can be modeled in detail or completely abstracted, depending on the purpose of the model. The following features of ABS are useful in creating behavioral models:

Asynchronous method calls and first-class futures: The essential feature of a distributed system is that communication (sending a method call) and execution (scheduling an incoming call) are decoupled. The caller can continue execution until the result of a call is needed, and the callee can schedule calls from multiple callers as needed.

Process suspension and boolean guards: Inside an ABS actor, many processes can execute in a cooperative manner, with only one process running at any given time. Processes suspend themselves when waiting for a method call result or waiting for a boolean condition over the actor state.

Data Structures and Functions: Algebraic datatypes are used to model actor state and data that is passed between actors via method calls. Functions that are calculated over such datatypes are side effect-free.

```
data StrategyEntry =
  StrategyEntry(String strategy_state, String strategy_action);

def List<StrategyEntry> strategy(String strategy_name)
  = builtin(sqlite3, "../data/journeys.sqlite",
      "SELECT state, action FROM strategies WHERE strategy_name = ?",
      strategy_name);
```

Fig. 1. Querying the "journeys.sqlite" database from within ABS, passing in an ABS value as query parameter.

Database Access. For the work presented in this paper, we use the recently added capabilities of ABS to import structured data stored in a SQLite database file into a running ABS model.

Table 1. ABS to SQL datatype mapping: the first and second columns show the SQL result to ABS datatype conversion; the second and third columns show how ABS datatypes are converted into query parameter values.

SQLite return value	ABS	SQLite query parameter
INTEGER	Int	INTEGER
INTEGER or REAL	Float	REAL
INTEGER or REAL	Rat	REAL
INTEGER (0 = False, otherwise True)	Bool	0 or 1
TEXT	String	TEXT
Row of the above	User-defined datatype	n/a

Structured data stored in an SQLite database can be directly read into ABS by converting query results into ABS datatypes. Executing a query inside ABS produces a list of ABS data, which can be used like any other list after the query has finished. If the query only returns rows of one value each, e.g. String, the type of the query result inside ABS will be List<String>. If, on the other hand, the query returns tuples containing more than one value, the query will name the ABS datatype that holds each resulting row. The constructor of this ABS datatype has to accept parameters of the same number and type as returned by the query. For example, the result from a query like SELECT name, age FROM persons, which returns (string, integer) tuples can be stored in an ABS datatype defined like data Person = Person(String, Int). Table 1 shows how SQL results are mapped to ABS values, and how ABS query parameters are mapped to SQL values.

Figure 1 illustrates how to import data into ABS from an SQLite file. For this example, let us assume that various strategies for a user journey game have been stored in the file journeys.sqlite containing entries that relate strategy_name, state, and action (See Sect. 4.1). It is possible to query such a

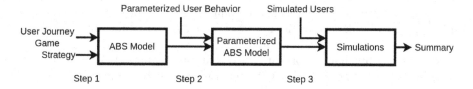

Fig. 2. Workflow pipeline.

file such that the records are stored in a list of strategy entries. In this example we define in ABS a datatype `StrategyEntry` that holds one entry from one strategy, and the function `strategy` that reads one full strategy from the SQLite table and stores it into a list `List<StrategyEntry>`.

Queries into the SQLite database can be parameterized in the standard way: parameters inside the query string are denoted by a question mark (`?`); values for these parameters are supplied as additional arguments to the query. Only basic datatypes (string, integer, float) can be supplied as parameters. The `strategy_name` parameter to the `strategy` function in Fig. 1 is used as such a query parameter; its value ends up in the corresponding `WHERE` clause in the SQL query sent to the database engine.

5   Workflow Pipeline

We now consider a pipeline for analyzing user journeys by means of simulations of an active object model of user journeys. The pipeline is depicted in Fig. 2 and consists of the following steps:

- *Step 1:* An ABS modeling framework imports user journey games and strategies from a database;
- *Step 2:* The model is adjusted by instantiating parameterized user behavior and modifying transitions to `finNeg` to be uncontrollable; and
- *Step 3:* Simulations are used to explore aspects of the user journey for given strategies of the service provider.

We develop an ABS model that implements users and service providers as active objects that communicate and run in parallel with each other. Additionally, a `WorkflowProvider` class that wraps all knowledge about strategies and available controllable and uncontrollable actions, serves as common knowledge base for both users and service providers. The model is parameterizable wrt. strategy, user behavior, and number of users. The output of a model run is the number and type of users in each final state, together with the average journey length and accumulated gas.

Generated games and strategies (see Sect. 4.1) are aggregated in an SQLite database that can be read from within ABS (see Sect. 4.2). In particular, strategies for user journey games can be generated from user journey games using UPPAAL STRATEGO and integrated in the ABS model to guide users in simulations. Since the generated strategies are memoryless, they can thus be exported as a mapping from states to actions. Refining a strategy corresponds to refining the mapping to be deterministic, i.e. there is at most one suggested action per state.

We now explain how to prepare data that can be imported into the ABS model in Sect. 5.1, then how the ABS model is constructed in Sect. 5.2.

5.1   Data Preparation for the Workflow Pipeline

In Step 1 of the workflow, we import user journey games and strategies into ABS. The workflow produces a single database file that contains all necessary information to simulate different scenarios.

The user journey game is transformed into a CSV format, that enumerates states and available actions in each state, as a series of entries (source state, action, target state, controllable or uncontrollable, cost) that are imported into a database, see Fig. 3. We export strategies from UPPAAL STRATEGO 10 by using export queries:

saveStrategy("strategy.xml", strategy).

Strategies are then also transformed into tabular CSV format, mapping states to actions, see Fig. 4, and we import the tables into the same SQLite database. Both imports cover Step 1 in Fig. 2. In the *start* state, the company assigns a virtual instance to the user, *AssignInstance*. When it is *Started*, the company has to wait for the user to work on the *TaskEvent*, expressed as a *Wait* action in the strategy and an uncontrollable action in the process model.

Source State	Action	Target State	Controllable	Cost
start	Registered	Registered	False	-1.9
start	AssignInstance	AssignInstance	True	-22
Started	TaskEvent	TaskEvent - 0	False	-2
ResultApproval	ResultsAccepted	ResultsAccepted	False	18

Fig. 3. Tables imported into the ABS model: The transition system as a list.

We adapt the user journey game to run simulations where users can give up in the middle of their journey (and hence, reach the unsuccessful final state). In the imported user journey game, actions leading to the unsuccessful final state were defined as controllable; otherwise, model checking could never guarantee to reach the successful final state (cf.

Source State	Action
start	AssignInstance
Started	Wait
ResultApproval	Wait

Fig. 4. Tables imported into the ABS model: The strategy as a state to action mapping.

Sect. 1). This restriction is not needed for simulation; in the adapted version, actions leading to the unsuccessful final state are modeled as uncontrollable actions. These adaptations cover Step 2.

Step 3 uses simulations to explore the model and possible service provider strategies. We simulate scenarios that combine the parameterized model with different users. In the ABS modeling framework, the model of the service provider and the user models are kept separate for easier construction and utilization.

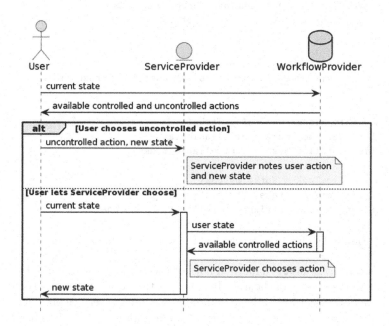

Fig. 5. Sequence diagram of one interaction in the simulation.

5.2   Modeling the User and the Service Provider

In the ABS model, the structure of the underlying user journey game is implemented via a component called *WorkflowProvider*, which is consulted by the user and the service provider objects. The ABS model contains one interface for users, one for service providers, and one for the workflow provider. Figure 5 shows the exchange of messages between the actors in the simulation.

Figure 6 shows the interfaces and data types of the simulation. As shown in the interaction diagram, the user is the "active" participant that initiates each round of choosing between actions. Consequently, the User interface offers no methods to be called from outside.

Since both the user and service provider need knowledge about the user journey game, the model encapsulates this knowledge in a common interface WorkflowProvider. Its method available_tasks returns all available controllable and uncontrollable actions, given a user identifier and the user's state. (The user identifier may be used to implement per-user strategies.)

The user chooses whether to perform a controllable or uncontrollable action and informs the service provider about its decision (see Fig. 5). The

```
interface User { }

interface ServiceProvider {
    Unit notifyUncontrolledAction(
        Int user_id, String uncontrolled_action, String new_state);
    Maybe<WorkflowTask> performControlledAction(
        Int user_id, String current_state);
}

interface WorkflowProvider {
    WorkflowTasks available_tasks(Int user_id, String state);
}

data WorkflowTasks = WorkflowTasks(
    List<WorkflowTask> controllable_tasks,
    List<WorkflowTask> uncontrollable_tasks);

data WorkflowTask = WorkflowTask(
    String origin_state, String target_state,
    String action, String controllable, Float cost);
```

Fig. 6. The internal structure of the workflow simulation model.

notifyUncontrolledAction method notifies the service provider about the chosen action and new state of the user. In contrast, the performControlledAction method leaves the decision of the action to be taken to the service provider, which in turn consults the workflow provider about its options. The chosen action is returned to the user, who updates its state accordingly.

The classes implementing these interfaces can be seen in the online repository,[1] which features the implementation of the workflow pipeline. The main variability is located in the implementations of the WorkflowProvider interface, where the modeler can set up workflow descriptions with varying strategies, or no strategy at all. The user class is parameterized with the likelihood of performing an uncontrollable action if applicable. The service provider class relies on the workflow provider for most of its behavior, but can be extended to implement resource-sensitive behavior (see the discussion of future work in Sect. 7).

5.3   Parameterized User Behaviour

User journey games aggregate the behavior of several users into one model, thereby assuming that all users are equally antagonistic; i.e., all users in the same state have the same available actions, and, when the service provider and the user both have available actions, all users have higher precedence than the service provider. These assumptions are captured in the strategies generated by UPPAAL STRATEGO: antagonistic users exploit their precedence over the service

---

[1] https://github.com/smartjourneymining/abs_journeys_aol-23/releases/tag/ AOL23.

provider when selecting the next action, and two different users in the same state can not be differentiated.

In reality, users differ based on individual properties which are abstracted away in user journey games. In our simulation framework, we would like the user model to capture structural differences between users that are not expressed through choices in the user journey game but are determined already at the beginning of the game.

For this purpose, we let the user model have *parameterized user behavior* by introducing a parameter to the user model that is unknown to the service provider but fixed at run-time, i.e. for every instantiated user. This user parameter p ranges from $[0, 1]$ and models the probability that the user waits for the service provider's guidance; with probability $1-p$ the user takes an uncontrollable action. This way, the parameter models the "compliance" of the user, changing the probability to wait for the service provider's actions or taking an arbitrary, uncontrollable transition. A non-compliant user, always taking uncontrollable actions, can be expressed with $p = 0$. A compliant user can be expressed with $p = 1$, waiting for the service provider's actions until its activity is required. All values between 0 and 1 express different levels of "compliance"; users that have a certain probability to wait for the service provider's action or to take an uncontrollable action. Additionally, to allow for a wider range of possible user behaviour, besides antagonistic users, we model users that decide their actions randomly. Figure 7 outlines the implementation of the parameterized user class. We discretized compliance probability p with integers ranging from 0 to 100. In the main block of our simulation, shown in Fig. 8, we generate a workflow object, `WorklfowProvider provider`, a company object for that workflow, `Company company` and several parameterized users, `List<User> users`. The user objects, which contain a `run()` method, start the simulation; their results are gathered in a map storing for each end state a triple over the total number of users in that state, the average number of steps and the average gas; further information about individual users is gathered in the background.

In our model, we differentiate users solely based on their compliance parameters. Remark that service providers may need to invest significant effort in determining their users' parameters to adjust their offers and fine-tune services. Discovering crucial user parameters is not trivial and requires extensive testing. Therefore, we investigate in the case study presented in Sect. 6 whether user compliance is a suitable way to capture realistic user behavior. Adjusting the compliance allows us to investigate different game settings without having to collect additional new data.

6 Case Study

6.1 Context

GrepS[2] is a company offering programming skill evaluations for Java programmers. GrepS is commissioned by external companies for recruiting, training, and

---

[2] See the webpage of GrepS for further details: https://www.greps.com/.

```
class ParametricUser(
    WorkflowProvider provider, Company company, Int compliance)
  implements User
{
    Bool finished = False;
    String current_state = "start";

    Unit run() {
      while (!finished) {
          WorkflowTasks possible_tasks =
              await provider!available_tasks(current_state);
          WorkflowTasks u_tasks = uncontrollable_tasks(possible_tasks);
          WorkflowTasks c_tasks = controllable_tasks(possible_tasks);
          if (u_tasks != Nil && c_tasks != Nil)
          {
              // Choose with the given probability whether to perform
              // an uncontrollable or controllable action.
              if (random(100) < compliance) {
                  this.offerControllableAction();
              } else {
                  this.uncontrollableAction(u_tasks);
              }
          } else if (u_tasks != Nil) {
              // Only uncontrollable actions available
              this.uncontrollableAction(u_tasks);
          } else if (c_tasks != Nil) {
              // Only controllable actions available
              this.offerControllableAction();
          } else {
              // No action available: User reached an end state
              finished = True;
          }
      }
    }

    Unit offerControllableAction() {
      Maybe<WorkflowTask> action =
          await company!controlledAction(current_state);
      switch (action) {
        Just(the_task) => {
          current_state = target_state(the_task);
        }
        Nothing => finished = True;
      }
    }
}
```

Fig. 7. Implementation of the parameterized user class.

```
// Main block.
{
  // Parameters to set for the chosen experiment
  Int n_users = ...
  Int obedience = ...

  // Instantiate the underlying workflow model
  WorkflowProvider provider  = new WorkflowProvider("non_det");
  // Create company object
  Company company = new Company(provider);

  // Create parameterized user objects
  List<User> users =
      await util!create_users(n_users, provider, company, obedience);

  // Aggregate results (end state => (count, avg. steps, avg. gas))
  Map<String, Triple<Int, Int, Float>> end_states =
      await util!collectUsersInMap(users, file);
}
```

Fig. 8. Creation of actors.

certification. The service that GrepS provides is based on prior research [6]. *Customers* of GrepS are typically companies that hire or train developers, which are the *users* of the service. Users are normally given one to two weeks to complete their programming skill evaluation.

A typical programming skill evaluation requires the user to complete three phases using GrepS: (1) sign-up, (2) solve a set of authentic programming tasks, and (3) approve to share the results (via a skill report) with the customer, i.e. the commissioning company. In a *successful* user journey, all three phases are completed in order and the customer receives the report. In an *unsuccessful* journey, the user permanently stops using the service at any phase, or does not approve the sharing of the results with the customer.

The data we analyze are system logs with recorded events from the interactions between users and the GrepS system. These system logs are an extended version of the logs published as part of the work of Kobialka *et al.* in [32], as the logs we use also contain the programming skill evaluations that are calculated by the GrepS system. An extract of the extended data is shown in Fig. 10. In this previous work, we report on the systematic generation and analysis of the GrepS user journey game. Figure 9 displays a simplified illustration of the task-solving and approval phase, leaving out the previously analyzed sign-up phase (states T0–T7). Controllable transitions are depicted as solid lines, uncontrollable transitions as dashed lines; transitions with positive weight are colored green, and those with negative weight are red. Each task during phase 2 consists of a pair of states: the first state is the solving of a task and the second is user feedback on the task. State T8 is a set-up task that is not used to evaluate skill, and T9 its corresponding user feedback. States T10–T17 are alternating tasks and feedback with T10 being the first practice task, T12 the second task, T14 the third task, and T16 the fourth task; the respective feedback is submitted after each single task. After each task has been submitted by the user, the system attempts to score the solution to the task and update the user's skill evaluation based on all solutions that have been scored so far. If the scoring process is successful, the log is updated ("Overall scores updated"). The increasing weights on edges along T8–T18 result from more users completing their tasks, i.e. users struggle with the first three tasks but from the third task on are all subsequent tasks completed [32]. In state T18, the user is informed that all tasks have been completed and explains the next steps that are to be completed within a specific number of workdays (as agreed with each GrepS customer in a service level agreement, SLA). States T21–T25 form the review phase, and T25 is the user approval for sharing the required report.

6.2   Evaluations of Users' Programming Skills by the GrepS System

The extended system logs capture many events with evaluated programming skills per user. We consider the last evaluation event as the *final* evaluated score (it captures the overall score of a user), and refer to the previous evaluation events as *tentative* scores. For each task solved by the user, the system evaluates the tentative skill level based on all available information (i.e., the current and any previous tasks that can be scored automatically). Note that the final score may involve partially human-graded tasks on dimensions such as readability, proper use of variable names, or other aspects that cannot be evaluated automatically. Thus, a user may have only one final skill score but can have many tentative skill scores during phase 2.

The unit of measurement used for the skill score is logits (i.e., the logarithm of the odds), which is frequently used within education or psychology to represent differences in skills and abilities on an interval scale using the Polytomous Rasch Model. A 5 on the scale used by GrepS is defined as the averagely skilled professional Java developer reported by Bergersen *et al.* [6], who also reported a standard deviation of skill scores of 1.3 logits. Note that this type of scale does not allow for ratio comparisons of skills (e.g., "someone is twice as

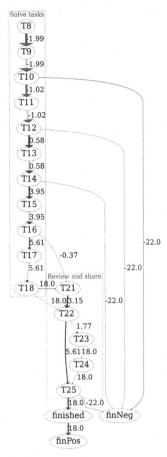

Fig. 9.   GrepS   user   journey   game (excerpt): task solving and approval phases.

skilled") because the number zero skill is not defined. However, the magnitude of differences is nevertheless constant across the range of the scale so that the magnitude of differences can be represented using a standardized effect size [17]. For example, a difference of 1.5 logits (i.e., a difference between 5.0 and 6.5, or 4.0 and 5.5) in skill would be considered a "large" effect by conventional standards (i.e., Cohen's $d = 0.8$).

Timestamp	⋯	Metadata
5245944	⋯	Registered
5780525	⋯	Registered
6104714	⋯	Activated
6104714	⋯	Logged in: Web page
6106191	⋯	Overall scores updated: [rasch.skill: 2.59 ...

Fig. 10. Extract of GrepS' system logs.

Skill evaluations in the provided system logs reveal an association between successful and unsuccessful journeys. Figure 11 compares the box-plots of skill scores for successful journeys, in orange, and unsuccessful journeys, in blue. We ignore all journeys without a skill evaluation[3] and only use the final evaluated score per user. The current comparison contains a *survival* bias since we ignore the skill levels of all users that did not receive any skill evaluation. For the 11 unsuccessful journeys, the median skill level is 4.2, thus about

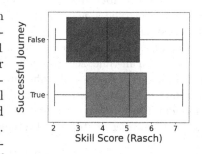

Fig. 11. Skill level comparison for successful and unsuccessful journeys from GrepS' system logs.

0.6 standard deviation for the less-than-average developer. For the 20 successful journeys, the median recorded skill level was about the same as an average developer (5.1). Both box-plots in Fig. 11 range from 2 to 7. Observe that the data distribution of unsuccessful journeys has more variance: its lower quartile reaches significantly lower than the lower quartile of the successful journeys. The upper quartile of the successful journeys reaches higher and is denser than the one of unsuccessful journeys.

Both box-plots indicate that the GrepS service is currently better suited for at-least average proficient developers. Developers below average, with a score of less than 3.5, have a clear disadvantage. The log also demonstrates that above-average developers fail and below-average developers succeed. The outcome of the journey is not determined by the skill level but also by other factors.

---

[3] We observed that system logs contain a large amount of very short unsuccessful journeys with no events containing scores. Including all these journeys would negatively bias the comparison and therefore we remove them from the comparison.

6.3   Simulation Analysis

We conduct several simulated scenarios in which we instantiate the parameterized user journey game, evaluate different service provider strategies, and test varying levels of user compliance, as a parametric behavior for users. We investigate the impact of different game strategies and the implications for the service provider to use the refined strategy to have a successful journey outcome and improve the user experience.

Building the Baseline of the Model. The initial model is constructed by modeling the GrepS user journey game and importing it into ABS, along with its corresponding UPPAAL game strategies for the service provider. We implement three strategies that the service provider can use: (1) a random one for a random selection between all available actions to the next transition in the game (no strategy), (2) a nondeterministic strategy, and (3) a refined strategy, minimizing the number of steps to reach a positive outcome, concretely, to reach the state finPos, see Fig. 9. Strategies (2) and (3) are exported from UPPAAL STRATEGO into ABS, as described in Sect. 5.1. The users are randomized; i.e., they take a random, uncontrollable actions.

We first check that our ABS model reproduces the results generated in UPPAAL. The user is parameterized in its compliance, instantiated with a fixed probability at run-time, see Sect. 5.3. We calibrate our ABS model with suitable user compliance settings and sufficient many simulated users, such that simulation results are aligned with the results from UPPAAL STRATEGO. By doing so, our model reproduces the average amount of gas when reaching a final state and the average number of steps for the nondeterministic and refined strategy each.

Exploring Alternative Scenarios. We experimented with a less restrictive model by adapting the underlying game, where we removed some of the assumptions that were needed for the game analysis in UPPAAL STRATEGO. In particular, in UPPAAL STRATEGO the analysis requires a guaranteeing strategy for the service provider, thus, users are not allowed to give up in the middle of their journeys and those actions (solid lines, representing transitions in the game to the final negative state finNeg, see Fig. 9) are controlled by the service provider. We adapt the model by making these interactions uncontrollable (therefore, controlled by users). Further, the UPPAAL STRATEGO game assumes that users always have precedence over the service provider. We additionally adapt our simulated users with a compliance parameter p, with probability $1 - p$ for each user to select a random, uncontrollable action, thereby lifting the assumption of adversary users. In the active object model, the generated strategies no longer guarantee a successful user journey outcome. However, the simulations still allow us to explore the GrepS user journey game, using one of the strategies. We observed that in the parameterized active object model with uncontrollable transitions to finNeg, the random strategy aligns with the nondeterministic strategy since there are no activities that the service provider is not allowed to select. Therefore, we only compare the random strategy with the refined strategy.

Figure 12 compares different aspects of the parameterized active object model with the two strategies, where all transitions leading to unsuccessful journey outcomes are user-controlled. The chance of taking such transitions (and therefore determining the outcome of the journey) is given by the compliance probabilities. Figure 12a displays the number of successful journeys for given compliance probabilities (the parameter p), we run simulations with a total of 1000 users, and with different probabilities for noncompliance or giving up $(1 - p)$, ranging from 0% to 100% and increasing p with 20% in each simulation. When comparing the mean user journey length, the refined strategy improves the random strategy drastically since user journeys are significantly shorter in the refined strategy, see Fig. 12b. Figure 12c compares the accumulated gas, revealing that the refined strategy reduces the accumulated gas for compliant users slightly. For noncompliant users with a short journey, the refined strategy improves the average accumulated gas from an average below -80 to -40.

Moreover, we investigate the different states where users give up their journey in the adapted ABS model, according to different compliance levels. Figure 13 shows the simulation results. With decreasing compliance levels, more users leave the journey, due to several states that allow users to give up, the number of users reaching the positive outcome shrinks rapidly, see Figs. 13a and 13b. For compliant users, see Fig. 13c, the service provider has good chances to guide the user to a successful outcome.

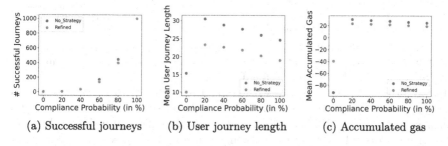

(a) Successful journeys   (b) User journey length   (c) Accumulated gas

Fig. 12. Comparison of different compliance probabilities and strategies.

Skill Level and Compliance. Observations from the system logs show that the average GrepS user is closely comparable with the simulations that consider 80% compliance, see Fig. 13c, and that $\frac{2}{3}$ of the users are successful. Concretely, in the provided log 18% of users gave up after the first task event, which aligns with the 20% decrease of users in the simulations, but only 9% gave up at the second and third tasks, which does not entirely align with the 16% and 12% decrease of users that is shown in the simulations, as well as 12% decrease of users at the reporting phase in the logs, with 6% decrease in the simulations.

We also investigate the relationship between the final skill score of users, detailed in Sect. 6.2, and the compliance parameter. Figure 14 shows the correspondence between the length of user journeys and the final skill level per

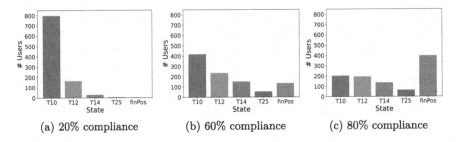

(a) 20% compliance   (b) 60% compliance   (c) 80% compliance

Fig. 13. Comparison of states where users stop in the simulated user journeys with different compliance probabilities; the company's goal is to maximize the reachability of finPos.

user. Results are grouped by skill level, where below or equal to 5 are sorted into the group of developers that are "below average", otherwise they are sorted into the group "above average". In comparison, Fig. 15 displays the simulated box-plots over user journey lengths for different compliance levels for the random strategy (Fig. 15a), and the refined strategy (Fig. 15b). While the length of user journeys vary from the user journey lengths observed in the logs when using the random strategy in the simulations, the refined

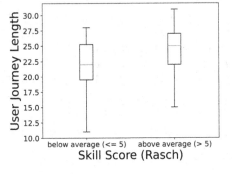

Fig. 14. Box-plots over user journey lengths per skill level in the system logs.

strategy produces user journeys with comparable lengths to those observed in the system logs. We further investigated the ratio of successful and unsuccessful journeys in the two skill groups. When ignoring users without a skill evaluation, 56% of unsuccessful user journeys belong to users that are scored "below average", and 73% of successful user journeys belong to users that are scored "above average". These values correspond to a compliance probability of about 85% for "below average" users and of more than 90% for "above average" users.

While not all aspects of the user-specific behavior could be replicated, our model is capable of differentiating different user groups as observed in the real-world system logs. By introducing one parameter for user compliance, we determine whether a user acts before the service provider and chooses an uncontrollable action. Whereas compliance appears to be a suitable notion to capture observed user behavior, users are in reality influenced by a wide range of parameters that are not independently recorded. We parameterized the modeling of user-specific behaviors and gained detailed insights into different kinds of users. The model adequately captured not only user journey lengths but also the distribution of final states and the number of successful journeys.

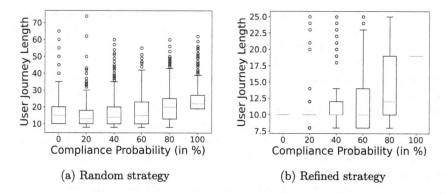

(a) Random strategy   (b) Refined strategy

Fig. 15. Box-plots over varying compliance levels and strategies in simulations.

6.4   Prescriptions

By using the simulation tool of the ABS active object language, we are able to adjust model details to conform to what is contained in the user logs. Previous game analysis required us to assume that users do not leave the journey, otherwise, no guaranteeing strategy could have been established. The active object model was adjusted to consider user parameters in the simulations, capturing various kinds of users. These adaptations allow service providers to evaluate the impact of possible changes on their services before implementing them. Several possible changes in either the strategy, the model, or both can be evaluated and the most promising ones can be implemented. Further, including user parameters in the model, allow us to adjust the simulation results towards the targeted users. In our case study, we compared different strategies and confirmed the suggestions from the model checker that the refined strategy is superior to the nondeterministic or random strategy. The strategies were generated in overapproximated games and tested in a more realistic setting. We could elaborate on differences between user groups and model them with proxy parameters, extracted from the system logs.

6.5   Evaluation

Our conclusions from the simulation analysis (Sect. 6.3) and new opportunities from exploring alternative scenarios (Sect. 6.4) can be summarised as follows:

1. more positive outcomes are related to "above average" skilled users,
2. compliance is a relevant proxy for user behavior (although with a still unresolved relation to programming skill), and
3. "what-if" scenarios may be used to simulate changes to the existing system for evaluating alternative directions for technical development in the future.

These insights have been further discussed with a long-term employee of the company, and third author of this paper, for their review. We summarize the feedback below.

Regarding point 1, more positive outcomes, GrepS is a user-focused service and is aware that different groups of users behave differently in their system. Depending on what a skill evaluation is used for, there are also situations where it is most sensible for a user to discontinue using the service. For example, if the first couple of programming tasks appear too difficult in a recruitment setting, a developer may opt out of the process and look for a different job. It is also known that less skilled developers are more resource-demanding in terms of needed support during the process, probably as a partial function of how well the user reads and understands the process and its requirements. At the same time, for a user-focused service, it is important to know which user groups are the key users, for which most of the resources should be used to keep satisfied with the service. Internally, the company is aware that less skilled users are less likely to complete all the programming tasks in Phase 2, or share an unsatisfying result during Phase 3.

Regarding point 2, compliance as a proxy of user behavior, companies need to challenge and further refine their own understandings of their key user groups. User parameters such as compliance—the willingness or capability to follow instructions—provide a more nuanced view than merely using programming skill evaluation to explain why some user journeys are unsuccessful. Compliant users tend to be more successful in their journey and have fewer problems solving the presented tasks, but it is at present unclear what the conceptual overlap is between "compliance" and factors such as technical skill or motivation.

Regarding point 3, the prescriptive analysis used to investigate "what-if" scenarios and to challenge assumptions that do not hold, GrepS is positive to evaluate such functionality more closely. For example, if a user in the present setup of the system stops solving a task, e.g. in states T10, T12, or T14, this user is unsuccessful. The simulation model could then attempt to answer the hypothetical question of what would happen if GrepS introduces a "user recovery" state where the sole goal is to bring the user back to the system, for example, by asking for feedback (is the user satisfied?), reminding the user (has the user forgot to continue?) or providing other kinds of targeted information (do the user know that valuable feedback is possible even though the report is not shared with GrepS' customer?). By estimating both expected costs (development time) and expected success (probabilities that users continue), such a simulation may yield better predictions of how many additional users would complete the analysis. If the simulation reveals that the additional users in the positive final state from a hypothetical intervention exceeds the cost of implementing it, such an intervention might be prioritized. Simulations of large and complex systems where relevant factors are parameterized, seem preferable to heavily relying on heuristics of what works (and doesn't) that require extensive experience to validate.

7   Conclusion and Future Work

This paper presents an active object simulation framework for user journeys. The framework can be combined with strategy analysis for service providers, based on model checking user journey games. We considered strategies generated in the model checker UPPAAL STRATEGO and showed that the results of model checking can be reproduced in our framework. Then, we extended the framework to parameterize the users' compliance with the intended user journey, and estimated how resilient different service provider strategies are to non-cooperating users. The active object framework allows prescriptive analysis, where the impact of changes can be evaluated before implementing them in the real system.

Previous analysis based on user journey games, using UPPAAL STRATEGO, over-approximates the service provider behavior, to establish strategies that guarantee a successful outcome. The active object simulation framework alleviates these assumptions, making the user journey model more realistic. The simulation framework uses two measures for the modeled user journeys: the total number of actions taken in the journey and the accumulated cost. When adapting the user journey game to the simulation framework, one has to evaluate if the strategy generated from the user journey game is compatible with the active object model. Otherwise, a random strategy might outperform a refined strategy. Therefore, it is important to compare refined strategies to a valid baseline, i.e. a random or nondeterministic strategy, and, if necessary, update the refined strategy to the new assumptions.

We present an industrial case study from GrepS, a small company offering programming skill evaluations to other companies. We investigated users with "below average" and "above average" proficiency. Our simulations reproduced findings from the Greps log, suggesting that GrepS is configured for "above average" proficient users. These users have a higher chance for a successful user journey with shorter user journeys than "below average" proficient users. In the case study, the active object model harmonized well with the refined strategy, user journey lengths were reduced and the final gas was kept at comparable levels in the system logs and simulations.

The presented active object simulation framework opens many interesting possibilities for future work. One obvious extension is to make the active object framework resource-sensitive, exploiting the resource-model of ABS [29]. The current model only considers gas as a resource, but every interaction between service provider and user has a duration and also requires physical resources, e.g. interactions with a GrepS employee. A time- and resource-sensitive model allows scenarios to be explored that show response times under various loads and "what-if" scenarios; e.g., whether adding personnel to answer user messages in a certain state of the user journey would increase overall completion rates. Such extension could consider load balancers that distribute or delegate activities in the service to workers with limited resources, mimicking resource management in cloud-based distributed systems, as previously modeled and analyzed using ABS with time and resources [28,35,37,47].

The current model is Markovian, as the next decision only depends on the current state. However, the model does provide access to the accumulated gas of users (i.e., the sum of the weights from previous interactions with the service provider). This allows richer models of decision-making to be investigated, where the current decision not only depends on the users' compliance parameter but also on past experiences by taking into account the accumulated gas, capturing how much "steam" the user has left to continue the journey. Accordingly, it would also be interesting to investigate further model parameters and their influence on successful user journeys (e.g., to fine-tune compliance or to capture other user behavior characteristics).

Conflict of Interest. The third author has financial interests in the company (GrepS) that owns the skill testing tool evaluated in the case study in this work.

References

1. van der Aalst, W.: Process Mining - Data Science in Action, 2nd edn. Springer, Heidelberg (2016). https://doi.org/10.1007/978-3-662-49851-4
2. Albert, E., et al.: Formal modeling and analysis of resource management for cloud architectures: an industrial case study using Real-Time ABS. Serv. Oriented Comput. Appl. **8**(4), 323–339 (2014). https://doi.org/10.1007/s11761-013-0148-0
3. Armstrong, J.: Programming Erlang: Software for a Concurrent World. Pragmatic Bookshelf, Raleigh (2007)
4. Behrmann, G., Cougnard, A., David, A., Fleury, E., Larsen, K.G., Lime, D.: UPPAAL-Tiga: time for playing games! In: Damm, W., Hermanns, H. (eds.) CAV 2007. LNCS, vol. 4590, pp. 121–125. Springer, Heidelberg (2007). https://doi.org/10.1007/978-3-540-73368-3_14
5. Berendes, C.I., Bartelheimer, C., Betzing, J.H., Beverungen, D.: Data-driven customer journey mapping in local high streets: A domain-specific modeling language. In: Pries-Heje, J., Ram, S., Rosemann, M. (eds.) Proceedings of International Conference on Information Systems - Bridging the Internet of People, Data, and Things (ICIS 2018). Association for Information Systems (2018). https://aisel.aisnet.org/icis2018/modeling/Presentations/4
6. Bergersen, G.R., Sjøberg, D.I.K., Dybå, T.: Construction and validation of an instrument for measuring programming skill. IEEE Trans. Software Eng. **40**(12), 1163–1184 (2014). https://doi.org/10.1109/TSE.2014.2348997
7. Bernard, G., Andritsos, P.: CJM-ex: goal-oriented exploration of customer journey maps using event logs and data analytics. In: Clarisó, R., et al. (eds.) Proceedings of BPM Demo Track and BPM Dissertation Award co-located with 15th International Conference on Business Process Modeling (BPM 2017). CEUR Workshop Proceedings, vol. 1920. CEUR-WS.org (2017). http://ceur-ws.org/Vol-1920/BPM_2017_paper_172.pdf
8. Bernard, G., Andritsos, P.: A process mining based model for customer journey mapping. In: Franch, X., Ralyté, J., Matulevicius, R., Salinesi, C., Wieringa, R.J. (eds.) Proceedings of Forum and Doctoral Consortium Papers at the 29th International Conference on Advanced Information Systems Engineering (CAiSE 2017). CEUR Workshop Proceedings, vol. 1848, pp. 49–56. CEUR-WS.org (2017). http://ceur-ws.org/Vol-1848/CAiSE2017_Forum_Paper7.pdf
9. Bernard, G., Andritsos, P.: CJM-ab: abstracting customer journey maps using process mining. In: Mendling, J., Mouratidis, H. (eds.) CAiSE 2018. LNBIP, vol. 317, pp. 49–56. Springer, Cham (2018). https://doi.org/10.1007/978-3-319-92901-9_5
10. Bernard, G., Andritsos, P.: Contextual and behavioral customer journey discovery using a genetic approach. In: Welzer, T., Eder, J., Podgorelec, V., Kamišalić Latifić, A. (eds.) ADBIS 2019. LNCS, vol. 11695, pp. 251–266. Springer, Cham (2019). https://doi.org/10.1007/978-3-030-28730-6_16

11. Bertolini, C., Liu, Z., Srba, J.: Verification of timed healthcare workflows using component timed-arc petri nets. In: Weber, J., Perseil, I. (eds.) FHIES 2012. LNCS, vol. 7789, pp. 19–36. Springer, Heidelberg (2013). https://doi.org/10.1007/978-3-642-39088-3_2

12. Bezirgiannis, N., de Boer, F., Johnsen, E.B., Pun, K.I., Tapia Tarifa, S.L.: Implementing SOS with active objects: a case study of a multicore memory system. In: Hähnle, R., van der Aalst, W. (eds.) FASE 2019. LNCS, vol. 11424, pp. 332–350. Springer, Cham (2019). https://doi.org/10.1007/978-3-030-16722-6_20

13. Bitner, M.J., Ostrom, A.L., Morgan, F.N.: Service blueprinting: a practical technique for service innovation. Calif. Manag. Rev. **50**(3), 66–94 (2008). https://doi.org/10.2307/41166446

14. de Boer, F., et al.: A survey of active object languages. ACM Comput. Surv. **50**(5), 76:1–76:39 (2017). https://doi.org/10.1145/3122848

15. Bouyer, P., Cassez, F., Fleury, E., Larsen, K.G.: Optimal strategies in priced timed game automata. In: Lodaya, K., Mahajan, M. (eds.) FSTTCS 2004. LNCS, vol. 3328, pp. 148–160. Springer, Heidelberg (2004). https://doi.org/10.1007/978-3-540-30538-5_13

16. Chen, T., Forejt, V., Kwiatkowska, M., Parker, D., Simaitis, A.: PRISM-games: a model checker for stochastic multi-player games. In: Piterman, N., Smolka, S.A. (eds.) TACAS 2013. LNCS, vol. 7795, pp. 185–191. Springer, Heidelberg (2013). https://doi.org/10.1007/978-3-642-36742-7_13

17. Chinn, S.: A simple method for converting an odds ratio to effect size for use in meta-analysis. Stat. Med. **19**(22), 3127–3131 (2000)

18. Crosier, A., Handford, A.: Customer journey mapping as an advocacy tool for disabled people: a case study. Soc. Mark. Q. **18**(1), 67–76 (2012). https://doi.org/10.1177/1524500411435483

19. David, A., Jacobsen, L., Jacobsen, M., Jørgensen, K.Y., Møller, M.H., Srba, J.: TAPAAL 2.0: integrated development environment for timed-arc petri nets. In: Flanagan, C., König, B. (eds.) TACAS 2012. LNCS, vol. 7214, pp. 492–497. Springer, Heidelberg (2012). https://doi.org/10.1007/978-3-642-28756-5_36

20. Daivd, A., et al.: On time with minimal expected cost! In: Cassez, F., Raskin, J.-F. (eds.) ATVA 2014. LNCS, vol. 8837, pp. 129–145. Springer, Cham (2014). https://doi.org/10.1007/978-3-319-11936-6_10

21. David, A., Jensen, P.G., Larsen, K.G., Mikučionis, M., Taankvist, J.H.: UPPAAL STRATEGO. In: Baier, C., Tinelli, C. (eds.) TACAS 2015. LNCS, vol. 9035, pp. 206–211. Springer, Heidelberg (2015). https://doi.org/10.1007/978-3-662-46681-0_16

22. Følstad, A., Kvale, K.: Customer journeys: a systematic literature review. J. Serv. Theory Pract. **28**(2), 196–227 (2018). https://doi.org/10.1108/JSTP-11-2014-0261

23. Fornell, C., Mithas, S., Morgeson, F.V., Krishnan, M.: Customer satisfaction and stock prices: high returns, low risk. J. Mark. **70**(1), 3–14 (2006). https://doi.org/10.1509/jmkg.70.1.003.qxd

24. Halvorsrud, R., Kvale, K., Følstad, A.: Improving service quality through customer journey analysis. J. Serv. Theory Pract. **26**(6), 840–867 (2016). https://doi.org/10.1108/JSTP-05-2015-0111

25. Halvorsrud, R., Mannhardt, F., Johnsen, E.B., Tapia Tarifa, S.L.: Smart journey mining for improved service quality. In: Carminati, B., et al (eds.) Proceedings IEEE International Conference on Services Computing (SCC 2021), pp. 367–369. IEEE (2021). https://doi.org/10.1109/SCC53864.2021.00051

26. Halvorsrud, R., Sanchez, O.R., Boletsis, C., Skjuve, M.: Involving users in the development of a modeling language for customer journeys. Softw. Syst. Model. **22**, 1–30 (2023). https://doi.org/10.1007/s10270-023-01081-w
27. Johnsen, E.B., Hähnle, R., Schäfer, J., Schlatte, R., Steffen, M.: ABS: a core language for abstract behavioral specification. In: Aichernig, B.K., de Boer, F.S., Bonsangue, M.M. (eds.) FMCO 2010. LNCS, vol. 6957, pp. 142–164. Springer, Heidelberg (2011). https://doi.org/10.1007/978-3-642-25271-6_8
28. Johnsen, E.B., Pun, K.I., Tapia Tarifa, S.L.: A formal model of cloud-deployed software and its application to workflow processing. In: 2017 25th International Conference on Software, Telecommunications and Computer Networks (SoftCOM), pp. 1–6 (2017). https://doi.org/10.23919/SOFTCOM.2017.8115501
29. Johnsen, E.B., Schlatte, R., Tapia Tarifa, S.L.: Integrating deployment architectures and resource consumption in timed object-oriented models. J. Logical Algebraic Methods Program. **84**(1), 67–91 (2015). https://doi.org/10.1016/j.jlamp.2014.07.001
30. Kamburjan, E., Hähnle, R., Schön, S.: Formal modeling and analysis of railway operations with active objects. Sci. Comput. Program. **166**, 167–193 (2018). https://doi.org/10.1016/j.scico.2018.07.001
31. Kobialka, P., Mannhardt, F., Tapia Tarifa, S.L., Johnsen, E.B.: Building user journey games from multi-party event logs. In: Montali, M., Senderovich, A., Weidlich, M. (eds.) ICPM 2022. LNCS, vol. 468, pp. 71–83. Springer, Cham (2022). https://doi.org/10.1007/978-3-031-27815-0_6
32. Kobialka, P., Tapia Tarifa, S.L., Bergersen, G.R., Johnsen, E.B.: Weighted games for user journeys. In: Schlingloff, B.H., Chai, M. (eds.) SEFM 2022. LNCS, vol. 13550, pp. 253–270. Springer, Cham (2022). https://doi.org/10.1007/978-3-031-17108-6_16
33. Lammel, B., Korkut, S., Hinkelmann, K.: Customer experience modelling and analysis framework a semantic lifting approach for analyzing customer experience. In: Proceedings of 6th Internetional Conferenc on Innovation and Entrepreneurship (IE 2016). GSTF (2016). https://doi.org/10.5176/2251-2039_IE16.10
34. Larsen, K.G., Pettersson, P., Yi, W.: UPPAAL in a nutshell. Int. J. Softw. Tools Technol. Transf. **1**(1–2), 134–152 (1997). https://doi.org/10.1007/s100090050010
35. Lin, J., Lee, M., Yu, I.C., Johnsen, E.B.: Modeling and simulation of spark streaming. In: Barolli, L., Takizawa, M., Enokido, T., Ogiela, M.R., Ogiela, L., Javaid, N. (eds.) Proc. 32nd IEEE International Conference on Advanced Information Networking and Applications (AINA 2018), pp. 407–413. IEEE Computer Society (2018)
36. Lin, J., Mauro, J., Røst, T.B., Yu, I.C.: A model-based scalability optimization methodology for cloud applications. In: Proceedings of 7th International Symposium on Cloud and Service Computing (SC^2 2017), pp. 163–170. IEEE Computer Society (2017). https://doi.org/10.1109/SC2.2017.32
37. Lin, J.-C., Yu, I.C., Johnsen, E.B., Lee, M.-C.: ABS-YARN: a formal framework for modeling Hadoop YARN clusters. In: Stevens, P., Wąsowski, A. (eds.) FASE 2016. LNCS, vol. 9633, pp. 49–65. Springer, Heidelberg (2016). https://doi.org/10.1007/978-3-662-49665-7_4
38. Maler, O., Pnueli, A., Sifakis, J.: On the synthesis of discrete controllers for timed systems. In: Mayr, E.W., Puech, C. (eds.) STACS 1995. LNCS, vol. 900, pp. 229–242. Springer, Heidelberg (1995). https://doi.org/10.1007/3-540-59042-0_76
39. Razo-Zapata, I.S., Chew, E.K., Proper, E.: VIVA: a visual language to design value co-creation. In: Proceedings of 20th Conference on Business Informatics (CBI 2018), vol. 01, pp. 20–29. IEEE (2018). https://doi.org/10.1109/CBI.2018.00012

40. Rosenbaum, M.S., Otalora, M.L., Ramírez, G.C.: How to create a realistic customer journey map. Bus. Horiz. **60**(1), 143–150 (2017). https://doi.org/10.1016/j.bushor.2016.09.010

41. Schlatte, R., Johnsen, E.B., Kamburjan, E., Tapia Tarifa, S.L.: Modeling and analyzing resource-sensitive actors: a tutorial introduction. In: Damiani, F., Dardha, O. (eds.) COORDINATION 2021. LNCS, vol. 12717, pp. 3–19. Springer, Cham (2021). https://doi.org/10.1007/978-3-030-78142-2_1

42. Schlatte, R., Johnsen, E.B., Kamburjan, E., Tapia Tarifa, S.L.: The ABS simulator toolchain. Sci. Comput. Program. **223**, 102861 (2022). https://doi.org/10.1016/j.scico.2022.102861

43. Schlatte, R., Johnsen, E.B., Mauro, J., Tapia Tarifa, S.L., Yu, I.C.: Release the beasts: when formal methods meet real world data. In: de Boer, F., Bonsangue, M., Rutten, J. (eds.) It's All About Coordination. LNCS, vol. 10865, pp. 107–121. Springer, Cham (2018). https://doi.org/10.1007/978-3-319-90089-6_8

44. Terragni, A., Hassani, M.: Analyzing customer journey with process mining: from discovery to recommendations. In: Proceedings of 6th International Conference on Future Internet of Things and Cloud (FiCloud 2018), pp. 224–229. IEEE (2018). https://doi.org/10.1109/FiCloud.2018.00040

45. Terragni, A., Hassani, M.: Optimizing customer journey using process mining and sequence-aware recommendation. In: Proceedings of 34th Symposium on Applied Computing (SAC 2019), pp. 57–65. ACM Press (2019). https://doi.org/10.1145/3297280.3297288

46. Tueanrat, Y., Papagiannidis, S., Alamanos, E.: Going on a journey: a review of the customer journey literature. J. Bus. Res. **125**, 336–353 (2021). https://doi.org/10.1016/j.jbusres.2020.12.028

47. Turin, G., Borgarelli, A., Donetti, S., Damiani, F., Johnsen, E.B., Tapia Tarifa, S.L.: Predicting resource consumption of kubernetes container systems using resource models. J. Syst. Softw. **203**, 111750 (2023). https://doi.org/10.1016/j.jss.2023.111750

48. Vandermerwe, S., Rada, J.: Servitization of business: adding value by adding services. Eur. Manag. J. **6**(4), 314–324 (1988). https://doi.org/10.1016/0263-2373(88)90033-3

49. Wong, P.Y.H., Albert, E., Muschevici, R., Proença, J., Schäfer, J., Schlatte, R.: The ABS tool suite: modelling, executing and analysing distributed adaptable object-oriented systems. Int. J. Softw. Tools Technol. Transf. **14**(5), 567–588 (2012). https://doi.org/10.1007/s10009-012-0250-1

Actors Upgraded for Variability, Adaptability, and Determinism

Ramtin Khosravi[1]([✉]), Ehsan Khamespanah[1], Fatemeh Ghassemi[1], and Marjan Sirjani[2]

[1] School of ECE, University of Tehran, Tehran, Iran
{r.khosravi,e.khamespanah,fghassemi}@ut.ac.ir
[2] School of IDT, Mälardalen University, Västerås, Sweden
marjan.sirjani@mdu.se

Abstract. The Rebeca modeling language is designed as an imperative actor-based language with the goal of providing an easy-to-use language for modeling concurrent and distributed systems, with formal verification support. Rebeca has been extended to support time and probability. We extend Rebeca further with inheritance, polymorphism, interface declaration, and annotation mechanisms. These features allow us to handle variability within the model, support non-disruptive model evolution, and define method priorities. This enables Rebeca to be used more effectively in different domains, like in Software Product Lines, and holistic analysis of Cyber-Physical Systems. We develop specialized analysis techniques to support these extensions, partly integrated into Afra, the model checking tool of Rebeca.

Keywords: Actor Languages · Variability Modeling · Cyber-Physical Systems · Model Checking

1 Introduction

The Actor model of computation was first proposed by Carl Hewitt in the 1970s [29], and further developed by Gul Agha [3], as a mathematical framework for concurrent and distributed computing systems. The model describes computation as a collection of autonomous entities called actors that encapsulate their states and communicate with each other by sending messages [30]. Actors have been used as a framework for theoretical understanding of concurrent and distributed computation, as the basis for designing many modeling and programming languages, and as a model for many practical implementations of concurrent systems [12, 26].

Rebeca (standing for *Re*active *Obj*ects *L*anguage) is an actor-based modeling language with model checking support designed in 1999–2001 [65, 66]. One of the main design decisions in creating Rebeca is to keep the core language as simple as possible. One can still use core Rebeca for modeling using a small set of features

---

The original version of the chapter has been revised. Reference [7] and the first name of the author in reference [8] has been corrected. A correction to this chapter can be found at https://doi.org/10.1007/978-3-031-51060-1_14

F. de Boer et al. (Eds.): *Active Object Languages: Current Research Trends*,
LNCS 14360, pp. 226–260, 2024.
https://doi.org/10.1007/978-3-031-51060-1_9

for coding. However, Rebeca is extended to work for timed systems [40] and address probability [32]. Timed Rebeca is used for the modeling and analysis of several applications [42,60,61,71]. In order to model complex systems the language is evolved in different directions [12]. A brief overview of Timed Rebeca language features is presented in Sect. 2. Rebeca is equipped with an integrated modeling and analysis tool, Afra, which provides LTL model checking for Rebeca as well as schedulability and deadlock-freedom analysis, and assertion check for Timed Rebeca [41].

In the new era of digitalization, smart factories, and systems of cyber-physical systems we are dealing with heterogeneous and dynamic systems. This introduces different types of variability in behavior, including those arising from different contexts in which the model is used (which is common in software product lines [51]), the need to dynamically adapt to the changes in the environment and in the system itself at runtime (like in self-adaptive and reconfigurable systems [70]), and the combination of these two types of variability (as in dynamic software product lines [4,31]). Hence, for a modeling language to address these requirements, it needs proper linguistic constructs to capture the variability in the behavior in a structured way. Current trends in the research community of software-intensive cyber-physical systems also confirm this [22,43,52].

When coping with systems of cyber-physical systems, we have to consider aspects of embedded and real-time systems together with complexities in concurrent and distributed systems[1]. In distributed and concurrent systems we are faced with uncertainties mainly caused by the network. The mainstream approach in the concurrency theory community uses nondeterminism to model concurrency. While the uncertainties in the environment may remain, we can aim for a deterministic design for the behavior of the system itself which is crucial for embedded and real-time systems communities. The recent work of Edward Lee and his group on the coordination language, Lingua Franca, shows one direction focusing on determinism [46,47] and PLC-like semantics [59].

Since its introduction, Rebeca has been used to model adaptive behavior in various domains, such as self-adaptive systems [38,39] and flow management systems [24]. Also, it has been used in [56] to model and analyze dynamic software product lines. However, until recently, Rebeca has not been equipped with special language features to support variable and adaptive behavior in a structured way.

The purpose of this paper is to demonstrate how the recent extensions of Timed Rebeca can be used by a wider community to model and analyze real-world applications, with a focus on how and where the language features can be used. The language extensions presented in this paper are summarized below.

Feature annotations as an explicit variability handling mechanism which are used to bind parts of the model to specific products in a software product line. This language extension is presented in this paper for the first time.

---

[1] Cyber-physical systems are also hybrid systems, bringing together cyber and physical components which are generally modeled differently. The interface between the cyber and the physical parts is also a source of complexity and an important research area that is not a topic of interest in this paper. This matter is addressed in Hybrid Rebeca introduced in [34].

Inheritance, Interfaces, and Polymorphism as language features that can
be used to support variability in model in a structured way. These features
have been added to Timed Rebeca in [71] and are used to support alternative
communication schemes among actors. In this paper, we present them as a
variability handling mechanism.

Priorities for actors and for message handlers to make the behavior of the
system more deterministic. This feature enables better modeling and verification of different types of cyber-physical systems. Priority in Timed Rebeca
has been introduced in [64] which illustrates through a few examples how Lingua Franca code can be naturally mapped to Timed Rebeca extended with
priorities.

We also provide three case studies to demonstrate the applicability of the above-
mentioned language extensions in modeling real-world systems in practice. We
have also verified the models for schedulability and deadlock-freedom and demonstrated how the Afra toolset is capable of analyzing systems for relatively large
state spaces (with more than 37 million states) on a personal computer in a
reasonable time (Sect. 3.6).

After a brief overview of Timed Rebeca we review the upgrades to the language (and the analysis tool) to support systematic variability management
(Sect. 3) and illustrates their applicability in a case study (Sect. 3.6). We explain
how Rebeca is extended to include priorities for actors and for message handlers
to address the need for determinism in the model (Sect. 4) and demonstrate its
applicability using a case study (Sect. 4.3). Afra provides complete support for
this feature in the modeling and analysis of Timed Rebeca models. In the last
section (Sect. 5), we explain how we can put together both features supporting
variability and priority and hence support the possibility of a holistic analysis for
modern cyber-physical systems. We may then formally verify the model to check
safety properties as well as schedulability and end-to-end timing properties.

2   Rebeca Overview

Rebeca [62, 67] is a class-based, imperative interpretation of the well-known actor
model of computation [3]. It describes the behavior of a system as a collection
of active objects with isolated states, communicating via asynchronous message
passing. Rebeca is a strongly typed modeling language with a Java-like syntax to make it easy to learn and use by practitioners. It is equipped with an
LTL model checker integrated into Åfra [2], an Eclipse-based development environment. The core Rebeca modeling language is intentionally kept simple, but
for various purposes, several extensions have been proposed, including Timed
Rebeca [63] for the domain of real-time systems, Hybrid Rebeca [34] for the
domain of cyber-physical systems, pRebeca [69] for modeling and analysis of
probabilistic systems, and PTRebeca [32] for probabilistic timed systems.

2.1   Running Example

To make our explanation of Rebeca and Timed Rebeca easier to follow, we explain the language features over a simple running example. The example is a highly simplified version of a Wireless Sensor LAN (WSLAN) system [42], in which a sensor periodically gathers and sends data to a computation unit. The computation unit buffers the received data and hands in a packet of data to a network whenever the buffer is full. The network transmits the data according to the TDMA network protocol [14].

2.2   Core Rebeca

A Rebeca model mainly consists of a number of *reactive class* definitions, which define the behavior of the classes of the actors in the model, as well as a `main` block that defines the instances of the actor classes. In the Rebeca model of the running example listed in Fig. 1, there are three classes of actors: `Sensor` (lines 1–16), `CompUnit` (lines 18–30), and `Network` (lines 32–37). The `main` block in lines 39–43 defines one instance of each class and specifies the arguments passed to their constructors. An instance of a reactive class is an actor in the system (which is also called a *rebec*).

The declaration of a reactive class starts with the keyword `reactiveclass`, followed by the reactive class name. The size of the queue is specified in the parentheses right after the reactive class name (e.g., line 1). A reactive class has a number of *state variables*, representing the local state of the actors. They

```
1  reactiveclass Sensor(3) {
2    statevars{
3      CompUnit cu;
4    }

6    Sensor(CompUnit cu1) {
7      cu = cu1;
8      self.gatherData();
9    }

11   msgsrv gatherData() {
12     byte data = ?(1,3);
13     cu.receiveData(data);
14     self.gatherData();
15   }
16 }

18 reactiveclass CompUnit(3) {
19   statevars {
20     Network network;
21   }
```

```
23   CompUnit(Network net) {
24     network = net;
25   }

27   msgsrv receiveData(byte data) {
28     network.send(data);
29   }
30 }

32 reactiveclass Network (3) {
33   msgsrv send(byte data) {
34     // Send data according
35     // to the TDMA protocol
36   }
37 }

39 main {
40   Sensor sensor():(cu);
41   CompUnit cu():(network);
42   Network network():();
43 }
```

Fig. 1. The Rebeca model of the running example (a simple sensor network)

may contain variables of basic data types, including booleans, integers, arrays, or references to other actors. The classes in the running example only contain state variables of the reference types. For example, every instance of Sensor has a reference to an instance of CompUnit (line 3). Each class can have a number of *constructors*, which are used to initialize instances of the class by initializing the state variables and possibly sending messages to other actors or themselves. For example, the constructor of Sensor (lines 6–9) initializes a sensor by setting its reference to CompUnit as well as sending itself a gatherData message. Each reactive class accepts a number of message types which are handled using *message servers*[2]. The message server gatherData of Sensor (lines 11–16) first chooses a data value in the range 1 to 3 nondeterministically (line 12) and sends a receiveData message to the associated CompUnit (denoted by the reference variable cu), passing the value of data as the argument (line 13)[3]. The effect of sending a message is appending the message to the message queue of the receiving actor (sometimes called its mailbox). Sending a gatherData to itself (line 14), the sensor exhibits a periodic behavior. In the definition of the message servers, well-known program control structures can be used, including *if-else* conditional statements, *for* and *while* loops, the definition of local variables, and assigning expressions built using usual arithmetic, logic, and comparative operators to local and state variables.

The general behavior of each actor is an infinite loop of taking a message from the mailbox and executing the corresponding message server. The actor waits if there is no message in the mailbox. The mailbox is a bounded FIFO queue. The queue size is bounded to prevent infinite state spaces during model checking. If a message is sent to an actor with a full mailbox, a *queue overflow* error happens and the state space generation is terminated. As we will see shortly in more detail, the model in Fig. 1 suffers from this problem when the sensor repeatedly sends itself gatherData messages. To remedy this, the sensor can send the next gatherData only after receiving some kind of acknowledgement message from the computation unit. Another solution is to use timing constraints introduced in Timed Rebeca.

It is important to note that in Rebeca there is no intra-actor concurrency, meaning that the execution of a message server must complete before the executing actor takes the next message from its mailbox. To make the behavior of the models more deterministic, we assume that two messages sent from one actor to another are delivered to the receiver's mailbox in order. The order of execution of enabled actors are arbitrary. An actor is enabled if it is not busy handling a message and its message queue is not empty. This arbitrary ordering of actors is a source of nondeterminism in the behavior of the model, requiring the model checker to inspect all possible interleavings of the message processing by different actors.

---

[2] In this paper we use the words *message server* and *method* interchangeably.

[3] Note that this data value has no effect on the behavior of the actors in this specific model and is only generated to demonstrate the use of nondeterministic choice expression.

2.3   Timed Rebeca

The models in core Rebeca are time abstract in the sense that the passage of time is not modeled explicitly. The nondeterminism in the processing of messages by different actors implicitly models the temporal ordering of events. For example, upon execution of gatherData, the sensor sends two messages: a receiveData to cu and another gatherData to itself. Now if the next message processed is receiveData, this indicates that the sensor gathers data in a time period relatively larger than the time needed by the computation unit to process the data (including the time needed to receive the message from the sensor). Conversely, if gatherData is processed first, it indicates that the sensor gathers data relatively faster. If this case happens routinely, both the sensor's and the computation unit's mailboxes quickly overflow.

To put constraints on the timings of delivering and processing of the messages, we can use an extension of Rebeca, named Timed Rebeca, which provides features for this purpose. Rewriting the two mentioned message servers as below fixes the queue overflow problem.

```
msgsrv gatherData() {                    msgsrv receiveData(byte data) {
    byte data = ?(1,3);                      delay(1);
    cu.receiveData(data);                    network.send(data);
    self.gatherData() after(2);          }
}
```

The clause after(2) after sending gatherData specifies the message needs two units of time to be delivered to the mailbox of the sensor, hence specifying the time period of two for gathering data. On the other hand, delay(1) statement in receiveData indicates that the computation unit needs one unit of time to process the message and send the data over the network. Timed Rebeca offers the following features to model the timed behavior of actors.

delay is a statement used to model computation times. Timed Rebeca assumes all statements other than delays are executed instantaneously. So, the computation time must be specified by the modeler using the delay statement. A statement delay(t) indicates the actor does not perform any action within the next t units of time.

after is a time tag attached to a message and defines the earliest time the message can be served, relative to the time when the message was sent. A clause after(t) may be added to a message send statement, indicating that the receiver can take the message from its mailbox only after t units of time.

deadline is a time tag attached to a message which determines the expiration time of the messages, relative to the time when the message was sent. A clause deadline(t) may be added to a message send statement, indicating that the message remains only t units of time in the receiver's mailbox, and purged afterward if its processing has not already started.

The same as Core Rebeca, the order of execution of enabled actors in Timed Rebeca are arbitrary. In Timed Rebeca, an actor is enabled if it is not busy handling a message and its message bag has a message whose time tag is less than the time tag of all the messages of other actors. This message is also called an enabled message. Timed Rebeca is also supported by Afra toolset for schedulability and deadlock freedom analysis. It makes use of special properties of the Timed Rebeca semantics (isolated actor states and serial execution within a single actor) to generate a data structure called *floating time transition system* which enables a coarse grain discretization of the state space [40].

2.4   Inheritance and Polymorphism

Like most other object-oriented programming and modeling languages, Rebeca provides mechanisms for reusing code through subclassing. A modeler is able to define a new reactive class as a subclass of an existing reactive class, using an inheritance mechanism. This is stated using the **extends** keyword followed by the name of the base reactive class, prior to the queue size declaration. This way, the new reactive class inherits all the state variables and message servers of the base reactive class. Rebeca also supports polymorphism through dynamic binding of the message servers. Since a subclass cannot remove any message server inherited from its superclass, its type is compatible with that of the superclass. Hence, it is possible to assign an instance of a subclass to a reference of the superclass. The actual message server invoked when processing a message is determined by the class of the receiving actor (not the type of the reference). This allows for improving code organization and readability as well as the creation of extensible programs [21]. An example of the usage of inheritance and dynamic binding in Rebeca is demonstrated in the Elevator case study (Sect. 3.6, Fig. 7).

An abstract reactive class is defined when a modeler wants to manipulate a set of classes through their common interface. Rebeca provides this by enabling **abstract** message server definition. An abstract message server has only a declaration and no implementation. A reactive class containing abstract message servers is called an abstract reactive class. Inheriting from an abstract reactive class requires providing definitions for all the abstract message servers in the base reactive class. Otherwise, the derived reactive class is also abstract, and the compiler forces the modeler to qualify that reactive class with the **abstract** keyword.

In some cases, there is a need for defining a completely abstract reactive class, i.e., a reactive class that provides no implementation at all. This is done by defining **interface** instead of reactive classes. It allows the modeler to determine message server names and their argument lists, but no bodies and no state variables. So, it provides only a type, not any implementation. In Rebeca, defining multiple interface implementation is allowed, which can be assumed as a kind of multiple inheritances. More details about the inheritance mechanism and polymorphism in Rebeca are presented in [71]. An example of using interfaces in Rebeca is illustrated in Fig. 3, lines 62–78.

3   Modeling Variability in Rebeca

In this section, we review the language features that can be used to capture variability in Rebeca models. At the finer level of granularity, we have feature annotations that can bind state variables, methods, and statements to feature expressions. On the other hand, polymorphism allows reactive classes to act as different implementations of abstract interfaces, hence providing a coarse-grained variability handling mechanism at the component level. Before going into the details of each language feature, we extend the running example with a few variable features.

3.1   Running Example with Variability

To demonstrate how variability is handled in Rebeca, we extend the running example with a few variable features. The feature diagram of the extended example is illustrated in Fig. 2. The whole system (represented by WSAN) has three sub-features Sensor, Computation Unit, and Network. The filled circle at the top of these features indicates that they are mandatory sub-features of WSAN, meaning that they must be included in every product configuration. There are three variation points in this example. The sensor can gather data with a fixed period, or sporadically. The arc between the edges to Periodic and Sporadic indicates that these sub-features are mutually exclusive. The computation unit can either immediately send the data received from the sensor, or decouple receiving and sending data. In the latter case, it buffers the received data and periodically sends a packet from the buffer (if available). Finally, the system can support the network protocols TDMA, MACB, or both (as indicated by the filled arc between the edges to the sub-features). The Timed Rebeca model of the extended running example is listed in Fig. 3. We will explain the details of the variability handling mechanisms in the following.

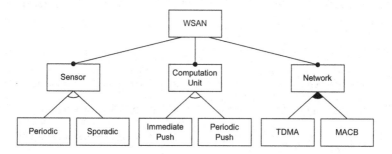

Fig. 2. The feature diagram of the running example of a simple sensor network with three variation points, periodic or sporadic for the sensor, immediate or periodic push for the computation unit, and two different protocols, TDMA and MACB, for the network

```
1  featurevar FT_PERIODIC_SENSOR;
2  featurevar FT_SPORADIC_SENSOR;
3  featurevar FT_IMMEDIATE_PUSH;
4  featurevar FT_PERIODIC_PUSH;
5  featurevar FT_SIMPLE_NETWORK;
6  featurevar FT_TDMA_NETWORK;

8  reactiveclass Sensor(3) {
9    statevars{
10     CompUnit cu;
11   }

13   Sensor(CompUnit cu1) {
14     cu = cu1;
15     self.gatherData();
16   }

18   msgsrv gatherData() {
19     cu.receiveData(0);
20     if (FT_PERIODIC_SENSOR)
21       self.gatherData() after(2);
22     else
23       self.gatherData()
               after(?(1,2,3));
24   }
25 }

27 env int BUFFER_SIZE = 4;

29 reactiveclass CompUnit(3) {
30   statevars {
31     Network network;
32     @feature(FT_PERIODIC_PUSH)
33     int[BUFFER_SIZE] buffer;
34     @feature(FT_PERIODIC_PUSH)
35     int cnt;
36   }

38   CompUnit(Network net) {
39     network = net;
40     @feature(FT_PERIODIC_PUSH)
41     self.process();
42   }

44   @feature(FT_IMMEDIATE_PUSH)
```

```
45   msgsrv receiveData(byte data) {
46     network.send(data);
47   }

49   @feature(FT_PERIODIC_PUSH)
50   msgsrv receiveData(byte data) {
51     buffer[cnt++] = data;
52   }

54   @feature(FT_PERIODIC_PUSH)
55   msgsrv process() {
56     for (int i=cnt; cnt>0; cnt--)
57       network.send(buffer[i]);
58     self.process() after(1);
59   }
60 }

62 interface Network {
63   msgsrv send(byte data);
64 }

66 reactiveclass MACBNetwork
             implements Network(3) {
67   msgsrv send(byte data) {
68     // Send data according
69     // to the MACB protocol
70   }
71 }

73 reactiveclass TDMANetwork
             implements Network(3) {
74   msgsrv send(byte data) {
75     // Send data according
76     // to the TDMA protocol
77   }
78 }

80 main {
81   Sensor sensor():(cu);
82   CompUnit cu():(network);
83   @feature(FT_SIMPLE_NETWORK)
84   MACBNetwork network():();
85   @feature(FT_TDMA_NETWORK)
86   TDMANetwork network():();
87 }
```

Fig. 3. The Timed Rebeca model of the running example extended by variability (the sensor network example extended with the variation points of Fig. 2)

3.2   Feature Annotations

In the context of software product line engineering, it is common to capture the variabilities in a separate variability model. Some well-known models for this purpose include the widely-used Feature Models [37], UML-based variability models [9], and Common Variability Language (CVL) [28]. We assume that the variability is captured in a feature model. The features are represented by global boolean *feature variables*. A *True* (resp. *False*) value for a feature variable indicates that the corresponding feature is included in (resp. excluded from) the product under analysis. In the running example (Fig. 3), the variables defined in lines 1 to 6 represent the 'leaf' features in the feature model of Fig. 2. Note that it is not necessary to define variables for the mandatory features included in every configuration.

We assume that the values for all feature variables are defined as parameters of the analysis process. Hence, Afra is currently capable of analyzing one product at a time. As we will see later, this limitation can be relaxed based on the existing theories for model checking several products at a time. We also assume that the values assigned to the feature variables are checked externally to satisfy the validity of the feature model (e.g., not including two alternatives in the configuration).

The feature variables can be used to define feature-specific behavior in two ways. The first is to use a feature variable as an ordinary global variable. Line 20 of Fig. 3 is an example of this type. It is possible to mix feature variables with state (or local) variables. The second way is to use *feature annotations*. The syntax @feature(*feature_expr*) may come before various language constructs which causes that construct to be included in the model only if *feature_expr* evaluates to *True*. As an example, the state variable `buffer` is included in the reactive class `CompUnit` only if the feature *Periodic Push* is present in the configuration (represented by the feature expression FT_PERIODIC_PUSH in the feature annotation of line 32). Note that the annotation only affects its immediately following declaration. Hence, the variable `cnt` in line 35 must be annotated separately (line 34). Other model elements can be annotated as well, e.g., statements (line 41), message servers (lines 44, 49, and 54), and actor instantiations (lines 83 and 85). As the Timed Rebeca syntax allows grouping of statements into blocks, which itself is a statement, one can annotate a group of statements within a message server:

```
...
@feature(SOME_FEATURE_EXPR) {
  statement 1;
  statement 2;
  ...
  statement n;
}
...
```

As illustrated by the feature annotations in lines 44 and 49, two alternative implementations of the same message server may be provided. However, in case the feature expressions of the annotations are not mutually exclusive, a duplicate definition error may be raised when compiling an individual product model which includes more than one definition for the same message server. In the case of verifying the whole product line without projecting the model onto an individual product configuration (Sect. 3.5), this check is more involved. Assuming that there are two definitions for the same message server, one annotated with the feature expression e_1 and another with e_2, an error must be raised if $e_1 \wedge e_2$ is satisfiable[4], which can be checked using a SAT solver.

3.3 Reactive Class Polymorphism

As stated in Sect. 2.4, the statically typed, class-based nature of Timed Rebeca allows polymorphic modeling with respect to the interfaces of the reactive classes. As an example, the `Network` interface defined in lines 62 to 64 of Fig. 3 specifies a single message server `send(byte)` without defining its behavior. Any class implementing `Network` must implement the message server, as illustrated by the classes `MACBNetwork` and `TDMANetwork`. To keep the running example as small as possible, the interface is defined in its simplest form and the implementations are omitted. However, the modeler can take advantage of more involved features of interfaces, e.g., by making classes implement multiple interfaces, defining inheritance hierarchies among interfaces, etc.

An interface can be used as the type of state variables (line 31) or parameters (line 38). An instance of any reactive class implementing that interface may be assigned to such a state variable or parameter (line 82). This use of polymorphic modeling provides a coarser-grained variability implementation mechanism (compared to feature annotations), where the variability is resolved by choosing among several components implementing the same interface.

3.4 Handling Reconfiguration

If we allow feature variables to change during execution, it is possible to change the configuration at runtime which allows the modeling of reconfigurable systems. The reconfiguration can take place using both variability mechanisms, feature annotation, and polymorphism. As an example, executing the following code will change the behavior of all sensors from periodic to sporadic[5].

```
if (someCondition) {
  FT_PERIODIC_SENSOR = false;
  FT_SPORADIC_SENSOR = true;
}
```

---

[4] More precisely, the satisfiability check must incorporate the constraints imposed by the feature model too. To this end, a feature expression F must be derived from the feature model (as explained in [5]), and the satisfiability of $e_1 \wedge e_2 \wedge F$ must be checked.

[5] Of course, since the two features are mutually exclusive, this could have been done using only one feature variable.

Note that this code can be placed at any reactive class, possibly other than **Sensor**. This allows the separation of reconfiguration logic from the actors' behavior. There is a limitation in using this type of reconfiguration where the feature variable is used to annotate some state variables or an entire reactive class (as opposed to a message server or a part of it). Since this changes the structure of the states of the system, it complicates the generation and analysis of the state space and thus is forbidden. If a reconfiguration of this type is required it is recommended to use polymorphism to handle the variability (as illustrated shortly in an example).

Moreover, a number of semantic issues arise when using annotative reconfiguration which are studied in [56]. The most important happens when a reconfiguration eliminates a message server, while there are messages of that type in some actor's mailbox. The solution proposed is to make the receiver actor perform a configuration check whenever it takes a message from its mailbox for execution and drop the message in case it is excluded from the model with respect to the configuration at the time of taking the message. In [56], a variability-aware semantics has been proposed for Rebeca supporting reconfiguration.

When using reactive class polymorphism, the reconfiguration can happen without the need to change the Rebeca semantics. As an example, the following method can be used to change the network protocol at runtime.

```
// in CompUnit:
statevars {
  Network defaultNet;
  Network alternativeNet;
  Network network;
}

CompUnit(Network def, Network alt) {
  defaultNet = def;
  alternativeNet = alt;
  network = def;
}

msgsrv switchNetwork() {
  network = alt;
}

// in reconfiguration logic (anywhere in the model):
if (someCondition) {
  cu.switchNetwork;
}

// in the main block:
MACBNetwork macb():();
TDMANetwork tdma():();
CompUnit cu():(macb, tdma);
```

Note that both network classes must be instantiated in the **main** block, as Rebeca does not support the dynamic creation of actors. It is possible that in

the implementation of the system the actors are instantiated just upon reconfiguration. In this case, special care must be taken during the implementation to
keep the verification results valid.

We also emphasize that the change of the network protocol happens whenever
the switchNetwork message is handled. So, the computation unit may work with
the default network for a while after the reconfiguration happens. If this makes
a problem, in Timed Rebeca, the reconfiguration logic should be given priority
over normal behavior using the technique explained in Sect. 4.

3.5   Model Checking in the Presence of Variability

When it comes to verification, one can derive the Rebeca model for each valid
configuration, and model check each model separately. However, this way we
cannot benefit from the commonalities among the behavior of the products. The
problem of model checking the whole product line at once has been the subject
of various studies, like [18]. In the context of Rebeca, [56] has addressed model
checking reconfigurable families of actor systems, based on a feature-annotated
state space generated for the whole product line.

One can statically analyze the product line model to detect the features whose
presence does not affect the satisfaction of a given property. For such features,
it suffices to verify the products that exclude those features. A similar technique
can be used regarding the alternative features (according to the feature model).
These improvements (as well as some others regarding evolving product lines)
have been studied in [57], using a variability-aware data and control dependency
graph generated from the model. The experimental results indicate a significant
reduction in the verification cost of the whole product line. Note that the model
checking of the whole product line at once has not been yet integrated into Afra
and is planned for future releases.

3.6   Case Study: Elevator Scheduling with Variability

To demonstrate how variability handling mechanisms can be used in practice to
enable an analysis of a real-time software product line, we studied an elevator
scheduling system which is originally defined in [55] and analyzed for schedulability using a Timed Automata Family. The feature model of the case study
is depicted in Fig. 4. The elevator system consists of three to five floors, as
indicated by the numeric feature Floors. A central controller is responsible for
scheduling the movement of the elevator. The time between two consecutive
requests on the same floor is assumed to be within a certain discrete range of
$[LOW, HIGH]$. The scheduling algorithm must guarantee a maximum waiting
time for each request ($TIMEOUT$). The system may support VIP floors (indicated by the optional feature VIP Floor), where the maximum waiting time is
less than normal floors ($TIMEOUT\_VIP$). On the other hand, the time between
two consecutive requests on a VIP floor may be different from non-VIP floors and
is assumed to be within the discrete range of $[VLOW, VHIGH]$. The elevator
system may be equipped with a weight sensor (indicated by the optional feature

Weight Sensor) which prevents the elevator from moving if the total weight in the cabin exceeds a limit. This increases the time the elevator waits at a floor in the worst case by *LVL_DELAY*.

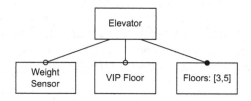

Fig. 4. The elevator case study feature model [55]

The Timed Rebeca model for the case study with four floors is listed in the Figs. 5, 6 and 7. To save space, we have omitted a few less important parts. The current implementation of Afra does not support the dynamic creation of actors, so the variability in the number of floors must be handled manually, by instantiating the desired number of actors in the main block (as in Fig. 7). The other two features are modeled by FT_VIP and FT_WEIGHT_SENSOR.

```
1  featurevar FT_VIP;                    19      @feature(FT_VIP)
2  featurevar FT_WEIGHT_SENSOR;          20      if (isVIP)
                                         21          timeout = TIMEOUT_VIP;
4  reactiveclass Floor(5) {              22      self.timeOut()
5    knownrebecs {                                   after(timeout);
6      Controller ctrl;                  23  }
7    }                                   24  msgsrv timeOut() {
8    statevars {                         25      assertion(!isWaiting);
9      int level;                        26  }
10     boolean isWaiting;                27  msgsrv served() {
11     @feature(FT_VIP)                  28      isWaiting = false;
12     boolean isVIP;                    29      int rqDly = ?(LOW, HIGH);
13   }                                   30      @feature(FT_VIP)
14   // constructor omitted              31      if (isVIP)
15   msgsrv makeReq() {                  32          rqDly = ?(VLOW, VHIGH);
16     ctrl.requestFor(level);           33      self.makeReq() after(rqDly);
17     isWaiting = true;                 34  }
18     int timeout = TIMEOUT;            35  }
```

Fig. 5. The elevator scheduling case study - Timed Rebeca model of the floors

Each floor actor, an instance of Floor reactive class (Fig. 5), knows its level, whether it is waiting for its request to be served, and if it is a VIP floor (only if VIP feature is on), modeled by the corresponding state variables (lines 9–12). Upon construction, a floor makes a request for the elevator. The body of the constructors are omitted to save space. When receiving a makeReq message (lines

15–23), the floor sends the controller a `requestFor` message along with its level number and sets itself in the waiting mode. To check the schedulability of the model, the floor schedules a `timeOut` message for either `TIMEOUT` or `TIMEOUT_VIP` to be sent to itself. Upon the timeout (lines 24–26), an assertion fails if the floor is still waiting. If the elevator arrives on a waiting floor (lines 27–35), the floor exits the waiting state and schedules the subsequent request for some time in the range [`LOW,HIGH`] (or [`VLOW,VHIGH`] for a VIP floor). To avoid the complexity of handling recurrent requests at a floor (i.e., a second request is made before the first one is served), we assume that *TIMEOUT* is reasonably smaller than *LOW*.

```
1  reactiveclass Controller(20) {            35   void stop() {
2    statevars {                             36     dir = NOT_MOVING;
3      Floor[LVL_CNT] floor;                 37   }
4      boolean[LVL_CNT] requested;           38   void handleArrival(int level) {
5      int dir;                              39     atLevel = level;
6      int atLevel;                          40     stopped = false;
7      boolean stopped;                      41     if (requested[level]) {
8    }                                       42       serve(level);
9    // constructor omitted                  43       stopped = true;
10   msgsrv requestFor(int dest) {           44     }
11     requested[dest] = true;               45   }
12     if (dir == NOT_MOVING)                46   void serve(int level) {
13       if (atLevel < dest)                 47     requested[level] = false;
14         move(UP);                         48     floor[level].served();
15       else if (atLevel > dest)            49   }
16         move(DOWN);                       50   boolean higherLevelsRq() ...
17       else                                51   boolean lowerLevelsRq() ...
18         serve(dest);                      52   void reschedule(int level) {
19   }                                       53     if (dir == UP)
20   msgsrv arrive(int level) {              54       if (higherLevelsRq())
21     handleArrival(level);                 55         move(UP);
22     reschedule(level);                    56       else
23   }                                       57         if (lowerLevelsRq())
24   void move(int direction) {              58           move(DOWN);
25     dir = direction;                      59         else
26     int next_arrival =                    60           stop();
           TIME_FOR_ONE_LEVEL;              61     else if (dir == DOWN)
27     @feature(FT_WEIGHT_SENSOR)            62       if (lowerLevelsRq())
28     if (stopped)                          63         move(DOWN);
29       next_arrival += LVL_DELAY;          64       else
30     if (direction == UP)                  65         if (higherLevelsRq())
31       self.arrive(atLevel + 1)            66           move(UP);
             after(next_arrival);           67         else
32     else if (direction == DOWN)           68           stop();
33       self.arrive(atLevel - 1)            69   }
             after(next_arrival);           70 }
34   }
```

Fig. 6. The elevator scheduling case study - the model of the controller in a non-VIP setting.

As its state variables, the (non-VIP) `Controller` (Fig. 6) knows the floors, whether there is a request for each floor, its direction (`NOT_MOVING`, `UP`, or `DOWN`), the level at which it just arrived, and whether it has stopped at that level (or just passed by). Upon receiving a request for a destination level (lines 10–19), the controller marks the floor as requested and starts to move the elevator toward the destination if it is not moving already. When the elevator arrives at a level (either as a destination or just passing by), it notifies the controller via `arrive` message (lines 20–23). The controller first handles the arrival, and then reschedules the elevator's movement if necessary. The movement (for one level) is handled in `move` method, whose function is to schedule an `arrive` message at the next visited floor (determined according to the current level and the direction). The time the elevator arrives on the next floor is `TIME_FOR_ONE_LEVEL`, plus the extra time needed to wait a the level if the weight sensor feature is included. This extra time is needed only if the elevator has been stopped to serve a request (hence the conditional statement in line 64). The functions of `handleArrival` and `server` are straightforward. After arrival, a rescheduling must happen if necessary (lines 52–69). If the elevator has been going up, and there are requests for upper levels, it continues in that direction. Otherwise, if there are requests for the lower directions, it changes direction downwards. If there are no other requests, it stops. A similar logic is followed if the elevator has been going down. The bodies of the two boolean methods `higherLevelsRq` and `lowerLevelsRq` are omitted to save space.

The weight sensor variability can be resolved in just a few annotations. To support VIP floors, special care must be taken when rescheduling to be able to meet the shorter waiting deadline of such floors. Hence, the basic controller is extended by `VIPController` to support VIP scheduling (Fig. 7). It inherits all members of the basic `Controller` and additionally knows which floors are of VIP type (line 4). The message server `arrive` is overridden in the way that it first determines its next direction considering only the requests for VIP floors. If no such request exists, the ordinary rescheduling algorithm is used by calling the (inherited) `reschedule` method. Again, the bodies of the two boolean methods `higherVIPLvlRq` and `lowerVIPLvlRq` are omitted to save space.

Each configuration of the model can be analyzed for schedulability using Afra. The results of the verification of a few products is reported in Table 1. To keep the size of the table small, we have only reported the configurations with four floors, and two configuration with five floors. For the configurations including VIP floors, only the topmost floor is considered as VIP.

The complexity of the analysis is greatly affected by the size of the intervals specifying the minimum and maximum amount of times between two consecutive requests for each floor (shown in the Rq.Int. column), as Afra checks for each value within the interval systematically. For the first four configurations, we set this parameter to three ($LOW = 20$, $HIGH = 22$, $VLOW = 22$, $VHIGH = 24$). The last two configurations have five floors, one with an interval of size two and the other with size three. The models are analyzed for schedulability and deadlock-freedom on a single core from a 3.6 GHz Core-i7 machine with 16 GB of RAM.

```
 1 | @feature(FT_VIP)                              25 |   boolean higherVIPLvlRq() ...
 2 | reactiveclass VIPController                   26 |   boolean lowerVIPLvlRq() ...
   |    extends Controller(20) {                   27 | }
 3 |   statevars {
 4 |     boolean[LVL_CNT] isVIP;                    29 | main {
 5 |   }                                            30 |   @feature(!FT_VIP) {
 6 |   // constructor omitted                       31 |     Controller ctrl():(f0, f1,
 7 |   msgsrv arrive(int level) {                      |         f2, f3);
 8 |     handleArrival(level);                      32 |     Floor f0(ctrl):(0);
 9 |     if (dir == UP)                             33 |     Floor f1(ctrl):(1);
10 |       if (higherVIPLvlRq())                    34 |     Floor f2(ctrl):(2);
11 |         move(UP);                              35 |     Floor f3(ctrl):(3);
12 |       else if (lowerVIPLvlRq())                36 |   }
13 |         move(DOWN);                            37 |   @feature(FT_VIP) {
14 |       else                                     38 |     VIPController ctrl():(f0,
15 |         reschedule(level);                        |         f1, f2, f3, false,
16 |     else if (dir == DOWN)                         |         false, false, false);
17 |       if (lowerVIPLvlRq())                     39 |     Floor f0(ctrl):(0, false);
18 |         move(DOWN);                            40 |     Floor f1(ctrl):(1, false);
19 |       else if (higherVIPLvlRq())               41 |     Floor f2(ctrl):(2, false);
20 |         move(UP);                              42 |     Floor f3(ctrl):(3, false);
21 |       else                                     43 |   }
22 |         reschedule(level);                     44 | }
23 | }
```

Fig. 7. The elevator scheduling case study - the model of the VIP controller and the instantiation of the actors.

Table 1. The number of states and transitions, and the time required to model check a few configurations of the elevator product line. Each row specifies a configuration by assigning values to the features Weight Sensor (WS), VIP Floor (VIP), and the number of floors (Floors). The parameter Rq.Int. specifies the size of the time interval between two consecutive requests ($[LOW, HIGH]$).

Config.	WS	VIP	Floors	Rq.Int	States	Transitions	Time (sec.)
1	✓		4	3	106,234	165,326	1
2	✓	✓	4	3	185,145	196,939	2
3			4	3	380,794	491,662	3
4		✓	4	3	1,221,333	1,543,755	10
5		✓	5	2	1,435,246	1,818,949	14
6		✓	5	3	37,178,658	48,576,931	384

Assuming the elevator waits for one time unit at each floor, and adds another time unit if it has a weight sensor, having the mentioned intervals between two consecutive requests yields in the smallest values for time outs as shown in Table 2. In case the time out values are infeasible to satisfy, Afra reports a schedulability violation and provides a counterexample trace as illustrated in Fig. 8.

Table 2. The smallest possible time out values for different configurations

Config.	WS	VIP	Floors	Rq.Int	*TIMEOUT*	*TIMEOUT_VIP*
1	✓		4	3	16	N/A
2	✓	✓	4	3	16	10
3			4	3	11	N/A
4		✓	4	3	11	8
5		✓	5	2	13	10
6		✓	5	3	13	10

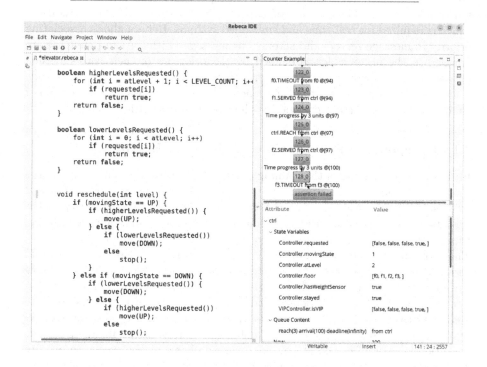

Fig. 8. The counterexample provided by Afra when a time out happens

4   More Deterministic Models Using Priorities

In concurrency theory, nondeterminism is used to model concurrency. Hewitt actors are designed for building distributed and network systems. There is a trend to add more determinism to the language models inspired from synchronous languages. Edward Lee and his team are proposing deterministic concurrency in [49]. Apart from that, in many applications, there is a predefined priority used for ordering the tasks in hand. Here we explain how priorities are added as annotations to Timed Rebeca to better support such applications.

In Rebeca, the semantics of the language is defined to order the execution of enabled actors nondeterministically. An actor is enabled if the actor is not busy handling a message and its message queue is not empty. Each actor has a message queue and the messages sent to an actor from another actor are put in the receiver's message queue with the same order that the messages are sent. So, in Rebeca, we have a point-to-point in-order message delivery, but we cannot have any assumptions about messages sent by different actors. For Timed Rebeca, the order of handling messages of an actor depends on the time tags of the messages. If there is more than one message with the same time tag then these messages are handled in a nondeterministic order (see [53] for a formal definition of the semantics). To make the behavior of actors in Rebeca models more deterministic, which is required for real-time and embedded systems, Rebeca allows associating priority to message servers and actors. The messages with the same time tag are handled in the order which is defined by the priorities of their corresponding message servers. Priorities for the actors are defined in the main part of the code where we instantiate actors from the reactive classes. This way, the execution of enabled actors takes place considering the associated priorities.

4.1   Incorporating Priorities into the Running Example

In the extended version of the running example in Fig. 10, we want to make sure that in each round of execution, all of the gathered data by Sensor is processed by CompUnit. So, there is a need for Sensor to have a higher priority in the execution in comparison with CompUnit. Figure 9 shows a diagram representing the program model of the running example, inspired from Lingua Franca [27]. The program is assembled from three actors, Sensor, CompUnit, and Network, shown as light gray boxes. The numbers in the top-left side of the boxes show the priorities of actors. Black triangles in the diagram show communication ports. In this model, both Sensor and CompUnit have output ports that are connected to corresponding input ports. In the diagram, methods are represented by dark gray chevrons. The order of defining methods in the figure shows the execution priority of methods, e.g., `receiveData` has a higher execution priority compared to `process` in the `CompUnit` actor. In Fig. 9, Sensor and CompUnit define methods that are triggered periodically.

As depicted in lines 50 to 55, of Fig. 10, three different priority levels are associated with instances of reactive classes using *priority annotations*. Having

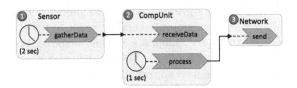

Fig. 9. A diagrammatic representation of the program model of the running example of sensor network with priorities, inspired with the Lingua Franca diagram notation

a smaller value for *priority annotations* means that the actor has a higher execution priority. Note that associating the same priority level with actors results in the nondeterministic choice among the actors when more than one of them are enabled.

In addition to the cases mentioned above, each reactive class is allowed to prioritize the execution of its message servers. It means that in the case of receiving two messages with the same time tag, the message server which is annotated with a higher priority will be executed first. In Fig. 10, we make sure that the method for receiving data from Sensor has a higher priority than the method for processing data in CompUnit. This decision is because CompUnit has to receive the data prior to processing it. This way, the priority among reactions 1 and 2 in Fig. 9 is addressed.

```
1  reactiveclass Sensor(3) {          29    @priority(1)
2    statevars{                       30    msgsrv receiveData(byte data) {
3      CompUnit cu;                   31      buffer[cnt++] = data;
4    }                                32    }

6    Sensor(CompUnit cu1) {           34    @priority(2)
7      cu = cu1;                      35    msgsrv process() {
8      self.gatherData(1);            36      for (int i=cnt; cnt>0; cnt--)
9    }                                37        network.send(buffer[i]);
                                      38      self.process() after(1);
11   msgsrv gatherData(byte data) {   39    }
12     cu.receiveData(1);             40  }
13     self.gatherData(1) after(2);
14   }                                42  reactiveclass Network (3) {
15 }                                  43    msgsrv send(byte data) {
                                      44      // Send data according
17 reactiveclass CompUnit(3) {        45      // to a protocol
18   statevars {                      46    }
19     Network network;               47  }
20     byte[4] buffer;
21     int cnt;                       49  main {
22   }                                50    @priority(1)
                                      51    Sensor sensor():(cu);
24   CompUnit(Network net) {          52    @priority(2)
25     network = net;                 53    CompUnit cu():(network);
26     self.process();                54    @priority(3)
27   }                                55    Network network():();
                                      56  }
```

Fig. 10. The Timed Rebeca model of the running example with priorities (the sensor network example with priorities for the actors and for the message servers)

In some cases, associating priorities to actors and methods within classes does not give us the order of execution of methods we are looking for. Hence, we also added another feature to Timed Rebeca, by which we can associate priorities with each method. This is a flat type of priority throughout the whole model which we call Global Priority (and is not shown in the examples). Note that using both `GlobalPriority` and `Priority` in one model is not allowed.

4.2 Analysis of Rebeca Models with Priorities

The model checking engine of Afra assumes that in the given model all of the actors and methods have priorities, if there is no priority associated to an actor or a method, then Afra assumes the lowest priority for it. At each step of the state space generation, Afra selects the highest priority enabled message from the enabled actor with the highest priority. In the case of having methods or actors with the same priority level, one of them is selected nondeterministically. During model checking, Afra generates the state space for all possible combinations.

Figure 11 compares the transition systems of the model of Fig. 10. As mentioned before, including priorities eliminates some nondeterministic choices which results in smaller transition systems. Two outgoing transitions of $S1\_0$ of Fig. 11(a) illustrates nondeterministic choice between executing the messages of `sensor` and `cu`. This nondeterminism is resolved by associating priorities to actor instances in $S1\_0$ of Fig. 11(b). Another kind of nondeterminism is depicted in $S2\_0$ for executing `receiveData` or `process` of the actor `cu`. In its corresponding state in Fig. 11(b), `receiveData` has a higher priority and there is no nondeterministic choice.

4.3 Case Study: Anti-lock Braking System, with Priority

We demonstrate the applicability of the priority feature of Rebeca on a simplified Brake-by-Wire (BBW) system with Anti-lock Braking System (ABS) [23,36,48]. To prevent uncontrolled skidding, ABS releases the brakes based on the slip rate, computed in terms of the torque and speed of wheels read by the wheel sensors. We previously specified and analyzed this case study within Hybrid Rebeca [33], an extension of Rebeca with continuous real variables that change over time, specified by ordinary differential equations (ODEs). Due to the absence of the priority feature, we handled the required priorities among the actors in the semantic model (this priority was hard-coded in the semantics). We revisit this example by replacing ODEs with simple expressions updating real-valued variables at discrete time intervals.

In this system, there is a wheel controller (WheelCtrl) for each wheel and a global brake controller (BrakeCtrl). Each wheel and the brake pedal are equipped with a sensor. The brake pedal sensor calculates the brake percentage based on the brake pedal's position and sends this value to BrakeCtrl. Each wheel sensor sends the speed of its wheel to its corresponding WheelCtrl which sends this value to BrakeCtrl. Then, BrakeCtrl computes the desired brake torque and the speed of all wheels and sends these values to each WheelCtrl to apply them. Depending on the slip rate, computed based on the current and desired speed, WheelCtrl releases the brake if the slip rate is greater than a specified value to prevent skidding.

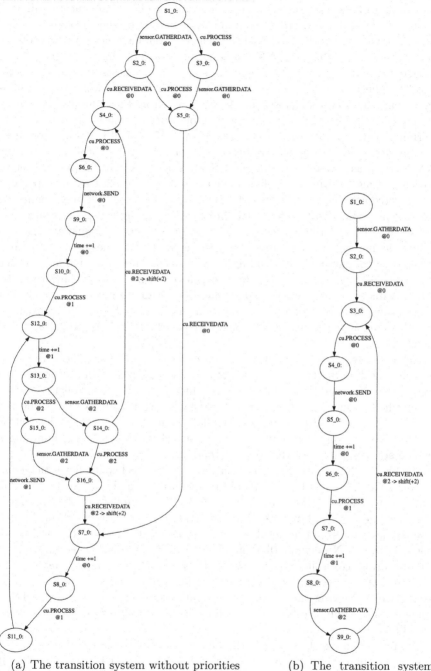

(a) The transition system without priorities

(b) The transition system with priorities

Fig. 11. Comparing transition systems of the model of Fig. 10 without priorities (a) and with priorities (b).

Each pair of a sensor and its corresponding controller are connected directly by a pair-to-pair link. All other communications are managed through a shared Controller Area Network (CAN) [50] which is a dominant networking protocol in the automotive industry. CAN is a serial bus network where nodes can send messages anytime. Upon multiple simultaneous send requests, only the message with the highest priority is accepted and sent through the network. After a message is sent, the network chooses another message from the requested messages. A CAN bus can be conceived as a single global priority-based queue [20] that deterministically dispatches messages based on their arrival times and for those messages arrived at the same time based on their priorities. Thus, we model the CAN network as a Rebeca class, called CANBusNetwork, with a message server for each message priority. We define an abstract class called Ent as the supertype for connected entities, e.g., ECUs in this example, over the CAN bus. Connected entities send their messages to CANBusNetwork by calling the appropriate message server corresponding to the message priority. Then, CANBusNetwork will transfer the message to the target entity by sending a rcv message. We assume that entities communicate by sending a pair of type and value, modeled as the parameters of rcv messages. We have considered three message priorities by defining three message servers sndH, sndM, and sndL as given in Fig. 12. For simplicity, we have considered two wheels in the model. The model consists of four other classes shown in Fig. 12: WheelSensor, WheelCtrl, BrakeSensor, and BrakeCtrl.

The WheelSensor class models the sensors and actuators of the wheel. The class has one known rebec of WheelCtrl. This class periodically updates the speed of the wheel and then sends the new value to the wheel controller (lines 33–35), specified by the message server sndSpeed. As each wheel sensor is connected via a pair-to-pair link to its wheel controller, we model this communication by directly sending a message setWspd to the wheel controller. Upon handling a message setTrq, it applies the effect of braking on the wheel speed (line 31).

The WheelCtrl class defines the behavior of the wheel controller which communicates via CAN bus by the global brake controller and via pair-to-pair link with its wheel sensors. So, this class has three known rebecs of WheelSensor, BrakeCtrl, and CANBusNetwork. Upon receiving the speed of the wheel through setWspd messages from the wheel sensor, it will send the speed to the brake controller via the CAN network (line 56). It receives the desired speed and torque from the brake controller via CAN bus through rcv messages (lines 46–52). We assume that the brake controller first sends the desired speed and then the torque. After receiving the torque, it computes the slip rate of the wheel and then decides to apply the brake by sending the appropriate torque to the wheel (lines 49–51).

The BrakeSensor class defines the behavior of the brake pedal sensor. The class has one known rebec BrakeCtrl which is the global brake controller. It has the state variable bpcnt which is the brake percentage and increased up to the value defined by the state variable max. This class sends the value of bpcnt periodically to BrakeCtrl via sndBrake message (lines 65–67). In the

```
1   env int TORQUE = 0;
2   env int SPEED = 1;
3   env int PERIOD = 1;
4
5   interface Ent{
6     msgsrv rcv(Ent entity,int
7                type, float value);
    }
8   reactiveclass CANBusNetwork(4){
9   CANBusNetwork(){}
10  @priority(1) //high
11  msgsrv sndH(Ent n,int t,float v)
12    {n.rcv((Ent)sender,t,v);}
13  @priority(2) //medium
14  msgsrv sndM(Ent n,int t,float v)
15    {n.rcv((Ent)sender,t,v) ;}
16  @priority(3) //low
17  msgsrv sndL(Ent n,int t,float v)
18    {n.rcv((Ent)sender,t,v) ;}
19  }
20  reactiveclass WheelSensor(1){
21    knownrebecs {
22      WheelCtrl wCtrl;}
23    statevars {
24      float spd; float trq;}
25    WheelSensor(float _s){
26      spd = _s;
27      self.sndSpeed();}
28    msgsrv setTrq(float _trq){
29      trq = _trq;}
30    msgsrv sndSpeed(){
31      spd = (float)spd-trq-0.1 ;
32      wCtrl.setWspd(spd);
33      if (spd>0)
34        self.sndSpeed() after(PERIOD);
35  }}
36  reactiveclass WheelCtrl
        implements Ent(2){
37    knownrebecs {
38      WheelSensor w;
39      BrakeCtrl bCtrl;
40      CANBusNetwork CAN;}
41    statevars {
42      float vspd;float wspd;}
43    WheelCtrl(){}
44    @priority(2)
45    msgsrv rcv(Ent n,int t,float v){
46      if (t==SPEED) vspd = v;
47      else{
48        if(((vspd-wspd*0.74)/vspd)>0.2)
49          w.setTrq(0);
50        else w.setTrq(v);
```

```
51  }}
52  @priority(1)
53  msgsrv setWspd(float spd){
54    wspd = spd;
55    CAN.sndM(bCtrl,SPEED,spd);}
56  }
57  reactiveclass BrakeSensor(1){
58    knownrebecs {
59      BrakeCtrl bCtrl;}
60    statevars {
61      float bpcnt;float max;}
62    BrakeSensor(float b,float m){
63      bpcnt = b; max = m;
64      self.Braking();}
65    msgsrv Braking(){
66      bpcnt = bpcnt + 1 ;
67      bCtrl.setBpcnt(bpcnt);
68      if (bpcnt<max)
69        self.Braking() after(PERIOD);
70  }}
71  reactiveclass BrakeCtrl
        implements Ent(4){
72    knownrebecs {
73      WheelCtrl wCtrlL;
74      WheelCtrl wCtrlR;
75      CANBusNetwork CAN;}
76    statevars {
77      float spdR;float rtrq;
78      float spdL;float rspd;
79      float bpcnt;}
80    BrakeCtrl(){
81      self.control();}
82    @priority(1)
83    msgsrv rcv(Ent n,int t,float v){
84      if (((WheelCtrl)n)==wCtrlR)
85        spdR = v;
86      else spdL = v;}
87    @priority(2)
88    msgsrv control(){
89      rtrq = bpcnt;
90      rspd = (spdR + spdL) / 2;
91      CAN.sndH(wCtrlR,SPEED,rspd);
92      CAN.sndH(wCtrlR,TORQUE,rtrq);
93      CAN.sndH(wCtrlL,SPEED,rspd);
94      CAN.sndH(wCtrlL,TORQUE,rtrq);
95      self.control() after(PERIOD);}
96    @priority(1)
97    msgsrv setBpcnt(float b){
98      bpcnt = b ;}
99  }
100 // main block in the next figure
```

Fig. 12. The specification of Brake-by-Wire system with Anti-lock Braking System

constructor, the actor sends a `sndBrake` message to itself to start the periodic communication.

The `BrakeCtrl` class is responsible for delegating the brake torque to wheel controllers. It defines three known rebecs, two for each wheel controller named `wCtrlL`, `wCtrlR`, and one for the network called `CAN`. This class has three state variables for the right and left wheels' speed and the brake pedal's brake percentage (`bpcnt`). It also has two auxiliary state variables for computing the desired speed and torque. The message server `control` is executed periodically to calculate the desired brake torque, calculated based on the brake percentage (lines 89–96). It also estimates the speed based on the speed of the wheels. Then, the estimated speed and global torque are sent to each wheel controller via the CAN network. The message server `setBpcnt` updates `bpcnt` based on the received value. The constructor sends a `control` message to itself to start the periodic execution.

The main block of the model is listed in Fig. 13. Figure 14 shows the LF's diagrammatic representation of the program model of the Brake-by-Wire system. As we considered two wheels in the system, the program is assembled from two instances of `WheelSensor` and `WheelCtrl`, one instance of `BrakeSensor`, `BrakeCtrl`, and `CANBusNetwork`. As depicted in Fig. 14, the values are received from `WheelCtrl` and `BrakeSensor` by `BrakeCtrl` to compute the desired brake torque and speed. `WheelCtrl` also receives its value from `WheelSensor`. To correctly compute the desired values in each period, we must guarantee that `BrakeCtrl` has received the most recent sensed values from the sensors. So, we assign the highest priority to the instances of `BrakeSensor` and `WheelSensors`. We assign the next priorities to the components over the path from `WheelSensor` to `BrakeCtrl`, i.e., instances of `WheelCtrls` and then `CANBusNetwork`. We also assign a lower priority to the message server `control` than `rcv` to be sure that it updates the values sensed for this period before its computation. If none of the priorities are considered, `WheelCtrl` may make the computation using stale values. This is in line with the policy of the order of execution of components "from upstream to downstream" in the design of CPS and used in Lingua Franca. We will explain this through a scenario in the following.

Consider the property that states "whenever the slip rate of a wheel exceeds 0.2, the brake actuator of that wheel must be immediately released". We imply from this property that at the end of each period if $(\text{rspd} - \text{WSL.spd} \times 0.75)/\text{rspd} > 0.2$ then `WSL.trq` must immediately become 0, where $\text{rspd} = (\text{WSL.spd} + \text{WSR.spd})/2$. Suppose that initially, the speed of the left and right wheels are 15 and 13, respectively and the initial brake percentage is 60. As only `WSL`, `WSR`, and brake sensor `BS` have messages in their queue, they first send the speed of wheels (i.e., 15 and 13) and brake percentage (i.e., 60) to their corresponding controllers upon handling their messages. Then, the wheel controllers and the brake controller handle `setWspd` and `setBpcnt` messages, respectively, to update their values. The wheel controllers send their speed values to the brake controller via `CAN` by sending a `sndM` message. Then, `CAN` handles its two `sndM` messages from the wheel controllers by sending `rcv` messages to the brake con-

```
93  │  main {
94  │      @priority(1)
95  │      WheelSensor WSL(WCL):(10,12);
96  │      @priority(2)
97  │      WheelCtrl WCL(WSL,BC,CAN):();
98  │      @priority(1)
99  │      WheelSensor WSR(WCR):(11,12);
100 │      @priority(2)
101 │      WheelCtrl WCR(WSR,BC,CAN):();
102 │      @priority(1)
103 │      BrakeSensor BS(BC):();
104 │      @priority(4)
105 │      BrakeCtrl BC(WCL,WCR,CAN):();
106 │      @priority(3)
107 │      CANBusNetwork CAN():();
108 │  }
```

Fig. 13. Actor instantiations for the Brake-by-Wire system with Anti-lock Braking System

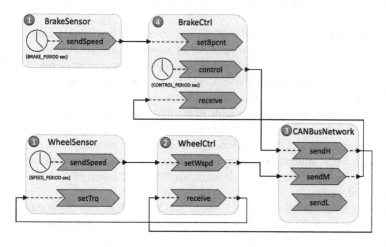

Fig. 14. A diagrammatic representation of the program model of the Brake-by-Wire system presented in Fig. 12, inspired from the Lingua Franca diagram notation

troller BC. Please note that CAN has a higher priority than the brake controller, so the brake controller BC first gets two rcv messages before handing its messages. BC has the next priority to be executed. It has three messages in its queue: two rcv messages and one control message. As the priority for handling rcv messages is higher than the control message, it first handles the rcv messages and updates the value speed of wheels, and then by handling the control message computes the desired torque and speed as 60 and 14 and sends them via two sequential rcv messages through CAN to each wheel controllers. The wheel controllers handle their rcv messages and compute the slip rate as 0.207 and 0.312 for the left and right wheels which indicates that the brake should be released by sending `setTrq(0)` to the wheels. This scenario satisfies the given property. Assume that no priority is defined for the message servers of the brake controller or the priority of the brake controller is not less than the others. So, the brake controller may handle `control` first while it has not received any values for the speeds (which are initially 0). Thus, the given property is wrongly violated.

The size of the state space generated by Afra has $10,088$ states and $12,732$ transitions. If we remove the priorities defined for the instances of actors, the resulting size is increased to $1,659,463$ states and $6,326,764$ transitions. If we also remove the priorities for the message servers within the `BrackCtrl` and `CANBusNetwork` classes, the resulting state space will have $2,523,309$ states and $10,313,561$ transitions. The priorities among the actors implicitly model a scheduling policy for executing actors to resolve nondeterminism due to their concurrent execution while the priorities among the message servers model a scheduling policy to resolve the nondeterminism caused by messages arriving at the same time.

5 Holistic Analysis of Cyber-Physical Systems

The two orthogonal features of variability handling mechanisms and priority can be used together. This combination of usage makes it possible to specify variability in the domain of embedded and cyber-physical systems. Using the features of upgraded Timed Rebeca, we may define different communication mechanisms, like broadcast or specific protocols like in a CAN bus in a more structured way and hence more usable and understandable for the engineers. We can model periodic and sporadic events and order their handling where necessary. This allows us to model different configurations for cyber-physical systems and perform a holistic analysis of safety and timing features. We revise our running example in Fig. 3 to extend its domain application, inspired from [11] in the automotive domain.

The extension to the Timed Rebeca model in Fig. 3 is brought by three modifications: 1) replacing the feature annotation by polymorphism and making `Sensor` and `ComptUnit` abstract classes, 2) adding another network type `CANBusNetwork`, similar to our case study in Sect. 4.3, and 3) adding variability to the abstract class `CompUnit` to communicate with entities over a CAN bus. As we need all the instances of `CompUnit` variations to either communicate over CAN or not, we add this variability by using a feature annotation (instead of defining two subclasses for each variant). The resulting model is shown in Fig. 15, with its main block listed in Fig. 16. We explain each modification in detail.

We remove the variables `FT_PERIODIC_SENSOR` and `FT_SPORADIC_SENSOR` and instead define `PeriodicSensor` and `SporadicSensor` as the subclasses of the abstract class `Sensor`. By making the superclass `Sensor` an abstract class, we can specify the common behavior between the two variant subclasses in the superclass as much as possible like the constructor. Substituting polymorphism for feature annotation allows having two variants of `Sensor` class within a model simultaneously. With the same discussion, we also remove the variables `FT_PERIODIC_PUSH` and `FT_IMMEDIATE_PUSH` and define `CompUnitPeriodic`

```
1  featurevar FT_SIMPLE_NETWORK;
2  featurevar FT_CAN_NETWORK;
3  featurevar FT_TDMA_NETWORK;

5  abstract Sensor{
6    statevars{CompUnit cu;}
7    Sensor(CompUnit cu1) {
8      cu = cu1;
9      self.gatherData();}
10     abstract msgsrv gatherData();
11 }
12 reactiveclass PeriodicSensor
        extends Sensor(3){
13   // constructor omitted
14   msgsrv gatherData() {
15     cu.receiveData(0);
16     self.gatherData()
              after(2);}
17 }
18 reactiveclass SporadicSensor
        extends Sensor(3){
19   // constructor omitted
20   msgsrv gatherData() {
21     cu.receiveData(0);
22     self.gatherData()
              after(?(1,2,3));}
23 }
24 abstract CompUnit {
25   statevars {
26     Network network;
27     @feature(FT_CAN_NETWORK)
28     int priority}
29   CompUnit(Network net, int pr){
30     network = net;
31     @feature(FT_CAN_NETWORK)
32     priority = pr;
33     init();}
34   abstract msgsrv
            receiveData(byte d);
35   abstract void init();
36   void transfer(byte data){
37     @feature(FT_CAN_NETWORK)
38     if (priority==1)
39       network.sendHigh(data);
40     else if (priority==2)
41       network.sendMedium(data);
42     network.send(data);}
43 }
```

```
45 env int BUFFER_SIZE = 4;
46 reactiveclass CompUnitPeriodic
        extends CompUnit(3){
47   statevars {
48     int[BUFFER_SIZE] buffer;
49     int cnt;}
50   // constructor omitted
51   void init(){self.process();}
52   msgsrv receiveData(byte d) {
53     buffer[cnt++] = d;}
54   msgsrv process() {
55     for(int i=cnt;cnt>0;cnt--)
56       transfer(buffer[i]);
57     self.process() after(1);}
58 }
59 reactiveclass CompUnitImmediate
        extends CompUnit(2){
60   // constructor omitted
61   void init(){}
62   msgsrv receiveData(byte d){
63     transfer(data);}
64 }
65 interface Network {
66   @feature(FT_CAN_NETWORK)
67   msgsrv sendHigh(byte data);
68   @feature(FT_CAN_NETWORK)
69   msgsrv sendMedium(data);
70   msgsrv send(byte data);
71 }
72 reactiveclass MACBNetwork
        implements Network(3) {
73   // constructor omitted
74   msgsrv send(byte data) { }
75 }
76 reactiveclass TDMANetwork
        implements Network(3) {
77   // constructor omitted
78   msgsrv send(byte data) { }
79 }
80 reactiveclass CANBusNetwork
        implements Network(3) {
81   // constructor omitted
82   @priority(1)
83   msgsrv sendHigh(byte data){}
84   @priority(2)
85   msgsrv sendMedium(data){}
86   @priority(3) //low
87   msgsrv send(byte data){}
88 }
```

Fig. 15. Extending the domain application of the sensor network running example shown in Fig. 3 by adding a CAN Bus and using the features of upgraded Timed Rebeca

```
82 | main {
83 |   @priority(1);
84 |   PeriodicSensor sr1():(cu1);
85 |   @priority(2);
86 |   CompUnitPeriodic cu1():(network, FT_CAN_NETWORK?2:0);
87 |   @priority(1);
88 |   SporadicSensor sr2():(cu2);
89 |   @priority(2);
90 |   CompUnitImmediate cu2():(network, FT_CAN_NETWORK?1:0);
91 |   @priority(3);
92 |   @feature(FT_SIMPLE_NETWORK)
93 |   MACBNetwork network():();
94 |   @feature(FT_TDMA_NETWORK)
95 |   TDMANetwork network():();
96 |   @feature(FT_CAN_NETWORK)
97 |   CANBusNetwork network():();
98 | }
```

Fig. 16. Actor instantiations for the upgraded sensor network running example shown in Fig. 15

and `CompUnitImmediate` as the subclasses of the abstract class `CompUnit`. The superclass `CompUnit` has one abstract function `init` which is called in the constructor. This abstract method contains the specific initialization needed for each variant subclass. In `CompUnitPeriodic`, this method must send a message to itself to start periodic execution while no initialization is required in `CompUnitImmediate`.

Thanks to the priority feature, we add another network type `CANBusNetwork`, suitable for modeling the network in the automotive domain. By using the feature expression `@feature(FT_CAN_NETWORK)`, we add variability to the abstract class `CompUnit`. This feature adds a `priority` state variable to the class. As messages are transmitted over a CAN bus based on their priorities, we define a message server for each message priority in `CANBusNetwork` and assign a priority to each message server using the priority feature. The `priority` variable of `CompUnit` indicates the priority of messages (received from the sensors). The method `transfer` of `CompUnit` sends messages to the network. If the network is a CAN bus, when the variable `FT_CAN_NETWORK` is set, then it calls the corresponding message server of `CANBusNetwork` based on the value of `priority`.

A configuration of the model where only the feature `FT_CAN_NETWORK` is present gives the model of two connected ECUs communicating over a CAN bus in a car. The first sensor instance `sr1` models the wheel sensor which periodically sends the speed of the wheel to its wheel controller, represented by `cu1`. The second sensor instance `sr2` is the gear sensor which sends the level of gear upon any change to its controller, represented by `cu2`.

6 Related Work

Apart from variability-aware extensions of modeling notations based on transition systems and process algebras (comprehensively surveyed in [10]), several formal modeling languages have been extended to support variability, including fPromela [16], fSMV [17], and an extension of Event-B [68]. Having our focus on formal modeling of asynchronously communicating distributed systems, the most notable language is Abstract Behavioral Specification (ABS) [1,35], which follows the concurrent object-oriented style of the actor model, and enables variability modeling using a delta-oriented approach [15,19,58]. Unlike ABS, our way to handle variability in Rebeca family of languages is through feature annotation and polymorphism which models the entire family behavior in one place. Verification of software product lines has a relatively long history. This includes the works based on modal I/O automata [45], PL-CCS [25], and early results based on Featured Transition Systems [18]. More recent advances on the verification of SPLs include a wide range of techniques such as static analysis [6,8], parity games [7], proof plans [44], and correct-by-construction approach [13].

Lee et.al. proposed Lingua Franca as a language for developing deterministic actors [46]. Lingua Franca resolve nondeterminisitc execution among actors using predefined order of executions for actors. The idea of associating priority to actors in Rebeca to make the model more deterministic is inspired from Lingua Franca. In comparison with [46], although actors can be deterministic in Rebeca, they are allowed to have nondeterministic behavior. This means that modelers are allowed to express the required level of nondeterminism in models.

7 Conclusion

In this paper, we presented an overview of the language features of Timed Rebeca to support variability management and modeling determinism. The approach to variability management is feature-oriented and is done using feature variables. By annotating parts of the model source code with feature expressions, we can bind model parts to a number of product configurations. Moreover, class polymorphism can be used to manage variability by providing alternative implementations of model components. This way, the whole product line can be modeled in a single artifact which explicitly models the variability in structure and behavior of the model. This enables the opportunity to analyze the whole product line model at once as opposed to analyzing every product individually. The theory behind verification of the whole product line has been developed and partially implemented and is a future step in the development of Afra, the Timed Rebeca model checker. Currently, Afra supports feature variables and verification of the individual products specified through a valuation of the feature variables. As a future work, we plan to study the feasibility of applying variability encoding [54] to defer the variability resolution time from compile-time to state-space generation time, which may increase the efficiency of whole-family verification.

We also showed how Timed Rebeca models can be made more deterministic by assigning priorities to message servers and actors. This enables the modelers to bring in assumptions about the execution environment or outside entities. In addition to making the model closer to a set of real world applications, this may result in (possibly significant) reduction in the size of the state space and make it more practical to analyze more complex systems. Both of these aspects enhance the practicality of the Timed Rebeca toolset to be used in industrial settings.

References

1. The ABS language. https://abs-models.org/
2. Afra toolset homepage. https://rebeca-lang.org/alltools/Afra
3. Agha, G.: Actors: A Model of Concurrent Computation in Distributed Systems. MIT Press, Cambridge (1986)
4. Ayala, I., Papadopoulos, A.V., Amor, M., Fuentes, L.: ProDSPL: proactive self-adaptation based on dynamic software product lines. J. Syst. Softw. **175**, 110909 (2021)
5. Batory, D.: Feature models, grammars, and propositional formulas. In: Obbink, H., Pohl, K. (eds.) SPLC 2005. LNCS, vol. 3714, pp. 7–20. Springer, Heidelberg (2005). https://doi.org/10.1007/11554844_3
6. ter Beek, M.H., Damiani, F., Lienhardt, M., Mazzanti, F., Paolini, L.: Efficient static analysis and verification of featured transition systems. Empir. Softw. Eng. **27**(1), 10 (2022)
7. ter Beek, M.H., van Loo, S., de Vink, E.P., Willemse, T.A.: Family-based SPL model checking using parity games with variability. In: Wehrheim, H., Cabot, J. (eds.) FASE 2020. LNCS, vol. 12076, pp. 245–265. Springer, Cham (2020). https://doi.org/10.1007/978-3-030-45234-6_12
8. ter Beek, M.H., Damiani, F., Lienhardt, M., Mazzanti, F., Paolini, L.: Static analysis of featured transition systems. In: Proceedings of the 23rd International Systems and Software Product Line Conference-Volume A, pp. 39–51 (2019)
9. Behjati, R., Yue, T., Briand, L., Selic, B.: SimPL: a product-line modeling methodology for families of integrated control systems. Inf. Softw. Technol. **55**(3), 607–629 (2013)
10. Benduhn, F., Thüm, T., Lochau, M., Leich, T., Saake, G.: A survey on modeling techniques for formal behavioral verification of software product lines. In: Proceedings of the Ninth International Workshop on Variability Modelling of Software-Intensive Systems, pp. 80–87 (2015)
11. Bengtsson, H.H., Hiller, M., Mattsson, F., Bengtsson, J.: Holistic analysis of task scheduling and message scheduling in automotive centralised E/E architecture. In: IEEE/SA Ethernet/IP@Automotive Techonology Day (2020)
12. Boer, F.D., et al.: A survey of active object languages. ACM Comput. Surv. (CSUR) **50**(5), 1–39 (2017)
13. Bordis, T., Runge, T., Schaefer, I.: Correctness-by-construction for feature-oriented software product lines. In: Proceedings of the 19th ACM SIGPLAN International Conference on Generative Programming: Concepts and Experiences, pp. 22–34 (2020)
14. Cionca, V., Newe, T., Dadârlat, V.: TDMA protocol requirements for wireless sensor networks. In: 2008 Second International Conference on Sensor Technologies and Applications (sensorcomm 2008), pp. 30–35. IEEE (2008)
15. Clarke, D., Muschevici, R., Proença, J., Schaefer, I., Schlatte, R.: Variability modelling in the ABS language. In: Aichernig, B.K., de Boer, F.S., Bonsangue, M.M. (eds.) FMCO 2010. LNCS, vol. 6957, pp. 204–224. Springer, Heidelberg (2011). https://doi.org/10.1007/978-3-642-25271-6_11

16. Classen, A., Cordy, M., Heymans, P., Legay, A., Schobbens, P.Y.: Model checking software product lines with SNIP. Int. J. Softw. Tools Technol. Transf. **14**, 589–612 (2012)
17. Classen, A., Cordy, M., Heymans, P., Legay, A., Schobbens, P.Y.: Formal semantics, modular specification, and symbolic verification of product-line behaviour. Sci. Comput. Program. **80**, 416–439 (2014)
18. Classen, A., Heymans, P., Schobbens, P.Y., Legay, A., Raskin, J.F.: Model checking lots of systems: efficient verification of temporal properties in software product lines. In: Proceedings of the 32nd ACM/IEEE International Conference on Software Engineering, vol. 1, pp. 335–344 (2010)
19. Damiani, F., Hähnle, R., Kamburjan, E., Lienhardt, M., Paolini, L.: Variability modules. J. Syst. Softw. **195**, 111510 (2023)
20. Davis, R.I., Burns, A., Bril, R.J., Lukkien, J.J.: Controller area network (CAN) schedulability analysis: refuted, revisited and revised. Real-Time Syst. **35**(3), 239–272 (2007)
21. Eckel, B.: Thinking in Java, 4th edn. Prentice Hall (2006)
22. Fadhlillah, H.S., Feichtinger, K., Meixner, K., Sonnleithner, L., Rabiser, R., Zoitl, A.: Towards multidisciplinary delta-oriented variability management in cyber-physical production systems. In: Proceedings of the 16th International Working Conference on Variability Modelling of Software-Intensive Systems, pp. 1–10 (2022)
23. Filipovikj, P., Mahmud, N., Marinescu, R., Seceleanu, C., Ljungkrantz, O., Lönn, H.: Simulink to UPPAAL statistical model checker: analyzing automotive industrial systems. In: Fitzgerald, J., Heitmeyer, C., Gnesi, S., Philippou, A. (eds.) FM 2016. LNCS, vol. 9995, pp. 748–756. Springer, Cham (2016). https://doi.org/10.1007/978-3-319-48989-6_46
24. Forcina, G., et al.: Safe design of flow management systems using Rebeca. J. Inf. Process. **28**, 588–598 (2020)
25. Gruler, A., Leucker, M., Scheidemann, K.: Modeling and model checking software product lines. In: Barthe, G., de Boer, F.S. (eds.) FMOODS 2008. LNCS, vol. 5051, pp. 113–131. Springer, Heidelberg (2008). https://doi.org/10.1007/978-3-540-68863-1_8
26. Haller, P.: On the integration of the actor model in mainstream technologies: the scala perspective. In: Proceedings of the 2nd Edition on Programming Systems, Languages and Applications Based on Actors, Agents, and Decentralized Control Abstractions, pp. 1–6 (2012)
27. von Hanxleden, R., et al.: Pragmatics twelve years later: a report on lingua franca. In: Margaria, T., Steffen, B. (eds.) ISoLA 2022, Part II. LNCS, vol. 13702, pp. 60–89. Springer, Cham (2022). https://doi.org/10.1007/978-3-031-19756-7_5
28. Haugen, Ø., Wasowski, A., Czarnecki, K.: CVL: common variability language. In: Kishi, T., Jarzabek, S., Gnesi, S. (eds.) 17th International Software Product Line Conference, SPLC 2013, Tokyo, Japan, 26–30 August 2013, p. 277. ACM (2013)
29. Hewitt, C.: Viewing control structures as patterns of passing messages. Artif. Intell. **8**(3), 323–364 (1977)
30. Hewitt, C.: Actor model of computation: scalable robust information systems. arXiv preprint arXiv:1008.1459 (2010)
31. Hinchey, M., Park, S., Schmid, K.: Building dynamic software product lines. Computer **45**(10), 22–26 (2012)
32. Jafari, A., Khamespanah, E., Sirjani, M., Hermanns, H., Cimini, M.: PTRebeca: modeling and analysis of distributed and asynchronous systems. Sci. Comput. Program. **128**, 22–50 (2016)

33. Jahandideh, I., Ghassemi, F., Sirjani, M.: An actor-based framework for asynchronous event-based cyber-physical systems. Softw. Syst. Model. **20**(3), 641–665 (2021)
34. Jahandideh, I., Ghassemi, F., Sirjani, M.: Hybrid Rebeca: modeling and analyzing of cyber-physical systems. In: Chamberlain, R., Taha, W., Törngren, M. (eds.) CyPhy/WESE -2018. LNCS, vol. 11615, pp. 3–27. Springer, Cham (2019). https://doi.org/10.1007/978-3-030-23703-5_1
35. Johnsen, E.B., Hähnle, R., Schäfer, J., Schlatte, R., Steffen, M.: ABS: a core language for abstract behavioral specification. In: Aichernig, B.K., de Boer, F.S., Bonsangue, M.M. (eds.) FMCO 2010. LNCS, vol. 6957, pp. 142–164. Springer, Heidelberg (2011). https://doi.org/10.1007/978-3-642-25271-6_8
36. Kang, E., Enoiu, E.P., Marinescu, R., Seceleanu, C.C., Schobbens, P., Pettersson, P.: A methodology for formal analysis and verification of EAST-ADL models. Reliab. Eng. Syst. Saf. **120**, 127–138 (2013)
37. Kang, K.C., Cohen, S.G., Hess, J.A., Novak, W.E., Peterson, A.S.: Feature-oriented domain analysis (FODA) feasibility study. Technical report, Carnegie-Mellon University, Pittsburgh, PA, Software Engineering Institute (1990)
38. Khakpour, N., Jalili, S., Talcott, C., Sirjani, M., Mousavi, M.: Formal modeling of evolving self-adaptive systems. Sci. Comput. Program. **78**(1), 3–26 (2012)
39. Khakpour, N., Khosravi, R., Sirjani, M., Jalili, S.: Formal analysis of policy-based self-adaptive systems. In: Proceedings of the 2010 ACM Symposium on Applied Computing, pp. 2536–2543 (2010)
40. Khamespanah, E., Sirjani, M., Kaviani, Z.S., Khosravi, R., Izadi, M.J.: Timed Rebeca schedulability and deadlock freedom analysis using bounded floating time transition system. Sci. Comput. Program. **98**, 184–204 (2015)
41. Khamespanah, E., Sirjani, M., Khosravi, R.: Afra: an eclipse-based tool with extensible architecture for modeling and model checking of Rebeca family models. In: Hojjat, H., Ábrahám, E. (eds.) FSEN 2023. LNCS, vol. 14155, pp. 72–87. Springer, Cham (2023). https://doi.org/10.1007/978-3-031-42441-0_6
42. Khamespanah, E., Sirjani, M., Mechitov, K., Agha, G.: Modeling and analyzing real-time wireless sensor and actuator networks using actors and model checking. Int. J. Softw. Tools Technol. Transf. **20**, 547–561 (2018)
43. Krüger, J., et al.: Beyond software product lines: variability modeling in cyber-physical systems. In: Proceedings of the 21st International Systems and Software Product Line Conference, vol. A, pp. 237–241 (2017)
44. Kuiter, E., Knüppel, A., Bordis, T., Runge, T., Schaefer, I.: Verification strategies for feature-oriented software product lines. In: Proceedings of the 16th International Working Conference on Variability Modelling of Software-Intensive Systems, pp. 1–9 (2022)
45. Larsen, K.G., Nyman, U., Wąsowski, A.: Modal I/O automata for interface and product line theories. In: De Nicola, R. (ed.) ESOP 2007. LNCS, vol. 4421, pp. 64–79. Springer, Heidelberg (2007). https://doi.org/10.1007/978-3-540-71316-6_6
46. Lohstroh, M., Menard, C., Bateni, S., Lee, E.A.: Toward a lingua franca for deterministic concurrent systems. ACM Trans. Embed. Comput. Syst. **20**(4), 36:1–36:27 (2021). https://doi.org/10.1145/3448128
47. Lohstroh, M., et al.: Actors revisited for time-critical systems. In: Proceedings of the 56th Annual Design Automation Conference 2019, DAC 2019, Las Vegas, NV, USA, 02–06 June 2019, p. 152. ACM (2019)
48. Marinescu, R., Mubeen, S., Seceleanu, C.: Pruning architectural models of automotive embedded systems via dependency analysis. In: 42th Euromicro Conference on

Software Engineering and Advanced Applications, pp. 293–302. IEEE Computer Society (2016)

49. Menard, C., et al.: High-performance deterministic concurrency using lingua franca. CoRR abs/2301.02444 (2023)

50. Pfeiffer, O., Ayre, A., Keydel, C.: Embedded Networking with CAN and CANopen, 1st edn. Copperhill Media Corporation (2008)

51. Pohl, K., Böckle, G., Van Der Linden, F.: Software Product Line Engineering, vol. 10. Springer, Heidelberg (2005). https://doi.org/10.1007/3-540-28901-1

52. Rabiser, R., Zoitl, A.: Towards mastering variability in software-intensive cyber-physical production systems. Procedia Comput. Sci. **180**, 50–59 (2021)

53. Reynisson, A.H., et al.: Modelling and simulation of asynchronous real-time systems using timed Rebeca. Sci. Comput. Program. **89**, 41–68 (2014)

54. von Rhein, A., Thüm, T., Schaefer, I., Liebig, J., Apel, S.: Variability encoding: From compile-time to load-time variability. J. Log. Algebraic Methods Program. **85**(1), 125–145 (2016)

55. Sabouri, H., Jaghoori, M.M., de Boer, F., Khosravi, R.: Scheduling and analysis of real-time software families. In: 2012 IEEE 36th Annual Computer Software and Applications Conference, pp. 680–689. IEEE (2012)

56. Sabouri, H., Khosravi, R.: Modeling and verification of reconfigurable actor families. J. Univers. Comput. Sci. **19**(2), 207–232 (2013)

57. Sabouri, H., Khosravi, R.: Reducing the verification cost of evolving product families using static analysis techniques. Sci. Comput. Program. **83**, 35–55 (2014)

58. Schaefer, I., Bettini, L., Bono, V., Damiani, F., Tanzarella, N.: Delta-oriented programming of software product lines. In: Bosch, J., Lee, J. (eds.) SPLC 2010. LNCS, vol. 6287, pp. 77–91. Springer, Heidelberg (2010). https://doi.org/10.1007/978-3-642-15579-6_6

59. Sehr, M.A., et al.: Programmable logic controllers in the context of industry 4.0. IEEE Trans. Industr. Inform. **17**(5), 3523–3533 (2021)

60. Sharifi, Z., Khosravi, R., Sirjani, M., Khamespanah, E.: Towards formal analysis of vehicle platoons using actor model. In: 2020 25th IEEE International Conference on Emerging Technologies and Factory Automation (ETFA), vol. 1, pp. 1820–1827. IEEE (2020)

61. Sharifi, Z., Mosaffa, M., Mohammadi, S., Sirjani, M.: Functional and performance analysis of network-on-chips using actor-based modeling and formal verification. Electron. Commun. Eur. Assoc. Softw. Sci. Technol. **66**, 1–16 (2013)

62. Sirjani, M., Jaghoori, M.M.: Ten years of analyzing actors: Rebeca experience. In: Agha, G., Danvy, O., Meseguer, J. (eds.) Formal Modeling: Actors, Open Systems, Biological Systems. LNCS, vol. 7000, pp. 20–56. Springer, Heidelberg (2011). https://doi.org/10.1007/978-3-642-24933-4_3

63. Sirjani, M., Khamespanah, E.: On time actors. In: Ábrahám, E., Bonsangue, M., Johnsen, E.B. (eds.) Theory and Practice of Formal Methods. LNCS, vol. 9660, pp. 373–392. Springer, Cham (2016). https://doi.org/10.1007/978-3-319-30734-3_25

64. Sirjani, M., Lee, E.A., Khamespanah, E.: Verification of cyberphysical systems. Mathematics **8**(7), 1068 (2020)

65. Sirjani, M., Movaghar, A.: An actor-based model for formal modelling of reactive systems: Rebeca. Technical report CS-TR-80-01, Tehran, Iran (2001)

66. Sirjani, M., Movaghar, A., Mousavi, M.: Compositional verification of an object-based reactive system. In: Workshop on Automated Verification of Critical Systems (AVoCS 2001) (2001)

67. Sirjani, M., Movaghar, A., Shali, A., De Boer, F.S.: Modeling and verification of reactive systems using Rebeca. Fund. Inform. **63**(4), 385–410 (2004)

68. Sorge, J., Poppleton, M., Butler, M.: A basis for feature-oriented modelling in event-B. In: Frappier, M., Glässer, U., Khurshid, S., Laleau, R., Reeves, S. (eds.) ABZ 2010. LNCS, vol. 5977, p. 409. Springer, Heidelberg (2010). https://doi.org/10.1007/978-3-642-11811-1_42

69. Varshosaz, M., Khosravi, R.: Modeling and verification of probabilistic actor systems using pRebeca. In: Aoki, T., Taguchi, K. (eds.) ICFEM 2012. LNCS, vol. 7635, pp. 135–150. Springer, Heidelberg (2012). https://doi.org/10.1007/978-3-642-34281-3_12

70. Weyns, D.: Software engineering of self-adaptive systems. In: Handbook of Software Engineering, pp. 399–443. Springer, Cham (2019). https://doi.org/10.1007/978-3-030-00262-6_11

71. Yousefi, F., Khamespanah, E., Gharib, M., Sirjani, M., Movaghar, A.: VeriVANca framework: verification of VANETs by property-based message passing of actors in Rebeca with inheritance. Int. J. Softw. Tools Technol. Transf. **22**(5), 617–633 (2020)

Analysis

Integrating Data Privacy Compliance in Active Object Languages

Chinmayi Prabhu Baramashetru$^{(\boxtimes)}$, Silvia Lizeth Tapia Tarifa$^{(\boxtimes)}$,
and Olaf Owe$^{(\boxtimes)}$

Department of Informatics, University of Oslo, Oslo, Norway
{cpbarama,sltarifa,olaf}@ifi.uio.no

Abstract. As users of digitalized services are more and more required
to share their personal data, it becomes increasingly important for applications to comply with users' consent for the handling of their personal
data. Ensuring compliance with such consent requires reasoning globally about both the flow of information and the interaction of different
parties handling personal data. In this direction, privacy by design principles cultivate a philosophy that endorses the development of systems
with built-in abilities to demonstrate compliance with data privacy to
guarantee the protection of personal data. However, there is an apparent mismatch in adopting such imprecise principles into explicit design
methods that support systematic solutions that integrates data privacy
in system design. In this paper, we propose an integration of privacy
concepts into a core active object language, to explore how the chosen
privacy-aware language semantics can ensure handling of personal data
according to users' privacy consent.

1 Introduction

Due to the rigorous modeling of the digital economy, companies nowadays are
tempted to treat users' personal data as enterprise-wide assets to gain insights
that benefit their businesses. The exchange of data through several online and
offline data sources and the proliferation of unlawful processing has resulted
in the enaction of personal data regulations to protect users against unlawful
business practices and retain their privacy rights. The General Data Protection
Regulations (GDPR) [7] is one such prime example that mandates transparent
data processing and enforces users' rights for their personal data to be handled according to their consent. The GDPR is an extensive text document, not
written by software designers or information engineers but by lawyers and policy-
makers. As a written text, the GDPR contains unclear terminology that can be
interpreted in different ways, contributing to the existing gap in what can be
enforced in practice for data privacy against what it required to be enforced by
the law. This problem is widely discussed and recognized by academia and industry researchers. However, well-understood concepts, models, and tools to support
GDPR enforcement are still controversial [20,22]. The GDPR hints towards privacy by design and default under Article 25, which envisions the support for

F. de Boer et al. (Eds.): *Active Object Languages: Current Research Trends*,
LNCS 14360, pp. 263–288, 2024.
https://doi.org/10.1007/978-3-031-51060-1_10

software development with built-in abilities to comply with data protection regulations [5,30].

Integrating privacy principles into the software development process is not a new challenge [8,25]. In particular, there have been several attempts to develop privacy by construction approaches [22]. However, many aspects of data privacy remain unexplored [13,29]. Since conventional languages do not have well-established support for privacy-specific properties, there is a need for new programming language primitives, preferably with methodology for proof of correctness to synthesize the program with privacy constructs.

In this paper, we discuss aspects of data privacy that have been little explored and have the potential to be addressed via language design principles [14], such as simplicity, expressiveness, transparency, and consistency. Using language design principles will help us enhance a core language for distributed systems with data privacy principles so that data privacy compliance can be easily expressed and checked. We consider a core active object language as our target, which provides a powerful mechanism to model distributed systems [6]. Active object languages combine the basic Actor model [1] with object-oriented concepts. Communication between active objects is realized asynchronously, allowing interleaved execution inside each object with its own processing thread. We first discuss the main abstractions that need to be considered in a language to address privacy awareness and later explore how language semantics can be used to enforce compliance for users' privacy consent. Concretely, we integrate privacy principles into a core active object language where 1) users can add or withdraw consent using special language constructs, 2) objects capture instances of entities, which are user-approved, and 3) the language semantics ensures that personal data is handled in accordance with the given users' privacy consent.

Paper Outline. We first identify the relevant GDPR requirements and technical challenges in Sects. 2 and 3. Then we focus on the language syntax in Sect. 4, motivating examples in Sect. 5 and semantics in Sect. 6. Reflections on the language are given in Sect. 7 and the correctness of the language is shown in Sect. 8, related work and discussion in Sect. 9 and conclusion and future work in Sect. 10.

2   The GDPR Requirements

The GDPR establishes a unified framework for data protection across the European Union. The GDPR is currently stretched over 11 chapters and consists of 99 articles. Across the chapters, it mentions several restrictions for personal data handling. In this section, we detail a few core principles of the GDPR that have the potential to be addressed via language design principles.

Purpose Limitation: Art. 5 Sect. 1(b) of the GDPR states purpose limitation as *"Personal data shall be collected for specified, explicit and legitimate purposes and not further processed in a manner that is incompatible with those purposes;*

...not be considered to be incompatible with the initial purposes". This requirement mainly imposes restrictions on systems for collecting a vast amount of data for ambiguous and broadly classified purposes. According to purpose limitation, data controllers are compelled to use personal data only for specific, well-defined purposes and cannot process further for alternative purposes. Additionally, Sect. 1(e) of Art. 5 mentions that personal data shall only be stored if necessary and imposes storage limitations based on purposes.

Conditions for Consent: Art. 6.1 (a) specifies that data subject's consent for handling their personal data for one or more purposes is essential for lawful processing. Under Art. 7 [7], the GDPR specifies various conditions for consent from data subjects. Consent needs to be informed and freely obtained before processing personal data. The terms and conditions presented to receive consent from data subjects should be clear, intelligible, and understandable. The GDPR also formulates that data subjects should be able to modify their consent at any time, and data controllers should facilitate this choice. If we rephrase this into a technical solution, any processing or collection of personal data should be attached to the individual consent from the users. Upon withdrawal, the personal data should no longer be used for any processing.

Data Subject Rights: Art. 12–21, specifies a set of rights that service providers must facilitate for data subjects while handling their personal data. Art. 15 remarks that a *"data subject shall have the right to access the purpose of processing categories of personal data, the recipients to whom personal data is disclosed or transferred, and the period for which the data will be stored."*. This is to say that users are an operative part of personal data processing. Exercising data subjects' rights allows users to access their personal data and have full decision rights on how it is handled.

3   The GDPR Technical Challenges

In this section, we discuss the main challenges related to GDPR requirements discussed in Sect. 2. In particular, we focus on the challenges with the potential to be addressed via language design principles. In contrast to well-explored problems for incorporating GDPR rules within a distributed system, the challenges discussed in this section are less explored by the research community [13].

Challenge 1: Contextual Awareness of Personal Data. The GDPR states that "personal data" is any information that is related to an identifiable person (data subject). In a technical context, this can be understood as data containing explicit identifiers such as name, identification number, physical identifier, online identifier, etc. In Sect. 2, we noticed that purpose plays a vital role in handling personal data. However, relating data handlers (entities) and purposes to identifiable personal data yields new challenges for information systems since data handling suddenly becomes highly contextual. For example, consider personal data D identified by entities E_1 and E_2. However, both entities can only handle D differently since they have access to D for different purposes.

Challenge 2: Data Processed as Personal Data. This can happen when non-personal data can be associated with an identifier or when such data is combined with other pieces of data to be associated with an individual. For example, entity E_1 can handle non-personal data D, which in the process of data handling is transformed into identifiable personal data D'. However, E_1 does not have authorization from the data owner to process such personal data (data leak), creating a violation of the users' consent preference.

Challenge 3: Personal Data with Multiple Owners. Although the GDPR never explicitly mentions how to process data owned by multiple data subjects, it is crucial to consider data handling when data concerns more than one data subject. As an example, let us consider a loan application that considers combined personal data D of two data subjects, Alice and Bob. If Alice allows the handling of her personal data for a set of purposes P_1 and Bob allows the handling of his personal data for a set of purposes P_2, it is unclear how to proceed with the handling of D.

Challenge 4: Unclear Terminology for Personal Data Handing. As shown in Sect. 2, the GDPR uses terminology that can have multiple interpretations, particularly for data handling. Vocabulary, such as collect, store, use, delete and transfer, is unspecified, and it is unclear how requirements directly related to such terminology should be enforced by services.

4   A Privacy-Aware Active Object Language

Active object languages [6] are considered suitable for distributed and service-oriented systems. We consider a core privacy-aware active object language (that we call P-AOL), that is extended with support for GDPR concepts, privacy policies, and notion of consent.

4.1   Privacy-Aware Aspects of P-AOL

In this section, we motivate the main privacy-related aspects that we will incorporate in P-AOL.

Data controllers (DC) and *data processors (DP)* can be understood as *entities*, which are identifiable organizations, organizational units, or roles in an organization that has or can handle data. P-AOL will include the declaration of a set of entities. In particular, an object can be associated with one declared entity to reflect the entity it represents (if any). An object associated with an entity may act as a DC or DP, and we formalize the transfer of rights from DC to DP. With this information, it is possible to enforce that only objects acting as authorized entities can access personal data. After that, we can check the access against the consent settings provided by the users.

Data subjects (DS) can be understood as *users* whose personal data is being handled by entities. As noted in Sect. 2, users should be able to express consent on their personal data handling. P-AOL will include unique objects that represent users so that we can check how a service behaves when interacting with the users' consent. In P-AOL, personal data will be associated with specific ids, transforming them into private values. P-AOL will be designed so that the language can handle non-private values freely and restrict the handling of private values. In particular, the language will handle private values with more than one owner (where each owner has different set-ups for their consent), e.g., personal data associated with bank loans for various legally accountable users.

Purposes can be understood as the reasons why personal data is being handled. P-AOL will include the declaration of a set of purposes. In particular, personal data will be associated with specific purposes. With this information, it is possible to enforce purpose-based processing. After that, we can check that personal data is handled according to the purposes stated in the users' consent.

Consent can be understood as an *informed agreement* that users give to allow the handling of their personal data. P-AOL will include the addition and removal of consent via *privacy policies* explicitly stating which entities can handle personal data, for what purposes, and what actions they can perform. Actions will be stated using the vocabulary in the GDPR (e.g., collect, transfer, use, store, etc.). The language used to capture consent is a simplified version of the language presented in [2].[1] Since consent is a runtime element, it cannot be assumed to be given all the time since users may modify it during the lifetime of a service. To capture such flexibility, P-AOL will include operations that users can perform to add and remove consent at any time, mimicking the enforcement of Article [7] in the GDPR. See Sect. 2.

Lawfulness of processing of personal data is a fundamental principle of the GDPR, as noted in Sect. 2. All the elements described above will help P-AOL to capture how personal data should be handled according to the consent given by users. As motivated in the introduction section, there exists a gap between ambiguous laws and concrete technical solutions. In particular, the GDPR uses the vocabulary of processing of personal data that includes, e.g., collect, transfer, use, store, etc., that can have different interpretations. In P-AOL we concretize an interpretation of such actions and explore how language semantics can enforce them. In this paper, we limit ourselves to only exploring the interpretation of use, collect, transfer, and store, which will be captured by the operational semantics of the language in Sect. 6. Concretely, we interpret: (1) *collection* of personal data as the action of creating new private values and possibly storing them in short-lived variables (e.g., local variables), (2) *transfer* of personal data as the action of sending private values to other entities, (3) *use* of personal data as the action of accessing private values without modifying them and (4) *storing* of personal data as the action of saving private values in long-lived variables (e.g., fields of objects). Similarly, other actions included in the GDPR, e.g., personal data deletion can be given an interpretation.

---

[1] The full policy language includes additional GDPR aspects such as location and retention time. For simplicity, we here only consider entities, purposes, and actions.

Synt. categories.			*Definitions.*
A	in	Type	$A ::= B \mid I \mid$ U
U	in	UserType	$B ::= T \mid \boxed{T}$
T	in	BasicType	
$\boxed{T}$	in	privType	$PR ::= E \; P \; \widehat{F} \; \widehat{IF} \; \widehat{CL} \; sc$
			$F ::= \textbf{def } B \; fn(\overline{B \; x}) = e;$
η	in	Entity	$E \; ::= \textbf{entities } \widehat{\eta};$
p	in	Purpose	$P \; ::= \textbf{purposes } \widehat{p};$
a	in	Action	$a \; ::= \textbf{use} \mid \textbf{collect} \mid \textbf{store} \mid \textbf{transfer}$
ρ	in	Policy	$IF ::= \textbf{interface } I \; \{\widehat{Sg}\}$
C,I,m,fn	in	Name	$CL ::= \textbf{class } C([\overline{A \; x}]) \textbf{ implements } \overline{I} \; \{[\; \overline{A \; x} \; ; \;] \; \overline{M}\}$
s	in	Stmt	$M ::= Sg \; sc$
x	in	Var	$Sg ::= A \; m([\overline{A \; x}])$
e	in	Expr	$sc ::= \{[\overline{A \; x};] \; s\}$
t	in	Tag	$s ::= \textbf{skip} \mid x := rhs \mid \textbf{if } e \; \{s\} \mid s; s \mid \textbf{await } g \mid$
			$\qquad \textbf{return } e \mid x.\textbf{addCon}(\rho) \mid x.\textbf{remCon}(\rho) \mid$
			$\qquad x.\textbf{addInst}(x) \mid x.\textbf{remInst}(x)$

$rhs ::= \alpha \mid \textbf{new } C(\overline{\alpha}) \; [\textbf{of } \eta] \mid e!m(\overline{\alpha}) \mid e.\textbf{get} \mid \textbf{new user}$

$g ::= x?$

$e ::= v \mid x \mid fn(\overline{e}) \mid e \; op \; e \mid \textbf{this}$

$\alpha ::= e \mid e \; \textbf{tag } t$

$\rho \;\; ::= \; (\widehat{\eta}, \widehat{a}, \widehat{p})$

$t \;\; ::= \; \langle \widehat{x}, \widehat{p} \rangle$

Fig. 1. Syntax of P-AOL. Constructs highlighted with grey background deal with privacy aspects. Terms like $\overline{e}$ denote (possibly empty) lists over the corresponding syntactic categories, terms like $\widehat{u}$ denote (possibly empty) sets over the corresponding syntactic categories. Square brackets [] denote optional elements.

4.2   Formal Syntax of P-AOL

The formal syntax of the language is given in Fig. 1. A type A is either a data type B, an interface I, or type U for users. Type B consists of basic types T, such as Bool, Int, product types (records), etc., as well as private types $\boxed{T}$ that extend the basic types with privacy-aware information (explained below). A program PR includes entities E, purposes P, a set of functions $\widehat{F}$, interfaces $\widehat{IF}$, classes $\widehat{CL}$, and a main block sc. Function declarations F have a return type B, a function name fn, a list of variable declarations $\overline{x}$ of types $\overline{B}$, and a function body given by an expression e. The type system allows functions to be defined over types B. Observe that functions can handle private values, however, freshly tagged values α are syntactically restricted. An interface IF has a name I and a set of method signatures $\widehat{Sg}$. A class CL has a name C, formal parameters and state variables (fields) $\overline{x}$ of types $\overline{A}$ and methods $\overline{M}$.

Observe that the *fields* of the class are defined as both its parameters and state variables. A method definition M consists of a signature Sg and a main block sc. A method signature Sg has a name m, and zero or more parameters

$\overline{A\ x}$ and a return type A. The main block consists of variable declarations $\overline{A\ x}$ and a method body with statements s.

The language includes standard statements s for sequential composition $s_1; s_2$, assignment, **if** statements, **skip** statement, **return** statement and a number of privacy specific statements. The statement **await** g enables co-operative scheduling; it conditionally suspends execution; the guard g controls processor release and consists of Boolean tests e? (explained below). Just like expressions e, the evaluation of guards g is side-effect-free. However, if g evaluates to false, the processor is released and the process is suspended. When the execution thread is idle, an enabled process may be selected from *the pool of suspended processes* by means of a default scheduling policy.

Right-hand-side expressions *rhs* include (possibly tagged) expressions α, a statement **new** to create an object, asynchronous method calls, future dereferencing **get** (explained below) and a statement to create new users. The expressions e of the language include variables x, values v, function expression $fn(\overline{e})$, and operations op on e (e.g., arithmetic and logical operations). The language includes non-assignable reserved variables, concretely and the self-reference **this**. Omitted from Fig. 1 are standard values of the basic types such as Bool and Int. The type $Unit$ has one value, $unit$. Communication in P-AOL is based on asynchronous method calls, denoted by assignments $f = e!m(\overline{\alpha})$ to future variables f. Here, o is an object expression, m a method name, and $\overline{\alpha}$ are (possibly tagged) expressions providing actual parameter values for the method invocation. (Local calls are written **this**!$m(\overline{\alpha})$). After calling $f = e!m(\overline{\alpha})$, the future variable f refers to the return value of the call, and the caller may proceed with its execution without blocking. Two operations on future variables control synchronization in P-AOL. First, the guard **await** f? suspends the active process unless a return to the call associated with f has arrived, allowing other processes in the object to execute. Second, the return value is retrieved by the expression f.**get**, which blocks all execution in the object until the return value is available.

Privacy Policies. The language includes the declaration of entities $\widehat{\eta}$ and purposes $\widehat{p}$. Privacy policies ρ are defined as the tuple $(\widehat{\eta}', \widehat{a}', \widehat{p}')$, where entities $\widehat{\eta}'$ are a subset of the declared entities $\widehat{\eta}$ in the system, purposes $\widehat{p}'$ are a subset of the declared purposes $\widehat{p}$ and actions $\widehat{a}'$ are a subset of the actions defined in the syntax of the language: **use, collect, store,** and **transfer**.

Users and Instances of Entities. New objects are created via the statement **new**. Each object is an instance of a class C with parameters α, and might be associated with an entity η. Such an association will allow us to guarantee that only authorized objects will be able to handle personal data. The language includes a statement **new user** to create special objects that represent users. Objects that are users can perform special operations in the language; such operations include add/remove consent via privacy policies and add/remove concrete instances of entities that can handle their own personal data. Consent can be added and removed with the statements x.**addCon**(ρ), respectively x.**remCon**(ρ). Here the consent is captured in the policy ρ and x evaluates to a user u that gives the consent. Instances can be added and removed with the statements $x.\textbf{addInst}(o)$, respectively $x.\textbf{remInst}(o)$. Here o evaluates to an object id that is authorized to handle the personal data of the user u (where x evaluates to u).

Personal Data and Purpose-Based Processing. We introduce tagged expressions α, with a constructor e **tag** t to associate personal data with identifiers and purposes. Here tags t of the form $\langle \widehat{x}, \widehat{p} \rangle$ (where $\widehat{x}$ evaluates to $\widehat{u}$) are attached to expressions e, so that they become private. Note that the tag $\langle \widehat{x}, \{p, q\} \rangle$ on some data entails that the data can be used for purpose p or q. The tag $\langle \widehat{x}, \emptyset \rangle$ entails that the data cannot be used for any purpose. We syntactically abuse this tag construct so that it can be applied on sets, lists and tuples, e.g., ("John Smith", 25, "Oslo") **tag** $\langle \{john\}, \{Registration\} \rangle$. This explicit tagging could be replaced by automatic and implicit tagging, given a strategy, e.g., for detecting users and purposes. However, such an extension is beyond the scope of this paper.

5   Motivating Examples

In this section, we consider two examples, a hospital information system and a bank loan system, to showcase the main data privacy-related aspects of P-AOL.

*A **Hospital Information System.*** Let us consider a hospital information system (HIS), drafted in P-AOL, and shown in Fig. 2. Doctors register new patients in the HIS. The HIS will communicate with a database DB, which stores the patients' personal data. Observe that in the code of the example, we have highlighted in blue how personal data flows along the system.

When a doctor registers a new patient via the method registerPatient, the doctor asks for the patient's data and connects it to an id and purposes via the **tag** construct, and from there on, non-personal data becomes personal data in the system. Then, the asynchronous call is assigned to future variable f1 and **await** f1? suspends the current task until the given guard becomes active or the future is resolved. To continue with the registration, the method registerPatient is further called in HIS and assigned to future f1 and awaits until f1 is resolved, which will further call the method setPersonalData in DB. When a doctor wants to access data from a patient, he calls the method requestPatientInfo, which in turn will call the method requestPatientInfo in HIS, which will further call the method requestPersonalData in DB. Once the future f2 is resolved and the personal data is available in the future, it is then retrieved via the **get** statement.

Let us assume the scenario described in the main block of our example, where we deploy an HIS called his, connected to the database db. We create a general practitioner (GP) gp, an emergency doctor (ED) ed, and two patients alice and bob. Observe that both patients alice and bob needed to consent to handle their personal data. In particular, alice has set up that the system and her GP can only handle her personal data. At the same time, bob has also given consent for his personal data to be handled in case of emergency. The semantics of P-AOL will internally check that private data handling is according to the declared consent

```
entities {Hosp, GP, ED, Lab}; purposes {Healthcare, Emergency};

interface IDB {Unit setPersonalData( D  d); D  requestPersonalData(U u); ... }
class DB() implements IDB {...}

interface IHIS {Unit registerPatient(U u, PD d); D  requestPatientInfo(U u); ...}
class HIS(DB db) implements IHIS {
     Unit registerPatient(U u, PD d {
          Fut <Unit> f1 := db!setPersonalData(d tag ⟨{u}, {Healthcare, Emergency}⟩);
          await f1; return unit; }
      D  requestPatientInfo(U u){ Fut < D > f2 := db!requestPersonalData(u);
          await f2?; d := f2.get ; return d; } ...}

interface IDoctor { Unit registerPatient(U u, PD d); Unit requestPatientInfo(U u); ... }
class Doctor(IHIS his) implements IDoctor {
     Unit registerPatient(U u, PD d){ Fut <Unit> f1 := his!registerPatient(u,d);
          await f1?; return unit; }
      D  requestPatientInfo(U u){ Fut < D > f2:= his!requestPatientInfo(u);
          await f2?; D  data := f2.get; return data; } ... }

{ // MAIN BLOCK
     IDB db := new DB() of Hosp; IHIS his := new HIS(db) of Hosp;
     IDoctor gp := new Doctor(his) of GP; IDoctor ed := new Doctor(his, nil) of ED;
     U alice := new user; U bob := new user;

     alice.addCon(({Hosp}, {store, transfer}, {Healthcare}));
     alice.addCon(({GP}, {collect, use, transfer}, {Healthcare}));
     alice.addInst(gp); alice.addInst(his); alice.addInst(db);

     bob.addCon(({Hosp}, {store, transfer}, {Healthcare}));
     bob.addCon(({Hosp}, {transfer}, {Emergency}));
     bob.addCon(({ED,GP}, {collect, use, transfer}, {Healthcare, Emergency}));
     bob.addInst(gp); bob.addInst(his); bob.addInst(db); bob.addInst(ed);

     // ... register users in the HIS ...
     Fut<Unit> f1 = gp!registerPatient(alice, d_a); ...
     Fut< D > f2 = ed!requestPatientInfo(bob); await f2?; D  d2 = f2.get ... }
```

Fig. 2. A hospital information system (HIS) example, drafted in P-AOL. Here non-private data (of type PD) becomes private (of type D) when associated with a particular user (patient), using an explicit tag construct.

of each user. We can, in principle, continue developing the scenario where both alice and bob change their consent, and doctors try to access their personal data, gaining a better understanding of how personal data is used in the HIS example. Such a modeling exercise can help understand and reason about what consent is needed from users, e.g., the information system might require the consent of all patients to handle their personal data in case of emergency.

B Bank Loan System. Let us consider a banking system with some procedures to apply for a bank loan. In particular, we look closer to a scenario where a couple applies together for a loan. Figure 3 shows the drafted version of the example in P-AOL, where the main block describes the scenario. We deploy a bank and its database, and we create a worker w and two users alice and bob. After registration in the system, alice and bob apply for a loan. As part of

```
entities {Bank, Officer}; purposes {Banking, Loan, Investment};

interface IDB {...} class DB() {...} // database

interface IBS { △ loanCapacity(( △ d1, △ d2) }
class BS(IDB db) implements IBS { △ loanCapacity ( △ d1, △ d2){...} ...}

interface IW { △ processLoanCouple( △ d1, △ d2) ...}
class W( IBS bank ) implements IW {
    △ processLoanCouple( △ d1, △ d2){ Fut < △ > f1= bank!loanCapacity(d1, d2);
    await f1?; △ d = f1.get; return d } ...}

{ // MAIN BLOCK
IDB db := new DB() of Bank; IBS b := new BS(db) of Bank; IW w := new W(b) of Officer;
U alice := new user; U bob := new user;

//...register consent for users...
alice.addCon(({Bank}, {use, collect, store}, {Banking}));
// Alice has given the officer full consent for Loan and Investment purposes.
alice.addCon({Officer}, {use, collect, transfer}, {Loan, Investment});
alice.addInst(bank); alice.addInst(db); alice.addInst(w);

bob.addCon(({Bank,Officer}, {use, collect, store, transfer}, {Banking,Loan}));
bob.addInst(bank); bob.addInst(db); bob.addInst(w);

Fut < △ > f = w!processLoanCouple($\delta_a$ tag ⟨{alice}, {Loan, Investment}⟩ ,
                                    $\delta_b$ tag ⟨{bob}, {Loan}⟩);
    await f?; Bool loanGranted:= f.get; if loanGranted { // give loan } ...}
```

Fig. 3. A bank loan system example, drafted in P-AOL. Here Δ abstracts away the type of records with personal data for the inputs and output of the function loanCapacity. Additionally, δ_a and δ_b abstract away the personal record values for alice and bob, respectively.

this procedure, the system must calculate their combined loan capacity via the function loanCapacity. Observe in the example that the function returns a value d (e.g., the maximum amount of money both alice and bob can request to the bank, given their current financial situation). This newly created value d belongs to both alice and bob and only for the purpose of Loan (to guarantee that this value can not be used for Investment since bob has not allowed his data to be used for such purpose). With this example, we want to showcase insights into how we envision tags for personal data should be combined to avoid data leaks. We will further detail how P-AOL deals with such cases in Sect. 6.

$$CN ::= \{cn\}$$

$$\sigma ::= x \mapsto {}_t v \mid \sigma \circ \sigma$$

$$\gamma ::= \{\sigma | s\}_\eta \mid idle$$

$$fut ::= f \mid f(v)$$

$$\chi ::= \varnothing \mid a \mapsto \widehat{\langle \eta, p \rangle} \mid \chi \circ \chi$$

$$v ::= o \mid f \mid u \mid \ldots$$

$$t ::= \emptyset \mid \langle \widehat{u}, \widehat{p} \rangle \mid \ldots$$

$$cn ::= \varepsilon \mid obj \mid msg \mid fut \mid \Sigma \mid cn\ cn$$

$$obj ::= o(\sigma, \gamma, q, \eta)$$

$$msg ::= m(o, o', \overline{{}_t v}, f, \eta)$$

$$q ::= \varepsilon \mid \gamma \mid q \circ q$$

$$\Sigma ::= u \mapsto \langle \chi, \widehat{o} \rangle \mid \Sigma \circ \Sigma$$

$$e ::= {}_t v \mid \ldots$$

$$\eta ::= \bot \mid \ldots$$

Fig. 4. Runtime syntax of P-AOL. Note that the empty tag values ${}_\emptyset v$ are equivalent to values v i.,e ${}_\emptyset v \cong v$ and syntax of expressions e, values v, and entities η extends the ones in Fig. 1 as indicated by "...".

6 An Operational Semantics for P-AOL

In this section, we detail the operational semantics of P-AOL. We first detail the runtime syntax, and then we focus on the evaluation of expressions and auxiliary functions to later focus on the SOS style rules. We will also discuss alternatives for error handling, which will be triggered when objects try to handle personal data without the right consent.

Runtime Syntax. Figure 4 shows the runtime syntax of P-AOL. A global *configuration CN* is a bracketed multiset of runtime elements: objects, invocation messages, futures, and user-specific consent. The associative and commutative multiset union operator on configurations is denoted by white space and the empty configuration by ε. For simplicity, classes are not represented explicitly in the semantics, but may be seen as static look-up tables of object layout and method definitions. An *object obj* is a term $o(\sigma, \gamma, q, \eta)$, where o is the object's identifier, σ is the state of the object and consists of the binding of the object's fields, γ is the process currently being executed, q a *pool of processes* waiting to be scheduled for execution, and η is the entity associated with the object. Note that entities η are extended with a special literal $\bot$, representing that no entity is associated to that object. An *invocation message* is a term $m(o, o', \overline{{}_t v}, f, \eta)$, consisting method name m, o the object callee, o' the object caller, $\overline{{}_t v}$ the call's actual parameter values, f the future to which the call's result is returned and η the entity associated with the object that called the method. A future *fut* has an identifier f and a reply value v. Consent Σ consists of $u \mapsto \langle \chi, \widehat{o} \rangle$, where u is a user, χ is a policy map represented as a set of bindings $a \mapsto \widehat{\langle \eta, p \rangle}$ that records for every action a, a set of pairs of entity and purpose, meaning that the entity is allowed to perform action a for the user u for purpose p. Here, empty policy map $\varnothing$ states that no entities or purposes are allowed for any action. The set $\widehat{o}$ are the instances that can handle the personal data of u, the semantics will check that only instances matching the declared consent will be able to handle the personal data of u (further details will be explained shortly). Here $\circ$ is the concatenation operator for states σ, process pools q, policy map χ and consent Σ.

$$\llbracket e \text{ tag } \langle \hat{x}, \hat{p} \rangle \rrbracket_\sigma = {}_t v, \quad \text{if } \llbracket e \rrbracket_\sigma = {}_{t_1} v \wedge \hat{u} = \llbracket \hat{x} \rrbracket_\sigma \wedge t = t_1 \oplus \langle \hat{u}, \hat{p} \rangle$$

$$\llbracket v \rrbracket_\sigma = v$$

$$\llbracket {}_{\langle \hat{u}, \hat{p} \rangle} v \rrbracket_\sigma = {}_{\langle \hat{u}, \hat{p} \rangle} v$$

$$\llbracket x \rrbracket_\sigma = \sigma(x)$$

$$\llbracket \text{this} \rrbracket_\sigma = \sigma(this)$$

$$\llbracket e_1 \text{ op } e_2 \rrbracket_\sigma = \begin{cases} {}_t v, & \text{if } e_1 = {}_{t_1} v_1 \wedge e_2 = {}_{t_2} v_2 \wedge t = t_1 \oplus t_2 \wedge v = v_1 \underline{op} \, v_2 \\ \llbracket \llbracket e_1 \rrbracket_\sigma \text{ op } \llbracket e_2 \rrbracket_\sigma \rrbracket_\sigma, & \text{otherwise} \end{cases}$$

$$\llbracket fn(\bar{e}) \rrbracket_\sigma = \begin{cases} {}_{t_{fn}} v_{fn} & \text{if } {}_{t_{fn}} v_{fn} = \llbracket e_{fn} \rrbracket_{[\bar{x} \mapsto {}_t v]} \wedge \bar{e} = \overline{{}_t v} \\ \llbracket fn(\llbracket \bar{e} \rrbracket_\sigma) \rrbracket_\sigma, & \text{otherwise} \end{cases}$$

Fig. 5. The evaluation of functional expressions. Here, $\underline{op}$ refers to the semantic operation corresponding to the syntax op.

A *process* $\{\sigma | s\}_\eta$ consists of a local state σ of local variable bindings, a list s of statements, and the entity η that made the call, or it is *idle*. (We identify any process with an empty statement list with the *idle* process). We let the fields of an object include *this*, denoting the identifier of the object.

The values from our program syntax are extended with runtime tags. In particular, ${}_t v$ represents (possibly empty) tagged values, where the tag t can be either $\emptyset$ or $\langle \hat{u}, \hat{p} \rangle$. If $\hat{u}$ is empty, the value is not considered private i.e., $\langle \emptyset, \hat{p} \rangle v = {}_\emptyset v$ and ${}_\emptyset v = v$; while values with non-empty tags are private. We also allow a runtime $\oplus$ operation on tags, letting the combination of an empty and a non-empty tag be the non-empty tag, and letting two non-empty tags be combined by unifying the users and intersecting the purposes to avoid tagging newly created values with purposes more than intended:

$$t_1 \oplus t_2 = \begin{cases} \langle \hat{u}, \hat{p} \rangle, & \text{if } t_1 = \emptyset \wedge t_2 = \langle \hat{u}, \hat{p} \rangle \\ \langle \hat{u}, \hat{p} \rangle, & \text{if } t_1 = \langle \hat{u}, \hat{p} \rangle \wedge t_2 = \emptyset \\ \langle \hat{u} \cup \hat{u}', \hat{p} \cap \hat{p}' \rangle, & \text{if } t_1 = \langle \hat{u}, \hat{p} \rangle \wedge t_2 = \langle \hat{u}', \hat{p}' \rangle \\ \emptyset & \text{otherwise} \end{cases}$$

The *initial configuration* of a program reflects its main block $\{\overline{A} \, \overline{x}; s\}$, which at runtime has the form $main(a, \{l | s\}_\perp, \varepsilon, \perp)$, where $main$ is an object. In the $main$ object, let a be the substitution $\varepsilon[this \mapsto main]$ and l be the substitution $\varepsilon[\overline{x} \mapsto default(\overline{T})]$. where $default(T)$ denotes the default value of type T. (We assume that for a well-typed program, the main block does not refer to the expression **this**).

Evaluation of Expressions. Let σ be a state which binds variables to values. The evaluation function for possible tagged expressions α for a given state σ is defined inductively over the syntax of the expressions in the language (see Fig. 5) and is mostly standard, i.e., $\llbracket \alpha \rrbracket_\sigma$ represents a confluent and terminating system, which reduces possible tagged expressions α to data values. The reduction of an expression always happens in the context of a given process, object state, and configuration. The program syntax provides an explicit **tag** construct to create private values when an argument e is tagged with t. The tag of the resulting value is formed by the $\oplus$ operation on the tag of the evaluated e combined with t. For binary operations op, we let $\underline{op}$ capture the actual arithmetic and logic operators that can directly be applied over values. If the operands are values, then we apply $\underline{op}$ and return the result; otherwise we syntactically distribute op until we reach values. The tags of the resulting value are combined in accordance to our tags combining operator $\oplus$, which is further showcased in the banking example in Sect. 5. For a (user-defined) function definition $\mathbf{def}\ B\ fn(\overline{B\ x}) = e_{fn}$, the evaluation of a function call $[\![fn(\overline{e})]\!]_\sigma$ reduces to the evaluation of the corresponding expression $[\![e_{fn}]\!]_{[\overline{x \mapsto {}_t v}]}$ when the arguments $\overline{e}$ have been reduced to ground terms $\overline{{}_t v}$. Note that the above evaluation is untyped: We assume that programs are well-typed such that evaluation produces type-correct values.

Evaluation of Guards. Given a substitution σ and a configuration cn, we can lift the evaluation of expressions to guards $[\![g]\!]_\sigma^{cn}$. Here we need the configuration cn to access future variables. Let $[\![x?]\!]_\sigma^{cn} = true$ if $[\![x]\!]_\sigma^{cn} = f$ and $f(v) \in cn$ for some value v (e.g., f is already resolved), otherwise if $f \in cn$ then $[\![x?]\!]_\sigma^{cn} = false$.

Auxiliary Functions. The function $scheduler(q)$ schedules an enabled process (if possible) from the process queue q of an object $o(\sigma, idle, q, \eta)$ in a configuration cn. The function $atts(C, \overline{{}_t v}, o)$ returns the initial state σ for the fields of a new instance o of class C, in which the formal parameters are bound to $\overline{{}_t v}$ and the field *this* is bound to the object identity o. The function $init(C)$ returns an activation (process) of the *init* method of C, if defined. Otherwise, it returns the *idle* process. The function $bind(m, o, o', \overline{{}_t v}, f, \eta)$ returns a process resulting from the activation of the method m on object o with actual parameters $\overline{{}_t v}$ and caller o', letting the caller o' be bound to a local system variable *caller* and the future reference f be bound to a local system variable *destiny*. If the binding succeeds, the method's formal parameters are bound to $\overline{{}_t v}$. The predicate $fresh(n)$ asserts that a name n is globally unique (where n may be an identifier for an object or a user). The definition of these functions is straightforward but requires that the class table is explicit in the semantics, which we have omitted for simplicity.

We now detail the functions that are used on the handling of data privacy. Following GDPR regulations, we allow the *transfer of processing rights* from DC to DP, provided that such transfer is not violating the user's privacy policies. We define a function $\mathcal{E}$ to select the entity and object responsible for the processing in each transition step that handles data, where $\perp$ indicates that the caller object does not represent a legal entity

$$\mathcal{E}(\langle o_{caller}, \eta_{caller} \rangle, \langle o_{cur}, \eta_{cur} \rangle) = \begin{cases} \langle o_{caller}, \eta_{caller} \rangle, & \text{if } \eta_{caller} \neq \perp \\ \langle o_{cur}, \eta_{cur} \rangle, & \text{otherwise} \end{cases}$$

Function $\mathcal{T}_\sigma(\alpha)$ extracts the (possibly empty) tags t from the expression α.

$$\begin{aligned} \mathcal{T}_\sigma({}_t v) &= t & \mathcal{T}_\sigma(e\ \mathbf{tag}\ \langle \hat{x}, \hat{p} \rangle) &= \mathcal{T}_\sigma(e) \oplus \langle \widehat{\sigma(x)}, \hat{p} \rangle \\ \mathcal{T}_\sigma(x) &= \mathcal{T}_\sigma(\sigma(x)) & \mathcal{T}_\sigma(e_1\ op\ e_2) &= \mathcal{T}_\sigma(e_1) \oplus \mathcal{T}_\sigma(e_2) \\ \mathcal{T}_\sigma(fn(\overline{e})) &= \oplus \overline{\mathcal{T}_\sigma(e)} & \mathcal{T}_\sigma(e) &= \emptyset \quad \text{otherwise} \end{aligned}$$

Functions $\mathcal{U}(t)$ and $\mathcal{P}(t)$ extract the users and purposes from tag t.

$$\mathcal{U}(t) = \{u \mid t = \langle \widehat{u}, \widehat{p} \rangle \wedge u \in \widehat{u} \wedge \widehat{u} \neq \emptyset \} \qquad \mathcal{P}(t) = \{p \mid t = \langle \widehat{u}, \widehat{p} \rangle \wedge p \in \widehat{p} \wedge \widehat{p} \neq \emptyset \wedge \widehat{u} \neq \emptyset\}$$

Let function $Inst(\widehat{u}, \Sigma)$ extract the common instances that can handle the data of the users $\widehat{u}$. Function $\mathcal{I}$ checks if the object is an authorized instance or not based on the user's consent. If the users $\widehat{u}$ are empty, meaning that the data in question is non-private, then the instance function will return true.

$$\mathcal{I}(\widehat{u}, \Sigma, o) = \begin{cases} true, & \text{if } \widehat{u} \neq \emptyset \wedge Inst(\widehat{u}, \Sigma) = \widehat{o} \ \wedge \ o \in \widehat{o} \\ true, & \text{if } \widehat{u} = \emptyset \\ false, & \text{otherwise} \end{cases}$$

Let function $Act(\Sigma, \eta, u, \widehat{p})$ return a set of allowed actions according to the consent Σ and entity η, particular user identifier u and purposes $\widehat{p}$.

$$Act(\Sigma, \eta, u, \widehat{p}) = \{a \mid \Sigma(u) = \langle \chi, \widehat{o} \rangle \ \wedge \ \exists p \in \widehat{p} \ \ (\eta, p) \in \chi(a)\}$$

We define function $\mathcal{A}(\Sigma, \eta, t)$ that for any given tags and entity extracts the allowed actions granted by the users in the consent Σ. If the tags t are empty implies that the data in question is non-private and all actions i.e., **use**, **collect**, **transfer**, **store**, are granted.

$$\mathcal{A}(\Sigma, \eta, t) = \begin{cases} \bigcap\limits_{i=1}^{n} (\Sigma, \eta, u_i, \widehat{p}), & \text{if } t = \langle \widehat{u}, \widehat{p} \rangle \wedge \widehat{u} = u_1 \ldots u_n \wedge \widehat{p} \neq \emptyset \\ \{\textbf{use}, \textbf{collect}, \textbf{transfer}, \textbf{store}\}, & \text{if } t = \emptyset \\ \emptyset, & \text{otherwise} \end{cases}$$

Monotonicity of Privacy Tags. We show that for non-empty tags t and t':

$$t \sqsubseteq t' \Rightarrow \mathcal{A}(\Sigma, \eta, t) \subseteq \mathcal{A}(\Sigma, \eta, t')$$

where $t \sqsubseteq t'$ expresses that t is more restrictive than t', defined by $\mathcal{U}(t') \subseteq \mathcal{U}(t) \wedge \mathcal{P}(t) \subseteq \mathcal{P}(t')$. Monotonicity implies that the more restrictive the tags are, the less actions are allowed, which in turn means that the privacy conditions of the operational semantics are violated more often (for given consent Σ). This supports the intuition that each user appearing in a tag comes with requirements to be fulfilled, so the less users the less requirements, and secondly the purposes provides processing rights, implying that the more purposes, the better (making more processing possible).

Monotonicity of Consent. A similar result holds for consent:

$$\Sigma \sqsubseteq \Sigma' \Rightarrow \mathcal{A}(\Sigma, \eta, t) \subseteq \mathcal{A}(\Sigma', \eta, t)$$

where $\Sigma \sqsubseteq \Sigma'$ expresses that Σ is more restrictive than Σ', in the sense that for each user u such that $\Sigma(u) = \langle \chi, \widehat{o} \rangle$ then $\Sigma'(u)$ is defined and for $\Sigma'(u) = \langle \chi', \widehat{o}' \rangle$ we have $\widehat{o} \subseteq \widehat{o}'$ and $(\eta, p) \in \chi \Rightarrow (\eta, p) \in \chi'$. The proof of these monotonicity results follows from our definitions in a straightforward manner.

$$\text{(SKIP)}$$
$$o(a, \{l \mid \textbf{skip}; s\}_{\eta'}, q, \eta) \to o(a, \{l \mid s\}_{\eta'}, q, \eta)$$

$$\text{(ACTIVATE)}$$
$$\frac{p = scheduler(q)}{o(a, idle, q, \eta) \to o(a, p, (q \setminus p), \eta)}$$

$$\text{(ASSIGN1)}$$
$$\frac{\langle o_0, \eta_0 \rangle = \mathcal{E}(\langle l(caller), \eta' \rangle, \langle o, \eta \rangle)}{\mathcal{I}(\mathcal{U}(\mathcal{T}_{aol}(\alpha)), \Sigma, o_0)}$$
$$\{\textbf{use}, \textbf{collect}\} \subseteq \mathcal{A}(\Sigma, \eta_0, \mathcal{T}_{aol}(\alpha))$$
$$x \in dom(l) \quad [\![\alpha]\!]_{aol} = {}_t v$$
$$\overline{\begin{array}{c} o(a, \{l \mid x = \alpha; s\}_{\eta'}, q, \eta)\ \Sigma \\ \to o(a, \{l[x \mapsto {}_t v \mid s\}_{\eta'}, q, \eta)\ \Sigma \end{array}}$$

$$\text{(ASSIGN2)}$$
$$\frac{\langle o_0, \eta_0 \rangle = \mathcal{E}(\langle l(caller), \eta' \rangle, \langle o, \eta \rangle)}{\mathcal{I}(\mathcal{U}(\mathcal{T}_{aol}(\alpha)), \Sigma, o_0)}$$
$$\textbf{use} \in \mathcal{A}(\Sigma, \eta_0, \mathcal{T}_{aol}(\alpha))$$
$$\mathcal{I}(\mathcal{U}(\mathcal{T}_{aol}(\alpha)), \Sigma, o)$$
$$\{\textbf{collect}, \textbf{store}\} \subseteq \mathcal{A}(\Sigma, \eta, \mathcal{T}_{aol}(\alpha))$$
$$x \notin dom(l) \quad [\![\alpha]\!]_{aol} = {}_t v$$
$$\overline{\begin{array}{c} o(a, \{l \mid x = \alpha; s\}_{\eta'}, q, \eta)\ \Sigma \\ \to o(a[x \mapsto {}_t v, \{l \mid s\}_{\eta'}, q, \eta)\ \Sigma \end{array}}$$

$$\text{(COND1)}$$
$$\frac{\langle o_0, \eta_0 \rangle = \mathcal{E}(\langle l(caller), \eta' \rangle, \langle o, \eta \rangle)}{\mathcal{I}(\mathcal{U}(\mathcal{T}_{aol}(e)), \Sigma, o_0)}$$
$$\textbf{use} \in \mathcal{A}(\Sigma, \eta_0, \mathcal{T}_{aol}(e))$$
$$[\![e]\!]_{aol} = true$$
$$\overline{\begin{array}{c} o(a, \{l \mid \textbf{if } e \{s_1\}; s\}_{\eta'}, q, \eta)\ \Sigma \\ \to o(a, \{l \mid s_1; s\}_{\eta'}, q, \eta)\ \Sigma \end{array}}$$

$$\text{(COND2)}$$
$$\frac{\langle o_0, \eta_0 \rangle = \mathcal{E}(\langle l(caller), \eta' \rangle, \langle o, \eta \rangle)}{\mathcal{I}(\mathcal{U}(\mathcal{T}_{aol}(e)), \Sigma, o_0)}$$
$$\textbf{use} \in \mathcal{A}(\Sigma, \eta_0, \mathcal{T}_{aol}(e))$$
$$[\![e]\!]_{aol} = false$$
$$\overline{\begin{array}{c} o(a, \{l \mid \textbf{if } e \{s_1\}; s\}_{\eta'}, q, \eta)\ \Sigma \\ \to o(a, \{l \mid s\}_{\eta'}, q, \eta)\ \Sigma \end{array}}$$

$$\text{(AWAIT1)}$$
$$\frac{[\![g]\!]_{aol}^{cn}}{\begin{array}{c} \{o(a, \{l \mid \textbf{await } g; s\}_{\eta'}, q, \eta)\ cn\} \\ \to \{o(a, \{l \mid s\}_{\eta'}, q, \eta)\ cn\} \end{array}}$$

$$\text{(AWAIT2)}$$
$$\frac{\neg[\![g]\!]_{aol}^{cn}}{\begin{array}{c} \{o(a, \{l \mid \textbf{await } g; s\}_{\eta'}, q, \eta)\ cn\} \\ \to \{o(a, idle, q \circ \{l \mid \textbf{await } g; s\}_{\eta'}, \eta)\ cn\} \end{array}}$$

Fig. 6. Execution rules for standard statements in P-AOL.

Transition System. Let $\to$ capture transitions between configurations. A run is a possibly terminating sequence of configurations $cn_0, cn_1, \ldots$ such that $cn_i \to cn_{i+1}$. When auxiliary functions are used in the semantics, these are evaluated in between the application of transition rules in a run. Rules apply to subsets of configurations (the standard context rules are not listed). For simplicity, we assume that configurations can be reordered to match the left-hand side of the rules, i.e., matching is modulo associativity and commutativity as in rewriting logic [16]. Transition rules transform configurations into new configurations and are given in Figs. 6, 7 and 8. We first present the transition rules for standard statement execution (Figs. 6 and 7) and later the rules for user interactions (Fig. 8).

For statement execution, we focus on the handling of personal data, following the current users' consent, where allowed actions are within the language constructs {use, collect, store, transfer} and the statement is executed under the right credentials. In particular, the semantics uses the function $\mathcal{E}$ to decide between checking the credentials of the caller object (and its entity) in the active process (emulating data handling delegation), or the credentials of the actual object (and its entity) processing the statement, in the sequel the chosen object

(New-Object)

$$\dfrac{\langle o_0, \eta_0 \rangle = \mathcal{E}(\langle l(caller), \eta' \rangle, \langle o, \eta \rangle) \quad \mathcal{I}(\mathcal{U}(\mathcal{T}_{aol}(\alpha)), \Sigma, o_0) \quad \mathcal{I}(\mathcal{U}(\mathcal{T}_{aol}(\alpha)), \Sigma, o')}{\begin{array}{c} \{\mathbf{use}, \mathbf{transfer}\} \subseteq \mathcal{A}(\Sigma, \eta_0, \mathcal{T}_{aol}(\alpha)) \quad \{\mathbf{collect}, \mathbf{store}\} \subseteq \mathcal{A}(\Sigma, \eta'', \mathcal{T}_{aol}(\alpha)) \\ \mathit{fresh}(o') \quad \{l' \mid s'\} = \mathit{init}(C) \quad a' = \mathit{atts}(C, \overline{\llbracket \alpha \rrbracket_{aol}}, o') \end{array}}$$

$$\begin{array}{l} o(a, \{l \mid x = \mathbf{new}\ C(\overline{\alpha})\ \mathbf{of}\ \eta''; s\}_{\eta'}, q, \eta)\ \Sigma \\ \rightarrow o(a, \{l \mid x = o'; s\}_{\eta'}, q, \eta)\ o'(a', \{l' \mid s'\}_\perp, \emptyset, \eta'')\ \Sigma \end{array}$$

(Async-Call)

$$\dfrac{\langle o_0, \eta_0 \rangle = \mathcal{E}(\langle l(caller), \eta' \rangle, \langle o, \eta \rangle) \quad \mathcal{I}(\mathcal{U}(\mathcal{T}_{aol}(\alpha)), \Sigma, o_0)}{\{\mathbf{use}, \mathbf{transfer}\} \subseteq \mathcal{A}(\Sigma, \eta_0, \mathcal{T}_{aol}(\alpha)) \quad \llbracket e \rrbracket_{aol} = o' \quad \mathit{fresh}(f) \quad \overline{\llbracket \alpha \rrbracket_{aol}} = \overline{\imath v}}$$

$$o(a, \{l \mid x = e!m(\overline{\alpha}); s\}_{\eta'}, q, \eta)\ \Sigma \rightarrow o(a, \{l \mid x = f; s\}_{\eta'}, q, \eta)\ m(o', o, \overline{\imath v}, f, \eta_0)\ f\ \Sigma$$

(Bind-Mtd)

$$\dfrac{\langle o_0, \eta_0 \rangle = \mathcal{E}(\langle o', \eta' \rangle, \langle o, \eta \rangle) \quad \mathcal{I}(\mathcal{U}(\mathcal{T}_{aol}(\imath v)), \Sigma, o') \quad \mathcal{I}(\mathcal{U}(\mathcal{T}_{aol}(\imath v)), \Sigma, o_0))}{\{\mathbf{use}, \mathbf{transfer}\} \subseteq \mathcal{A}(\Sigma, \eta', \mathcal{T}_{aol}(\imath v)) \quad \mathbf{collect} \in \mathcal{A}(\Sigma, \eta_0, \mathcal{T}_{aol}(\imath v))}$$

$$o(a, \gamma, q, \eta)\ m(o, o', \overline{\imath v}, f, \eta')\ \Sigma \rightarrow o(a, \gamma, q \circ \mathit{bind}(m, o, o', \overline{\imath v}, \eta'), \eta)\ \Sigma$$

(Return)

$$\dfrac{\langle o_0, \eta_0 \rangle = \mathcal{E}(\langle l(caller), \eta' \rangle, \langle o, \eta \rangle) \quad \mathcal{I}(\mathcal{U}(\mathcal{T}_{aol}(e)), \Sigma, o_0)}{\{\mathbf{use}, \mathbf{transfer}\} \subseteq \mathcal{A}(\Sigma, \eta_0, \mathcal{T}_{aol}(e)) \quad f = l(\mathit{destiny})}$$

$$o(a, \{l \mid \mathbf{return}(e); s\}_{\eta'}, q, \eta)\ f\ \Sigma \rightarrow o(a, \mathit{idle}, q, \eta)\ f(\llbracket e \rrbracket_{aol})\ \Sigma$$

(Read-Fut)

$$\dfrac{f = \llbracket e \rrbracket_{aol}}{o(a, \{l \mid x = e.\mathbf{get}; s\}_{\eta'}, q, \eta)\ f(\imath v) \rightarrow o(a, \{l \mid x = \imath v; s\}_{\eta'}, q, \eta)\ f(\imath v)}$$

Fig. 7. Execution rules for standard statements in P-AOL.

will be called the accountable object. In the standard execution rules, all checks related to data privacy are highlighted in grey. Observe that such checks for non-private values will return *true* since the tags associated with the values would be empty. If any of the premises in the rules do not hold, the execution in the object will be blocked. We conventionally write a to denote the object state, which maps fields to values in an object and l to denote local state, which maps local variables to values in a process. In the sequel, the variable s will match any (possibly empty) statement list.

Rule SKIP consumes a **skip** in the active process. Rule ACTIVATE schedules a process from the waiting process queue, when there is no current process executing. Rule ASSIGN1 assigns (private) values to local variables; it validates the accountable object by checking against user-allowed instances. Since the statement is using the values in expression α and creating a new private value $\imath v$

that is temporarily collected in a local variable, the rule checks the allowance for actions **use** and **collect** for α by its valid tags. Rule ASSIGN2 assigns the (private) value of expression α to a field in an object o, it validates the accountable object by checking against user allowed instances, and the allowance for action **use** for α since the statement is using the values in expression α. Then it validates for the current object o the allowance for actions {**store**, **collect**} for collecting and long-term storing the newly created private value $_tv$ in the field of object o.

Rules COND1 and COND2 cover the two cases of conditional statements, validating the accountable object by checking against user-allowed instances and the allowance for action **use** for e. Rule AWAIT1 consumes the **await** g statement if g evaluates to true in the current state of the object. Rule AWAIT2 suspends the active process into the process pool, leaving the active process *idle* if the guard g evaluates to false. Note that no privacy checks are done in these rules since guards are associated with futures. Rule NEW-OBJECT creates a new object with a unique identifier o' and entity η''. The object's fields a' are given default values and are extended with the actual values $[\![\alpha]\!]_{aol}$ for the class parameters (evaluated in the context of the creating process), and o' for *this*. The process $init(C)$ will be active (this function returns *idle* if the *init* method is unspecified in the class C, and it asynchronously calls *run* if the latter is specified). The rule validates the accountable object by checking against user-allowed instances and the allowance for actions {**use**, **transfer**} for $\overline{\alpha}$ since the statement is using and transferring the (private) values in expression $\overline{\alpha}$, to the newly created object. Similarly, it checks the credentials for the newly created object and the allowance for actions {**collect**, **store**} for $\overline{\alpha}$ since these new (private) values are collected and stored long-term in the fields of the created object.

Rule ASYNC-CALL sends an invocation message with the method name m and the actual parameters $\overline{_tv}$, to $[\![e]\!]_{aol}$, which return value is associated to a freshly created future f. It validates the accountable object by checking against user-allowed instances and the allowance for actions {**use**, **transfer**} for $\overline{\alpha}$ since the statement is using the values in expression $\overline{\alpha}$, and transferring the values $\overline{_tv}$ to $[\![e]\!]_{aol}$. In Rule BIND-MTD, the invocation message is consumed, and the function $bind(m, o, o', \overline{_tv}, f, \eta')$ binds a method call in the class of the callee o. This results in a new process $\{l \mid s\}'_\eta$ which is placed in the queue of o, where the formal parameters of m are bound in l to $\overline{_tv}$, the reserved variable *caller* is bound to o', and a reserved variable *destiny* is bound to f. The rule validates the caller object by checking against user allowed instances and allowance of action {**use**, **transfer**} to check if the respective consent exists for the caller object in the configuration since the call. It then validates the accountable object and the allowance for action **collect** for $\overline{_tv}$ since the statement is temporarily collecting them in the local variables of the new process.

Rule RETURN places the return value into the associated future of the process that was stored in the reserved variable *destiny*. It validates the accountable object and the allowance for actions {**use**, **transfer**} for e since the statement is using and transferring e to the associated future. Rule READ-FUT deferences a future on the form $f(v)$. Note that if the future lacks a value, it is of the form

$$(\textsc{New-User})$$
$$fresh(u)$$

$$o(a, \{l \mid x = \textbf{new user} ; s\}_{\eta'}, q, \eta) \; \Sigma \rightarrow o(a, \{l \mid x = u; s\}_{\eta'}, q, \eta) \; \Sigma \circ u \mapsto \langle \varnothing, \{o\} \rangle$$

$$(\textsc{Add-Consent})$$
$$[\![x]\!]_{aol} = u \quad \chi' = InsrtPol(\chi, \rho)$$

$$o(a, \{l \mid x.\textbf{addCon}(\rho); s\}_{\eta'}, q, \eta) \; \Sigma \circ u \mapsto \langle \chi, \hat{o} \rangle \rightarrow o(a, \{l \mid s\}_{\eta'}, q, \eta) \; \Sigma \circ u \mapsto \langle \chi', \hat{o} \rangle$$

$$(\textsc{Withdraw-Consent})$$
$$[\![x]\!]_{aol} = u \quad \chi' = RmvPol(\chi, \rho)$$

$$o(a, \{l \mid x.\textbf{remCon}(\rho); s\}_{\eta'}, q, \eta) \; \Sigma \circ u \mapsto \langle \chi, \hat{o} \rangle \rightarrow o(a, \{l \mid s\}_{\eta'}, q, \eta) \; \Sigma \circ u \mapsto \langle \chi', \hat{o} \rangle$$

$$(\textsc{Add-Instance})$$
$$[\![x]\!]_{aol} = u \quad [\![e]\!]_{aol} = o'$$

$$\frac{o(a, \{l \mid x.\textbf{addInst}(e); s\}_{\eta'}, q, \eta)}{o'(a', \gamma', q', \eta'') \; \Sigma \circ u \mapsto \langle \chi, \hat{o} \rangle \rightarrow o(a, \{l \mid s\}_{\eta'}, q, \eta)} \\ o'(a', \gamma', q', \eta'') \; \Sigma \circ u \mapsto \langle \chi, \hat{o} \cup \{o'\} \rangle$$

$$(\textsc{Remove-Instance})$$
$$[\![x]\!]_{aol} = u \quad [\![e]\!]_{aol} = o'$$

$$o(a, \{l \mid x.\textbf{remInst}(e); s\}_{\eta'}, q, \eta) \\ o'(a', \gamma', q', \eta'') \; \Sigma \circ u \mapsto \langle \chi, \hat{o} \rangle \\ \rightarrow o(a, \{l \mid s\}_{\eta'}, q, \eta) \\ o'(a', \gamma', q', \eta'') \; \Sigma \circ u \mapsto \langle \chi, \hat{o} \setminus \{o'\} \rangle$$

Fig. 8. User interactions semantics for AOL.

f and the reduction in this object is blocked. Note that no privacy checks are done in this rule, since they will be done by the corresponding assignment rule.

In Fig. 8, rule NEW-USER creates a new user with a unique identifier u and assigns it to variable x. The user u is then added to the global consent Σ. Rule ADD-CONSENT allows user u to add policy $\rho = (\hat{\eta}, \hat{a}, \hat{p})$ to his/her consent, here the function $InsrtPol(\chi, \rho)$ adds to the binding χ the new elements in ρ. Let cp be the Cartesian product of the sets $\hat{\eta}$ and $\hat{p}$, this creates a set of pairs $\overbrace{\langle \eta, p \rangle} \in cp$. Each action in $\hat{a}$ is then mapped to cp, creating a binding χ'', which updates χ, such that $InsrtPol(\chi, \rho)$ returns an updated binding χ'. Rule WITHDRAW-CONSENT allows user u to respectively remove the element in the policy ρ in the binding χ, by using the function $RmvPol(\chi, \rho)$, updating the global consent Σ. Similarly, rules ADD-INSTANCE and REMOVE-INSTANCE allow user u to add, respectively remove, instance o' to the consent in Σ.

7   Reflection on P-AOL Semantics

We now reflect on the formal syntax and semantics of P-AOL and frame the discussion toward the challenges presented in Sect. 3. Challenge 1 is related to contextual awareness for handling personal data. To meet this challenge, we introduce new program constructs, i.e., entities, and purposes. We use data tags to associate data with user identities and purposes (to capture purpose-based processing). Challenge 2 is related to data becoming personal data. Our language captures such scenarios by a special **tag** construct that associates expressions to user ids and purposes. During the evaluation of such expression, the system reduces the expression to a private value, such that the privacy-related checks in the standard execution rules will apply. Challenge 3 is related to personal data with multiple owners. This scenario is clearly explained by the bank loan system example in Sect. 5, which is further discussed in the evaluation of expressions (see Fig. 5): When private values are associated with two or more users, we consider the union of users and intersection of purposes, such association is further used to check consent in the standard execution rules to guarantee that the handling of private values associated with multiple users considers the consent of each of them. Challenge 4 is related to unclear terminology for personal data handling in the GDPR. Our formal language considers a concrete interpretation of the terminology and enforces them in the transition rules for standard execution so that corresponding checks are done according to the consent of each user, as shown in the scenarios of the motivating examples in Sect. 5.

7.1   Thoughts on Error Handling in P-AOL When Lacking Consent

The semantics of P-AOL does not include runtime error handling. If a runtime error occurs in one of the objects, the execution in the active process will stop and the object will be blocked, yet the object stays alive. One particular case in which errors might occur in P-AOL is caused by the lack of consent for handling personal data. One alternative to overcome such errors is the use of a *dynamic consent interaction dialogue with the user*, where a dialogue mechanism is introduced asking for the required consent from the user. Regarding GDPR, this could be reflected by opt-in/opt-out requests, allowing users to opt in or opt out dynamically at runtime. We can further refine the options to:

Allow-once: for temporary consent, with a new dialogue next time needed,
Allow-always: for changing the consent so that it is kept for further processing.

However, this requires users to be available whenever the data is processed, which is not always reasonable. Hence, there is a need for other complementary mechanisms such as:

- *Suspension points*, allowing the current process to be suspended until a Boolean condition is satisfied or a return value is available. (e.g., extend guards in the **await** statement to handle Boolean expressions). Then if the condition or return value are not available at that point (e.g., the user has not yet given the required consent), we can introduce a release point and suspend execution in the active process until the needed results are available, meanwhile, letting other (enabled) processes from the waiting queue be scheduled, unblocking the execution in the object.
- *Exception handling*, where exceptions are raised at the process level and handled for e.g. using try and catch block locally in the process.
- *Process finalizers*, which will terminate the process gracefully, possibly undoing some actions and sending messages to the involved parties. This is similar to roll-backs and fall-back functions in Solidity [24] and finalizers in other language settings [3].

8   Correctness

P-AOL's operational semantics results in a possible non-terminating state transition system. We prove that any execution of a program in our language will satisfy compliance at every step. Compliance in our setting expresses that any personal data handling should follow the user's privacy consent. Intuitively, handling personal data is allowed via actions *use*, *collect*, *store*, and *transfer*. Hence, we formalize actions to check if valid consent exists for every action and user in any state and then check against program premises required to execute any statement. We use first-order logic to reason about the correctness of our program since we need predicates, function symbols, and quantifiers. Our formulas are typically defined for each state of an object o in a given configuration cn.

Below, we define action formulas where we check if the appropriate action exists in the consent Σ for the data in question.

Definition 1 (Use). *Given a state cn, consent Σ, private tags t, object ids o, o_0 and entity η_0, we define the following formula (use), expressing consented usage of private data:*

$$use(cn, o, t, \Sigma, o_0, \eta_0) = \exists \sigma, l, \eta, \eta', q, s, s' \ . \ o(\sigma, \{l \mid s; s'\}_{\eta'}, q, \eta) \in cn \ \wedge$$
$$\forall u \in \mathcal{U}(t) \ \exists \hat{o}, \chi \ . \ u \mapsto \langle \chi, \hat{o} \rangle \in \Sigma \wedge \exists p \in \mathcal{P}(t) \ . \ \langle \eta_0, p \rangle \in \chi(use) \wedge o_0 \in \hat{o}$$

Definition 2 (Collect). *Given a state cn, consent Σ, private tags t, object ids o, o_0 and entity η_0, we define the following formula (col), expressing consented collection of private data:*

$$col(cn, o, t, \Sigma, \eta_0, o_0) = \exists \sigma, l, \eta, \eta', q, s, s' \ . \ o(\sigma, \{l \mid s; s'\}_{\eta'}, q, \eta) \in cn \ \wedge$$
$$\forall u \in \mathcal{U}(t) \ \exists \hat{o}, \chi \ . \ u \mapsto \langle \chi, \hat{o} \rangle \in \Sigma \wedge \exists p \in \mathcal{P}(t) \ . \ \langle \eta_0, p \rangle \in \chi(collect) \wedge o_0 \in \hat{o}$$

Definition 3 (Store). *Given a state cn, consent Σ, private tags t, object ids o, o_0 and entity η_0, we define the following formula (store), expressing consented storing of private data:*

$$store(cn, o, t, \Sigma, o_0, \eta_0) = \exists \sigma, l, \eta, \eta', q, s, s' \ . \ o(\sigma, \{l \mid s; s'\}_{\eta'}, q, \eta) \in cn \ \wedge$$
$$\forall u \in \mathcal{U}(t) \ \exists \hat{o}, \chi \ . \ u \mapsto \langle \chi, \hat{o} \rangle \in \Sigma \wedge \exists p \in \mathcal{P}(t) \ . \ \langle \eta_0, p \rangle \in \chi(store) \wedge o_0 \in \hat{o}$$

Definition 4 (Transfer). *Given a state cn, consent Σ, private tags t, object ids o, o_0 and entity η_0, we define the following formula (trans), expressing consented transfer of private data:*

$$trans(cn, o, t, \Sigma, o_0, \eta_0) = \exists, \sigma, l, \eta, \eta', q, s, s' \ . \ o(\sigma, \{l \mid s; s'\}_{\eta'}, q, \eta) \in cn \ \wedge$$
$$\forall u \in \mathcal{U}(t) \ \exists \hat{o}, \chi \ . \ u \mapsto \langle \chi, \hat{o} \rangle \in \Sigma \wedge \exists p \in \mathcal{P}(t) \ . \ \langle \eta_0, p \rangle \in \chi(transfer) \wedge o_0 \in \hat{o}$$

In all the above formulas, $\mathcal{P}(t)$ extracts the purposes and $\mathcal{U}(t)$ extracts the users from tags t. We check the compliance against rules that can access private data at any state. This is to say that, in our operational semantics, the rules accessing personal data through actions are New-object, Assign1, Assign2, Cond1, Cond2, Async-Call, Bind-Mtd, and Return. Other rules from the semantics do not constitute any compliance check and are therefore omitted in the proof. We check if the program permission to execute any statements is in accordance with the appropriate consent by the user in that state.

Definition 5 (Compliance). *To check compliance with respect to user consent for executing any program statement, we define the following formula,* comp:

$$comp(cn, o, \Sigma) = \exists \sigma, x, e, \alpha, \overline{\alpha}, l, m, q, \eta, \eta', s, s', o_0, \eta_0 \ .$$
$$o(\sigma, \{l \mid s \ ; s'\}_{\eta'}, q, \eta) \in cn \wedge \langle o_0, \eta_0 \rangle = \mathcal{E}(\langle l(caller), \eta' \rangle, \langle o, \eta \rangle)$$
$$\wedge \ (s = (x := \alpha) \wedge x \in dom(l) \Rightarrow$$
$$\quad use(cn, o, \mathcal{T}_{aol}(\alpha), \Sigma, o_0, \eta_0) \wedge col(cn, o, \mathcal{T}_{aol}(\alpha), \Sigma, \eta_0, o_0))$$
$$\wedge \ (s = (x := \alpha) \wedge x \notin dom(l) \Rightarrow$$
$$\quad use(cn, o, \mathcal{T}_{aol}(\alpha), \Sigma, o_0, \eta_0) \wedge col(cn, o, \mathcal{T}_{aol}(\alpha), \Sigma, o_0, \eta_0) \ \wedge$$
$$\quad store(cn, o, \mathcal{T}_{aol}(\alpha), \Sigma, o_0, \eta))$$
$$\wedge \ (s = (x := \text{new } C(\overline{\alpha}) \text{ of } \eta'') \Rightarrow$$
$$\quad use(cn, o, \overline{\mathcal{T}_{aol}(\alpha)}, \Sigma, o_0, \eta_0) \wedge col(cn, o, \overline{\mathcal{T}_{aol}(\alpha)}, \Sigma, \eta'', o_0) \ \wedge$$
$$\quad store(cn, o, \mathcal{T}_{aol}(\alpha), \Sigma, o_0, \eta'') \wedge trans(cn, o, \overline{\mathcal{T}_{aol}(\alpha)}, \Sigma, o_0, \eta_0))$$
$$\wedge \ (s = (x := \text{if } e \ \{s_1\}) \Rightarrow use(cn, o, \mathcal{T}_{aol}(e), \Sigma, o_0, \eta_0))$$
$$\wedge \ (s = (x := e!m(\overline{\alpha})) \Rightarrow$$
$$\quad use(cn, o, \mathcal{T}_{aol}(\alpha), \Sigma, o_0, \eta_0) \wedge trans(cn, o, \overline{\mathcal{T}_{aol}(\alpha)}, \Sigma, o_0, \eta_0)) \ \wedge$$
$$\quad (bind(m, o, o', \overline{t\overline{v}}, \eta') \in q \Rightarrow col(cn, o, \overline{\mathcal{T}_{aol}(\alpha)}, \Sigma, o_0, \eta''))$$
$$\wedge \ (s = (x := return(e) \ ) \Rightarrow use(cn, o, \mathcal{T}_{aol}(e), \Sigma, o_0, \eta_0)) \ \wedge$$
$$\quad trans(cn, o, \overline{\mathcal{T}_{aol}(e)}, \Sigma, o_0, \eta_0))$$

Definition 6 (Compliance property). *We define an execution as a sequence of execution steps, possibly non-terminating, where each step is made according to the operational semantics. An execution is said to be* privacy compliant *if each step in the execution satisfies* comp(cn, o, Σ) *where* cn *is the configuration at the start of the step,* o *is the object performing the step, and* Σ ∈ cn *is the consent.*

Theorem 1 (Compliance). *All executions following our operational semantics are privacy compliant.*

Proof. We prove the compliance property by case analysis on the rules. We prove that each execution step, between the configurations $cn_i \mapsto cn_{i+1}$, satisfies the compliance property, which again implies that all executions in our transition system satisfies compliance.

To prove this, let's assume that the current state is *cn* in our execution.

- CASE ASSIGN1. We may assume that the current program statement is $x := \alpha$ and $x \in dom(l)$ in object $o(\sigma, \{l \mid x := \alpha; s'\}_{\eta'}, q, \eta)$. Rule Assign1 is used, and we have $\langle o_0, \eta_0 \rangle = \mathcal{E}(\langle l(caller), \eta' \rangle, \langle o, \eta \rangle)$. The premises imply $use(cn, o, \mathcal{T}_{aol}(\alpha), \Sigma, o_0, \eta_0)$, $col(cn, o, \mathcal{T}_{aol}(\alpha), \Sigma, \eta_0, o_0))$.
  Hence the compliance formula $comp(cn, o, \Sigma)$ holds for the current execution step.

- CASE NEW-OBJECT. We may assume that the current program statement is $x :=$ **new** $C(\overline{\alpha})$ **of** η'' in object $o(\sigma, \{l \mid x = $ **new** $C(\overline{\alpha})$ **of** $\eta''; s\}_{\eta'}, q, \eta)\}$.
  The rule used is New-object, and we have $\langle o_0, \eta_0 \rangle = \mathcal{E}(\langle l(caller), \eta' \rangle, \langle o, \eta \rangle)$. The premises together imply $col(cn, o, \overline{\mathcal{T}_{aol}(\alpha)}, \Sigma, o_0, \eta'')$, $store(cn, o, \overline{\mathcal{T}_{aol}(\alpha)}, \Sigma, o_0, \eta'')$, $use(cn, o, \overline{\mathcal{T}_{aol}(\alpha)}, \Sigma, o_0, \eta_0)$, and $trans(cn, o, \overline{\mathcal{T}_{aol}(\alpha)}, \Sigma, o_0, \eta_0)$.
  Hence the compliance formula $comp(cn, o, \Sigma)$ holds for the current execution step.
- CASE ASYNC-CALL. We may assume the current program statement is $x = e!m(\overline{\alpha})$ in object $o(\sigma, \{l \mid x:=e!m(\overline{\alpha}) ; s'\}_{\eta'}, q, \eta)$. The rule used is Async-call, and we have $\langle o_0, \eta_0 \rangle = \mathcal{E}(\langle l(caller), \eta' \rangle, \langle o, \eta \rangle)$. The premises imply $use(cn, o, \overline{\mathcal{T}_{aol}(\alpha)}, \Sigma, o_0, \eta_0)$ and $trans(cn, o, \overline{\mathcal{T}_{aol}(\alpha)}, \Sigma, o_0, \eta_0))$.
  Hence the compliance formula $comp(cn, o, \Sigma)$ holds for the current execution step.

Analogous proofs can be done for all the other statements. However, the requirement of $comp(cn, o, \Sigma)$ concerning method binding is stronger than the last two premises of rule BIND-MTD, since there could be changes to the consent while methods are in the process queue. If we assume that the consent is not strengthened for a user u while there are pending invocations with private data about u, we can also conclude that method binding is compliant. This is a reasonable assumption, assuming such updates on Σ may be temporarily delayed. Thus in all execution steps, we conclude that the compliance property holds, thereby proving that all executions in our transition system are privacy compliant.

9   Related Work and Discussion

Notions such as privacy by design (PbD) [5], data protection by design and default [18], and legal compliance appear quite often in the literature; despite much ongoing work in this direction, the research community agrees about the need of practical guidance on such notions [13,29]. Schneider indicates that privacy principles, such as PbD, go through various levels of abstraction from their conceptual models during design time until software implementation and do not entirely guarantee privacy [22]. Hence, there is a need of privacy-aware languages that help capture software design models with data privacy constructs that facilitate the check of privacy principles. Purpose is vital to privacy, and role-based access control (RBAC) models enriched with purpose-awareness [4,15,32] for enterprise data handling have been previously well-explored; these authorization models fail to capture the current regulatory requirements and consider only organizational interests and not user preferences. Researchers have previously explored information flow analysis to comply programs against privacy policies, many of these approaches use static techniques [17,23,27]. It is essential to highlight that in all of these prior works, static analysis alone will not be enough to fully automate GDPR compliance since elements, such as consent, change at runtime. Complementary to our line of work, Hjerppe et al. [10] presents a static source code analysis to detect personal data; their focus is on the developers perspective rather than on the users' perspective. Hayati and Abadi [9] describe an approach to model and verify aspects of privacy policies with a focus on entities and purpose, ignoring other aspects of GDPR. Closer to our work, Tokas et al. [26] and Karami et al. [12] explore language-based GDPR compliance. The former [26] considers a core active object language with runtime updates of user consent, presents an operational semantics, and shows that the semantics guarantees compliance. User policies consider entity, purpose, and access rights; however, different from our approach, access rights are less GDPR-oriented and understood in terms of read, append, and write accesses. The latter [12] considers a sequential Java-like language and uses opt-in/opt-out requests to relevant users. Consent management operations are built into the language. In contrast to our work, we capture data privacy consents, in particular, a predefined user interface for the adjustment of the consent settings.

In the direction of a general study of GDPR and legal compliance, Ranise and Siswantoro [21] propose an approach for privacy-aware automated legal compliance checking by using tools for policy analysis on efficient SMT solvers. Unfortunately, this was proposed before GDPR and did not consider crucial elements like consent, actions, entities, and other GDPR requirements. Piras et al. [19] propose the design of an architecture abiding by GDPR requirements. However, this approach lacks implementation details on compliance and does not address data interoperability at lower system operations, unlike our approach, where enforcement of data subjects' preferences and monitoring inconsistency with consent is handled on a data level, guaranteeing a concrete notion of compliance. Further away from the techniques shown in this paper, there is a line of research that explores compliance checking through blockchain technology; Vargas [31] proposes a blockchain-based automated tool for compliance that considers consent operations and the purpose of processing. Similarly, Truong et al. [28] propose a Blockchain-based personal data management compliance with the GDPR platform, guaranteeing GDPR requirements like transparency and accountability. However, blockchain's immutability, i.e., ledgers can never be erased, clashes with GDPR's "right to be forgotten", and even if personal data is stored off-chain, any record on the chain will result in violation of GDPR in the platform.

10 Conclusions and Future Work

This paper proposes integrating privacy concepts into a core active object language to explore how language syntax and semantics can be used to ensure personal data handling by design and default. We first motivate the privacy constructs that must be included in the language to address privacy awareness and enforcement of compliance with personal data handling according to users' consent. Then, we propose a semantics that integrates such abstractions. Finally, we prove the correctness of the semantics with respect to users' consent.

Our current proposed semantics is fixed to a concrete interpretation of GDPR terminology. It would be interesting to explore how to parametrize the transition rules with respect to desired personal data handling checks according to different data privacy legislations and domain expertise. The proposed data privacy checks introduce heavy runtime overheads for every transition rule that is handling data.

An interesting next step will be to look into how to reduce the checkpoints so that we still guarantee compliance by using, e.g., behavioural types [11] that can statically approximate the required checks so that they occur less often. We have addressed some fine-grained personal data handling concepts for GDPR in the proposed transition rules. However, we omitted concepts like data deletion (for the right to be forgotten) and data retention time (for storage limitation), which have a temporal flavor in the analysis. It would be interesting to further extend the semantics to include such concepts in the compliance checks.

We formalized the transfer of rights between data controllers (DC) and data processors (DP) by the notion of *accountable entity*. We want to extend the compliance checks such that DCs also restrict the processing rights for processors and sub-processors. GDPR mentions contractual agreements between DC and DP and the processor's liability towards the DC. Hence, we may need to add privacy rules for DCs to restrict the information exchange between controllers and (sub)processors, e.g., by keeping track of the approved processors for each controller. Finally, we want to build a proof of concept tool to make the semantics of P-AOL executable and evaluate it via case studies and use cases.

Acknowledgment. We would like to thank Nils Gruschka for his feedback related to data privacy, the GDPR requirements and its challenges, and Paola Giannini for her feedback related to the language semantics.

References

1. Agha, G.A.: ACTORS: A Model of Concurrent Computations in Distributed Systems. The MIT Press, Cambridge (1986)
2. Baramashetru, C.P., Tapia Tarifa, S.L., Owe, O., Gruschka, N.: A policy language to capture compliance of data protection requirements. In: ter Beek, M.H., Monahan, R. (eds.) IFM 2022. LNCS, vol. 13274, pp. 289–309. Springer, Cham (2022). https://doi.org/10.1007/978-3-031-07727-2_16
3. Boehm, H.: Destructors, finalizers, and synchronization. In: Conference Record of POPL 2003: The 30th SIGPLAN-SIGACT Symposium on Principles of Programming Languages, New Orleans, Louisisana, USA, 15–17 January 2003, pp. 262–272. ACM (2003)
4. Byun, J.-W., Bertino, E., Li, N.: Purpose based access control of complex data for privacy protection. In: Proceedings of the tenth ACM Symposium on Access Control Models and Technologies, Stockholm, Sweden, pp. 102–110. ACM (2005)
5. Cavoukian, A., Chibba, M.: Advancing privacy and security in computing, networking and systems innovations through privacy by design. In: Proceedings of the 2009 Conference of the Centre for Advanced Studies on Collaborative Research, pp. 358–360. ACM (2009)
6. de Boer, F.S., et al.: A survey of active object languages. ACM Comput. Surv. **50**(5), 76:1–76:39 (2017)
7. European Parliament and Council. Regulation (EU) 2016/679 of the European parliament and of the council of 27 April 2016 on the protection of natural persons with regard to the processing of personal data and on the free movement of such data, and repealing directive 95/46/EC (general data protection regulation) (text with EEA relevance) (2016). http://data.europa.eu/eli/reg/2016/679/oj/eng

8. Gürses, S., Troncoso, C., Diaz, C.: Engineering privacy by design. Comput. Priv. Data Protect. **14**(3), 25 (2011)
9. Hayati, K., Abadi, M.: Language-based enforcement of privacy policies. In: Martin, D., Serjantov, A. (eds.) PET 2004. LNCS, vol. 3424, pp. 302–313. Springer, Heidelberg (2005). https://doi.org/10.1007/11423409_19
10. Hjerppe, K., Ruohonen, J., Leppänen, V.: Annotation-based static analysis for personal data protection. In: Friedewald, M., Önen, M., Lievens, E., Krenn, S., Fricker, S. (eds.) Privacy and Identity 2019. IAICT, vol. 576, pp. 343–358. Springer, Cham (2020). https://doi.org/10.1007/978-3-030-42504-3_22
11. Hüttel, H., et al.: Foundations of session types and behavioural contracts. ACM Comput. Surv. **49**(1), 1–36 (2016)
12. Karami, F., Basin, D.A., Johnsen, E.B.: DPL: A language for GDPR enforcement. In: 35th IEEE Computer Security Foundations Symposium, CSF 2022, Haifa, Israel, 7–10 August 2022, pp. 112–129. IEEE (2022)
13. Kutyłowski, M., Lauks-Dutka, A., Yung, M.: GDPR – challenges for reconciling legal rules with technical reality. In: Chen, L., Li, N., Liang, K., Schneider, S. (eds.) ESORICS 2020. LNCS, vol. 12308, pp. 736–755. Springer, Cham (2020). https://doi.org/10.1007/978-3-030-58951-6_36
14. MacLennan, B.J.: Principles of Programming Languages: Design, Evaluation, and Implementation, 2nd edn. Holt, Rinehart & Winston, USA (1986)
15. Masoumzadeh, A., Joshi, J.B.D.: PuRBAC: purpose-aware role-based access control. In: Meersman, R., Tari, Z. (eds.) OTM 2008. LNCS, vol. 5332, pp. 1104–1121. Springer, Heidelberg (2008). https://doi.org/10.1007/978-3-540-88873-4_12
16. Meseguer, J.: Conditional rewriting logic as a unified model of concurrency. Theoret. Comput. Sci. **96**, 73–155 (1992)
17. Myers, A.C., Liskov, B.: Protecting privacy using the decentralized label model. ACM Trans. Softw. Eng. Methodol. **9**(4), 410–442 (2000)
18. Network, E., Agency, I.S.: Privacy and data protection by design: from policy to engineering. Publications Office (2014)
19. Piras, L., et al.: DEFeND architecture: a privacy by design platform for GDPR compliance. In: Gritzalis, S., Weippl, E.R., Katsikas, S.K., Anderst-Kotsis, G., Tjoa, A.M., Khalil, I. (eds.) TrustBus 2019. LNCS, vol. 11711, pp. 78–93. Springer, Cham (2019). https://doi.org/10.1007/978-3-030-27813-7_6
20. Politou, E., Alepis, E., Patsakis, C.: Forgetting personal data and revoking consent under the GDPR: challenges and proposed solutions. J. Cybersecur. **4**(1), tyy001 (2018)
21. Ranise, S., Siswantoro, H.: Automated legal compliance checking by security policy analysis. In: Tonetta, S., Schoitsch, E., Bitsch, F. (eds.) SAFECOMP 2017. LNCS, vol. 10489, pp. 361–372. Springer, Cham (2017). https://doi.org/10.1007/978-3-319-66284-8_30
22. Schneider, G.: Is privacy by construction possible? In: Margaria, T., Steffen, B. (eds.) ISoLA 2018. LNCS, vol. 11244, pp. 471–485. Springer, Cham (2018). https://doi.org/10.1007/978-3-030-03418-4_28
23. Sen, S., Guha, S., Datta, A., Rajamani, S.K., Tsai, J., Wing, J.M.: Bootstrapping privacy compliance in big data systems. In: 2014 IEEE Symposium on Security and Privacy, San Jose, CA, pp. 327–342. IEEE (2014)
24. soliditylang.org. Solidity documentation (2023). https://docs.soliditylang.org/_/downloads/en/latest/pdf/
25. Spiekermann, S.: The challenges of privacy by design. Commun. ACM **55**(7), 38–40 (2012)

26. Tokas, S., Owe, O.: A formal framework for consent management. In: Gotsman, A., Sokolova, A. (eds.) FORTE 2020. LNCS, vol. 12136, pp. 169–186. Springer, Cham (2020). https://doi.org/10.1007/978-3-030-50086-3_10
27. Tokas, S., Owe, O., Ramezanifarkhani, T.: Static checking of GDPR-related privacy compliance for object-oriented distributed systems. J. Log. Algebraic Methods Program. **125**, 100733 (2022)
28. Truong, N.B., Sun, K., Lee, G.M., Guo, Y.: GDPR-compliant personal data management: a blockchain-based solution. IEEE Trans. Inf. Forensics Secur. **15**, 1746–1761 (2020)
29. Utz, C., Degeling, M., Fahl, S., Schaub, F., Holz, T.: (Un) informed consent: studying GDPR consent notices in the field. In: Proceedings of the 2019 ACM SIGSAC Conference on Computer and Communications Security, pp. 973–990 (2019)
30. van Lieshout, M., Kool, L., van Schoonhoven, B., de Jonge, M.: Privacy by design: an alternative to existing practice in safeguarding privacy. Info **13**(6), 55–68 (2011)
31. Vargas, J.C.: Blockchain-based consent manager for GDPR compliance. Open Identity Summit 2019 (2019)
32. Yang, N., Barringer, H., Zhang, N.: A purpose-based access control model. In: Third International Symposium on Information Assurance and Security, pp. 143–148 (2007)

Context-Aware Trace Contracts

Reiner Hähnle[1]([⊠]), Eduard Kamburjan[2], and Marco Scaletta[1]

[1] Technical University of Darmstadt, Darmstadt, Germany
{reiner.hahnle,marco.scaletta}@tu-darmstadt.de
[2] University of Oslo, Oslo, Norway
eduard@ifi.uio.no

Abstract. The behavior of concurrent, asynchronous procedures depends in general on the call context, because of the global protocol that governs scheduling. This context cannot be specified with the state-based Hoare-style contracts common in deductive verification. Recent work generalized state-based to trace contracts, which permit to specify the internal behavior of a procedure, such as calls or state changes, but not its call context. In this article we propose a program logic of context-aware trace contracts for specifying global behavior of asynchronous programs. We also provide a sound proof system that addresses two challenges: To observe the program state not merely at the end points of a procedure, we introduce the novel concept of an observation quantifier. And to combat combinatorial explosion of possible call sequences of procedures, we transfer Liskov's principle of behavioral subtyping to the analysis of asynchronous procedures.

1 Introduction

Contracts [16,35] are a cornerstone of the rely-guarantee paradigm for verification [25], as it enables the decomposition of a program along naturally defined boundaries. A well-established example are procedure contracts which encapsulate the behavior of the execution of a single procedure in terms of pre- and post-condition.[1] Traditionally, a pre-condition describes the state at the moment a procedure is called, and the post-condition describes the state at the moment the procedure terminates. The contract-based approach to deductive verification permits to verify a program in a *procedure-modular* manner and so makes it possible to conduct correctness proofs of sequential programs of considerable complexity and size in real programming languages [10,17].

A concurrent setting poses a completely different challenge, because concurrently executing procedures may interfere on the state, causing a myriad of possibly different behaviors, even for small programs. Contracts in the presence of fine-grained concurrency tend to be highly complex, because they have to encode substantial parts of the invariants of the whole system under verification [4]. It was rightly argued since long that a suitable *granularity* of interference is key to arrive at manageable specifications of concurrent programs [26].

---

[1] Additional specification elements, such as frames or exceptional behavior, can be considered as syntactic sugar to achieve concise post-conditions.

F. de Boer et al. (Eds.): *Active Object Languages: Current Research Trends*,
LNCS 14360, pp. 289–322, 2024.
https://doi.org/10.1007/978-3-031-51060-1_11

Main Contribution. The present paper constitutes an effort to generalize the contract-based approach to the verification for concurrent programs. Generalization involves two aspects: First, it is necessary to specify sets of *traces* of a verified program, not merely sets of pre-/post states, to be able to refer to the context of a program and to internal events, such as other procedure calls. Trace-based logics, such as temporal logic, are standard to specify concurrent programs. Here, we use a recent trace logic [7] that is exogenous [40] (i.e., allows judgments involving explicit programs) and can characterize procedure calls. Second, and this is our central contribution, not merely the procedure under verification is specified by traces, but *pre-/postconditions are generalized to traces*. This permits to specify the context in which a contract is supposed to be applied without ghost variables or other auxiliary constructs. As we are going to show, this approach admits a *procedure-modular* deductive verification system for concurrent programs, where the correctness of each procedure contract implies the correctness of the conjunction of all contracts, i.e. of the whole program.

Setting. There is an important limitation: our current approach does not work for preemptive concurrency, but is targeted at the *active object* paradigm [9]. With asynchronous procedures and syntactically explicit suspension points, active objects are a good trade-off between usability and verifiability, and they feature appropriate *granularity* to render contract-based specification useful.

Earlier research [12,15] showed that active objects are amenable to deductive verification, however, that work suffered from limitations: Asynchronous procedure calls, even with explicit suspension points, cannot be encapsulated in a big-step abstraction using pre-/post-conditions to describe state. Instead, a specification must at least partially describe the possible *traces* resulting from procedure execution, including (procedure-)*internal* events, such as synchronization, to reason about concurrency. Because of this, the state-based approach of [12,15] turned out to be problematic in two aspects: First, it necessitates the use of ghost variables, in this case for recording event histories during symbolic execution. This, in turn, requires to reason about histories as a data structure, hindering proof search automation. Second, *specification* of a procedure's context is done in terms of *state*. This makes it impossible to specify the history and future wherein a procedure is expected to operate correctly. For example, a procedure relying on a given resource may require that certain operations to prepare that resource were completed once it starts. Dually, it might expect that its caller cleans up afterwards. In particular, properties that stipulate the existence of global traces, such as liveness, cannot be expressed with state-based contracts. The context-aware trace contracts we define below do not require ghost variables and they let one specify the history and future of a called procedure.

Approach. The sketched limitations of state-based approaches to specification of concurrent programs suggest to explore *trace-based* specification contracts. We present *context-aware trace contracts* (CATs). Syntactically, these are formulas of a logic for symbolic traces [7], generalizing first-order pre- and post-conditions. One immediate consequence is that trace elements, such as events, become first-class citizens and need not be modeled with ghost variables. The possible traces of a given procedure m are specified with a CAT C_m in the form of a judgment $m : C_m$, meaning that all possible traces of m, *including their context*, are described by C_m.

Our main contribution is to fashion these contracts as *context-aware*. This means that a CAT for a procedure m consists of three parts: A generalized pre-condition describing the assumed *trace* up to the moment when m starts; the possible traces produced by executing m; and a post-condition that again is a trace describing the assumed operations taking place after termination of m. The generalization of pre-/post-conditions to traces requires careful examination of allocation of guarantees: A procedure *guarantees* only its *post-state* but it *assumes* the system continues in a certain fashion—this is, however, not guaranteed by the procedure, but by the *caller*.

Let us illustrate CATs with an example. Consider a procedure work that operates on a file. Its pre-condition is that the file was opened. Its internal specification is that the file may be read or written to, but nothing else. Its post-condition is that (A) in the final state of work, a flag indicating that it has finished is set, and that (B) after work terminated, the file will be closed. While the procedure assumes that the file has been opened upon start, itself it can only guarantee (A), while it is the caller's obligation to ensure (B).

Summary of Contributions and Structure. Our main contribution is the generalization of state-based procedure contracts to the context-aware, trace-based CAT model that permits not merely to specify the behavior of a procedure, but also its context. We apply the CAT theory to a simplified active object concurrency model, where trace specification involves communication events, and the proof calculus must keep track of when a procedure may start execution and when its pre-condition must hold.

To render specification and verification practical, we add two further ingredients: the novel concept of an *observation quantifier* lets one record the (symbolic) value of a program variable at a given point in a CAT. This can be seen as a generalization of old references in state-based contract languages [33] and lets one compare the symbolic values of program variables at different points within a CAT. Second, to reduce the specification and verification effort, we generalize Liskov's behavioral subtyping principle [34] to CATs.

We first discuss the state of the art in Sect. 2, before we introduce our programming model in Sect. 3. The CAT concept is based on a trace logic, described in Sect. 4, and CATs themselves are described in Sect. 5. The proof calculus is given in Sect. 6, before we give an example in Sect. 7, describe the Liskov principle in Sect. 8 and conclude in Sect. 9.

Formal proofs of our results are given in our technical report [18].

2   State of the Art

Traces and Contracts. Specifying traces in logic has a long tradition, for example, using Linear Temporal Logic (LTL) [42] for events. We focus here on trace logics used for deductive verification. Our use of traces for internal specification is based on work by Bubel et al. [7], which is following a line of research going back to Dynamic Logic with Co-Inductive traces [6] that focused on a sequential while language and is not connected to contracts.

Dynamic Trace Logic (DTL) [5] is an extension of dynamic logic that uses LTL formulas as post-conditions. DTL was investigated for a fragment of Java without concurrency and implemented as a prototype in th KeY system. It only specifies changes of the state and no events, and is targeting internal behavior of methods.

ABSDL [12,15] uses first-order logic and a ghost variable to keep track of events. As discussed in the introduction, the use of a ghost variable to encode trace properties in state predicates leads to complex specification patterns. ABSDL was implemented in KeY-ABS [12] for the Active Object language ABS [24]. As specification, however, it only supports object invariants, procedure contracts must be encoded. This specification principle does not scale to complex systems and protocols and, as it keeps track of events, but not of states, it cannot handle specifications for internal state change. The specifications are also procedure-local: one cannot express global system properties or even liveness.

Behavioral Program Logic (BPL) [27] is a parametric logic with trace-based semantics, that has been instantiated for a calculus that supports behavioral procedure contracts [30]. A behavioral procedure contract supports limited specification of context, by specifying which procedures are allowed to run before execution starts, but it does so in a dedicated specification pattern called *context set*, which is not uniform for trace logic. The approach is implemented in the Crowbar tool [31] for ABS and based on *Locally Abstract, Globally Concrete (LAGC)* semantics [13,14], a bilayered trace semantics that differentiates between local traces of statements and global traces of programs. Local traces are parameterized with a concurrent context and combined into a concrete global trace once that context becomes known due to scheduling decisions. In the end, a set of concrete traces is produced for a given program.

Context and Contracts. With *context* we mean the execution trace before and after a procedure is executed, as specified from the perspective of the procedure. In the following, we discuss approaches that view traces from a similar perspective. Behavioral contracts for Active Objects are discussed above.

Session types are a typing paradigm for specification and verification of event traces in concurrent systems [22], which was adapted to active objects [29]. Session types have a projection mechanism that generates a local specification from a global one. Projection is re-interpreted as generation of proof obligations within BPL, where *global* soundness relies on the *implicit* context of the global specification [27,28].

Typestate [3,11] is an approach, where a trace of procedure calls is specified at the object level. In terms of the file example in the introduction, the order of opening, writing/reading, and closing a file would be part of the specification of the file class. Typestate has recently been integrated in deductive verification [36], but is complementary to contracts: it specifies traces from the

$$P \in Prog ::= \overline{M} \{d\ s\} \qquad\qquad e \in Expr ::= f \mid \cdots$$
$$M \in ProcDecl ::= m()\,\{s;\ \texttt{return}\} \qquad d \in VarDecl ::= \varepsilon \mid x;\ d$$
$$s \in Stmt ::= \texttt{skip} \mid x = e \mid m() \mid !m() \mid \texttt{if}(e)\{s\} \mid s; s \mid$$
$$\texttt{open}(f) \mid \texttt{close}(f) \mid \texttt{read}(f) \mid \texttt{write}(f)$$

Fig. 1. Syntax of Async

point of view of the entities that are the target of events, while contracts specify traces from the point of view of the origin of events. In particular, it presupposes object-like structures. As we can see later, this is unnecessary for contracts, which merely require *procedures*.

In this article, we focus on specifying the *temporal* context of a procedure call, i.e., the preceding and subsequent events. Orthogonal to this, and not our concern here, is the *spatial* context, where one specifies the relation between different parts of the heap memory, such as in Separation Logic [39,41], Dynamic Frames [32], Permission Logic [37], etc. These are *state*-based formalisms. To combine them with CATs is future work.

3   Program Semantics

3.1   The Async Language

Syntax. We define the Async language, a small, imperative language that features asynchronous as well as synchronous procedure calls, and a tree-like concurrency model. It slightly simplifies typical Active Object languages [9], but it is close enough to expose the challenges of trace-based semantics and contracts for languages with cooperative scheduling. We permit recursion only for synchronous calls, which is sufficient in practice. For the sake of being able to present relevant examples, we add a small domain-specific language extension with file operations (second line of statement rule in Fig. 1).

Definition 1 (Syntax). *The syntax of programs P and their elements is given by the grammar in Fig. 1. A program P consists of a set of procedures given by* procedures(P) *and an init block that declares the global variables and the initial statement to start execution. The global lookup table $\mathcal{G}$ is defined by $\mathcal{G} = \langle m()\,\{s; \texttt{return}\}\rangle_{m \in \text{procedures}(P)}$. Let* PVar *be the set of program variables with typical value x. Let m range over procedure names and f over file descriptors.*

There are no type annotations and no local variables in Async. A procedure M has a name m, and a procedure body for execution. Each procedure ends with a **return** statement, serving merely as a syntactic marker to simplify the semantics of process termination: There are neither return values, nor procedure parameters, all of which can be encoded as global variables. A statement

s is either a standard imperative construct, like assignment or sequential composition, a synchronous call $m()$, an asynchronous call $!m()$ or a file operation for opening, closing, reading and writing a file[2]. We underspecify the set of expressions, but require that file identifiers are literals. We assume expression evaluation to be total.

To guide the presentation and motivate our approach we use the following running example.

Example 1. The following program writes to two files using the do procedure. This procedure opens the file stored in the global variable file, asynchronously issues its closing, and then calls operate.

```
do() { open(file); !closeF(); operate(); return; }
operate() { write(file); return; }
closeF() { close(file); return; }
{file; file = "file1.txt"; do(); file = "file2.txt"; do(); }
```

Concurrency Model. Before we formalize the semantics of Async, we point out its cooperative tree-like scheduling for concurrency. By cooperative, we mean that a process is preemption-free: Once a procedure starts, it runs until the end of its code before another procedure can be scheduled. This is standard in both Actor and Active Object languages [9]. By tree-like, we mean that all asynchronously called procedures by a process p, are guaranteed to run *directly after* p terminates. This ensures that from the point of view of the caller of p, these processes are hidden and do not interleave with other caller processes.

Example 2. Consider a program where procedure m asynchronously calls m1 and m2, while m1 asynchronously calls m3 and m4.

```
m() { !m1(); !m2(); return }
m1() { !m3(); !m4(); return }
{ m() }
```

The tree-like semantics ensures the following scheduling constraints:

- The processes for m1 and m2 run directly after the one for m terminates, and before any other process is scheduled (of a potential caller of m).
- The processes for m3 and m4 run directly after the one for m1 terminates, and before any other process is scheduled.
- Assume that m1 is scheduled before m2, then the processes for m3 and m4 run before the one for m2.

Synchronous calls are handled via inlining and are a special case of this model.

---

[2] We do not add the value to be written as a parameter, again for simplicity. This can be easily modelled with a global variable, if desired.

Example 3. Consider the following program:

```
m1() { !m3(); return }
m2() {...}
m3() {...}
{ m1(); m2() }
```

Since the body of m1 is inlined before the one of m2, under the tree-like semantics all the procedures called in m1 (synchronous or not) run before m2. Therefore, is ensured that m3 runs before m2.

Example 4. The tree-like concurrency model guarantees that in Example 1, procedure operate is executed before closeF, because the two calls occur in the same scope, and the first one is synchronous while the second is asynchronous.

3.2 States and Traces

We define the program semantics formally, following mostly [7], except for file operations, some aspects of call identifier management, and tree-like concurrency. First, we require some technical definitions.

Definition 2 (State, State Update). *A state $\sigma \in \Sigma$ is a partial mapping $\sigma :$ PVar $\rightharpoonup$ Val from variables to values. The notation $\sigma[x \mapsto v]$ expresses the update of state σ at x with value v and is defined as $\sigma[x \mapsto v](y) = v$ if $x = y$ and $\sigma[x \mapsto v](y) = \sigma(y)$ otherwise.*

There is a standard evaluation function val_σ for expressions, for example, in a state $\sigma = [x \mapsto 0, y \mapsto 1]$ we have $\text{val}_\sigma(x + y) = \text{val}_\sigma(x) + \text{val}_\sigma(y) = 0 + 1 = 1$.

Call scopes inside events keep track of active and called processes for procedures. This simplifies the semantics as one does not need an explicit process pool or stack frames.

Definition 3 (Scope). *A (call) scope is a pair $scp = (m, id)$, where m is a procedure name and id is a call identifier.*

Events keep track of side effects, in particular they keep track of asynchronous calls, process scheduling and termination, and file interactions.

Definition 4 (Event Marker). *Let m be a procedure name, id a call identifier, and scp a scope. Event markers ev are defined by the grammar:*

$$ev ::= \text{call}(m, id) \mid \text{invoc}(m, id) \mid \text{ret}(id) \mid \text{push}(scp) \mid \text{pop}(scp) \mid$$
$$\text{open}(f) \mid \text{close}(f) \mid \text{read}(f) \mid \text{write}(f)$$

We denote with $ev(\overline{e})$ a generic event marker over expressions $\overline{e}$. Event markers $\text{call}(m, id)$, $\text{invoc}(m, id)$, and $\text{ret}(id)$ are associated with a synchronous call, an asynchronous call, and a return statement, respectively. Event markers $\text{push}(scp)$ and $\text{pop}(scp)$ are associated with the start (process activation after a call) and end of a computation in a procedure (termination of a process after the return statement has been executed) in scope *scp*, respectively. These events are similar to, but simpler than the ones in [14,15] due to the absence of futures, call parameters, and return values. In addition, in [14,15] *invocation reaction* events are used only for asynchronous calls, while we use push for synchronous calls as well to achieve greater uniformity.

We define dedicated event markers open(f), close(f), read(f), and write(f) associated with operations on a file f. These are a domain-specific extension of the framework, added for the benefit of having examples.

Definition 5 (Trace). *A trace τ is defined by the following rules (where ε denotes the empty trace):*

$$\tau ::= \varepsilon \mid \tau \curvearrowright t \qquad t ::= \sigma \mid ev(\overline{e})$$

We define a singleton trace *as $\langle\sigma\rangle = \varepsilon \curvearrowright \sigma$. When an event $ev(\overline{e})$ is generated we need to uniquely associate it with the state σ in which it was generated. To do so we define the corresponding* event trace *$ev_\sigma(\overline{e}) = \langle\sigma\rangle \curvearrowright ev(\text{val}_\sigma(\overline{e})) \curvearrowright \sigma$.*

Traces are finite sequences over events and states, where every event is encapsulated in an event trace triple. Events do not change a state. States and events do not need to be constantly alternating, there can be arbitrarily many state updates between the occurrence of two events.

Sequential composition "r;s" of statements is semantically modeled as trace composition, where the trace from executing r ends in a state from which the execution trace of s proceeds. Thus the trace of r ends in the same state as where the trace of s begins. This motivates the *semantic chop* "**" on traces [20,21,38] that we often use, instead of the standard concatenation operator ".".

Definition 6 (Semantic Chop on Traces). *Let τ_1, τ_2 be non-empty and finite traces. The semantic chop $\tau_1 {**} \tau_2$ is defined as $\tau_1 {**} \tau_2 = \tau \cdot \tau_2$, where $\tau_1 = \tau \curvearrowright \sigma$, $\tau_2 = \langle\sigma'\rangle \cdot \tau'$, and $\sigma = \sigma'$. When $\sigma \neq \sigma'$ the result is undefined.*

Example 5. Let $\tau_1 = \langle\sigma\rangle \curvearrowright \sigma[\text{x} \mapsto 1]$ and $\tau_2 = \langle\sigma[\text{x} \mapsto 1]\rangle \curvearrowright \sigma[\text{x} \mapsto 1, \text{y} \mapsto 2]$, then $\tau_1 {**} \tau_2 = \langle\sigma\rangle \curvearrowright \sigma[\text{x} \mapsto 1] \curvearrowright \sigma[\text{x} \mapsto 1, \text{y} \mapsto 2]$.

Our trace semantics evaluates an individual statement "locally". Obviously, it is not possible to fully evaluate composite statements in this manner. Therefore, local semantic rules perform one evaluation step at a time and defer evaluation of the remaining statements, which are put into a *continuation*, to subsequent rule applications. Syntactically, continuations are simply statements s wrapped in the symbol K. To achieve uniform definitions we permit the case that no further evaluation is required (it has been completed) and use the "empty bottle" symbol for this case.

Definition 7 (Continuation Marker). *Let s be a program statement, then K(s) is a continuation marker. The empty continuation is denoted with K$(\emptyset)$ and expresses that nothing remains to be evaluated.*

3.3   Semantics of Async

The semantics of Async is two-layered: a local semantics for small-step evaluation of a single process, and a global semantics for the evaluation of the whole state, in particular scheduling and other concurrency operations.

As our language is locally deterministic[3], we define local small-step evaluation $\mathrm{val}_\sigma(s)$ of a statement s in state σ to return a *single* trace: The result of $\mathrm{val}_\sigma(s)$ is of the form $\tau \cdot \mathrm{K}(s')$, where τ is an initial (small-step) trace of s and $\mathrm{K}(s')$ contains the remaining, possibly empty, statement s' yet to be evaluated.

To distinguish different calls of the same procedure, we generate fresh call identifiers. This cannot be done locally, so the most recently used call identifier is passed as a "counter" id to the local evaluation rules. Yet another context parameter of the local evaluation rules is the identifier of the currently executing scope cId. It is passed down from a global rule. Both parameters appear as superscripts in $\mathrm{val}_\sigma^{id,cId}(s)$.

Definition 8 (Small-Step Local Evaluation). *The local evaluation rules defining* $\mathrm{val}_\sigma^{id,cId}(s)$ *are given in Fig. 2.*

$$\mathrm{val}_\sigma^{id,cId}(\texttt{skip}) = \langle \sigma \rangle \cdot \mathrm{K}(0)$$

$$\mathrm{val}_\sigma^{id,cId}(x = e) = \langle \sigma \rangle \curvearrowright \sigma[x \mapsto \mathrm{val}_\sigma(e)] \cdot \mathrm{K}(0)$$

$$\mathrm{val}_\sigma^{id,cId}(\texttt{return}) = \mathsf{ret}_\sigma(cId) \cdot \mathrm{K}(0)$$

$$\mathrm{val}_\sigma^{id,cId}(\texttt{if } e \texttt{ \{ } s \texttt{ \}}) = \begin{cases} \langle \sigma \rangle \cdot \mathrm{K}(s), & \text{if } \mathrm{val}_\sigma(e) = \mathsf{tt} \\ \langle \sigma \rangle \cdot \mathrm{K}(0) & \text{otherwise} \end{cases}$$

$$\mathrm{val}_\sigma^{id,cId}(r;s) = \tau \cdot \mathrm{K}(r';s), \quad \text{where } \mathrm{val}_\sigma^{id,cId}(r) = \tau \cdot \mathrm{K}(r') \text{ and } 0; s \rightsquigarrow s$$

$$\mathrm{val}_\sigma^{id,cId}(m()) = \mathsf{call}_\sigma(m, id+1) \cdot \mathrm{K}(0)$$

$$\mathrm{val}_\sigma^{id,cId}(!m()) = \mathsf{invoc}_\sigma(m, id+1) \cdot \mathrm{K}(0)$$

$$\mathrm{val}_\sigma^{id,cId}(\texttt{open}(f)) = \mathsf{open}_\sigma(f) \cdot \mathrm{K}(0) \qquad \mathrm{val}_\sigma^{id,cId}(\texttt{close}(f)) = \mathsf{close}_\sigma(f) \cdot \mathrm{K}(0)$$

$$\mathrm{val}_\sigma^{id,cId}(\texttt{read}(f)) = \mathsf{read}_\sigma(f) \cdot \mathrm{K}(0) \qquad \mathrm{val}_\sigma^{id,cId}(\texttt{write}(f)) = \mathsf{write}_\sigma(f) \cdot \mathrm{K}(0)$$

Fig. 2. Local Program Semantics.

The rules for asynchronous calls, synchronous calls, and return emit suitable event traces. The difference between call and invoc is that the former directly triggers execution of a procedure in the trace composition rules below. In both cases a new call identifier is generated based on id, therefore any two calls, no matter whether synchronous or not, always have different call identifiers.

The rule for sequential composition assumes empty leading continuations are discarded, the remaining rules are straightforward. Local evaluation of a statement s yields a small step τ of s plus a continuation $\mathrm{K}(s')$. Therefore,

---

[3] Evaluation of a single process, in a known context.

traces can be extended by evaluating the continuation and stitching the result to τ. This is performed by trace *composition rules* that operate on configurations of the form τ, K(s). To formulate the composition rules we need to introduce auxiliary structures to keep track of scopes and the call tree.

We define *schematic traces* that allow us to characterize succinctly sets of traces (not) containing certain events via matching. The notation $\overset{\overline{ev}}{\cdots}$ represents the set of all non-empty, finite traces *without* events of type $ev \in \overline{ev}$. Symbol $\cdots$ is shorthand for $\overset{\emptyset}{\cdots}$. With $\tau_1 \overset{\overline{ev}}{\cdots} \tau_2$ we denote the set of all well-defined traces $\tau_1 \text{**} \tau \text{**} \tau_2$ such that $\tau \in \overset{\overline{ev}}{\cdots}$.

Maintaining the stack of call scopes is handled by the composition rules with the help of events push(scp) and pop(scp) that are added to the generated trace τ. To find the current call scope in τ, one simply searches for the most recent pushed scope that was not yet popped:

Definition 9 (Current Call Scope, Most Recent Call Identifier). *Let* τ *be a non-empty trace. The* current call scope *is defined as*

$$currScp(\tau) = \begin{cases} scp & \tau \in \cdots \text{push}_\sigma(scp)^{\overset{\text{push,pop}}{\cdots}} \\ currScp(\tau') & \tau \in \tau' \underline{\text{**}} \text{push}_\sigma(scp) \cdots \text{pop}_{\sigma'}(scp)^{\overset{\text{push,pop}}{\cdots}} \end{cases}$$

The most recent call identifier *of a trace is retrieved with*

$$id(\tau) = \max\{i \mid \tau \in \cdots \text{invoc}(\_,i)\cdots \text{ or } \tau \in \cdots\text{call}(\_,i)\cdots\} \ .$$

If τ *is not empty then we define the function* $last(\tau) = last(\tau' \curvearrowright \sigma) = \sigma$, *for some state* σ *and possibly empty trace* τ'.

To retrieve the most recent call identifier it suffices to consider events that introduce fresh call identifiers, i.e. call and invoc.

To define the processes in a given trace that are eligible for scheduling, we define the call tree of a trace that records the dependencies of the call scopes. Each node in the call tree is a scope in the given trace, where an edge (v_1, v_2) denotes that v_1 called or invoked v_2.

Definition 10 (Call Tree). *A call tree for a trace* τ *is an ordered tree*

$$(V(\tau), E(\tau), <)$$

with vertices $V(\tau) = \{(m,i) \mid \tau \in \cdots\text{invoc}(m,i)\cdots \text{ or } \tau \in \cdots\text{call}(m,i)\cdots\}$, *edges*

$$\begin{aligned} E(\tau) = \{&(currScp(\tau'), (m,i)) \mid (\tau \in \tau'\underline{\text{**}}\text{call}_\sigma(m,i)\cdots) \\ &\vee (\tau \in \tau'\underline{\text{**}}\text{invoc}_\sigma(m,i)\cdots)\} \end{aligned}$$

and order $(m_1,i_1) < (m_2,i_2) \iff i_1 < i_2$. *We define the set of* idle nodes $V_{idle}(\tau) \subseteq V(\tau)$ *as those asynchronous calls having not yet started to execute:*

$$V_{idle}(\tau) = \{(m,i) \mid \tau \in \cdots\text{invoc}(m,i)^{\overset{\text{push}(m,i)}{\cdots}}\}$$

We also define a function to retrieve all children of a given call scope:

$$children(scp, \tau) = \{child \mid (scp, child) \in E(\tau)\}$$

Observe that V_{idle} can never coincide with V, since the main scope is never idle, i.e. $(init, 0) \notin V_{idle}$.

To define the tree-like semantics mentioned in Sect. 3.1, we introduce implicit barriers for the execution of asynchronously called procedures: a procedure that was invoked in scope *scp* must be scheduled before the scope *scp* is exited. We do not allow pending procedure invocations in a closed call scope. This is formalized in the following definition.

Definition 11 (Schedule Function). *Given a trace τ we define*

$$schedule(\tau) = children(currScp(\tau), \tau) \cap V_{idle}(\tau)$$

The above scheduling function realizes tree-like concurrency, but can be easily adapted to other concurrency models. For example, $schedule(\tau) = \{\min(V_{idle}(\tau))\}$ defines a deterministic scheduler (as does any instantiation that returns a singleton or empty set), while $schedule(\tau) = V_{idle}(\tau)$ is the usual fully non-deterministic scheduler.

$$\tau = \mathsf{call}_\sigma(init, 0)\underline{**}\mathsf{push}_\sigma((init, 0))$$
$$\underline{**}\mathsf{call}_\sigma(\mathtt{m}, 1)\underline{**}\mathsf{push}_\sigma((\mathtt{m}, 1))$$
$$\underline{**}\mathsf{invoc}_\sigma(\mathtt{m1}, 2)\underline{**}\mathsf{invoc}_\sigma(\mathtt{m2}, 3)$$
$$\underline{**}\mathsf{push}_\sigma((\mathtt{m1}, 2))$$
$$\underline{**}\mathsf{invoc}_\sigma(\mathtt{m3}, 4)\underline{**}\mathsf{invoc}_\sigma(\mathtt{m4}, 5)$$
$$\underline{**}\mathsf{ret}(2)$$

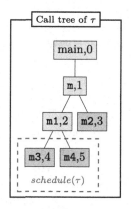

Fig. 3. Trace and call tree for an incomplete execution of program from Example 2.

Example 6. Consider an incomplete execution of the program in Example 2, with m1 scheduled before m2 and ending with the return statement of m1. We show in Fig. 3 on the left the trace τ generated by the composition rules that we introduce later in Definition 12, as well as its call tree on the right. As described in Example 2, m3 and m4 are executed before m2(). At this point, m3 and m4 can be scheduled according to the tree semantics, but not m2.

Definition 12 (Trace Composition Rules). *One global evaluation step of a configuration τ, K(s) is given by the* trace composition rules *in Fig. 4.*

Rule PROGRESS. This rule uses the local small-step semantics $\mathrm{val}_\sigma^{id(\tau),i}(s)$ to evaluate s in the continuation in the currently active process i. The local evaluation function is passed the most recent call id $id(\tau)$ and the id i of the current call scope. It is triggered whenever the current trace does not end in a call event (which would require starting the execution of a synchronously called procedure) and no return event for the current scope has been yet generated (which would require scheduling of asynchronously called procedures). The first two premises exclude these options, respectively.

Rule CALL. This rule schedules the execution of a synchronously called procedure: If the trace ends in a call event, then the body s' of the procedure m that has just been called is *prepended* to the current continuation s.

Rule RUN. This rule schedules the execution of an asynchronously called procedure: If the current scope id finished execution of its return statement (presence of return event with id in τ), but was not de-scheduled (no pop event emitted yet), and at least one of its remaining asynchronous calls (to m) is not scheduled, then the body s' of m is *prepended* to the body of the continuation s and the new scope is pushed on the current trace.

Rule RETURN. This rule de-schedules a process, which is the case if it has terminated, and has no asynchronous calls left to execute.

$$(\text{PROGRESS}) \quad \frac{\begin{array}{cc} \tau \notin \cdots \mathsf{call}_\sigma(\_,\_) & \tau \notin \cdots \mathsf{ret}_\sigma(i)\cdots \\ \sigma = \mathrm{last}(\tau) \quad currScp(\tau) = (m,i) & \mathrm{val}_\sigma^{id(\tau),i}(s) = \tau' \cdot \mathrm{K}(s') \end{array}}{\tau, \mathrm{K}(s) \to \tau \underline{**} \tau', \mathrm{K}(s')} \quad (1)$$

$$(\text{CALL}) \quad \frac{\tau \in \cdots \mathsf{call}_\sigma(m,id) \qquad \mathrm{lookup}(m,\mathcal{G}) = m()\ \{s';\ \mathtt{return}\}}{\tau, \mathrm{K}(s) \to \tau \underline{**}\mathsf{push}_\sigma((m,id)), \mathrm{K}(s';\ \mathtt{return};\ s)} \quad (2)$$

$$(\text{RUN}) \quad \frac{currScp(\tau) = (\_,id) \quad \mathrm{lookup}(m,\mathcal{G}) = m()\ \{s';\ \mathtt{return}\}}{\tau \in \cdots \mathsf{ret}_\sigma(id)^{\ \mathsf{pop}_\sigma(\_,id)}\cdots \quad (m,id_2) \in \mathrm{schedule}(\tau) \quad \sigma = \mathrm{last}(\tau)}{\tau, \mathrm{K}(s) \to \tau \underline{**}\mathsf{push}_\sigma((m,id_2)), \mathrm{K}(s';\ \mathtt{return};\ s)} \quad (3)$$

$$(\text{RETURN}) \quad \frac{\tau \in \cdots \mathsf{ret}_\sigma(id)^{\ \mathsf{pop}_\sigma(m,id)}\cdots \quad currScp(\tau) = (m,id) \quad \mathrm{schedule}(\tau) = \emptyset}{\tau, \mathrm{K}(s) \to \tau \underline{**}\mathsf{pop}_\sigma((m,id)), \mathrm{K}(s)} \quad (4)$$

Fig. 4. Global Small-Step Semantics of `Async`.

We say that a rule is applied with a call identifier i, if it is applied in a state $\tau, \mathrm{K}(s)$ with $currScp(\tau) = (\_,i)$.

Finally, we define the traces of a program, as well as the big-step denotational semantics of statements and programs.

Definition 13 (Program Trace). *Given a statement s (with implicit lookup table) and a state σ, the* traces *of s are all the possible maximal sequences* *obtained by repeated application of composition rules starting from* $\langle \sigma \rangle, \mathrm{K}(s)$. *If finite, a maximal sequence has the form*

$$\langle \sigma \rangle, \mathrm{K}(s) \rightarrow \cdots \rightarrow \tau, \mathrm{K}(\emptyset) \ ,$$

also written $\langle \sigma \rangle, \mathrm{K}(s) \xrightarrow{*} \tau, \mathrm{K}(\emptyset)$.

Let τ *be a trace and* $(\_, i) = currScp(\tau)$. *A maximal sequence without using the rule* RUN *with* i *is denoted*

$$\tau, \mathrm{K}(s) \xrightarrow{X} \tau', \mathrm{K}(\emptyset)$$

The traces defined by $\xrightarrow{X}$ are those, where the asynchronously called procedures of the outermost statement s are not resolved, but those of synchronously called methods within s are.

We define two program semantics, the global one represents the execution of a program taking into account the execution of asynchronous calls. The local one represents the execution of a program without doing so.

Definition 14 (Program Semantics). *The* global semantics *of a statement* s *is only defined for terminating statements as*

$$[\![s]\!]_\tau^G = \{\tau' \mid \tau, \mathrm{K}(s) \xrightarrow{*} \tau \underline{**}\tau', \mathrm{K}(\emptyset), \ schedule(\tau \underline{**}\tau') = \emptyset\}$$

The local semantics *of a statement* s *is defined, again for terminating statements, as*

$$[\![s]\!]_\tau^L = \{\tau' \mid \tau, \mathrm{K}(s) \xrightarrow{X} \tau \underline{**}\tau', \mathrm{K}(\emptyset)\}$$

The semantics of a program P *with initial block* $\{d; s\}$ *is defined as follows, assuming no procedure is called "init". State* σ_d *initializes all variables in* d *to default values.*

$$[\![P]\!]_d^G =$$

$$\{\tau \mid \mathsf{call}_{\sigma_d}(init, 0)\underline{**}\mathsf{push}_{\sigma_d}(init, 0), \mathrm{K}(s; \mathtt{return}) \xrightarrow{*} \tau, \mathrm{K}(\emptyset), \ schedule(\tau) = \emptyset\}$$

The local and global semantics are connected[4] as follows. Recall that we permit only synchronous recursive calls and only terminating programs have a semantic value.

Proposition 1. *Let* s *be a statement without synchronous method calls,* s' *any procedure body and* τ *a trace, then:*

$$[\![s; s']\!]_\tau^G = \bigcup_{\tau' \in [\![s]\!]_\tau^L} [\![s]\!]_\tau^L \underline{**} [\![s']\!]_{\tau \underline{**}\tau'}^G \ .$$

A special case is $[\![s]\!]_\tau^G = \bigcup_{\tau' \in [\![s]\!]_\tau^L} [\![s]\!]_\tau^L \underline{**} [\![\emptyset]\!]_{\tau \underline{**}\tau'}^G \ .$

---

[4] The split between local and global is inspired by the LAGC semantics for Active Objects [14]. There are some technical differences between our semantics and LAGC, most prominently that both our local and global semantics are only defined on concrete traces: We do not evaluate symbolically.

Our trace contracts are used to specify functional properties, but are also able to express generic properties. To keep formalities manageable, we do not introduce exceptions and verify exception-freedom, but merely specify what it means that the sequence of file operations is correct.

Definition 15 (File Correctness). *A trace τ is file correct, if for every file descriptor f occurring in τ and any position i in τ with an event $\mathsf{write}_\sigma(f)$, $\mathsf{read}_\sigma(f)$ or $\mathsf{close}_\sigma(f)$ for some σ, there is a position j with in τ with the event $\mathsf{open}_{\sigma'}(f)$ for some σ' and for no k with $j < k < i$, there is a $\mathsf{close}_{\sigma''}(f)$ event at position k for some σ''.*

4   A Logic for Trace-Based Specification

The trace logic is based on [7], however, instead of modeling program variables as non-rigid symbols in trace formulas, we define a quantifier to bind values of program variables to logical variables at a specific position in the trace.

4.1   Syntax

Formulas are constructed over a set LVar of first-order observation variables and a set RecVar of recursion variables.

Definition 16. *Let P range over first-order predicates, X over recursion variables RecVar, x over program variables PVar, and y over logical variables LVar. The syntax of the logic is defined by the following grammar:*

$$\Phi ::= \lceil P \rceil \mid X \mid Ev \mid \Phi \wedge \Phi \mid \Phi \vee \Phi$$
$$\mid \Phi \cdot \Phi \mid \Phi \ast\ast \Phi \mid (\mu X.\Phi) \mid \mho x \text{ as } y.\Phi$$

We forbid any occurrence of recursion variables X in the scope of $\mho$.

Events Ev related to the beginning, return, and end of a procedure m in scope (m, i) have the form $\mathsf{start}(m, i)$, $\mathsf{ret}(i)$, $\mathsf{pop}(m, i)$, respectively. Events Ev related to manipulation of a file f have the form $\mathsf{open}(f)$, $\mathsf{close}(f)$, $\mathsf{read}(f)$, or $\mathsf{write}(f)$. It is not necessary that events in the trace logic exactly follow the events in the trace semantics. In fact, a certain degree of abstraction is usually desirable. The event structure Ev of our logic is parameterizable. The semantics of events in the logic relative to events in traces is defined in Sect. 4.2.

The novel aspect of our logic is the *observation quantifier* $\mho$. It addresses the problem that, unlike in state-based Hoare-style contracts, in the asynchronous setting it is necessary to observe the value of program variables at arbitrary points inside a trace specification. This could be achieved with non-rigid variables, but to control their visibility is technically complex already in the sequential case [1]. An intuitive version of scoping is provided by quantifiers of the form $\mho x$ as $y.\Phi$, where a *logical* variable y observes the value of a *program* variable x at the position in the trace, where the quantifier occurs. This observed snapshot is available within the scope Φ of the quantifier, but not outside.

Example 7 (Notation for generic finite traces). The expressive power of fixed points can be used to define transitive closure. Let the predicate $NoEv(\overline{ev})$ be true in any state that is not one of the events occurring in a set of events $\overline{ev}$. We define the trace formula

$$\overset{\overline{ev}}{\cdot\cdot} \;=\; \mu X.\,(NoEv(\overline{ev}) \vee NoEv(\overline{ev}) \cdot X)$$

that characterizes all non-empty, finite traces that do not contain an event occurring in $\overline{ev}$. If $\overline{ev} = \emptyset$, we simply write "$\cdot\cdot$".

Finally, we take the convention to omit writing the $*\!*$ operator between $\overset{\overline{ev}}{\cdot\cdot}$ and any adjacent trace formula. For example, the expression "$\lceil P \rceil \,\cdot\cdot$" denotes all finite traces that begin with a state, where P is true. Another useful pattern is $\Phi \overset{\overline{ev}}{\cdot\cdot} \Psi$, which expresses that any finite trace *not* involving an event in $\overline{ev}$ may occur between the traces specified by Φ and Ψ.

The $\cdot\cdot$ notation is the syntactic equivalent of $\cdots$ defined in Sect. 3.3 and extremely useful to write concise specifications. Thanks to the expressive power of fixed points, it is *definable* in our logic.

4.2 Semantics

We use a fixed[5] first-order interpretation I for predicate and function symbols, an environment $o : \mathsf{LVar} \rightarrow \mathsf{PVar} \times \Sigma$ for observation quantifiers, and a recursion variable assignment $\rho : \mathsf{RecVar} \rightarrow 2^{\mathsf{Traces}}$ that maps each recursion variable to a set of traces. The (finite-trace) semantics $[\![\Phi]\!]_{\rho,o}$ of formulas as a set of traces is inductively defined in Fig. 5.

The observation environment o records for a logic variable y introduced by an observation quantifier the program variable x and program state σ it keeps track of. Hence, for a given y one can construct a first-order variable assignment $\beta : \mathsf{LVar} \rightarrow \mathsf{Val}$ via the following definition:

$$\beta(o)(y) = \sigma(x) \text{ with } o(y) = (x, \sigma)$$

Our language does not include equality over logical observation variables.

Definition 17. *The semantics of our logic is given in Fig. 5, where $\sqsubseteq$ and $\sqcap$ denote point-wise set inclusion and intersection, respectively, and $\mathsf{I}, \beta \models P$ is first-order satisfiability under interpretation I and variable assignment β.*

By a *trace formula* we mean a formula of our logic that is closed with respect to both first-order and recursion variables. Since the semantics of a trace formula does not depend on variable assignments, we sometimes use $[\![\Phi]\!]$ to denote $[\![\Phi]\!]_{\rho,o}$ for arbitrary ρ and o.

Example 8. The following formula describes all traces, where the value of program variable x decreases after a call to decr with call identifier 1:

$$\cdot\cdot\, \mho\, x \text{ as } y_1.\,(\mathsf{start}(\mathsf{decr}, 1) \,\cdot\cdot\, \mathsf{ret}(1) *\!* \mho\, x \text{ as } y_2.\lceil y_1 > y_2 \rceil) \,\cdot\cdot$$

---

[5] This can be generalized as usual, if needed.

$$[\![\lceil P \rceil]\!]_{\rho,o} = \langle \Sigma \rangle \text{ if } \mathsf{I}, \beta(o) \models P \qquad [\![\lceil P \rceil]\!]_{\rho,o} = \emptyset \text{ if } \mathsf{I}, \beta(o) \not\models P$$

$$[\![X]\!]_{\rho,o} = \rho(X)$$

$$[\![\mathsf{start}(m,i)]\!]_{\rho,o} = \{\mathsf{call}_\sigma(m,i) \underline{**} \mathsf{push}_\sigma((m,i)) \mid \sigma \in \Sigma\}$$

$$[\![\mathsf{ret}(i)]\!]_{\rho,o} = \{\mathsf{ret}_\sigma(i) \mid \sigma \in \Sigma\} \qquad [\![\mathsf{pop}(m,i)]\!]_{\rho,o} = \{\mathsf{pop}_\sigma((m,i)) \mid \sigma \in \Sigma\}$$

$$[\![\Phi_1 \wedge \Phi_2]\!]_{\rho,o} = [\![\Phi_1]\!]_{\rho,o} \cap [\![\Phi_2]\!]_{\rho,o} \qquad [\![\Phi_1 \vee \Phi_2]\!]_{\rho,o} = [\![\Phi_1]\!]_{\rho,o} \cup [\![\Phi_2]\!]_{\rho,o}$$

$$[\![\Phi_1 \cdot \Phi_2]\!]_{\rho,o} = \{\tau_1 \cdot \tau_2 \mid \tau_1 \in [\![\Phi_1]\!]_{\rho,o} \wedge \tau_2 \in [\![\Phi_2]\!]_{\rho,o}\}$$

$$[\![\Phi_1 ** \Phi_2]\!]_{\rho,o} = \{\tau_1 \underline{**} \tau_2 \mid \tau_1 \in [\![\Phi_1]\!]_{\rho,o} \wedge \tau_2 \in [\![\Phi_2]\!]_{\rho,o}\}$$

$$[\![\mho x \text{ as } y.\Phi]\!]_{\rho,o} = \{\langle \sigma \rangle \underline{**} \tau \mid \tau \in [\![\Phi]\!]_{\rho,o[y \mapsto (x,\sigma)]} \wedge \sigma \in \Sigma\}$$

$$[\![\mu X.\Phi]\!]_{\rho,o} = \sqcap\{F \mid [\![\Phi]\!]_{\rho[X \mapsto F],o} \sqsubseteq F\}$$

Fig. 5. Semantics of Trace Formulas.

5 Contracts

5.1 The Concept of Trace-Aware Contracts

Our goal is to generalize contracts, where the pre- and post-conditions are state formulas, to contracts, where initial and trailing *traces* may occur.

For example, consider a procedure operate that works on a file. First it prepares the file in some way, then it computes something with the data in it, finally it tidies the file up. In addition, operate assumes the file was opened before it starts and that someone takes care to close it after it finishes.

The internal actions of operate are specified as a *trace* over suitable events. However, its pre- and post-conditions are also *traces*, as they do not specify the moment *when* the procedure is called and when it terminates, but operations performed *sometime before* and *after*. The *global* trace has the following shape:

$$assume ** \overbrace{work}^{operate} ** continue \qquad (5)$$

In the following we abbreviate the trace formulas with their first letter, that is a for *assume*, etc. *State* pre- and post-conditions are the states where the assume and work traces (work and continue) overlap, so we can refine (5) into:

$$assume ** \lceil Pre \rceil ** work ** \lceil Post \rceil ** continue \qquad (6)$$

Formula $\lceil Pre \rceil$ describes the states a caller must be in when operate is called, which are the states that operate can assume to be started in. Dually, $\lceil Post \rceil$ describes the states operate ensures upon finishing, which are the states the caller expects to be in, after the call to operate. We say that the trace formulas assume and continue are the *context* described by the above trace specification. Contexts pose a challenge to modularity: For a Hoare-style contract, the caller is responsible for the pre-condition, while the callee is responsible for the post-condition. The temporal dimension of the procedure (first call, then termination) and the temporal dimension of the contract (first pre-condition, then post-condition) coincide. This is not the case for the trace contexts: The trace *continue* occurs *after* the call, but must be established by the caller. Moreover, the context is not local to the call site of the procedure, it describes arbitrary actions before and after the call.

Consider Fig. 6, with procedure m_{orig}, containing a synchronous call to m, which in turn contains another synchronous call to ma. From the perspective of ma the post-condition ($\theta_{c_{ma}}$, using the notation we introduce in Definition 18) describes the actions of the caller (procedure m) *and the complete call stack*, i.e., the caller's callers such as m_{orig}, which are unaware of the call to ma.

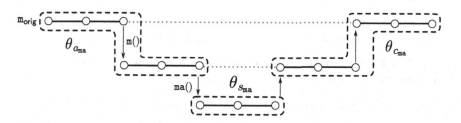

Fig. 6. Scope of the post-condition.

Before we turn our attention to the solution of these difficulties in verification, let us formalize the syntax and semantics of a trace contract.

5.2   Formal Trace Contracts

Definition 18 (Trace Contract, Pre-/Post-Trace). *Let $\mho_{\overline{x},\overline{y}}$ denote a possibly empty list of observational quantifiers over program variables $\overline{x}$ and logic variables $\overline{y}$. A trace contract C_m for a procedure m has the form*

$$C_m = \ll \theta'_{a_m} \cdot \mho_{\overline{x_1,y_1}}.\lceil q_{a_m}\rceil \mid \lceil q_{a_m}\rceil \cdot \theta'_{s_m} \cdot \mho_{\overline{x_2,y_2}}.\lceil q_{c_m}\rceil \mid \lceil q_{c_m}\rceil \cdot \theta'_{c_m} \gg ,$$

where $\lceil q_{a_m}\rceil$, $\lceil q_{c_m}\rceil$ are first-order predicates[6] and θ'_{a_m}, θ'_{s_m}, θ'_{c_m} are trace formulas. We call $\theta_{a_m} = \theta'_{a_m} \cdot \mho_{\overline{x_1,y_1}}.\lceil q_{a_m}\rceil$ the pre-trace, $\theta_{s_m} = \lceil q_{a_m}\rceil \cdot \theta'_{s_m} \cdot \mho_{\overline{x_2,y_2}}.\lceil q_{c_m}\rceil$ the internal behavior, and $\theta_{c_m} = \lceil q_{c_m}\rceil \cdot \theta'_{c_m}$ the post-trace of the contract.

We impose the following restrictions that express that all observation variables in the pre-trace are bound, all free logical variables in the internal behavior are bound by the observation variables of the pre-trace, and all free logic variables in the post-trace are bound by the observation variables of the pre-trace or internal behavior:

---

[6] $\lceil q_{a_m}\rceil$ and $\lceil q_{c_m}\rceil$ correspond to $\lceil Pre\rceil$ and $\lceil Post\rceil$ above. Of course, it is redundant that these formulas occur twice in C_m, but we want each part of a trace contract to be readable on its own.

- $\mathsf{fv}(\theta_{a_m}) = \emptyset$
- $\mathsf{fv}(\theta_{s_m}) \subseteq \overline{y_1}$
- $\mathsf{fv}(\theta_{c_m}) \subseteq \overline{y_1} \cup \overline{y_2}$

A possible contract of procedure `operate` in Example 1 is as follows. It expects the file was opened, has not been closed or opened again, and has not been written to yet. Then `operate` ensures not to open or close it, abstracting away from the actual work. Finally, the contract stipulates that the file will be closed by one of the callers, while not having been opened, closed, or written to.

$$\lll \cdot\cdot\ \mho\ \texttt{file as}\ f.\ \mathsf{op}(f)\ \overset{\mathsf{op}(f),\mathsf{cl}(f),\mathsf{w}(f)}{\cdot\cdot}\ \Big|\ \overset{\mathsf{op}(f),\mathsf{cl}(f)}{\cdot\cdot}\ \Big|\ \overset{\mathsf{op}(f),\mathsf{cl}(f),\mathsf{w}(f)}{\cdot\cdot}\ \mathsf{cl}(f)\ \cdot\ggg$$

We classify trace contracts according to the trace formulas they contain. A contract is context-aware if it has a non-trivial pre- or post-trace:

Definition 19 (Context-Aware Contract). *Let C_m be a trace contract as in Definition 18:*

$$C_m = \lll \theta'_{a_m} \cdot \mho_{\overline{x_1,y_1}}.\lceil q_{a_m}\rceil \mid \lceil q_{a_m}\rceil \cdot \theta'_{s_m} \cdot \mho_{\overline{x_2,y_2}}.\lceil q_{c_m}\rceil \mid \lceil q_{c_m}\rceil \cdot \theta'_{c_m}\ ,\ggg$$

Contract C_m is context-aware *if at least one of $\theta'_{a_m} \not\equiv \cdot\cdot$ or $\theta'_{c_m} \not\equiv \cdot\cdot$ holds. Contract C_m is a* state contract *if $\theta'_{s_m} \equiv \cdot\cdot$. Otherwise, it is a* proper trace contract.

Thus, a Hoare-style contract is a non context-aware state contract, while the contracts in [7] are non context-aware proper trace contracts. The previously introduced cooperative contracts [30] are context-aware state contracts, however, with a non-uniform treatment of the context.

As a final note, before we turn to the technical machinery behind trace contracts, we stress that they naturally extend to asynchronous communication. Consider Fig. 7, with procedure $\mathtt{m_{orig}}$, containing a synchronous call to m, which now contains two *asynchronous* calls to ma and mb. Analogous to Fig. 6, the post-trace of ma ($\theta_{c_{ma}}$) describes the actions of the caller (m) and the complete call stack, including the *asynchronous* callers, and subsequently running methods such as mb.

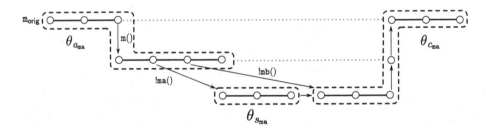

Fig. 7. Scope of the post-trace with asynchronous calls.

The same setup from m's point if view is shown in Fig. 8: Its inner specification contains the traces of the methods it asynchronously calls.

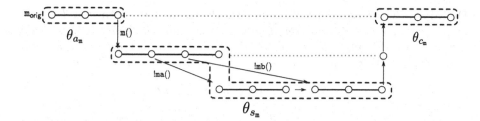

Fig. 8. Scope of the inner trace with asynchronous calls.

5.3   Events Versus Predicates

The style of specification in Example 1 relies on op(f) and cl(f) being events—
if they were predicates, then op(f) would be evaluated as "it is true that f is
open". The following contract cannot be fulfilled, because $isOpen(f)$ cannot be
true and false at the same time (f is a *logical*, rigid variable):

$$\ll \cdot \, \mho\, \texttt{file as } f.\; \lceil isOpen(f)\rceil \;|\; \lceil isOpen(f)\rceil \;\cdot\cdot\; \lceil !isOpen(f)\rceil \;|\; \lceil !isOpen(f)\rceil \cdot\gg$$

If we want to express without events that f was open before and is closed
later, then we need to introduce a second observation.

$$\ll \cdot \, \mho\, \texttt{file as } f.\; \lceil isOpen(f)\rceil$$
$$|\; \lceil isOpen(f)\rceil \;\cdot\cdot\; \mho\, \texttt{file as } f'.\; \lceil !isOpen(f')\rceil$$
$$|\; \lceil !isOpen(f')\rceil \cdot\gg$$

This contract still lacks the information that f and f' refer to the same file.
This can be addressed with a function id that retrieves the id of a file descriptor.

$$\ll \cdot \, \mho\, \texttt{file as } f.\lceil isOpen(f)\rceil \;|\; \cdots \;|\; \mho\, \texttt{file as } f'.\lceil id(f) \doteq id(f') \wedge !isOpen(f')\rceil \cdot\gg$$

5.4   Semantics of Trace Contracts

We formalize what it means for a contract to hold for a given procedure m.
Intuitively, a contract for m holds in a global trace τ, if it the trace can be
chopped along the events related to m, such that each part of the contract
holds. We formalize this intuition as *trace adherence*.

Definition 20 (Trace Adherence). *Let C_m be a contract for procedure m with*

$$C_m = \ll \theta'_{a_m} \cdot \mho_{\overline{x_1,y_1}}.\lceil q_{a_m}\rceil \;|\; \lceil q_{a_m}\rceil \cdot \theta'_{s_m} \cdot \mho_{\overline{x_2,y_2}}.\lceil q_{c_m}\rceil \;|\; \lceil q_{c_m}\rceil \cdot \theta'_{c_m} \gg .$$

We say that trace τ adheres to C_m for call identifier i of m if

$$\tau \in [\![\theta'_{a_m} \cdot \mho_{\overline{x_1,y_1}}.(\lceil q_{a_m}\rceil \cdot \mathsf{start}(m,i) \cdot \lceil q_{a_m}\rceil \cdot \theta'_{s_m} \cdot$$
$$\mho_{\overline{x_2,y_2}}.(\lceil q_{c_m}\rceil \cdot \mathsf{pop}(i) \cdot \lceil q_{c_m}\rceil \cdot \theta'_{c_m}))]\!]_{\emptyset,\emptyset}$$

We write this as $\tau, i \models C_m$

Definition 21 (Procedure Adherence, Program Correctness). *Let $P = \overline{m}\ \{d\ s\}$ be a program containing a procedure $m \in \overline{m}$ with contract C_m. Given a trace τ, let $\mathsf{idOf}(m,\tau)$ be the set of all call identifiers in τ occurring in a call scope with m. We say that m adheres to C_m in s, written $m \models C_m$, if*

$$\forall \tau \in [\![P]\!]_d^G.\ \forall i \in \mathsf{idOf}(m,\tau).\ \tau,i \models C_m\ .$$

Consider the init block of program P as an implicitly declared procedure and part of $\overline{m}$, so it is uniformly handled in $\overline{m}$. Then P is correct, written $\models P$, if

$$\forall m \in \overline{m}.\ m \models C_m\ .$$

Definitions 20, 21 are based on the pop event, not ret, meaning that the call scope is completed. In consequence, they specify the final state of a procedure and *all of its asynchronously called* procedures.

Context-aware contracts preserve a decisive degree of modularity for verification, because a contract can still replace inlining the procedure body during verification—and this is crucial for inter-procedural verification to scale. However, as shown in the next section, one needs additional machinery to keep track of the post-trace. To make this precise, we need a weaker form of adherence: A procedure *weakly* adheres to its contract, if it adheres to its pre-trace and the specification of its inner behavior. Later we show that weak adherence of all procedures, together with the design of the proof system, ensures (strong) adherence.

Definition 22 (Weak Adherence). *Let C_m be the contract of a procedure m as in Definition 18. Let $\widehat{C_m}$ be the contract that is like C_m, except $\theta'_{c_m} = \cdots$. We say that m weakly adheres to C_m, if it adheres to $\widehat{C_m}$.*

6   Proof Calculus

The proof calculus for context-aware contracts is based on symbolic program execution, while tracking the symbolic trace with the help of *updates* [1]. In contrast to previous work [7], here we perform *eager* symbolic execution, but *lazy* weakest precondition computation: The rules for symbolic execution connect an update prefix, the executed program, and a trace specification, and manipulate all three of them. This simplifies rules for trace logics that specify behavioral properties (cf. [27]).

6.1   Trace Updates

During symbolic execution we eagerly generate *trace updates* consisting of state updates and event updates, to keep track of the trace in terms of changes of the program state and of the generated events. One can think of a trace update as a sequence of symbolic state changes and symbolic events that resulted from symbolic execution of the program under verification until the current state.

Definition 23 (Trace Update). *The syntax of trace updates is defined by the following grammar, where ϵ is the empty sequence of updates*

$$u::= \{v:=e\} \mid \{\mathsf{Ev}(\bar{e})\}$$
$$\mathcal{U}::= \epsilon \mid u\mathcal{U}$$

$\mathrm{val}_\sigma^{id,cId}(u\mathcal{U}s) = T \cdot \mathrm{K}(\mathcal{U}s)$, if $\mathrm{val}_\sigma^{id,cId}(u) = T \cdot \mathrm{K}(\text{\DH})$

$\mathrm{val}_\sigma^{id,cId}(\{v := e\}) = \{\langle\sigma\rangle \curvearrowright \sigma[v \mapsto e]\} \cdot \mathrm{K}(\text{\DH})$

$\mathrm{val}_\sigma^{id,cId}(\{\mathrm{run}(m,i,sy)\}) = \mathrm{call}_\sigma(m,i)\underline{**}[\![\mathtt{s};\ \mathtt{return}]\!]_{\mathrm{call}_\sigma(m,i)}^{\mathcal{G}} \cdot \mathrm{K}(\text{\DH})$,

$\qquad$ where $\mathrm{lookup}(m,\mathcal{G}) = m()\{\mathtt{s};\ \mathtt{return}\}$

$\mathrm{val}_\sigma^{id,cId}(\{\mathrm{run}(m,i,as)\}) = [\![\mathtt{s};\ \mathtt{return}]\!]_{\mathrm{call}_\sigma(m,i)}^{\mathcal{G}} \cdot \mathrm{K}(\text{\DH})$,

$\qquad$ where $\mathrm{lookup}(m,\mathcal{G}) = m()\{\mathtt{s};\ \mathtt{return}\}$

$\mathrm{val}_\sigma^{id,cId}(\{\mathrm{invoc}(m,i)\}) = \{\mathrm{invoc}_\sigma(m,i)\} \cdot \mathrm{K}(\text{\DH})$

$\mathrm{val}_\sigma^{id,cId}(\{\mathrm{start}(m,i)\}) = \{\mathrm{call}_\sigma(m,i)\underline{**}\,\mathrm{push}_\sigma((m,i))\} \cdot \mathrm{K}(\text{\DH})$

$\mathrm{val}_\sigma^{id,cId}(\{\mathrm{ret}(i)\}) = \{\mathrm{ret}_\sigma(i)\} \cdot \mathrm{K}(\text{\DH})$

$\mathrm{val}_\sigma^{id,cId}(\{\mathrm{pop}(m,i)\}) = \{\mathrm{pop}_\sigma((m,i))\} \cdot \mathrm{K}(\text{\DH})$

Fig. 9. Local evaluation of statements with update prefixes.

The local evaluation rules for statements **s** prefixed with updates $\mathcal{U}$ are given in Fig. 9. In contrast to the local semantics, here the returned configuration consists of a *set of* traces and a continuation marker. The reason is that in the calculus we abstract away from the execution of procedure calls by means of procedure contracts. Therefore, the body of a called procedure is never actually inlined, so its evaluation cannot be local, but it must be global, resulting in a *set of* traces representing every possible execution of the procedure body which may contain asynchronous calls. Here we overload the $\underline{**}$ operator to work on sets of traces. The non-obvious rules are those for $\mathrm{run}(m,i,sy)$ and $\mathrm{run}(m,i,as)$, where sy and as are literals that mark the call mode. Run events represent the set of all possible executions of a procedure in the context (m,i) after synchronous (sy) and asynchronous (as) scheduling, respectively. In contrast to the semantics of $\mathrm{run}(m,i,as)$, the one of $\mathrm{invoc}(m,i)$ is simply a trace event that keeps track of the asynchronous invocation of m.

With these rules we integrate the semantics of updates directly into the local semantics, extending Definition 13, via

$$[\![\mathcal{U}]\!]_\tau = \{\tau' \mid \tau, \mathrm{K}(\mathcal{U}) \xrightarrow{\mathsf{X}} \tau\underline{**}\tau', \mathrm{K}(\text{\DH})\}\ ,$$

where, the PROGRESS rule is generalized such that, given $\mathrm{val}_\sigma^{id,cId}(\mathcal{U}s) = T \cdot \mathrm{K}(s')$, any of the traces $\tau' \in T$ is considered for extending the current trace.

6.2   Judgments

We define a sequent calculus based on four different forms of judgment that express the connection between updates, statements and trace formulas. A sequent has the form $\Gamma \vdash \gamma$, where γ is one of the judgements defined below, and Γ a set of such judgements. $\Gamma \vdash \gamma$ means: It holds for all states σ that if σ is a model for all formulas in Γ, then it is also a model for γ.

The first judgment form expresses that a procedure weakly adheres to its contract. When it occurs as a premise, it can be used to assume the contract during symbolic execution. When it occurs in a conclusion, it is the proof obligation that must be established by verification. This judgment is independent of a given state.

Definition 24 (Contract Judgment). *The judgment* $m : C_m$ *expresses that a procedure* m *weakly adheres to its contract* C_m:

$$\models m : C_m \iff m \models \widehat{C_m}$$

We cannot use (strong) adherence here, because a procedure cannot control, whether its caller guarantees the post-trace. Strong adherence will emerge later as a global property of the calculus.

The second judgment form expresses that an update $\mathcal{U}$ describes traces that are models for some trace formula Φ. It is relative to a state σ.

Definition 25 (Local Update Judgment). *The judgment* $\mathcal{U} : \Phi$ *holds in a state* σ *if all traces of* $\mathcal{U}$, *prefixed with* σ *are specified by* Φ:

$$\sigma \models \mathcal{U} : \Phi \iff [\![\mathcal{U}]\!]_{\langle \sigma \rangle} \subseteq [\![\Phi]\!]$$

The next two judgments forms are similar to the previous ones, but have a *global* nature in the sense that they do not only consider the traces described by the local semantics of a statement or update, but also include the traces generated by calls in the updates and statements. This means that any unresolved invoc event leads to execution of the associated procedure.

Definition 26 (Update and Statement Global Judgments). *The global judgments* $\mathcal{U}s :_G \Phi$ *and* $\mathcal{U} :_G \Phi$ *hold in a state* σ *if all traces described by* $\mathcal{U}$ *and* s, *respectively, and starting in* σ *are specified by* Φ:

$$\sigma \models \mathcal{U}s :_G \Phi \iff \bigcup_{\tau' \in [\![\mathcal{U}]\!]_{\langle \sigma \rangle}} [\![\mathcal{U}]\!]_{\langle \sigma \rangle} \underline{**} [\![s]\!]_{\tau'}^G \subseteq [\![\Phi]\!]$$

$$\sigma \models \mathcal{U} :_G \Phi \iff \bigcup_{\tau' \in [\![\mathcal{U}]\!]_{\langle \sigma \rangle}} [\![\mathcal{U}]\!]_{\langle \sigma \rangle} \underline{**} [\![0]\!]_{\tau'}^G \subseteq [\![\Phi]\!]$$

A subtle point is that $[\![0]\!]_{\tau'}^G$ still generates the traces of the non-resolved procedures in τ', even though it executes the empty context.

Please observe that the global judgements are global with relative to their scope, not the whole program. Regarding the difference between local and global update judgments, consider update $\mathcal{U} = \{\text{invoc}(m,i)\}\{\text{ret}(i')\}$ and trace specification $\Phi = \cdots \text{invoc}(m,i)\cdot\text{ret}(i')\cdot\text{start}(m,i)\cdots$. Locally, Φ is not a valid specification for $\mathcal{U}$, because for any σ:

$$\sigma \models \{\text{invoc}(m,i)\}\{\text{ret}(i')\} : \cdots \text{invoc}(m,i)\cdot\text{ret}(i')\cdot\text{start}(m,i)\cdots$$
$$\iff [\![\{\text{invoc}(m,i)\}\{\text{ret}(i')\}]\!]_{\langle\sigma\rangle} \subseteq [\![\cdots \text{invoc}(m,i)\cdot\text{ret}(i')\cdot\text{start}(m,i)\cdots]\!]_\sigma$$
$$\iff \{\text{invoc}_\sigma(m,i)\underline{**}\,\text{ret}_\sigma(i')\} \subseteq [\![\cdots \text{invoc}(m,i)\cdot\text{ret}(i')\cdot\text{start}(m,i)\cdots]\!]_\sigma$$

This is obviously not the case. However, it is true as a global judgment, because in this case the invocation event starts procedure m, which adds the required event:

$$\sigma \models \{\text{invoc}(m,i)\}\{\text{ret}(i')\} :_G \cdots \text{invoc}(m,i)\cdot\text{ret}(i')\cdot\text{start}(m,i)\cdots$$

We override the *schedule* function of Definition 11 to accept also trace updates.

Definition 27 (Schedule Function over Trace Updates).

$$schedule(\mathcal{U}) = \{(m,i)\,|\,\mathcal{U} = \mathcal{U}_1\{\text{invoc}(m,i)\}\mathcal{U}_2\,\{\text{ret}(oId)\}\,\mathcal{U}_3$$
$$where\ \mathcal{U}_3\ does\ not\ contain\ \text{run}(m,i,as)\}$$

Lemma 1 (Soundness of Scheduling).

$$schedule(\mathcal{U}) = \bigcup_{\tau\in[\![\mathcal{U}]\!]} schedule(\tau)$$

The proof is in the technical report [18]. The tree-like concurrency model is crucial: The traces in the semantics of $\mathcal{U}$ contain *more* call scopes, but the tree-like concurrency model ensures that they are all closed, and hence cannot be scheduled.

6.3 Proof Rules

We have four classes of proof rules: (1) for procedure contract judgments, (2) for symbolic execution of the sequential part of the language, i.e., straight-line programs and synchronous calls under the global judgment, (3) for asynchronous calls under the global judgment, and (4) to reduce updates in a global judgment to a local judgment. We do not consider the rules for updates in local judgments. These are an open research question orthogonal to context-aware contracts. All given rules for procedure calls use contracts, we refrain from providing rules that resolve calls by inlining.

Procedure Contracts. The rule for procedure contracts requires to prove the global judgment that the body of a procedure, starting when the pre-trace holds, generates a trace where the pre-trace, the internal behavior and the state postcondition hold. Being global, this trace includes all asynchronously called procedures. To model the trace at the moment when the procedure starts, a fresh, uninterpreted update symbol $\mathcal{V}$ is used as the update prefix to describe *locally* the pre-trace.

The observation variables $\overline{y}$ are skolemized into constant symbols $\overline{c^y}$. This substitution is denoted $[\overline{y}\backslash\overline{c^y}]$. Notation inline$(m)$ retrieves the body of procedure m. Judgments C must all be contract judgments. For simplicity, and without loss of generality, we set the identifier of the current scope to a fixed constant oId.

$$\text{Contract}\ \frac{\mathcal{V},\overline{c_1^y},\overline{c_2^y},oId\ \text{fresh} \qquad \theta_{pre} = \left(\theta'_{a_m}\cdot\lceil q_{a_m}\rceil\right)\left[\overline{y_1}\backslash\overline{c_1^y}\right]}{\begin{array}{c}\theta_{post} = \left(\theta'_{a_m}\cdot\lceil q_{a_m}\rceil\cdot\theta'_{s_m}\cdot\lceil q_{c_m}\rceil\right)\left[\overline{y_1}\backslash\overline{c_1^y}\right]\left[\overline{y_2}\backslash\overline{c_2^y}\right]\\ C,\mathcal{V}\{\text{start}(m,oId)\}:\theta_{pre}\vdash\mathcal{V}\{\text{start}(m,oId)\}\,\text{inline}(m):_G\theta_{post}\\ \hline C\vdash m:\!\ll\!\theta'_{a_m}\cdot\mathcal{U}_{\overline{x_1,y_1}}\!\cdot\!\lceil q_{a_m}\rceil\mid\lceil q_{a_m}\rceil\cdot\theta'_{s_m}\cdot\mathcal{U}_{\overline{x_2,y_2}}\!\cdot\!\lceil q_{c_m}\rceil\mid\lceil q_{c_m}\rceil\cdot\_\!\gg\end{array}}$$

It is worth pointing out that the post-trace θ'_{c_m} in the contract (see Definition 18) is not used here. Indeed it is out of the scope of the procedure and occurs as an additional obligation to the *caller* in the rules below. It is essential that $\lceil q_{c_m}\rceil$ does not describe the state after the final statement of m, rather it describes the final state after the last asynchronously called procedure terminates.

Symbolic Execution of Straight-Line Programs. The schematic rules of the symbolic execution calculus for straight-line programs are in Fig. 10, with the core language on the left and the domain-specific extension on the right. The Assign rule generates a state update for the assigned variable. Rule Cond branches a proof according to guard e and rule Return generates the eponymous event update. The rules for operations on a file f generate the associated events. The rules Close, Read, and Write require that the file was opened and not closed intermittently.

$$\text{Assign}\ \frac{\Gamma\vdash\mathcal{U}\{v:=e\}s:_G\Phi}{\Gamma\vdash\mathcal{U}\,v=e;s:_G\Phi}$$

$$\text{Cond}\ \frac{\Gamma,\mathcal{U}:\!\cdots\lceil e\rceil\vdash\mathcal{U}s;s':_G\Phi \qquad \Gamma,\mathcal{U}:\!\cdots\lceil!e\rceil\vdash\mathcal{U}s':_G\Phi}{\Gamma\vdash\mathcal{U}\,\text{if}\,e\,\{s\};s':_G\Phi}$$

$$\text{Return}\ \frac{\Gamma\vdash\mathcal{U}\{\text{ret}(oId)\}:_G\Phi}{\Gamma\vdash\mathcal{U}\,\text{return}:_G\Phi}$$

$$\text{AsyncCall}\ \frac{i\ \text{fresh}}{\dfrac{\Gamma\vdash\mathcal{U}\{\text{invoc}(m,i)\}s:_G\Phi}{\Gamma\vdash\mathcal{U}\,!m();s:_G\Phi}}$$

$$\text{Open}\ \frac{\Gamma\vdash\mathcal{U}\{\text{open}(f)\}s:_G\Phi}{\Gamma\vdash\mathcal{U}\,\text{open}(f);s:_G\Phi}$$

$$\text{Close}\ \frac{\Gamma\vdash\mathcal{U}:\!\cdots\,\text{open}(f)\,\overset{\text{close}(f)}{\cdots}\quad\Gamma\vdash\mathcal{U}\{\text{close}(f)\}s:_G\Phi}{\Gamma\vdash\mathcal{U}\,\text{close}(f);s:_G\Phi}$$

$$\text{Read}\ \frac{\Gamma\vdash\mathcal{U}:\!\cdots\,\text{open}(f)\,\overset{\text{close}(f)}{\cdots}\quad\Gamma\vdash\mathcal{U}\{\text{read}(f)\}s:_G\Phi}{\Gamma\vdash\mathcal{U}\,\text{read}(f);s:_G\Phi}$$

$$\text{Write}\ \frac{\Gamma\vdash\mathcal{U}:\!\cdots\,\text{open}(f)\,\overset{\text{close}(f)}{\cdots}\quad\Gamma\vdash\mathcal{U}\{\text{write}(f)\}s:_G\Phi}{\Gamma\vdash\mathcal{U}\,\text{write}(f);s:_G\Phi}$$

Fig. 10. Sequent rules for straight-line programs.

Synchronous Procedure Calls. The pattern in the conclusion of the Call rule below matches the antecedent (to retrieve the contract for the called procedure m), the executed statement (to ensure the next statement to be executed is a synchronous call) and the trace specification. The latter splits into three parts: Φ is the specification of the trace until the call to m, θ is the specification for the part of the trace that is generated by m, and Ψ specifies the remaining trace.[7]

The rule has three premises. The first corresponds to establishing the condition for the contract to apply: both, the pre-trace θ_{a_m} of the procedure contract and the prefix Φ of the specification of the currently executed code must be valid for the current trace update $\mathcal{U}$. The second premise checks that the internal behavior θ_{s_m} specified in the contract is contained in the given specification θ, i.e. the contract is suitable to achieve the claimed specification. In the last premise update $\mathcal{U}$ is extended with a run event to mark that the contract was used, and specification is strengthened by the contract, obtained from the proof of the first two premises. Symbolic execution continues on s in the succedent, where not only Ψ needs to be established, but also θ_{c_m}, because as the caller of m we are also responsible to ensure the post-trace of the contract.

$$
\text{Call}\ \frac{
\begin{array}{c}
\Gamma \vdash \mathcal{U} : (\Phi \wedge \theta_{a_m}) \qquad [\![\theta_{s_m}]\!] \subseteq [\![\theta]\!] \qquad i \text{ fresh} \\
\Gamma, \mathcal{U}\{\mathsf{run}(m,i,sy)\} : (\Phi \wedge \theta_{a_m}) \mathbin{**} \theta_{s_m} \vdash \\
\mathcal{U}\{\mathsf{run}(m,i,sy)\}\, s :_G (\Phi \wedge \theta_{a_m}) \mathbin{**} \theta_{s_m} \mathbin{**} (\Psi \wedge \theta_{c_m})
\end{array}
}{
\Gamma, m :\!\ll\!\theta_{a_m} \mid \theta_{s_m} \mid \theta_{c_m}\!\gg\, \vdash \mathcal{U}\, m();s :_G \Phi \mathbin{**} \theta \mathbin{**} \Psi
}
$$

The remaining call rules follow the pattern established above with variations due to scheduling.

Deterministic Asynchronous Procedure Calls. The rule for deterministic scheduling applies when exactly one asynchronously called procedure, here m, can be scheduled, according to the first premise. The lookup of the contract for m in Γ now becomes the second premise. The remaining premises are analogues to the Call rule, with the difference that the call identifier i is not fresh, but it matches the identifier of the asynchronous invocation to be scheduled.

$$
\text{ScheduleD}\ \frac{
\begin{array}{c}
schedule(\mathcal{U}) = \{(m,i)\} \qquad \Gamma \vdash m :\!\ll\!\theta_{a_m} \mid \theta_{s_m} \mid \theta_{c_m}\!\gg \\
\Gamma \vdash \mathcal{U} : (\Phi \wedge \theta_{a_m}) \qquad [\![\theta_{s_m}]\!] \subseteq [\![\theta]\!] \\
\Gamma, \mathcal{U}\{\mathsf{run}(m,i,as)\} : (\Phi \wedge \theta_{a_m}) \mathbin{**} \theta_{s_m} \vdash \\
\mathcal{U}\{\mathsf{run}(m,i,as)\} :_G (\Phi \wedge \theta_{a_m}) \mathbin{**} \theta_{s_m} \mathbin{**} (\Psi \wedge \theta_{c_m})
\end{array}
}{
\Gamma \vdash \mathcal{U} :_G \Phi \mathbin{**} \theta \mathbin{**} \Psi
}
$$

Non-deterministic Asynchronous Procedure Calls. The rule generalizes the deterministic version, by adding the last four premises not just once, but for each possible scheduling decision. This ensures that symbolic execution considers all possible traces. We suffer from a blow-up in the size of the proof tree here, but

---

[7] In practice, this split shape must be obtained by suitable weakening rules on trace formulas. The details are future work.

the use of contracts provides at least a suitable mechanism to abstract over the scheduling decisions of the called procedures.

$$\text{ScheduleN} \quad \cfrac{(m,i) \in schedule(\mathcal{U}) \begin{cases} \Gamma \vdash m : \ll \theta_{a_m} \mid \theta_{s_m} \mid \theta_{c_m} \gg \\ \Gamma \vdash \mathcal{U} : (\varPhi \wedge \theta_{a_m}) \qquad [\![\theta_{s_m}]\!] \subseteq [\![\theta]\!] \\ \Gamma, \mathcal{U}\{\mathsf{run}(m,i,as)\} : (\varPhi \wedge \theta_{a_m}) \mathbin{**} \theta_{s_m} \vdash \\ \qquad \mathcal{U}\{\mathsf{run}(m,i,as)\} :_G (\varPhi \wedge \theta_{a_m}) \mathbin{**} \theta_{s_m} \mathbin{**} (\varPsi \wedge \theta_{c_m}) \end{cases}}{\Gamma \vdash \mathcal{U} :_G \varPhi \mathbin{**} \theta \mathbin{**} \varPsi}$$

We can observe a substantial degree of uniformity among the different call rules. This is possible, because the use of events allows us to separate *scheduling* from *contract application*.

Other Rules. The following inconspicuous rule reduces global to local reasoning: When no invocation event is left to be resolved, then the local and global judgments are equivalent and the final pop event is added. We assume that the identifier and name of the procedure we are considering are globally known as m, oId.

$$\text{Finish} \quad \cfrac{\Gamma \vdash \mathcal{U}\{\mathsf{pop}((m, oId))\} : \varPhi \qquad schedule(\mathcal{U}) = \emptyset}{\Gamma \vdash \mathcal{U} :_G \varPhi}$$

6.4 Properties of the Proof Rules

Our rules are sound in the usual sense of sequent calculi. As for the compositionality, we get that all procedures behave as specified and that files are treated correctly.

Proposition 2. $[\![\mathcal{U}\mathcal{U}']\!]_\tau = \bigcup_{\tau' \in [\![\mathcal{U}]\!]_\tau} [\![\mathcal{U}]\!]_\tau \mathbin{**} [\![\mathcal{U}']\!]_{\tau \mathbin{**} \tau'}.$

Theorem 1 (Soundness). *Rules* ScheduleD, ScheduleN, Call, Contract, Finish, *and the rules in Fig. 10 are sound.*

The following theorem states a sufficient condition for a program without asynchronous self-calls to be correct.

Theorem 2 (Global Adherence). *Let P be an always terminating program with procedures $\overline{m}$. Let $C^{\overline{m}} = \{m : C_m\}$ denote the set of all contract judgments and $C^{\overline{m}}_{m'} = C^{\overline{m}} \setminus \{m' : C_{m'}\}$ the set of contract judgments for all procedures but m'. If for all $m \in \overline{m}$ the following sequent is valid*

$$C^{\overline{m}}_m \vdash m : C_m$$

then (1) All traces of P are file-correct (Definition 15), and (2) $\models P$ (Definition 21).

The proofs can be found in the technical report [18]. The only detail we point out here is that to show program correctness, we need strong procedure adherence. which we obtain from the proof of θ_{c_m} demanded by the succedent of the final premise of the call rules.

7 Case Study

We verify the procedures described in Example 1 to illustrate the working of the calculus. First we specify a set of contracts for Example 1, in slightly prettified syntax. The init block is, as discussed above, regarded as a procedure (with a trivial contract). Obviously, this contract cannot have a non-trivial context:

$$C_{\mathtt{main}} = \ll \lceil \mathsf{true} \rceil \mid \, \cdot\cdot \, \mid \lceil \mathsf{true} \rceil \gg$$

Regarding procedure do, we specify that it assumes that the file stored in f was not opened so far, and it closes it internally.

$$C_{\mathtt{do}} = \ll \cdot\cdot \, \mho \; \mathtt{file} \; \mathtt{as} \; f. \overset{\mathsf{open}(f)}{\cdot\cdot} \lceil \mathsf{true} \rceil \mid \, \cdot\cdot \, \mathsf{close}(f) \, \cdot\cdot \, \mid \lceil \mathsf{true} \rceil \cdot\cdot \gg$$

Procedure closeF specifies that it closes the file and does not reopen it. To prove this modularly, we must specify that the file was opened before.

$$C_{\mathtt{closeF}} = \ll \cdot\cdot \, \mho \; \mathtt{file} \; \mathtt{as} \; f. \; \mathsf{open}(f) \overset{\mathsf{close}(f)}{\cdot\cdot} \lceil \mathsf{true} \rceil \mid$$
$$\lceil \mathsf{true} \rceil \cdot \mathsf{close}(f) \overset{\mathsf{open}(f)}{\cdot\cdot} \mid \lceil \mathsf{true} \rceil \cdot\cdot \gg$$

Finally, we specify that operate just writes to the file, but doesn't close it, which is expected to be done by the caller.

$$C_{\mathtt{operate}} = \ll \cdot\cdot \, \mho \; \mathtt{file} \; \mathtt{as} \; f. \; \mathsf{open}(f) \overset{\mathsf{close}(f)}{\cdot\cdot} \lceil \mathsf{true} \rceil \mid$$
$$\lceil \mathsf{true} \rceil \cdot \mathsf{write}(f) \overset{\mathsf{close}(f)}{\cdot\cdot} \mid \lceil \mathsf{true} \rceil \cdot\cdot \, \mathsf{close}(f) \cdot\cdot \gg$$

Proving closeF. Let M be the set of all procedures. We use, for readability, the following abbreviations:

$$\mathcal{U} = \mathcal{V}\{\mathsf{start}(\mathtt{closeF}, oId)\}$$
$$\phi_1 = \mathcal{U} : \mathsf{open}(f) \overset{\mathsf{close}(f)}{\cdot\cdot} \lceil \mathsf{true} \rceil$$

We apply the Contract rule and skolemize away all observation quantifiers. In the antecedent we have the assumption that the pre-trace holds, and must show that the trace specification is globally fulfilled. Next, we apply the Close rule and show that the file is not closed yet. For simplicity, we map the variable f directly to the Skolem constant from the observation quantifier. To show the left premise, we observe that ϕ_1 occurs on both sides of the sequent if we use the simple observation $[\![\cdot\cdot]\!] \Leftrightarrow [\![\cdot\cdot \lceil \mathsf{true} \rceil]\!]$.

$$\mathrm{Close} \, \frac{C_{\mathtt{closeF}}^{\overline{m}}, \phi_1 \vdash \mathcal{U} :\cdot\cdot \, \mathsf{open}(f) \overset{\mathsf{close}(f)}{\cdot\cdot} \qquad \vdots \, (1)}{\mathrm{Contract} \, \frac{C_{\mathtt{closeF}}^{\overline{m}}, \phi_1 \vdash \mathcal{U}\mathsf{close}(\mathtt{f}); \; \mathtt{return}; :_G \mathsf{open}(f) \overset{\mathsf{close}(f)}{\cdot\cdot} \lceil \mathsf{true} \rceil \cdot \mathsf{close}(f) \overset{\mathsf{open}(f)}{\cdot\cdot}}{C_{\mathtt{closeF}}^{\overline{m}} \vdash \mathtt{closeF} :_G C_{\mathtt{closeF}}}}$$

We symbolically execute `return`, adding the corresponding event to the update, and apply the Finish rule, because we obviously cannot schedule any other procedure. Clearly, this relies on proof obligation generation and the concurrency model: No event *this process* can schedule is pending.

$$
\text{Finish} \;\frac{schedule(\mathcal{U}\{\mathsf{close}(f)\}\{\mathsf{ret}(oId)\}) = \emptyset \qquad \vdots \, (2)}{C^{\overline{m}}_{\mathsf{closeF}}, \phi_1 \vdash \mathcal{U}\{\mathsf{close}(f)\}\{\mathsf{ret}(oId)\} :_G \mathsf{open}(f) \stackrel{\mathsf{close}(f)}{\cdots} \lceil \mathsf{true} \rceil \cdot \mathsf{close}(f) \stackrel{\mathsf{open}(f)}{\cdots}}
$$

$$
\text{Return} \;\frac{}{C^{\overline{m}}_{\mathsf{closeF}}, \phi_1 \vdash \mathcal{U}\{\mathsf{close}(f)\}\mathsf{return}; \; :_G \mathsf{open}(f) \stackrel{\mathsf{close}(f)}{\cdots} \lceil \mathsf{true} \rceil \cdot \mathsf{close}(f) \stackrel{\mathsf{open}(f)}{\cdots}}
$$

$$
\vdots \, (1)
$$

The remaining sequent is straightforward to show: The antecedent is $\mathcal{U}$: $\mathsf{open}(f) \stackrel{\mathsf{close}(f)}{\cdots} \lceil \mathsf{true} \rceil$, so we need to show $\{\mathsf{close}(f)\}\{\mathsf{ret}\{oId\}\} : \mathsf{close}(f) \stackrel{\mathsf{open}(f)}{\cdots}$. This reduces to $\{\mathsf{ret}\{oId\}\} : \stackrel{\mathsf{open}(f)}{\cdots}$, which is clearly the case.

$$
\frac{}{\mathcal{U} : \mathsf{open}(f) \stackrel{\mathsf{close}(f)}{\cdots} \lceil \mathsf{true} \rceil \vdash \mathcal{U}\{\mathsf{close}(f)\}\{\mathsf{ret}(oId)\} : \mathsf{open}(f) \stackrel{\mathsf{close}(f)}{\cdots} \lceil \mathsf{true} \rceil \cdot \mathsf{close}(f) \stackrel{\mathsf{open}(f)}{\cdots}}
$$

$$
\vdots \, (2)
$$

Proving `do`. Proving the contract of `do`, which we show in full detail in the technical report [18], requires to prove an asynchronous call. At the end of symbolic execution, the *schedule* function returns a singleton set (the call to `closeF`), which must be taken care of. It is the contract of this very rule that adds the information about a $\mathsf{close}(f)$ event that is used to prove the final post-trace.

Proving `operate`. Proving the correctness of `operate` is completely analogous to proving correctness of `closeF`, except that a write event instead of a close event is added.

Proving the Init Block. The init block is trivial to prove: It does not restrict its own behavior, thus the only failure could stem from file operations or not fulfilling the contract of called procedures. There are no file operations and the only called procedure has trivial pre- and post-traces.

8   Liskov Principle

Having introduced context-aware contracts and a calculus to verify them, we turn our attention towards a different approach to handle contracts: behavioral subtyping in the form of a Liskov principle [34]. In its original formulation, it states that if some property is provable for elements of a class C, then it must be provable for all elements of any class D that is a subclass of C.

It can, however, also be understood on a contract-level [23] by focusing on the property to be proven, not the classes. This means that instead of focusing on (well-behaving of) subclasses, we focus on (well-behaving of) their *contracts*: For state contracts the Liskov principle states that if a procedure m in class C has a contract $Contr_m$, and a procedure n overrides m in some subclass D of C, then n must also satisfy $Contr_m$. Moreover, we can weaken this condition to allow for a stronger specification of n: the contract $Contr_n$ of n must be a *subcontract* of $Contr_m$. We detail the notion of a *subcontract*

Thus, the Liskov principle can be expressed as an order on contracts over procedures of the same signature, it does not require a language involving classes, objects or even subtyping.[8] We only need to formalize the notion of a sub-contract: For *state* contracts $Contr_1 = (\text{pre}_1, \text{post}_1)$, $Contr_2 = (\text{pre}_2, \text{post}_2)$ this is obvious: $Contr_2$ is a sub-contract of $Contr_1$ if these two conditions hold:

1. Pre-Condition pre_2 is weaker than pre_1: $\text{pre}_1 \rightarrow \text{pre}_2$.
2. Post-Condition post_2 is stronger than post_1: $\text{post}_2 \rightarrow \text{post}_1$.

Equivalently, we say $Contr_1$ is *more general than* $Contr_2$ and write $Contr_1 \succeq Contr_2$. The sub-contract may define *additional* pre-conditions and a stronger, more specific *post-condition*.

We reformulate the above definition for trace contracts. A sub-contract may weaken the pre-condition, which is the responsibility of the *caller*. It may give the caller more possibilities, but restricts its own post-condition, which it can control. The principle is that sub-contracts *weaken* the part of the contract they cannot control, and strengthen the part of the contract they can control.

For trace contracts, the central issue are the formulas of the traces q_a and q_c that are at the border between the assume/continue context and the internal behavior (see Definition 18). The subtyping principle for context-aware contracts considers q_a as part of the pre-trace because it describes a state the procedure *cannot control*. In contrast, q_c is considered part of the post-trace, because the specified procedure *can control* it.

For simplicity, we formulate context-aware behavioral subtyping for contracts without observation variables, whose addition is straightforward, but technically distracting.

Definition 28 (Behavioral Subtyping for Context-Aware Contracts).
We define the more general than *relation $\succeq$ between two context-aware contracts distinguished by superscripts 1, 2:*

$$\ll \theta'_{a^1} \cdot \lceil q_{a^1} \rceil \mid \lceil q_{a^1} \rceil \cdot \theta'_{s^1} \cdot \lceil q_{c^1} \rceil \mid \lceil q_{c^1} \rceil \cdot \theta'_{c^1} \gg$$
$$\succeq \ \ll \theta'_{a^2} \cdot \lceil q_{a^2} \rceil \mid \lceil q_{a^2} \rceil \cdot \theta'_{s^2} \cdot \lceil q_{c^2} \rceil \mid \lceil q_{c^2} \rceil \cdot \theta'_{c^2} \gg$$
$$\Longleftrightarrow$$

$$[\![\theta'_{a^1} \cdot \lceil q_{a^1} \rceil]\!] \subseteq [\![\theta'_{a^2} \cdot \lceil q_{a^2} \rceil]\!] \tag{L1}$$
$$\wedge \, [\![\theta'_{s^1} \cdot \lceil q_{c^1} \rceil]\!] \supseteq [\![\theta'_{s^2} \cdot \lceil q_{c^2} \rceil]\!] \tag{L2}$$
$$\wedge \, [\![\theta'_{c^1}]\!] \subseteq [\![\theta'_{c^2}]\!] \tag{L3}$$

---

[8] This insight was used already in [19] to formulate a Liskov principle for feature-oriented programming.

When all traces θ'_a, θ'_c, and θ'_s are empty, this definition boils down to the Liskov principle for state contracts stated above. The first condition (L1, for pre-trace and -condition) and the last condition (L3, for the post-trace) are concerned with the context of a procedure, which it cannot control. Hence, we permit weakening here. The second condition (L2, for the internal behavior and post-condition of the procedure) is under its control. Thus, we permit strengthening.

In our setting without inheritance, we can use the Liskov principle to specify a procedure with a set of contracts, and use the above subtyping principle to order them. First, we introduce the idea of a maximal contract.

Definition 29 (Maximal Procedure Contract). *Given a finite set $\mathcal{N}$ of procedure contracts for a procedure ordered by $\succeq$, let $Max(\mathcal{N})$ be the set of maximal elements in $\mathcal{N}$.*

We permit a procedure to be specified with multiple contracts, for different situations according to different usages. Using *maximal* procedure contracts, we need only a subset of them to be proven. The following rule is straightforward: Given an invocation event on m, it computes all maximal (most general) contracts and applies all of them.

$$\text{actOrder} \frac{\begin{cases} \Gamma \vdash m : \ll \theta_{a_m} \mid \theta_{s_m} \mid \theta_{c_m} \gg \\ \Gamma \vdash \mathcal{U} : (\Phi \wedge \theta_{a_m}) \qquad [\![\theta_{s_m}]\!] \subseteq [\![\theta]\!] \\ \Gamma, \mathcal{U}\{\mathsf{run}(m,i,as)\} : (\Phi \wedge \theta_{a_m}) **\theta_{s_m} \vdash \\ \qquad \mathcal{U}\{\mathsf{run}(m,i,as)\} :_G (\Phi \wedge \theta_{a_m}) ** \theta_{s_m} ** (\Psi \wedge \theta_{c_m}) \end{cases}}{\Gamma \vdash \mathcal{U} :_G \Phi ** \theta ** \Psi} \quad \begin{array}{l} schedule(\mathcal{U}) = \mathcal{P} \\ \\ (m,i) \in Max(\mathcal{P}) \end{array}$$

Remark 1. We proposed behavioral subtyping as a technique to reduce the number of different call sequences of asynchronous procedures that need to be considered during verification. Techniques to combat combinatorial explosion of instruction sequences are standard in model checking [8], but they are at the level of *code* not at the level of specifications (i.e., contracts). This holds even for a partial-order reduction technique that was adapted to asynchronous procedures [2].

9   Conclusion

We extended state contracts and trace contracts to *context-aware trace contracts* (CATs). This permits to specify the behavioral context in which a procedure is executed, i.e., not merely the static pre-condition, but the actions and states reached before its execution begins and also those after it ends. Such a specification of the *call context* as part of a procedure contract is essential to specify the global behavior of concurrent programs is a succinct manner. We instantiated the CAT methodology to a language with asynchronous calls, where the context is of uttermost importance, and gave a proof-of-concept using a file handling scenario.

To combat combinatorial explosion in verification proofs, we stated a Liskov principle for CATs that has the potential to reduce the effort dramatically.

We hope our work will enable new specification patterns to overcome the long-standing specification challenge in deductive verification for trace properties and concurrent programs.

Future Work. In future work, we plan to investigate richer concurrency models, in particular full Active Objects with suspension, futures and multiple objects [9]. One question that we did not investigate here, is the relation of CATs to object and system invariants.

Our observation quantifiers permit to connect programs and traces in a reasonably abstract, yet fine-grained and flexible manner. However, their proof theory is an open question: In rule Contract in Sect. 6.3 we approximated the semantics of observation quantifiers in a fairly crude manner by Skolemization. This makes it difficult to relate different observations to each other and draw conclusions from them. The axiomatization of observation quantifiers and their comparison to existing logics with observation constructs should be studied in its own right.

Obviously, the CAT framework must be implemented so that larger case studies can be performed. This involves to complete the existing rule set with rules for update simplification in local judgments.

Acknowledgements. This work was partially supported by the Research Council of Norway via the SIRIUS Centre (237898) and the PeTWIN project (294600), as well as the Hessian LOEWE initiative within the Software-Factory 4.0 project.

We profited enormously from the detailed and constructive remarks of the reviewers.

References

1. Ahrendt, W., Beckert, B., Bubel, R., Hähnle, R., Schmitt, P.H., Ulbrich, M. (eds.): Deductive Software Verification - The KeY Book - From Theory to Practice. LNCS, vol. 10001. Springer, Cham (2016). https://doi.org/10.1007/978-3-319-49812-6
2. Albert, E., de la Banda, M.G., Gómez-Zamalloa, M., Isabel, M., Stuckey, P.J.: Optimal context-sensitive dynamic partial order reduction with observers. In: Zhang, D., Møller, A. (eds.) Proceedings 28th ACM SIGSOFT International Symposium on Software Testing and Analysis, ISSTA, pp. 352–362. ACM (2019)
3. Aldrich, J., Sunshine, J., Saini, D., Sparks, Z.: Typestate-oriented programming. In: OOPSLA Companion, pp. 1015–1022. ACM (2009)
4. Baumann, C., Beckert, B., Blasum, H., Bormer, T.: Lessons learned from microkernel verification - specification is the new bottleneck. In: Cassez, F., Huuck, R., Klein, G., Schlich, B. (eds.) Proceedings 7th Conference on Systems Software Verification. EPTCS, vol. 102, pp. 18–32 (2012)

5. Beckert, B., Bruns, D.: Dynamic logic with trace semantics. In: Bonacina, M.P. (ed.) CADE 2013. LNCS (LNAI), vol. 7898, pp. 315–329. Springer, Heidelberg (2013). https://doi.org/10.1007/978-3-642-38574-2_22

6. Bubel, R., Din, C.C., Hähnle, R., Nakata, K.: A dynamic logic with traces and coinduction. In: De Nivelle, H. (ed.) TABLEAUX 2015. LNCS (LNAI), vol. 9323, pp. 307–322. Springer, Cham (2015). https://doi.org/10.1007/978-3-319-24312-2_21

7. Bubel, R., Gurov, D., Hähnle, R., Scaletta, M.: Trace-based deductive verification. In: Piskac, R., Voronkov, A. (eds.) Proceedings of 20th International Conference on Logic for Programming, Artificial Intelligence and Reasoning (LPAR), Manizales Colombia. EPiC Series in Computing. EasyChair (2023)

8. Clarke, E.M., Grumberg, O., Minea, M., Peled, D.A.: State space reduction using partial order techniques. Int. J. Softw. Tools Technol. Transf. **2**(3), 279–287 (1999)

9. de Boer, F., et al.: A survey of active object languages. ACM Comput. Surv. **50**(5), 76:1–76:39 (2017)

10. De Gouw, S., De Boer, F.S., Bubel, R., Hähnle, R., Rot, J., Steinhöfel, D.: Verifying OpenJDK's sort method for generic collections. J. Autom. Reason. **62**(1), 93–126 (2019)

11. DeLine, R., Fähndrich, M.: Typestates for objects. In: Odersky, M. (ed.) ECOOP 2004. LNCS, vol. 3086, pp. 465–490. Springer, Heidelberg (2004). https://doi.org/10.1007/978-3-540-24851-4_21

12. Din, C.C., Bubel, R., Hähnle, R.: KeY-ABS: a deductive verification tool for the concurrent modelling language ABS. In: Felty, A.P., Middeldorp, A. (eds.) CADE 2015. LNCS (LNAI), vol. 9195, pp. 517–526. Springer, Cham (2015). https://doi.org/10.1007/978-3-319-21401-6_35

13. Din, C.C., Hähnle, R., Henrio, L., Johnsen, E.B., Pun, V.K.I., Tarifa, S.L.T.: LAGC semantics of concurrent programming languages. CoRR, abs/2202.12195 (2022)

14. Din, C.C., Hähnle, R., Johnsen, E.B., Pun, K.I., Tapia Tarifa, S.L.: Locally abstract, globally concrete semantics of concurrent programming languages. In: Schmidt, R.A., Nalon, C. (eds.) TABLEAUX 2017. LNCS (LNAI), vol. 10501, pp. 22–43. Springer, Cham (2017). https://doi.org/10.1007/978-3-319-66902-1_2

15. Din, C.C., Owe, O.: Compositional reasoning about active objects with shared futures. Formal Aspects Comput. **27**(3), 551–572 (2015)

16. Guttag, J.V., Horning, J.J., Garland, S.J., Jones, K.D., Modet, A., Wing, J.M.: Larch: Languages and Tools for Formal Specification. Springer, New York (1993). https://doi.org/10.1007/978-1-4612-2704-5

17. Hähnle, R., Huisman, M.: Deductive software verification: from pen-and-paper proofs to industrial tools. In: Steffen, B., Woeginger, G. (eds.) Computing and Software Science. LNCS, vol. 10000, pp. 345–373. Springer, Cham (2019). https://doi.org/10.1007/978-3-319-91908-9_18

18. Hähnle, R., Kamburjan, E., Scaletta, M.: Context-aware trace contracts. CoRR, abs/2310.04384 (2023)

19. Hähnle, R., Schaefer, I.: A liskov principle for delta-oriented programming. In: Margaria, T., Steffen, B. (eds.) ISoLA 2012. LNCS, vol. 7609, pp. 32–46. Springer, Heidelberg (2012). https://doi.org/10.1007/978-3-642-34026-0_4

20. Halpern, J.Y., Shoham, Y.: A propositional modal logic of time intervals. J. ACM **38**(4), 935–962 (1991)

21. Harel, D., Kozen, D., Parikh, R.: Process logic: expressiveness, decidability, completeness. In: 21st Annual Symposium on Foundations of Computer Science, Syracuse, New York, USA, 13–15 October 1980, pp. 129–142. IEEE Computer Society (1980)

22. Honda, K., Yoshida, N., Carbone, M.: Multiparty asynchronous session types. In: Proceedings of the 35th ACM SIGPLAN-SIGACT Symposium on Principles of Programming Languages, POPL 2008, pp. 273–284 (2008)
23. Huisman, M., Ahrendt, W., Grahl, D., Hentschel, M.: Formal specification with the java modeling language. In: Deductive Software Verification – The KeY Book. LNCS, vol. 10001, pp. 193–241. Springer, Cham (2016). https://doi.org/10.1007/978-3-319-49812-6_7
24. Johnsen, E.B., Hähnle, R., Schäfer, J., Schlatte, R., Steffen, M.: ABS: a core language for abstract behavioral specification. In: Aichernig, B.K., de Boer, F.S., Bonsangue, M.M. (eds.) FMCO 2010. LNCS, vol. 6957, pp. 142–164. Springer, Heidelberg (2011). https://doi.org/10.1007/978-3-642-25271-6_8
25. Jones, C.B.: Developing methods for computer programs including a notion of interference. Ph.D. thesis, University of Oxford, UK (1981)
26. Jones, C.B.: Granularity and the development of concurrent programs. In: Brookes, S.D., Main, M.G., Melton, A., Mislove, M.W. (eds.) 11th Annual Conference on Mathematical Foundations of Programming Semantics, MFPS, New Orleans, LA, USA. ENTCS, vol. 1, pp. 302–306. Elsevier (1995)
27. Kamburjan, E.: Behavioral program logic. In: Cerrito, S., Popescu, A. (eds.) TABLEAUX 2019. LNCS (LNAI), vol. 11714, pp. 391–408. Springer, Cham (2019). https://doi.org/10.1007/978-3-030-29026-9_22
28. Kamburjan, E., Chen, T.-C.: Stateful behavioral types for active objects. In: Furia, C.A., Winter, K. (eds.) IFM 2018. LNCS, vol. 11023, pp. 214–235. Springer, Cham (2018). https://doi.org/10.1007/978-3-319-98938-9_13
29. Kamburjan, E., Din, C.C., Chen, T.-C.: Session-based compositional analysis for actor-based languages using futures. In: Ogata, K., Lawford, M., Liu, S. (eds.) ICFEM 2016. LNCS, vol. 10009, pp. 296–312. Springer, Cham (2016). https://doi.org/10.1007/978-3-319-47846-3_19
30. Kamburjan, E., Din, C.C., Hähnle, R., Johnsen, E.B.: Behavioral contracts for cooperative scheduling. In: Ahrendt, W., Beckert, B., Bubel, R., Hähnle, R., Ulbrich, M. (eds.) Deductive Software Verification: Future Perspectives. LNCS, vol. 12345, pp. 85–121. Springer, Cham (2020). https://doi.org/10.1007/978-3-030-64354-6_4
31. Kamburjan, E., Scaletta, M., Rollshausen, N.: Deductive verification of active objects with crowbar. Sci. Comput. Program. 226, 102928 (2023)
32. Kassios, I.T.: The dynamic frames theory. Form. Asp. Comput. 23(3), 267–288 (2011)
33. Leavens, G.T., et al.: JML Reference Manual (2013). Draft revision 2344
34. Liskov, B., Wing, J.M.: A behavioral notion of subtyping. ACM Trans. Program. Lang. Syst. 16(6), 1811–1841 (1994)
35. Meyer, B.: Applying "design by contract". IEEE Comput. 25(10), 40–51 (1992)
36. Mota, J., Giunti, M., Ravara, A.: On using verifast, vercors, plural, and key to check object usage. CoRR, abs/2209.05136 (2022)
37. Müller, P., Schwerhoff, M., Summers, A.J.: Viper: a verification infrastructure for permission-based reasoning. In: Jobstmann, B., Leino, K.R.M. (eds.) VMCAI 2016. LNCS, vol. 9583, pp. 41–62. Springer, Heidelberg (2016). https://doi.org/10.1007/978-3-662-49122-5_2
38. Nakata, K., Uustalu, T.: A Hoare logic for the coinductive trace-based big-step semantics of While. Log. Methods Comput. Sci. 11(1), 1–32 (2015)
39. O'Hearn, P.W.: Resources, concurrency and local reasoning. In: Gardner, P., Yoshida, N. (eds.) CONCUR 2004. LNCS, vol. 3170, pp. 49–67. Springer, Heidelberg (2004). https://doi.org/10.1007/978-3-540-28644-8_4

40. Pnueli, A.: The temporal logic of programs. In: 18th Annual Symposium on Foundations of Computer Science, Providence, Rhode Island, USA, pp. 46–57. IEEE Computer Society (1977)
41. Reynolds, J.C.: Separation logic: a logic for shared mutable data structures. In: LICS, pp. 55–74. IEEE Computer Society (2002)
42. Wolper, P.: Temporal logic can be more expressive. Inf. Control **56**, 72–99 (1983)

Type-Based Verification of Delegated Control in Hybrid Systems

Eduard Kamburjan[1]([✉])[ID] and Michael Lienhardt[2][ID]

[1] University of Oslo, Oslo, Norway
eduard@ifi.uio.no
[2] ONERA, Palaiseau, France
michael.lienhardt@onera.fr

Abstract. We present a post-region-based verification system for distributed hybrid systems modeled with Hybrid Active Objects. The post-region of a class method is the region of the state space where a physical process must be proven safe to ensure some object invariant. Prior systems computed the post-region locally to a single object and could only verify systems where each object ensures its own safety, or relied on specific, non-modular communication patterns. The system presented here uses a *type-and-effect system* to structure the interactions between objects and computes post-regions globally, but verifies them locally. Furthermore, we are able to handle systems with *delegated* control: the object and method that shape the post-region change over time. We exemplify our approach with a model of a cloud-based hybrid system.

1 Introduction

Cyber-physical systems are notoriously difficult to design, maintain and analyze, and major innovation drivers such as the Internet-of-Things or Digital Twins pose additional challenges for formal modeling and verification. For one, such systems are inherently distributed. For another, the controlling software may, contrary to classical control, use *delegation* for the controlled process: parts of the controlling software may run on a cloud infrastructure which may restart the controlling processes, as well as reallocate to a different instance. Thus, the obligation for part of the control can be delegated to another instance. Formal guarantees are of critical importance, yet distributed hybrid models and delegation remain an open theoretical challenge.

In this work, we present a system for modular deductive verification of distributed hybrid systems, which is able to handle delegated control. Our approach is based on *hybrid programs*: programs that contain constructs to express continuous evolution of their state. Programming languages-based approaches for modeling of hybrid systems have recently gained increased research attention [24,27,30] and aim to provide a theory for hybrid systems that combines simulation, verification and usability. One of their advantages over low-level formalisms, such as hybrid automata [6] or process algebras [16], is the rich theory of

F. de Boer et al. (Eds.): *Active Object Languages: Current Research Trends*,
LNCS 14360, pp. 323–358, 2024.
https://doi.org/10.1007/978-3-031-51060-1_12

modularity and structure available for programming languages that allows one to capture and analyze the adaptive structure of modern distributed cyber-physical systems. We show that hybrid programs can indeed provide the necessary structure to handle loose coupling and delegation, by integrating verification with a *type-and-effect* system [51], a lightweight analysis technique for programs to keep track of side-effects in computational units.

Hybrid Active Objects. We use the Hybrid Active Object (HAO) concurrency model, which is one hybrid programming paradigm for distributed systems and extends Active Objects [17] and is implemented in the *Hybrid Abstract Behavioral Specification* (HABS) language [34].

A Hybrid Active Object o is an Active Object that additionally encapsulates a physical process. Only the discrete processes of o may interact with the physical process of o. A discrete process reacts on changes in the physical process using its suspension guards. While the discrete process is active, the fields of the physical process can be accessed as normal fields, but when time advances such fields change their value according to the physical dynamics.

Previous work [30, 34] introduced two verification systems for Hybrid Active Objects that verify object invariants: Kamburjan [30] gives a generalization of post-condition reasoning for object-oriented languages [1] to hybrid systems. However, the system has one major drawback: it computes post-regions based on single classes – it cannot handle interactions between multiple objects beyond checking conditions on the passed parameters. Thus, it is not able to use global information about the overall system to aid verification. On the other hand, an alternative system [34] can handle more complex interactions, but suffers from a lack of modularity: To make use of global structure, it only uses a small, rigidly defined syntactic subset of HABS. In particular, the structure of the overall system may not change and delegation is not possible.

Type-Based Deductive Verification. In this work we present a novel verification system for HABS that goes beyond previous systems for object invariants: we use a type-and-effect system to enable *post-regions* to be computed based on interactions between multiple objects. By using the structure provided by the type system, we are able to integrate deductive verification systems with the modeling and analysis of cloud systems.

Given an object invariant I, we verify for each method m that when it suspends, I holds until the next process runs. The *post-region pr* of a method is the part of the state space where the dynamics must satisfy I for this property to hold. For example, if another method mctrl executes every n time units, then the post-region of m can be restricted to the next n time units. It must, however, be ensured that mctrl is indeed called as specified. We say that mctrl is controlled if the global structure indeed ensures that it is called every n time units. The caller of a controlled method is a *controlling* method.

Our system can verify *delegated* control, where the controlling method changes during the lifetime of a controlled object. Consider again the method mctrl from above. It can be called every n time units *by another object* and the object calling `mctrl` may change over time. To use the post-region of `m`, we must ensure that there is *always* some controller for `mctrl`. To do so, for each object and each method that is specified as being externally controlled, we keep track of the current controller using a type-and-effect system.

A type-and-effect system is a generalization of data type systems, which are defined for some specific side-effect. It checks the correctness of evaluation for a certain set of objects with respect to this side-effect. In our case, the side-effect of interest is time advance. By keeping track of how much time each statement takes, we can verify whether `mctrl` is called frequently enough. Additionally, we keep track of *ownership* [15] to ensure that every method that requires to be frequently called is indeed always owned by somebody who does. A main feature of our behavioral type system is its parametricity: while we do keep track of effects and ownership, we do not compute how long a certain communication pattern takes. Systems for that kind of property are available [23,37] or are straightforward to extend; we integrate them through oracles that encapsulate their analysis. That drastically simplifies our system and allows us to focus on the presentation of the novel features of the type-and-effect system.

Contributions. Our main contribution is a modular deductive verification system for Hybrid Active Objects with *delegated* control that uses a type-and-effect system to govern interactions (1) between multiple Hybrid Active Objects and (2) between Hybrid Active Objects and cloud-models using Timed Active Objects.

Proofs for our theorems are given available in the technical report [33].

2   Hybrid Active Objects and Post-regions

In this section we present the preliminiaries for the rest of the article. First, we present the HABS language that implements Hybrid Active Objects. It is introduced, and fully described, by Kamburjan et al. [34]. Here, we only present the language parts that are relevant for post-region based verification and omit, e.g., inheritance, method visibility and variability.

A Hybrid Active Object (HAO) is a strongly encapsulated object, i.e., no other object, not even from the same class, may access the fields of an instance. Communication between HAOs is only possible through asynchronous method calls and synchronization: each method call generates a container called *future* for the caller that uniquely identifies the (to be) started process at callee side. The future may be passed around and permits to synchronize (i.e., wait until the called process terminates) with it and read the return value of the associated process. HAOs implement *cooperative scheduling*: Inside an object, only one process is active at a time. This process cannot be preempted by the scheduler—it must explicitly release control by either terminating or suspending (via **await**). These two properties make (Hybrid) Active Objects easy to analyze: Approaches for sequential program analyses can be applied between two **await** statements (and method start and end).

Hybrid Active Objects differ from standard Active Objects by a **physical** block and **physical** fields. A **physical** field is a field that has some dynamics, while

```
1  class Tank(Log log){            //class header with field declaration
2    physical Real level = 5;      //physical field declaration
3    Real drain = -1;              //field declaration
4    physical{ level' = drain; }   //dynamics
5    { this!up(); this!down(); }   //constructor
6    Unit down(){                  //method header
7      await diff level <= 3 & drain <= 0;
8      log!triggered(); drain =  1; this!down();
9    }
10   Unit up(){                    //method header
11     await diff level >= 10 & drain >= 0;
12     log!triggered(); drain = -1; this!up();
13   }
14 }
```

Fig. 1. A water tank in HABS with event-based control.

the **physical** block describes the very dynamics of all **physical** fields as ODEs. These dynamics are used to update the state whenever time advances. Inside a method, an imperative language is used, which has special statements to advance time or to wait until some condition on the state holds. These conditions define an urgent transition: The method is reactivated as soon as possible once the condition holds (and no other process is active).

Example 1. Consider the water tank model in Fig. 1. The tank keeps a water level between 3 liters and 10 liters. The pictured class, Tank has two discrete fields (log and drain) and a **physical** field level. A physical field is described by its initial value and an ODE in the **physical** block, which models that the water level is linear with respect to the drain. Line 5 gives the constructor in form of an initialization block where the two methods up and down are called. Each method starts with a statement that has as its guard the condition when the process will be scheduled (for up, at the moment the level reaches 10 while water rises). This is logged by calling the external object log on method triggered. This method call is asynchronous, i.e., the execution of the up (or down) continues without waiting for it to finish. No future is used in this example. Then, the drain is adjusted and the method calls itself recursively to react the next time.

Example 1 illustrates *event-based* control, as the guard of the **await diff** statement define an event boundary. Alternatively, one may use *time-based* control, as the following example illustrates.

Example 2. The controller in Fig. 2 checks the water level of a tank once every time unit by using the **await duration** statement to suspend the ctrl process for the required amount of time. We use JML style [39] comments for specification.

```
1 /*@ requires 4 <= inVal <= 9 @*/
2 /*@ invariant 3 <= level <= 10 && −1 <= drain <= 1 @*/
3 class TankTick(Real inVal){
4    physical Real level = inVal;
5    Real drain = -1;
6    physical{ level' = drain; }
7    { this!ctrl(); }
8    Unit ctrl(){
9       await duration(1);
10      if(level <= 4) drain =  1;
11      if(level >= 9) drain = -1;
12      this!ctrl();
13   }
14 }
```

Fig. 2. A specified water tank in HABS with time-based control.

2.1 Syntax

The syntax of HABS is given by the grammar in Fig. 3. Standard expressions e are defined over fields f, variables v and operators !, |, &, >=, <=, +, -, *, /. Ordinary differential expressions (ODE) are equalities over expressions extended with a derivation operator e'. Types T are all class names, type-generic futures Fut<T>, Real, Unit and Bool.

Prgm ::= $\overline{CD}$ {s} CD ::= class C $[(\overline{T\ f})]$ {$\overline{FD}$ [Phys] [{s}] $\overline{Mt}$}		Classes
Mt ::= T m($\overline{T\ v}$) {s;return e;}		Methods
FD ::= T f[= e]; | physical Real f = e;		Fields
Phys ::= physical {$\overline{ODE}$}		Physical Block
s ::= while (e) {s} | if (e) {s} [else {s}] | s;s		
| await$_p$ g | [[T] e] = rhs | duration(e)		Statements
g ::= e? | duration(e) | diff e		Guards
rhs ::= e | new C($\overline{e}$) | e.get | e!m($\overline{e}$)		RHS Expressions

Fig. 3. HABS grammar. Notation [·] denotes optional elements and $\overline{\cdot}$ lists.

A program consists of a set of classes and a main block. Each class may have a list of discrete fields that are passed as parameters on object creation and a list of internally declared fields with. An internally declared field[1] may be declared as **physical**. In this case it must be of Real type and must be initialized. Furthermore, a class has a physical block, which defines the dynamics of **physical** fields and

---

[1] *All* fields, independent of where they are declared, are accessible only from their object.

must be present if at least one field is **physical**. An optional initialization block is executed directly after object creation and serves as the constructor. Lastly, a class has a set of methods.

Methods, initializing and main blocks consist of statements. Besides the asynchronous method calls (`e!m()`) described above, only the following constructs are non-standard:

- The **duration(e)** statement advances time by e time units. No other process may execute in that object during this time lapse.
- The **e.get** right-hand side expression reads from a future. A future is a container that is generated by an asynchronous call. Afterwards a future may be passed around. With the **get** statement one can read the return values once the called process terminates. Until then, the reading process blocks and no other process can run on the object (that is attempting to read).
- The **await$_p$ g** statement suspends the process until the guard g holds. A guard is either (1) a future poll **e?** that waits until the process for the future in e has finished its computation, (2) a **duration** guard that advances time, or (3) a differential guard **diff e** that holds once expression e evaluates to true. Each such statement has a (program-wide unique) suspension point identifier p, which we use to identify the most recent suspension in a trace.

We assume that all methods are suspension-leading, i.e., each method starts with an **await** statement. This is easily achieved by adding **await diff true** if a method is not suspension-leading without significant changes to the behavior[2]. Concerning the **physical** block, we only admit blocks describing trivial behavior for all non-**physical** fields. Finally, we only consider well-typed (w.r.t. data types) programs, where differential guards contain only `Real`-typed variables.

2.2 Semantics

The runtime semantics is a transition system of the form $tcn_1 \rightarrow tcn_2$, where the configurations tcn have the form $\mathsf{clock}(t)$ cn for some $t > 0$ and a configuration cn, which consists of objects and processes. For readability's sake, we give the full formal definition in the technical report [33], as the exact formalization of state adds no further insights here, and only define runtime objects formally.

Definition 1 (Runtime Objects). *A runtime object has the form*

$$(o, \rho, \mathsf{ODE}, f, prc, q)$$

An Object has an identifier o, an object store ρ that maps the object fields to their values, the current dynamic f, an active process prc and a set of inactive processes q as its parameters. The physical behavior description ODE is taken from the class declaration.

---

[2] The difference is that the process is scheduled and descheduled immediately at its start.

Runs. The semantics of a programs is expressed as a set of *runs*. A run generated by the operational semantics. For each run, we also generate a set of traces, one per object.

A trace θ is a mapping from $\mathbb{R}^+$ to states, meaning that at time t the state of the program is $\theta(t)$. A trace is extracted from a run by interpolating between two configurations resulting from discrete steps using the last solution. We say that clock(t_i) cn_i is the final configuration at t_i in a run, if any other timed configuration clock(t_i) cn'_i is before it.

Definition 2 (Traces). *The initial configuration of a program* Prgm *is denoted* cn_0 *[11]. A run of* Prgm *is a (possibly infinite) reduction sequence*

$$\mathsf{clock}(0)\ cn_0 \rightarrow \mathsf{clock}(t_1)\ cn_1 \rightarrow \cdots$$

A run is time-convergent *if it is infinite and* $\lim_{i\rightarrow\infty} t_i < \infty$. *A run is* locally terminated *if every process occurring within the run terminates normally.*

For each object o occurring in the run, its trace *is defined as* θ_o:

$$\theta_o(x) = \begin{cases} \textit{undefined} & \textit{if o is not yet created} \\ \rho & \textit{if } \mathsf{clock}(x)\ cn \textit{ is the final configuration at } x \\ & \quad \textit{and } \rho \textit{ is the store of o in cn.} \\ adv_{heap}(\rho, f, x - y) & \textit{if there is no configuration at } \mathsf{clock}(x) \\ & \quad \textit{and the last configuration was at } \mathsf{clock}(y) \\ & \quad \textit{with state } \rho \textit{ and dynamic } f \end{cases}$$

with the following auxiliary function to advance the store ρ by t time units according to dynamics f.

$$adv_{heap}(\rho, f, t)(\mathtt{f}) = \begin{cases} \rho(\mathtt{f}) & \textit{if } \mathtt{f} \textit{ is not physical} \\ f(t)(\mathtt{f}) & \textit{otherwise} \end{cases}$$

The full definition is given in the technical report [33] and illustrated there. We normalize all traces and let them start with 0 by shifting all states by the time the object is created.

Example 3. Consider Example 1 and an object where the initial value is 5, i.e., inVal = 5. It evaluation has the first discrete steps at time 0, 1. The state after the transition is as follows:

$$t = 0 \quad \{\mathtt{level} = 5, \mathtt{drain} = -1\}$$
$$t = 1 \quad \{\mathtt{level} = 4, \mathtt{drain} = 1\}$$
$$t = 8 \quad \{\mathtt{level} = 10, \mathtt{drain} = -1\}$$

The trace θ thus has the following properties at these times (as per the second case in the above definition:

$$\theta(0) = \{\mathtt{level} = 5, \mathtt{drain} = -1\}$$
$$\theta(1) = \{\mathtt{level} = 4, \mathtt{drain} = 1\}$$
$$\theta(8) = \{\mathtt{level} = 10, \mathtt{drain} = -1\}$$

The general solution of the dynamics is

$$\texttt{level}(t) = \texttt{level}(t_0) + \texttt{drain}(t_0) * t$$
$$\texttt{drain}(t) = \texttt{drain}(t_0)$$

This is used to define the value of θ in between. For example for $0 < x < 1$ we have $\texttt{level}(t_0) = \texttt{level}(0) = 5$ and, thus

$$\theta(x)(\texttt{level}) = \texttt{level}(x - 0) = 5 + \theta(x - 0)(\texttt{drain}) * x = 5 - 1 * x$$

As we will see later, we must be able to soundly overapproximate the states after a suspension and before the next process is scheduled. To make this precise, we use the notion of *suspension-subtraces*.

Definition 3 (Suspension-Subtraces). *Let* C.m *be a method in some program* Prgm. *Let* θ_o *be a trace, stemming from some run of* Prgm *for some object o of class* C. *Let i be the index in* θ_o *where some process of* m *suspends and terminates. We say that* θ_o^i *is the suspension-subtrace of* θ_o, *if it starts at i and ends at (including) the time where the next non-trivial[3] process is scheduled. If there is no such time, then* θ_o^i *is infinite. Additionally,* θ_o^i *has a variable* t *with* $\theta_o^i(0)(\texttt{t}) = 0$ *and* $\texttt{t}' = 1$. *I.e., a clock that keeps track of the length of* θ_i.
The set of all suspension-subtraces of m *in* Prgm *is denoted* $\Theta(\texttt{m}, \texttt{Prgm})$.

Suspension subtraces are exactly the traces between two discrete steps with length > 0. They contain the states where time advances and no process is active (for a given object). In the above example, θ has one suspension-subtraces. It defined by the restriction of the domain to $0 \le t \le 1$. For $\theta(1)$.

2.3 Differential Dynamic Logic

To verify HABS, we generate proof obligations that encode that a certain statement or physical process has a certain post-condition. Our logic of choice is differential dynamic logic $(d\mathcal{L})$ [45,47], a first-order dynamic logic embeds *hybrid algebraic programs* into its modalities. Hybrid algebraic programs are defined by a simple imperative language, extended with a statement for ordinary differential equations. Such a statement evolves the state according to some dynamics for a non-deterministically chosen amount of time.

Definition 4 (Syntax of $d\mathcal{L}$). *Let p range over predicate symbols (such as $\doteq, \ge$), f over function symbols (such as $+$) and x over variables. Hybrid algebraic programs α, formulas φ and terms t are defined by the following grammar.*

$$\varphi ::= p(\bar{t}) \mid \neg\varphi \mid \varphi \wedge \varphi \mid \exists \texttt{x}.\ \varphi \mid [\alpha]\varphi \qquad t ::= f(\bar{t}) \mid \texttt{x} \qquad dt := f(\overline{dt}) \mid t \mid (t)'$$
$$\alpha ::= \texttt{x} := t \mid \texttt{x} := * \mid \alpha \cup \alpha \mid \alpha^* \mid ?\varphi \mid \alpha; \alpha \mid \{\alpha\} \mid \overline{\texttt{x} = dt} \& \varphi$$

---

[3] I.e., a process that performs any action instead of descheduling immediately.

In the following, we use the usual derived connectives $(\rightarrow, \vee, \forall)$ for brevity. Modalities $[\cdot]$ contain hybrid algebraic programs and may be nested using the ? operator. All ODEs are autonomous. The semantics of hybrid programs is as follows: Program $\mathsf{x} := t$ assigns the value of t to x. Program $\mathsf{x} := *$ assigns a non-deterministically chosen value to x. Program $\alpha_1 \cup \alpha_2$ is a non-deterministic choice. Program α^* is the Kleene star. Program $?\varphi$ is a test or filter. It either discards a run (if φ does not hold) or performs no action (if φ does hold). Program $\alpha_1; \alpha_2$ is sequence and $\{\alpha\}$ is a block for structuring. Finally, the statement $\mathsf{x} = dt \& \varphi$ evolves the state according to the given ODE in the evolution domain φ for some amount of time. The evolution domain describes where a solution is allowed to evolve, not the solution itself. The semantics of the first-order fragment is completely standard. The semantics of $[\alpha]\varphi$ is that φ has to hold in *every* post-state of α if α terminates. We stress that if α is an ODE, then this means that φ holds throughout the *whole* solution.

Example 4. The following formula expresses that the position of a bouncing ball with initial position x below $10\,\mathrm{m}$ and initial null velocity v is below 10 before reaching the ground (given that the gravity is $9.81\,\mathrm{m/s}$).

$$0 \le \mathsf{x} \le 10 \wedge \mathsf{v} \doteq 0 \rightarrow [\mathsf{x}' = \mathsf{v}, \mathsf{v}' = -9.81 \& \mathsf{x} \ge 0]\mathsf{x} \le 10$$

Events can be expressed as usual by an event boundary created between a test and an evolution domain. The following program models that the ball repeatedly bounces back exactly on the ground.

$$\left(\{\mathsf{x}' = \mathsf{v}, \mathsf{v}' = -9.81 \& \mathsf{x} \ge 0\}; ?\mathsf{x} \le 0; \mathsf{v} := -\mathsf{v} * 0.9\right)^*$$

We identify HABS variables and fields with $d\mathcal{L}$ variables and denote with $\mathsf{trans}(\mathsf{e})$ the straightforward translation of HABS expressions into $d\mathcal{L}$ terms. Standard control flow constructs (while, if) are encoded using the operators above [46].

Weak negation $\tilde{\neg}$ is needed to define event boundaries. It is defined analogously to normal negation, except for weak inequalities:

$$\tilde{\neg}(t_1 \ge t_2) \equiv t_1 \le t_2$$

2.4 Post-region Invariants

To verify an object invariant, one generates a proof obligation in dynamic logic for each method, and one for the constructor. If all proof obligations can be closed, i.e., the dynamic logic formulas are all valid, then the object invariant holds at every point a process starts, ends, suspends or regains control. This approach is modular, as changes is one method do not require to reprove other methods.

There are such systems for numerous discrete object-oriented languages, e.g., Java (in the KeY-system using Java Dynamic Logic [1]) and ABS (in KeY-ABS [18] using ABS Dynamic Logic [19] and in Crowbar [35] using Behavioral

Program Logic [29]). In the most basic case the proof obligations for an invariant I take the following form for discrete languages:

$$I \rightarrow [\mathsf{s}]I$$

where s is the method body of the method in question; and for the constructor

$$\mathsf{true} \rightarrow [\mathsf{s}]I.$$

The main idea is that the constructor always establishes the object invariant and each method preserves it. Each method may assume the invariant, because the last process established it and in discrete system, *state does not change* when no process is active. This is not the case for hybrid systems, the above proof obligation scheme is *not* sound.

To accommodate hybrid systems the proof obligation scheme must incorporate the dynamics in the post-condition, as a so called *post-region invariant* [30]. The case for methods is the following:

$$I \rightarrow [\mathsf{s}]\big(I \wedge [\mathsf{dyn}\&\varphi]I\big)$$

where dyn are the dynamics and φ is the *post-region*. The post-region is the region where the dynamics must be safe. We say that I is the post-region invariant for φ and stress that it is necessary to establish I as a pure post-condition as well – it may be the case that $\varphi \equiv \mathsf{false}$, i.e., that the next process starts *without* time advance[4]. To ensure that this next process can also assume I, it is necessary to add I without dynamics to the post-condition.

If e *basic* post-region is just true, i.e., the dynamics must stay safe forever. In general, basic post-regions are not sufficient – consider the two models in Example 2 and Example 1: these systems are not safe for an unlimited time, instead there are internal control loops that define when a discrete computation will start. I.e., it suffices to restrict φ to the region where it is *not* guaranteed that another method will take over. One can easily extend the precondition, if the method starts with a guard, by adding the guard to the left-hand side of the implication.

Two further possible ways to soundly compute more precise *internal* post-regions were proposed: structural control and (method-)local control [30]. They have in common that they are local – the post-region is computed based on information derived from a single class. They cannot, however, verify the above examples.

Next, we define the formalization of general soundness for post-regions [31], which parameterizes the proof obligation scheme with post-region generators. In the following, we denote the specified invariant for a class c with I_c. For initialization, a constraint on the initial values of the externally initialized fields may be specified. This *creation condition* is denoted pre_c and used a precondition for the constructor.

---

[4] The post-region is a part of the state space of the object, with time as a dimension.

2.5   General Proof Obligation Scheme

A proof obligation scheme defines a set of $d\mathcal{L}$-formulas, such that validity of all these formulas implies safety of the program. The scheme we give here is parametric in the notion of post-region, as well as in the specification. Method contracts, in the sense of pre-/postcondition pairs, are not of interest here, we only use a precondition $\mathsf{pre}_{\mathsf{C.m}}$, which is a first-order formula over the method parameters, and a postcondition $\mathsf{post}_{\mathsf{C.m}}$, which is a first-order formula over the fields of the class. Similarly, $\mathsf{init}_{\mathsf{C}}$ is the precondition of the initial block/constructor and I_{C} is the class invariant.

Before we define the proof obligation scheme, we must establish some auxiliary structures.

- We assume two variables t and cll. Variable t keeps track of time and variable cll keeps track of contract violations. This is necessary, because the postcondition is evaluated at the end of the methods and intermediate failures must be remembered until then.
- The fail statement sets cll to 1, i.e., records a contract violation.

$$\mathsf{fail} = \mathsf{cll} \; := 1$$

- The havoc statement sets all fields, including all physical fields, *but not local variables* to new values. This is used to approximate suspension, where another process can run, but only change fields.

$$\mathsf{havoc} = \mathsf{f}_1 := *; \ldots \mathsf{f}_n := *; \quad \text{for all fields } \mathsf{f}_i$$

- The $\mathsf{havoc}^{\mathsf{ph}}$ statement sets all *physical* fields to new values.

$$\mathsf{havoc}^{\mathsf{ph}} = \mathsf{f}_1 := *; \ldots \mathsf{f}_n := *; \quad \text{for all physical fields } \mathsf{f}_i$$

- The post-region formula $\mathsf{pr}(\varphi, I, \mathsf{ode})$ expresses that a certain invariant I holds for dynamics ode under post-region φ:

$$\mathsf{pr}(\varphi, I, \mathsf{ode}) = I \wedge \big[\mathsf{t} := 0; \{\mathsf{ode}, \mathsf{t}' = 1 \& \varphi\}\big] I$$

Whenever I and ode are understood, we just write $\mathsf{pr}(\varphi)$. Next, we define the proof obligation scheme itself.

Definition 5 (Proof Obligation Scheme). *Let* Prgm *be a program. For each class* c *in the program, let* $\mathsf{ode}_{\mathsf{C}}$ *be its dynamics and* $\mathsf{s}_{\mathsf{C.init}}$ *the code of the constructor. For every method* C.m *let* $\mathsf{s}_{\mathsf{C.m}}$ *be the method body. Let* ψ *be a family of post-regions, i.e., formulas over the physical fields of a class and* t, *indexed with (1) method names including the constructor, and (2) suspension point identifiers. Let* $\mathsf{s_{main}}$ *be the statement of the main block. The proof obligation scheme* ι^ψ *for family* ψ *is a function from methods and initial block to formulas, defined as follows. We use the subscript notation for* ι. *For every class* C, *there is one formula*

$$\iota^\psi_{\mathsf{C.init}} \equiv \mathsf{init}_{\mathsf{C}} \wedge \mathsf{cll} \doteq 0 \rightarrow \big[\mathsf{trans}(\mathsf{s_{init}})\big]\big(\mathsf{cll} \doteq 0 \wedge \mathsf{pr}(\psi_{\mathsf{C.init}}, I_{\mathsf{C}}, \mathsf{ode}_{\mathsf{C}})\big)$$

for each method m *in* C *one formula*

$$\iota_{C.m}^{\psi} \equiv I_C \wedge \mathsf{pre}_{C.m} \wedge \mathsf{cll} \doteq 0 \rightarrow \big[\mathsf{trans}(s_{C.m})\big]\big(\mathsf{cll} \doteq 0 \wedge \mathsf{post}_{C.m} \wedge \mathsf{pr}(\psi_{C.m}, I_C, \mathsf{ode}_C)\big)$$

and for the main block the formula

$$\iota_{\mathbf{main}}^{\psi} \equiv \mathsf{cll} \doteq 0 \rightarrow \big[\mathsf{trans}(s_{\mathbf{main}})\big]\mathsf{cll} \doteq 0.$$

The translation trans *of* HABS *statements into* $d\mathcal{L}$ *statements is given in Fig. 4.*

$$\mathsf{trans}(s_1; s_2) = \mathsf{trans}(s_1); \mathsf{trans}(s_2)$$
$$\mathsf{trans}(\mathsf{if}(e)\{s_1\}\mathsf{else}\{s_2\}) = \mathsf{if}(\mathsf{trans}(e))\{\mathsf{trans}(s_1)\}\mathsf{else}\{\mathsf{trans}(s_2)\}$$
$$\mathsf{trans}(\mathsf{while}(e)\{s\}) = \mathsf{while}(\mathsf{trans}(e))\{\mathsf{trans}(s)\}$$
$$\mathsf{trans}(v = e) = v := \mathsf{trans}(e)$$
$$\mathsf{trans}(\mathsf{return}\ e) = \mathtt{result} := \mathsf{trans}(e)$$

$$\mathsf{trans}(v = e.\mathsf{get}) = \{\{?\mathsf{pr}(\mathsf{true})\}; \mathsf{havoc}^{\mathsf{ph}}; ?I_C; v := *\} \cup \{\{?\neg\mathsf{pr}(\mathsf{true}); \mathsf{fail}\}; \mathsf{havoc}^{\mathsf{ph}}; v := *\}$$
$$\mathsf{trans}(\mathsf{await}_p\ g) = \{?\mathsf{pr}(\psi_p \wedge \ulcorner\mathsf{trans}(g))\}; \mathsf{havoc}; ?\mathsf{trans}(g) \wedge I_C\}$$
$$\cup \{?\neg\mathsf{pr}(\psi_p \wedge \ulcorner\mathsf{trans}(g)); \mathsf{fail}\}; \mathsf{havoc}; ?\mathsf{trans}(g)\}$$

$$\mathsf{trans}(v = e!m(e_1, \dots)) = \{\{?\mathsf{pre}_m(e_1, \dots)\} \cup \{?\neg\mathsf{pre}_m(e_1, \dots); \mathsf{fail}\}\}; v := *$$
$$\mathsf{trans}(v = \mathsf{new}\ C(e_1, \dots)) = \{\{?\mathsf{init}_C(e_1, \dots)\} \cup \{?\neg\mathsf{init}_C(e_1, \dots); \mathsf{fail}\}\}; v := *$$
$$\mathsf{trans}(\mathsf{duration}(e)) = t := 0; \{\{?\mathsf{pr}(t \le e)\} \cup \{?\neg\mathsf{pr}(t \le e); \mathsf{fail}\}\};$$
$$t := 0; \{\mathsf{ode}, t' = 1 \& t \le \mathsf{trans}(e)\}; ?t \ge \mathsf{trans}(e)$$

$$\mathsf{trans}(\mathtt{f}) = f, \text{ where } f \text{ is the } d\mathcal{L} \text{ variable representing field } \mathtt{f}$$
$$\mathsf{trans}(\mathtt{v}) = v, \text{ where } v \text{ is the } d\mathcal{L} \text{ variable representing variable } \mathtt{v}$$
$$\mathsf{trans}(e_1\ op\ e_2) = \mathsf{trans}(e_1)\ op\ \mathsf{trans}(e_2)$$
$$\mathsf{trans}(\mathsf{diff}\ e) = \mathsf{trans}(e)$$
$$\mathsf{trans}(g) = \mathsf{true} \text{ if } g \text{ does not have the form } \mathsf{diff}\ e$$

Fig. 4. Translation of HABS-statements into $d\mathcal{L}$ programs.

If $\psi_{C.m}$ is the same for all methods and the class is understood, then we drop the index. We first examine the proof obligation for normal methods. The precondition $I_C \wedge \mathsf{pre}_{C.m} \wedge \mathsf{cll} \doteq 0$ expresses that the object invariant and the method precondition hold. The last term initializes the special variable cll. The first term of the post-condition (of the modality) expresses that no intermediate check failed the proof and cll is still 0. The second term checks the method post-condition and the last term ensures safety in the post-region. As previously discussed, it takes the form $I_C \wedge [\mathtt{t}:=0; \{\mathsf{ode}, t' = 1 \& \varphi\}]\,I_C$. It expresses that the invariant holds when the method terminated and that it is an invariant for the dynamics in a defined post-region.

The proof obligation for constructors is analogous but (1) does not assume the invariant, as it has not been established yet, and (2) assumes the creation condition as its precondition. A constructor has no post-condition. The proof obligation for the main block is *only* checking that all calls and object creations adhere to the respective precondition, as it runs outside of any object and, thus, has no additional specification.

The translation of statements into $d\mathcal{L}$-programs works as follows. We consider all fields as variables for the translation. The translation of sequence, branching, loops and assignment of side-effect free expressions to location is straightforward. We can ignore the expression of **return** statements as invariants cannot specify return values. The other statements are translated as follows:

- Synchronization with **get** first checks pr(true), if the formula does not hold, then verification fails. This models that during synchronization, time may pass and the invariant must, thus, hold. It is *not* sound to assume the post-region ψ here: synchronization blocks, so no other process can run. Furthermore, it may stay blocked for an unbound amount of time, so the invariant must hold for an unbound amount of time as well. Afterwards, v is set to a new, unknown value, as the return value in a future is not specified. Additionally, havoc^ph is used to model that the physical fields may have changed during the synchronization. In case the check succeeds, the invariant is known to hold for the new values of the fields.
- Suspension with **await** is similar, but uses both the post-region ψ *and* the guard. We use havoc?;trans(g) to set all fields (but not variables) to new values – contrary to the case of **get**, the non-physical fields may have been changed by another process. For the new values only the guard is known to hold. The invariant is also known to hold, but only if the check succeeds. We stress again that time advancement is modeled in the contained modality.
- Method calls check the precondition of the called method. Again, v is set to a new, unknown value to model a fresh future.
- Object creation is analogous to method calls.
- Finally, blocking time advance is similar to synchronization using **get**, with two differences: First, while it is still not sound to use ψ, we may limit the time spent executing this statement. Second, instead of causing havoc, we can precisely simulate the state change by advancing the dynamics for the amount of time given in the **duration** statement.

A scheme generates one formula per entity. Its ultimate aim, however is to establish a safety property for the overall system. Indeed, if we use the post-region **false** for all methods, we may be able to show validity of all formulas – yet it does mean that the system is safe. We, thus, need a formalization of the conditions when the validity of all proof obligations generated by a scheme imply safety.

Formally, a scheme is sound if validity of all generated formulas is sufficient to prove safety of all class with respect to their invariants, and safety of all methods with respect to their contracts. We consider partial correctness [26], i.e., we do not consider deadlock and non-terminating programs.

Definition 6 (Sound Proof Obligation Scheme). *If the validity of all proof obligations from ι^ψ implies that for all locally terminating, time-divergent runs, inv_C holds in every state of every trace of every object o realizing any class* C, *whenever (1) o is inactive or (2) time advances, and that the pre-condition of a method holds in every prestate and the post-condition in every poststate, then we say that ι^ψ is sound.*

Condition (2) expresses that the object stays safe whenever time advances, even if a method is already active. This is critical, as otherwise an object would be in an unsafe state, but would still be considered safe if it, for example, performs a non-suspending **duration**.

We can break down soundness of the scheme into two parts: it must describe the discrete transitions correctly, and it must describe the suspension-subtraces correctly. For the former, we observe that this property can be shown by reasoning about the translation function **trans** – we, thus, only need a formalization for the later.

We remind that suspension-subtraces contain the states where time advances and no process is active, and that (non-trivial) post-regions are not used when time advances and a process is active, for example during the execution of an **get** statement.

Definition 7 (Sound Post-Regions). *Let* **Prgm** *be a set of programs, all containing a class* C *with a method* m. *Let ψ be a first-order formula over the fields of* C *and the variables of* m. *We say that ψ is* **Prgm**-*sound for* C.m, *if every state of every suspension-subtrace of every program in* **Prgm** *is a model for ψ:*

$$\forall \texttt{Prgm} \in \textbf{Prgm}. \ \forall \theta \in \Theta(\texttt{m}, \textbf{Prgm}). \ \forall i \leq |\theta|. \ \theta[i] \models \psi$$

This is indeed sufficient – to show soundness of the proof obligation scheme, it suffices that the used post-region generator is sound: The following theorem [31] states that soundness of post-regions implies soundness of proof obligation schemes.

Theorem 1 ([31]). *If $\psi_{C.m}$ is* **Prgm**-*sound for all* C.m, *then the proof obligation scheme of Definition 5 is sound for* **Prgm** *in the sense of Definition 6.*

Basic post-regions are obviously sound. A slightly more complex notion is the one of locally controlled post-regions [30]. For a simple example, consider a method m without branching or suspension that calls another method **called**. Method **called** has the leading guard x >= 0. Then the post-region for m is x <= 0 – it describes all suspension-subtraces until another process runs, namely the one it called itself. Thus, a post-region generator that assigns x <= 0 to m is sound.

Concrete examples of post-regions that are able to verify Example 1 are described in prior work [30]. In the next section, we introduce a similar system that is not verifiable with those post-regions.

3   Externally Controlled Timed Post-regions

In the following we consider timed control, where the controlling discrete process is *outside* the object of the controlled physical process where the post-region is to be used. To retain modularity of the proof system, we aim to keep the proof obligations the same as before, but instead of *deriving* that a method implements a timed controller, we require the user to *specify* it. The overall system then has to ensure that this method is indeed *globally* called with the required frequency. This property in turn, is handled by a type system – it is a structural property of the whole program, and as such inherently non-local. By using a lightweight type analysis, we keep the required user interactions during the analysis low.

As we target a more volatile situation of IoT systems, which often come with cloud components, we allow the controlling discrete process to change. For example, we allow one controller to shut down and another to take over. We also allow multiple controlling discrete processes to control different aspects of a physical controller, e.g. an internal controller for event-based properties and an external controller for timed-based ones.

Before we come to the formal details, we illustrate the targeted kind of system with a smaller example. We use again JML style comments for specification.

Example 5. Consider the upper code in Fig. 5, a variation of the timed water tank of Example 2. The /*@ *requires* ... @*/ clause specifies the creation condition and /*@ *invariant* ... @*/ specifies the safety invariant. The Tank class has the same physical behavior as before, but the ctrl method is replaced by localCtr which does *not* repeatedly perform the check on its own. Instead, it is specified with /*@ *timed_requires 1* @*/ that the method must be called at least once per time unit.

In this example, there is only one object of class Tank, line 25, and the responsibility of calling localCtrl on this object is then shared between the methods Mobile.run and Controller.timer. Since the method Mobile.run creates the tank, it become by default the initial controller to all its controlled methods. On the other hand, the Controller.timer method is annotated with the /*@ *time_control* : t.localCtrl = [1, 0] @*/ clause, which means that this method takes control of the method localCtrl of its parameter t, waits for 1 unit of time (with the **await duration**(1) statement line 16), calls localCtrl line 18, recursively calls itself line 19 and stops, leaving 0 unit of time until the next call to t.localCtrl.

Hence, upon calling Mobile.run, the Tank object t is created, a Controller object c is created, and the control of t.localCtrl is directly transferred to c.timer. After 40 time units, the Mobile instance synchronizes with c.timer and a new Controller takes over the control of t.localCtrl forever.

There is subtle, timing related bug in this code. At $t = 40$, the final call to timer does not result in a call to localCtrl, but the **await** statement is still executed making time advancing to $t = 41$ before the method's termination. As the newly created controller also waits for one second at the beginning of its execution, localCtrl next call is a $t = 42$: the required call at $t = 41$ is skipped. The lower code in Fig. 5 gives a solution: by only advancing time when a call is made afterwards, the gap at $t = 41$ can be avoided.

Note that this bug can be identified in the specification of the faulty version of timer method. Indeed this specification states that the method: i) waits 1 unit of time at the beginning of its execution before calling t.localCtrl; and ii) concludes its execution with t.localCtrl having to be called right away. Hence it is unsound to delegate the control of the tank to sequences of calls to timer. The fixed version of the timer method concludes it execution with t.localCtrl having to be called after 1 time unit, and so sequences calls to timer do correctly control the tank.

Such subtle bugs illustrate both the need for tool support in the analysis of distributed hybrid and timed systems, as well as the value of specification.

Let us call ceid a pair of a location (a variable or a field) and a method, such as t.localCtrl or c.timer in our example. There are several structural requirements that need to be checked to ensure that a control pattern such as the one presented in our example works: (1) for each controlled ceid, there is always a controlling ceid; (2) the controlling ceid is indeed observing the specified time behavior and (3) if the controlling ceid changes, there are no gaps in control. If all these properties can be ensured, then the specification of the marked timed controller method can be used in the post-region.

The proof obligations do not change: the post-region for the methods in Tank are defined by the frequency of the timed controller. The proof obligations needed for the specification of Controller are not hybrid (as the class contains no **physical** block) and can be handled by discrete approaches to Active Object verification.

Example 6. For Tank, the formulas in Fig. 6 are generated. Let I be the invariant specified in Fig. 5, ψ the mapping from each method to t $\leq$ 1 and $dyn \equiv$ level' = drain.

3.1   Type System

As discussed previously, this type system has one unique goal: check that methods are called correctly with respect to their *timed_requires* annotation. It is thus entirely independent from the physical aspects of HABS and focuses only on the time aspect of a HABS program. In particular, this type system must, to reach its goal, perform a *time analysis* of the input program, i.e., compute how much time each statement can take (in particular the **await** and **duration** statements). Then it must use the information provided by this time analysis to keep track of the ceid control relationship and ensure that all ceid are correctly called.

```
1  /*@ requires 4 <= inVal <= 9  @*/
2  /*@ invariant 3 <= level <= 10 && -1 <= drain <= 1 @*/
3  class Tank(Real inVal){
4    physical Real level = inVal;
5    Real drain = -1;
6    physical{ level' = drain; }
7    /*@ timed_requires 1 @*/
8    Unit localCtrl(){
9      if(level <= 4) drain =  1;
10     if(level >= 9) drain = -1;
11   }}
12
13 class Controller(){
14   /*@ requires t!= null && time_control: t.localCtrl = [1, 0] @*/
15   Unit timer(Tank t, Int time){
16     await duration(1);
17     if(time != 0) {
18       t!localCtrl();
19       Fut<Unit> f = this.timer(t, time - 1);
20       await f?;
21   }}}
22
23 class Mobile {
24   Unit run() {
25     Tank t = new Tank(4);
26     Controller c = new localCtrl(); Fut<Unit> f = c.timer(t, 40);
27     await duration(40);      await f?;
28     c = new Controller(); f = c.timer(t, -1);
29 }}
```

```
1  class Controller(){
2    /*@ requires t!= null && time_control: t.localCtrl = [1, 1] @*/
3    Unit timer(Tank t, Int time){
4      if(time != 0) {
5        await duration(1);
6        t!localCtrl();
7        Fut<Unit> f = this.timer(t, time - 1);
8        await f?;
9    }}}
```

Fig. 5. An externally controlled tank with mobile control. The upper version of `Controller.timer` contains a subtle bug regarding timing, which is fixed in the lower version.

$\iota_{\mathtt{Tank}.\mathtt{init}}^{\psi}$

$\equiv\ 4 \leq \mathtt{inVal} \leq 9 \rightarrow \big[\mathtt{level} := \mathtt{inVal}; \mathtt{drain} := -1;\big]\,(I \wedge [\mathtt{t} := 0\{dyn, \mathtt{t}' = 1 \& \mathtt{t} \leq 1\}]I)$

$\iota_{\mathtt{Tank}.\mathtt{localCtrl}}^{\psi}$

$\equiv\ I \rightarrow \big[\mathtt{if}(\mathtt{level} \leq 4)\mathtt{drain} := 1; \mathtt{if}(\mathtt{level} \geq 9)\mathtt{drain} := -1;\big]\,(I \wedge [\mathtt{t} := 0\{dyn, \mathtt{t}' = 1 \& \mathtt{t} \leq 1\}]I)$

Fig. 6. Proof obligations for Tank in Example 6.

Time Analysis. Designing a time analysis is a difficult task, since such an analysis is undecidable in general (it includes the halting problem), yet the concrete design choices are not central to this work. Many such design choices must be made to decide which behaviors of a program is abstracted away by the analysis, and possibly many complex structures and algorithms must be defined to precisely analyze the rest of the program. Interestingly, resource analysis, and time analysis in particular, have already been defined for ABS [2,4,37] and it is reasonable to imagine that other time analysis, with different capabilities, will be defined in the future. In order to take advantage of the existing (and possibly future) time analysis, we design our type system to be able to use any of them: our type system is thus parametric, and given any correct time analysis, ensures that methods are called correctly. The following definition informally describes the different features of a time analysis that are needed by our type system:

Definition 8. *A* Time Analysis *for a given program* Prgm *is a triplet* (CF, TC, TA) *where:*

- CF *are expressions used to describe how time passes. Since explicit time advance is expressed with rationals in* HABS, CF *must include* $\mathbb{Q}$, *and since some computation can take infinite time, expressions in* CF *must be comparable to* ∞.
- TC *is a function that gives information about the* execution context *of methods and statements. Indeed, since the behavior of a method can change depending on its parameters and the state of the callee, it might be relevant for the time analysis to be sensitive to such execution context and give how much time lapses in a statement depending on an execution context.*
- *Finally,* TA *is the function giving how much time a method or a statement takes depending on the current execution context.*

The coreid Control Relationship. Within a method, a ceid can be controlled in two ways:

1. either a ceid is locally controlled (i.e., the current method is the one responsible to call the ceid), in which case we store how much time is left until a call to the ceid is required;
2. either the control of a ceid has been delegated (i.e., the current method passed the control of ceid to a different process and might get the control back later), in which case we keep track of which future controls the ceid, and when that future terminates.

Consequently, a typing statement for HABS statements has the form $\Gamma_l, \Gamma_d \vdash_c s :$ Γ_l', Γ_d' where: Γ_l registers the ceid locally controlled; Γ_d registers the ceid whose control has been delegated; c is the execution context given by and forwarded to the time analysis (with the TC and TA functions); s is the typed statement; and Γ_l' (resp. Γ_d') is the locally controlled ceid (resp. delegated ceid) obtained after executing s. The context Γ_l maps ceids to the maximum amount of time that can lapse before the method must be called. The context Γ_d maps ceids to tuples $(\mathit{fid}, t_{\min}, t_{\max}, t)$ where: fid is the future to which the ceid has been delegated; $t_{\min}$ (resp. $t_{\max}$) is the minimum (resp. maximum) amount of time before the future is resolved; and t is the maximum amount of time between fid is resolved and the next time ceid must be called.

Remark 1. To keep the presentation of our type system simple, we suppose two restrictions on the syntax of the input program Prgm:

- Prgm does not contain any loop, and
- every assignment in Prgm declares a new variable.

These restrictions do not limit the expressivity of HABS, since loops can be translated into recursive method calls, and variables can always be renamed in fresh variables, following a *Static Single Assignment* pattern.

Example 7. To get a first impression of how this control relationship works, let us look at the method Mobile.run in Fig. 5, and look at how its execution using the faulty version of the Controller.timer method shape the Γ_l and Γ_d contexts. Since the Mobile class does not have any field and Mobile.run does not have any parameter, we can consider that this method does not control anything when it starts: Γ_l and Γ_d are both empty. Then, after the creation of the tank t, which contains a method annotated with *time_requires*, that method must be locally controlled: Γ_l now maps the ceid t.localCtrl to 1 (i.e., the content of the *time_requires* annotation), and Γ_d is still empty. After the creation of the controller c, does not not contain any method annotated with *time_requires*, Γ_l and Γ_d are left unchanged. The call to c.timer(t,40) does change the contexts however: the timer method states in its annotation that it takes over the control of t. Here, our type system must first check that the control transfer is sound (i.e., that the timer method will not call ceid too late), and then registers the transfer in the contexts: Γ_l becomes empty and Γ_d now states that the future f controls ceid. We use the time analysis to check that f controls ceid for 40 units of time, and so the various **await** statements are correct w.r.t. the control of ceid. After the **await** f statement, the control of ceid is once again local: Γ_l now maps ceid to 0 (i.e., the content of the *time_control* annotation of the timer method), and Γ_d is now empty. Finally, the creation of a new controller c and the call c.timer(t,-1) is different from before: here the check that the control transfer is sound fails since Γ_l states that ceid must be called right away and the annotation on c.timer states that ceid will not be called sooner than after 1 unit of time.

342   E. Kamburjan and M. Lienhardt

The rest of this Section first introduces the definition giving what we consider
to be a well-typed program, and presents the different rules defining our type
system.

Definition 9. *A program* Prgm *is* well-typed *iff all its methods and its* **main** *can
be validated with the rules presented in the following paragraphs.*

Typing Rules. The first rule we present is to check method declaration:

$$\frac{tctrl(\text{C.m}) = [\text{x}_i.\text{m}_j \mapsto [t_j, t'_j]]_{i \in I, j \in J_i} \quad \forall i \in I, \forall j \in J_i, \ treq(\text{T}_i.\text{m}_j) \geq t_j}{\forall c \in \text{TC}(\text{C.m}), \ \begin{pmatrix} [\text{x}_i.\text{m}_j \mapsto t_j]_{i \in I, j \in J_i}, \emptyset \vdash_c \text{s} : [\text{x}_i.\text{m}_j \mapsto t''_j]_{i \in I', j \in J'_i}, \emptyset \\ I' \subseteq I \quad \forall i \in I', \ J'_i \subseteq J_i \wedge \forall j \in J_i, \ t'_j \leq t''_j \end{pmatrix}}{\text{C} \vdash \text{T m}(\text{T}_1 \ \text{y}_1, \dots, \ \text{T}_n \ \text{y}_n) \ \{\text{s};\text{return e};\}}$$

The concluding statement of the rule means that we check the definition of
method m in class C. In the premise, we first check the annotation of the method.
We use two functions to access a method's annotation: *tctrl* returns the information related to the *time_control* annotation, i.e., a mapping from controlled ceids
to their pair $[t, t']$ in the annotation; and *treq* returns the information related to
the *timed_requires* annotation, i.e., how often the method must be called. Using
these two functions, the premise controls that for each controlled ceid $\text{x}_i.\text{m}_j$, the
time t_j that will lapse between the beginning of the method and the first call to
the ceid is correct, i.e., it is less than the maximum time between two calls of
ceid.

The second part of the premise checks the validity of the method's body. It
collects (with TC(C.m)) all the execution contexts c registered by the time analysis
for that method, and analyses the validity of the method's body for each of these
context individually, as stated in the validation predicate $\vdash$ indexed with c. To
do that, it first constructs the initial contexts Γ_l and Γ_d where Γ_l corresponds
to the method's annotation (i.e., for each ceid $\text{x}_i.\text{m}_j$, the time left before the
next call is at most t_j) and Γ_d is empty; then it analyses the method's body,
which returns new contexts Γ'_l and Γ'_d; and check the validity of these resulting
contexts, i.e., the ceids in Γ'_l are correct w.r.t. the annotation (for each ceid
$\text{x}_i.\text{m}_j$, the time left before the next call is at least t'_j at the end of the method)
and Γ'_d is empty, meaning that no delegated ceid need to be controlled anymore.

Example 8. Consider for instance the method timer of the Controller class in
the upper part of Fig. 5. In the first part of the rule's premise, the *tctrl*(C.m) call
gets the method's *time_control* annotation which states that the method: takes
control of the ceid t.localCtrl; calls ceid after 1 unit of time; and finishes its
execution with ceid that must be called with no delay. Then the premise of the
rule checks that this annotation is correct w.r.t. the annotation of the method
Tank.localCtrl: since ceid will not be called after 1 unit of time, Tank.localCtrl
must not require to be called more often that this. As Tank.localCtrl requires
to be called every 1 unit of time, this check is validated.

The second part of the premise checks that the method's body holds w.r.t. the
method's annotation for every execution context identified by the time analysis:

we can safely consider in this example that there is only one execution context. Here, we initialize the Γ_l context to the mapping [ceid ↦ 1] and the Γ_d context to the empty mapping. We will see in detail with the next rules how these contexts are used and updated while type-checking statements. But informally, we can follow the reasoning presented in Example 7, to see that after executing the timer method's body, the resulting context Γ_l' is [ceid ↦ 0], and the resulting context Γ_d' is empty (as expected by the rule). Moreover, since Γ_l' is not empty, the last line of the premise is triggered: the only key in the mapping Γ_l' is ceid, which is declared in the method's annotation, and its image is 0 (i.e., the time left before the next required call to ceid), which is consistent to the method's annotation.

Typing Statements. We next present the rules to handle statements within methods, based on the following judgment, which is introduced above.

$$\Gamma_l, \Gamma_d \vdash_c \mathbf{s} : \Gamma_l', \Gamma_d'$$

The first such rule deals with infinite computation. Indeed, it is possible to delegate the control of a ceid to a method that will never finish. In that case, there is no need to take back the control of ceid: we know it will be safely handled forever and we can thus simply forget about it.

$$\frac{\Gamma_l, \Gamma_d \vdash_c \mathbf{s} : \Gamma_l', \Gamma_d' \uplus [\text{ceid} \mapsto (\textit{fid}, t_{\min}, t_{\max}, t)] \quad t_{\min} = \infty}{\Gamma_l, \Gamma_d \vdash_c \mathbf{s} : \Gamma_l', \Gamma_d'}$$

This is what is written in this rule: if while typing a statement, we end up with a ceid that have been delegated to a method call $\textit{fid}$ that will run forever (i.e., the minimum computation time $t_{\min}$ of $\textit{fid}$ is infinite), then we can remove ceid from the delegated context.

Example 9. This rule is suited to type-check methods similar to run of the Mobile class in Fig. 5. Indeed, as stated in Example 7, that method creates a new controller in line 28 and forever delegates the control of t.localCtrl to that controller. Hence there is no need to keep information about that ceid anymore: it can safely be removed from Γ_d', which in turn makes the typing rule for method declaration hold as it requires for Γ_d' to be empty.

The following rule deals with conditional statements:

$$\frac{\Gamma_l, \Gamma_d \vdash_c \mathbf{s}_1 : \Gamma_{l,1}, \Gamma_d' \quad \Gamma_l, \Gamma_d \vdash_c \mathbf{s}_2 : \Gamma_{l,2}, \Gamma_d' \\ \text{dom}(\Gamma_{l,1}) = \text{dom}(\Gamma_{l,2}) \\ \Gamma_l' = [\text{ceid} \mapsto \min(\Gamma_{l,1}(\text{ceid}), \Gamma_{l,2}(\text{ceid}))]_{\text{ceid} \in \text{dom}(\Gamma_{l,1})}}{\Gamma_l, \Gamma_d \vdash_c \mathbf{if(e)} \ \{ \ \mathbf{s}_1 \} \ \mathbf{else} \ \{ \ \mathbf{s}_2 \ \} : \Gamma_l', \Gamma_d'}$$

In this rule, we type-check the two branches of the if statement individually and require that: the two resulting delegated contexts are the same (i.e., they are both equal to Γ_d'); and that the two resulting local contexts $\Gamma_{l,1}$ and $\Gamma_{l,2}$ declare the same ceids. Finally, to ensure the validity of the if statement, we state that its resulting local context maps every ceid to its minimum value in $\Gamma_{l,1}$ and $\Gamma_{l,2}$, and leave unchanged Γ_d'.

The following rule checks sequential composition:

$$\frac{\Gamma_l, \Gamma_d \vdash_c s_1 : \Gamma_l', \Gamma_d' \quad \Gamma_l', \Gamma_d' \vdash_c s_2 : \Gamma_l'', \Gamma_d''}{\Gamma_l, \Gamma_d \vdash_c s_1; \; s_2 : \Gamma_l'', \Gamma_d''}$$

That rules simply checks first the first statement, which gives some resulting contexts Γ_l' and Γ_d', and then the second using Γ_l' and Γ_d' as initial contexts. The result of checking the sequential composition is then the result of checking the second statement.

The **await** statement is a single instruction whose only effect (of interest to our type system) is to make time pass. This is what is written in the following rule: we use a specific rule, identified with the typing predicate $\vdash_c^t$, to manage time passing, and typing the **await** statement is identical to only managing the time consumed by that statement.

$$\frac{\Gamma_l, \Gamma_d \vdash_c^t \text{ await } g : \Gamma_l', \Gamma_d'}{\Gamma_l, \Gamma_d \vdash_c \text{ await } g : \Gamma_l', \Gamma_d'}$$

We will describe the rule for time passing using the $\vdash_c^t$ judgment later.

The following rule checks the assignment statement.

$$\frac{\Gamma_l, \Gamma_d \vdash_c \text{ rhs} : [m_i \mapsto t_i]_{i \in I}, \Gamma_l', \Gamma_d' \quad \Gamma_l'' = \Gamma_l' \uplus [x.m_i \mapsto t_i]_{i \in I} \quad \Gamma_l'', \Gamma_d' \vdash_c^t \text{ T } x = \text{rhs} : \Gamma_l''', \Gamma_d''}{\Gamma_l, \Gamma_d \vdash_c \text{ T } x = \text{rhs} : \Gamma_l''', \Gamma_d''}$$

This rule first checks the right hand side of the assignment. Since a right hand side can create an anonymous object with methods that must be controlled, the result of typing a rhs includes, in addition to the contexts Γ_l' and Γ_d', a mapping $[m_i \mapsto t_i]_{i \in I}$ corresponding to the newly created anonymous ceids. Then the rule names these ceids and includes them into the local context Γ_l'' by simply adding their name x. Finally, the rule manages the possibility of time passing, resulting in the two final contexts Γ_l''' and Γ_d''.

Example 10. In the method run of the Mobile class in Fig. 5, line 25 creates a new tank t that has the method localCtrl that needs to be controlled. To apply the assignment statement rule to that line, let first recall that the initial Γ_l and Γ_d contexts of that method is empty. We will see later that the right hand side new Tank(4) is typed

$$\emptyset, \emptyset \vdash_c \text{ new Tank(4)} : [\text{localCtrl} \mapsto 1], \emptyset, \emptyset$$

Hence, Γ_l'' in the rule is equal to $[t.\text{localCtrl} \mapsto 1]$. Finally, since object creation is instantaneous, we have that $\Gamma_l''' = \Gamma_l''$ and $\Gamma_d'' = \Gamma_d$: the rule thus correctly registers $t.\text{localCtrl} \mapsto 1$ to Γ_l and keeps Γ_d empty.

The following rule, for typing the **duration** statement, is identical to the one used to type the **await** statement. Indeed, the only effect of these two statements is only to make time pass, the only difference is that the **duration** statement also blocks other processes, which is managed by the time analysis.

$$\frac{\Gamma_l, \Gamma_d \vdash_c^t \textbf{duration(e)} : \Gamma_l', \Gamma_d'}{\Gamma_l, \Gamma_d \vdash_c \textbf{duration(e)} : \Gamma_l', \Gamma_d'}$$

The following rule deals with time passing.

$$\frac{\begin{array}{c} \texttt{TA}(c, \mathbf{s}) = [t_{\min}, t_{\max}] \\ \Gamma_{l,1} = [\texttt{ceid} \mapsto \Gamma_l(\texttt{ceid}) - t_{\max}]_{\texttt{ceid} \in \text{dom}(\Gamma_l)} \\ C = \{i \mid i \in I \wedge t_{i,\max} \leq t_{\min}\} \\ \Gamma_{l,2} = [\texttt{ceid}_i \mapsto t_i + (t_{\max} - t_{i,\min})]_{i \in C} \\ \Gamma_d' = [\texttt{ceid}_i \mapsto (\mathit{fid}_i, t_{i,\min} - t_{\max}, t_{i,\max} - t_{\min}, t_i)]_{i \in I \setminus C} \\ \Gamma_l' = \Gamma_{l,1} \uplus \Gamma_{l,2} \quad \forall \texttt{ceid} \in \text{dom}(\Gamma_l'), \Gamma_l'(\texttt{ceid}) \geq 0 \end{array}}{\Gamma_l, [\texttt{ceid}_i \mapsto (\mathit{fid}_i, t_{i,\min}, t_{i,\max}, t_i)]_{i \in I} \vdash_c^t \mathbf{s} : \Gamma_l', \Gamma_d'}$$

With the function call $\texttt{TA}(c, \mathbf{s})$, this rule first queries the time analysis to know, given the current execution context c, what is the minimum time $t_{\min}$ and maximum time $t_{\max}$ that the current statement $\mathbf{s}$ can take. Then the rule updates the two contexts Γ_l and Γ_d to include this passing of time. Updating the local context Γ_l is quite simple, we just state that now the remaining time before each $\texttt{ceid}$ must be called has been decreased by $t_{\max}$. Updating the delegated context Γ_d is more subtle, since during this passing of time some method calls might have finished and we must retake local control of the related delegated $\texttt{ceids}$. The set C corresponds to all the delegated $\texttt{ceids}$ whose control is given back to the local computation, since the corresponding method call is known to have finished. We collect all these $\texttt{ceids}$ in a new local context $\Gamma_{l,2}$, and for all of them, since the maximum time that lapsed between the end of the method and now is $t_{\max} - t_{i,\min}$, we say that the maximum amount of time that can pass until their next call is $t_i + (t_{\max} - t_{i,\min})$. For the $\texttt{ceids}$ whose control stays delegated, we simply store them in Γ_d' and update the execution time of the related method call.

Finally, the rule checks that the locally controlled $\texttt{ceids}$ are safe by ensuring that the time left until their next call is positive, i.e., no specified frequency is violated so far.

Example 11. Consider for instance the method `timer` of the `Controller` class in the upper part of Fig. 5. We already saw in Example 8 that the initial Γ_l context of this method is $[\texttt{ceid} \mapsto 1]$ with $\texttt{ceid} = \texttt{t.localCtrl}$, while Γ_d is empty. The first statement of that method is **await duration(1)** which clearly takes 1 unit of time: we can thus suppose that the time analysis states that

$$\texttt{TA}(c, \textbf{await duration(1)}) = [1, 1]$$

Hence, $\Gamma_{l,1}$ in the rule is $[\texttt{ceid} \mapsto 0]$: $\texttt{ceid}$ must be called without delay. Then, since Γ_d is empty, so are $\Gamma_{l,2}$ and Γ_d' in the rule. We can then conclude the application of the rule: Γ_l' is thus equal to $[\texttt{ceid} \mapsto 0]$, that validates the last constraint of the rule's premise.

Example 12. Another interesting application of the time passing rule is the **await duration**(40) statement line 27 in the upper part of Fig. 5. At that point of the method's execution, the future f is running and controlling the ceid t. localCtrl. We can suppose that the time analysis correctly identified f's information, and so before line 27 Γ_l is empty, and Γ_d is $[\texttt{ceid} \mapsto (\texttt{f}, 41, 41, 0)]$, stating that ceid is controlled by f, that f will take exactly 41 units of time to complete, and that once this future completed, ceid must be called right away. Similarly to the previous example, we suppose that the time analysis for the await statement is precise:

$$\text{TA}(c, \textbf{await duration}(40)) = [40, 40]$$

Hence, the set C is empty. Following the definition of the different contexts in the rule, we have that $\Gamma_{l,1}$ and $\Gamma_{l,2}$ are empty, and Γ_d' is $[\texttt{ceid} \mapsto (\texttt{f}, 1, 1, 0)]$. We can then conclude the application of the rule: Γ_l' is thus the empty set, and so the last constraint of the rule's premise is validated.

Example 13. A last interesting application of the time passing rule is the **await f** statement line 27 in Fig. 5. As we saw in the previous example, here Γ_l is empty, and Γ_d is $[\texttt{ceid} \mapsto (\texttt{f}, 1, 1, 0)]$, stating that ceid is controlled by f, that f will take exactly 1 units of time to complete, and that once this future completed, ceid must be called right away. Similarly to the previous example, we suppose that the time analysis for the await statement is precise:

$$\text{TA}(c, \textbf{await f?}) = [1, 1]$$

Hence, the set C is the rule is $\{\texttt{ceid}\}$. Following the definition of the different contexts in the rule, we have that $\Gamma_{l,1}$ is empty, $\Gamma_{l,2}$ is $[\texttt{ceid} \mapsto 0]$ (the Mobile object takes back control of ceid and must call it right away), and Γ_d' is empty. We can then conclude the application of the rule: Γ_l' is thus equal to $[\texttt{ceid} \mapsto 0]$, that validates the last constraint of the rule's premise.

Typing Right Hand Sides and Expressions. The following (axiomatic) rule deals with side effect-free expression which do not have any effect by construction. The resulting contexts are identical to the initial ones.

$$\Gamma_l, \Gamma_d \vdash_c \texttt{e} : \emptyset, \Gamma_l, \Gamma_d$$

Similarly, the following rule deals with the **get** right hand side, whose only effect is to pass time. Since time passing is handled in our type system with a rule on statements (as previously described), no other effect is registered in this rule and the resulting contexts are identical to the initial ones.

$$\Gamma_l, \Gamma_d \vdash_c \texttt{e}.\textbf{get} : \emptyset, \Gamma_l, \Gamma_d$$

The following rule checks object creation:

$$\frac{M = \{\text{m} \mid \text{C.m} \in \text{dom}(treq)\} \quad S = [\text{m} \mapsto treq(\text{C.m})]_{\text{m} \in M}}{\Gamma_l, \Gamma_d \vdash_c \text{new } \text{C}(\text{e}_1, \ldots, \text{e}_n) : S, \Gamma_l, \Gamma_d}$$

This expression does not have any effect on the contexts Γ_l and Γ_d, but might add new ceids corresponding to the newly created object. These unnamed ceids are stored and returned in the mapping S.

The last rule of our type system deals with method call. This rule is responsible of two main features in our type system: if the method call corresponds to a ceid, we must reset the time counter in the local context Γ_l; and we must transfer the ceids delegated to this method call from Γ_l to Γ_d.

$$\frac{\begin{array}{c} \forall 1 \leq i \leq n, \ type(\text{e}_i) = \text{T}_i \quad tctrl(\text{T}_1.\text{m}) = [\text{x}_i.\text{m}_j \mapsto [t_j, t'_j]]_{i \in I, j \in J_i} \\ \forall i \in I, \forall j \in J_i, \ \Gamma_l[\text{e}_i.\text{m}_j] \geq t_j \\ \Gamma'_l = \Gamma_l \setminus \{\text{e}_i.\text{m}_j \mid i \in I, j \in J_i\} \quad \Gamma''_l = \begin{cases} \Gamma'_l[\text{e}_1.\text{m} \mapsto treq(\text{T}_1.\text{m})] & \text{if } \text{e}_1.\text{m} \in \text{dom}(\Gamma_l) \\ \Gamma'_l & \text{else} \end{cases} \\ \text{TC}(c, \text{e}_1!\text{m}(\text{e}_2, \ldots, \text{e}_n)) = c' \quad \text{TA}(c', \text{T}_1.\text{m}) = [t_{\min}, t_{\max}] \quad \textit{fid} \text{ fresh} \end{array}}{\Gamma_l, \Gamma_d \vdash_c \text{e}_1!\text{m}(\text{e}_2, \ldots, \text{e}_n) : \emptyset, \Gamma''_l, \Gamma_d[\text{e}_i.\text{m}_j \mapsto (\textit{fid}, t_{\min}, t_{\max}, t'_j)]_{i \in I, j \in J_i}}$$

This rule works as follows. First, it gets the type of every expression involved in the method call, and gets the information related to the *time_control* annotation of the callee. Then it checks that the method call is correct w.r.t. the control annotation, i.e., the times given in Γ_l for all the delegated ceid are valid w.r.t. the specification of the method. Then, it extract from Γ_l the ceids that are still local in Γ'_l and updates Γ'_l into Γ''_l if the callee is a locally controlled ceid. And finally, it computes using the function TC the execution context of this method call to obtain its minimum and maximum execution time to generate all the relevant information in Γ_d for the newly delegated ceids.

Example 14. Consider for instance the call to t.localCtrl line 18 in the method timer of the Controller class in the upper part of Fig. 5. Let define ceid = t.localCtrl: we previously discussed that before the call, Γ_l is [ceid $\mapsto$ 0] and Γ_d is empty. Then, following the first line of the premise of the rule, we have that $n = 1$, $\text{T}_1 = $ Tank and $I = \emptyset$ (since the method Tank.localCtrl does not control anything). The second line of the premise only checks the validity of the control delegation, which is empty in our case. Then, following the third line of the premise, we have that $\Gamma'_l = \Gamma_l$ and $\Gamma''_l = $ [ceid $\mapsto$ 1] since ceid is the method being called. And finally, we can consider that the time analysis correctly identifies that ceid does not take any time to execute (i.e., TA(c', Tank.localCtrl) = $[0,0]$); but since ceid does not control anything, the context for delegated control stays empty after the method call.

Example 15. Another interesting application of the method call rule is the c .timer(t, 40) call line 26 in the upper part of Fig. 5. Let define ceid = t.localCtrl: we previously discussed that before the call, Γ_l is [ceid $\mapsto$ 1] and Γ_d is empty. Then, following the first line of the premise of the rule, we have that $n = 1$, $\text{T}_1 = $ Controller and $I = \{2\}$: Controller.timer takes control of ceid. The second line of the premise checks the validity of the control delegation, i.e., that $\Gamma_l[\text{ceid}]$ (the maximum time allowed before calling ceid) is longer than or equal to the time `Controller.timer` takes to call it: since both numbers are 1, the check passes. Then, following the third line of the premise, we have that $\Gamma'_l = \emptyset$ since ceid is delegated, and so $\Gamma''_l = \emptyset$. And finally, we can consider like in Example 12 that the time analysis correctly identifies that this call to `Controller.timer` takes exactly 41 units of time to execute (i.e., $TA(c', \texttt{Controller.timer}) = [41, 41]$), which means that context for delegated control after the method call has the form $[\texttt{ceid} \mapsto (\texttt{f}, 41, 41, 0)]$.

Example 16. An last interesting application of the method call rule is the `c.timer` (t, -1) call line 28 in the upper part of Fig. 5. Let define ceid = t.localCtrl: we previously discussed that before the call, Γ_l is $[\texttt{ceid} \mapsto 0]$ and Γ_d is empty. Then, following the first line of the premise of the rule, we have that $n = 1$, $T_1 = \texttt{Controller}$ and $I = \{2\}$: `Controller.timer` takes control of ceid. The second line of the premise checks the validity of the control delegation, i.e., that $\Gamma_l[\texttt{ceid}]$ (the maximum time allowed before calling ceid) is longer than or equal to the time `Controller.timer` takes to call it: this check fails since $\Gamma_l[\texttt{ceid}]$ is 0. Hence, this rule correctly identifies the subtle timing error in Fig. 5.

If instead we use the fixed version of the `timer` method, before the call Γ_l becomes $[\texttt{ceid} \mapsto 1]$ (and Γ_d stays empty). Here, like in Example 15, the checks in the second line of the premise would be validated: our analysis would correctly validate our proposed fix.

Then, following the third line of the premise, we would have that $\Gamma'_l = \emptyset$ since ceid is delegated, and so $\Gamma''_l = \emptyset$. And finally, we can consider that the time analysis correctly identifies that this call to `Controller.timer` will never finish (i.e., $TA(c', \texttt{Controller.timer}) = [\infty, \infty]$), which means that context for delegated control after the method call has the form $[\texttt{ceid} \mapsto (\texttt{f}, \infty, \infty, 0)]$.

3.2   Proof System

For the proof system itself, we can now safely assume the specification as a post-region for the class, as long as the program is well-typed.

Theorem 2 (Soundness of Timed External Control). *Let* C *be a class with a an externally timed* m *with frequency* l. *The externally controlled timed post-region of* cm *is defined as follows:*

$$\psi^{\text{et}}_{\texttt{C.cm}} \equiv \texttt{t} \leq l$$

Let $\mathbf{Prgm}^{\Vdash}$ *be the set of well-typed programs according to Definition 9. The post-region* $\psi^{\text{et}}_{\texttt{C.cm}}$ *is* $\mathbf{Prgm}^{\Vdash}$*-sound for all methods* m *in* C.

There can be multiple externally timed methods and it is sound to combine their corresponding post-region generators [31]. Using the theorem, we can see that `Tank` in Fig. 5 is safe, if the formulas in Example 6 are valid and the type checker succeeds. The proof obligations are the same as the ones in Example 2; they can be automatically closed by KeYmaera X [21] and are available [30].

4   Modeling Cloud-Aware Hybrid Systems

Equipped with the type-and-effect system, we now investigate a bigger example to show how Hybrid Active Objects can,be used to model cyber-physical systems using a cloud infrastructure.

Scenario. We model the cloud infrastructure that is shown in Fig. 7. A, possibly growing, set of nodes, must be controlled by a central instance. To do so, the control instance can create new controller tasks and assign them to virtual machines (VM). Each controller task controls one node for a certain amount of time. Once it finishes controlling, a new task must be started, possibly on another VM. When a new task is created, one must pick a VM with enough free resources and, if no such VM exists, create a new one. As a VM may also run other tasks, e.g., accessing some other mechanism of the nodes, the set of VMs may grow and shrink, depending on the resource consumption.

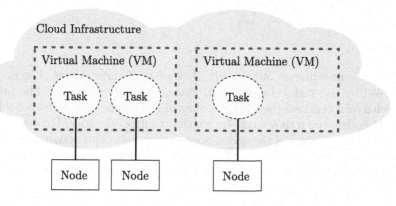

Fig. 7. Cloud infrastructure to control nodes.

Resource-Modeling. Modeling cloud infrastructure requires the use of *resource-sensitive* actors and *deployment components* [28] to model the cloud infrastructure. We do not allow Hybrid Active Objects to run on deployment components, so the resource model is not relevant for our verification system. However, we consider resource-*aware* HAOs, i.e., HAOs that communicate with (and are controlled by) resource-*using* Timed Active Objects, which are allowed to consume resources. Communication is handled via method calls and Cooperative Contracts [32]. A detailed introduction to resource-aware modeling with Active Objects is given by Schlatte et al. [50], we give a short introduction into the core concepts next.

A deployment component (DC) is an abstraction over some *location* that posses some *resources*, that are refilled once per time unit. Any object may run on at most one DC and each statement may consume some resource. If the DC

350   E. Kamburjan and M. Lienhardt

has not enough resources to perform a resource-consuming statement, than the clock must be advanced by one time unit until the resource is refilled and can be consumed again. The process blocks the object for that time. The following code creates a DC with 3 units of the speed resource (line 4) and creates an object on it (line 5) using the [DC: dc] annotation. It then calls the m method which consumes 10 resources (modeled by the [Cost: 10] annotation. Thus, the method takes (at least) 4 time units to complete. Annotations are specific to resource modeling in ABS. They can be ignored *for our verification*, if it can be shown that the resource model does not influence the time behavior.

```
1 class C() { Unit m(){ [Cost: 10] skip; } }
2 class D() {
3   Unit setup() {
4     DC dc = new DeploymentComponent(map[Pair(Speed, 3)]);
5     [DC : dc] C c = new C();
6     Fut<Unit> f = c!m();
7     f.get;
8   }
9 }
```

Model. We now discuss our model[5]. It consists of three classes. The nodes are modeled by the Tank class in Fig. 5, that we already discussed. The tasks are modeled by a CtrlTask (non-hybrid) class in Fig. 8. The sole method of this class takes a node n and a time until for which it controls the node. For controlling, it calls the ctrl method of the node once per time unit. This action consumed one resource (through the [Cost: 1] annotation) – it must, thus, be ensured that there are always enough resources to perform this action without delay.

```
1 class CtrlTask() {
2   /*@ time_control: n.ctrl = [0,0] @*/
3   Unit ctrl(Node n, Int until){
4     Rat start = timeValue(now());
5     while (timeValue(now()) <= until + start) {
6       [Cost: 1]Fut<Unit> f = n!ctrl();
7       duration(1,1);
8     }
9   }
10 }
```

Fig. 8. A resource-aware model of a controlling task.

---

[5] Available at https://formbar.raillab.de/wp-content/uploads/2021/10/nodecloud.zip.

Finally, the managing instance is modeled as a `Manager` (non-hybrid) class, shown in Fig. 9 and 10. The manager keeps a list of its DCs, corresponding to VMs, and maps each of its DCs to the number of tasks assigned to it. Periodically, here, every 10 time units, it removes all DCs which have no tasks assigned (`cleanup`). It may create a new DC with the capacity for 3 tasks (`createNewDc`) and it is able to return a DC with below 2 tasks if a new task arrives (`getFreeDc`). This is done in the `manage` method: it takes a uncontrolled node and a time `d > 0`. It selects a fitting DC and creates a task on it. It then increases the number of tasks assigned to this DC and waits until the control task is finished. Once the task is finished, the number of tasks assigned to the chosen DC is reduced and after 1 time unit the procedure is repeated.

```
11 class Manager() {
12    Map<DeploymentComponent, Int> freeMap = map[];
13    Unit run(){ await duration(10); this!cleanup(); this!run(); }
14
15    DeploymentComponent createNewDc(){
16       DC dc = new DeploymentComponent(map[Pair(Speed, 3)]);
17       freeMap[dc] = 0;
18       return dc;}
19    DeploymentComponent getFreeDc(){
20       foreach (dc in keys(freeMap)){ if(freeMap[dc] <= 2) return dc; }
21       return this.createNewDc();}
22    /*@ time_control: n.ctrl = [0,∞] @*/
23    Unit manage(Node n, Int d){/* See next figure */ }
24    Unit cleanup(){ /* removes all DC with freeMap[dc] == 0 */ }}
```

Fig. 9. A resource-aware model of a cloud infrastructure.

```
25    /*@ time_control: n.ctrl = [0,∞] @*/
26 Unit manage(Node n, Int d){
27    DeploymentComponent target = this.getFreeDc();
28    [DC : target] CtrlTask ctrlTask = new CtrlTask();
29    Fut<Unit> f1 = ctrlTask!ctrl(n, d);
30    freeMap[freeMap[target]]++; await f1?;
31    freeMap[freeMap[target]]--;
32    Fut<Unit> f2 = this!manage(n,d); await f2?; }
```

Fig. 10. A resource-aware model of a cloud infrastructure.

Finally, we need a scenario to set up a number of nodes and connect them to the infrastructure. The following code sets up 10 nodes that start over 10 time units and uses each controlling task for 3 time units:

```
35 { Manager manager = new Manager();
36   for(i in 1..10){
37     Node n = new Node(i); manager!manage(n, 3, i);
38     await duration(1);
39   }}
```

Analysis. To verify the described model, we need to perform two steps: first, we need to close all generated proof obligations, second, we need to ensure that it is typable. The proof obligations are already given in the previous section, so we must merely describe the typing and why the time and alias analysis succeeds.

To check that the model is typable, we first need to identify a time analysis for it. For simplicity, we informally describe such a TA. First, it is easy to see that the resource are correctly used in the model and do not cause time passing. Indeed, three units of speed are declared in a deployment component, and each of them host the computation of at most 3 CtrlTask.ctrl processes, each of them costing 1 unit of speed each unit of time. Then it is easy to see that only the methods CtrlTask.ctrl, Manager.run, Manager.manage and the main block take time. Since CtrlTask.ctrl is only called with its parameter until equal to 3, this method always takes 3 units of time to complete (each iteration of its **while** loop taking 1 unit of time). The method Manager.run runs for 10 units of time and then stops. Since Manager.manage synchronizes with its recursive call, it runs forever. Finally, the main block takes 10 units of time and then concludes.

Interestingly, since every methods always has the same behavior w.r.t. time, we do not need to consider execution context for this time analysis.

We can now apply the type system to the model, and check if a valid type statement can be derived from the rules given in Sect. 3.1. Since we considered in Sect. 3.1 that all loops have been translated away, we will consider here that the three loops in the models implicitly correspond to anonymous methods.

First, the class Node contains only one method, ctrl with $tctrl(\mathtt{Tank.ctrl}) = \emptyset$. Hence the initial local and delegated context for typing this method are both empty. Moreover, the two **if** statements in the method do not create any controlled object, so the method is clearly well typed, with the type derivation of its body being:

$$\emptyset, \emptyset \vdash \mathtt{if(level <= 4) \ drain = 1; \ if(level >= 9) \ drain = -1;} : \emptyset, \emptyset$$

The three other methods Manager.run, Manager.createNewDc and Manager.getFreeDc have the same feature of Tank.ctrl (their controlling annotation is empty, and they do not create any controlled object), and so they are trivially well-typed, with a type derivation similar to the one of Tank.ctrl.

Let now consider the method CtrlTask.CtrlTask as shown in Fig. 8. Correspondingly to its annotation, the local environment used to type this method's body is $\Gamma_l = [\mathtt{n.ctrl} \mapsto 0]$. The statement of line 4 in Fig. 8 does not take any time and does not have any effect on the domain of Γ_l, so after that statement (correspondingly to the typing rule for assignment and time passing), the local context is still equal to Γ_l. Since the parameter until is always equal to 3, we can consider for simplicity that the **while** loop Line 5 in Fig. 8 have been flattened into three copies of its body[6]. Each copy starts with $\Gamma_l = [\text{n.ctrl} \mapsto 0]$ and $\Gamma_d = \emptyset$; calls n.ctrl right away, resulting in $\Gamma_l = [\text{n.ctrl} \mapsto 1]$ and $\Gamma_d = \emptyset$; and executes **duration(1,1);**, resulting in $\Gamma_l = [\text{n.ctrl} \mapsto 0]$ and $\Gamma_d = \emptyset$; So, since $0 \leq 0$ (the end time of n.ctrl in the annotation is smaller or equal to the one in Γ_l), the concluding premises of the *method declaration* typing rule are validated, and so the method is well-typed.

Let now consider the method Manager.manage. Correspondingly to its annotation, the local environment used to type this method's body is $\Gamma_l = [\text{n.ctrl} \mapsto 0]$. The statements in Lines 27–29 in Fig. 10 does not take any time and does not have any effect on the domain of Γ_l, so after that statement (correspondingly to the typing rule for assignment and time passing), the local context is still equal to Γ_l. Line 29 in Fig. 10 delegates the control of n.ctrl to the method call, which takes exactly 3 units of time, as stated in our discussion of TA. Hence, after Line 29, the local context Γ_l is empty, and the delegated context is $\Gamma_d = [\text{n.ctrl} \mapsto (\mathit{fid}, 3, 3, 0)]$ for some future name fid. Line 30 in Fig. 10 contains two statement. The first one is a simple increment, and has no effect on time or on control: after it the local and delegated contexts are unchanged. The second statement synchronizes with fid: three units of time pass, and fid finishes, giving the control of n.ctrl back to the local context. Hence, since no time passed between the end of fid and the end of the **await** statement, that statement is well typed and results in Γ_l being back equal to $[\text{n.ctrl} \mapsto 0]$ and Γ_d being empty. Line 31 has not effect on time or control, so Γ_l and Γ_d are kept unchanged after it. Finally, Line 32 contains two statements. The first statement delegates the control of n.ctrl to another instance of the Manager.manage method. After this statement, we thus obtain that the local context Γ_l is empty, and the delegated context is $\Gamma_d = [\text{n.ctrl} \mapsto (\mathit{fid}, \infty, \infty, \infty)]$ (recall that TA states that the computation time of Manager.manage is infinite). We can thus apply the *infinite computation* typing rule, to state that n.ctrl is forever well manage and remove it from Γ_d. Hence, before the await in Line 32, we get that both the local and delegated contexts are empty. We can thus type check the await statement, that waits for an infinite amount of time without causing any control issue, and conclude the typing of the method.

The last instruction set we need to type check is the main block. Similarly to the CtrlTask.CtrlTask method, since the loop body is executed exactly 10 times, we suppose for simplicity that the loop has been flattened away, its body being copied 10 times in the main. Typing the main starts with the local and delegated contexts, Γ_l and Γ_d, being empty. Then Line 35 has not effect on time or control,

---

[6] As stated in Sect. 3.1, our type system can manage arbitrary loop statements by implicitly and automatically replacing them with dedicated method calls and synchronization. We don't use this approach in our informal explanation of the type system because even though this automatic approach always works (i.e., it is correct and complete), it adds new methods, calls and synchronization that obfuscate our explanations. Note that we do not require the recursion to be bounded.

so Γ_l and Γ_d are kept unchanged after it. Line 37 first creates a new Node which has the controlled method ctrl. That control is given to the main, and so after this statement, $\Gamma_l = [\text{n.ctrl} \mapsto 1]$ (Γ_d is still empty). The second statement in Line 37 calls the method Manager.manage, and thus delegates the control of n. ctrl to it. This method call is well typed, since the annotation of Manager.manage stipulates that n.ctrl will be called right away. After this method call, we thus obtain that Γ_l is empty, and Γ_d is $[\text{n.ctrl} \mapsto (\text{fid}, \infty, \infty, \infty)]$ for some future name fid. Like during the typing of method Manager.manage, we can apply the *infinite computation* typing rule to state that n.ctrl is forever well manage and remove it from Γ_d. Hence, after Line 37, we get back an empty local context and and empty delegated context. Line 38 makes 1 unit of time pass, which has no effect on the main, since it has no registered controlled element.

This concludes the typing of this model: every methods in it are well-typed, as well as the main, and so, following Theorem 2, we can soundly use the specified post-region ($\text{t} \leq 1$) in the proof obligation.

Note the modularity enforced by our system: a change in the HAO does not require us to rerun the type system, a change in the cloud system does not requires us to reprove the HAO.

5   Related Work

Deductive Verification of Hybrid Programming Languages. We already discussed $d\mathcal{L}$, which is a simple algebraic programming language. For distributed systems, $d\mathcal{L}$ has been extended to $\mathcal{Q}d\mathcal{L}$ [44,45], which is implemented in the KeYmaeraD tool [48]. $\mathcal{Q}d\mathcal{L}$ introduces concurrency by extending the $d\mathcal{L}$-program variables to *indexed* variables, which are manipulated using array-style statement. The concurrency model is essentially shared memory and it does not add structuring elements or special constructs to deal with concurrency.

Hybrid Rebeca [27] is a language that has both constructs for discrete systems and hybrid automata, i.e., it separates these two concepts. Its semantics is not based on classical program semantics, but on a translation into a single hybrid automaton. For verification, only model checking has been investigated. Thus, the system is neither modular nor is it able to handle unbounded systems.

Process algebras are minimalistic programming languages that have spawned several formalisms for distributed hybrid systems. None of them has been considered for type systems. The CCPS system [38] is an extension of timed process algebra TPL [25] and CCS [42] uses an inbuilt notion of sensor and actuators. The φ-calculus [49] is an extension of the π-calculus. It has no physical processes but considers them as a part of the environment. The work of Khadim [36] gives a detailed comparison on the process algebras HyPA [16], Hybrid χ [14], both extending ACP [9], the φ-calculus and another extension of ACP [10]. The HYPE calculus [22] is an approach that focuses on the composition of continuous behavior, less so on the interaction through discrete actions.

Compositional Deductive Verification of Hybrid Systems. For deductive verification of hybrid models, besides $d\mathcal{L}$, only Hybrid CSP, another process algebra, has been considered [40]. In its basic formulation, neither $d\mathcal{L}$ nor Hybrid CSP have structuring mechanisms for composition or modularity, and additional systems to provide a proof structure on to have been proposed. All these systems have in common that they structure the proof of a hybrid model and do not use structuring mechanisms on the language layer. Mitsch et al. [43] give a methodology for composition based specific patterns used to encode components into $d\mathcal{L}$. Bohrer and Platzer [13] give a proof language for Constructive Differential Game Logic, a variant of $d\mathcal{L}$. The HHL prover [52] for Hybrid CSP embeds Hoare triples into Isabelle/HOL and can use its structuring mechanisms, such as lemmata. Baar and Staroletov [8] give a system to decompose $d\mathcal{L}$ proofs by transforming hybrid programs into control-flow graphs and annotating contracts to the edges.

Behavioral Type Systems. Bocchi et al. [12] describe timed session types for a minimalistic timed process calculus with channels, based on the π-calculus. Their work checks protocol adherence and uses clock variables for time. These clocks are specified and kept track of by using linear predicates.

Majumdar et al. [41] use session types to coordinate *robotic programs*. Robotic programs do not isolate the dynamics as hybrid objects, instead all physical processes share the same geometric space. A focus of their work is the correct partition of the geometric space and the correctness of protocols between parties in disjoint subspaces.

Avanzini and Dal Lago [7] present a type system for complexity classes of functional programs, which is at its core a time analysis. In a similar direction, there is a long line of work of cost analysis, which intersects with time analysis. For Active Objects, cost analysis has been considered by Flores-Montoya [20] and Albert et al. [3]. Albert et al. [5] also discuss computing t_{min}. Time analysis has been used directly for deadline analysis by Laneve et al. [37].

6   Conclusion

We presented a verification system for distributed hybrid systems that combines deductive verification to verify object invariants with a type-and-effect system to use the global structure of the overall system. Our system is highly modular and more expressive than prior approaches: only one proof obligation is generated per method and local changes do not require to reprove the whole system. Global analysis is performed using a lightweight type system. We can express and verify patterns with delegated control, a pattern crucial for modeling cloud-aware hybrid systems.

This work as a further indication that hybrid programming languages are a useful modeling technique in the volatile environment of modern cyber-physical systems, and that it is possible carry over analyses techniques, such as type-and-effect systems or method-based rely-guarantee reasoning, to a hybrid setting.

Concerning the language model, we observe that an object must stay safe forever and cannot be shut down explicitly. It would be convenient, and make hybrid active objects more suitable for digital twin applications, to have some life cycle management with explicit life phases for starting, running, maintaining and shutting down a HAO.

Acknowledgments. This work was partially supported by the Research Council of Norway via the SIRIUS center (Grant Nr. 237898) and the PeTWIN project (Grant Nr. 294600). We thank Reiner Hähnle and Richard Bubel for extensive and constructive feedback on early drafts of this paper.

References

1. Ahrendt, W., Beckert, B., Bubel, R., Hähnle, R., Schmitt, P.H., Ulbrich, M. (eds.): Deductive Software Verification - The KeY Book - From Theory to Practice. LNCS, vol. 10001. Springer, Cham (2016). https://doi.org/10.1007/978-3-319-49812-6

2. Albert, E., Arenas, P., Genaim, S., Gómez-Zamalloa, M., Puebla, G.: COSTABS: a cost and termination analyzer for ABS. In: Kiselyov, O., Thompson, S.J. (eds.) PEPM. ACM (2012)

3. Albert, E., Correas, J., Johnsen, E.B., Pun, V.K.I., Román-Díez, G.: Parallel cost analysis. ACM Trans. Comput. Log. **19**(4) (2018)

4. Albert, E., et al.: Formal modeling and analysis of resource management for cloud architectures: an industrial case study using real-time ABS. Serv. Oriented Comput. Appl. **8**(4) (2014)

5. Albert, E., Genaim, S., Martin-Martin, E., Merayo, A., Rubio, A.: Lower-bound synthesis using loop specialization and Max-SMT. In: Silva, A., Leino, K.R.M. (eds.) CAV 2021. LNCS, vol. 12760, pp. 863–886. Springer, Cham (2021). https://doi.org/10.1007/978-3-030-81688-9_40

6. Alur, R., Courcoubetis, C., Henzinger, T.A., Ho, P.-H.: Hybrid automata: an algorithmic approach to the specification and verification of hybrid systems. In: Grossman, R.L., Nerode, A., Ravn, A.P., Rischel, H. (eds.) HS 1991-1992. LNCS, vol. 736, pp. 209–229. Springer, Heidelberg (1993). https://doi.org/10.1007/3-540-57318-6_30

7. Avanzini, M., Lago, U.D.: Automating sized-type inference for complexity analysis. Proc. ACM Program. Lang. **1**(ICFP) (2017)

8. Baar, T., Staroletov, S.: A control flow graph based approach to make the verification of cyber-physical systems using KeYmaera easier. Model. Anal. Inf. Syst. **25**(5) (2019)

9. Bergstra, J.A., Klop, J.W.: Algebra of communicating processes with abstraction. Theor. Comput. Sci. **37** (1985)

10. Bergstra, J.A., Middelburg, C.A.: Process algebra for hybrid systems. Theor. Comput. Sci. **335**(2–3) (2005)

11. Bjørk, J., de Boer, F.S., Johnsen, E.B., Schlatte, R., Tapia Tarifa, S.L.: User-defined schedulers for real-time concurrent objects. Innov. Syst. Softw. Eng. **9**(1) (2013)

12. Bocchi, L., Yang, W., Yoshida, N.: Timed multiparty session types. In: Baldan, P., Gorla, D. (eds.) CONCUR 2014. LNCS, vol. 8704, pp. 419–434. Springer, Heidelberg (2014). https://doi.org/10.1007/978-3-662-44584-6_29

13. Bohrer, B., Platzer, A.: Structured proofs for adversarial cyber-physical systems. CoRR, abs/2107.08852 (2021)

14. Bos, V., Kleijn, J.J.T.: Redesign of a systems engineering language: formalisation of X. Formal Aspects Comput. **15**(4) (2003)

15. Clarke, D., Wrigstad, T., Östlund, J., Johnsen, E.B.: Minimal ownership for active objects. In: Ramalingam, G. (ed.) APLAS 2008. LNCS, vol. 5356, pp. 139–154. Springer, Heidelberg (2008). https://doi.org/10.1007/978-3-540-89330-1_11

16. Cuijpers, P.J.L., Reniers, M.A.: Hybrid process algebra. J. Log. Algebraic Methods Program. **62**(2) (2005)
17. de Boer, F.S., et al.: A survey of active object languages. ACM Comput. Surv. **50**(5) (2017)
18. Din, C.C., Bubel, R., Hähnle, R.: KeY-ABS: a deductive verification tool for the concurrent modelling language ABS. In: Felty, A.P., Middeldorp, A. (eds.) CADE 2015. LNCS (LNAI), vol. 9195, pp. 517–526. Springer, Cham (2015). https://doi.org/10.1007/978-3-319-21401-6_35
19. Din, C.C., Owe, O.: Compositional reasoning about active objects with shared futures. Formal Asp. Comput. **27**(3) (2015)
20. Flores-Montoya, A.: Upper and lower amortized cost bounds of programs expressed as cost relations. In: Fitzgerald, J., Heitmeyer, C., Gnesi, S., Philippou, A. (eds.) FM 2016. LNCS, vol. 9995, pp. 254–273. Springer, Cham (2016). https://doi.org/10.1007/978-3-319-48989-6_16
21. Fulton, N., Mitsch, S., Quesel, J.-D., Völp, M., Platzer, A.: KeYmaera X: an axiomatic tactical theorem prover for hybrid systems. In: Felty, A.P., Middeldorp, A. (eds.) CADE 2015. LNCS (LNAI), vol. 9195, pp. 527–538. Springer, Cham (2015). https://doi.org/10.1007/978-3-319-21401-6_36
22. Galpin, V., Bortolussi, L., Hillston, J.: HYPE: hybrid modelling by composition of flows. Formal Aspects Comput. **25**(4) (2013)
23. Giachino, E., Johnsen, E.B., Laneve, C., Pun, K.I.: Time complexity of concurrent programs. In: Braga, C., Ölveczky, P.C. (eds.) FACS 2015. LNCS, vol. 9539, pp. 199–216. Springer, Cham (2016). https://doi.org/10.1007/978-3-319-28934-2_11
24. Goncharov, S., Neves, R., Proença, J.: Implementing hybrid semantics: from functional to imperative. In: Pun, V.K.I., Stolz, V., Simao, A. (eds.) ICTAC 2020. LNCS, vol. 12545, pp. 262–282. Springer, Cham (2020). https://doi.org/10.1007/978-3-030-64276-1_14
25. Hennessy, M., Regan, T.: A process algebra for timed systems. Inf. Comput. **117**(2) (1995)
26. Hoare, C.A.R.: An axiomatic basis for computer programming. Commun. ACM **12**(10) (1969)
27. Jahandideh, I., Ghassemi, F., Sirjani, M.: An actor-based framework for asynchronous event-based cyber-physical systems. Softw. Syst. Model. **20**(3) (2021)
28. Johnsen, E.B., Schlatte, R., Tarifa, S.L.T.: Integrating deployment architectures and resource consumption in timed object-oriented models. J. Log. Algebraic Methods Program. **84**(1) (2015)
29. Kamburjan, E.: Behavioral program logic. In: Cerrito, S., Popescu, A. (eds.) TABLEAUX 2019. LNCS (LNAI), vol. 11714, pp. 391–408. Springer, Cham (2019). https://doi.org/10.1007/978-3-030-29026-9_22
30. Kamburjan, E.: From post-conditions to post-region invariants: deductive verification of hybrid objects. In: HSCC. ACM (2021)
31. Kamburjan, E.: Modular analysis of distributed hybrid systems using post-regions (full version). CoRR, abs/2309.10470 (2023)
32. Kamburjan, E., Din, C.C., Hähnle, R., Johnsen, E.B.: Behavioral contracts for cooperative scheduling. In: Ahrendt, W., Beckert, B., Bubel, R., Hähnle, R., Ulbrich, M. (eds.) Deductive Software Verification: Future Perspectives. LNCS, vol. 12345, pp. 85–121. Springer, Cham (2020). https://doi.org/10.1007/978-3-030-64354-6_4
33. Kamburjan, E., Lienhardt, M.: Type-based verification of delegated control in hybrid systems (full version). CoRR, abs/2309.01370 (2023)

34. Kamburjan, E., Mitsch, S., Hähnle, R.: A hybrid programming language for formal modeling and verification of hybrid systems. Leibniz Trans. Embed. Syst. **8**(2), 04:1–04:34 (2022)
35. Kamburjan, E., Scaletta, M., Rollshausen, N.: Deductive verification of active objects with crowbar. Sci. Comput. Program. **226** (2023)
36. Khadim, U.: A comparative study of process algebras for hybrid systems. Computer science reports. Technische Universiteit Eindhoven (2006)
37. Laneve, C., Lienhardt, M., Pun, K.I., Román-Díez, G.: Time analysis of actor programs. J. Log. Algebraic Methods Program. **105** (2019)
38. Lanotte, R., Merro, M.: A calculus of cyber-physical systems. In: Drewes, F., Martín-Vide, C., Truthe, B. (eds.) LATA 2017. LNCS, vol. 10168, pp. 115–127. Springer, Cham (2017). https://doi.org/10.1007/978-3-319-53733-7_8
39. Leavens, G.T., et al.: JML Reference Manual (2013). Draft revision 2344
40. Liu, J., et al.: A calculus for hybrid CSP. In: Ueda, K. (ed.) APLAS 2010. LNCS, vol. 6461, pp. 1–15. Springer, Heidelberg (2010). https://doi.org/10.1007/978-3-642-17164-2_1
41. Majumdar, R., Yoshida, N., Zufferey, D.: Multiparty motion coordination: from choreographies to robotics programs. Proc. ACM Program. Lang. **4**(OOPSLA) (2020)
42. Milner, R.: A Calculus of Communicating Systems. LNCS, vol. 92. Springer, Cham (1980). https://doi.org/10.1007/3-540-10235-3
43. Müller, A., Mitsch, S., Retschitzegger, W., Schwinger, W., Platzer, A.: Tactical contract composition for hybrid system component verification. STTT **20**(6) (2018)
44. Platzer, A.: Quantified differential dynamic logic for distributed hybrid systems. In: Dawar, A., Veith, H. (eds.) CSL 2010. LNCS, vol. 6247, pp. 469–483. Springer, Heidelberg (2010). https://doi.org/10.1007/978-3-642-15205-4_36
45. Platzer, A.: A complete axiomatization of quantified differential dynamic logic for distributed hybrid systems. LMCS **8**(4) (2012)
46. Platzer, A.: The complete proof theory of hybrid systems. In: LICS. IEEE (2012)
47. Platzer, A.: Logical Foundations of Cyber-Physical Systems. Springer, Cham (2018). https://doi.org/10.1007/978-3-319-63588-0
48. Renshaw, D.W., Loos, S.M., Platzer, A.: Distributed theorem proving for distributed hybrid systems. In: Qin, S., Qiu, Z. (eds.) ICFEM 2011. LNCS, vol. 6991, pp. 356–371. Springer, Heidelberg (2011). https://doi.org/10.1007/978-3-642-24559-6_25
49. Rounds, W.C., Song, H.: The Ö-calculus: a language for distributed control of reconfigurable embedded systems. In: Maler, O., Pnueli, A. (eds.) HSCC 2003. LNCS, vol. 2623, pp. 435–449. Springer, Heidelberg (2003). https://doi.org/10.1007/3-540-36580-X_32
50. Schlatte, R., Johnsen, E.B., Kamburjan, E., Tapia Tarifa, S.L.: Modeling and analyzing resource-sensitive actors: a tutorial introduction. In: Damiani, F., Dardha, O. (eds.) COORDINATION 2021. LNCS, vol. 12717, pp. 3–19. Springer, Cham (2021). https://doi.org/10.1007/978-3-030-78142-2_1
51. Talpin, J.-P., Jouvelot, P.: The type and effect discipline. In: LICS. IEEE (1992)
52. Wang, S., Zhan, N., Zou, L.: An improved HHL prover: an interactive theorem prover for hybrid systems. In: Butler, M., Conchon, S., Zaïdi, F. (eds.) ICFEM 2015. LNCS, vol. 9407, pp. 382–399. Springer, Cham (2015). https://doi.org/10.1007/978-3-319-25423-4_25

Enforced Dependencies for Active Objects

Violet Ka I Pun$^{(\boxtimes)}$ and Volker Stolz

Western Norway University of Applied Sciences, Bergen, Norway
{Violet.Ka.I.Pun,Volker.Stolz}@hvl.no

Abstract. We present an active object-based language that records required and provided method completions ahead of method invocations. With this language, a programmer can use method declarations to specify the dependencies between different types of tasks. The type system makes sure that the programmer declares how to fulfil the prerequisites. An operational semantics defines non-deterministic program execution with the necessary synchronisations.

We present the grammar, dynamic semantics in the form of operational semantics rules, and a rule-based type system that checks the dependencies. The absence of cyclic task dependency can be checked at the level of method declaration.

1 Introduction

In the recent decades, business process workflows have been significantly digitalised and automated using various process aware information systems (PAIS) [8], e.g., workflow management systems (WMS), which is regarded as among the most effective systems for facilitating cooperative business operations [7]. Planning workflows requires domain specific knowledge which gives an overview of how different tasks interact with each other with respect to not only the resources shared among them, but also to the their task dependency. This is particularly challenging for planning workflows that are across organisations, where one or more tasks in a workflow local in an organisation are depending on tasks in the concurrent workflows running in different organisations. Existing tools often lack such domain specific knowledge and also suffer from inflexible support for cross-organisational workflows [14], which make workflow planning still largely a manual process relying on human experts.

One way to facilitate workflow planning would be to automate the coordination of tasks based on the dependency of their execution order provided by domain experts. Ali et al. have developed the workflow modelling language $\mathcal{R}$PL [2] which supports the notion of the dependency of task execution order as well as resources shared among tasks. In this language, task dependency is modelled at the level of method invocations, but not specified at the level of method definition. This mismatch means that no validation between required and provided task dependencies can be made, leading to imprecise, or sometimes even incorrect, models and no means of validation.

F. de Boer et al. (Eds.): *Active Object Languages: Current Research Trends*,
LNCS 14360, pp. 359–374, 2024.
https://doi.org/10.1007/978-3-031-51060-1_13

In this paper, we explore a variation of the language proposed in [2] with the support of specifying task dependencies in the form of *contracts* at the level of method declarations. In our proposed workflow model, there are two options for synchronisation, instead of the only one in the original: after an asynchronous call, as before, we can either *await/get* the result of the call through its associated *future* before proceeding, or we defer synchronisation until some later method call with the new **after**-construct. This construct provides more flexibility than **await** (though conceptually also **await** could be adapted to the more flexible dependencies), and the explicit recording of how obligations are fulfilled eliminates the need for an expensive static analysis of whether requirements are met.

Apart from the dynamic effect of synchronisation, **await** alone does not allow us to capture dependencies in the business-domain: a future of a particular type may be provided through one of many different method calls (all returning values of the same type), whereas we would like to specify that a future must have been obtained in a particular way (through a specific method call).

To this end, we augment *method declarations* with dependencies (DPs): annotations that specify *how exactly* (through which method call) a future must have been obtained. Then, we define a simple type system, which performs an additional static check, to for each method invocation with an **after**-clause that the futures have been acquired in the prescribed way. The dynamic semantics presented in [2] remains unaffected: a program with dependency annotations behaves exactly as the program with the annotations removed from method declarations. The augmentation and construct in method declarations and invocations proposed in this language are intended to be the stepping stone of capturing richer dependencies and more complex control-flow patterns, e.g., [15], that are common in the domain of business process modelling in the future.

In the following, we first present the syntax and semantics, as well as a summary of the behaviour of our workflow modelling language in Sect. 2. We then augment the type system with conformance checking for the correct use of dependencies in Sect. 3. We show common properties of type systems such as subject reduction, and discuss some observations in Sect. 4, for example, whether it is possible to statically check for circular dependencies. We explore the related work in Sect. 5, and in Sect. 6, we conclude the paper with a summary and identify potential future work.

2   Core Language

In this section, we propose a core language for modelling workflows featuring task dependency. Both the syntax and semantics are based on a typical active object language [3]. The language adopts a Java-like syntax inspired by the abstract behavioural specification language ABS [11] and is similar to our earlier work on workflow modelling language [2].

$$P ::= \overline{CD} \ \{\overline{T \ x} \ ; \ s\}$$
$$CD ::= \textbf{class} \ C \ \{\overline{T \ x} \ ; \ \overline{M}\}$$
$$M ::= Sg \ \{\overline{T \ x} \ ; \ s\}$$
$$Sg ::= T \ m(\overline{T \ x}) \ \overline{DP}$$
$$DP ::= C.m \mid DP \wedge DP$$
$$T ::= B \mid \textbf{Fut}\langle B \rangle$$
$$B ::= C \mid \textsf{Bool} \mid \textsf{Int} \mid \textsf{Unit} \mid \cdots$$

$$e ::= x \mid b \mid fs \mid \textbf{this}$$
$$fs ::= f? \mid fs \wedge fs$$
$$s ::= x = rhs \mid \textbf{skip} \mid \textbf{if} \ e \ \textbf{then} \ s \ \textbf{else} \ s$$
$$\mid \textbf{await} \ f? \mid \textbf{return} \ e \mid s \ ; \ s$$
$$rhs ::= e \mid \textbf{new} \ C \mid f.\textbf{get}$$
$$\mid e.m(\overline{e}) \ \textbf{after} \ \overline{fs} \mid e!m(\overline{e}) \ \textbf{after} \ \overline{fs}$$

Fig. 1. Abstract Syntax.

2.1 Syntax

Figure 1 presents the abstract syntax of our language. A program P consists of a main method and a set of class declarations $\overline{CD}$, each of which has a set of fields and a set of methods. A method M has a signature Sg and a method body with a set of local variables and a statement. A signature Sg indicates the return type T, a set of formal parameters $\overline{x}$ as well as the task dependency $\overline{DP}$ of a method with the name m. Types are standard, where the type constructor for a future, denoted as $\textbf{Fut}\langle B \rangle$, is like any explicit future construct. The task dependency $\overline{DP}$ specified in the signature of a method m is a (possibly empty) set of conjunctions of methods whose completion m is depending on. For methods that do not depend on any other method, that is, do not have any constraint on the task dependency, we use $T \ m(\overline{T \ x})$ as the method signature. With empty dependencies, as we will see later in the semantics, method calls behave exactly as before in $\mathcal{R}$PL. Each depending method is denoted as $C.m$, where C refers to the class of the method. Example 1 shows how a task dependency can be specified in the signature of method declarations.

Example 1. Let $\overline{DP} = \{DP_1, DP_2\}$, $DP_1 = C_1.m_1$ and $DP_2 = C_2.m_2 \wedge C'_2.m'_2$. The signature $T \ m(\overline{T \ x}) \ \overline{DP}$ states that method m has the task dependency $\overline{DP}$ specifying that m depends on the completion of either method m_1 of class C_1 or method m_2 of class C_2 *and* method m'_2 of class C'_2.

Statements are standard, where the cooperative scheduling is enabled using **await** $f?$, which suspends a process until the condition $f?$ is validated, i.e., the method associated to the future f returns. Note that we could easily extend the condition to regular boolean expressions. The right hand side of an assignment can be an expression e, creating a new object of class C, retrieving the value stored in a future f, as well as synchronously or asynchronously invoking a method m.

Methods can only be invoked after a (possibly empty) set of methods has returned, which is specified with an **after** clause in the method invocation statement. The clause **after** $\overline{fs}$ is used to indicate the completion of depending method calls in the form of a set of conjunctions of return tests $\overline{fs}$. If the set $\overline{fs}$ is empty, it is evaluated to *true*, which means that the method can be invoked without any restriction; otherwise, at least one of the conjunctions must be evaluated to

```
1   class Hospital(e,s)
2   { Unit receivePatient() {
3       Fut⟨Unit⟩ f₁=this!registerPatient();
4       Fut⟨Unit⟩ f₂=e!call() after f₁?;
5       Fut⟨Unit⟩ f₃=s!call() after f₁?;
6       Fut⟨Unit⟩ f₄=this!examinePatient() after f₂? ∨ f₃?; }
7
8       Unit registerPatient() { ... }
9       Unit examinePatient() Expert.call ∨ Surgeon.call { ... }
10  }
11
12  class Expert() { ... Unit call() Hospital.registerPatient { ... } ... }
13
14  class Surgeon() { ... Unit call() Hospital.registerPatient { ... } ... }
15
16  { ...
17    Expert e = new Expert();
18    Surgeon s = new Surgeon();
19    Hospital h = new Hospital(e,s);
20
21    while (true) {Fut⟨Unit⟩ f=h!receivePatient() after {}; await f?}
22    ... }
```

Fig. 2. Illustrative example.

true in order to invoke the method. Example 2 illustrates the idea of the **after** clause as follows:

Example 2. Let $\overline{fs} = \{fs_1, fs_2\}$, $fs_1 = f_1?$ and $fs_2 = f_{21}? \wedge f_{22}?$. The method call $x!m(\overline{e})$ **after** $\{\}$ does not have any restriction on the invocation, while the call $x!m(\overline{e})$ **after** $\overline{fs}$ is depending on the completion of the method call associated with f_1 or on completion of the two invocations associated with $f_{21}? \wedge f_{22}?$.

By observing Examples 1 and 2, a task dependency stated in the method signature can be seen as a *contract* of method invocations. Thus, ideally, the depending methods specified in the form of return tests in the **after** clause should conform with the task dependency specified in the signature. We perform such a conformance check with a simple type system introduced in Sect. 3.

Next, we briefly explain the syntax with a simple example shown in Fig. 2. Note that we write $fs_1 \vee fs_2$ instead of $\{fs_1, fs_2\}$ and $C_1.m_1 \vee C_2.m_2$ instead of $\{C_1.m_1, C_2.m_2\}$ for the clarity of the code. Lines 1–10 define the class Hospital, while Line 12 and 14 define the classes Expert and Surgeon, respectively. Lines 16–22 specify the main method of the workflow model, which first creates the objects of class Expert, Surgeon and Hospital, where the Hospital is staffed with Expert and Surgeon, and continuously receives patients on Line 21. Note that receiving patients does not have any task dependency. This is also reflected in the signature of the method receivePatient declared on Line 2 where no task dependency is specified.

To receive a patient, the Hospital first needs to do the registration without any constraint (Line 8). Only after the patient is registered, an expert (Line 4) and a surgeon (Line 5) will be called, corresponding to the method declarations on Line 12 and on Line 14, respectively. Either the expert or the surgeon has to

(a) Original language	(b) New construct	(c) Potential equivalent formulation
$f_1 = \dots$ $f_2 = \dots$ **await** f_1? $f_A = o!m()$ **await** f_2? $f_B = p!n()$	$f_1 = \dots$ $f_2 = \dots$ $f_A = o!m()$ **after** f_1? $f_B = p!n()$ **after** f_2?	$f_1 = \dots$ $f_2 = \dots$ $f_A = o!m()$ **after** f_1? $f_B = p!n()$ **after** f_1? $\wedge$ f_2?

Fig. 3. Different formulations of explicit dependencies.

$$cn ::= obj\ invoc\ F$$
$$obj ::= \overline{o(a, p, q)}$$
$$invoc ::= \overline{invoc(o, f, m, \overline{v})}$$
$$F ::= \overline{fut(f, val)}$$
$$p ::= \text{idle} \mid \{l \mid s\}$$
$$q ::= \emptyset \mid \{l \mid s\} \mid q\ q$$

$$a, l ::= [\dots, x \mapsto v, \dots]$$
$$val ::= v \mid \bot$$
$$v ::= o \mid f \mid b \mid k$$
$$s ::= \textbf{cont}(f) \mid \textbf{suspend} \mid \dots$$
$$rhs ::= e.m(\overline{e}) \mid e!m(\overline{e}) \mid \dots$$

Fig. 4. Runtime syntax of the core language.

return the call before the patient can be examined (Line 6), as it is specified in the signature of the method on Line 9.

Observation. Note that the explicit dependencies in method calls come in addition to the general sequential composition: in the case of the first pair of actions (Lines 4 and 5) in the Hospital example in Fig. 2, which both synchronise on the completion of the initial call to registerPatient(), they are virtually started in parallel as soon as f_1 becomes available. In the case that the second call would have synchronised on a different future, the statement order matters and subsequent **after** constraints essentially become *conjunctions*. We capture this behaviour through the three equivalent fragments in Fig. 3. Note that variant (c) is only type-correct if the declaration corresponding to p!n() indeed declares *both* requirements.

2.2 Semantics

In this section, we describe the operational semantics of the language that handles method invocations with task dependency. The rest of the semantics are classical for an active object language [5,11] and can be found in Appendix A.1.

The runtime syntax of the core language is defined in Fig. 4. A configuration is an unordered set of objects, invocation messages, and futures, respectively written as *obj*, *invoc* and F. Each object is denoted as $o(a, p, q)$ where o refers to the object identifier, a stores the value of object fields, p is the currently running process and q is a (possibly empty) pool of suspended processes. The currently running process p can either be idle or consist of a set of local variables l

$$(\textsc{Sync-Call-After})$$
$$o(a, \{l \mid x = e.m(\overline{e}) \textbf{ after } \overline{fs} \; ; \; s\}, q)$$
$$\to o(a, \{l \mid \textbf{if } \overline{fs} \; \{x = e.m(\overline{e}) \; ; \; s\} \textbf{ else } \{\textbf{suspend} \; ; \; x = e.m(\overline{e}) \textbf{ after } \overline{fs} \; ; \; s\}\}, q)$$

$$(\textsc{Async-Call-After})$$
$$o(a, \{l \mid x = e!m(\overline{e}) \textbf{ after } \overline{fs} \; ; \; s\}, q)$$
$$\to o(a, \{l \mid \textbf{if } \overline{fs} \; \{x = e!m(\overline{e}) \; ; \; s\} \textbf{ else } \{\textbf{suspend} \; ; \; x = e!m(\overline{e}) \textbf{ after } \overline{fs} \; ; \; s\}\}, q)$$

$$(\textsc{Self-Sync-Call})$$
$$\frac{o = [\![e]\!]_{aol} \quad \overline{v} = [\![\overline{e}]\!]_{aol} \quad f' \text{ fresh} \quad f = l(\text{destiny})}{\{l' \mid s'\} = \text{bind}(o, f', m, \overline{v}, \text{class}(o))}{o(a, \{l \mid x = e.m(\overline{e}) \; ; \; s\}, q)}$$
$$\to o(a, \{l' \mid s' \; ; \; \textbf{cont}(f)\}, q \cup \{l \mid x = f'.\textbf{get} \; ; \; s\}) \; fut(f', \bot)$$

$$(\textsc{Self-Sync-Return})$$
$$\frac{f = l(\text{destiny})}{o(a, \{l' \mid \textbf{cont}(f)\}, q \cup \{l \mid s\})}$$
$$\to o(a, \{l \mid s\}, q)$$

$$(\textsc{Sync-Call})$$
$$\frac{o' = [\![e]\!]_{aol} \quad o \neq o' \quad f \text{ fresh}}{o(a, \{l \mid x = e.m(\overline{e}) \; ; \; s\}, q)}$$
$$\to o(a, \{l \mid f = e!m(\overline{e}) \; ; \; x = f.\textbf{get} \; ; \; s\}, q)$$

$$(\textsc{Async-Call})$$
$$\frac{o' = [\![e]\!]_{aol} \quad \overline{v} = [\![\overline{e}]\!]_{aol} \quad f \text{ fresh}}{o(a, \{l \mid x = e!m(\overline{e}) \; ; \; s\}, q)}$$
$$\to o(a, \{l \mid x = f \; ; \; s\}, q) \; invoc(o', f, m, \overline{v}) \; fut(f, \bot)$$

$$(\textsc{Invoc})$$
$$\frac{\{l \mid s\} = \text{bind}(o, f, m, \overline{v}, \text{class}(o))}{o(a, p, q) \; invoc(o, f, m, \overline{v})}$$
$$\to o(a, p, q \cup \{l \mid s\})$$

$$(\textsc{Return})$$
$$\frac{v = [\![e]\!]_{aol} \quad f = l(\text{destiny})}{o(a, \{l \mid \textbf{return } e \; ; \; s\}, q) \; fut(f, \bot)}$$
$$\to o(a, \{l \mid s\}, q) \; fut(f, v)$$

Fig. 5. Semantics related to method invocations.

and a statement s, denoted as $\{l \mid s\}$. Each invocation message $invoc(o, f, m, \overline{v})$ comprises the identifier of the callee object o, the name m and the actual parameters $\overline{v}$ of the called method, as well as the identifier of the future f associated to the invocation. A future $fut(f, val)$ in a configuration consisting of a future identifier f and a value val which is v if the future is resolved or $\bot$ otherwise. Statements extend the static syntax with $\textbf{cont}(f)$ for returning control to the caller process and $\textbf{suspend}$ to put a running process into the pool of pending processes. The right hand side of assignments is the same as the static syntax with the extension of method invocations without the $\textbf{after}$ clause.

To invoke a method that has constraints regarding task dependency, the semantics needs to check whether the methods this invocation is depending on have completed, that is, the futures associated to these methods are resolved. This check is handled by rules SYNC-CALL-AFTER and ASYNC-CALL-AFTER. The rules rewrite a method invocation to a conditional statement which checks the value of the set of conjunctions of future tests $\overline{fs}$. If the value is true, it

$$\llbracket \overline{fs} \rrbracket_F = \begin{cases} \llbracket \overline{fs}'' \rrbracket_F \vee \llbracket fs' \rrbracket_F & \text{if } \overline{fs} = \overline{fs}'' \cup fs' \\ \text{True} & \text{if } \overline{fs} = \emptyset \end{cases}$$

$$\llbracket fs \rrbracket_F = \begin{cases} \llbracket f? \rrbracket_F & \text{if } fs = f? \\ \llbracket f? \rrbracket_F \wedge \llbracket fs' \rrbracket_F & \text{if } fs = f? \wedge fs' \end{cases}$$

$$\llbracket f? \rrbracket_F = \begin{cases} \text{True} & \text{if } fut(f, v) \in F \wedge v \neq \bot \\ \text{False} & \text{otherwise.} \end{cases}$$

Fig. 6. Evaluating conjunctions of futures.

means that either $\overline{fs}$ is empty or at least one conjunction in $\overline{fs}$ is evaluated to true, implying that all the futures in at least one conjunction are all resolved. The method invocation will then be transformed into a call without any dependency; otherwise, a **suspend** statement will be prepended to the method invocation such that the process will be moved to the pool of pending processes. The evaluation of the set of conjunctions of futures $\overline{fs}$ is defined in Fig. 6, where the function returns a boolean value, and the evaluation is based on the set of futures F in the runtime configuration.

The treatment of method calls without task dependency and their returns are standard, and are handled by rules SELF-SYNC-CALL, SYNC-CALL, SELF-SYNC-RETURN and RETURN. The auxiliary function bind$(o, f, m, \overline{v}, C)$ activates method m of class C with actual parameters $\overline{v}$, callee o and associated future f, and returns a process as the method activation. This process contains a local variable *destiny* bound to future f and has the formal parameters bound to $\overline{v}$. For the case of synchronous self-calls, the statement **cont**(f) is appended to the statement list of the new process in rule SELF-SYNC-CALL, which is later used in rule SELF-SYNC-RETURN to return the control to the caller process. Whereas for the case of asynchronous calls, an invocation message is generated, which is later consumed in rule INVOC by placing the process associated to method invocation in the callee's process pool. Note that synchronous calls are treated as asynchronous calls followed by a blocking **get** statement.

3 Type System

In this section, we present a type system for our language. While it is mostly standard for a language with active objects and futures, this simple type system allows us to statically check whether or not method invocations are made according to the contract, i.e., the task dependencies specified in the method signature.

Figure 7 shows a subset of rules for static type checking, with the focus on typing method invocations and method and class declaration, as well as programs. The rest of the typing rules are typical and we refer the readers to Fig. 11 in Appendix A.2. We use Γ as the typing environment. The typing rules have the

$$\text{(T-Sync-Call)}$$
$$conform(\overline{fs}, DP) \quad \forall f_{m'}^{C'} \in \overline{fs}.\ \Gamma \vdash f_{m'}^{C'} : \mathbf{Fut}\langle B'\rangle$$
$$\Gamma \vdash e : C \quad \Gamma \vdash \overline{e} : \overline{T} \quad \Gamma(C)(m) = \overline{T} \to B :: DP$$
$$\overline{\Gamma \vdash e.m(\overline{e})\ \mathbf{after}\ \overline{fs} : B}$$

$$\text{(T-Async-Call)}$$
$$\frac{\Gamma \vdash e.m(\overline{e})\ \mathbf{after}\ \overline{fs} : B}{\Gamma \vdash e!m(\overline{e})\ \mathbf{after}\ \overline{fs} : \mathbf{Fut}\langle B\rangle}$$

$$\text{(T-Method)}$$
$$\forall C.m' \in DP.\ m' \in \Gamma'(C) \quad \nexists T \in \overline{T}.T = \mathbf{Fut}\langle B\rangle$$
$$\Gamma' = \Gamma[\overline{x} \mapsto \overline{T}, \overline{y} \mapsto \overline{T'}] \quad \Gamma'[\text{destiny} \mapsto \mathbf{Fut}\langle T\rangle] \vdash s$$
$$\overline{\Gamma \vdash T\ m(\overline{T\ x})\ DP\ \{\overline{T'\ y}\ ;\ s\}}$$

$$\text{(T-Class)}$$
$$\frac{\Gamma[\text{this} \mapsto C, \text{fields}(C)] \vdash \overline{M}}{\Gamma \vdash \mathbf{class}\ C\ \{\overline{T\ x}\ ;\ \overline{M}\}}$$

$$\text{(T-Program)}$$
$$\frac{\Gamma[\overline{x} \mapsto \overline{T}] \vdash s \quad \forall CD \in \overline{CD}.\ \Gamma \vdash CD}{\Gamma \vdash \overline{CD}\ \{\overline{T\ x}\ ;\ s\}}$$

Fig. 7. Type system.

form of $\Gamma \vdash s$ for statements, $\Gamma \vdash e$ for expressions, $\Gamma \vdash M$ for methods, $\Gamma \vdash CD$ for class declarations and $\Gamma \vdash P$ for programs.

Each program is typed by the initial typing environment Γ, which associates each class name to a mapping from method names to method signatures. Consider a method m of class C that is defined as $T''\ m(\overline{T\ x})\ DP\ \{\overline{T'\ x'};\ s\}$, to derive the signature of the method, we use

$$\Gamma(C)(m) = \overline{T} \to T'' :: DP\ .$$

Annotating Futures. To facilitate type checking task dependency, we annotate each future with the class and method to which the future is associated as follows: Given a program P, for each $f = e!m(\overline{e})$ in P, if method m is of class C, we rewrite all occurrences of f to f_m^C. Such annotation requires statically identifying the method invocation which a future is associated to, we therefore use the type system to restrict futures from being passed as parameters (see rule T-Method). Note that the intermediate future for synchronous calls (see rules Self-Sync-Call and Sync-Call in Fig. 5) will not be used in the **after** clause, thus, does not need to be annotated.

Type Checking Task Dependency. For static type checking, the only complex cases are method calls where methods can only be invoked after the completion of some specific methods, as identified in the signature of the methods. In the case of synchronous method calls, rule T-Sync-Call ensures that the variables in the return tests $\overline{fs}$ in the **after** constraints are futures, and these futures are associated to the methods stated in the task dependency of the method signature. The auxiliary function *conform* that the rule uses to perform such a conformance check is defined as follows:

(T-Config)
$$\frac{\forall o(a,p,q) \in obj.\Delta \vdash_R o(a,p,q)}{\begin{array}{c}\forall invoc(o,f,m,\overline{v}) \in invoc.\Delta \vdash_R invoc(o,f,m,\overline{v})\\ \forall fut(f,val) \in F.\Delta \vdash_R fut(f,val)\end{array}}{\Delta \vdash_R obj\ invoc\ F}$$

(T-Invoc)
$$\frac{\Delta(f) = \mathsf{Fut}\langle T\rangle \quad \Delta(\overline{v}) = \overline{T}}{match(m, \overline{T} \to T::\_, \Delta(o))}{\Delta \vdash_R invoc(o,f,m,\overline{v})}$$

(T-Object)
$$\frac{\begin{array}{c}fields(\Delta(o)) = [\overline{x \mapsto T}] \quad \Delta' = \Delta[\overline{x \mapsto T}]\\ \forall x \in dom(a).\Delta' \vdash_R a(x) : \Delta'(x)\\ \forall\{l\mid s\} \in \{p\} \cup q.\Delta' \vdash_R \{l\mid s\}\end{array}}{\Delta \vdash_R o(a,p,q)}$$

(T-Process)
$$\frac{\Delta \vdash_R \overline{v} : \overline{T}}{\Delta[\overline{x \mapsto T}] \vdash_R s}{\Delta \vdash_R \{[\overline{x \mapsto v}]\mid s\}}$$

(T-Fut)
$$\frac{\Delta(f) = \mathsf{Fut}\langle T\rangle}{val \neq \bot \Rightarrow \Delta(val) = T}{\Delta \vdash_R fut(f,val)}$$

(T-Cont)
$$\frac{\Delta(f) : \mathsf{Fut}\langle T\rangle}{\Delta \vdash_R \mathsf{cont}(f)}$$

(T-Suspend)
$$\frac{}{\Delta \vdash_R \mathsf{suspend}}$$

(T-Idle)
$$\frac{}{\Delta \vdash_R \mathsf{idle}}$$

Fig. 8. Type system for runtime configurations.

$conform(\overline{fs}, \overline{DP})$
$$= \begin{cases} conform(\overline{fs}\backslash fs, \overline{DP}\backslash DP) & \text{if } \exists fs \in \overline{fs}, \exists DP \in \overline{DP}.\ confm(fs, DP)\\ \mathtt{True} & \text{if } \overline{fs} = \overline{DP} = \emptyset\\ \mathtt{False} & \text{otherwise.}\end{cases}$$

$confm(fs, DP)$
$$= \begin{cases} confm(fs', DP') & \text{if } fs = f_m^C \wedge fs' \text{ and } DP = C.m \wedge DP'\\ \mathtt{True} & \text{if } fs = f_m^C \text{ and } DP = C.m\\ \mathtt{False} & \text{otherwise.}\end{cases}$$

Observe that the task dependency specified in DP in the signature of a method needs to be equivalent to the return tests of the depending methods stated in the **after** clause of the corresponding method invocations. In other words, in order to fulfil the conformance check, the dependency used in a method invocation *cannot be weaker or stronger* than the contract, that is, the task dependency specified in the method signature. Type checking the rest of the synchronous call is standard. The case of asynchronous method calls is straightforward: rule T-Async-Call reduces the call to a synchronous call for further type checking.

To ensure the correct identification of the origin of a future f, on which the conformance check relies, futures cannot be passed as parameters. It is restricted by rule T-Method, which type checks a method by adding a fresh name *destiny* to typing context binding to the type of the future associated to the method. The typing rules for class declarations and programs in Fig. 7 are also standard.

Typing Runtime Configurations. The type system is extended for typing runtime configurations $\Delta \vdash_R cn$, which is shown in Fig. 8. A typing environment gives the type of each active object, future and invocation message. Each component of the configuration is checked individually in a standard manner. Rule T-Object checks each element of an object, rule T-FUT checks futures and rule T-INVOC type checks invocation messages where the auxiliary function match$(m, \overline{T} \to T :: \_, \Delta(o))$ ensures that, for a method m that has return type T with its actual parameters of type $\overline{T}$, whether or not the signature $\overline{T} \to T :: \_$ matches the signature for method m of the callee o.

Properties of the Type System. Our type system has the property of subject reduction.

Theorem 1 (Subject Reduction). *If $\Delta \vdash_R cn$ and $cn \to cn'$, then there exists a typing context Δ' such that $\Delta \subseteq \Delta'$ and $\Delta' \vdash_R cn'$.*

Proof (Sketch). The proof is by straightforward induction over the application of transition rules. The proof is standard and thus omitted from the paper. In particular, the task dependency annotation does not affect the subject reduction. □

4   Observation and Discussion

Next, we make a useful observation about our dependency analysis. Cyclic, and hence unsatisfiable, dependencies can be declared for sets of methods, e.g. as shown in Fig. 9. As methods are type-checked individually, the type system does not directly report cycles. However, a type-correct program cannot call either of these methods, and we can easily report a cycle or dead code in general through a simple additional analysis.

```
1  class A {
2      T method1() B.method2 { ... }
3  }
4  class B {
5      T method2() A.method1 { ... }
6  }
```

Fig. 9. Circular dependency.

Proposition 1. *A cycle in the transitive closure of the dependency graph of a well-typed program implies that no method call to any member of a cycle (within the strongly connected component, SCC) can be made in this program.*

Given a method declaration/signature Sg, let $\Sigma : Sg \to 2^{C.m}$ denote the set of all used dependencies, i.e.,

$$\Sigma(T\ m(..)\ \overline{DP}) := \{C.m \mid C.m \in \overline{DP}\}.$$

This gives rise to the relation of all *direct* dependencies $(C.m, D.n)$ in a program P ("calls to method C.m must complete method D.n first"):

$$R_P := \{\{(m, n) \mid n \in \Sigma(m)\} \mid m \in P\},$$

of which we can compute the transitive closure R_P^+ in the usual way.

Every method in the SCC of the transitive closure must effectively be dead code, unreachable from anywhere—especially the *main* entry point to the program: Given a well-typed program P such that $\emptyset \vdash P$. Let us assume that a first (and possibly only) call to some member $C.m$ of the SCC exists in some method $D.n$ in P. Since the program is well-typed, $D.n$ must be well-typed and every call in $D.n$ must fulfil its requirements, hence also the call to $C.m$ must be preceded by the necessary calls to obtain the required futures. Any member in the SCC (also $C.m$), has at least one of its requirements also from the SCC, and hence one of these calls in $D.n$ preceding the call to $C.m$ must have eventually a call to $C.m$ as a dependency. Correspondingly, the call that we started our consideration from cannot have been the first call to $C.m$.

Comparing await and after

As we can see there is some overlap between the functionalities of **await** statements and **after** clauses – both of them either suspend the currently running process if the return test of some given futures is evaluated to false or allow the process to continue its execution if it is evaluated to true.

Compared to **await** statements, **after** clauses allow more complex dependency structure, namely a set of conjunctions of return tests $\overline{fs}$, where the relation among the set elements is interpreted as a disjunction. The valuation of return tests in the disjunction is purely used to control method invocations. In contrast, after an **await** statement, it is clear that any involved futures can be used without incurring another suspension (on another **await**) or even blocking (on a **get**). Although **await** statements can be easily extended to support a conjunction of return tests fs, it is unclear if it is reasonable to extend the **await** statement to express disjunctive relation among return tests.

Multiple Dependencies of Same Type

Our system already allows the specification of multiple dependencies stemming from identical calls, e.g., as in T Class.method() **after** $C.m \wedge C.m$. Currently, there is no mechanism to enforce that these two obligations must be fulfilled via two different futures. A model can hence fulfil both obligations with a single future. It is not yet clear to us if a repeat occurrence of a requirement should imply that both occurrences in a conjunct *must* be distinct, or if we may need the expressivity of either variant. This could be achieved through an annotation mechanism expressing which pairs or sets of requirements need to be disjoint.

Such a mechanism would enable us to request a constant number of calls, e.g., to allocate resources. A similar approach for an actor-model with explicit resource allocation (and deallocation) has been discussed by Ali et al. [2]. Their dependencies are expressed in an orthogonal dimension as integer values, unrelated to the object-based workflow models. We plan to investigate a streamlined solution that integrates both approaches, giving the modeler better granularity in declaring dependencies and obligations on how they must be fulfilled.

Alternative Semantics for after-Construct

As observed in Sect. 2.1, care must be taken to select the right means of synchronisation. Whereas synchronisation through **await** can always be introduced on existing futures, **after**-clauses must match exactly their declarations and cannot contain additional futures. Any additional synchronisation before a call must be done via an **await**.

A potential change in the runtime semantics for ASYNC-CALL-AFTER could easily make the statement non-suspending by deferring the implicit **await** from the calling task to the called task. In a sequence such as $f_o = o!m()$ **after** f?; s, the evaluation of statement s would then directly continue as the suggested form of sequential composition would no longer **await** f? in the caller. We see here some potential for our new language as otherwise a similar effect could only be achieved by moving the pair of prerequisite future and subsequent call into a new method without any dependency, and then invoking this new method asynchronously. This workaround comes at the cost of, in our opinion, decreased readability of the program. The proposed way would be similarly (syntactically) light-weight as e.g., the Go language's go { ... } construct for concurrency, albeit on the level of individual statements.

5   Related Work

Numerous workflow modelling languages and approaches have been proposed to facilitate workflow planning, including UML-AD [9], BPMN [6], BPEL [13], CPN [10] and YAWL [1].

While UML-AD compares well to existing WMS, the language does not fully capture advanced synchronisation patterns, e.g., N-out-of-M joins [4]. In addition, it does not allow communication among workflows, thus cannot capture the dependency between them.

BPEL and BPMN provide ample expressivity to model the control flows and synchronisation patterns in business workflows. While BPEL does not allow inter-workflow communication, different workflows can communicate through messages in BPMN. Nonetheless, the dependencies of the global control flow cannot be specified by means of semantics [4] in the language.

The expressivity of high-level Petri nets, including CPN and YAWL, is in general comparable with the many workflow modelling languages; however, control flow modelling for, e.g., multiple instances or advanced synchronisation patterns, is not entirely satisfactory [1]. Inter-workflow communication is illustrated to some extent with the help of hierarchical models in CPN based modelling languages.

In contrast to these works, our language is expressive enough to model the organisation of control flows, complex decisions, exclusive event-based decisions and parallel event-based decisions in business process workflows. In addition, it allows formally specifying and modelling task dependencies in workflow models, and supports inter-workflow communication by joining different workflow models using explicit notions task dependencies.

Kamburjan et al. [12] introduce the concept of a resolvedBy annotation for **get** requests that they use in a contract-based proof-system that can reason about the guarantees the value of a future can give. The annotation declares the potential origins of a future. Their concern is orthogonal to ours, as they are concerned with return values for proofs, whereas we are concerned with statically checked dependencies that need to be dynamically resolved for a method call. It should be possible to encode our dependencies e.g., through additional boolean variables communicated through futures (indicating which asynchronous calls have been resolved), and hence a static dependency check through the proof system, although allowances would have to be made to make the checks on **await**, not necessarily **get**.

6 Conclusion

We have presented a workflow modelling language that features explicit declaration of dependencies for method calls: in addition to the formal parameters, the modeller provides an optional **after** clause to specify which methods in which classes have to be called (and returned) before the call can proceed. The caller of such a method has to provide evidence of their requisite calls by passing their corresponding futures in addition to any actual parameters. The type system ensures that a correct program fulfils all dependencies, and that the program cannot encounter circular dependencies.

We believe that our language fills a gap in workflow modelling, where designers would like to encode more domain-knowledge, and have a means of automatically using that knowledge, here through verification via a type system.

Our language is based on the workflow modelling language with resources $\mathcal{RPL}$ [2] which has the **after** clause implemented. We plan to consolidate our work into a single version with both resources and dependencies, and extend the implementation of the $\mathcal{RPL}$ with annotation of dependencies. We also plan to evaluate our approach on the workflows at our project partner (the Pathology department at the Haukeland University Hospital).

Another natural extension is to enhance the expressiveness of the augmentation and construct in method declarations and invocations in the language to capture richer dependencies and more complex control-flow patterns for workflow modelling.

Further future investigations include studying the effect of relaxing the provided dependencies on the caller side by permitting to just provide a set of return tests that will satisfy one of the disjuncts instead of all of them, as well as moving the suspension of **after** clauses from the caller into the callee's context. We also want to investigate in how far an annotation of futures in parameters, e.g., derived from their use in **after** clauses in the body, can preserve soundness while still remaining useful.

Acknowledgements. This work is part of the CROFLOW project: Enabling Highly Automated Cross-Organisational Workflow Planning, funded by the Research Council of Norway (grant no. 326249).

A   Appendix

In this appendix, we present the remaining of the semantics in Fig. 10 in Appendix A.1 and the additional typing rules for static type system in Fig. 11 in Appendix A.2 of the core language.

A.1   Semantics

$$
\frac{(\text{If-True})}{[\![e]\!]_{aol,F} = \text{True}}{o(a, \{l \mid \text{if } e \text{ then } s_1 \text{ else } s_2 \text{ ; } s\}, q) \; F \;\to o(a, \{l \mid s_1 \text{ ; } s\}, q) \; F}
\qquad
\frac{(\text{If-False})}{[\![e]\!]_{aol,F} = \text{False}}{o(a, \{l \mid \text{if } e \text{ then } s_1 \text{ else } s_2 \text{ ; } s\}, q) \; F \;\to o(a, \{l \mid s_2 \text{ ; } s\}, q) \; F}
$$

$$
\frac{(\text{Await-True})}{v \neq \perp}{o(a, \{l \mid \text{await } f? \text{ ; } s\}, q) \; \mathit{fut}(f, v) \;\to o(a, \{l \mid s\}, q) \; \mathit{fut}(f, v)}
\qquad
\frac{(\text{Await-False})}{v = \perp}{o(a, \{l \mid \text{await } f? \text{ ; } s\}, q) \; \mathit{fut}(f, v) \;\to o(a, \{l \mid \text{idle}, q \cup \{l \mid \text{await } f? \text{ ; } s\}) \; \mathit{fut}(f, v)}
$$

$$
\frac{(\text{Get})}{v \neq \perp}{o(a, \{l \mid x = f.\textbf{get} \text{ ; } s\}, q) \; \mathit{fut}(f, v) \; z \to o(a, \{l \mid x = v \text{ ; } s\}, q)x \; \mathit{fut}(f, v)}
\qquad
\frac{(\text{New})}{o' = \text{fresh} \quad a' = \text{atts}(C, o')}{o(a, \{l \mid x = \textbf{new } C \text{ ; } s\}, q) \;\to o(a, \{l \mid x = o' \text{ ; } s\}, q) \; o'(a', \text{idle}, \emptyset)}
$$

$$
\frac{(\text{Activate})}{p = \text{select}(a, q, cn)}{o(a, \text{idle}, q) \; cn \;\to o(a, p, q \backslash p) \; cn}
\quad
\frac{(\text{Context})}{cn \to cn'}{cn \; cn'' \;\to cn' \; cn''}
\quad
\frac{(\text{Skip})}{o(a, \{l \mid \textbf{skip} \text{ ; } s\}, q) \;\to o(a, \{l \mid s\}, q)}
\quad
\frac{(\text{Suspend})}{o(a, \{l \mid \textbf{suspend} \text{ ; } s\}, q) \;\to o(a, \text{idle}, q \cup \{l \mid s\})}
$$

Fig. 10. Semantics in addition to the rules in Fig. 5 (assignments for fields and local variables are omitted). The auxiliary function atts(C, o') returns the default values of the fields of class C and o' is the value for **this**; the function select selects a process from the process pool for execution if it is ready to execute.

A.2   Type System

$$\frac{\text{(T-VAR)}}{\Gamma \vdash x : T}$$

$$\text{(T-BOOL)} \quad \Gamma \vdash b : \text{Bool}$$

$$\frac{\text{(T-FUTTEST)}}{\Gamma \vdash e : \text{Fut}\langle B \rangle} \quad \Gamma \vdash e? : \text{Bool}$$

$$\frac{\text{(T-AND)}}{\Gamma \vdash g_1 : \text{Bool} \quad \Gamma \vdash g_2 : \text{Bool}}{\Gamma \vdash g_1 \wedge g_2 : \text{Bool}}$$

$$\frac{\text{(T-OR)}}{\Gamma \vdash g_1 : \text{Bool} \quad \Gamma \vdash g_2 : \text{Bool}}{\Gamma \vdash g_1 \vee g_2 : \text{Bool}}$$

$$\frac{\text{(T-SEQ)}}{\Gamma \vdash s \quad \Gamma \vdash s'}{\Gamma \vdash s \, ; \, s'}$$

$$\frac{\text{(T-COND)}}{\Gamma \vdash e : \text{Bool} \quad \Gamma \vdash s \quad \Gamma \vdash s'}{\Gamma \vdash \text{if } e \text{ then } s \text{ else } s'}$$

$$\text{(T-SKIP)} \quad \Gamma \vdash \text{skip}$$

$$\frac{\text{(T-AWAIT)}}{\Gamma \vdash e : \text{Bool}}{\Gamma \vdash \text{await } e}$$

$$\frac{\text{(T-RETURN)}}{\Gamma \vdash e : B}{\Gamma \vdash \text{return } e}$$

$$\frac{\text{(T-ASSIGN)}}{\Gamma \vdash rhs : \Gamma(x)}{\Gamma \vdash x = rhs}$$

$$\text{(T-NEW)} \quad \Gamma \vdash \text{new } C : C$$

$$\frac{\text{(T-GET)}}{\Gamma \vdash e : \text{Fut}\langle B \rangle}{\Gamma \vdash e.\text{get} : B}$$

Fig. 11. Typing rules in addition to the type system presented in Fig. 7.

References

1. van der Aalst, W.M., ter Hofstede, A.H.: YAWL: yet another workflow language. Inf. Syst. **30**(4), 245–275 (2005)
2. Ali, M.R., Lamo, Y., Pun, V.K.I: Cost analysis for a resource sensitive workflow modelling language. Sci. Comput. Program. **225**, 102896 (2023). https://doi.org/10.1016/j.scico.2022.102896
3. de Boer, F., et al.: A survey of active object languages. ACM Comput. Surv. **50**(5), 76:1–76:39 (2017). https://doi.org/10.1145/3122848
4. Bouchbout, K., Alimazighi, Z.: Inter-organizational business processes modelling framework. In: Proceedings of II 15th East-European Conference on Advances in Databases and Information Systems, ADBIS 2011, vol. 789, pp. 45–54. CEUR-WS.org (2011)
5. Caromel, D., Henrio, L.: A Theory of Distributed Objects. Springer, Heidelberg (2005). https://doi.org/10.1007/b138812
6. Chinosi, M., Trombetta, A.: BPMN: an introduction to the standard. Comput. Stand. Interfaces **34**, 124–134 (2012)
7. Dourish, P.: Process descriptions as organisational accounting devices: the dual use of workflow technologies. In: Proceedings of the 2001 International ACM SIG-GROUP Conference on Supporting Group Work, pp. 52–60. ACM (2001)

8. Dumas, M., van der Aalst, W.M.P., ter Hofstede, A.H.M. (eds.): Process-Aware Information Systems: Bridging People and Software Through Process Technology. Wiley, Hoboken (2005)
9. Dumas, M., ter Hofstede, A.H.M.: UML activity diagrams as a workflow specification language. In: Gogolla, M., Kobryn, C. (eds.) UML 2001. LNCS, vol. 2185, pp. 76–90. Springer, Heidelberg (2001). https://doi.org/10.1007/3-540-45441-1_7
10. Jensen, K.: A brief introduction to coloured petri nets. In: Brinksma, E. (ed.) TACAS 1997. LNCS, vol. 1217, pp. 203–208. Springer, Heidelberg (1997). https://doi.org/10.1007/BFb0035389
11. Johnsen, E.B., Hähnle, R., Schäfer, J., Schlatte, R., Steffen, M.: ABS: a core language for abstract behavioral specification. In: Aichernig, B.K., de Boer, F.S., Bonsangue, M.M. (eds.) FMCO 2010. LNCS, vol. 6957, pp. 142–164. Springer, Heidelberg (2011). https://doi.org/10.1007/978-3-642-25271-6_8
12. Kamburjan, E., Din, C.C., Hähnle, R., Johnsen, E.B.: Behavioral contracts for cooperative scheduling. In: Ahrendt, W., Beckert, B., Bubel, R., Hähnle, R., Ulbrich, M. (eds.) Deductive Software Verification: Future Perspectives. LNCS, vol. 12345, pp. 85–121. Springer, Cham (2020). https://doi.org/10.1007/978-3-030-64354-6_4
13. Ouyang, C., Dumas, M., ter Hofstede, A.H., van der Aalst, W.M.: From BPMN process models to BPEL web services. In: Proceedings of 2006 IEEE International Conference on Web Services, ICWS 2006, pp. 285–292. IEEE (2006)
14. Reichert, M., Weber, B.: Enabling Flexibility in Process-Aware Information Systems - Challenges, Methods. Technologies. Springer, Heidelberg (2012). https://doi.org/10.1007/978-3-642-30409-5
15. Russell, N., van der Aalst, W.M.P., ter Hofstede, A.H.M.: Workflow Patterns: The Definitive Guide. MIT Press, Cambridge (2016)

Correction to: Actors Upgraded for Variability, Adaptability, and Determinism

Ramtin Khosravi, Ehsan Khamespanah, Fatemeh Ghassemi, and Marjan Sirjani

Correction to:
Chapter 9 in: F. de Boer et al. (Eds.): *Active Object Languages:*
Current Research Trends, **LNCS 14360,**
https://doi.org/10.1007/978-3-031-51060-1_9

The original version of the book was inadvertently published with an incorrect/incomplete form of reference [7] in Chapter 9. This has been corrected.

The original version of the book was inadvertently published with an incorrect author name in reference [8] in Chapter 9. This has been corrected.

The updated version of this chapter can be found at
https://doi.org/10.1007/978-3-031-51060-1_9

Author Index

Printed in the United States
by Baker & Taylor Publisher Services